W9-COL-767

INTRODUCTION TO EDUCATIONAL RESEARCH

To the memory of Walter and Thalia, in gratitude for their education values and support

INTRODUCTION TO EDUCATIONAL RESEARCH

A Critical Thinking Approach

W. NEWTON SUTER
University of Arkansas at Little Rock

For information:

Sage Publications, Inc.
2455 Teller Road
Thousand Oaks, California 91320
E-mail: order@sagepub.com

Sage Publications Ltd.
1 Oliver's Yard
55 City Road
London EC1Y 1SP
United Kingdom

Sage Publications India Pvt. Ltd.
B-42, Panchsheel Enclave
Post Box 4109
New Delhi 110 017 India

Printed in the United States of America

Library of Congress Cataloging-in-Publication Data

Suter, W. Newton, 1950-
Introduction to educational research: A critical thinking approach / W. Newton Suter.
p. cm.
Includes bibliographical references and index.
ISBN 1-4129-1390-X (cloth)
1. Education—Research. 2. Critical thinking. I. Title.
LB1028.S944 2006
370.′7′2—dc22

2005008161

This book is printed on acid-free paper.

05 06 07 08 09 10 9 8 7 6 5 4 3 2 1

Acquiring Editor: Diane McDaniel
Editorial Assistant: Marta Peimer
Production Editor: Diana E. Axelsen
Copy Editor: Jamie Robinson
Typesetter: C&M Digitals (P) Ltd.
Indexer: David Luljak
Cover Designer: Audrey Snodgrass

Brief Contents

Detailed Contents

PART V: CONSUMER TO PRODUCER 373

List of Features

Critical Perspectives

Highlight and Learning Checks

Critical Thinker Alerts

List of Tables and Figures

Tables

Figures

PREFACE

These are exciting times in education—particularly in educational research. The importance of research in education was elevated significantly by the No Child Left Behind Act of 2001, the federal legislation that squarely placed a spotlight on educational research. The law requires that educational programs and practices be grounded in scientifically based evidence. Hunches and traditions are to be replaced by data-driven decisions that follow logically from rigorous research completed in schools.

In the spirit of the No Child Left Behind Act of 2001, the purpose of *Introduction to Educational Research: A Critical Thinking Approach* is to enable clear and astute thinking—critical reasoning—about the scientific process of research in all its diversity. What is important in today's changing education landscape is the ability to think clearly about research methods, reason through complex problems, and evaluate published research. This is why the textbook is titled *Introduction to Educational Research: A Critical Thinking Approach.* It is a pleasure to share this useful information with other educators and equip them with the thinking skills needed to transform education into a truly research-based scientific discipline.

Educational practitioners using critical thinking are in the best position to ask the right questions about research, read published research reports with comprehension, offer suggestions for implementation, create a proposal to evaluate a program or answer a research question, and carry out the proposed research. The effect of research on teaching and learning is potentially profound, dependent in many ways on teachers' ability to understand, critique, and apply findings from high quality studies in education.

Learning how the research process—the very heart of science—can supplant less trustworthy ways of knowing can be thrilling indeed. It is liberating to understand the process of research in education and develop skills in evaluating published research reports. This text embodies many reasons why the study of research can be exciting.

Students often enter a research methods course with little background knowledge in and understanding of this area. Because of their limited exposure to research, students may feel insecure having few personal linkages to relate to new information. They probably have struggled to comprehend published research reports they have read in other classes. But now the research process is the focus, and what students don't always realize is that learning about research methods and techniques (such as the statistical analysis of data) is far more conceptual than technical. Courses in which these research methods are explored often become the most enjoyable and interesting. Part of that interest stems from changing ways of thinking and reasoning about research—from foggy to clear. I wrote this text to capture that interest in the study of research methods in education.

I also wrote the book to make research *accessible* to education students and practitioners by equipping them with the reasoning and thinking skills needed to understand and critically evaluate published research. This text is appropriate for a first or intermediate course in educational research methods at the undergraduate or graduate level. Its orientation is toward *consumers* of educational research. The major components of the research process and the principles of sound methodology are introduced for the eventual *producer* of research. Because many instructors of courses in educational research methods require the completion of a research proposal, the last chapter focuses on the practical aspects of completing this capstone requirement. I hope that many students' proposals will, upon approval and funding, generate new data and culminate in a formal report worthy of publication. Other instructors may forgo the proposal and end a course with one or more critiques of published educational research—the topic of the second-to-last chapter. Above all else, students using this book will *understand how and why researchers think like they do.*

Features

The chapters of this book are loaded with many examples and illustrations culled from premiere journals that publish educational research. Each chapter includes an **Outline**, **Overview**, and **Chapter Summary**. Additionally, each chapter contains many features that enable the goal of helping students understand how and why researchers think like they do.

Critical Thinker Alerts are spread throughout the 15 chapters. Each one describes a key concept in research coupled with a discussion question designed to enable clear thinking.

Highlight and Learning Checks provide conceptual recaps and opportunities for student engagement.

Critical Perspectives present "Critical Thinking Toolboxes" (and associated questions) within a context that describe key concepts (e.g., control, sampling, etc.) across three major research traditions in education: *quantitative, qualitative,* and *action research.*

Critical Terms are defined throughout.

More Examples direct students to the Web-based student study site, which includes guided tours of published articles highlighting the major concepts of a chapter in the context of published research.

Application Exercises can be used for additional learning checks, student projects, or optional enrichment.

On Your Own provides many options for Web-based learning activities and additional resources that facilitate the learning objectives of each chapter.

Organization

The text is organized in a manner that heightens interest and systematically eases students into the process of thinking like a researcher. Experience has proven this sequential organization maximizes students' engagement and understanding. The 15 chapters are organized logically into five parts.

Part I: Foundations is an introduction to thinking critically about research and its great diversity. Chapter 1 describes the value of research in education and views educators as reflective practitioners and teacher researchers as critical thinkers. Chapter 2 piques interest about scientific reasoning and sharpens students' thinking about research with a presentation of powerful ideas. Chapter 3 describes different perspectives across approaches to contemporary research in education.

Part II: Research as Process introduces the research problem, the language and process of research, and how theory is linked to practice. Chapter 4 focuses on the research problem, the research hypothesis, and the issues that surround the research question. Chapters 5 and 6 describe the language of research (including basic terms such as *constructs, variables, hypotheses,* and *theories*) and how theory-based and problem-based research are integrated processes.

Part III: Data Collection includes Chapter 7, which focuses on control in research; Chapter 8, which focuses on sampling designs and sample size; and Chapter 9, which focuses on measurement soundness and instrumentation.

Part IV: Design and Analysis includes Chapter 10 with coverage of common experimental research designs, Chapter 11 with common nonexperimental research designs, Chapter 12 with qualitative research designs and analysis, and Chapter 13 with statistical analysis of quantitative designs.

Part V: Consumer to Producer includes practical guides to research analyses and critiques in Chapter 14 and writing research proposals in Chapter 15.

Supplements

Instructor Resource CD

This CD contains keyed answers and discussion points for Critical Thinker Alerts, keyed answers to Highlights and Learning Checks, keyed answers to the objective Application Exercises, and a test bank of multiple-choice questions (with answers). Instructors will find other resources on the CD, including assignments and suggested activities appropriate for different models of teaching.

Web-Based Student Study Site

This site provides access to many full-text research reports in Sage journals carefully linked to concepts and questions in each chapter of the text. The site also links to further learning exercises, additional descriptions of research concepts and applications, chapter objectives and quizzes, and samples of research critiques and proposals.

Acknowledgments

My approach to teaching research methods with a focus on thinking skills evolved through a process of fine-tuning after many years of teaching this subject to students at the University of Arkansas at Little Rock. These students' patience and feedback after many field trials enabled my instructional objectives to be met. We got it right together and I thank them.

Portions of this book were adapted from my text *Primer of Educational Research* (1998), published by Pearson Education, Inc., and I thank them for their reversion of rights to me.

I also thank the many reviewers for their help with preliminary drafts of this textbook. Their praise was welcome, and although the criticism was sometimes searing, it was always constructive. Their suggestions resulted in many improvements and strengthened the book immeasurably. They include the following:

Becky Kochenderfer Ladd, Arizona State University

Tandra L. Tyler-Wood, University of North Texas

Alan D. Moore, University of Wyoming

Rita C. Kolody, Idaho State University

Namok Choi, University of Louisville

David K. Pugalee, University of North Carolina, Charlotte

Larry C. Loesch, University of Florida

Yvonne Bui, University of San Francisco

Lisa Keller, University of Massachusetts, Amherst

Suzanne Young, University of Wyoming

Stephen C. Enwefa, Jackson State University

John Gardner, Queen's University, Belfast, Northern Ireland

Nedra Atwell, Western Kentucky University

MaryAnn Byrnes, University of Massachusetts, Boston

Kimberly Eretzian Smirles, Emmanuel College

Ricardo Cornejo, San Diego State University

I thank Diane McDaniel, Education Acquisitions Editor at Sage Publications, for her wisdom and leadership. She always steered me in the right direction and masterfully inspired creative work. I also thank Production Editor Diana E. Axelsen, Copy Editor Jamie Robinson, and Editorial Assistant Marta Peimer for skillfully transforming a manuscript into a book. Finally, thanks extend to Associate Editor Katja Werlich Fried, who assisted with the supplements that enhance the instructional and learning value of this book.

Part I Foundations

Every structure needs a solid foundation for support, including the metaphorical structure of educational research. Part I provides a foundation to buttress the powerful ideas and critical thinking that enhance your understanding of the process of educational research. The foundation, which supports your thinking about central topics in research, includes problems in and questions about research, major concepts embedded within the specialized language of research, how theory is related to practice, issues related to data collection (such as control, sampling, and measurement), common designs used by researchers, and how researchers analyze and interpret educational data. Your clear thinking about the entire structure and process of educational research enables you to critically evaluate research, and ultimately, to construct educational studies by completing a proposal (blueprint) that answers your own researchable questions.

Never has so much attention been focused on the findings of educational research, and never has the need for critical evaluation of that research been so strong. The three chapters in Part I form an underpinning by introducing ways of thinking about research in education and honoring the creative variations in approaches to research that exist across the educational landscape. Chapter 1 describes the value of research in education, the need for astute judgments about problems in education, and the importance of educators taking on the role of reflective practitioners. In addition to providing an understanding and appreciation of critical thinking, this chapter also makes clear why the art and science of teaching and learning often yield inconsistent research findings.

Chapter 2 introduces more powerful foundational ideas to sharpen concept formation in research. Many of these ideas, such as those related to interpreting data, establishing control, and assessing relationships, support objectives in later chapters. Chapter 2 also reinforces the notion that thinking like a researcher is an acquired skill that is enhanced by practice.

Chapter 3 lays more reinforcing foundation by revealing how research questions in education can be answered by many different approaches and perspectives rather than just one approach. Contemporary research in education is often described by its "mixed methods." Chapter 3 reveals that there is a wide selection of research designs and ways of thinking about them that create very useful mixes. What all these different approaches to research in education have in common is an elegance that can be fully appreciated by exploring the ideas and principles described in the remaining twelve chapters.

1

Educators as Critical Thinkers

Outline

Overview

Many students are surprised to learn that the study of research methods in many fields of inquiry, particularly education, is far more conceptual than technical. Learning about research involves new ways of thinking, and in one sense, students of research could easily believe they are studying within a department of philosophy. These new ways of thinking are indeed intriguing to students. Some find them counterintuitive; others find them downright fascinating. Most would agree that thinking like a researcher is elegant, in a sense, and is ultimately a very comfortable experience.

Astute thinking about research can greatly enhance your ability to understand published educational research and communicate effectively with other educational practitioners. Sharing your ideas about research findings is one step toward improving learning for others. Your ability to understand research in education is greatly enhanced by critical thinking skills. A thinking-skills approach to educational research views teacher researchers as critical, reflective practitioners.

The Value of Research in Education

Educational researchers are committed to improving the quality of education by increasing their knowledge of the art and science of teaching and the process of learning. Educational practitioners, such as teachers, counselors, administrators, and curriculum specialists, become most effective when their skills and classroom wisdom are combined with their knowledge of educational research. The goal of this book is to make educational research accessible to practicing educational professionals, those ultimately responsible for improving learning in the classrooms. Making research accessible requires the ability to read and critique published educational research—and think clearly about the entire process. Clearly, the effect of research on teaching and learning—a potentially profound influence—is dependent on teachers' ability to understand, critique, and apply findings from high quality published studies.

Each chapter of this book is concerned with an important facet of educational research, one that enables you to read research reports with greater comprehension and critical appraisal. By the time you reach the end of this book, you will understand the most important principles and concepts of educational research, those that will enable you to read and evaluate research reports. This will put you in a good position to make sound decisions about applying educational research in your practice. The final chapter will introduce you to the next level—preparing to conduct your own research. Learning how to think critically about the research process and how to evaluate published research will enable you to prepare a clearly written research proposal in any area of education.

Practitioners' ability to understand the process of educational research—and be able to evaluate it—became especially important with the No Child Left Behind Act of 2001. This is because the Act placed great emphasis on using scientific research to determine what works best in our schools. The idea that science can contribute to our understanding of teaching and learning is decades old (see Gage's 1978 classic, *The Scientific Basis of the Art of Teaching*). But what is new is that scientific research applied to education is now mandated by law with the passage of No Child Left Behind. This legislation shifts educators' focus to scientific research for help in determining best practices in our schools. The scientific emphasis highlights the value of empirical, systematic, rigorous, and objective procedures to obtain valid knowledge about teaching and learning. The Act favors true experimental research for guidance, the type of research best suited for uncovering cause-and-effect relationships. Yet, as you will see, there are many other scientific approaches to research that are valuable for practicing educators.

The influence of the Act on education is enormous. Educators who are in a position to evaluate scientific research in education (the focus of this book) are in the best position to understand the requirements of the law—and carry them out responsibly.

Conducting research is the most reliable method for acquiring new knowledge about teaching and learning. All the alternative "ways of knowing" (like common sense, intuition, authority, tradition, etc.) have proven less useful for advancing our understanding of the complex process of learning. Educational research in recent years has revealed information that is quietly changing the way we teach. Research by Howard Gardner (1993, 1999, 2000), for example, supports our asking "How are you smart?" instead of "How smart are you?" His notion is that multiple intelligences applied in classrooms engage students who benefit from alternatives to the traditional verbal (lecture) approach to teaching. Such classrooms, with the backing of research, capitalize on abilities aligned with music, movement, social interaction, introspection, and spatial (visual) relations, among others.

HIGHLIGHT AND LEARNING CHECK 1-1

Science and Wisdom

Studying the art and science of teaching and learning can be viewed as a melding of scientific principles and personal craft knowledge. Explain how both science and experiential wisdom can help us understand the personal, creative, and scientific bases of education.

Other recent research reveals that passivity and learning do not mix well, for learners of all ages seem to learn best through real-life, meaningful activity (such as hands-on projects and social interaction). In fact, much contemporary research in neuroscience and cognitive psychology supports the early progressive methods of learning popular nearly 100 years ago (see, e.g., Schunk, 2004). Today, many of the progressive ideas of John Dewey have been rebadged and are commonly referred to under the label of *constructivism,* to highlight the fact that learners must actively construct, or build, an understanding for meaningful retention. Other examples of the illuminating value of research are the teaching of reading (National Institute of Child Health and Human Development, 2000), the understanding of learning disabilities and teaching to "rewire" the brain (Temple et al., 2003), and the preparation of highly qualified teachers (Darling-Hammond & Youngs, 2002). You will find many other examples of programs and practices in education that meet the criterion of solid research support at the What Works Clearinghouse (http://www.w-w-c.org/) and at the Promising Practices Network http://www.promisingpractices.net/).

The scope of research problems in education is indeed huge, and the value of applying research findings in the classroom to improve learning and retention cannot be overstated. Useful research findings stem from large-scale scientific experiments to very local, small-scale teacher action research in the classroom—and everything in between. The same research principles, like controls to minimize bias and measurements that minimize error, are used across the full spectrum of research approaches in education. These important principles—and how to think clearly about them—are described in the chapters that follow.

Reading journal articles that report research results is not easy. (It does get easier with practice.) The scholarly literature in any field is often dense and filled with jargon; it is always slow reading. But I believe understanding and applying research holds the key to improving the art and science of teaching and learning. You could probably go to easier sources for information about "what works," like the popular but biased media (magazines, television, etc.), devotees of pendulum swings, or tidbits off the Internet. (I am reminded of the confused man who lost his wallet in the dark alley but searched under the street lamp because the light was better.) However, the simplicity of these sources greatly distorts the complex reality. The *scientific* basis of the art of teaching is revealed only by research literature. Understanding published scientific literature involves bringing new light to previously dim areas (to continue the lost wallet metaphor). This book will illuminate the process of educational research so you are in a better position to read, understand,

and apply research in your own practice. You can also begin the process of conducting your own research. These tasks involve critical thinking. Many classroom teachers develop the skill of critical thinking when reflecting on their practice. The value of critical thinking, reflective teaching, and teacher action research is explored in the following sections.

Critical Thinking in Educational Research

Although there is little debate over the value of critical thinking in our complex society, different disciplines (e.g., cognitive psychology, philosophy, behavioral psychology) focus on different definitions by highlighting a variety of abilities and processes (Huitt, 1998). Most definitions of critical thinking center on analyzing and evaluating ideas using reasoned reflection. The cognitive process of analysis involves breaking up complexity into its constituent components to see how they are connected—tightly, loosely, or not at all. The process of evaluation involves examining a process and making a judgment using one or more standards as a context or benchmark. Research is often evaluated against the scientific standard, yet there is variance of opinion about what constitutes "science." This is especially true in education. One person might argue that scientific research in education is defined by its specific methods (e.g., intervention, random assignment, rigorous controls, etc.), while another might argue science is defined by systematic inquiry and an explicit chain of reasoning.

CRITICAL THINKING: Careful, astute reasoning that includes conceptualization, synthesis, analysis, and evaluation. Critical thinkers reach sound conclusions about the connections between ideas and observations.

There is bountiful opportunity for critical thinking in educational research—and much room for debate among the sharpest critical thinkers. The No Child Left Behind Act of 2001, undoubtedly the most sweeping federal reform of public education in our history, demands educators' attention to critical thinking about research and data-driven decisions. Thinking critically involves evaluating research conclusions by first analyzing the research process that led to those conclusions. Merely having data is not a sufficient condition for making sound conclusions.

Here is an example. Suppose a sample of homeschooled high school students outperformed a sample of public school students on a standardized achievement test of reading and mathematics. Does one conclude that parents are better instructors than certified teachers? Hardly. The research process might reveal ample opportunities for distortion of data combined with a faulty chain of logic rather than reasoned reflection. One common illogical argument might lead one to conclude that because two events occur together, one causes the other (e.g., that a concurrent sharp increase in the homeschooling of high school students and rise in SAT or ACT scores are directly related). If homeschooled students did outperform public school students, one might reasonably ask, Would the homeschooled students have performed even higher had they been in public school? Might a different subsample of homeschooled students, perhaps more representative, score lower than public school students? Would a different measure of achievement lead to different findings? The point is that educational data can be completely misinterpreted using noncritical thinking. Sound conclusions require reasoned reflection, that is, using logical reasoning while attending to alternative explanations (ones that can be ruled out with additional data). The use of noncritical thinking leaves us vulnerable to the misunderstandings favored by those who push pseudoscience, whereby claims are offered that *appear* to have a scientific basis but do not.

In addition to the cognitive skills of analysis and evaluation, Facione (1998) described several other abilities involved in critical thinking, including interpretation, inference, explanation, and self-regulation. *Interpretation* involves other skills, such as determining meaning and significance, and is itself aided by the clear formation of categories. Critical consumers of educational research can read published reports and sort the information rapid-fire into mental categories (e.g., qualitative case study, experimental intervention, etc.) supporting its interpretation (e.g., the study means that math skills often erode over the summer) and its significance (e.g., there is need for refresher sessions). *Inference* is a skill that requires identifying relevant information and drawing appropriate conclusions. Critical consumers of educational research might determine, for example, that all available evidence suggests that reducing class size does not necessarily lead to changes in students' achievement. *Explanation* involves describing and justifying reasoning. Critical consumers of educational research can describe valid findings and state the procedures used to determine such findings' validity (e.g., a generalized, widening achievement gap using multidimensional measures of achievement on representative samples). *Self-regulation* involves thinking about thinking (self-examination) and making appropriate corrections (self-correction). Critical consumers of educational research may ask themselves, "Does my bias influence my reactions to these findings?" or "Did I understand the implications of their research design?"

Overall, critical thinking in educational research involves examining research ideas and assessing the credibility of data-driven conclusions. One must judge the quality of the information gathered and weigh the evidence presented. Clear thinking and logic prevail, regardless of the astonishing variation in types of educational research. Quantitative ("statistics") research, for instance, involves deductive and inductive reasoning from theory toward verification (but never veering too far from theory). Qualitative (text or "metaphor") research, by comparison, involves "reasoning toward meaning" (or formal abduction), as described by Shank (2002). He believes that this type of practical reasoning in qualitative research is evident when we "make hunches, read clues, discern omens, diagnose symptoms, formulate patterns, and concoct explanations" (p. 119). Shank believes that clear "metaphorical thinking" (the use of the metaphor in reasoning) is especially valuable in qualitative research. Further, Shank believes that research is nothing more than "applied logic" with reasoning being "clear and careful." He offered three "visions" of critical thinking about research: (1) the "mirror," where critical thinking is sharp and reflective; (2) the "window," where critical thinking is simple and elegant; and (3) the "lantern," where critical thinking is flexible and creative (Shank, 2002, p. 125).

Critical thinking in education is one guard against the susceptibility to common fallacies, or errors in reasoning. Trochim (2000), for example, described two common ones: ecological fallacies and exception fallacies. *Ecological fallacies* occur when group data are used to make an inference about an individual. That a school has the highest reading scores does not suggest that every student at that school is a strong reader. Concluding that Bob, a student at the school, must not have reading difficulties would be an ecological fallacy. *Exception fallacies* result from generalized conclusions based on a single case. An observation of Bob's astonishing reading gains would not suggest that the teacher's approach works similarly for all students. There are many other fallacies that threaten the value of research in education, and these are explored in the chapters that follow. Diverse approaches to educational research and the clear thinking of educators hold the greatest promise for advancing the scientific basis of education.

HIGHLIGHT AND LEARNING CHECK 1-2

Careful Reasoning

Critical thinking in education involves careful reasoning about research and its implications. This includes being on watch for alternative explanations and possible misinterpretations of findings. Explain how the question "What else might explain these findings?" illustrates qualities of critical thinking.

In summary, we know that critical thinking is *careful* (watchful, cautious), *astute* (sharp, clear), and *analytical* (logical in the sense of examining interrelating elements to draw conclusions). Educators need critical thinking to assess the worth of claims about our understanding of a phenomenon (such as a widening achievement gap or increasing drop out rate). Most researchers in education would agree that critical thinking involves *conceptualization* (idea building), *synthesis* (putting together), *analysis* (pulling apart), and *evaluation* (judgment) of information obtained from reflection and observation (or experience), all leading to reasoned conclusions and implications. Such reasoning guards against fallacious thinking.

Educators as Reflective Practitioners

Educational administrators, counselors, and teachers are making steady progress in their own brand of research and critical thinking. Often dubbed *action research,* this approach to improving classrooms and schools centers on school professionals who use a variety of research methods with the intent of learning more about their practice and making immediate improvements based on the implications of data analysis. The potential to affect positive change is huge for classroom teachers who study their classroom learning processes. Teachers who adopt a "practice as inquiry" approach to their work find it natural to systematically examine their teaching by recording what was done (and why) and how it might be improved, collecting data to learn more about the practice, analyzing the data, and reflecting on the implications of findings for change. Few would argue that teachers are in the best position to institute data-driven improvements

REFLECTIVE TEACHING: Teachers thinking critically about the art and science of teaching, collecting data to test ideas, and revising their practice to solve classroom problems or improve learning.

in practice immediately. However, to do so they must understand the research process, how to take advantage of it, and ways to think clearly about the meaning of educational data.

Lest you remain unconvinced that teachers benefit from an understanding of research in education, consider one example of a reflective practitioner. High school chemistry teacher Carolyn Csongradi (1996) wondered how she might encourage more female students to enter the physical sciences. Her project involved integrating history, science, religion, and philosophy by asking students to read about the origins of scientific thought and the changing roles of women in science. Her review of the literature revealed that the pursuit of science by females might be hindered by a perception of male domination, fewer appropriate role models, possible test bias, and a historical trend that generally denied females an influence in the evolution of scientific thinking. Csongradi specifically structured an assignment "to take advantage of areas in which females have traditionally performed well—philosophy, history, and relationships." This was done in two phases. Phase I was an assignment that students were to complete using pen and paper. It required them to construct a comparative chart of Plato and Aristotle. Phase II involved a larger project answering five essay questions about the origins of scientific ideas, two of which required "female points of view." Students could work alone or in pairs. Csongradi collected various achievement data and used keen observations to shed light on how this educational practice might affect her male and female students.

What did she find with her 42 male and 48 female students? The data from Phase I (the comparative charts on paper) revealed that females scored significantly higher than males. Further, though not part of the formal analysis, an incidental finding was nonetheless interesting: Seven males versus one female failed to submit the assignment. Phase II data revealed no major differences between males and females, yet the highest scores overall (91%) were earned by females working alone and the lowest were earned by males and females working together in pairs (77%). Also of interest: Csongradi found males outperformed females on the final examination—100 multiple-choice questions. She noted that males and females had equal grades prior to the multiple-choice final exam.

Csongradi's working hypothesis suggested that females should outperform males on a project emphasizing writing, philosophy, and history. She concluded "in the main, this hypothesis was not supported" (Csongradi, 1996). Perhaps her most interesting (and unanticipated) finding emerged while reading students' work when "an additional variable became apparent." This variable was related to computer and peripheral equipment. Her follow-up survey of technology use for the Phase II project revealed that most students found online sources helpful. Yet Csongradi wondered whether computers, especially in the context of math and science courses, might foster a sense of "male domination." Her concluding observation is thought-provoking: "When the assignment [Phase I] did not involve computer use, the females not only had superior scores, but 16% of the males failed to do the work." Other teachers are prompted to investigate their own classroom dynamics by the title of Csongradi's action research, *How Technology Cheats Girls*, which leads back to the question, "Does technology cheat girls?"

I caught up with Carolyn Csongradi, who teaches at Palo Alto High School in California. We had a chance to talk about action research, and a portion of an interview appears on page 10.

INTERVIEW WITH CAROLYN CSONGRADI

1. Question: You were using online research tools via the Internet well before the Web became commonplace in many schools. You were also conducting classroom research well before the teacher action research and reflective practitioner movement became widely known. What is your vision for the next decade or so? Will teacher research become commonplace?

Answer: [It is important] to encourage teachers to be active as practitioners—that is, to routinely engage in action research on a regular basis. Action research can be a simple as my asking questions about a teaching practice, gathering data informally, and then reflecting on what I've learned from the student data. Sometimes when I read what another teacher has published in an action research journal I think "I don't have time to do that." The reality is that good teachers do action research informally on a small scale many times during the year, and in fact, on a daily basis. We just need to be more conscious of what we are doing so that we can see the outcomes more clearly. For instance, as a science teacher I'm constantly trying new labs, redesigning them as I discover what works and what doesn't in terms of achieving particular content objectives. That's action research on a small scale.

Changing teaching practices in my experience is something I do by a process of self-discovery in my own classroom. Teacher action research is accomplished in diverse formats, sometimes unconsciously and sometimes more formally. When I teach three sections of the same subject, I will modify a new lesson plan throughout the day until I find what works best. In a way, this is teacher action research. When presented in this way, it sounds so much less intimidating.

By 2015 our classrooms will be addressing a more diverse population, creating opportunities for us to explore in a systematic way via action research what teaching strategies are more effective in improving students' learning. The classroom teacher will have a profound role in this bigger picture.

2. Question: In what ways can teacher action research not only improve classroom practice but enhance the whole profession of teaching?

Answer: Teachers believe college and professional development is often limited to what is offered by school districts. Action research represents a way in which teachers can renew their education and continue to grow both intellectually and professionally without formal courses.

3. Question: Many teachers are probably thinking "I can barely accomplish my own instructional tasks. Now they want me to do classroom research on top of it all. No way!" Can you think of ways to encourage classroom research in view of all the other teaching demands?

Answer: We are doing this every day. What we need to do is recognize that is what is happening and have some time to reflect on it.

4. Question: Teacher action research is said to be collaborative—students and teachers working together. How can this type of collaboration be useful for your own students?

Answer: I think the collaboration happens both formally and informally. Sometimes it is merely a question-and-answer discussion. Other times, it's reading lab notebooks or an essay.

(Continued)

5. Question: Can you describe any other benefits of reflective teachers conducting classroom research?

Answer: One of the key benefits for me is one of relieving what has been the inevitable burnout and boredom that comes from working with adolescents and being somewhat academically isolated. I have left the classroom more than once because the job has grown stale. Action research has enabled me to stay enthusiastic and engaged in the profession of teaching.

6. Question: Your research revealed that some female high school students may be less interested [than their male counterparts] in online interactive computer research tools. Does your recent experience suggest that females are less likely to enter physical science fields such as chemistry?

Answer: My classes are evenly balanced with respect to males and females; females do well in the course. However, I am careful to test with a variety of instruments. Consistently, females do better on free-response items and less well on multiple-choice items than do males. This was true in 1996 and remains true in 2005. If one designs all test instruments as multiple choice, I imagine that would discourage female students. My tests use a variety of formats.

My last unit test in honors chemistry had the usual combination of multiple-choice and free-response test items. Once again, I observed a disparity: Females score lower on multiple-choice items but higher on free-response items. I interviewed several tenth-grade girls and discovered that the multiple-choice format has an either-or character about it. One issue seems to be the difficulty eliminating incorrect distractors. What I suspect is that some of my girls lack a good test-taking strategy for a multiple-choice format. It is very intriguing to ask why this is so, and whether it is true in other subjects or more so in physical science. I remain convinced that we often pursue careers in which we are successful because they offer psychological rewards. If students do poorly on tests, I suspect they are less likely to pursue that subject area as a career.

Teacher Researchers as Critical Thinkers

Because critical thinking involves keen observation and reflection plus the cognitive skills associated with analysis and evaluation, it can be said that teacher action researchers are critical thinkers. Examples of their work reveal why this is the case. Diane Painter (2000), for example, studied how students who use higher order thinking skills developed expanded expectations of their learning. She stated,

> I decided to conduct a teacher research project to investigate what happens when students have the opportunity to set their own goals and objectives, and work together to research a topic of their own choosing . . . I wanted to look closely at the student interactions, the literacy and cooperative learning skills the student exhibit, and reflect upon [their work] within the realm of the constructivist philosophy of teaching.

Painter's review of the literature on brain research suggested that educators "provide many opportunities for varied learners to make sense of ideas and information" in a context where challenge is moderate. Painter's after-school computer club provided the ideal study site where students were challenged to develop their own knowledge rather than receiving prepackaged information in a workbook. She observed that the school's computer club was a social activity forming a knowledge-building community as well as a medium for "storing, organizing, and reformulating" ideas. This description conforms to a constructivist model of learning. By looking at Painter's results and analysis of the after-school program, other teachers may easily recognize how key components of extracurricular activities might be incorporated into daily lessons as a means to encourage all students in creative problem solving.

Reflective teacher Kristina Hedberg (2002) also provided an illustration of critical thinking in the classroom. As a fourth-grade teacher of English for Speakers of Other Languages (ESOL), Hedberg was intent on developing a strategy to enhance students' comprehension and retention of content in a social studies curriculum. Her analysis of the complex learning process convinced her of the "importance of tapping into students' prior knowledge." After carefully considering the factors that impact her students' reading comprehension, she decided on a method (SQ3R, meaning survey, question, read, recite, and review) that capitalized on students' using their background knowledge to attach meaning to new information, hence increasing its retention. Hedberg used multiple sources of data (*triangulation*) to answer several research questions, and after inspecting patterns and trends, she carefully drew conclusions based on her observations. She concluded that "the data collected while using SQ3R method show evidence of affecting these ESOL students' content reading behavior in a positive manner." Hedberg also provided data to support her interpretation that students' comprehension increased in large part because they were "interacting with the text in a more meaningful way."

HIGHLIGHT AND LEARNING CHECK 1-3

Practice as Inquiry

Teacher action researchers are scientists in their classrooms. They use critical thinking to test ideas by collecting data and revising their practice. Explain how you could adopt a "practice as inquiry" philosophy in the classroom to illustrate an educator's role as a reflective practitioner with skill in critical thinking.

Here is another example of one teacher's critical thinking in the classroom. Kindergarten and first-grade teacher Gail Ritchie (2000) thought about ways to meet state history standards of learning in a play-based classroom. Her data collection included careful observations in the form of student interviews, surveys, responses to open-ended questions, and products that revealed learning; parent questionnaires; photographs and videotapes; and field notes and reflective memories. Ritchie's critical thinking was revealed by her reflective journals and her analysis of the entries that noted the significance of her data. Her evaluation of the efforts to teach required objectives through play led not only to her conclusion that play-based strategies were effectively meeting required history objectives but also to her discovery of the value of "spiraling" to help her young students build stronger mental connections among abstractions.

Other teachers also use critical thinking in action research to advantage. Sally Bryan (2000) compared learning outcomes in a traditional classroom and an inquiry-oriented, project-based classroom that focused on student-centered utilization of knowledge. Angie McGlinchey (2002) wondered how nutrition instruction and student knowledge affected the eating habits of fifth graders. Barbara Poole and

Kerry Smith (2000) wondered, "What motivates children to read independently?" Curran Roller (1998) asked, "How is the learning process affected by the inclusion of graphing calculators in the trigonometry & math analysis curriculum?" Finally, Tonya Baskerville and Tamie Campbell (1999) wondered whether students would learn better if they were aware of their strongest learning styles.

Especially noteworthy are critical thinking teachers Karen Dellett, Georgene Fromm, and Susan Karn and advisor Ann Cricchi (1999), who developed critical thinking skills among their own third- and fourth-grade students. Here is a portion of their research summary (or abstract):

> Our research was designed to investigate what happens when third and fourth grade students learn and apply strategies to develop metacognitive behaviors. Data analysis focused on student responses in thinking journals. Additional data was gathered from such sources as surveys, reflective chats, and field notes. By incorporating thinking strategies in our classrooms we observed a shift in student behavior. Students demonstrated increased self-reliance, a new awareness of thinking capabilities, an ability to make connections to prior knowledge, the ability to take a risk as they explored solutions to particular problems, and an emerging awareness of thinking strategies. Through this process we realized that our professional practice was impacted as much, if not more, than our students' emerging understanding of how they think.

All of the teacher research projects described in this section were culled from the Teacher Research Home Web site of the Graduate School of Education at George Mason University in Fairfax, Virginia. This entire collection displays how teachers reflect on and evaluate their practice, pose a researchable question, analyze collected data to uncover patterns, consider alternative explanations, and reach sound conclusions given the data at hand. Teacher action researchers use a large variety of research strategies to answer their questions. These diversified research methods and techniques—and the scientific thinking that accompanies them—are covered in some detail in the remaining chapters.

HIGHLIGHT AND LEARNING CHECK 1-4

Teacher Action Researchers

The claim is made that teacher action researchers are critical thinkers. Explain how data collection in the classroom illustrates many components of critical thinking.

Inconsistencies in Research

Teacher action researchers, reflective practitioners, and critical consumers of research are often frustrated by the simple fact that scientists appear to constantly change their minds! Making sense of inconsistencies in research is a challenge for researchers and reflective practitioners alike. The challenged is lessened by astute, critical thinking.

It is quite common for two research studies, both designed to answer the same question, to yield different findings and opposite conclusions. The most likely explanation can be found in the *design* and *procedural* differences between the two studies.

Consider a clear example from the field of medicine. In 1985, the *New England Journal of Medicine* published back-to-back studies designed to answer the question "Does estrogen use in post menopausal women affect the risk of heart disease?" One study involving more than 1200 women reported that estrogen use increases the risk of heart disease (Wilson, Garrison, & Castelli, 1985), while the second study, involving more than 32,000 women, reported that estrogen use decreases the risk of heart disease (Stampfer et al., 1985). How can these contradictory findings be explained? By a catastrophic error in analysis? No, not usually. By fundamental differences in the methods used to answer the question? Yes, very likely. And what differences are the most likely explanations? The answer to this question is explored in the following paragraphs.

DISCREPANT FINDINGS: Research outcomes that are inconsistent (or in opposition) across studies. Such findings are often explained by differences in research methods and procedures.

Very often, one finds differences in *instrumentation*, or the process of collecting data in a research study. In the estrogen research, one study used mailed questionnaires to collect data, while the other study used physical examinations and "brass instruments." Faced with a questionnaire, you might check "No" to the question, "Have you had any cardiac disorders in the past 5 years?" A physician checking an EKG recording, however, may have a very different answer to that question. And what about chest pain? It may be interpreted as indigestion on a questionnaire but as angina by a doctor who asks other questions.

Other differences in the estrogen studies included the period of follow up (4 versus 8 years). Estrogen might decrease the risk of heart disease when used for a short period of time and then increase the risk when used for a longer period of time.

Another explanation for opposing conclusions may be found in *sampling*, or the process used to select research participants. This is a likely explanation because estrogen use might lower the risk of heart disease in one group of people but increase it in another group with different characteristics. One study collected data from women aged 30 to 55, while the other used women aged 50 to 83. Estrogen use may have a protective effect for nonsmokers but a harmful effect for smokers. Does estrogen affect diabetics differently? Might it affect differently those with a family history of heart disease? The list of intervening sample characteristics is almost endless.

Yet another explanation for opposing conclusions may be found in the *intervention*, or the process of manipulating the treatment conditions. In the estrogen example, its influence may depend on the type (natural versus synthetic) or dosage of estrogen, with small amounts showing a protective effect and larger amounts showing a harmful effect. The research of hormone replacement therapy on women's health has had a particularly rocky road. Early studies of its influence on breast cancer risk were, as expected, mixed, yet one large study at Stanford University was halted prematurely due to the dramatic but clear emerging finding: Hormone replacement therapy increases breast cancer risk (Richter, 2002). The reason for this single study's influence on recommendations was its large scope and unprecedented level of control over potentially contaminating influences.

Contradictory studies abound in the health sciences—and in education. Opposing results in a drug study, for example, are due to differences in administration, dose, frequency, length of time on the drug, patient differences (age, sex, health, etc.), when measures are collected, the type of measures collected, the follow-up interval, definitions (e.g., how pain, fatigue, menopause, etc. are defined), the reason for exclusion, statistical methods, biases, placebo influences, and so on. The same research question, three different studies, three different outcomes, three different conclusions—it is all very common. Just look at the variation in diet research if you need more convincing. And this is an example where there are fewer complications surrounding the outcome measure, that is, the simple recording of pounds lost. Imagine the added complexity in education where there is often little agreement (huge variation) in measured outcomes like achievement. So what does lead to weight loss, according to the research? Well, it depends, of course, on all the factors built into the research study itself, such as time frame (short-term versus long-term weight loss), subject characteristics, and co-occurring activities like exercise.

These differences in instrumentation, sampling, and intervention (among others) have counterparts in educational research. For example, cooperative learning efforts as implemented by one particular teacher may have positive effects on a very specific outcome with only one type of student. A change in any one of these factors may offset or possibly reverse the positive effect. The truth, which is often frustrating, seems to be that there are few, if any, educational interventions that influence all types of students equally. That is why the most common answer to the question "What is the effect of ______ on students?" is probably "It depends." (You can fill in the blank with all sorts of variables in education such as class size, teacher training, homework, scheduling, teaching style, and on and on.) Other areas of "frustrating" educational research (discrepant findings) include learning to read, charter school influences on achievement, teacher preparation programs and its outcomes, and class size and its relationship to learning (among many others). The learning-to-read research, in fact, has boiled over to what is commonly called the "reading research wars."

HIGHLIGHT AND LEARNING CHECK 1-5

Opposing Data

Research findings on many, if not most, topics in education are "inconsistent." Explain why researchers answering the same research question can produce opposing data and reach different conclusions.

CRITICAL THINKER ALERT 1-1

Inconsistent Research

Research results are often contradictory. Research inconsistencies are to be expected because results are a function of how research is designed, conducted, and analyzed. Further, even similar findings are subject to different interpretations, sometimes radically so.

Discussion: How might three studies of, for example, class size and student achievement, show that reduction in class size increases achievement, decreases achievement, and leaves achievement unaffected? What study differences might explain these discrepant findings? Try another research topic, such as the impact of charter schools on student achievement.

Chapter Summary

Making educational research accessible is the goal of this book, and learning about research involves new ways of thinking. Researchers improve the quality of education by increasing their knowledge of the art and science of teaching and the process of learning. Practitioners acquire this knowledge by reading published research reports. Evaluating research enables one to make sound decisions about applying educational research to practice. Critical thinking about research is a developed skill. A thinking-skills approach to educational research views educators as reflective practitioners and teacher researchers as critical thinkers. Many educators' ideas about research are challenged by a deeper understanding of its process, and as a result, they begin to understand why research results can be so maddeningly contradictory and inconclusive. Critical thinkers understand that inconsistent or opposing research findings in education are largely a function of methodology—how research is designed and carried out. Other factors that explain research discrepancies are topics explored in the remaining chapters.

Application Exercises

1. Visit the What Works Clearinghouse (WWC), "the trusted source for what works in education" (http://www.w-w-c.org/). The What Works Clearinghouse was founded in 2002 by the U.S. Department of Education's Institute of Education Sciences (IES) to provide a central source for information on program and practice effectiveness in education. It uses the most rigorous standards of scientific research applied to education in its evaluations and recommendations. You might also visit the RAND Corporation's Promising Practices Network (http://www.promisingpractices.net/). It also describes programs and practices that credible research suggests are effective in improving learning and adjustment outcomes for students and families. Because both sites are fully grounded in scientific evidence, the importance of this information can be linked directly to the value of research. What programs and practices described at one or both of these sites strike you as especially significant, ones that highlight the value of research? Why?

2. Using the same resources in your library or on the Internet, find two studies that present findings that contradict each other. Then try to explain how it is possible that the two studies could yield contradictory results. Hint: This is not as difficult as you might think. Two studies could be located by reading a third study in an area of interest. Authors of the third study in their review of previous research in the beginning of their article will often cite several studies revealing one outcome and several others that reveal a different outcome. Find one in each opposing group and examine the study differences carefully in an attempt to explain the opposition.

Log on to the Web-based student study site at http://www.sagepub.com/eic for more information about the materials presented in this chapter, suggestions for activities, study aids such as electronic flashcards and review quizzes, a sample research proposal, and research recommendations that include journal article links (with discussion questions and an article evaluation guide) and questions related to this chapter.

2

Thinking About Research

Outline

Overview

Chapter 1 introduced a thinking-skills approach to educational research, one that views teachers as critical, reflective practitioners poised to apply findings from research in education. Chapter 1 also revealed that thinking like a researcher is an acquired skill enhanced by practice. This chapter introduces some powerful concepts that critical consumers of educational research can use to understand the research process. This chapter also begins to demystify the process and provides several clues to answering the puzzling question "Why are research findings so discrepant?" One major clue is found in the powerful concept of control (or lack of it).

Sharpen Your Thinking About Research: Powerful Ideas

As educators, you probably have your own ideas about research, even though you may not think about them in a formal way. Your ideas were probably garnered from all types of scientific research in diverse fields of study, not solely from education. Medical research, it seems, attracts more news media than many other fields of study, so some of what you already know about the research process may be the result of widely disseminated medical or health-related research findings. Many principles in research, like control, are in fact broadly applicable, as they are embedded in the scientific research process in general and shared by the fields of education, psychology, nursing, business, communications, sociology, neuroscience, political science, biology, and hundreds of other fields. As you will see in this chapter, however, education poses unique challenges for scientific researchers. Educational research requires developing new methods of inquiry and adjusting our thinking somewhat from the simplistic ideas conveyed by news reports of findings in the area of health and medicine.

Are Biases in Research Obvious?

The Amazing Randi

Consumers of research in many fields of inquiry mistakenly believe that biases in empirical studies are usually obvious and can nearly always be detected, even by those without special training. Consider a dramatic example from medicine, but one with direct implications for research in education. In 1988, the journal *Nature* published a celebrated research study (Davenas et al., 1988) with remarkable claims made in support of a discredited branch of medicine known as homeopathy (the use of very dilute substances to cure a disease which, at full strength, would cause the disease in healthy people). *Nature* agreed to publish these findings if a team assembled by the journal could observe a *replication* (or repetition) of the experiments. One member of the observation team was particularly interesting: James Randi, also known as The Amazing Randi, a professional psychic debunker. A magician by training, The Amazing Randi successfully uncovers the tricks used by frauds who claim to have psychic powers. The homeopathic researchers never claimed to have such powers, but the *Nature* team believed that the researchers may have been less than careful, and without the researchers' knowledge or awareness may have allowed a source of bias to creep in and somehow influence the findings in unintentional ways. The real issue was not fraud but contaminating bias so subtle that it was beyond the researchers' level of awareness.

RESEARCH BIAS: Distortion of data collected in a research study that is explained by unwanted influences stemming from observers, research participants, procedures and settings, or researchers themselves.

The homeopathic experiments were replicated under the watchful eyes of The Amazing Randi with the appropriate controls for experimenter bias such as *blinding* (or being "in the dark"), whereby the researchers were kept unaware of which conditions were supposed to (according to homeopathic theory) result in higher measurements. With these controls (and others) in place, the *Nature* observers found that the homeopathic effects disappeared and concluded that the original, positive findings were the result of experimenter bias. The scientific community, including educational researchers, benefited from the reminder that some contaminating biases are so subtle that their discovery requires keen perception, like that of the caliber of James Randi's. All consumers of research, it seems, must be aware of the perils of "wishful science."

Clever Hans

The introduction of subtle influences beneath the awareness of those responsible is not a new discovery. About 100 years ago in Germany, a horse named Hans bewildered spectators with displays of unusual intelligence, especially in math (Pfungst, 1911). The horse's owner, von Osten, tested Hans in front of an audience by holding up flash cards. Hans would, for example, see "4 + 5" and commence to tap his hoof 9 times for a correct answer. Hans would even answer a flash card problem showing, say, "1/4 + 1/2" by tapping 3 times then 4 times. Amazing! said the crowds and reporters. Worldwide fame was bestowed on the animal now known as "Clever Hans."

CONTROL: The idea that procedures used in research can minimize bias, neutralize threats to validity, rule out alternative explanations, and help establish cause-and-effect relationships.

This remarkable display lasted several years before the truth was uncovered by Oskar Pfungst, a psychologist with training in—you guessed it—the scientific method. Pfungst revealed that Clever Hans responded to very subtle cues from von Osten—cues that von Osten himself was oblivious to. Body posture and facial cues (like raised eyebrows, widened eyes, flared nostrils) were the inevitable result of the owner's excitement as the hoof tapping approached the correct number. When the right number was tapped, the height of excitement was displayed all over von Osten's face. This, then, became the signal to stop tapping. Once the research-oriented psychologist put in place the appropriate controls, like showing the flash cards to the horse only (not to von Osten, who was therefore "blind"), then the hoof tapping began to look more like random responses. Clever Hans didn't seem so clever after all. Von Osten himself was never accused of

HIGHLIGHT AND LEARNING CHECK 2-1

Overlooking Bias

The history of science in many fields, including education, reveals numerous examples of biases that created significant distortions in data leading to erroneous conclusions. Explain how biases, either subtle or not, can be overlooked by researchers.

being a fraud, for the communication was below his awareness (and imperceptible to spectators). Although the Clever Hans phenomenon was not discovered in a research setting, it is a valuable reminder that one cannot be too careful when investigating all types of effects, from magic in medicine to genius in horses.

Little Emily

Good science with careful controls requires clear thinking—not necessarily adulthood and a Ph.D. in rocket science. This was shown by 9-year-old Emily Rosa in a fourth-grade science project (Lemonick, 1998). In fact, her study was published in the prestigious *Journal of the American Medical Association* (Rosa, Rosa, Sarner, & Barrett, 1998). Journal editor George Lundberg reminds us that age doesn't matter: "It's good science that matters, and this is good science." Her newsworthy study debunked therapeutic touch (TT), a medical practice that claims to heal by manipulating patients' "energy fields." Lemonick (1998) reported that many TT-trained practitioners wave their hands above the patient's body in an attempt to rearrange energy fields into balance in order to heal wounds, relieve pain, and reduce fever. Emily's study was simple. A sample of TT therapists placed their hands out of sight behind a screen. Emily then flipped a coin, its outcome to determine which TT therapist's hand (left or right) she would place her own hand over. She reasoned that the TT practitioners should have the ability to feel her own energy above one of their hands. Each practitioner was then asked to report which hand was feeling her energy. After she tallied her results, it was determined that the therapists did no better than chance, suggesting it was all guesswork.

Lemonick (1998) also reported that Emily, being a young scientist, knew that her test must be generalized, by being repeated under varying situations and with other subjects, before its results would be considered definitive. Nevertheless, her findings do cast doubt on TT advocates' claims about how TT works and, by contrast, do support the power of the placebo effect (i.e., wishful thinking while receiving special medical attention). Simply, one of the most important ingredients to good science is control. Emily's one well-controlled yet simple study was more valuable than a hundred studies with poor control. In this case, Emily's "special training" was clear thinking about science.

CRITICAL THINKER ALERT 2-1

Bias

Research results are never 100% free and clear of bias. Culture, prior experiences, beliefs, attitudes, and other preconceived ways of thinking about the research topic influences how a research project is designed and how the results are interpreted. No interpretation occurs on a neutral "blank slate."

Discussion: Do you believe that research in education and its interpretation can be influenced by political factors? In what ways might political orientation influence research in education and its impact?

Interpretations or Misinterpretations?

Consumers of research might believe that sloppy reasoning and misinterpretations of data occur rarely. This is not correct. Misinterpretations of data are actually quite common, and instances of flawed reasoning abound. Let's consider a few examples.

Iowa First

In an attempt to show the waste of simply throwing money at education to increase educational productivity (such as higher achievement test scores), a nationally known columnist recently cited the "Iowa first phenomenon" in support of his argument. Iowa, the argument goes, scored highest in the nation on the SAT (according to the columnist's latest reports), but did not rank high in terms of state per-pupil expenditure. Is this a meaningful comparison? No, according to Powell (1993), especially when you consider that *only about 5% of the high school seniors in Iowa took the SAT.* Most took the ACT (the American College Testing program is headquartered in Iowa). A select few took the SAT in pursuit of universities beyond their borders—such as Stanford, Yale, and Harvard. This academically talented group inflated the SAT average, which is meaningless when compared with, for example, the SAT average of students in New Jersey (home of the ETS, which administers the SAT). New Jersey at that time ranked high in per-pupil expenditure but relatively low in SAT scores. It was no surprise, then, that according to research reports at the time, the majority (76%) of New Jersey high school seniors, including the less academically able, took the SAT. Simply, state-by-state rankings of score averages make little sense when the composition of the population taking the tests varies so widely.

Pygmalion

Some of the most widely known and influential studies conducted in the social sciences also illustrate the problem of data misinterpretation. In education, perhaps the most dramatic example is Robert Rosenthal and Lenore Jacobson's experiment with teachers' self-fulfilling prophecies. This study, described in their book *Pygmalion in the Classroom: Teacher Expectation and Pupils' Intellectual Development* (1968), received a tremendous amount of media coverage and remains one of the most frequently cited studies ever conducted in the broad social sciences. The study suggested that children's intelligence can increase merely in response to teachers' *expectation* that it will do so.

Unfortunately, the media frenzy over this experiment overshadowed the scientific criticism occurring in less accessible outlets (Elashoff & Snow, 1971; Wineburg, 1987). Richard Snow (1969), for example, observed that in Rosenthal and Jacobson's original data, one student whose IQ was expected to increase moved from 17 to 148! Another student's IQ jumped from 18 to 122! Because IQs hover around 100 and rarely exceed the boundaries of 70 to 130, one can only conclude that the original set of data was flawed and meaningless. The idea of teachers' self-fulfilling prophecies took hold despite the data errors, however, and continues to the present day. (There is ample evidence that teachers do have expectations of student performance based on seemingly irrelevant characteristics and that they may behave in accordance with those expectations. There is less evidence, however, that students' measured intelligence can spurt in the manner originally suggested by Rosenthal and Jacobson's interpretation of the data.)

Hawthorne

One of psychology's best known research biases—the Hawthorne effect—is also a case study in the misinterpretation of data. The Hawthorne effect was "discovered" during a series of experiments at the Hawthorne Western Electric plant from 1924 to 1932. This effect refers to a subject's exhibiting a change in behavior as a result of simply being studied. It is also referred to as the *novelty* effect or the *guinea pig* effect and is generally believed to stem from the increased attention that research subjects receive during the course of a study. The Hawthorne effect suggests that an increase in workers' production levels attributed to, for example, the installation of a conveyer belt, could actually stem from the attention they received from being studied in response to a change (any change). Whatever the cause, the Hawthorne experiments are believed to be a major impetus in the launching of industrial psychology as a discipline.

The major findings of this study (Roethlisberger & Dickson, 1939) were interpreted *impressionistically* by the researchers, and because the Hawthorne effect became so entrenched in the minds of other researchers, it wasn't until 50 years later that the original data were analyzed objectively and statistically (Franke & Kaul, 1978). Remarkably, Chadwick, Bahr, and Albrecht (1984) reported that "the findings of this first statistical interpretation of the Hawthorne studies are in direct and dramatic opposition to the findings for which the study is famous" (p. 273). In other words, an objective analysis revealed (at least in these "data") that the Hawthorne effect was a myth. In truth, there may be a Hawthorne effect in other contexts, but we know that its existence is not supported by the original Hawthorne data. Research "findings" sometimes take on a life of their own, often having little or no connection to the original data.

Reading Wars

Perhaps the most contemporary (and controversial) instances of claims related to data misinterpretation and misuse are found in the 2000 publication of the National Reading Panel Report (National Institute of Child Health and Human Development, 2000). Congress in 1997 requested a national panel to convene and evaluate the scientific literature on different approaches used to teach beginning readers. The National Reading Panel (NRP) spent 2 years assessing the research-based knowledge on reading instruction, and in 2000 published its conclusions in the "Report of the National Reading Panel: Teaching Children to Read." The report, which was intended to be useful to the Reading First initiative of the 2001 No Child Left Behind federal legislation, was instantly controversial due to charges that data were grossly misinterpreted (among other factors).

HIGHLIGHT AND LEARNING CHECK 2-2

Different Interpretations

Data collected in educational research do not interpret themselves. Explain how two reasonable researchers may offer different interpretations of the same data.

The title of one critic's article in *Education Week* provides a glimpse into the source of controversy: "I Told You So! The Misinterpretation and Misuse of the National Reading Panel Report" (Yatvin, 2003, p. 56).

Other Examples

Yet another example of data misinterpretation in the area of reading was described by Coles (2004) who claimed that the "brain glitch" research connecting brain activity and learning to read had been thoroughly misunderstood. He reported "danger" in classrooms applying this research, fueled by "political power" aligned with "shame science" and "brainless instruction."

This misinterpretation of data reminds me of an old story about the psychologist who trained a flea to jump on command. This psychologist then investigated what effect removing a leg from the flea, one at a time, would have on its ability to jump. He found that even with one leg, the flea could jump at the command "Jump!" Upon removing the flea's last leg, he found that the flea made no attempt to jump. After thinking about this outcome for awhile, he wrote up his findings and concluded, "When a flea has all legs removed, it becomes deaf." His finding was indeed consistent with that interpretation, but it is simply not the most reasonable one.

CRITICAL THINKER ALERT 2-2

Misinterpretation

Misinterpretation of research results occurs all the time—and not just by the popular media. Every research finding requires cautious and tentative interpretations. Different interpretations of the same finding are common.

Discussion: Presume a researcher finds that a new program in all county high schools is linked to higher standardized math scores but higher dropout rates and more time spent teaching to the test. Is this evidence of the program's effectiveness?

Control in Experimentation: Compared to What?

One might believe incorrectly that control groups in research are considered a luxury and are not needed to evaluate the effectiveness of new interventions. Control groups serve a vital function by enabling researchers who test new methods to answer the question "Compared to what?" Let's consider a dramatic example in medicine once again to illustrate this point. Assume a researcher wanted to test the effectiveness of acupuncture on lower back pain. She recruited 100 patients with such pain and asked them to rate their pain on a 1 to 10 scale before undergoing acupuncture 3 times a week for 10 weeks. At the end of the 10 weeks, the patients rated their back pain once again, and, as expected by the researcher, the pain was greatly reduced. She concluded that acupuncture was effective for reducing low back pain.

Are there other explanations for this finding? You bet, and the researcher should have *controlled* for these alternative, rival explanations with appropriate control groups before any conclusions were drawn. For starters, what about the mere passage of time? Is not time one of the best healers for many conditions? Maybe these patients would have had greatly reduced back pain 10 weeks later if they had done nothing. (Have you ever had a backache? Did it go away without any treatment? Undoubtedly, yes.) A good control for this explanation would be a 10-week "waiting list" control group which simply waited for the acupuncture in the absence of any treatment.

HIGHLIGHT AND LEARNING CHECK 2-3

Comparison Groups

Researchers often use comparison groups to answer the question "Compared to what?" This is because a change in a "treatment" group by itself is often difficult to interpret. Explain why a treatment group's scores may change over time without the influence of any "treatment." Can *no* change in a treatment group be evidence of a treatment effect? Explain.

What about the effect due to simply resting 3 times a week for 10 weeks? Or an effect due to the awareness of undergoing an alternative treatment? Or an effect due to lying down on a special acupuncture table? Or an effect due to simply piercing the skin? An appropriate control in these instances would be a group treated *exactly* the same as the acupuncture group, including having their skin pierced superficially while lying down 3 times a week on a special acupuncture platform. In fact, members of this group should not be aware that they are in the control group. In the jargon of research, this is referred to as *blinding* the control to the influence stemming from the awareness of special treatment. This control group, then, controls for the influence of time, resting prone during the day, receiving special attention, and many other factors as well, including the simple *expectation* that pain will go away. (In this book, the labels *control group* and *comparison group* are used interchangeably since no attempt is made to differentiate between them. The labels *experimental group* and *treatment group* are used interchangeably for the same reason.)

The value, or necessity, of placebo groups as a control is most obvious in medical research. New treatments in medicine must be compared to something; they are often compared to traditional treatments or placebo groups. Thompson (1999) reported how medical researchers tested the usefulness of implanting cells harvested from embryos into the brains of those with Parkinson's disease to replace those cells killed by the disease. Imagine being in the placebo group for this study: You are prepped for surgery and sedated. A hole is then drilled through your skull. Without receiving any embryonic cells, your surgeons sew you up and send him you home. Controversial, yes, but not from the perspective of control.

We know that the *placebo effect,* an effect resulting from the mere thought (like wishful thinking) that co-occurs with receiving a drug or some other treatment, can exert powerful influences in pain, sleep, depression, and so on. The effect was discovered on the World War II battlefields when injured soldiers experienced pain relief after they mistakenly thought they were getting morphine; in fact, they were simply getting saline solution. But can there be a placebo effect in Parkinson's disease? Evidently so. Most medical societies do indeed endorse the use of such fake surgeries as a necessary means for learning about cause and effect. How else can we learn about a treatment's effectiveness? There is often a tension between research ethics and tight scientific controls, as in the case of the Parkinson's disease study. The researchers' need to control for patients' wishful thinking was met by the "sham" (placebo) surgery, but the patients also got a chance for real help. After the study was completed, the sham surgery patients received the embryo cells in the same manner as the treatment patients. The Parkinson's study should convince you that good medical science is not possible without control. The same is true for educational research, as you'll see in this textbook.

Consider another example of the value of a control group (again in medicine). Arthroscopic knee surgery is supposed to relieve arthritic pain for about 300,000 Americans each year. The only problem, according to Horowitz (2002), is that it does no good. This conclusion is based on what Horowitz referred to as a "rarely used but devastatingly effective test: sham surgery." She reported that researchers "randomly assigned some patients to undergo the surgery while other patients were wheeled into the operating room, sedated, given superficial incisions (accompanied by the commands and operating room noises they would hear if the real surgery were taking place), patched up and sent home." The result, she reported, is that fake surgery worked as well as the real one, given that 2 years later there was no difference between the two groups in terms of pain, mobility, and so on (Moseley, 2002).

CRITICAL THINKER ALERT 2-3

Control Groups

Control groups allow researchers to answer the question "Compared to what?" Because the mere passage of time is a great healer in medicine and patient expectations influence outcomes, untreated ("placebo") groups are needed to assess treatment effects above and beyond time and expectations. The same concept applies in educational research, although time and expectations are combined with hundreds of other extraneous factors.

Discussion: Why is it so difficult in education to utilize a classic control group, the kind used, for example, in clinical trials to assess a drug's influence? Is the clinical drug trial in research the most appropriate model to use in education?

Can You Trust Intuition?

Most people, including researchers, have poor intuitive abilities when it comes to estimating the probability of random outcomes, hence there is an obvious need for statistical tests that calculate the probability of chance events. Intuitive guesses are often wrong, and sometimes incredibly so. Consider these two well known paradoxical puzzles:

1. I bet that in a room with 25 people there are at least 2 with the same birthday. Want to bet?

2. There are three closed doors, with a new car behind one and nothing behind the others. I know which door hides the car. You choose a door, then I open another one that shows there is nothing. Do you want to stick with your original choice, or do you want to switch to the other closed door?

Because statistical judgments are often way off, you are better off not betting in the birthday problem. The odds are 50-50—even odds—for a birthday match with 23 people in a room. With 25 people, the odds slightly favor a birthday match. And with 35 people, for example, the odds are overwhelming that there will be a match. Here's an explanation using 23 people: Imagine Person 1 having 22 chances for a birthday match, Person 2 having 21 chances for a match, Person 3 having 20 chances for a match, Person 4 having 19 chances for a match, and so on. The chances mount up quickly, don't they? These additive chances will equal about 50-50 with 23 people. Many people make intuitive judgments that lead to a losing bet, thinking erroneously that there must be 365 people (or perhaps half that number) for equal odds. A fraction of that number, like 50, yields a match with close to 100% certainty (but you can never be 100% sure!). (Over the years, I've noticed that teachers in the lower grades, like kindergarten and first grade, are not at all surprised by the birthday matching problem. The reason, I believe, is that teachers at these levels tend to recognize birthdays in the classroom, and with classes of over 20 students, there are often days when two birthdays are celebrated.)

INTUITION: A belief without an empirical basis. Research findings often contradict intuitive beliefs.

In the door problem above, you'd better switch. If you stay with your original choice, the chance of winning is .33. If you switch, the chance is .66. Honestly. Think of it this way. You either pick one door and stay with it for good (1/3 chance), or you can pick the other two doors (as a bundle) and I'll even show you which one of the other two it isn't before you make your selection (obviously avoiding the one it isn't). Put that way, the choice is obvious. I'll take that bundle of two. Rephrasing a problem, without changing the problem itself, often leads to more intelligent decisions. Much more information about this problem, termed the "Monty Hall Dilemma," can be found in vos Savant (2002), who was responsible for bringing this problem to light and generating great interest among scientists and lay readers.

Here's another counterintuitive problem: Among women aged 40 to 50, the probability that a woman has breast cancer is .8% (8/10 of 1%). If she has breast cancer, the probability is 90% she will have a positive mammogram. If she does not have breast cancer, the probability is 7% that she will still have a positive mammogram. If a woman does have a positive mammogram, then the probability she actually does have breast cancer is indeed very high. True or False? (This problem is adapted from Gigerenzer, 2002.) The answer is False. Think in frequencies, with rounding over the long run. Of 1,000 women, 8 will have breast cancer. Of these 8, 7 will have a positive mammogram. Of the remaining 992 who don't have breast cancer, some 70 will still have a positive mammogram. Only 7 of the 77 women who test positive (7 plus 70) have cancer, which is 1 in 11, or 9%. Many people are way off, guessing probabilities like 90%. Natural frequencies make the problem so much easier, don't you think?

I believe this is also counterintuitive: What is the probability of correctly guessing on five (just five) multiple-choice questions, each with only four choices? Most people grossly underestimate this probability (especially students who believe they can correctly guess their way through a test!). The probability is 1 out of 1024. Thus, you will need over 1,000 students blindly guessing on a test before one would be expected to score 100%.

HIGHLIGHT AND LEARNING CHECK 2-4

Data Impressions

Researchers do not analyze statistical data impressionistically or intuitively, fearing a wrong interpretation and conclusion. How does this common intuitive "disability" explain, for instance, being impressed with psychic readings or losing money in Las Vegas?

While we're at it, try another: A man on a motorcycle travels up a mountain at 30 miles per hour. He wants to travel down the other side of the mountain at such a speed that he averages overall 60 mph for the entire trip. What is the speed that he must travel down the other side to average 60 mph overall? (Assume no slowing down or speeding up at the top—no trick there). One may guess 90 mph, thinking 30 + 90 = 120 and 120/2 = 60. That's the wrong answer. There is no speed fast enough, really. The guess involves the mistake of thinking there is only one kind of mean—the arithmetic mean, whereby 30 + 90 = 120 divided by 2 = 60. What is needed here is the *harmonic* mean. Here is the explanation: The size of the hill doesn't matter, right? It is not irrelevant. Assume it is 30 miles up and 30 miles down. Going up will take an hour (30 miles going 30 miles per hour). To travel 60 mph overall, the motorcycle must go 60 miles in an hour (obviously, 60 mph). Well, the motorcycle driver has already spent that hour going up! Racing down a million miles an hour will take a few seconds; that will still put his speed under 60 mph overall. Research and statistics use many different types of means. Fortunately, the one used in educational research is almost always the simple arithmetic mean, that is, the sum of scores divided by the number of scores.

Here is one last problem (Campbell, 1974, p. 131), which is especially relevant to pregnant women. Assume I sponsored the following ad that appeared in a tabloid newspaper:

> Attention expectant mothers: Boy or girl—what will it be? Send $20 to Professor Suter along with a side-view photo of pregnant mother. Money-back guarantee if at least 5 months pregnant. I'll tell for sure—this is research based.

Does spending $20 sound like a smart thing to do? No, it doesn't. I'd get rich for the simple reason I'd be right half the time, keeping $10 on average, even while honoring the guarantee. I won't mind returning $20 half the time since it's not mine, as long as I keep $20 the other half of the time (presuming those for whom I am correct won't ask for a refund). Flaws and fallacies abound in statistical thinking (and in research designs). Our inability to "think smartly" about statistical problems explains, in part, how the unscrupulous can get rich.

CRITICAL THINKER ALERT 2-4

Intuition

Intuition might work well for personal decisions but not for statistical ones. Researchers need to know what is—and is not—an outcome that could have easily arisen from chance factors.

Discussion: How might a teacher resolve the conflict between their gut feeling (intuition) and what science might suggest works best in education? Should educational practices be dominated by scientific findings, or is there a place for other ways of knowing?

Relationships: Do We Have Sufficient Information?

Autism

Clear thinking in research involves knowing which group comparisons are relevant and which ones are not. Consider this sentence: From a research perspective, when symptoms of autism appear shortly after the measles/mumps/rubella (MMR) vaccine, then we know the evidence for "vaccine damaged" children is pretty strong. Is that true? Definitely not, for symptoms of autism typically appear in children at around the same age at which the MMR vaccine is given. So far, in Table 2.1 we have information only in the cell marked "X" (representing MMR children with autism). This is insufficient. You must consider three other groups (marked "?" in Table 2.1): (1) MMR children who are not autistic (lower left); (2) Non-MMR children who are autistic (upper right); and (3) Non-MMR children who are not autistic (lower right).

RELATIONSHIP: Any connection between variables—though not necessarily cause and effect—whereby values of one variable tend to co-occur with values of another variable.

TABLE 2.1 **Fourfold Table Relating MMR and Autism**

		MMR	
		Yes	*No*
Autistic?	*Yes*	X	?
	No	?	?

Note: Only one cell provides information (X). Information in all four cells is needed to establish a relationship.

A relationship can be established only when all the cells in a table are filled in with information like the original finding (X). The assessment of relationships, or associations, requires at least two variables (MMR and Autism, in this case), each with at least two levels of variation (Yes versus No for MMR; Yes versus No for Autism).

Grade Retention

Here is a similar problem, one made concrete with fictional data. True or False: From a research perspective, if it is found that most high school dropouts in a study were not retained (i.e., held back), then we know that retention is not linked to dropping out (disproving the retention-dropout connection).

I hope you chose False, for this problem conveys the same idea as the MMR and autism problem. We need a fourfold table to establish the relationship among the data. Let's say we found 100 high school dropouts after sampling 1,100 participants, 70 of whom had not been retained (70 out of 100, that's "most," right?). Then we studied 1,000 high school students who had not dropped out and found that 930 had also not been retained. The remaining 70 had been retained. The fourfold table (two variables, each with two levels of variation) is shown in Table 2.2.

FOURFOLD TABLE: A method of displaying data to reveal a pattern between two variables, each with two categories of variation.

TABLE 2.2 **Fourfold Table Relating Student Retention and Dropout**

		Retention	
		Yes	*No*
Dropout?	*Yes*	30	70
	No	70	930

This table reveals a very strong relationship among the data. If students are retained, the chance of their dropping out is .3 (30 out of 100); without retention, it is .07 (70 out of 1000). A very common mistake in thinking is wrongly concluding that there is (or is not) a relationship on the basis of incomplete information (only one, two, or three cells within a fourfold table).

SAT Preparation

Consider another example. Evaluate this claim: Because most of the students who score high on the SAT don't enroll in any type of test preparation program, we know that there is no connection between test preparation and SAT scores. Is this conclusion sound and logical? No, it is faulty and improper, representing a type of statistical fallacy. It might be based on data such as this: Of the 100 high scorers, only 20 enrolled in a test preparation program. Yet we need two more groups: those low SAT scorers who did and did not enroll in such programs. Perhaps only 5 of the 100 low scorers enrolled in a course, leaving 95 low scorers who did not. With four groups, it is clear there is relationship between the two variables, for there is a .80 chance (20 out of 25) of scoring high for those who took the course, but only about a .46 chance (80 out of 175) for those who did not take the course. (There were 100 low and high scorers overall; 25 total who took the course and 175 total who did not take the course.) Reaching false conclusions based on incomplete data is common. The four cells, or fourfold table, for this problem are shown in Table 2.3.

TABLE 2.3 Fourfold Table Relating SAT Scores and Course Preparation

		SAT Scores	
		Low	*High*
Course?	*Yes*	5	20
	No	95	80

College Admission

Sometimes a relationship found in combined groups will disappear—or even reverse itself—when separated into subgroups. This problem is known as Simpson's puzzle, and Moore (2001) provided an interesting illustration of it. Consider his fourfold table, which is presented in Table 2.4.

TABLE 2.4 Fourfold Table Relating Sex of Applicant and College Admission Decision

		Male	*Female*
Decision	*Admit*	35	20
	Deny	45	40

Source: *Statistics: Concepts and Controversies* (5th ed.) by D. S. Moore, 2001, New York: W. H. Freeman.

HIGHLIGHT AND LEARNING CHECK 2-5

Fourfold Tables

Assessing relationships in education often involves collecting data using a fourfold table. What four groups (at least) would be needed to determine a link between late enrollment in kindergarten and placement in special education later on?

Moore wondered whether given this hypothetical data, there was discrimination in college admissions. It sure appears to be the case given that 44% (35/80) of the males but only 33% (20/60) of the females were admitted. But when Moore presented the same data broken out by Engineering and English fields, it became clear that exactly half of all Engineering applicants, both male and female, were admitted; and a quarter of all English applicants, both male and female, were admitted. This is shown in Table 2.5.

It becomes clear that some relationships are revealed best by three rather than two variables considered together.

Table 2.5 **Three-Way Table Relating Sex of Applicant, Field, and College Admission Decision**

		Field			
		Engineering		*English*	
		Male	*Female*	*Male*	*Female*
Decision	*Admit*	30	10	5	10
	Deny	30	10	15	30

Source: *Statistics: Concepts and Controversies* (5th ed.) by D. S. Moore, 2001, New York: W. H. Freeman.

CRITICAL THINKER ALERT 2-5

One-Group Study

A one-group study is often impossible to interpret. Comparison groups establish control and permit one to discover relationships between variables, the first step toward learning about cause and effect.

Discussion: Can you think of one-group research used in advertising, the kind that is designed to sound convincing but clearly is not? From a research perspective, what important piece of information is lacking in the claim?

Contrasting Groups: Are They Meaningful?

Researchers often make use of contrasting (or paradoxical) groups, like the French who consume wine (and cheese) but have low heart disease. Is that conclusive in showing that wine lowers heart disease? No. Similarly, if people who eat fish twice a week live longer than those who don't, can we conclude that eating fish results in greater longevity? Hardly. Cheese-gobbling, wine-stoking French also may bicycle to the market, eat slowly, consume a lot of fresh vegetables, even floss often, any one of which may lower heart disease. And perhaps those who eat fish also eat vegetables with the fish, exercise, or have better health insurance. (Far-fetched? Fish is expensive and probably consumed by wealthier people, and wealth is linked to occupation, which is linked to health insurance coverage. In addition, those with comprehensive health insurance may live longer than those without it as a result of the better care such coverage provides.)

In education, researchers are faced with the same problem when they compare groups that are not comparable at the outset. Recall the homeschooling example presented earlier. If homeschooled students outperform their public school counterparts on achievement tests, can we conclude that parents make the best teachers? Hardly, since we are faced with many plausible rival explanations. Perhaps more able students are homeschooled. And if these homeschooled students had entered public education, might they have scored even higher on achievements tests? Or perhaps only those homeschooled students who excel in achievement are tested? Perhaps a different picture would emerge if all homeschooled students were tested. What if Montessori-schooled children outperform their public school counterparts? Perhaps those Montessori students also had private tutors. Or perhaps their families were simply wealthier, wealth itself being linked with test scores. (This is often called the "Volvo effect," to reflect the finding that the price of vehicles in a driveway can be linked to students' test scores.) Once again, we are faced with an interpretive dilemma due to the fact that relationships are usually easy to find—but hard to interpret.

HIGHLIGHT AND LEARNING CHECK 2-6

Interpreting Differences

Research in education often involves contrasting groups, those chosen because of a difference on one dimension but presumed to be similar on all others. But sometimes they are not. Explain the interpretative problems involved with comparing the achievement differences of students who were breast fed and those who were not.

CRITICAL THINKER ALERT 2-6

Contrasting Groups

The use of contrasting groups, those formed without random assignment, poses serious problems of interpretation. Groups formed on one dimension (e.g., exercise) may also be different in other ways (e.g., diet). Finding faster mental reaction times among those who exercise–and who have better diets–does not disentangle the influences of exercise and diet.

Discussion: Why is it difficult to interpret a research finding, for example, that shows students who sleep longer (on average) in high school also earn better grades?

Statistical Logic: How Can Inference Help?

Inferential statistics and their underlying logic are very useful to all researchers, removing much of the guesswork about relationships. Very practical indeed, these types of statistics include hundreds of what are commonly called *inferential tests,* like the *t* and the *F,* all of which have in common the determination of *p,* or probability. This *p* value allows one to figure out whether a relationship, as opposed to a number of random chance factors, is likely to exist in the population represented by the data in the sample. For example, to determine whether there is a connection between fat in the blood (lipids) and short-term memory span (the capacity to hold items like those in a grocery list in memory for a brief time without forgetting), a researcher might collect data on 100 subjects' cholesterol levels, divide the subjects into two groups (lower versus higher cholesterol), and then compute the average memory span (after its assessment) for both groups. The researcher knows that chance factors will cause a mean difference between the two groups *even if cholesterol and memory were in no way related.*

INFERENTIAL STATISTICS: Statistical reasoning that permits generalization beyond the sample to a larger population. Central to this reasoning is the notion of statistical significance, meaning that a relationship found in the sample is probably not due to the workings of chance.

Let's presume the two groups' average memory spans were 7.1 (for the low cholesterol group) and 6.4 (for the high cholesterol group). Is this difference greater than what one might expect after assigning 100 people into two random (not different) groups and testing their memory spans? Enter the *p* value for final determination. If the *p* value is low, like .01, one would conclude that chance influence is unlikely, and that there probably exists a relationship or connection between cholesterol and memory span in the population of people similar to those in the sample. This is the essence of reasoning in statistics, and why the *p* value is so prominent. Fortunately, we do not calculate the actual *p* values by hand. That's what statistical software does for us.

HIGHLIGHT AND LEARNING CHECK 2-7

Chance Factors

Statistical significance suggests that chance factors are not likely explanations of research results. It does not necessarily suggest that the statistics are *important* or *substantial.* Explain why the use of statistical reasoning in research is vital to evaluating claims made by those with ambiguous data.

One of the first statistical tests ever developed, and almost certainly one of the most commonly used tests today, was created in about 1900 in an Irish brewery. Known as the *t* test and used to determine the statistical significance of one mean difference (that is, two means), its developer was a chemist who wanted to develop a better tasting beer. He needed information about comparisons between two recipes, not so much in the sample but in the population of beer drinkers represented by the sample. His new creation, the *t* test, provided information about the population given only data from a sample. Because many research scenarios call for comparing two means, you can see why the *t* test is so commonly used.

The history of statistics, then, is connected to the history of beer making, a fact that should convince you of the practical nature of inferential statistics. Other commonly used statistical tests, such as the *F* test (named after Sir Ronald Fisher, its developer), were developed in the United States on the farm, so to speak, to solve agricultural problems. Fisher needed a method for comparing complex groupings (based on different methods of irrigation or fertilizing) in an attempt to maximize crop production. Once again, we see how statistical techniques were developed to solve applied, practical problems opposed to settling theoretical debates. Many other statistical tests were also developed in business and industry.

Contemporary educational researchers might use the *t* test to compare two different methods of teaching reading or the *F* test to compare the four groups that combine when essays are written by hand versus computer and by girls versus boys. The applications are almost endless.

CRITICAL THINKER ALERT 2-7

Inferential Statistics

The use of inferential statistics via the famous *p* value permits cautious researchers to reach conclusions about members of a population in general (not just a sample), conclusions that must be carefully tempered yet *still* might be wrong. The *p* refers to a level of probability, not proof.

Discussion: Presume a researcher reported that students born in the fall were earning slightly higher achievement scores than students born in other seasons. What information is missing that might help interpret and evaluate this finding?

Muddied Thinking About Important Ideas

Research in many fields, and particularly in education, is loaded with terms that are poorly understood. This concluding section samples a few common misconceptions. Clear ways to think about these ideas are elaborated in the chapters that follow.

Misunderstood Statistical Significance

Consider once again the term *statistically significant,* which many might incorrectly believe means roughly the same as *important* or *substantial.* Probably the single best phrase to capture the meaning of *statistically significant* is "probably not due to chance." It carries no connotation like "important" or "valuable" or "strong." Very small effects, for example, training in test-taking skills that "boost" a group's achievement scores—from, say, 54 to 56—might be statistically significant but trivial and of little practical importance.

The term *statistically significant* does not in any way suggest an explanation of findings either—it suggests only that an observed relationship is probably not due to chance. For example, let's pretend that your friend claims to have psychic powers, that is, to be able to affect the outcome of a coin toss. As the coin is tossed, your friend can "will" more heads as an outcome than would be expected by chance. After

100 tosses, the results are in: The coin turned up heads 60 times. Is this statistically significant? Yes, because a coin tossed 100 times would be expected to land on heads with a frequency of about 43 to 57 most of the time. ("Most of the time" means 95% of the time, hence if you were to toss a coin 100 times and repeat this for 100 trials, 95 of the trials would probably produce between 43 and 57 heads.) Notice that 60 heads was a statistically significant outcome since it was beyond the limits imposed by chance 95% of the time. But also notice that no explanation is offered by the term *statistically significant.*

There are many explanations other than "psychic ability." Perhaps there was something wrong with the coin (it did not average 50/50 heads-tails in the long run), or mistakes were made in the tally of heads, or the "psychic" was a cunning trickster. Also, there always exists the possibility that the outcome of the coin toss was indeed a chance occurrence, although this explanation is correct less than 5% of the time. (Note: The concept of statistical significance is undoubtedly the single most difficult one in the introductory study of educational research. Don't worry how those numbers were determined in the coin toss example. This will be fully explained in Chapter 13, where it is discussed far more conceptually than mathematically.)

HIGHLIGHT AND LEARNING CHECK 2-8

Statistical Thinking

Statistical thinking permits researchers to disentangle what could reasonably be attributed to chance factors and what could not. Explain why researchers need statistical help with interpreting a small (or large) difference between two groups in a study.

The famous expression $p < .05$ means statistically significant, or the probability is less than 5 out of 100 that the findings are due to chance. In this sense, the word *probably* in science refers to a 95% likelihood. As 5 out of 100 is 1 out of 20, there are 19 or more chances out of 20 that a relationship uncovered by statistical methods is "real" (or not due to chance). It sounds arbitrary; it is. Scientists, I suppose, could have agreed on 18 out of 20. But they did not. It was 19 out of 20 that stuck as the scientific standard. Keep in mind that for every 20 studies completed that show statistical significance, 1 study is probably "fluky." That's another reason why a single study by itself is suggestive only, and any definitive conclusion about it would be premature until replications reveal that fluke as an explanation is incredibly unlikely.

Knowing more about statistics enables us to critically evaluate research claims. This is especially important because meaningless statistics are often presented in support of an argument. Wonderful examples of this can be found in the book *Damned Lies and Statistics: Untangling Numbers From the Media, Politicians, and Activists* (Best, 2001). The author considers well-known, often-cited statistics and shows that they are senseless, yet may take on lives of their own. One famous statistical claim tells us that since 1950, there has been a doubling every year of the number of American children gunned down. The problem with this claim is its impossibility, for if 1 child was gunned down in 1950, by 1970, the number of children gunned down would have exceeded a million. By 1980, the number would have surpassed a billion, and by 1990, the number would have topped the recorded population throughout history. Best (2001) shows that the hilarious number would have reached 35 trillion in 1995, and soon after become a number only encountered in astronomy. Clearly, many "well known" statistics in the social sciences can be wildly wrong.

CRITICAL THINKER ALERT 2-8

Statistical Significance

Statistical significance is related to probability; it does not carry any implication about practical value. Nor does it relate to the importance or strength of a connection among the factors being investigated. *Significance* in the statistical sense is more closely related to, for example, likely or unlikely outcomes of chance events.

Discussion: If a researcher reported a statistically significant link between students' college entrance examination (SAT) scores and the size of the students' high schools (smaller schools were associated with higher scores on average), does this suggest changes in policy regarding the construction of new schools? Why or why not?

Misunderstood Proof

It is a mistaken belief that educational researchers can prove theories by collecting data in order to prove hypotheses. *Prove* is a word that is best dropped from your vocabulary, at least during your study of educational research. Unlike those who prove theorems in geometry, those who conduct educational research will most likely *test* theories by finding *support* for a specific hypothesis born from the theory. For example, constructivist theory predicts that students who *construct* meaning, for example, by creating a metaphor to increase their understanding, will learn new material better than students who passively receive new material prepackaged in a lecture. If, in fact, a researcher found that the "constructed" group learned the new material faster than the "lectured" group did, it would prompt the conclusion that the research hypothesis was supported (not proven), and the theory which spawned the hypothesis would, in turn, become more credible. *Testing, supporting,* and *adding credibility* are all more suitable terms in educational research than *proving.*

HIGHLIGHT AND LEARNING CHECK 2-9

Research Support

Support is a far better word than *proof* in the study of educational research. (Proofs are better suited for geometry and physics.) The term is used when the data gathered are consistent with (*support*) a theory that predicted the outcome. Explain how research support (not proof) is tied to the ever-present concern about alternative explanations for research findings.

There are at least two reasons why educational researchers cannot prove hypotheses or theories. First, research findings are usually evaluated with regard to their statistical significance, which involves the computation of a *p* value, referring to the *probability* (not proof) that a certain finding was due to chance factors. Although the *p* values can be extraordinarily low (e.g., .000001, or 1 chance out of a million that the findings were due to chance), they cannot drop to zero. So there is always the possibility—however small—that research findings could be attributable to chance.

Second, no matter how well controlled a study is, there always exists the possibility that the findings could be the result of some influence other than the one systematically studied by the researcher. For example, a researcher might compare the relative effectiveness of learning to spell on a computer versus the "old-fashioned" way of writing words by hand. If the computer group learned to spell better and faster than the handwriting group, might there be reasons other than the computers for the better performance? Yes, there might be several. For example, maybe the teachers of the computer group were different, possibly more enthusiastic or more motivating. It might be that the enthusiasm or motivation by itself resulted in better spelling performance. If the more enthusiastic and motivating teachers had taught the handwriting method, then the handwriting group might have outperformed the computer group.

Consider another explanation. The computing group was taught in the morning, and the handwriting group in the afternoon. If the computing group outperformed the handwriting group, how would you know whether the better performance was a teaching-method effect or a time-of-day effect? You wouldn't know. Perhaps students could choose the computer group or handwriting group. If higher achieving students (hence better spellers) chose the computer group, the findings would tell us nothing about the relative effectiveness of the two methods of learning (only that better spellers prefer to work on a computer).

CRITICAL THINKER ALERT 2-9

Proof

Theories are supported, not proven. They are developed to enhance our current understanding and guide research. A good theory may outlive its usefulness and never be proven; it may be replaced with a more useful one. The words *research* and *prove* usually don't belong in the same sentence.

Discussion: What famous theorists come to mind from your studies of education and/or psychology? Freud? Skinner? Jung? Dewey? What happened to the theory? Did the theory evolve into a different one?

I hope that some of these research concepts have stimulated your interest in the process of scientific research in general and educational research in particular. In the next chapter, we will examine the great diversity of approaches to educational research.

Chapter Summary

A few powerful concepts go far in helping educators unravel the complexities of the research process. A sampling of these ideas includes the following: how bias can be subtle, why data require interpretation (and the related notion that misinterpretation of results is common), why control is vital, why intuition is often unreliable, why associations in research require sufficient information, the meaningfulness of contrasting groups, the power of statistical inference, and how thinking becomes muddied. Critical thinking about research is a developed skill that helps clear the muddied waters of research in education.

Application Exercises

1. Locate an author's opinion about an issue or topic in education (perhaps it is a letter to the editor or story about education in a magazine, blog, or newspaper). Analyze the arguments carefully, paying particular attention to sloppy reasoning or fallacious thinking. Which conclusions seem astute? Which ones seem faulty?
2. Locate an example of teacher action research in your library or on the Internet. (Search Google for "teacher action research.") Summarize the research report and describe why you think it reveals reflective practice and critical thinking about research.
3. Visit your library and locate a journal that publishes the findings of research studies, such as the *American Educational Research Journal, Journal of Educational Psychology,* or *Journal of Educational Research.* Alternatively, use the Internet and locate an online journal that publishes full-text reports of research, such as *Education Policy Analysis Archives.* Other online journals that publish educational research can be found at the Web site of the American Educational Research Association's Special Interest Group, Communication of Research (http://aera-cr.asu.edu/links.html). Find a study that uses a control group and explain its function. In other words, what is it that the control group controls?
4. Using the same resources in your library or on the Internet, locate a study and focus on one or more ideas introduced in this chapter, including bias, misinterpretations, counterintuitive findings, assessing relationships via fourfold tables (or similar group comparisons), the use of contrasting groups, statistical significance, and the notion of proof. Are any ideas in this chapter also conveyed in the published research report?
5. One might argue that research in education is too easily influenced by current politics. Discuss ways in which political orientation might affect, even bias, research in education. To get started, think about how politics might influence the very definition of science, what qualifies as rigorous evidence, how federal research funds are awarded, or how research findings might be disseminated. Do you feel that politics can influence the research base in education? How might this occur?

ON YOUR OWN

Log on to the Web-based student study site at http://www.sagepub.com/eic for more information about the materials presented in this chapter, suggestions for activities, study aids such as electronic flashcards and review quizzes, a sample research proposal, and research recommendations that include journal article links (with discussion questions and an article evaluation guide) and questions related to this chapter.

3

Diversity of Educational Research

Outline

Overview

Chapter 1 described why educational researchers value critical thinking, the core activity that permits the questioning and inquiry needed to understand and evaluate teaching and learning. John Dewey (1933) believed that critical thinking was "active, persistent, and careful consideration" of evidence that supports our current understanding (p. 118). Educational researchers have many choices regarding the type of inquiry they can use to investigate their researchable problems. Given the large variation in approaches to research, careful consideration in selection is indeed required.

Once a researcher focuses on a topic, answers to several questions determine whether or not to proceed (such as those relating to ethics, which are discussed in Chapter 4). If the researcher proceeds, then another series of decisions must be made with regard to the type of research best suited to the research needs. The type of research selected is crucial since it directly affects the conclusions which are possible after the analysis of data. We will see, for example, that logic will not permit cause-and-effect interpretations without the use of very special types of research designs (and controls). Other approaches to research will not permit a new level of understanding based on, for example, a highly memorable and theory-spawning metaphor.

What type of research is best suited to answer a research question? There are literally hundreds of different types of educational research, but this section will not belabor all of the fine distinctions. Instead, it will focus on the major research classifications, those which have implications for the researcher's conclusions. For organizational purposes, seven distinctions are described. None of these distinctions carry implications for defining science. Richard Shavelson, past dean of Stanford University's School of Education, emphasized the point that no one research method is by definition scientific (or unscientific). He stated, "How one applies the method to a particular problem determines the quality of the research. The research question should always drive the design of the study, and not the other way around" (quoted in Hass, 2004, p. 4).

Research Perspectives

Educational researchers approach their work from many different perspectives using many different methods. They often arrange variables in a single study to function in complex configurations. It is a misleading oversimplification to pigeonhole the vast array and complexity of educational research and discuss only seven different types of research. Thus, instead of artificially oversimplifying and compartmentalizing educational research, I will present the most important distinctions that occur in educational research. Labeling educational research as a "type" is not as important as understanding the implications of a study's most distinctive features. Above all else, the research, whatever its distinctive features, must answer the research question. I believe that describing the distinctive features of educational research, and thus avoiding contrived typologies, captures the complexity of the research and does not place imposing restraints on researchable questions. This implies that a research question need not be rejected because it does not conform to a standard classification of research.

The seven distinctions described here are as follows:

- Quantitative versus qualitative
- Descriptive versus inferential
- True experimental versus quasi-experimental
- Causal comparative versus correlational
- Single-subject versus group
- Teacher versus traditional
- Large-scale policy versus small-scale evaluation

Quantitative Versus Qualitative

At the risk of oversimplification, this distinction may be described as concerned with numbers versus words. A quantitative study tests specific hypotheses, usually stated in advance, and incorporates measures which can be analyzed statistically. This type of research uses tables or charts to display findings that can (it is hoped) be generalized beyond the sample to a wider population. The researcher is distant in a sense, and guards against bias and other influences which may skew the results. Qualitative studies, by contrast, frequently allow a hypothesis to emerge after careful exploration, observation, or interaction. Qualitative researchers often use narratives to describe their observations. These stories capture a rich understanding which may not generalize beyond the research setting and unique characteristics of the sample. Researchers often opt for this approach when they believe that the educational outcomes are too complex to reduce to a number. They might argue that pinning numbers on students and applying statistical maneuvers is akin to averaging musical notes. Qualitative researchers are inclined to "paint a portrait" or describe teaching as orchestration, whereas quantitative researchers are more inclined to plug in the numbers, summarize the results, or describe effective teaching in terms of percentages, ratings, and students' percentile scores on achievement tests.

QUANTITATIVE RESEARCH: Research aimed at testing hypotheses with numerical values rather than explaining complex phenomena through verbal descriptions.

Once again at the risk of oversimplification, it could be said that if you agree with the statement "Teaching is a science," you are probably more inclined toward quantitative (numbers) research. By contrast, if you agree with the statement "Teaching is an art," you are probably more inclined toward qualitative (words) research. A quantitative study of teacher style might describe effective teachers in the following way: They waited an average of 6 seconds before answering, asked 7.2 questions per 5-minute interval, and deviated from the prescribed model only once or twice during each lesson." A qualitative study of teacher style might describe an effective teacher in the following way: Her control over the class made it seem as though she had eyes in the back of her head, and yet all the while she maintained a quick tempo and displayed an artistry not usually seen in beginning teachers.

QUALITATIVE RESEARCH: Research aimed at explaining complex phenomena through verbal descriptions rather than testing hypotheses with numerical values.

One memorable illustration of the distinction between quantitative research and qualitative research was provided by Johnson (2005). He offered the hypothetical "Coffee Study" as an example of a quantitative study, with its hypothesis that "drinking coffee improves students' ability to perform on standardized tests" (a "numbers" outcome). He contrasted the Coffee Study with the hypothetical "Coffee House Study," an example of a qualitative study. By observing naturally occurring social interactions and studying the cultural milieu of a campus coffee house, he was able to learn more about his original curiosity: What is the nature, quality, and function of a campus coffee house?

CRITICAL THINKER ALERT 3-1

Mixed Data

Many research questions in education are best answered with a combination of quantitative and qualitative data. The use of one type does not exclude the use of the other within the same study.

Discussion: Consider the construct "motivation." Can you think of motivation's *qualities* (essential characteristics) and *quantities* (levels or amounts of something)? If so, describe why this two-pronged approach to research on motivation might lead to greater understanding.

HIGHLIGHT AND LEARNING CHECK 3-1

Numbers and Words

Quantitative ("numbers") research usually focuses on statistical maneuvers to reach conclusions; qualitative ("words") research usually focuses on narrative descriptions and pattern seeking in language to reach conclusions. In a study of school climate and dropout rates, what aspect of the study is most likely quantitative? What aspect is most likely qualitative?

It is not true that all educational research is either quantitative *or* qualitative in nature. Increasingly, researchers are incorporating both approaches in a single study (often a measure of good research), and as a consequence, current educational research is as valuable as it has ever been. Blending the two approaches might, for example, involve a study of the *scientific* basis of the *art* of teaching. Today, a purely quantitative study may be criticized for its lack of attention to qualitative analysis.

Examples of quantitative and qualitative research findings in published reports are presented in Table 3.1.

Descriptive Versus Inferential

This distinction is concerned with the generalization of research findings. If data are collected for the single purpose of describing a specific group with no intention of going beyond that group, then the study is considered to be *descriptive.* Examples here would include a study of teachers' attitudes toward the integration of computers in

Table 3.1 Examples of Quantitative and Qualitative Research

Quantitative Research Findings

- "The means and standard deviations for the measures used in this study . . . are shown in Table 2 . . . This sample showed significant negative correlations with age for all four SCWT scores" (Johnson, Bouchard, Segal, Keyes, & Samuels, 2003, p. 61).
- "Table 2 includes internal reliability alpha scores for all scales. Except for the score for the variable reflective disposition . . . alpha scores were all considerably above the minimum acceptable level of .60" (Giovannelli, 2003, pp. 299–300).
- "Table 6 presents the mean scores, adjusted mean scores, and standard deviations by time and condition on general and domain-specific metacognitive knowledge. As one can see from Table 6, no significant differences were found between conditions on any aspect of the metacognitive measures before the beginning of the study (. . . all p values > .05). Yet at the end of the study, significant differences were found . . . $p < .01$" (Kramarski & Mevarech, 2003, p. 299).
- "We examined performance trends of the kindergarten students with regard to listening comprehension and behavior . . . [and this] indicated a significant difference ($p = .02$) between treatment and comparison group students on the listening posttest; no significant interaction was found" (Brigman & Webb, 2003, p. 289).
- "A positive and significant correlation ($r = .669$, $p < .001$, $n = 177$) existed between parents and students reports of family involvement in science homework" (Van Voorhis, 2003, p. 329).
- "The statistical analysis of data support the four hypotheses. Subjects instructed in the Model of Generative Teaching comprehended more economics ($p < .0001$)" (Kourilsky & Wittrock, 1992, p. 873).
- "The means presented in Table 1 suggest that 4-year-olds in same-sex classrooms were more likely to engage in solitary dramatic play" (Roopnarine et al., 1992, p. 765).
- "Abecedarian children earned higher average scores than did the Perry Preschool Project subjects: Mean CAT percentile scores ranged between 38 and 41" (Campbell & Ramey, 1995, p. 764).
- "Altogether, readers made 3,003 oral reading errors in the 72 lessons. Table 1 presents error rates by story for students in low, middle, and high groups" (Chinn, Waggoner, Anderson, Schommer, & Wilkinson, 1993, p. 372).
- "The results of the multivariate and univariate analyses of the reading data are summarized in Tables 2-4. In the tables, grade equivalents are shown for each outcome measure. . . . In addition, effect sizes are shown for each experimental-control comparison" (Madden, Slavin, Karweit, Dolan, & Wasik, 1993, p. 132).

Qualitative Research Findings

- "The story revealed that children may be aware of the precursors or associated symptoms of their learning disability by early childhood, and definitely by school age. They may feel different, or as if 'something's wrong with me,' earlier than is usually considered" (McNulty, 2003, p. 378).
- "Thus, whereas teachers configured groups on the basis of a difference, students frequently desired a compatibility rooted in sameness . . . the clash between teachers' official practices and the students' unofficial interpretation and navigation of those practices sometimes had unfortunate consequences for student learning and academic identity" (Rubin, 2003, pp. 558, 566).
- "Interview data and field notes indicated . . . peer conditions typically started the problem-solving process by brainstorming ideas, which were presented in the form of questions or suggestions. . . . Evidence from observations . . . showed that working collaboratively gave students a chance to ask questions, offer suggestions, elaborate thinking, and provide feedback . . . videotaped observations . . . indicated that there tended to be more agreement than disagreement among members, and few constructive suggestions were made" (Ge & Land, 2003, pp. 32–33).
- "Clearly, Carmen brought to the classroom a belief and value system, imbedded in her experiences as a person of color. Foremost was a belief in the value of her own cultural heritage and an understanding and appreciation of how it shaped her as a person. She then attempted to translate this understanding into pedagogical methods that would help her students find links between their lives and the content they were studying. She did this in several ways" (Kauchak & Burbank, 2003, p. 68).

(Continued)

TABLE 3.1 (Continued)

- "Four themes of technology use emerged: (1) technology as a knowledge source, (2) technology as a data organizer, (3) technology as information presenter, and (4) technology as facilitator" (Pringle, Dawson, & Adams, 2003, p. 48).
- "Our subsequent interviews show that naive but imaginative accounts persisted in some children even after direct instruction designed to change them. Thus, despite their fanciful qualities, these ideas apparently acquire a 'ring of truth' for those children who are prone to construct and believe in them" (Van Sledright & Brophy, 1992, p. 854).
- "Our analysis of field notes and videotapes suggested that all students did in fact participate meaningfully in science activities and class discussion" (Scruggs & Mastropieri, 1994, p. 794).
- "Thus, interactions from a transactional perspective seemed to emphasize the processes important for children to learn, rather than particular products or skills" (Neuman, Hagedorn, Celano, & Daly, 1995, p. 814).
- "Interview transcripts were coded as categories emerged from the data. Each classification is explained in depth, and illustrative teacher comments are provided. . . . The majority of teachers were classified as remediationists" (Tomchin & Impara, 1992, pp. 210, 213–214).
- "The microanalysis revealed five interactive strategies that seemed to be used quite naturally by African-American parent-teachers to assist and extend children's literacy activity" (Neuman & Roskos, 1993, p. 115).
- "A third theme that emerged from the interviews was the juxtaposition of two cultures: that of the elementary school and that of the university" (Kagan, Dennis, Igou, Moore, & Sparks, 1993, p. 439).

CRITICAL THINKER ALERT 3-2

Qualitative Data

Qualitative data in education are often far more complex than quantitative data. The proper analysis of such data is usually challenging and time consuming and often requires creative talents.

Discussion: Imagine two definitions of *motivation,* one derived from the time spent completing 25 lessons and the other derived from analyzing 20-minute interviews about career goals. Further, imagine the spreadsheet of recorded times from 100 students and a box full of written transcripts of 100 interviews. Describe how the tasks of analyzing these two types of data will require different challenges.

the curriculum at Polytechnic High School or a study of how students in Mr. Alonzo's class use probability to solve everyday problems. Such descriptive studies could be undertaken for very practical reasons, like how to best prepare teachers for computers in their classrooms and how to best introduce a lesson that builds on students' prior knowledge. Clearly, data from these studies do not test any theory, nor are they used to learn about teachers or students in general. No attempt is made to infer what other teachers might think or what other students might know. This type of inference that extends beyond the sample studied is referred to as *generalization.*

DESCRIPTIVE RESEARCH: Research aimed at describing the characteristics of a population without generalizing or testing statistical hypotheses.

This distinction is important because, among other reasons, it determines the type (and even calculation) of statistics used in the analysis of data.

In contrast to descriptive studies, *inferential* studies attempt to go beyond those people and settings studied by making generalized statements about a larger population—specifically, the one that supplied the people for the sample. Such generalized statements are warranted only to the extent that the sample is representative of the larger population from which it was drawn. These generalized statements are known as *inferences*, hence the name *inferential* for this research. Political pollsters provide an example of research that is clearly inferential. The pollsters are not so much concerned with the responses from the sample—their primary focus is the population that is represented by the sample. A typical research finding in this case might be that 75% (plus or minus 3%) of parents support the idea of year-round schooling. The plus or minus figure illustrates an inference about the population, in the sense that the true percentage in the population of all parents is most probably between 72% and 78%. To use inference in a logical argument involves reaching a conclusion about something larger from something smaller, such as about a larger population from a smaller sample.

INFERENTIAL RESEARCH: Research aimed at generalizing to a larger population with data collected from samples of the population.

Inferential studies are also identified by statements regarding statistical significance. For example, assume a researcher wanted to know whether sixth-grade girls have a greater vocabulary than sixth-grade boys. To test this hunch, 500 boys and 500 girls were randomly selected from large public school districts in Seattle and were given a test of vocabulary knowledge. Let's assume that the girls scored an average of 86%, while the boys scored an average of 81%. The researcher reported that this difference was statistically significant. This means that there is most likely a "true" difference in the vocabulary levels of girls and boys in the population represented by the sample. (The population in this case might be all sixth graders in Seattle public schools. These findings may also apply to sixth graders in general across the nation, but this would have to be confirmed by a nationwide sample.) The researcher could have also reported, given a smaller gap, that the obtained difference was not statistically significant, in which case the difference would be interpreted as chance (not meaningful) and the conclusion would be that there is likely no difference among girls' and boys' vocabulary knowledge in the population.

HIGHLIGHT AND LEARNING CHECK 3-2

Description Versus Inference

Descriptive research in education focuses on details or characteristics of a population without making inferences beyond those who are studied. Inferential research attempts to generalize from a sample which provides data to a larger population of interest via the use of statistical maneuvers. Is a study of middle-school boys' versus girls' interest in science more likely to be descriptive or inferential? What about a study of retention practices at Washington Elementary School?

In summary, the most salient feature of inferential studies is the use of a sample in order to make generalized statements about a larger population. Descriptive studies, by contrast, merely describe a group characteristic with no intention of making statements that extend beyond the group being studied.

Other examples of descriptive versus inferential studies are presented in Table 3.2.

TABLE 3.2 Examples of Descriptive and Inferential Research

Descriptive Research

- A researcher interviews all recent graduates of a teacher education program to learn more about their perceptions of program quality.
- A researcher develops a new test of computer literacy and administers it to ninth graders in one school district to determine their level of background knowledge.
- A researcher measures the school climate at Evergreen High and makes recommendations for improving teachers' morale.
- A researcher in special education observes Cindy for a week in an attempt to understand her reading difficulties.

Inferential Research

- A researcher samples 1300 adults to learn more about the nation's attitudes toward public education.
- A researcher samples 100 boys and 100 girls and tests them to learn about gender differences in emotional intelligence in the population.
- A researcher samples 60 schools in the state for 3 years to see whether the student absenteeism rate has significantly shifted over time.
- A researcher samples 100 top scoring high school students on the Advanced Placement tests to learn more about the study habits of high achievers in general.

CRITICAL THINKER ALERT 3-3

Descriptive Studies

Descriptive studies in education often generate ideas that others may investigate with inferential methods in order to determine whether findings generalize. Understanding complex relationships often begins by a process aimed at providing complete descriptions.

Discussion: Presume my description of a local high school (via surveys, interviews, student and teacher profiles, test scores, etc.) reveals an at-risk student population (defined by demographics such as income level) that matches outcomes associated with private schools in affluent suburbs. I wonder whether the qualities and outcomes of this particular school generalize beyond its borders to other states. How do you suppose I could learn whether or not this combination of qualities and outcomes is representative of others around the country?

True Experimental Versus Quasi-Experimental

True Experimental: Manipulation Plus Random Assignment

True experimental research is characterized by two essential features: manipulation and random assignment. An *experimental manipulation* is the creation of groups that reflect different categories of one unifying dimension, such as class sizes of 10, 15, and 20 students. Another manipulation might involve creating two different methods of learning (such as online versus offline). The groups formed by the researcher are referred to as an *independent variable*, which is described more fully in Chapter 5. The independent variables in this case are class size and type of learning. The second feature of true experimental research, *random assignment*, is accomplished by a random number table (described in Chapter 8) and assures that the different groups forming categories of the independent variable are roughly comparable to begin with (the variation in students is scattered across the groups). This type of true experimental research may also be called *intervention* research for the obvious reason it involves the experimenter's intervention in the creation of groups. Often, true experimental research involves random assignment of participants to either a treatment group or a control (comparison) group. The treatment may be as simple as instructions to breathe deeply during a test (or no specific instructions at all—a control group). True experimental research is strongest for ferreting out cause-and-effect relationships, and for this reason experimental research is the first choice—if it's practical—when the research question concerns causal relationships.

TRUE EXPERIMENTAL RESEARCH: Research involving the use of a manipulated independent variable (an intervention) coupled with random assignment of subjects to groups. Such designs are strong for testing cause-and-effect relationships (e.g., randomized posttest control group design, randomized pretest-posttest control group design, and randomized matched control group design).

Consider another example of true experimental research: A researcher wanted to determine whether learning how to spell with the use of a computer or by handwriting resulted in higher spelling achievement. To this end, the researcher sampled 120 third graders and randomly assigned them to one of two created groups: a computer group or a handwriting group. The computer group learned and practiced the spelling of words with a computer 3 times a week for 10 weeks. The handwriting group learned and practiced the same words for the same amount of time. Then both groups were tested on the same sample of words chosen from the pool of words that were practiced during the 10 weeks.

Let's pretend the results revealed the handwriting group scored significantly higher than the computer group. Assuming that all biases were held in check and there existed no rival explanations for this finding, this researcher would be entitled to conclude that learning to spell via handwriting (versus the computer) results in (causes) higher spelling achievement (at least among students similar to those in this study). This type of cause-and-effect interpretation is possible only because the research is truly experimental; the independent variable (type of learning: computer versus handwriting) was manipulated (groups were created by the researcher) and subjects were assigned randomly to groups. It is precisely this type of research that the No Child Left Behind legislation prefers since it leads to identifying educational practices supported by rigorous scientific evidence.

HIGHLIGHT AND LEARNING CHECK 3-3

Manipulation and Random Assignment

True experimental research is defined by a manipulation, or creation of group differences, coupled with random assignment of participants to groups. Quasi-experimental research includes a manipulation without the coupling of random assignment of participants to groups. What are the implications of random assignment for control and cause-and-effect conclusions?

CRITICAL THINKER ALERT 3-4

The "Gold Standard"

The simple process of random assignment of research participants to groups has huge implications for the control of extraneous variables. A true experiment, whenever feasible, is the best method for uncovering cause-and-effect relationships.

Discussion: Why do you suppose that true experiments are dubbed the "gold standard" in research? Do you think it is reasonable to consider schools as appropriate field settings for educational experiments? What practical problems might be encountered in school settings?

Consider one more example. A researcher suspects that excessive fat in a diet is linked to lowered cognitive functioning. As a test of this idea, 300 high school students are randomly assigned to one of three diet groups: high fat, low fat, and control. Students in the high fat group are required to eat a balanced diet consisting of a minimum of 100 grams of fat per day. Students in the low fat group are required to eat a balanced diet of a maximum of 10 grams of fat per day. Control students function as a type of baseline by eating what they normally eat. The prescribed diets are followed for 6 months before several tests of cognitive functioning are collected (these include simple measures of reaction time in an associative learning task to more complex tasks such as solving logic problems). After tabulating the results, the researcher finds enhanced performance across the board for the low fat group (relative to the controls) and lowered performance for the high fat group (relative to the controls).

RANDOM ASSIGNMENT: Assignment of research participants to groups such that all members have an equal and independent chance of being assigned to each group.

The study described above qualifies as a true experiment because an independent variable was *manipulated* (the investigator created the three conditions) and students were *randomly* assigned to the three conditions. If the researcher was certain that extraneous influences were neutralized and there were no competing alternative explanations, then the researcher is entitled to a causal interpretation. In this case, a reasonable interpretation of the data might be that fat in the diet impacts our ability to remember, think, and reason.

The power of random assignment to equate groups is truly remarkable. Such a simple procedure accomplishes so much, for groups formed via random assignment are roughly equivalent on hundreds, if not thousands, of important but extraneous and potentially confounding variables. Group comparability formed by random assignment even applies to variables that have not yet been discovered. Imagine randomizing two groups right now, then peer into your crystal ball to discover that Factor Q, discovered in the year 2050, is believed to be the most important determinant of school success. This doesn't present a problem even today, or in any way invalidate current true experimental research. This is because these two random groups would have roughly equivalent levels of Factor Q. This equivalence, as you'll see in Chapter 7, controls for countless extraneous influences.

CRITICAL THINKER ALERT 3-5

Random Selection

Random *selection* (not assignment) of subjects has no bearing on the type of study conducted (e.g., true experimental or quasi-experimental). It only influences how well the results, whatever the type of study, might generalize to the whole population.

Discussion: One might argue that changes in educational practices will happen one classroom at a time and under the direct control of teachers. What does this view of educational reform suggest about the value of random selection and generalized statements about the population? Are reforms so localized that generalized statements are not relevant?

Quasi-Experimental: Manipulation Without Random Assignment

Quasi-experiments are so named because they resemble experiments to some degree (*quasi* in this sense means "somewhat"). They employ some type of manipulation, but a critical feature, however, is lacking: random assignment. Because of this limitation, quasi-experiments are not especially strong with regard to uncovering cause-and-effect relationships. This is because quasi-experiments cannot capitalize on the incredible power of random assignment.

QUASI-EXPERIMENTAL RESEARCH: Research involving the use of a manipulated independent variable (an intervention) *without* random assignment of participants to groups, weakening the researchers' ability to ferret out cause-and-effect relationships.

Consider an example of a researcher who wanted to learn about the achievement effects of year-round schooling. Many schools were contacted to learn whether they would be interested in participating in the study, and 10 schools were found having the resources and commitment needed to fairly answer this research question. As a comparison, 10 other schools were selected to function as a control group. Note that the schools were not assigned randomly to the two conditions. Follow-up testing revealed that the year-round schools achieved significantly higher than the control (9-month) schools. The researcher must carefully temper the interpretation of these data because schools comprising the two groups may have been different from the start—perhaps the year-round schools would have achieved higher *without* the year-round intervention. Recall that these schools were unique in the sense that they were able to participate in the first place. Might some other factor co-occur in schools with the year-round calendar? Might they have better facilities, teachers with higher morale, or different student populations? If so, perhaps this co-occurring factor itself was the cause of the observed effect.

Without random assignment, one can never assume that two or more groups are comparable. This problem could be offset, however, if the control schools were *matched*, or equated, with the year-round schools. Matched schools would be chosen for their similarity based on one or more characteristics, such as facilities, teacher morale, student backgrounds, and so forth. Matching falls short (far short) of randomization, however, since there always exists the possibility of a difference on a critical but unmatched variable—one that explains away the presumed effects. Matching equates groups only on matched variables and nothing more. (There is another type of matching, a statistical maneuver used in the analysis of data called the *analysis of covariance,* that can also offset some of the problems due to lack of randomization.) When individual students cannot be assigned randomly, as is frequently the case, researchers often invoke alternative types of randomization. They may, for example, randomly assign *entire classrooms* to receive a treatment while others are reserved as controls. Simply, the power of random assignment, the cornerstone of true experiments, lies in its ability to equate groups over countless extraneous variables.

Time Series Quasi-Experiments and Rival Explanations

Consider another example of a quasi-experiment, a *time series* design. As is true with all quasi-experiments, a time series study uses an intervention or treatment without random assignment. With this design, a group is observed (or some measure collected) over a period of time followed by an intervention. Observation or measurement continues, and a treatment effect is presumed if the post-treatment observations differ significantly from the pretreatment observations. For example, assume that a researcher tracked a school's student absenteeism rate daily for 60 days and found a fairly steady rate of .15 over this time period. Next, the researcher implemented an automatic computer-controlled home telephone calling device. The rate of absenteeism was then tracked for 60 days after the installation of the new system. The researcher observed a steadily decreasing rate which appeared to level off at about .06 and concluded that the new system of home calling was responsible for (that is, caused) the decline. Notice that researchers who use quasi-experimental designs are intent on making cause-and-effect claims (they often conclude that their treatment or intervention resulted in a change in the trend). Such cause-and-effect claims, however, are more risky without the use of a randomized control group.

How can the researcher be certain that the computer calling system, not some other factor, was responsible for the effect? Maybe the calling system was put into effect in early February, and absenteeism might have improved without *any* intervention during March because of better weather. Or possibly a new principal was hired in February, one that vowed to lower absenteeism using other methods. Or maybe new computers were introduced in the school in February, enhancing student interest, and consequently lowering absenteeism. Or maybe the pre-intervention rate of .15 in the preceding months was unusually high due to a flu epidemic, so the "improved" rate of .06 represented a return to normal during February and March (and hence there was no treatment effect at all). The point is that other interpretations are plausible without a randomized comparison group, one that would be affected similarly by weather, flu, new policies, new computers, and the like. Ideally, one would also want to track a randomized control group within the same school, forming a controlled basis for comparison (in other words, redesign the quasi-experiment into a true experiment).

Educational research that is quasi-experimental is not flawed simply because it is quasi-experimental, for it may be that techniques such as group or case-by-case matching successfully produced comparable groups. Group matching involves selecting a comparison *group* that is similar on average to a treatment group on the matched variables; case-by-case matching involves repeatedly selecting a comparison *subject* who is similar to a treatment subject on each of the matched variables. (More will be said about matching in Chapters 7 and 11.) It may be that nonrandom groups are, for all practical purposes, essentially similar and do function as adequate controls in the same way as randomized groups. It is unwarranted to automatically assume, however, that they are similar. Quasi-experimental research is common in education, and good quasi-experimental research is marked by the use of clever control procedures to circumvent some of the problems associated with lack of randomization.

HIGHLIGHT AND LEARNING CHECK 3-4

Time Series Quasi-Experiments

Time series quasi-experiments examine patterns and trends by repeated observations or measures over time. Why are such designs prone to difficulties in establishing cause-and-effect connections and to rival explanations?

Several common applications of true experiments and quasi-experiments are shown in Table 3.3.

Table 3.3 Examples of True and Quasi-Experimental Research

True Experimental Research

- A researcher randomly assigned 100 students to either an experimental group (with exercise 4 times a week) or a control group (with no exercise) and after 6 months tested their memory spans.
- A researcher pretested students' ability to reason with logic and then randomly assigned 100 to a group that received a daily dose of ginseng or a control group that received placebo. All the students were posttested 6 months later.
- A researcher measured the "baseline" level of hyperactivity in 100 hyperactive third graders. The two students (one pair) with the highest level of hyperactivity were randomly assigned to either an experimental group (given Ritalin) or a control group (given a placebo). Then all of the other pairs were similarly assigned, until the pair with the lowest level of hyperactivity was randomly assigned. The researcher collected hyperactivity measures after 3 months.

Quasi-Experimental Research

- A researcher implemented year-round schooling in one district and found a similar one to serve as a control. After 3 years, students' average achievement scores were compared.
- A researcher found 50 7-year-old identical twins who were all tested in their mathematical reasoning aptitude. One member of each pair volunteered to have piano lessons weekly for 2 years (the other member did not). Eight years later, all the twins were tested in their math ability.
- A researcher measured the dropout rate in a large urban school district for 4 years before implementing a mentoring program in the district. The dropout rate was then monitored for another 4 years.

Causal Comparative Versus Correlational

CAUSAL COMPARATIVE RESEARCH: Nonintervention research aimed at uncovering relationships by comparing groups of people who already differ on a variable of interest. It uses designs that search for causes or effects of a preexisting factor of interest. The preexisting factor differentiates groups and permits a meaningful comparison (e.g., examining achievement differences between children in one-parent and two-parent families).

Causal comparative and correlational research both stand in stark contrast to true experimental and quasi-experimental research. As we have seen, experimental research involves some type of manipulation or intervention in order to comfortably make cause-and-effect statements. Causal comparative and correlational research involve *no intervention, manipulation, or random assignment* of any sort, and consequently, pose challenges for researchers intent on discovering cause-and-effect relationships. These research approaches involve the examination of relationships that exist "naturally," meaning without any intervention by the researcher. Let's examine causal comparative research first.

Causal Comparative Research: Group Classifications

A researcher might explore the relationship between the amount of television watching and academic achievement in a causal comparative study. Students might be classified into one of four groups based on how much television they watch (0 to 5 hours per week, 6 to 15 hours per week, 16 to 25 hours per week, and 26 or more hours per week). Then academic achievement scores would be collected and compared across the four classifications. Notice that students were *classified* in accordance with their television habits; they were not assigned randomly to watch a prescribed number of hours per week (a manipulation). This classification procedure is the hallmark of causal comparative research, and as such involves studying "the world the way it is." Causal comparative research might be better retitled "group self-classification" research. (In a sense, subjects assign *themselves* to a group on the basis of a characteristic, hence the term *classification.*) Causal comparative research, then, uses one or more attribute variables in its search for relationships.

HIGHLIGHT AND LEARNING CHECK 3-5

Existing Group Differences

Causal comparative research focuses on participant attribute variables, searching for relationships by comparing groups classified by existing differences. Explain why finding higher academic achievement in students who sleep 10 hours nightly compared to those who sleep 5 hours nightly is weak evidence that sleep by itself aids retention of learned material.

Another example of this approach would involve exploring the relationship between early music lessons and later math achievement. Two groups of sixth-grade children might be formed: those who had piano lessons prior to age 7 and those who did not. Then the math achievement of the two groups would be compared. There is no intervention or manipulation here, and no random assignment to music conditions. This type of causal comparative study is more like a "natural" experiment. Even if the children who had piano lessons were higher achievers in math, the explanation could be related to some other extraneous factor, for example, socioeconomic status (wealthier families could afford music lessons *and* math camp).

Many issues in educational research can only be studied in this passive (nonexperimental) manner because to do so in any other way would be impractical or unethical. The influence of divorce on children's achievement, interests, and aspirations could only be studied with the causal comparative method. (Can you imagine assigning parents randomly to the "bitter divorce group"? Of course not.) Another example of causal comparative research might be the link between style of parenting and outcomes such as academic achievement, self-esteem, and disruptive behavior. In this case, parents would be classified (not assigned) into one of several groups based on their parenting style. Then measures of achievement and self-esteem would be compared across the parenting styles.

Tempered Conclusions

In the preceding examples of television, music, divorce, and parenting, we see that researchers must temper their interpretations about cause and effect. If frequent television watching is associated with lower achievement, one does not know whether television was responsible for the decline in achievement; possibly, the low achievement was a consequence of lower scholastic ability, which led to a lack of interest in school, and more television watching to fill the void left by that lack of interest (not doing homework and the like). Similarly, if children of divorced parents have more behavior problems at school, one would not know what caused what (or even whether one caused the other). Maybe the behavior problems were a result of the divorce; maybe the divorce was the result of behavior problems. Quite possibly, both the divorce and behavior problems were a consequence of some other cause entirely (like socioeconomic factors). Further, if an authoritarian style of parenting is associated with more disruptive behavior at school, could it not be the case that children who are disruptive to begin with might foster a specific type of authoritarian parenting? This problem is akin to the old chicken and egg problem—which came first?

Consider another hypothetical study aimed at comparing IQs of adolescents who were breast fed versus bottle fed as infants. This would qualify as a causal comparative study because groups were formed on the basis of an attribute variable or preexisting difference (they could not be randomly assigned, and, in a sense, the adolescents assigned themselves). Let's presume that the IQs of breast-fed infants were significantly higher than the IQs of their bottle-fed counterparts. It can be concluded, quite correctly, that there exists a relationship between type of feeding and IQ measures. It may not be warranted to conclude that breast-feeding *results* in higher IQs, however, because of the inherent limitations imposed by causal comparative research. This is because breast-feeding mothers may be different from other mothers in many important ways. For example, breast-feeding mothers might be older and have a higher socioeconomic status. They might be healthier, less likely to have consumed alcohol while pregnant, less likely to live in homes with lead paint (assuming this is linked to socioeconomic status), or more likely to expose their preschool children to music. All of these other reasons, plus hundreds more, could easily be the causal mechanism underlying the type-of-feeding and IQ connection.

Causal comparative studies using attribute variables are common in other fields, and their interpretations are also fraught with difficulties. Consider a hypothetical finding that vegetarians live longer than meat eaters. Is this longevity the result of diet? We simply would not know because, for example, the vegetarians may also exercise more and this exercise might be the direct cause of their longevity. Or maybe the vegetarians smoke less, and this difference is the real cause of the longevity effect. If this is true, then smokers who become vegetarians would not increase their longevity in any way. (I am reminded of early reports that premature male baldness is linked to heart attacks among the middle aged. If a man were balding, would it then be wise for him to have hair transplants to ward off a heart attack?)

Consider one more example. Let's assume that it is discovered that those who have headaches also have high levels of muscle tension in their neck and shoulders. Would you interpret this to mean that muscle tension in the neck and shoulders causes headaches? Isn't it just as likely that headaches lead to muscle tension in response to pain? Or might a third factor, like pollen, cause both the headache and the "achy all over feeling" that triggers muscle tension? Clearly, causal comparative studies, despite the name, are not as well suited to study cause and effect as are experimental studies. This approach to research is better titled "attribute studies" or "comparative studies," dropping the inference about cause altogether. (The word *cause* is undoubtedly included in this label because of researchers' ultimate interest in cause.)

HIGHLIGHT AND LEARNING CHECK 3-6

Casual Comparative Caution

Causal comparative studies are common in education, creating the need to be overly cautious when interpreting findings and reaching conclusions. Presume a study revealed that the lowest quartile (25%) rank of high school students were also in the lowest quartile in birth weight. What cautions are needed before concluding that there is a causal connection between birth weight and academic performance?

Search for Causes

Causal comparative studies are valuable, though, because they do uncover relationships rather easily which could be studied further with different, preferably experimental, methods to learn more about the basis (cause) of the relationship. If experimental methods are not possible (e.g., studying the influence of divorce on children) or impractical (e.g., studying the effects of different styles of parenting), then clever researchers who use causal comparative methods must rely on other techniques to help illuminate uncovered relationships. One technique is the investigation of *time sequence.* For example, if it is found that divorce is related to misbehavior at school, a time sequence could differentiate the divorce-causes-misbehavior interpretation from the misbehavior-causes-divorce interpretation. Since the cause of an effect must occur first, the divorce should *precede* the misbehavior if it is the causal mechanism. But if divorce is the effect of a misbehavior cause, then the misbehavior should come first. The reality, of course, is certainly not that simple. Both divorce and behavior problems at school may themselves be the complex effects of many other complex causes.

HIGHLIGHT AND LEARNING CHECK 3-7

Causal Comparative Techniques

Some topics in education can only be studied using non-intervention, causal comparative designs (e.g., influence of divorce, size of family, socioeconomic status, etc.). There are, however, strategies for learning more about causal connections. What techniques enable researchers to learn more about the bases of relationships uncovered by causal comparative designs?

Causal comparative researchers use other strategies to infer cause. One might be called the method of "common prior antecedents." This method involves focusing on a presumed effect, say, skill at teaching. After groups of highly skilled and less skilled teachers have been identified, one begins a systematic search for prior differences that distinguish the two groups. For example, one might find no differences between the two groups on college grade point average, highest degree (bachelor's versus master's), educational philosophy, whether or not they have children, and many other prior variables. By contrast, it might be found that the highly skilled teachers regularly enrolled in continuing education courses and attended workshops, whereas the less skilled teachers did neither. If such dramatic differences did exist (and they seem to make sense), then one would have some degree of assurance that the variable on which the two groups differ (continuing education) is probably related in some causal way to the difference which formed the basis of the two groups in the first place (more versus less skilled teachers). At the very least, this finding supports the causal interpretation, though a true experiment would constitute far more rigorous evidence. One alternative hypothesis is that skilled teachers are simply "born to teach." And they are also more interested in education issues because of their skills, with their continuing education merely reflecting this interest.

Establishing cause is clearly a proposition not of all or none but of more or less, and so it is with different approaches to research: Some approaches are better suited than others for establishing cause. A well designed and executed causal comparative study, to be sure, may establish stronger causal connections than a weak, confounded experiment. Also, it makes little sense to search for *the* cause, as if there were one and only one. It seems reasonable to conclude that most relationships in the teaching and learning process are complex; an experiment could shed light on one aspect of a multifaceted causal chain, and a causal comparative study could illuminate another facet.

CRITICAL THINKER ALERT 3-6

Causal Comparative

Causal comparative studies (also called ex-post-facto studies) are common in educational research. These studies use attribute variables, not independent variables, and although causal comparative findings are difficult to interpret, they often suggest ideas that might be tested experimentally.

Discussion: How do you interpret a finding that shows elementary students who were held back (not promoted) in first or second grade have a much higher probability than promoted students of dropping out of high school? Does this finding (and your interpretation) suggest an experimental test to determine cause and effect? Is this feasible or practical? Is it a meaningful research question?

Correlational Research

Correlational research is also a type of nonintervention research, one that measures the world the way it is in search of relationships. But correlational studies do differ from causal comparative ones in several ways. Let's examine these more closely.

Individual Differences

The most salient difference between causal comparative and correlational research is whether subjects are classified into groups (causal comparative) or measured as individuals (correlational). Consider a typical correlational study, one examining the relationship between television watching and scholastic achievement. (Recall that the same relationship was assessed earlier as an example of a causal comparative study.) Assume that a sample of 100 students was available for this study. Each student (subject) would be measured and scaled on a continuum revealing the number of hours per week (on average) spent watching television. All the subjects would also be measured on a scale designed to assess scholastic achievement. Finally, a statistical maneuver would be applied to reveal in the data the extent to which the two variables are related. (There will be more about this statistic, called the *correlation coefficient* or *r,* in Chapter 11.) Notice that no groups were formed with the correlational approach; the individual scores were not clumped in any way. The subjects were analyzed statistically as individuals.

CORRELATIONAL RESEARCH: A type of nonexperimental research using one of several designs that measure individual differences in an attempt to uncover relationships between variables.

Correlational ("individual") researchers are keenly interested in the vast array of differences in people that need explanation, such as the rich differences in intelligence, personality, home environments, teaching styles, learning styles, leadership styles, and temperaments, to name just a few. Differences in constructs like these cry out for explanations. Consider the complex variation in "happiness," a focus of correlational researchers. (Psychologists who study individual differences via correlations are often called *differential psychologists.*) In order to explain differences in people's levels of happiness, one might begin by determining what other differences are correlated (and *un*correlated) with happiness. Correlational researchers, such as psychologists David Lykken and Auke Tellegen of the University of Minnesota, are finding that happiness is related to individual differences in optimism but apparently *not* correlated with "logical" factors such as wealth, education, family, job status, and professional achievement. Happiness is apparently best understood as a trait (Lykken & Tellegen, 1996), probably in part genetically based, whose level seems to be randomly predetermined and relatively immune to the vicissitudes of daily life. Like a biological set point that partly determines weight, people tend to hover around a constant happiness level that may only temporarily shift (for maybe 3 to 6 months at most) after an event such as winning a lottery or losing a loved one.

This theory suggests that someone with many problems may be happier than someone who "has it all." The point is that individual differences need explaining, and that they are best explained by determining what other differences they are correlated with. Correlational researchers welcome differences, and they design their measuring instruments to be sensitive to very small differences. This is because in a correlational study, greater variation (a larger spread

HIGHLIGHT AND LEARNING CHECK 3-8

Correlational Designs

Correlational research, like causal comparative research, involves no intervention, and it is conceptually similar to causal comparative research. The major difference between causal comparative and correlational research is that participants are classified (grouped) in causal comparative research but measured on a continuum (ungrouped) in correlational research. This distinction has statistical, not interpretative, implications. Explain how a study of age at entrance to kindergarten and its link to later special education placement could be approached using both causal comparative and correlational designs.

in scores) is more likely to correlate with other measured differences. Simply, if you want to show that happiness is correlated with optimism, you want the full range of people—happy and sad, optimistic and pessimistic, and those in the middle.

Correlation Is Not Causation

Virtually all of the cautionary statements made about causal comparative research with regard to cause and effect are equally applicable and important with correlational research. When a correlation is found between the amount of sugar consumed by first graders and their level of hyperactivity, it might be tempting to conclude that sugar consumption causes hyperactivity. This type of reasoning is faulty because associations do not prove cause. The sugar and hyperactivity correlation could be explained by some other causal mechanism; for example, high sugar consumption might be linked to a poor diet, and the lack of vitamin D found in a poor diet might be the real trigger for hyperactivity. (This illustration is merely hypothetical.) If so, then simply reducing the first graders' sugar consumption would have no affect on their hyperactivity. Consider reports from Sweden that reveal a correlation between the number of babies born and the population of storks around the calendar year. We would not conclude that storks cause babies! (The causal mechanism is likely related to climate.)

HIGHLIGHT AND LEARNING CHECK 3-9

Links, Not Cause

Correlational research establishes links between variables. A link may or may not be causal in any way. Explain how a correlational link between television watching and class rank in high school may and may *not* be causal in origin.

Consider a correlation between the speed of test taking and scores on a test (let's pretend that faster speed is associated with higher scores). Does this correlation suggest that speed causes better performance? If so, then simply encouraging the lower scorers to go faster should raise their scores. (This is unlikely.) Or consider the correlation between foot size and spelling ability among elementary school children. One does not cause the other; development explains both (older children have bigger feet and they are better spellers). Finally, what about the correlation between the number of churches and the number of liquor stores in a sampling of American cities? Does church drive people to drink? Hardly. The causal mechanism is simply city size—larger cities have more churches and more liquor stores as a function of population size.

CRITICAL THINKER ALERT 3-7

Correlation

Correlational findings do not imply cause-and-effect relationships, though they often uncover relationships that might be tested experimentally.

Discussion: How do you interpret a finding that shows a positive correlation between physical exercise and grade point average among high schoolers? What other interpretations are possible? How would you test this relationship using true experimental research?

Summary of the Differences Between Causal Comparative and Correlational Research

Causal comparative research is differentiated from correlational research because subjects are *grouped* on the basis of a shared or common characteristic or attribute variable (e.g., whether they had early training in music). The classification (not random assignment) into groups and their comparison on some other measure (e.g., math aptitude) are the defining characteristics of causal comparative research. Such research is focused on the effects or causes of these "clumped" group differences, though the basic design is rather weak for disentangling cause and effect (or establishing cause in any sense). This design does not ignore individual differences, to be sure, but research questions are directed at cause-and-effect relationships and answered with group contrasts (hence the name *causal comparative* for this research). The question of the effects of authoritarian versus permissive styles of parenting, for example, would be answered by contrasting groups of children with parents of both styles while searching for influences on behavior, such as occupational aspirations, self-esteem, or whatever the researchers' hunches might be. Both causal comparative and correlational research reveal associations, and because of the nonmanipulated nature of their variables, cannot conclusively establish cause and effect. Cause-and-effect relationships are best discovered with experimental research. Remember that association does not imply cause.

Correlational research, by contrast, measures individual differences (unclumped) on two or more variables, and describes their linkage with a statistical summary. Correlational researchers are often interested in the full range of people's differences and their explanations. They may seek to explain variation in occupational aspirations, for example, by correlating it with measures of tolerance to frustration or even height. Their focus is the explanation of human variation; they are less interested in isolating the one-and-only cause or effect.

Examples of causal comparative and correlational research are shown in Table 3.4.

Single-Subject Versus Group

In some fields in education, such as special education or counseling, researchers often use designs that require a single subject (or a small group). The goal of single-subject research is to determine if interventions designed to change some aspect of behavior are, in fact, effective (at least for a single individual). Single-subject research designs achieve their control through a system that uses the individual as his or her own control if a control group is not available. For example, let's assume that Sam shows clear signs of hyperactivity and his teacher wants to "experiment" in an attempt to find the best strategy (at least for Sam) for bringing about behavior that is more conducive to learning. The teacher might record the frequency of hyperactivity by sampling behavior every hour (several 5-minute blocks could be randomly chosen each hour). This systematic observation functions as a baseline against which treatments may be compared.

SINGLE-SUBJECT RESEARCH: Research aimed at studying a single individual (or very small group) to learn more about relationships among variables or trends over time.

Next, the teacher might introduce a system for praising instances of Sam's behavior judged to be counter hyperactive. The teacher might continue praising Sam for a

Table 3.4 Examples of Causal Comparative and Correlational Research

Causal Comparative Research

- A researcher measured the mathematical reasoning ability of young children who had enrolled in Montessori schools and compared the scores with those of a group of similar children who had not been to Montessori schools.
- A researcher compared the weights of students at schools with and without structured physical education.
- A researcher compared the high school dropout rates of students who had been retained (held back) in elementary school and similar students who had not been retained.
- A researcher formed three groups of preschoolers–those who never watched Sesame Street, those who watched it sometimes, and those who watched it frequently–and then compared the three groups on a reading readiness test.

Correlational Research

- A researcher measured students' self-esteem and linked these scores to ratings of their physical attractiveness.
- A researcher measured how quickly students completed a test to see if their speed was associated with test scores.
- A researcher investigated the relationship between age and reaction time in a simple task (push the left button to a red light, the right button to a green light).
- A researcher studied a group of 5-year-olds by examining the association between their current height and the age (in weeks) when they first began walking.

HIGHLIGHT AND LEARNING CHECK 3-10

Group and Single-Subject Tradeoff

Both single-subject and group research investigate relationships of interest to researchers in education. Group research often yields more generalizable findings, yet single-subject research may yield very useful findings without widespread application. What type of research is more likely to incorporate time as a factor to establish control? Why?

GROUP RESEARCH: Research aimed at studying one or more large groups to learn more about relationships among variables or trends over time.

period of time while carefully observing his hyperactivity and recording his progress. If his hyperactive behavior declines during the praising sessions, then this would be taken as evidence that the treatment is effective. Greater support for its effectiveness would be found if Sam's hyperactivity increased when the treatment (praise) was withdrawn (this is usually called a *return to baseline*). Furthermore, when the treatment is reinstated, one would expect to find a concomitant reduction in hyperactivity. These return-to-baseline and reinstated-treatment phases may continue until the evidence for the treatment's effectiveness is so strong that a return to baseline is no longer needed as evidence.

The design described above is relatively simple, but simplicity is not characteristic of all single-subject designs. Some are very sophisticated indeed, and these will be described in Chapter 10. Single-subject research, as you may suspect, is not appropriate when a researcher intends to make widely generalized statements about the relative effectiveness of educational interventions.

In education, group research is far more common than single-subject research, since many researchers want to test broadly generalizable theories about school learning. Group research designs are the focus of Chapters 10 and 11. They appear in many different configurations, all intended to produce meaningful interpretations of

TABLE 3.5 Examples of Single-Subject and Group Studies

Single-Subject Studies

- Jim's frequency of stuttering was observed for 1 week, followed by 1-week observations during which classical music was played quietly in the background. Observations were then made for 1 week with no music in the background; finally, music was reinstated for 1 week before final observations.
- Sam and Ted, two very aggressive fifth graders, were placed on special diets and observed intensely for six 1-week sessions to determine if their diet was related to their behavior. The design was as follows, where D = diet and C = control:

Week:	1	2	3	4	5	6
Sam	C	D	C	D	C	D
Ted	D	C	D	C	D	C

Group Studies

- Two hundred low-achieving third graders were tutored for 1 hour after school by high school volunteers. After 6 months, their achievement was compared to that of a random control group which did not receive training.
- Three groups of 500 high school seniors (including first born, second born, and later born individuals) were tested to determine their level of occupational aspiration. The researcher then compared the levels across birth orders.

data that have been gathered according to a specific plan (design). The number of subjects required to form a group is discussed in Chapter 8.

Here are two examples to clarify this distinction. A finding from a single-subject research design might be, "Paul's social interactions increased, compared to baseline, when these behaviors were reinforced with tokens." By contrast, a group research finding might be, "The 30 classes that were taught rules for sharing had fewer conflicts than the 30 control classes." Other examples of single-subject versus group studies are shown in Table 3.5.

HIGHLIGHT AND LEARNING CHECK 3-11

Classroom Self-Reflection

Teacher research is self-reflective inquiry, that is, the study of one's own teaching. Traditional research is far more formal, often aimed at testing hypotheses generated from theories. What other differences describe these two approaches?

Teacher Versus Traditional

Teacher research is often described as self-reflective inquiry, and as such, refers to classroom teachers who study their own practice of teaching. Recall from Chapter 1 that this general concept was referred to as *action research.* Teacher research can be viewed as a type of action research. Teachers who favor this approach to research understand the complex nature of the teaching and learning process in the classroom, but at the same time, they are intent on studying their professional craft in a personalized, intimate, empowering way.

Teacher research also represents an attitude. Teacher-researchers often question the value of outside experts who collect data without any personal experience and issue directives to the passive implementers (teachers) about the best methods of pedagogy. Teacher research assumes that teachers are reflective practitioners who have an obligation to study their own work, in spite of the institutional bureaucracy that may appear to deny teachers some of their intellectual and professional rights. Teacher-researchers are more likely to use their field notes, work samples, or journals instead of standardized test scores. They may use shared teacher stories and metaphors as a way of understanding classrooms.

TEACHER RESEARCH: Self-reflective inquiry whereby teachers study their own practice, collect data, and attempt to solve a problem or improve learning in their classrooms.

Some call teacher research a "movement," and it is clear that the movement is gaining momentum, most likely because it recognizes that "teaching belongs to teachers, and that, as experts about their own practice, teachers are the ones most able to understand and refine their work" (Oberg & McCutcheon, 1987). It would be ill-advised to think of this approach to research as substandard. Newer standards for the validity of classroom research (see, e.g., Eisenhart & Borko, 1993) are in fact more inclusive than conventional ones and in many ways create a more level playing field. Teacher research offers an alternative method for gaining knowledge and reforming our schools and should not be perceived as merely a small-scale version of traditional research.

TRADITIONAL RESEARCH: Formal scientific research using accepted guidelines and an integrated process aimed at testing hypotheses.

Traditional research, by contrast, is far more formal. Traditional researchers strive toward theory building and generalized knowledge. Such research is "colder" than teacher research in the sense that data gathering is detached, standardized, and designed to be relatively free from bias. Traditional research usually builds on prior research, as revealed by a review of the literature, and its findings are more remote, often "hidden" in journals, couched in statistical terms, and embedded within research jargon that few practitioners can understand. Standardized test scores may be transformed in arcane ways. Critics say that the academic authors writing such reports may be promoted to full professors within their institutions, but classrooms may be left in the dark.

Examples of teacher research and traditional research appear Table 3.6.

CRITICAL THINKER ALERT 3-8

Action Research

At the same time that the No Child Left Behind agenda emphasizes the traditions of rigorous scientific research, there is a movement toward teacher ("action") research in classrooms. Both approaches to research have value (depending on the purpose of the research).

Discussion: Do you think that the traditions of rigorous scientific research (treatments, controls, randomization, etc.) are necessarily at odds with teacher action research in the classroom? Can you think of a research question that is best answered using a model of teacher action research? Can you think of one best answered using experimentation and large-scale sampling designed to maximize generalization?

TABLE 3.6 Examples of Teacher Research and Traditional Research

Teacher Research

- Mrs. Goetz wondered whether cooperative learning strategies would help students learn about division using fractions. She arranged for her third period math class to complete the exercise sheets while working together in groups of four to five students. She compared their final test scores with those of her fourth period "control" group that worked on the exercises individually. Because the cooperative group did so well, she took "action" and used cooperative learning strategies in her other math classes.
- Upon reflection, Mr. Shepherd realized that seventh graders would learn German faster if only German (and no English) were spoken in his classes after the midterm. He tried this for a semester and compared the students' test scores against the scores of students in his classes the previous semester. The results favored the German-only method, the method he now uses.

Traditional Research

- In order to test the effectiveness of computer-assisted instruction in physics (developed from generative models of learning), 60 schools were selected to use the courseware for 1 year. A randomized control group of 60 schools which used traditional "talk-and-chalk" methods was used as a comparison.
- In a multisite longitudinal study of the effects of early childhood education, 200 "at-risk" preschoolers participated in a special intervention program from the age of 1 to 4. They were tracked for 10 years and assessed yearly on a battery of different measures. A control group not receiving any intervention was also tracked and measured as a comparison.

Large-Scale Policy Versus Small-Scale Evaluation

Much research in education is directed toward forming public policy or creating new legislation affecting a large population of students and teachers. Because of the potential to impact hundreds of thousands of students and teachers, this type of research is large scale, often involving thousands of schools within a state or hundreds of thousands of students nationwide. As you might expect, this type of research is associated with organizations designed for this task and requires ample funding. The data collection is massive, the analysis is complex, and the public policy implications are often dramatic.

LARGE-SCALE POLICY RESEARCH: Research using large data sets (often standardized measures) with the intention of shaping public policy and influencing reform.

SMALL-SCALE EVALUATION RESEARCH: Research aimed at evaluating local programs or procedures for the purpose of improvement or decision making.

Many schools (or districts) need programs evaluated on a much smaller scale. The impact is largely local, although the success of a local program might easily spread beyond its borders with time. This type of research is often referred to as *evaluation research* and is distinguished by a "need to know" whether a program as currently implemented is achieving its goals or whether (and how) it might be improved. In contrast to large-scale policy research, the impact of evaluation research tends to be rather localized (within a school or district).

Table 3.7 presents several examples that contrast large-scale policy research and small-scale evaluation research.

HIGHLIGHT AND LEARNING CHECK 3-12

Large-Scale Useful Data

Large-scale policy research often uses standardized achievement measures and focuses on shaping public policy or suggesting reform. Small-scale evaluation research focuses on local programs and practices with the intent of improving outcomes or deciding on continuance. Is large-scale policy research intended for public use? Where might one find useful large-scale data?

Table 3.7 Examples of Large-Scale Policy and Small-Scale Evaluation Research

Large-Scale Policy Research

- Researchers used the National Assessment of Educational Progress (NAEP) data to compare the white-minority gap in achievement over the past 6 years in 20 large urban districts.
- Researchers sampled 400 charter schools (and 12,000 students) in seven western states and compared their reading achievement gain to a matched sample in noncharter public schools.

Small-Scale Evaluation Research

- Researchers at a local high school compared students' going-to-college rate before and after implementing a new program that centered on students visiting local colleges during their senior year.
- Researchers at a local middle school surveyed students to learn more about their reactions to a longer day but shorter week school schedule.

CRITICAL THINKER ALERT 3-9

Policy Research

Although large-scale policy research often uses national data sets managed by federal agencies and institutions with federal support, students of educational research may access portions of these large repositories of data under the guidance of others (often faculty members who have been trained in the access and analysis of such data).

Discussion: The National Center for Education Statistics (NCES) manages a large data set referred to as the National Assessment of Educational Progress, or NAEP. It is also called "The Nation's Report Card" and is available on the NCES Web site (http://nces.ed.gov/nationsreportcard/). Much of these data are for public use and are available for secondary analyses using simple tools online. In 2003, for example, nearly 350,000 students (in fourth and eighth grades) in over 70,000 schools were assessed in reading. Subgroup analyses included breakdowns by gender, race and/or ethnicity, school location, type of school, and eligibility for free or reduced cost lunch. Researchers use many other background and situational variables in their analyses. What other variables do you think might provide especially useful information about reading achievement in our nation's schools? Why do you think this?

Thinking Beyond Dichotomies

It is probably not productive to think about the previous seven pairs of research approaches as dichotomies, that is, in the either-or terms suggested by the presence of *versus* between the approaches. (Sorting the types of research into dichotomies

HIGHLIGHT AND LEARNING CHECK 3-13

Multiple Approaches

Research in education is seldom an instance of one pure type of research. A single study often mixes multiple approaches. Explain how a mixed method study might yield greater understanding of a problem in education.

functioned here as an organizational scheme, but this scheme will undoubtedly break down somewhat when applied to published research.) Many researchers believe that valuable educational research should be a mix, as needed, across these distinctions. Such mixed studies are sometimes referred to as *mixed methodologies* (see "Mixed Methodologies in Educational Research: A Conclusion" below). Clever mixed methodologies often function to increase our understanding of the teaching and learning process in ways that a single method cannot.

Mixed Methodologies in Educational Research: A Conclusion

This chapter revealed the great diversity in approaches to educational research. Education is fortunate to have great variation in modes of inquiry, opening up research potential in every corner of its discipline. There is no compelling reason for research in education to be single-minded, and indeed, premiere journals in education publish with increasing frequency what is often called *mixed method* research. The usual meaning of this term suggests research that combines both quantitative and qualitative approaches within a single study. A study of cheating, for example, might use a statistical model to estimate the incidence of cheating based on the similarity of answers to multiple-choice questions of students sitting in close proximity. This measure of cheating might be supplemented by richer information obtained from focus groups or video surveillance (with permission). Teacher action research often illustrates the advantages of mixed method research, for test scores are often analyzed in concert with classroom observations or informal interviews.

The study of educational research is nevertheless aided by the imposition of some simplifying structure on the diversity and complexity of research designs. One reasonable conclusion is that contemporary educational research is influenced most heavily by three major traditions: qualitative, quantitative, and action research. These distinct traditions have greatly influenced educational research over the years, sometimes forming research "camps." These three traditions, in fact, represent very different perspectives across many steps in the research process, such as hypothesis formation, sampling, measurement, and data analysis (to name a few). For these reasons, the three approaches to educational research—quantitative, qualitative, and action—will be compared and contrasted in each of the remaining chapters. This will function as a constant reminder that educational researchers approach their work in very different ways. There is no one best method; each method is

HIGHLIGHT AND LEARNING CHECK 3-14

Mixed Method

The usual meaning of *mixed method* research in education suggests an approach that combines both quantitative and qualitative types of data and designs. Explain how a study of teaching effectiveness might use mixed methods.

CRITICAL THINKER ALERT 3-10

Blended Research

There are many different approaches to educational research. Many times a single study cannot be labeled as one type to the exclusion of others. Most research studies have blended characteristics of several different dimensions, making pigeonholing them difficult and not very useful.

Discussion: Browse current issues of the journal *Education Policy Analysis Archives* (http://epaa.asu.edu/). What aspects of the reported research are most convincing of the blending of different types of research?

more or less useful for a particular purpose. As the quantitative, qualitative, and action approaches to research are revealed in the remaining chapters, try to imagine how two—or all three—might be combined into mixed methodologies. Mixed method research in education has great potential to influence ways of thinking about problems and practices in the teaching and learning process.

MORE EXAMPLES

Additional descriptions of published research may help to solidify your knowledge of important ideas related to different types of studies educational researchers use to test their research hypotheses and answer their research questions. You will recognize aspects of the seven dimensions previously described. You will find additional descriptions on the Web-based student study site for this textbook (www.sagepub.com/eic).

Chapter Summary

The research hypothesis is tested within the context of prior research (the "literature") in an area using many different approaches. These alternative forms of educational research can be differentiated in terms of *quantitative* orientation (analysis with numbers) or *qualitative* orientation (analysis with words). They can *describe* characteristics within the sample or use the sample in order to make *inferences* about a larger population. They may use *experimental* or cause-and-effect methods (manipulation, or creation, of an independent variable with the use of random assignment) or *quasi-experimental* methods (a manipulated intervention without random assignment).

Further, research may involve comparing groups that already differ (e.g., children in one-parent versus two-parent families) with the hope of learning about cause and effect, as in *causal comparative* research; it may also involve measuring individual characteristics and statistically linking them to other measures with the hope of discovering and explaining relationships, as in *correlational* research. Researchers may also study *single cases* or (more typically) larger *groups*. Practitioners may conduct action research for the purpose of learning more about their practice, as in *teacher* research; others may carry out more formal research, often guided by theory with the intent of generalizing to a larger population, as in *traditional* research. Finally, researchers may conduct large-scale studies, often involving thousands of schools (statewide or nationwide) with very large data sets. Findings from such large-scale studies often shape policy and influence legislation. These massive studies are contrasted with small-scale, localized studies often completed for the purpose of learning more about students, teachers, programs, or curricula within a district or school. *Mixed method* research in education usually suggests a research approach that is both qualitative and quantitative.

Application Exercises

1. Decide whether each of the research summaries below is a better example of quantitative or qualitative research.
   a. Researchers concluded that students often perceive school as The Big Game.
   b. Researchers found that standardized achievement measures have steadily declined.
   c. Researchers found that students' stories reflected strong achievement motivation.
   d. Researchers concluded that the time spent on homework predicted final examination performance.

2. Decide whether each of the research summaries below is a better example of descriptive or inferential research.
   a. Researchers found that teachers at Henderson High favored the concept of year-round schooling.
   b. Researchers concluded that males have less electrical activity in the emotional centers of the brain.
   c. Researchers concluded that the general public perceives teaching to be one of the most important occupations.
   d. Researchers found that very few students in Chicago schools studied Latin as a foreign language.

3. Decide whether each of the research summaries below is a better example of true experimental or quasi-experimental research.
   a. Researchers compared the treatment group receiving low-fat meals with a randomized control group and found faster mental processing in the low-fat group.
   b. Researchers compared students' scores under the "less is more" curriculum with a matched comparison group and found better achievement under "less is more."
   c. Researchers observed the trends in teenage smoking before and after the advertising ban and concluded that the ban effectively reduced the incidence of smoking.
   d. Researchers manipulated the length of lecture time in six randomized groups and concluded that the optimum length is 20 minutes.

4. Decide whether each of the research summaries below is a better example of causal comparative or correlational research.
   a. Smokers were compared with nonsmokers and it was found that smokers have shorter attention spans.
   b. Delinquents were compared with nondelinquents and it was found that delinquents were less likely to have grown up with fathers.
   c. Students' scores on the Inference Ability Test were significantly linked to hours of sleep.
   d. Children's weight at birth was found to be unrelated to their IQ scores 10 years later.

5. Decide whether each of the research summaries below is a better example of single-subject or group research.
   a. It was found that music influenced John's behavior more than other treatments did.
   b. Respondents' test scores were positively related to length of time allowed.
   c. Researchers found that females recognized subtle expressions more than males did.
   d. It was found that the key to Mrs. Smith's outstanding class performance was the frequent use of metaphor.

6. Decide whether each of the research summaries below is a better example of teacher or traditional research.
   a. Mr. Smith discovered that his students greatly benefited from brainstorming before writing.

b. Researchers found that the evolutionary theory of happiness was supported.
c. Professor Ortega found that students' understanding was enhanced with the use of 2 rather than 10 concrete examples.
d. Researchers found that extroversion as a trait is largely inheritable.

7. Decide whether each of the research summaries below is a better example of large-scale policy research or small-scale evaluation research.
   a. Researchers studied the driving records of nearly 50,000 high school seniors in seven populated states and correlated the number of violations with class ranking based on the students' grade point averages. They found a positive relationship between "clean" driving records and class ranking (higher achieving students were safer drivers, after adjusting for total miles driven) and recommended that major insurance companies adjust rates according to academic standing.
   b. Researchers found in a sample of over 1,000 schools in the Southwest that there were fewer student absences in those schools that employed a full-time school nurse.
   c. Researchers at Blue Ridge High School found that a new program designed to increase students' going-to-college rates was not having its intended effects.
   d. Researchers at Red Rock Elementary School found far fewer missing assignments after teachers began posting all assignment schedules on the school's Web site.

8. Following the recommendations in Application Exercise 3 in Chapter 2, visit your library or use the Internet to locate published research that you would classify as mixed method research. Describe why you think the study uses a mixed method approach to research.

9. Browse current online journals that publish educational research in your field of interest (as described in the preceding paragraph). Set a reasonable time frame in which to locate studies that illustrate as many of the following approaches to research as you can find: quantitative, qualitative, descriptive, inferential, true experimental, quasi-experimental, causal comparative, correlational, single-subject, group, teacher, traditional, large-scale policy, and small-scale evaluation. Which approaches seem to dominate the field? Were any approaches to research not represented in your collection of studies? Can you offer any conclusions about approaches to research in your field after browsing? Are any patterns apparent?

ON YOUR OWN

Log on to the Web-based student study site at http://www.sagepub.com/eic for more information about the materials presented in this chapter, suggestions for activities, study aids such as electronic flashcards and review quizzes, a sample research proposal, and research recommendations that include journal article links (with discussion questions and an article evaluation guide) and questions related to this chapter.

Part II Research as Process

The three chapters in Part II contribute to the structural integrity of educational research by revealing its process. Part II may be viewed as framework supported by the foundation. Chapter 4 addresses the major issues related to the research question being posed, including those related to ethics, the meaningfulness of the research problem, and its context within prior research. Once the researcher focuses on a research question, there are a series of important decisions that must be made. Chapter 4 reveals that critical thinking about different types of data has consequences for the value of exposed findings. Many studies in educational research venture beyond the answer to a single research question. They also raise new questions, which often are within a different framework.

Chapter 5 describes the terms used to build the framework that will answer the research question. Researchers investigate constructs (as in *construction*) by using tools designed by at least four types of variables and three types of hypotheses. This chapter reveals that researchers are constantly looking out for sources of influence that may challenge the validity of their claims. (They become watchful inspectors.) Critical thinking about variables and hypotheses sharpens researchers' conclusions.

Chapter 6 describes research as a process of integrated steps (the connecting structural hardware). This chapter makes clear that some educational research is geared toward explanation (i.e., theory based), while other research targets applied problems (e.g., action research). Increasingly, a new style is emerging: a practical blend. All three chapters in Part II reveal how both research and clear thinking can be understood as a process.

4

The Research Problem

Outline

Overview

Research in education is a process, or series of integrated steps. The whole purpose of the research, whatever the approach taken (as described in the previous chapter), is to learn more about the problem being investigated. Researchers hope that their qualitative or quantitative data will enable them to better understand the phenomenon or relationship that spurred their initial interest in the research. Not all problems in education open themselves for scientific inquiry. And even when problems do, that the data are available does not necessarily mean that they will enlighten the researcher. For these reasons, it is vital that researchers think clearly about the purpose of the research and know for certain what might, or might not, be learned from the involved process that extends from the research question to implications based on the obtained data. There is no sense in collecting data that cannot answer a research question.

Given the importance of the research question and its implications for the entire research process, this chapter addresses the major issues surrounding the research problem being investigated and the central questions which logically follow. As it turns out, once the researcher focuses on a research problem, there are a series of questions that must be answered. The answers to these questions determine whether the researcher should proceed.

The Research Hypothesis Versus the Research Question

First, let us make a distinction between a research hypothesis and a research question. Generally, researchers reserve the term *research hypothesis* for a study that is closely linked to a theory (usually called *theory based* and sometimes called *basic*). A *theory* is merely an explanation for a phenomenon or set of established empirical findings. (The value of theories is described further in Chapter 6.) It is the *theory* which produces a research hypothesis, and if supported by the research, the theory is given credibility. In a published research article, the research hypothesis frequently takes the form "It is predicted that . . ." or "It is expected that . . ." or "It is anticipated that . . ." or some similar statement. Almost all research hypotheses can be recast into the familiar form If A, then B, where A details a variation presumed to cause some effect, and B details the predicted outcome. This form (If A, then B) is helpful for distinguishing cause from effect, but it often produces awkward syntax. Hence, the research hypothesis frequently appears in the "It is expected that . . ." format. The hypothesis in a qualitative study may be reformatted and referred to as a *foreshadowed question.*

RESEARCH HYPOTHESIS: A predicted outcome based on theory or understanding, often stated as If A, then B. It may also be stated as a foreshadowed question in qualitative research.

The *research question,* by contrast, is usually (but not always) associated with studies that are more problem based, applied, or practical (less theoretical). In this case, the research question may arise from a practical rather than theoretical need to know something. For example, a school may evaluate a new system in place for decreasing absenteeism. The system involves an automatic computer-calling device that informs parents at home when a particular student is not in attendance. Does this system reduce absenteeism? Is it

RESEARCH QUESTION: The purpose of research stated in the form of a question.

worth the cost? Or consider a case where a superintendent wants to know whether the magnet or incentive schools in the district are successful at reducing or eliminating a prior mathematics achievement difference between male and female students. Notice that no theory is being tested in these applied situations; there is simply a real-world need for more information. In this case, the purpose of the research is usually stated in the form of a research question such as "Do magnet schools eliminate a math achievement gap between males and female students?" The research question is sometimes referred to by researchers as a *research objective,* and if so, is expressed in a format such as "The purpose of this study is to . . ."

RESEARCH PROBLEM: The state of affairs or context for research that make clear why data are being collected.

HIGHLIGHT AND LEARNING CHECK 4-1

No Research Vacuum

Research is not conducted within a vacuum. There is a context (problem) and purpose (hypothesis or question). Why do educational researchers avoid collecting isolated data without a reasoned outcome?

Many research reports precede a statement of the research hypothesis (or question) with a *problem statement.* This statement merely describes the reasons for research, such as lack of knowledge or conditions that need improvement. A problem statement provides a context for the research and makes clear why data were collected and analyzed. Problem statements in educational research are often focused on factors that impede optimal learning conditions.

Sources of the Hypothesis

Whether the purpose of research is stated as a hypothesis or question often tells us how closely the research is linked to a theory or model. The research hypothesis is usually (but not always) stated in a *directional* form, which means that the researcher can speculate about the direction of differences (higher or lower) or the direction of a relationship (positive or negative). It is the theory which spawned the hypothesis that provides the guidance about which direction the results might take. For example, the constructive theory of learning suggests that learners who take notes themselves during a lecture will remember more than those who follow along with notes that have been provided. The directional hypothesis might be, "If students take notes during a lecture rather than follow notes that have been supplied, then they will remember more after the lecture."

It turns out that research hypotheses can be formulated in several ways. One common way is via *deductive* reasoning, that is, reasoning from general to specific (general theories produce specific hypotheses). Constructivist learning theory (general) suggests that, for example, authentic learner-centered activities like discussions and group projects (specific) will result in greater learning than passive teacher-centered strategies like lecture and worksheets (for some types of learning objectives). It is also possible to reason in the other direction, or *inductively,* where specific ideas or experiences could lead to general conclusions in the form of a theory. Classroom teachers observe countless phenomena and experience countless specific interactions in their learning environments. These specific but recurring instances may provide good ideas for general teaching practices. A general model, or theory, may summarize

CRITICAL PERSPECTIVES 4-1

THE HYPOTHESIS

Critical Thinking Toolbox

Critical thinking is enhanced by trying to identify *unstated assumptions.* One trick to identifying unstated assumptions is to ask yourself "What is presumed true but not explicitly stated?" A problem in thinking exists when the unstated assumptions, once revealed, have questionable validity. Critical thinking is also enhanced by an awareness and avoidance of faulty *circular reasoning.* Circular reasoning occurs when the claim is the same as the evidence. It is usually apparent when the meaning of what precedes the word *because* is the same as the meaning of what follows the word (thus providing no new information). For example, the statement "Achievement is lower in large classes because there are too many students" is circular, since "large classes" and "too many students" mean the same thing, hence providing no explanation. "This is true because it is true" is hardly compelling.

The Hypothesis in Quantitative Research

The hypothesis in quantitative research is specific and set in stone for the duration of the study. It often appears as an If A, then B statement and is typically imposed on the research design by a theory. It is supported (or not) indirectly by a statistical test aimed at the null hypothesis. (As described in Chapters 5 and 13, this statistical hypothesis called the "null hypothesis" presumes there is no relationship among variables in the population represented by those in the study.) "Rejecting" the null hypothesis supports (rather than proves) the theory that generated the hypothesis in the first place.

The Hypothesis in Qualitative Research

A research hypothesis in qualitative research is permitted to "emerge" or "evolve" during data collection. Researchers' initial ideas about patterns among data are indeed fluid, and unless there exists an imposing and restrictive set of expectations that may cloud perceptions and search methods, the hypothesis at the conclusion of a study may be very different from the one at the beginning. Ongoing data collection shapes the working hypothesis. The research hypothesis may eventually generate a theory itself.

The Hypothesis in Action Research

An action research hypothesis is often born from a question aimed at solving a problem. One example might be, "How do I encourage students to read the short story *before* coming to class?" The reflective question itself suggests that perhaps engaging students' interest before assigning the reading might make a difference. This idea suggests further that perhaps making the story personally relevant to students' lives might also make a difference. In this sense, the research hypothesis is akin to a practical classroom question. It is not designed to generate a theory or understanding (as in qualitative research), nor is it typically generated from a theory and tested statistically (as in quantitative research). It presents itself upon reflection as the real-life demands of the classroom and needs of learners suggest alternatives to ongoing practices.

Critical Thinking Questions

The claim "Educational researchers should agree on a single function for a research hypothesis because there is one function that is best" contains both an unstated assumption and a circular argument. Can you describe these examples of faulty reasoning embedded within the claim?

CRITICAL THINKER ALERT 4-1

Theories

Formal theories in education are sources for testable research hypotheses. But so are teachers' experiences in the classroom. Teachers' craft knowledge and practical wisdom generate ideas that may be tested more formally by the research process.

Discussion: Your craft knowledge, practical wisdom, and clear thinking about education is sure to generate testable hypotheses. For example, knowledge of teaching research courses might lead to this hypothesis: "If students enroll in a research course early in their program (as opposed to late), then they are more likely to choose a thesis option over a comprehensive examination as an exit requirement." Follow-up research might then compare students' longer-term retention of research concepts as a function of their choice for the exit requirement (a thesis or an exam). What are your ideas for a testable research hypothesis given your practical knowledge about education?

the induced hypotheses which arose from specific observations. Teachers may also arrive at induced hypotheses from reading the published research literature in an area. The major point is that some research hypotheses are not theory based; they may be theory producing. Deductively generated hypotheses tend to be investigated using quantitative research methods; inductively generated hypotheses tend to be investigated with qualitative research methods.

DEDUCTIVE REASONING: A chain of logic progressing from general (e.g., theory) to specific (e.g., hypothesis) that is often used in quantitative research.

INDUCTIVE REASONING: A chain of logic progressing from specific (e.g., observations) to general (e.g., theory) that is often used in qualitative research.

Consider an example. A teacher might notice that her young students learn best when they are having fun and are happy. The teacher might wonder whether there is a connection between emotion and learning and test this idea by measuring learning under varying emotion-laden conditions. Sure enough, the teacher finds that this research hypothesis is supported—children made happy by singing funny songs learned to spell a list of words faster than control children did. Support for this specific hunch about the learning-emotion link might lead to tests of its generalization among adults. For example, it might be predicted that adults who are emotionally "flat" have more trouble learning how to solve several puzzles. Further support might lead to the beginning formulation of a new (or revised) theory of learning, possibly a biochemical one that links emotion, neurochemical changes associated with emotion, and learned outcomes. In summary, keen classroom observations, specific personal experiences, or careful reading of applied research results may generate educated hunches in the form of research hypotheses, which, if supported, form the basis for a more general understanding or explanation of the teaching and learning process.

HIGHLIGHT AND LEARNING CHECK 4-2

Deduction and Induction

Deductive reasoning involves a chain of logic progressing from general to specific; inductive reasoning involves a chain of reasoning progressing from specific to general. How do researchers use both types of logic to arrive at testable hypotheses?

In addition to deduction and induction, there is another, indeed famous, method for arriving at hypotheses. Let's call it *creative visualization,* which is best illustrated by James Watson and Francis Crick's discovery of the double helix structure of DNA (Watson, 1968). Their training as biochemical scientists was apparently supplemented by dozing before a fireplace in the living room. Here in this hallucinatory state, the structure revealed itself in the flames. It was a hypothesis-to-discovery journey worthy of a Nobel Prize. Of course, this flash of insight was preceded (and followed) by logical induction and deduction while intensively testing hypotheses in the laboratory.

Keen, reliable *observations* over time are also sources for research hypotheses. Classroom teachers are well positioned to notice patterns and trends that can be investigated more formally. They also learn from countless experiences those strategies that could be developed more completely and tested via empirical methods.

Intellectual curiosity also leads to research hypotheses. Natural wonder leads to learning about research on a given topic. This knowledge forms the basis of a literature review, and it is hard to imagine a thorough review of the literature that does not culminate in a meaningful research hypothesis. (More discussion of literature reviews can be found later in this chapter and in Chapter 15.) A literature review also reveals that researchers often suggest ideas for future research in the concluding section of a published research article.

Once the researcher has formulated a question or hypothesis, a series of follow-up questions usually arises that demand attention. These questions will be described in the following sections.

CRITICAL THINKER ALERT 4-2

Research Ideas

Researchers are generous with their research ideas. A great source for testable hypotheses may be found in published research studies, where authors often offer suggestions for future research. Don't think every idea must be your own. Just be sure to properly cite sources and acknowledge references!

Discussion: Browse current issues of an online journal in education research such as *Education Policy Analysis Archives* (http://epaa.asu.edu/). Locate the suggestions for future research, which are often near the closing discussion section of the article. Are they good ideas? Why do you think that?

Is the Hypothesis or Question Researchable?

This question may seem obvious, but it is not. There are many truly important and fascinating questions that can be asked about education, but in fact some of them are simply not researchable because it is not possible to collect data to answer them. For example, the question, "Should moral or character education be taught in school along with reading, writing, and arithmetic?" is a very reasonable and important question. But what type of data will actually answer it? Questions that are concerned with "should," "ought," or something similar are outside the realm of scientific research; they are more closely aligned with philosophy, ethics, morality, or some other intellectual discipline, maybe even theology. But don't think that research must therefore ignore all questions related to character education. The question "Do children who receive formal instruction in character education have higher levels of moral reasoning?" is directly answerable, since a researcher could compare the levels of moral reasoning from one group of children given specific instruction in morality with another control group which had received no such instruction. Doing this would require using a specially designed instrument to scale children's thinking along a morality dimension from low to high (its operational definition).

RESEARCHABLE: A research hypothesis (or question) that can be tested (or answered) directly by the collection and analysis of data.

Consider another important question: "What is the best way to teach problem solving skills?" No amount of data collected will answer this question either, since a better teaching method could always be found. What *is* answerable is a question such as "What method—lecture versus discussion—is most effective for increasing students' problem solving skills?" Answering this might involve measuring students' skills, then placing some in a lecture format and others in a discussion format (the manipulation), followed by a reassessment of skills.

CRITICAL THINKER ALERT 4-3

Publications

Very readable professional publications such as *Phi Delta Kappan* and *Educational Leadership* are also rich sources for researchable ideas in education. Don't think they are written only for academic scholars!

Discussion: Both of these resources make available online one or two articles from each issue. Links to these publications can be found on their Web sites (http://www.pdkintl.org/ and http://www.ascd.org/). Browse online articles from recent issues of each publication and search for researchable ideas. What did you find?

HIGHLIGHT AND LEARNING CHECK 4-3

Answering a Question

A question in education is researchable to the extent that data can be collected to answer it. Decide whether this question is researchable: "Can the No Child Left Behind Act solve teaching problems?" Why or why not?

Other questions may just need refining before they are researchable. For example, consider the question "Why do some students 'rise to the challenge' when facing an obstacle, while others simply give up or withdraw?" This type of general question is best answered by a theory which explains the underlying construct (trait) believed to be responsible for the difference. Maybe the trait is "psychological hardiness" or "educational optimism." The theory behind the trait would have to explain its basic qualities, like how it manifests itself in the classroom, how it develops, how it is nurtured, why it is stunted, what its consequences are, and many others. A more specific, refined question might be, "Do children who delay gratification when they are young tend to pursue more difficult tasks when they are older?" The answer to this question helps us solve the bigger puzzle: "Why are some students the way they are?" This information can then be incorporated into a more credible theory of hardiness. And, as we have seen, the prevailing theory will then be able to address general questions such as "Why?"

Other examples of researchable and nonresearchable questions appear in Table 4.1.

CRITICAL THINKER ALERT 4-4

Professional Organizations

Professional organizations such as the American Educational Research Association and the American Psychological Association and their affiliated regional associations (with discounted student membership fees) afford many opportunities and avenues to learn about current research (e.g., annual conventions and prestigious journals). Don't think professional organizations aren't for students!

Discussion: Visit the Web sites of these two organizations (www.apa.org and www.aera.net) and explore the links that are well suited for students and educators. What interesting information did you find?

TABLE 4.1 **Examples of Nonresearchable and Researchable Questions**

Nonresearchable	Researchable
Is No Child Left Behind (NCLB) good for education?	Is the adequate yearly progress (AYP) different in economically disadvantaged students and others?
How did public education get like this?	What trends are apparent in National Assessment of Educational Progress (NAEP) reading and math scores over the past decade?
Should all children wear uniforms in public school?	Do children in schools requiring uniforms achieve higher than children in schools not requiring uniforms?
What is the best way to teach reading?	Which group of third graders has higher reading achievement: phonics-based learners or whole language-based learners?
Does research prove that watching violence on TV leads to aggression?	Do children who watch more violence on TV behave more aggressively?
Do people unconsciously repress traumatic memories?	Is memory for emotional events more likely to be more distorted than memory for nonemotional events?

CRITICAL THINKER ALERT 4-5

Researchable Questions

The question "Will the achievement gap ever be closed?" is not researchable. The question "Is school size related to the achievement gap?" is researchable.

Discussion: Consider this question: "Is the homeschooling movement good for American education?" Is this question researchable? If not, what related questions are, in fact, researchable?

Is the Research Legal and Ethical?

RESEARCH ETHICS: Established guidelines that encourage responsible research practices and assure the protection of human research participants.

All researchers in education must adhere to legal codes and conform to ethical guidelines in the conduct of their research. All responsible researchers adhere to these standards with "zero tolerance." From a legal standpoint, research participants are protected under the National Research Act of 1974 from mental, physical, and emotional injury. Also, no responsible researcher can collect personal data without the *informed consent* of the participants. Furthermore, the 1974 Buckley Amendment assured legal safeguards would be in place to guarantee *confidentiality* (where sensitive information would be held in strict confidence). The law also assured *anonymity* whenever possible (unless permission was granted to the contrary).

Most schools ensure compliance with the law through the establishment of a review board to make certain research participants' legal rights under the law are not violated. Researchers may be exempt from formal review by these boards under a variety of situations, including doing research using existing and publicly available data, doing research using routine educational tests that do not identify individual names, and doing research in usual settings (e.g., classrooms) involving usual practices (e.g., teaching strategies)—as long as confidentiality is maintained.

Researchers also conduct their business with the full recognition of morality. They know that some practices, although not illegal, would be contrary to ethical guidelines. Ethical treatment of research participants would not, for example, involve deception, denial of opportunity, or the deliberate withholding of educational interventions believed to be beneficial. Unethical behaviors include failing to disclose the general nature of research (its purpose) to all participants, treating participants with disrespect, and being less than honest or responsible in the handling and reporting of collected data. There are few charges more serious than the charge which suggests a researcher may have violated ethical concerns in the conduct of research with human participants. All research participants should have a clear understanding of what the research involves, be informed that they are free to withdraw at any time for any reason, and understand clearly how to reach the researcher with questions. A summary code of ethics governing educational researchers appears in Table 4.2.

TABLE 4.2 Summary of Basic Ethical Guidelines for Educational Researchers

- Clarify that participation in a research study is *voluntary*; no coercion of any kind should be tolerated; participants may *freely* withdraw at any time.
- Obtain *informed* consent from participants; all aspects which might affect the decision to participate must be explained, including all risks.
- Avoid *deception*, cause no harm, and avoid invasion of privacy.
- Maintain *confidentiality* and *integrity* of data; maintain *anonymity* of participants.
- *Debrief* participants and provide information or explanation about the research.
- *Benefits* should outweigh *risks* after careful consideration.

The American Educational Research Association (2000) has created guidelines for educational researchers called *Ethical Standards.* Its most relevant guiding standards are concerned with research populations, educational institutions, and the public. As you would expect, their standards are concerned with obtaining informed consent, assuring confidentiality or anonymity, discouraging deception, guaranteeing participants' right to withdraw from a study, minimizing negative consequences, and avoiding coercion. There are also standards that extend beyond the protection of human participants, including those concerned with sensitivity to local institutional guidelines and ongoing practices, avoidance of exploitation for personal gain, responsibility to be "mindful" of cultural differences among participants, and communication of findings (including their *practical* significance) in clear, straightforward language.

CRITICAL THINKER ALERT 4-6

Ethics

Breaches of legal and ethical guidelines in research are not tolerated. A blunder in this area has more serious consequences than, say, a blunder in sampling. Researchers think carefully about ethical guidelines and professional responsibilities prior to their decision making at each step in the research process.

Discussion: For ethically responsible researchers, some topics in education–such as cheating, sexual harassment, and students' home environments–appear to be more challenging than others. Think about how a researcher might attempt to answer these questions: "Is the incidence of cheating higher in online or traditional courses?"; "What student attributes are associated with cheating?" Or this question: "Does the threat of failure increase or decrease students' motivation for learning?"

Protection of Human Participants

The code of ethics governing educational researchers—the protection of human subjects—is the primary concern of a school's Institutional Review Board (IRB). Although each IRB has unique requirements, there are generalities common to nearly all IRBs. Approval from an IRB starts with a request for review. The University of Arkansas at Little Rock, for example, requires that authors of research proposals (see Chapter 15) provide descriptions of the following:

- The purpose of research
- The method of participant recruitment
- The tasks required for participants
- The type of data collected
- The procedures to assure anonymity or confidentiality

Most IRB requests for review seek the researcher's letter of consent and copies of the proposed instruments used to gather data (questionnaires, interview questions, etc.) and other relevant documents. Consent to participate is usually satisfied with a form signed by participants once they understand the nature of the research. As you would expect, the consent form varies depending on the peculiarities of the proposed research. An important part of any consent letter is a clear statement of volunteer rights. The sample form in use at the University of Arkansas at Little Rock includes this statement:

> Your participation in this study is completely voluntary, and you may choose not to participate. You are free to withdraw from this study at any time with no penalty to you. Your responses will be confidential. If the results of this study were to be written for publication, no identifying information will be used.

Participant consent forms also encourage subjects to ask questions about the study once they learn more about its purpose and why the collection of data will help our understanding of a particular topic or bring us closer to a solution for a specific problem. The consent form also describes the procedures used by the researcher, how confidentiality will be assured (and its limits, if any), and the duration of the study. Participants must also know in advance about the discomforts, risks (however slight), and inconveniences stemming from their participation. They also must be made aware of anticipated benefits from their participation. It is important that participants receive a signed copy of their consent form, which includes contact information should they have lingering questions for the principal investigator or supervisor (in the case where the researcher is a student). Much of the same information is contained in a cover letter that seeks volunteers once the study (including its purpose, procedures, duration, etc.) has been approved by the IRB.

Ethics and Responsibility

Ethics in research extends beyond the protection of human participants. The American Psychological Association (2002) has described general ethical principles and responsible codes of conduct for psychologists. These apply well to educational practitioners and researchers. Their five general principles cluster around the following concepts:

- Beneficence and nonmaleficence
- Fidelity and responsibility
- Integrity
- Justice
- Respect for people's rights and dignity

Extracting these key ideas and applying them to the field of education suggests that researchers safeguard the rights of others, respect their dignity and worth, establish their trust, and guard against all factors that lead to misuse of influence. Further, educational researchers seek to "promote accuracy, honesty, and truthfulness in the science, teaching, and practice" of education. They are well aware that "fairness and justice entitle all persons to access to and benefit from" their research

HIGHLIGHT AND LEARNING CHECK 4-4

Protection of Participants

Research ethics focuses on the protection of human participants and the responsible conduct of researchers. Ethical practices include the use of informed consent and assuring fairness. What are other components of research ethics?

in education. Finally, application of these principles to educational researchers suggests that researchers attend to individual differences including "age, gender, gender identity, race, ethnicity, culture, national origin, religion, sexual orientation, disability, language, and socioeconomic status. . . ." These are precisely the important attribute variables (see Chapter 5) that researchers seek to incorporate into their research hypotheses and build into their designs. From this perspective, it becomes easy to understand what is lacking from research in any field that does not generalize (e.g., using only white males in their 60s when studying heart disease).

Is the Hypothesis or Question Meaningful?

MEANINGFUL RESEARCH: Research conducted with clear value, which is often assessed in terms of positive impact in areas such as social and educational influence. It may also change ways of thinking or suggest new directions for research and theory.

This is probably the most difficult question researchers must answer, and probably the one that prompts the most disagreement, which is undoubtedly a function of the ambiguity of the term *meaningful.* For our purpose, this term means "value," as in the worth of a question in terms of the meaning that could be extracted from its answer. Reviewers of research who are left wondering "So what?" or "Who cares?" would seriously question its meaningfulness. Meaningful research questions yield answers that are often valued in terms of their impact or social value. Some research questions, in fact, do produce answers that are "blockbusters" and are truly groundbreaking. This category would undoubtedly fit the research question posed in "The Oak School Experiment" and described in detail by Rosenthal and Jacobson (1968). The research question was "Within a given classroom [will] those children from whom the teacher expected greater intellectual growth show such greater growth?" (p. 61). The answer was a qualified "Yes." This answer had great meaning for many educators and researchers. For teachers, it meant that they should recognize their expectations of individuals' intellectual potential and harness the energy surrounding those beliefs in ways that foster growth. For researchers, it meant that complex patterns of communication between students and teachers, however subtle, should be studied in order to learn more about how expectations manifest themselves in the classroom. The researchers' job essentially was to develop new theories to help explain the self-fulfilling prophecy in the classroom.

The decade of the sixties also witnessed another research question and answer that can only be described as a "blockbuster." The question posed by James Coleman and his associates (1966) can be paraphrased as "What factors best explain the variation in academic achievement among school children?" (The answer, oversimplified, was "socioeconomic status.") The answer had great influence because it shifted attention away from preconceived ideas that were not supported by research data (e.g., that achievement was a function of school expenditures).

Other stimulating research questions asked more recently have had great meaning for researchers and practitioners because they have shifted the direction of research and resulted in widespread changes in classroom practices. A brief sampling of these questions includes the following:

- Will classroom practices designed to increase motivation also reduce discipline problems?
- What are the effects of cooperative learning strategies on achievement and attitude?
- Does a model of teaching based on cognitive science result in better comprehension and longer retention than traditional instruction?
- Will portfolio assessments result in better achievement than traditional assessments?
- Will teaching that is tuned into students' multiple intelligences result in higher achievement and changes in motivation?
- Will teaching strategies based on students' learning styles result in stronger motivation and higher achievement?

Other examples of meaningful research questions are provided in Table 4.3.

Table 4.3 Examples of Potentially Meaningful Research Questions in Education

- What school factors and instructional methods reduce the socioeconomic achievement gap between students?
- How might differences in the culture of learning (attitudes toward schooling) explain persistent achievement differences among groups?
- What achievement and socio-emotional effects can be linked to students who are home schooled or attend online public schools?
- What important educational outcomes can be linked to the charter school movement?
- What factors tend to shorten the careers of exemplar teachers?
- What are the effects of high-stakes testing programs on students' ability to think creatively?
- What student achievement effects can be linked to teachers with alternative certification?
- How does the revision of the SAT college entrance exam influence the high school curriculum?
- What is the relationship between the implementation of No Child Left Behind and high school dropout rates?
- How are early childhood education programs related to later achievement in school?
- How are qualities of the home environment related to children's achievement in school?
- What is the relationship between children's excessive viewing of television and their academic achievement?
- What is the relationship between school expenditures and students' achievement?
- What teaching behaviors are most strongly associated with high achievement in mathematics?
- How do American students compare to students from other industrialized nations in terms of achievement?
- How do changes in self-esteem relate to educational outcomes?
- How do socioeconomic status, ethnicity, race, and sex affect students' school experiences?
- How does prior knowledge affect new learning?
- How does a student's cultural background influence the school experience?
- What factors are most strongly associated with high school dropout rates?
- Is teachers' use of constructivist techniques of teaching related to ease of learning?
- How does ability grouping affect students' outcomes?
- How does the practice of mainstreaming influence the achievement of students with special needs?

HIGHLIGHT AND LEARNING CHECK 4-5

Meaningful Research

Meaningful research in education is judged to be valuable for some reason and often measured by its positive influence. Choose which of the following two questions you judge to be more meaningful: (1) "Will mentoring and progressive teaching methods reduce the socioeconomic achievement gap?" or (2) "What portion of IQ variance is explained by hereditary factors?" Why do you think this?

These research questions have had great meaning for most people involved in education, for they have influenced the thinking of many educators and have resulted in significant changes in the focus of many educational researchers. Generally, meaningful research questions not only have implications for classroom practice but also often influence policy makers as well. Research on the effects of the "standards movement" (and its consequences such as high-stakes testing), effects of alternative certification paths for beginning teachers, influences of the charter school movement, and linkages between early childhood education programs and later achievement (including beyond high school and college) may have direct bearing on policies and legislation statewide (or even nationwide, as witnessed by the No Child Left Behind Act of 2001).

Replicate and Extend

Research questions do not, of course, have to be groundbreaking or highly influential in terms of practice or policy making to be "meaningful." Most educational research, in fact, appears to follow a *replication and extension* model. What this means is that a great deal of research is conducted to test the limits and extend the general work already done. *Replication* suggests that the research is basically a "repeat" of earlier work—essentially the same hypothesis is tested or the same research question is asked but with a design that provides for an additional piece of information. For example, Kiewra, DuBois, Christian, and McShane (1988) tested whether students who use a matrix type of study notes before a test outperform those who use the more traditional outline study notes. Their study (which is described more fully in the student study guide at www.sagepub.com/eic) was done with a 19-minute videotaped lecture on types of creativity with college students who were not allowed to take notes themselves (they could only review the notes supplied by the researchers 1 week later, prior to the test). An example of the replication and extension model would involve a replication in the sense that the research hypothesis would still maintain that matrix notes are superior to traditional notes. It would involve an extension in the sense that the follow-up study might use a 40-minute videotape on a different topic, or a live lecturer as opposed to a videotape, or high school students instead of college students, or a 3-week instead of 1-week test interval. Notice that these extensions would test the general application of the original finding, or the extent to which the finding holds up under somewhat different situations using different participants.

REPLICATE AND EXTEND: A model of research favoring the repetition of an earlier study with an additional feature that enhances its generalization.

Another logical follow-up to the study on matrix study notes described above would involve training students to take matrix study notes, then comparing their

> **HIGHLIGHT AND LEARNING CHECK 4-6**
>
> ### Replication
>
> *Replication and extension* is a common model of research in education and involves repeating an earlier study with an additional feature that permits wider application and generalization. Describe how you might replicate and extend this research finding: Tenth graders' retention of learned material from a 20-minute lecture on the dynamics of psychoanalysis was greatly enhanced by a 30-second advance organizer related to the forces of household plumbing.

test scores with the scores of those who take traditional notes. This research is probably regarded as being beyond the limits of replication and extension, however, for the original hypothesis tested whether higher test scores were yielded by students' *review* of matrix notes (recall they were written by the researcher and simply given to students for review). A follow-up study, on the other hand, would test the effect of matrix notes *written* and reviewed by students. This study would test a different, albeit related, research hypothesis and would be considered more an extension than a replication of the original.

The important point is that educational research is nearly always linked, more or less, to research that has already been done. In this sense, each research study provides a small piece to a much larger puzzle and should, in some way or another, fit into a larger scheme. This leads us to yet another question.

Has It Already Been Answered?

This question is answered by what is called the *review of literature*, a term referring to a description of the prior research that is related to the study (what other researchers have done) and its conceptual basis (relevant theories and constructs). The theoretical underpinning or conceptual framework of a study provides a context for the findings and helps organize the important empirical information that is known about a particular phenomenon.

> **REVIEW OF LITERATURE:** A summary of past and current research and thinking on a specific researchable topic.

The obvious source of information in the review of literature is the library—increasingly online. Libraries on many college and university campuses can change quickly and dramatically in response to technological advances in information science. In fact, universities may be built without a library building, since many library holdings can be accessed electronically from the desktop or laptop of researchers from almost any location.

Reports of published research are most often found in periodicals—the professional journals in the field of education which are organized around common interests, such as learning, motivation, assessment, and so on. Some journals are specialized (e.g., *Journal of Educational Psychology*), while others are more general or broad in scope (e.g., *American Educational Research Journal, or AERJ*). (*AERJ* is published by the American Educational Research Association and is considered one of the premiere journals in the field.) Some journals, such as *Educational Researcher*, are considered to be very scholarly while others, such as *Educational Leadership* and *Phi Delta Kappan*, reach many more readers with far broader interests (including many classroom teachers and school administrators).

Online journals in education are appearing with increasing frequency. Many are available without charge or registration and include full-text reports (e.g., *Education*

Policy Analysis Archives), while many other full-text journal contents are available for a nominal fee. Several publications with wide circulation (e.g., *Educational Leadership* and *Phi Delta Kappan*) include the full texts of some articles online with every issue without charge. Many scholarly journals in education offer a table of contents online, coupled with an online summary or abstract of the article or study, though securing the article in its entirety often requires a subscription or membership fee. Perhaps the best source for finding online journals is the Web site of the American Educational Research Association (http://www.aera.net).

There is a daunting, nearly overwhelming amount of educational research published in scholarly journals. Fortunately, there are educational indexes available which enable researchers to locate from the vast amount of educational research those studies of particular interest to the researcher describing the context for research. The *Education Index* is one such index, allowing researchers to locate (by topic and author) empirical research reports published in nearly 400 journals since 1929. Skill in using the *Education Index* only comes with firsthand practice and requires consultation with a reference librarian.

ERIC Resources

Another index is the *Current Index to Journals in Education (CIJE)* published by a national information center and clearinghouse known as ERIC (Education Resources Information Center). *CIJE*, dating back to 1969, is especially useful since it presents a summary of the research in an area in addition to where it may be found in hundreds of journals. The most efficient way of searching for relevant research reports is through the use of computers. Computer searching of *CIJE* is made possible by searching *ERIC descriptors*, or key words and phrases that allow rapid scanning of topics. These descriptors are found in the publication *Thesaurus of ERIC Descriptors*. A learn-by-doing visit to the reference section of a library is the best way to understand *CIJE* and the ways of accessing it. Searching is quick, painless, free, and often done for the first time without any assistance, thanks to technology advances in storage and retrieval. The World Wide Web, of course, affords easy access to the ERIC database, and many students prefer searching the research literature at the ERIC Web site (www.eric.ed.gov/). The Department of Education reengineered and enhanced ERIC in 2004, adding many new no-cost, full-text resources.

ERIC: Education Resources Information Center, a database (clearinghouse) of journal and nonjournal education literature and documents.

HIGHLIGHT AND LEARNING CHECK 4-7

ERIC on the Net

ERIC via the Internet remains a first-stop source for much research in education. What other Internet sources are available for locating and retrieving reports of educational research?

Many researchers make valuable contributions to education by reviewing the vast amount of research done in an area, making sense of it, and presenting it in a useful, newly organized (synthesized) format. These reports can be found in some journals (e.g., *Review of Educational Research*) and comprehensive, scholarly books such as the *Review of Research in Education, Handbook of Research on Teaching, Handbook of Educational Psychology*, and *Encyclopedia of Educational Research*.

A selected sampling of education journals appears in Table 4.4.

TABLE 4.4 A Sample of Journals in Education

Action in Teacher Education	*Journal of Applied Behavioral Sciences*
Action Research	*Journal of Child Psychology and Psychiatry and Applied Disciplines*
Active Learning in Higher Education	*Journal of Counseling Psychology*
Adult Education	*Journal of Curriculum Studies*
Adult Education Quarterly	*Journal of Early Childhood Literacy*
American Educational Research Journal	*Journal of Early Childhood Research*
American Journal of Health Education	*Journal of Educational Measurement*
American Journal of Mental Deficiency	*Journal of Educational Psychology*
American Secondary Education	*Journal of Educational Research*
Arts and Humanities in Higher Education	*Journal of Experimental Child Psychology*
British Journal of Educational Psychology	*Journal of Experimental Education*
Catholic Education	*Journal of General Psychology*
Child Development	*Journal of Genetic Psychology*
Clearing House	*Journal of Hispanic Higher Education*
College Student Journal	*Journal of Instructional Psychology*
Current Issues in Middle Level Education	*Journal of Learning Disabilities*
Developmental Psychology	*Journal of Legal Education*
Education	*Journal of Personality Assessment*
Education and Urban Society	*Journal of Physical Education, Recreation and Dance*
Educational Administration Quarterly	*Journal of Research in International Education*
Educational and Psychological Measurement	*Journal of Research in Science Teaching*
Educational Forum	*Journal of School Health*
Educational Management Administration and Leadership	*Journal of School Psychology*
Educational Leadership	*Journal of Studies in International Education*
Educational Perspectives	*Journal of Teacher Education*
Educational Policy	*Journal of Transformative Education*
Educational Psychology Review	*Kappa Delta Pi Record*
Educational Researcher	*Language Learning*
Educational Technology	*Learning and Leading with Technology*
Elementary School Journal	*Measurement and Evaluation in Guidance*
Emotional and Behavioral Difficulties	*Mental Retardation*
European Physical Education Review	*Middle School Journal*
Exceptional Children	*Monograph of the Society for Research in Child Development*
Harvard Educational Review	*NASSP Bulletin*
Health Education	*New Teacher Advocate*
High School Journal	*Perceptual and Motor Skills*
Human Development	*Personnel and Guidance Journal*
Instructional Science	
Journal of Applied Behavioral Analysis	

(Continued)

TABLE 4.4 (Continued)

Phi Delta Kappan	*Scholar-Practitioner Quarterly*
Planning and Changing	*School Administrator*
Presidency	*School Public Relations*
Principal Magazine	*School Review*
Professional Educator	*School Science and Mathematics*
Psychological Reports	*Social Education*
Psychology in the Schools	*Social Studies*
Reading Improvement	*Teacher Educator*
Reading Research and Instruction	*Teachers College Record*
Reading Research Quarterly	*Theory and Research in Education*
Reading Teacher	*Theory Into Practice*
Review of Educational Research	*Urban Education*

Source: Adapted from "Writing for Professional Publication: Some Myths and Some Truths," by K. T. Hensen, 2003, *Phi Delta Kappan, 84*(10), p. 791 and "Structural Characteristics and Citation Rates of Education Journals," by J. C. Smart and C. F. Elton, 1981, *American Educational Research Journal, 18*(4), p. 406.

CRITICAL THINKER ALERT 4-7

ERIC

A search of ERIC via the Internet is a fast, efficient method for learning about research in any area of education. The American Educational Research Association Web site maintains a list of online journals. Some publishers (e.g., Sage Publications) and many university libraries also provide online access to many of their journals.

Discussion: Access the ERIC search engine on the Internet and spend a few minutes (it's fast!) learning about research outcomes on achievement effects of "block scheduling." What did you find out?

Yet another tool for locating and retrieving published research in education is Google Scholar (http://scholar.google.com/). Launched in late 2004, it is likely to become increasingly useful for researchers and students of research alike.

Meta-Analysis

Appearing with increasing frequency are published reports of meta-analysis studies, a type of *quantitative* summary of the literature on one topic. *Meta-analysis* is a statistical summary of a body of empirical studies, all of which were conducted to answer one research question (or test one research hypothesis). These studies are very helpful for researchers wanting to learn about research on a topic, since the meta-analyst must compile (and cite) dozens or even hundreds of studies before a meta-analysis can be performed. Meta-analysis is best suited for research questions that can be answered "Yes" or "No." For example, one of the earliest meta-analyses was done in psychology by researchers trying to answer the question "Does psychotherapy work?" Each study conducted earlier by researchers trying to answer this question thus became a *data point* in a meta-analysis. Of course, each of the hundred or more individual studies was not a perfect replication of any other; researchers may have studied different outcomes, types of therapy, length of therapy, types of patients, and the like (in the same mode as replication and extension described earlier). Nevertheless, all of the studies had in common that they all searched for an answer to the same basic question.

META-ANALYSIS: A statistical summary of many studies conducted to answer the same research question.

HIGHLIGHT AND LEARNING CHECK 4-8

Meta-Analysis

Meta-analysis is a quantitative summary of research designed to answer similar research questions. It provides a "big picture." What types of research questions are best answered with meta-analysis?

Meta-analysis, when applied to a large collection of studies, is an overall test in the sense that it attempts to report the "big picture." Meta-analysis also is able to uncover relationships across studies that would not be apparent to the single researcher testing one relationship. For example, a meta-analysis might reveal that therapy is effective, but only if administered over 16 weeks or more using one specific approach with only one particular type of illness. A meta-analytic counterpart in education might be any of the following questions: "Does retention help students?"; "Is bilingual education effective?"; "Does corporal punishment reduce misbehavior?"; "Do mainstreamed students hinder the progress of other students?"; "Does homework in elementary school lead to higher achievement?"; or "Does class size reduction affect the achievement gap?" Needless to say, the report of a carefully executed meta-analysis would be a welcome finding for anyone wanting to review the literature in a particular area. The criteria for evaluating published meta-analyses are provided by Chambers (2004). Examples of published meta-analysis reports are provided in Table 4.5.

CRITICAL THINKER ALERT 4-8

Meta-Analysis

A meta-analysis of research on a specific researchable question in education is a realistic project for students (often with no budget); it may also lead to a publishable thesis or dissertation. Others' meta-analyses help to provide comprehensive reviews of the literature.

Discussion: Think about a question in education, such as "Do homeschooled students score higher on college entrance examination scores?" or "Is there a link between teenage depression and achievement outcomes?" or "Is the drug education program DARE effective?" (or any other question that might capture your interest). Use the ERIC database and determine whether a meta-analysis has been conducted on that question (or a related one). What did you find?

TABLE 4.5 Examples of Published Meta-Analyses of Educational Research

- "Meta-Analysis of Experimental Research Based on the Dunn and Dunn Model" (Lovelace, 2005).
- "How Does Distance Education Compare With Classroom Instruction? A Meta-Analysis of the Empirical Literature" (Bernard et al., 2004).
- "The Effects of School-Based Writing-to-Learn Interventions on Academic Achievement: A Meta-Analysis" (Bangert-Downs, Hurley, & Wilkinson, 2004).
- "Effectiveness of Consultation on Student Ratings Feedback: A Meta-Analysis" (Penny & Coe, 2004).
- "Comprehensive School Reform and Achievement: A Meta-Analysis" (Borman, Hewes, Overman, & Brown, 2003).
- "Mathematics Interventions for Children With Special Needs: A Meta-Analysis" (Kroesbergen & van Luit, 2003).
- "Instructing Adolescents With Learning Disabilities: Converting a Meta-Analysis to Practice" (Swanson & Deshler, 2003).
- "Comparing Student Satisfaction With Distance Education to Traditional Classrooms in Higher Education: A Meta-Analysis" (Allen, Bourhis, Burrell, & Mabrey, 2003).
- "A Meta-Analysis of the Effectiveness of Computer-Assisted Instruction in Science Education" (Bayraktar, 2001-2002).
- "Meta-Analyses of Big Six Interests and Big Five Personality Factors" (Larson, Rottinghaus, & Borgen, 2002).
- "Validity of IQ-Discrepancy Classifications of Reading Disabilities: A Meta-Analysis" (Stuebing, Fletcher, LeDoux, Lyon, Shaywitz, & Shaywitz, 2002).
- "The Self-Concept of Students With Learning Disabilities: A Meta-Analysis of Comparisons Across Different Placements" (Elbaum, 2002).
- "Research on Interventions for Adolescents With Learning Disabilities: A Meta-Analysis of Outcomes Related to Higher-Order Processing" (Swanson, 2001).
- "School-Based Interventions to Enhance the Self-Concept of Students With Learning Disabilities: A Meta-Analysis" (Elbaum & Vaughn, 2001).
- "Systematic Phonics Instruction Helps Students Learn to Read: Evidence From the National Reading Panel's Meta Analysis" (Ehri, Nunes, Stahl, & Willows, 2001).
- "A Meta-Analysis of Studies Examining the Effect of Whole Language Instruction on the Literacy of Low-SES Students" (Jeynes & Littell, 2000).
- "Predicting Children's Competence in the Early School Years: A Meta-Analytic Review" (La Paro & Pianta, 2000).
- "Reading Research for Students With LD: A Meta-Analysis of Intervention Outcomes" (Swanson, 1999).
- "A Meta-Analysis of the Relationship Between Anxiety Toward Mathematics and Achievement in Mathematics" (Ma, 1999).
- "Experimental Intervention Research on Students With Learning Disabilities: A Meta-Analysis of Treatment Outcomes" (Swanson & Hoskyn, 1998).
- "Effects of Instruction in Deriving Word Meaning From Context: A Meta-Analysis" (Fukkink & de Glopper, 1998).
- "The Effects of School-Based Interventions for Attention Deficit Hyperactivity Disorder: A Meta-Analysis" (DuPaul & Eckert, 1997).
- "Meta-Analysis of Cross-Cultural Comparisons of Cognitive Test Performance" (Van de Vijver, 1997).
- "The Effect of School Resources on Student Achievement" (Greenwald, Hedges, & Laine, 1996).
- "Within-Class Grouping: A Meta-Analysis" (Lou, Abrami, Spence, Poulsen, Chambers, & d'Apollonia, 1996).
- "The Efficacy of Computer Assisted Instruction (CAI): A Meta-Analysis" (Fletcher-Flinn & Gravatt, 1995).
- "Gender Differences in Learning Styles: A Narrative Review and Quantitative Meta-Analysis" (Severiens & Ten Dam, 1994).
- "An Investigation of the Effectiveness of Concept Mapping as an Instructional Tool (Horton, McConney, Gallo, Woods, Senn, & Hamelin, 1993).

What Type of Data Will Answer It?

This question is concerned with the nature of educational data and whether it is possible to collect data that are relevant to the research question or hypothesis. There are many different types of educational data and many different methods used to gather such data. Probably the best known type of educational data is standardized achievement test scores. These are well known because of their widespread use in this country and because their results are usually made public, sometimes in the form of national or international rankings on the evening news.

Although there is much current national debate about the value of standardized tests such as the SAT (formerly the Scholastic Assessment Test and the Scholastic Aptitude Test), the debate is nothing new. Standardized achievement testing, in fact, is believed to be about 3,000 years old! (For an interesting account of this history see DuBois, 1966.) In about 1,000 BCE the ancient Chinese tested their citizenry in seven basic areas in order to select those most talented for positions of ruling authority (called mandarins). Scholars believe that the individuals being tested used clay tablets and private cubicles and were threatened with serious penalties for cheating (cheaters were beheaded!). These ancient civil service exams tested the following core "arts": music, archery, horsemanship, writing, arithmetic, and the rites and ceremonies of public and private life.

Incidentally, history has a way of reinventing itself. One immensely popular theory of intelligence is described by Howard Gardner (1993) in *Frames of Mind: The Theory of Multiple Intelligences.* This theory of "multiple intelligences" is currently the basis of many attempts at curricular reform and posits seven (you guessed it) intelligences: music, spatial, bodily/kinesthetic, linguistic, logical/mathematical, interpersonal, and intrapersonal. Can you match these with their ancient Chinese counterparts? (They are listed in corresponding order.) The theory of multiple intelligences has spawned hundreds of research studies, all aimed at understanding how students learn best. One mark of a good theory is the extent of research it stimulates. Gardner's theory would score very high in this regard. The theory, like all good ones, is constantly evolving. Gardner (1999) described additions to the original seven intelligences, one being the interesting talent of understanding our natural environment (or the "naturalist" intelligence). There may be others as well, including existential, spiritual, and moral intelligences.

There are other important outcomes beyond those measured by standardized tests, and they may be assessed with questionnaires, essay tests, oral interviews, behavioral observations, portfolios, performance measures, and many others. These assessments may be used to measure, for example, attitudes, motivation, persistence, creativity, optimism, emotional adjustment, ability to form an argument or think critically, or character formation. All of these outcomes are measurable, although some may not "measure up" to the standards using the criteria of reliability and validity (see Chapter 9).

Examples from the myriad educational measures that can be applied in a research study are presented in Table 4.6.

CRITICAL THINKER ALERT 4-9

Standardized Tests

All standardized tests are just that: standardized. To the extent that learners' minds and ways of thinking are supposed to conform to a predefined standard, then standardized tests are appropriate. Their long history of use does not suggest that they are valid for future use, especially if learner diversity is honored and creativity is encouraged.

Discussion: What is the impact of using standardized test scores as outcome measures in educational research? Does this lead to standardized curricula and standardized minds? What might be the consequences?

TABLE 4.6 **Examples of Common Measures and Sources of Educational Data**

- **Standardized national surveys** (e.g., National Longitudinal Survey of Youth or NLSY)
- **Standardized performance test scores**
  - National and International Assessments (e.g., National Assessment of Educational Progress or NAEP, Trends in International Mathematics and Science Study or TIMSS)
  - Intelligence (e.g., Otis-Lennon School Ability Test, Wechsler Intelligence scales)
- **Achievement tests**
  - Norm-referenced (e.g., Stanford Achievement Test Series, Iowa Tests of Basic Skills, ACT college entrance exams)
  - Criterion-referenced (e.g., General Educational Development or GED test)
- **Aptitude tests** (e.g., SAT college entrance exam, Seashore Measures of Musical Talent)
- **Diagnostic tests** (e.g., Diagnostic Math Inventory)
- **Standardized affective measures**
  - General personality (e.g., Adjective Checklist)
  - Interest (e.g., Strong-Campbell Interest Inventory)
  - Self-concept (e.g., Piers-Harris Children's Self-Concept Scale)
  - Attitudes (e.g., Attitudes Toward Mathematics)
- **Style and preference measures** (e.g., Learning Style Inventory)
- **Teacher-made or researcher-made achievement tests**
  - Essay tests
  - Objective tests (multiple choice, true-false, matching, completion, short-answer, etc.)
  - Portfolio assessments (e.g., judgments of learning gain, attitude shifts, etc.)
- **Questionnaires and surveys** (often with rating scales or rankings)
- **Interviews** (often unstructured, open-ended)
- **Observational measures** (e.g., tallies, frequencies, ratings)
- **Unobtrusive measures** (e.g., "hidden" record keeping such as attendance rates)
- **Field notes and logs** (e.g., perceptions, reactions, accounts)
- **Content analyses** (e.g., narrative themes within documents)

Types of Educational Measures

Cognitive Measures

The complexity of educational research can be explained, in part, by the daunting variety of measures used to answer research and evaluation questions. The variation of measures shown in Table 4.6 is no surprise when one considers the inherent complexities in the teaching process and its learning outcomes (from "bubbling" behavior on standardized tests to free-spirited creative thinking). The No Child Left Behind (NCLB) Act of 2001, mandating that all states develop an accountability system to assure students' achievement levels reach proficiency in reading and math by 2014, compounds the variation in outcome measures. Further, NCLB requires states to demonstrate their academic performance levels via an index known as Adequate Yearly Performance (AYP). Because the methods of assessments and curriculum standards vary from state to state, educational researchers are faced with even greater variation in achievement measures under NCLB. The AYP, however, across states does share the commonality of standardization: The achievement assessment within states is based on instruments developed by testing experts to assure sound, fair measurement of the states' curriculum "frameworks" and is administered and scored under controlled conditions. Many of these "high-stakes" measures of achievement are multiple-choice formats (with the exception of tests for writing skills). A sampling of recently released standardized test items from the California Achievement Test (CAT) and the California Standards Test (CST) used as measures of AYP under NCLB in California can be found on the Web site of the California Department of Education (http://www.cde.ca.gov/).

COGNITIVE MEASURES: Educational tests that measure mental abilities and school achievement.

Naturally, educational researchers and teachers are also interested in many other types of cognitive measures. Achievement tests are used for many purposes other than the AYP function. There are specialized standardized achievement tests (e.g., Gates-McGinitie Reading Test) and many other instruments used for diagnostic purposes in remedial instruction (e.g., Stanford Diagnostic Reading Test). These achievement "batteries" may be norm-referenced (with their scores interpreted in reference to scores in the comparison group) or *criterion-referenced* (with their scores interpreted in reference to a specific level of mastery). This difference is captured by a comparison between two types of scores: a percentile score, which is norm-referenced, and a pass/fail score, which is criterion-referenced. Aptitude, or intelligence, tests also capture the interest of educational researchers. These include the individually administered Stanford-Binet and Wechsler scales of intelligence and the group administered Otis-Lennon School Ability Test and Differential Aptitude Test, as well as the SAT used in college admissions (which was revised in 2005). There are many different ways to classify the large variety of cognitive tests, a task made much easier by the Buros Institute of Mental Measurements (http://www.unl.edu/buros/). The Institute publishes *Mental Measurements Yearbooks* and *Tests in Print,* both containing critical reviews to support informed selection of tests and measures of all types. Description of more than 20,000 tests and other measuring devices may also be found in the *ETS Test Collection* (http://www.ets.org/testcoll/).

HIGHLIGHT AND LEARNING CHECK 4-9

Standardized Cognitive Measures

Standardized cognitive measures of achievement are important measures under the mandates of the No Child Left Behind Act, especially as they relate to Adequate Yearly Performance (AYP). Where does one gather information on cognitive measures used in education?

Teacher action researchers who reflect on their practice construct a variety of achievement measures for use in their classrooms, including the familiar multiple-choice, true-false, fill-in-the-blank, short-answer, and matching formats. But other teacher-made and researcher-made classroom achievement measures take the form of essays, projects, or portfolios. Assessment using these more complicated approaches to tapping achievement involves secondary measures, often using rubrics in the form of rating scales and multiple raters. A *rubric* takes the form of a matrix with specific skills or components forming one axis and a ranking of evidence or evaluation as a measure of proficiency forming the other. Rubrics usually specify a scoring formula, one that determines item *weighting* (whether one item should be counted more than another) as well as a system for totaling points.

The Misunderstood Percentile

The percentile score is often schools' preferred method of reporting standardized achievement tests results. Educational researchers have different preferences. Percentile scores are all bunched up near the middle, creating a "natural" distortion among relative rankings. Very small changes in raw scores near the middle (like 5 raw score points) will result in large percentile shifts (like the 50th to 84th percentile, or 34 percentile ranks). But 5 more raw score points beyond that will move you up only 14 percentile ranks. At the extreme high end, yet another 5 raw score points will improve your percentile score by only 1 percentile rank. (This example assumes a test with a mean of 70 and a standard deviation of 5. There will be more about means and standard deviations in Chapter 8.) You can see how people can misinterpret the extent of improvement (or decline) or classroom differences. The changes might look very large in terms of percentile differences but represent only a small difference in raw scores (or the other way around).

I remain convinced that very few people understand the concept of percentiles, despite its heavy use in the schools. Percentiles are really 1 of 99 points. Think of taking thousands of scores, rank ordering them high to low, and then putting an equal number of scores into 1 of 100 shoe boxes. The lowest, say, 25 scores go into Box 1, the next lowest 25 scores go into Box 2, and so on, until the 25 highest scores go into Box 100. The percentile rank then becomes the "divider" number between boxes. (Think of three shoe boxes pushed together; there are now only two dividers that separate the boxes.) Hence, the percentile scale ranges between 1 and 99. It refers to the percentage of scores at or below the raw score. The natural bunching near the middle has been flattened as all scores are "pushed" into 100 boxes of equal size, creating a distortion and common misinterpretation.

Another reporting score, called the *normal curve equivalent* (NCE), also uses a 1 to 99 scale, but NCE scores are not distorted like percentiles. Although many people think NCEs are interpreted like percentiles, they are in fact interpreted differently. An NCE of 90, for example, is not the same as a percentile rank of 90. Generally, NCEs should not be interpreted with regard to an individual's score. (Why they are reported on individual score reports is a mystery to me.) Standardized score reports appear to be misinterpreted routinely, or never interpreted at all.

CRITICAL THINKER ALERT 4-10

Percentiles

Percentiles remain one of the most widely used—and abused—statistics in education. They have been largely replaced with other measures less distorted and more useful over time (e.g., scale scores).

Discussion: Why do you suppose the percentile has dominated testing in education for so long? Do researchers have alternatives that are better than ranking students?

The NCE, however, does have several advantages that explain its widespread use. Like other standardized test scores (e.g., SAT, ACT, IQ, T, Z), the NCE score transformation permits uniform interpretability. Once scores from tests that have widely different score ranges (such as 0 to 20 or 1 to 200) are converted to NCE scores, they can be interpreted similarly. This is because all NCEs have a mean of 50 and a standard deviation of 21. (There will be more about these statistics in later chapters.) It is immediately apparent that an NCE of 30 is considerably below the group's average. (It is also possible to approximate its percentile—below the 20th. This is explained in Chapter 8.) One can readily see the advantages of moving "raw" scores from different tests onto a common yardstick, that is, if the concern is relative standing (comparison with others).

HIGHLIGHT AND LEARNING CHECK 4-10

Percentiles

Percentiles are widely used but often misinterpreted in educational research and assessment because they are "naturally" distorted. Describe why other measures used by educational researchers are more useful than the "raw" percentile.

Fashola (2004) cited yet another advantage of the NCEs. When educational programs cite gain scores as evidence of effectiveness, critical consumers of research can interpret an NCE gain score of 9 or higher as evidence of effectiveness. This value of 9, according to Fashola (2004, pp. 536–537), must be set against "the average NCE expected gain of 8," a type of control comparison.

Affective Measures

Affective measures are targeted toward traits, feelings, values, attitudes, interests, beliefs, and perceptions. These may be self-directed (e.g., self-esteem) or other directed (attitudes towards school, feelings toward classmates, etc.). Commonly, these traits and psychological constructs are measured via Likert and rating scales. *Likert* scales use an agree-disagree continuum, often with 5 scale points (agree strongly, agree, neutral, disagree, strongly disagree) and sometimes with 7 scale points. Frequently a series of related statements (perhaps 5 to 10) form a subscale that is scored by summing total points (1 to 5 for each item, presuming a 5-point agree-disagree scale). Items are often written to minimize response biases such as a tendency to use only lower or upper portions of a scale (or its midpoints). For example, in an instrument designed to measure teaching effectiveness, the statement "Instructor is well organized" might be counterbalanced with "Instructor lacks preparation." Care must be taken to recode Likert values so that they refer to the same uniform direction (e.g., negative item values might be flipped—5 becomes 1—so that disagreement on a negative item becomes a favorable response). The use of similar items (in the same direction or otherwise) also helps establish the consistency of the measure, as there should be convergence of ratings on conceptually similar items (ratings on an "organization" item should be related to ratings on a "planning" item if the scales are being responded to carefully).

AFFECTIVE MEASURES: Educational tests that measure noncognitive constructs such as traits, attitudes, and beliefs.

An alternative to the familiar Likert scale is a *rating scale*, in which a continuum of choice is provided, but it is not an agree-disagree continuum. For example, two items might ask respondents about an instructor's grading procedures, with one rating item (returns tests promptly) using a 1 to 5 scale of never to always, and the other rating item (provides useful feedback) using a three-choice response (tests graded with good feedback; test graded without feedback; tests not graded). Both Likert and rating scales, among others, are often found bundled in affective instruments called *inventories*, a common one being the Strong-Campbell Interest Inventory. Scaled items may also be combined to form affective instruments called *questionnaires* and *surveys*, two examples being the Sixteen Personality Factor Questionnaire and the Kuder Occupational Interest Survey. Examples of different scales of measurement, often used to assess attitudes, are shown in Table 4.7.

HIGHLIGHT AND LEARNING CHECK 4-11

Affective Measures

Affective measures in education permit researchers to investigate opinions, attitudes, or emotions (e.g., fear of math); interests (e.g., occupational); and traits (e.g., self-esteem). What are some commonly used affective measures in education?

The use of *interviews* ("vocal questionnaires") is also a mainstay of educational research in both quantitative and qualitative paradigms. The structure of an interview can vary from respondents selecting among several choices to their providing open-ended reactions. Care must be taken during the planning and conduct of *interview schedules* (as they are sometimes called) due to the possibility of bias, given that the "instrument" is human. Bias may result from preconceived expectations, stereotypes, halo influences, interviewer characteristics (e.g., age, sex, etc.), verbal and nonverbal cues, and reactive procedures such as the use of a video or audio recorder, to name only a few. Further, the wording of a question may influence the response, as in a *leading question* that cues an answer (often an "appropriate" one).

Observational Measures

The cognitive and affective measures described above are examples of *active* measures in the sense that the research participants provide responses via paper-and-pencil or computer. These are contrasted with *observational* measures, whereby the researcher becomes more active in the recording of data. Educational researchers use many different types of recording procedures in observational studies, including a focus on frequency, duration, or intensity of behaviors. Observations may also be taken continuously or after a fixed or random interval of time. Many instruments, including rating scales, have been developed for use in observation studies.

OBSERVATIONAL MEASURES: Researcher-recorded data based on personal perceptions of research participants or objects.

TABLE 4.7 Examples of Scales Commonly Used in Educational Measurement

Likert Scale

This course was well organized

1	2	3	4	5
Disagree Strongly	Disagree	Neutral	Agree	Agree Strongly

Rating Scales

The instructor returns tests promptly

1	2	3	4	5
Never	Rarely	Sometimes	Often	Always

Forced Choice

a. I learned a great amount
b. I became interested in the subject

Semantic Differential

Compared to other instructors, this one is . . .

Worse ____ ____ ____ ____ ____ ____ ____ Better

Thurstone Scale

1. Cooperative classrooms are too noisy.
   ______ true ______ false ______ can't decide

Adjective Checklist

______ enthusiastic

______ organized

______ fair

HIGHLIGHT AND LEARNING CHECK 4-12

Observational Measures

Observational measures permit the recording of information based on the researchers' perceptions (not participant responses). What precautions are necessary to ensure useful observational data?

Care must be taken, however, to avoid the possibility of observational techniques themselves, causing change in the very behavior being recorded (a *reactive* measure). Other potential problems include observer bias such as changing perceptions over time, interpretations consistent with personal beliefs or expectations (contamination), and a "halo" effect where generalized perceptions influence specific observations. A halo effect may be evident when an observer judging a teacher's use of questioning during a discussion is influenced by an initial positive impression of the high quality of that teacher's work in general. This is how a master teacher (of overall high caliber) who might not be so spectacular in the use of questioning can nevertheless receive high ratings in that specific dimension of teaching. Adequate training, testing, and "recalibration" of observers to ensure accuracy can reduce many of the problems inherent in observational measures.

Types of Data and Philosophy

The type of data used by researchers often reflects an orientation (or philosophy) about education and how to best proceed toward meeting research objectives. An example may be found in the debate about teaching reading. Should children be taught using a phonics approach (an emphasis on letter-sound correspondence with skills building on each other) or a whole language approach (immersion in meaningful literature with an emphasis on discovery)? This debate, one might think, would be resolved by examining the research on this issue. The problem is that the advocates of *both* approaches point to research that supports their view.

HIGHLIGHT AND LEARNING CHECK 4-13

Philosophy and Data

One's philosophy of education may influence that type of research data judged to be most valuable. How can researchers' beliefs about teaching and learning explain, in part, inconsistencies in the research literature?

How can educational research produce two sets of findings that support opposing approaches and are therefore inconsistent with each other? Simply, advocates of the approaches use different types of data for evaluation. Phonics advocates point to "decontextualized" skills that are assessed easily by standardized multiple-choice tests. Whole language advocates tend to believe that more global, qualitative measures of meaning and comprehension (not multiple-choice tests) are most appropriate in the study of emerging literacy in language rich environments. Because the focus of whole language instruction is not sub-skill mastery, assessments (like standardized tests) that are designed to determine how well beginning readers break language into its components are simply not appropriate. Clearly, the choice of one particular type of data does not represent a search for "the truth" as much as it does an inclination toward one preferred method of teaching. It is no surprise, therefore, that when phonics is compared with whole language using standardized multiple-choice tests, phonics appears better; but when the two approaches are pitted against each other using students' reading diaries, whole language appears better. To be sure, the choice of a particular type of educational data is one reason for the seemingly weak conclusion that research shows "mixed results."

CRITICAL THINKER ALERT 4-11

Self-Reporting

Self-reporting that does not match the "truth" reflects human motivations, perceptions, and coping mechanisms, among other factors (not character flaws). Self-reports in research should be substantiated with other sources of evidence.

Discussion: How might a researcher substantiate, for example, high school students' self-reports of hours of television watched per week? How might they adjust for problems such as the television being on but not being watched?

The mixed-results phenomenon in educational research is also fueled by weak instrumentation such as "self-reports," known to be notoriously inaccurate. What research respondents report often does not match reality, in large part due to respondents' desire to provide socially acceptable answers or to please researchers (tell them what they want to hear). Many respondents are hesitant to admit that they did not follow instructions, to admit to embarrassing events, or to admit to less socially acceptable behavior. With a bias toward responses favoring a positive light, researchers struggle to disentangle objective accuracy from subjects' wishful thinking and delusions. Often, this is impossible, and research relying heavily on self-reports is sometimes dismissed as not credible. For example, studying alcoholism by measuring blood alcohol levels, or by searching through participants' garbage, might reveal findings about alcohol consumption very different from those obtained via verbal self-reports. Self-reports of cheating or smoking on high school campuses, for example, are not likely to match findings from video surveillance.

CRITICAL THINKER ALERT 4-12

Types of Data

There are many different types of useful methods of measurement in education. Each method leads to a different type of data. This wide variation in data is another explanation for puzzling inconsistencies among research findings.

Discussion: Consider this research question: "Is there a connection between attitudes toward school and daily exercise among high school students?" *Attitude* requires careful definition. What type of data shown in Table 4.6 would you gather to assess attitude? Why did you choose this type of data? Does it appear that your research will be more closely aligned with qualitative or quantitative outcomes?

CRITICAL THINKER ALERT 4-13

No Best Type of Data

There is no single type of educational data that is inherently best for all purposes. The type most suitable depends on the specific purpose to which the data are put. Field notes may be as suitable as standardized test scores.

Discussion: Choose the types of educational data you think are most appropriate for investigating these topics: school climate in a local charter school, AYP (Adequate Yearly Progress) as defined by the No Child Left Behind Act, math and science aptitude and interest among middle school boys and girls, trends in homework assignment and parents' role in its completion, and reading outcomes among second graders. Why did you reach the conclusions that you did?

Research Hypotheses in the Literature

Important issues surrounding the research hypotheses and research question (and the research process itself) are found easily in published research reports. (Other important components of the research process are described in Chapters 5 and 6.) Research hypotheses are often wrapped around several different types of variables (these are described more completely in the following chapter). Researchers distinguish between these four types of variables:

- Independent (the presumed cause or treatment)
- Dependent (the presumed effect or measured outcome)
- Attribute (the important characteristics of the research participants)
- Extraneous (other influences that need to be controlled)

Consider the following published study as an example of a research hypothesis.

Web-Based Learning

Uribe, Klein, and Sullivan (2003) derived their research questions from several meta-analyses in the areas of collaborative learning, problem-based learning, and computer-mediated learning. (Recall from this chapter that meta-analysis is an analysis of many research studies considered together.) Their reviews of prior studies in the area of collaborative learning suggested it was a more effective learning structure than individual learning. This was revealed by research using a large number of learning outcomes (dependent variables). They also noted that problem solving is one of the most important cognitive tasks in everyday life, and that collaborative learning appears well suited to problem solving tasks. Their conclusion that the characteristics of the Internet and computer-mediated instruction (such as Web-based learning) are "ideal" for problem-based learning led them to wonder, "Do the positive effects of collaborative learning in a face-to-face environment transfer to computer-mediated collaborative learning?" Deeper searches of the research literature (including other meta-analyses) and the identification of relevant variables (namely, ability grouping) enabled them to focus on the effects of two learning structures (individual Web-based learning and collaborative Web-based learning) and of ability grouping on students' performance in solving complex problems.

Their first research question was "Does learning structure affect learner performance in problem-solving tasks and time on task?" "Learning structure" was their single independent variable, with two categories being compared: individual Web-based learning and collaborative Web-based learning. "Learner performance" as an outcome was operationally defined as points earned on the solution to a military problem scenario using a scoring rubric for each of four steps in the problem. Another research question was "Does learning structure affect learner attitudes?" "Attitudes" as a construct was operationally defined by a 10-item survey using a Likert rating scale (an agree-disagree continuum); this functioned as a second dependent variable. A third research question was "Does ability grouping affect learner performance in problem-solving tasks and time on task?" Notice that "ability grouping" was an attribute variable (subjects classified themselves based on a characteristic). It was operationally defined by students' academic composite with two levels (higher, lower) being formed by a median split (half above, half below) on GPA.

Uribe and colleagues' (2003) research participants were 59 students enrolled in an aerospace studies course. Because each student was *randomly* assigned to the individual or collaborative condition, their independent variable (learning structure) was what is called a *true* independent variable, hence their research design was true experimental (experimental research designs are described in Chapter 10). Collaborative *dyads* (groups of two) were formed by randomly assigning a higher ability and lower ability student to each pair. (Uribe and colleagues' review of the research literature suggested that heterogeneous groups are associated with more positive outcomes.) Members of the dyad were able to collaborate on the problem solution using a virtual classroom set up by the researchers.

Uribe and colleagues' analysis of the data revealed answers to their three research questions. The answer to their first question was "Yes, learning structure affected problem solving performance and time on task, with collaborative Web learners scoring significantly higher than individual Web learners on the problem-solving task and spending more time on task." The answer to their second research question was "Yes, learning structure affected learning attitudes; there was a preference for working with a partner opposed to alone, yet those working alone generally felt they had more time available and that the computer-mediated tasks were easier to use." The answer to their third question was "No, ability grouping was not related to performance on the problem-solving task or on time on task."

Uribe and colleagues (2003) concluded that "the benefits of face-to-face collaboration on problem-solving tasks transfer to a computer-mediated environment" (p. 14). Their supplemental analysis of interactive communication patterns also enabled their conclusion that "participants who worked with a partner appeared to have benefitted from the ability to discuss the problem and possible solutions" and "were able to access more information related to the problem" (p. 14). Their finding related to ability grouping (no difference) also enabled a speculative conclusion: Lower ability students in the dyads may have benefitted by being paired with higher ability students. Another conclusion is possible: GPA may not be a good indicator of ability or a specific problem-solving skill. GPA might be a better operational definition of "motivation" or some other related construct.

Most meaningful research questions, once answered, carry important implications, the most obvious one in this study being the value of computer-mediated collaborative instruction. At least in the context tested (the specific setting, research participants, outcome measures, etc.), the researchers found that collaborative learning in a computer-mediated environment appears superior to individual learning in the same environment. The researchers also noted that instructors "should keep in mind the increased time necessary in a computer-mediated collaborative environment" (p. 17). In addition to the clear practical orientation of this research, the study is noteworthy for its attention to theory as well. The researchers referred to the theory of "transactional distance" (Moore & Kearsley, 1996), which predicts that if course structure is held constant but dialogue is increased, the decrease in transactional distance will positively affect learner performance. The dyad's promotion of dialogue in the collaborative condition appeared to improve task understanding and increase information retrieval. Because this is what the underlying theory predicted, it can be said that the theory was supported by this empirical evidence.

Answers to good research questions always suggest meaningful additional research questions, as was the case with Uribe and colleagues (2003). For example, future research could investigate the optimal group size in Web-based collaborative learning structures (only groups of size two were investigated by these researchers). What about the formation of groups? Does whether self-selection or arbitrary assignment is used make a difference in communication and performance? These researchers also wondered, "Do students learn a process better, as they appear to do in this study, if they are able to discuss with a peer online?" (p. 17). Further research could also focus on different types of tasks (not only problem solving) using Web-based collaborative learning.

Uribe and colleagues' (2003) study illustrates several important facets of a research question. They derived their questions from an extensive review of the research literature, capitalizing on others' meta-analyses. Their questions were clearly answerable given the data collected, and no breaches of research ethics were apparent. The questions were meaningful given their clear implications for practice and attention to at least one theory. Several types of data were collected, including performance measures, time, attitudes, and patterns of communication. Their research questions had not been answered before, as revealed by their search of prior studies, and the questions represented a clear extension of our knowledge about the application of collaborative learning in a computer-mediated environment.

MORE EXAMPLES

Additional descriptions of published research may help to solidify your knowledge of important ideas related to issues surrounding research hypotheses and questions. You will find additional descriptions on the Web-based student study site (www.sagepub.com/eic).

Chapter Summary

Because of its central importance, much attention is focused on the research hypothesis (or research question) so that it is researchable, legal and ethical, and meaningful. The research hypothesis is tested within the context of prior research (or literature) in the area using numerous types of educational data. Two researchers testing the same hypothesis may arrive at different conclusions, explained in part by differences in methodology and inclination to use different types of data. Widely different approaches to research methodology are possible in the quest for knowledge and understanding. Many studies in educational research venture beyond the answer to a research question—they raise new questions as well.

Application Exercises

1. Browse the online journals as described in the Application Exercises in Chapter 2. Locate a published research report in your field of interest. Zero in on the hypothesis being tested. How would you describe the source for this hypothesis? Does it match any of the sources described in this chapter? Does it illustrate a strategy for hypothesis formation not described in this chapter?
2. Decide whether you think each of the following questions is researchable.
   a. Should the school year be lengthened to include most of the summer months?
   b. How should the history of the Nazi Holocaust be taught in high schools?
   c. Are students more creative in groups or working alone?
   d. How can students' creativity be maximized?
   e. Does research prove students learn to read best by phonics instruction?
3. Make a judgment about whether or not you think each of the following research proposals would pass an ethics review committee. If not, state what ethical violation is apparent.
   a. A random sample of students at Carver Junior High School will be told that their performance on an intelligence test was far below average; then their achievement a year later will be compared to that of a control group to see how beliefs about intelligence affect learning.
   b. Students will be required to wear beepers; when beeped by the researchers, they will write down their private thoughts.
   c. Students will each be given $2500 for their participation in a year-long study; to decrease the chance of dropping out, they will be paid only after their participation is complete.
   d. In order to minimize their embarrassment, students will not be told before or after the experiment that the study is related to cheating.
   e. College students who volunteered to participate will not be told that the "brain food" diets may cause impotence in rare situations, since the very suggestion may cause the problem.
   f. Tiny hidden cameras will be installed in the rest rooms to see if the educational program actually reduced smoking between classes.
   g. Researchers will use 100 schools to norm a new achievement test; names of the lowest scoring third will be sold to private tutoring companies with the highest bids.
   h. SAT scores with names will be used by the researchers; they will contact each test taker for permission to use the scores in a test of the relationship between achievement and month of birth.
4. Browse several online journals in your field of interest (see #1 above). Select a published report that you think represents a meaningful research question. What is the rationale for your selection?
5. Access the ERIC collection of resources in education (http://www.eric.ed.gov/) and key in a search term related to the article selected in #4 above. Select one of the journal articles returned in the search. Focus on the type of data collected and analyzed. Do you recognize any cognitive, affective, or observational measures? If not, what type of data was collected? Does this educational measure fit into a scheme described in this chapter? Can you think of yet another classification for educational measures that might fit these data?

ON YOUR OWN

Log on to the Web-based student study site at http://www.sagepub.com/eic for more information about the materials presented in this chapter, suggestions for activities, study aids such as electronic flashcards and review quizzes, a sample research proposal, and research recommendations that include journal article links (with discussion questions and an article evaluation guide) and questions related to this chapter.

5
RESEARCH LANGUAGE

OUTLINE

OVERVIEW

Clear thinking about research is enhanced to the extent that you view the conduct of educational research as a process, or series of integrated steps. Understanding this process requires familiarity with several terms, namely *constructs, variables,* and *hypotheses.* These basic concepts will be introduced with many concrete examples. They are part of the "language" of research. Understanding the research language is sometimes demanding, but the language is fundamental. Your ability to critically evaluate published research requires the knowledge that the research process forms an integrated whole. This chapter will lay some groundwork for your acquisition of this knowledge and ability.

Constructs and Operational Definitions

The challenge of educational research is especially difficult in part because educators are interested in complex abstractions, such as "motivation," "self-esteem," or "creativity." Other researchers might study soil samples under the microscope, distances with a telescope, or tumors with a magnetic resonance imaging machine. The abstract dimensions that interest educational researchers are called *constructs* because they are *constructed* or invented labels—a shorthand way of describing many interrelated behaviors, all of which are postulated to represent the same trait or ability. For example, all of the behaviors and skills believed to reflect intelligence may be bundled conceptually and referred to collectively as "intelligence." The underlying dimension inferred by a construct such as intelligence (or self-esteem, motivation, etc.) is only postulated to exist. We cannot see or touch it directly. It is "in the head," so to speak. Simply, think of a construct as a label for a presumed trait or ability.

CONSTRUCT: A label for an abstract trait or ability (such as creativity or intelligence) that is only presumed to exist, as it cannot be measured directly.

Although we cannot see a construct, we can test the theory (explanation) behind a construct by directly studying the presumed indicators of the construct. These indicators (i.e., behavioral or overt manifestations) are referred to as the operational definition of the construct. "Intelligence" (the construct) may be inferred from "intelligent behaviors" (the indicators), like correctly solving a logic problem, answering questions about word meanings, repeating backwards a string of eight numbers, solving a math problem, using "street smarts" to achieve a goal, starting a new business, paraphrasing the theme of a written paragraph, solving an equation, or executing a triple lutz.

HIGHLIGHT AND LEARNING CHECK 5-1

Constructs as Labels

A *construct* is a label for an abstract trait or ability; an *operational definition* is (presumably) an observable and measurable (empirical) indicator of the construct. Presume a researcher studied birth weight and its relation to later stress resiliency (using scores on the Hardiness Scale). What is the construct and what is its operational definition?

Another example of a construct is "anxiety," which is only presumed to exist by observing and measuring its presumed indicators, like heart rate. Heart rate (average beats per minute), then, becomes the operational definition of the construct "anxiety." The major point is this: Abstract constructs must be defined in a way that makes them observable and measurable (operational definitions). Such constructs may be defined in many different ways, some of which are more appropriate than others.

Some operational definitions clearly do not reflect the rich complexity of the presumed construct. Consider the construct "love," for example. Just as people who have intelligence are expected to act in predictable ways, people who have love (or are "in love," as they say) are expected to act in predictable ways, or at least have predictable characteristics. "Love," with all its complex emotions, could be operationally defined as the level of an endorphin-like chemical found in the blood. (Increases in this chemical, also found in chocolate, are believed to be responsible for the euphoric "high" that falling in love brings. Its decrease is believed to be responsible for the "honeymoon is over" feeling.) Or "love" could be operationally defined by the frequency of romantic kissing, a self-report (on a 1 to 10 metric rating scale, ranging from "I'm indifferent" to "I'm going crazy with love"), or even by the credit limit that one partner imposes on the other's charge card at Dillard's.

OPERATIONAL DEFINITION: An empirical measure of the presumed indicator of a construct or state, such as heart rate as an indicator of "anxiety."

In any case, these abstract constructs must be measurable in some form or another. Researchers can't perform their job by simply talking about constructs; they must observe and measure them. That task requires making important decisions about how to operationally define the construct in measurable terms, terms that hopefully reflect the complex construct. School learning is an important, and complex, outcome of education. It is often simplified by the term *achievement,* which in turn is operationally defined by scores on standardized achievement tests such as the Stanford Achievement Test series.

CRITICAL THINKER ALERT 5-1

Operational Definitions

Although operational definitions permit researchers to study constructs, an operational definition may not reflect the construct's true qualities. Placing a label on an operational definition is a convenience. Be on guard for operational definitions that may not match the essence of a construct. One example is helmet size as a measure of the intelligence of soldiers during World War I.

Discussion: Can you think of an operational definition of "motivation," one that reflects what is commonly believed to be true for that construct? What about "interest in school learning"? What about "ability to get along with others"?

Operational Definitions as Empirical Indicators

Perhaps the best way to think about the operational definition is this: It is the *rule for putting numbers or codes next to names* in a research study. Consider the construct "test anxiety," for example. Most people know what this means, and the label itself has allowed us to communicate fairly well about test anxiety. But how would you know if an intervention designed to lower test anxiety was effective? General impressions are not acceptable, because they are especially prone to bias. Researchers usually find more empirical indictors of test anxiety. *Empirical,* in this sense, means objective, firsthand, and verifiable. Scientists find unacceptable statements such as "The subjects just kinda looked less uptight." More empirical measures might include subjects' heart rate, average number of eye blinks per minute, level of perspiration, number of fidgets, or blood pressure. But does heart rate, for example, really capture the essence of test anxiety in the same way that an endorphin-like chemical captures the essence of love? Hardly. Here is the troubling tradeoff: Constructs often (but not always) lose their meaning when they are operationalized, that is, when numbers are put next to names.

Consider an example such as "creativity." People generally understand what is meant by this term, and because of this, we can talk about classroom ideas that foster creativity, home environments that are most conducive for enabling creative behavior to flourish, and many other factors that might be linked to creativity in students. Let us pretend that a biochemical theory of creativity posits that babies who were breast fed tend to be more creative in high school than babies who were bottle fed. One hundred students were located and classified into the breast-fed group or the bottle-fed group. However difficult that may have been, consider the harder part—how to measure creativity. Can creativity be measured by teachers' ratings on a 1 to 10 scale, by number of award-winning science projects, by number of unusual uses for a brick named within 1 minute, by ratings of students' short stories as judged by a creativity "expert," or by scores on a researcher-developed Test of Creativity? Do any of these measures really capture the essence of creativity? Needless to say, the method chosen for *putting numbers next to names* has great implications for the value and meaning of the research.

HIGHLIGHT AND LEARNING CHECK 5-2

Operational Definitions

That a construct is defined operationally does not necessarily suggest that the definition is meaningful. What might be lacking if "teaching effectiveness" is defined by students' scores on standardized tests?

Some systems for putting numbers next to names could render the research meaningless, since a researcher might be testing a hypothesis very different from what was intended. For example, a researcher might test the hypothesis "The quality of the home environment before school age is linked to intelligence 10 years later." The researcher decides to use high school rank (based on GPAs) and SAT scores as

CRITICAL THINKER ALERT 5-2

Different Definitions

Two equally reasonable researchers may have very different operational definitions for the same construct. Although the researchers intend to measure the same "thing," their different definitions raise the possibility that one (or both) may not be measuring the construct being investigated.

Discussion: What are the consequences of researchers having very different definitions of the same construct (e.g., "intelligence")? Is this a good thing? What are the implications for discrepant or confusing research findings?

measures of intelligence, but these measures may be—more appropriately—indicators of *motivation*, not intelligence. And then there is the problem of operationally defining the "quality of the home environment." Can it be defined by the number of educational toys accessible, by the frequency of verbal interaction between parents and children, by the type of verbal interaction, by the frequency of parents' reading to their children, by the sheer variety of daily stimulation, by the number of hours that the television is turned on per week, by the frequency of parents' punitive and restrictive behaviors, or by the simple presence of two parents? When operational definitions do not accurately reflect the construct being investigated, the research results are, at best, open to competing interpretations.

I hope you can see that the decisions made regarding the operational definitions of constructs are among the most far reaching. Chapter 9 reveals that decisions about operational definitions have important implications for the *validity* of measures. Other examples of constructs and operational definitions appear in Table 5.1. It is important to notice that abstract labels (constructs) must be transformed into concrete, observable indicators (operational definitions).

TABLE 5.1 Examples of Constructs and (Not Necessarily Good) Operational Definitions

Construct	Examples of Operational Definitions
Intelligence	
	Score on SAT (Educational Testing Service assessment)
	Score on Stanford-Binet Scale
	Score on Wechsler Adult Intelligence Scale (WAIS)
	Reaction time (average) on perceptual naming task
	Head circumference (in inches)
	Score on Pedigrees Test (in which the test taker uses a schematic family tree to answer questions about familial relationships)
	Score on test of short-term memory
	Grade point average (GPA)
	Score on test of vocabulary knowledge
Anxiety	
	Heart rate
	Blood pressure
	Self-report rating (1–7 scale)
	Galvanic Skin Response (GSR, measures the amount of perspiration)
Motivation	
	Grade point average (GPA)
	Observers' ratings (1–7 scale) during an interview about career plans
	Number of Advanced Placement courses taken

(Continued)

TABLE 5.1 **(Continued)**

Construct	Examples of Operational Definitions
Self-Esteem	
	Score on scales such as Coopersmith or Piers-Harris
	Number of positive self-statements during an interview
Creativity	
	Number of novel uses for a paper clip described in 3 minutes
Hyperactivity	
	Number of gross motor movements in 15 minutes
	Teacher's ratings on a 1–5 scale
Stress	
	Number of eye blinks per minute
	Ounces of alcohol consumed
	Blood pressure
Charisma	
	Rating on a 7-point scale
	Number of leadership positions held
Aggression	
	Observers' tallies of hits and kicks
	Number of days suspended from school
Teaching Effectiveness	
	End-of-course student ratings
	Principal's rating
	Students' standardized achievement test scores
	Students' reflective ratings after graduation

CRITICAL THINKER ALERT 5-3

Old Constructs

Sometimes old constructs resurface with new labels, generating initial interest until research reveals the "new" construct is hardly new at all. "Self-perceptions of ability," for example, have been given different labels over the years (with subtle differentiation). The same is true for "intelligence" (or "aptitude").

Discussion: What are the implications of new labels for generally old constructs or ideas? What does this suggest for a researcher's review of the literature? Should constructs be confined to narrowly defined terms at the risk of missing very relevant information?

Types of Variables

All educational research involves the description or explanation of *variables*, those changing qualities or characteristics of learners, teachers, environments, teaching methods, instructional materials, assessment instruments, and virtually all factors related to education in the broadest sense. A *variable*, then, refers to any dimension that has two or more changing values. Examples of learner variables are sex (male or female), achievement (1 of 99 percentile ranks), self-esteem (low, average, high), socioeconomic status (lower, middle, upper), prior knowledge (none, some, extensive), learning style preference (visual, auditory, tactile/kinesthetic), and the amount of musical experience prior to age 8. Examples of teacher variables include experience (1 year, 2 years, 3 years, 4 or more years), educational background (bachelor's versus master's degree), and grade level taught (kindergarten through twelfth grade). Examples of environments include class size (ranging from 1 to 40 students) and setting (inner city, rural, suburban). Examples of instructional or classroom variables include level of technological support (none versus a computer at every desk) and the size of cooperative learning groups (3, 5, or 7 students). Prominent instructional materials include the use of color on musical scores (yes or no) and the number of analogies found in a physics lesson (zero, one, or two). And finally, examples of assessment variables include type of test (multiple choice versus essay), type of grading (pass/fail versus A–F letter grades), and type of graduation requirement (portfolio versus standardized achievement test). As you you can see, the number of variables of interest to educational researchers is almost limitless.

VARIABLE: Any dimension with two or more changing values, such as age or sex.

HIGHLIGHT AND LEARNING CHECK 5-3

Variables and Constants

Researchers use both variables and constants in their research. Variables are dimensions with changing values; constants have one value. Presume a researcher studied tenth-grade girls' interest in science to determine whether it was related to different science experiences in middle school. What are the researcher's variables and constants?

CRITICAL THINKER ALERT 5-4

Variables

Research in education seeks to uncover relationships, ones that might enable a better understanding of the teaching and learning process. Relationships are uncovered by studying variables–those qualities or characteristics that change (vary) across learners, teachers, schools, and so on. A characteristic that does not change is called a *constant* (e.g., the use of only males in a research study). Although researchers use variables to find relationships, they also use constants to control for unwanted sources of extraneous influence.

Discussion: In what sense might one researcher's constant be another one's variable? Is it possible for one researcher's "nuisance" factor to be another's primary focus in a search for a relationship? Can you think of an example?

Independent, Dependent, Attribute, and Extraneous Variables

The practice of research requires that variables be clearly identified and categorized. The following categories are common and represent a generally accepted system for distinguishing types of variables:

- Independent
    - True independent
    - Quasi-independent
- Dependent
- Attribute
- Extraneous

Independent Variables

Variables categorized here are under the command of the researcher and usually reflect a treatment or intervention of some type. They are "free" to vary (hence *independent*) in the sense that the researcher can determine the conditions or categories that define the variable. For example, "size of learning group" might be an independent variable with levels determined by the researcher to be three, five, or seven students. Independent variables are believed to be the *cause* of some resultant effect. The researcher might suspect that small learning groups result in better learning. Here's another example. A researcher might believe that preschoolers' training in music leads to better math reasoning in adolescence. The independent variable would be type of musical training, with categories being no training, piano lessons once a week, and piano lessons twice a week.

INDEPENDENT VARIABLE: A variable reflecting a presumed cause and the conditions created (manipulated) by the researcher for comparison (e.g., type of teaching method). It is the A in the If A, then B hypothesis.

Here's an example from a published research study. Kramarski and Mevarech (2003) observed that the National Council of Teachers of Mathematics emphasizes the importance of mathematical reasoning as a part of doing mathematics. But what instructional strategies are best for enhancing students' abilities to reason mathematically? The researchers' review of literature led them in two directions: cooperative learning (using small-group activities) and metacognitive training (in which teachers monitor and explain their own thinking). Most prior investigations of these strategies combined both into a single method, but Kramarski and Mevarech wondered about the unique, or separate, contribution of each to students' reasoning skills in mathematics, transfer of mathematics knowledge, and metacognitive knowledge itself. To investigate these relationships between instruction and learning, these researchers

HIGHLIGHT AND LEARNING CHECK 5-4

Independent Variable

An *independent variable* is an intervention, the presumed cause of some effect. It is *manipulated* by the researcher, meaning that the conditions defining the variable are actively created by the researcher. (Words such as *treatment, implementation,* and *intervention* are often used to describe an independent variable.) Presume a researcher studied the influence of three different types of mentoring programs on career aspiration. What is the independent variable?

arranged for four instructional methods: (1) cooperative learning combined with metacognitive training, (2) cooperative learning without metacognitive training, (3) individualized learning combined with metacognitive training, and (4) individualized learning without metacognitive training.

Their independent variable was therefore instructional method, with the levels (or categories) being the four different types of instruction (what they referred to as COOP+META, COOP, IND+META, and IND). It is important to understand that their research used one independent variable and that the variation which created this one independent variable consisted of four different groups (not four independent variables).

True Independent Versus Quasi-Independent Variables

Two types of independent variables exist: true independent and quasi-independent. The true independent variable (1) is manipulated by the researcher, meaning that the variable and its categories are created by the researcher; and (2) involves the *random* assignment of research participants to any one of the categories. For example, I might believe that students learn to spell words faster by handwriting spelling practice than by computer keyboard practice. Notice that I created this variation in spelling practice and could also create whatever differences between the groups that I want. I might settle on three groups: handwriting only, keyboarding only, and combination handwriting and keyboarding. I could also assign learners randomly to conditions since each student could practice in any one of the three groups. This is a true independent variable because I believe it will cause differences in the rate of spelling acquisition, I created it by determining which conditions would exist, and I am free to assign students randomly to the three different conditions.

TRUE INDEPENDENT VARIABLE: An independent variable that permits random assignment of research participants.

QUASI-INDEPENDENT VARIABLE: An independent variable that does not permit random assignment of research participants.

LEVEL OF AN INDEPENDENT VARIABLE: The categories or conditions that define an independent variable (e.g., 10-, 20-, and 30-minute lectures if the independent variable is lecture length).

The interrelated notions of *presumed cause* and *created conditions* are referred to as a *manipulation* of an independent variable by researchers. The fact that the manipulation was coupled with random assignment defines the independent variable as a *true* one.

Consider a different type of independent variable referred to as a *quasi-independent variable.* (*Quasi* means "having a likeness or resemblance to something.") Quasi-independent variables are believed to be the cause of some effect, and their created conditions qualify as a manipulation, but restrictions are in place which prohibit the random assignment of subjects to groups. For example, let's presume that a school purchased 100 computers for use in its classrooms. Teachers believe that the use of these computers results in faster spelling achievement, hence they encourage students to practice spelling via the computer as often as they can. In order to assess the effectiveness of the computers for this purpose, a school is found that is not using computers but is as similar as possible in other respects to the school that is using them. Notice that these two conditions were not created in a truly independent way; the students who used the computers (or did not use them) could not be determined randomly. (Quasi-independent variables are more akin to "natural" interventions where the researcher has less control over conditions and their assignments.)

True independent variables have researcher-determined conditions *with* random assignment. Quasi-independent variables have researcher-determined conditions *without* random assignment. *This distinction is critical.* The simple technique of random assignment will determine in large part how confident you can be that, for example, the computer was the cause of observed differences in spelling. As you will see in Chapter 10, the use of quasi-independent variables will define *quasi-experimental* research designs, which are less persuasive in establishing cause-and-effect relationships than their true experimental design counterparts, those with random assignment.

Here is another example of this true independent versus quasi-independent variable distinction. A researcher wants to test the influence of a mentor on high school students' career aspirations. One hundred twelfth graders are selected as research participants. Of those 100 students, 50 are randomly assigned to mentors who provide mentoring relationships during their senior year. The other random 50 function as comparison (control) students. Just prior to graduation, all 100 students are assessed on their level of career aspiration. (You'll recall that "career aspiration" is a construct that must be operationally defined.) Mentoring in this case is a true independent variable since it was manipulated by the researcher (it was a presumed cause of some effect and the researcher created the two conditions that defined the variable) and subjects could be assigned to conditions randomly. Remember that manipulation coupled with random assignment defines a true independent variable.

Contrast this situation with a researcher who also believes mentoring is related to aspirations, begins a mentoring program at one high school for students who are interested, and then selects students from a similar high school across town to function as a comparison group. Students from both schools are measured to assess their level of career aspiration just prior to graduation. Although mentoring was manipulated by the researcher, students could not be randomly assigned to conditions. This is an example of the use of a quasi-independent variable. As you'll see shortly, the distinction has great implications for the researcher's ability to make inferences about cause and effect.

The use of true independent variables permits much stronger conclusions about cause, whereas the use of quasi-independent variables forces the researcher to temper cause-and-effect conclusions. It might be, for example, that control students at the crosstown high school were really not similar at all, perhaps having lower overall aspirations to begin with. The use of random assignment with true independent variables, by contrast, creates groups that are known, or at least presumed, to be similar (comparable) except, of course, regarding the manipulation itself (the use of mentors). The power of random assignment to equate groups is stunning, as revealed in Chapter 7.

Sometimes researchers can use true independent and quasi-independent variables in the same study. Flowerday and Schraw (2003), for example, in a study of the effect of choice on cognitive and affective "engagement," randomly assigned students to a choice condition (choice of task versus no choice of task), but students were "self-selected" with respect to the type of task (essay versus crossword puzzle), meaning that they assigned themselves, so to speak, to one task or another. This distinction (which is fully explained in Chapter 10) is important because the two groups formed by random assignment to the choice independent variable were comparable (due to the random process), whereas the groups formed by self-selection (type of task) were not. Flowerday and Schraw reminded readers of this distinction by noting that the influence due to type of task "should be viewed as quasi experimental, whereas the [influence of] choice constitutes a true experimental effect that is not confounded by self-selection" (p. 209). (The question being posed by these researchers was whether choice affected effort and performance. It may be that essay performance, for example, is superior only when chosen as a task.)

Dependent Variables

Variables categorized as dependent are also called *outcome* variables or measures. (Sometimes they are called *criterion* measures.) The values of this variable are presumably *dependent* on the particular condition of the independent variable (hence the name). Using the computer versus handwriting study described previously, one reasonable dependent variable might be the number of practice sessions needed to spell words correctly or the number of words spelled correctly on a final spelling test.

DEPENDENT VARIABLE: A variable reflecting the presumed effect of the manipulation of an independent variable (e.g., score on achievement test). It is the B in the If A, then B hypothesis.

HIGHLIGHT AND LEARNING CHECK 5-5

Dependent Variable

A *dependent variable* is the measured outcome, the presumed effect of some cause. Presume a researcher studied the influence of class size on teacher absenteeism. What is the dependent variable?

The dependent variables are the *effects* of the causal variation induced by the independent variable, and in this sense, they could also be called the *effect* variables (though this is not customary). A research study may indeed have several dependent variables. In the example of spelling practice through the use of a computer, other possible dependent variables include the spelling score on a standardized achievement test (spelling subtest), the number of recognized spelling errors in a short story, or students' levels of enjoyment or satisfaction during spelling lessons.

An Example: Cooperative Learning

Consider an example from a published research study mentioned earlier, the Kramarski and Mevarech (2003) investigation of four different instructional methods (a combination of cooperative learning and metacognitive training). Their interest centered on how these four types of instructional strategies affected these constructs: "mathematical reasoning," "ability to transfer mathematical knowledge," and "metacognitive knowledge." It comes as no surprise that they used three measures to assess these outcomes: a graph interpretation test, a graph construction test, and a metacognitive questionnaire. These instruments, when scored, yielded three separate dependent variables. Because these measuring devices contained subscales in addition to a total score (such as general strategies versus specific strategies and fluency versus flexibility), it is more precise to say that their research used 10 dependent variables (although much of the analysis was directed at the three total scores from the three different instruments). It is very common in educational research to have more dependent variables than independent variables, given the interest in multiple outcomes.

Dependent variables often take the form of operationally defined constructs, as discussed earlier in this chapter. They are the "blank" in the expression ". . . as measured by _________." For example, if a research study investigated the influence of school size on overall achievement, the dependent variable would be ". . . as measured by the Stanford Achievement Tests." Or if a research study investigated the influence of greater autonomy on teacher morale, the dependent variable would be ". . . as measured by the rate of absenteeism." Or if a research study investigated the influence of cooperative learning groups on self-esteem, the dependent variable would be ". . . as measured by the Coopersmith Self-Esteem Inventory." Or if a study investigated the influence of sugar on hyperactivity, the dependent measure might be ". . . as measured by the duration of fidgeting." Of course, observers would have to be trained to recognize what constitutes a fidget, that is, the label "fidget" itself must be operationally defined by the presence of specific behaviors.

Another Example: Engagement

Consider another example, the study of choice on cognitive and affective engagement by Flowerday and Schraw (2003) described previously. "Engagement" was the construct being studied, specifically motivation to learn ("cognitive engagement") and positive attitude ("affective engagement") as revealed through satisfaction and effort. The operational definitions of these two constructs become the dependent variables, or outcome measures. The instruments used to collect these measures included the 13-item Desire-for-Control Scale, a 10-item Interest Questionnaire, and a 12-item Attitude Checklist. The first two instruments were scored and used as dependent variables to measure the operational definition of the construct "cognitive engagement." Similarly, the Attitude Checklist was scored and used as a dependent variable to measure the operational definition of "affective engagement." This checklist "assessed different aspects of participants' affective engagement, including enjoyment, satisfaction, effort, deeper processing, motivation, fairness, and sense of control" (p. 210).

The major concern over how *well* these dependent variables measure the construct being investigated is covered in Chapter 9. The fact that a construct has been operationally defined and measured as a dependent variable, that is, with numbers placed next to names, tells us nothing about whether the definition is accurate or meaningful. (That separate focus is the concern of reliability and validity, as you'll see in Chapter 9.)

One More Example: Readiness to Learn

Consider one more example of a construct, operational definitions, and the distinction between independent and dependent variables in a published research study. Brigman and Webb (2003) investigated the construct "readiness to learn"—defined as the prerequisite learning skills of attending, listening, and cooperating—in kindergartners. These skills, of course, are merely words or labels and must themselves be operationally defined in measurable terms. Listening was operationalized as the score on the Listening Comprehension Subtest of the Stanford Early School Achievement Test (SESAT2). The other two skills were operationalized as the scores on the Comprehensive Teacher Rating Scale (ACTeRS). (The ACTeRS contains two subscales labeled Attention and Social Skills.) For reasons that are unclear, these researchers combined the Attention and Social Skills subscales into one total score (probably because they were highly correlated) and labeled this the Behavior Rating Total. Their two dependent variables, therefore, were the Listening Comprehension score and the Behavior Rating Total score. These measures, then, became the operation definition of the construct "readiness to learn."

Their manipulated independent variable was instructional method, which was implemented over 12 weeks with two conditions—the "Ready to Learn" (RTL) curriculum versus a traditional instruction comparison group (or treatment versus control). (The RTL curriculum involves five teaching strategies designed to impart school success skills among kindergartners.) This was a true independent variable because the students were randomly assigned to classes, and the classes were randomly assigned to teachers. Six classes were then randomly chosen to participate in the RTL curriculum; six were retained as comparison classes. The independent variable, then, may also be described as type of curriculum, with the conditions being RTL and traditional (control). This research study, therefore, used one independent variable (with two conditions) and two dependent variables. The study's results supported the use of the RTL curriculum. The researchers concluded that teachers can increase kindergartners' readiness to learn beyond that of comparison students, equip them with skills needed to succeed in school, and perhaps prevent future failure.

Dependent and Independent Variables Contrasted

Knowledge of the distinction between independent and dependent variables is vitally important for understanding the research process. Do you remember the old adage "An apple a day keeps the doctor away"? If this were tested empirically, can you determine the independent and dependent variables? The independent variable would be whether or not an apple was eaten each day, and the dependent variable might be how many doctor visits were needed by the apple eaters and non-apple eaters. Or more generally and less literally, the independent variable might be type of diet (good versus poor), and the dependent variable would be the frequency of colds, flu, or whatever index of health was chosen. And if subjects could be assigned randomly to the apple eating conditions, the independent variable would be a true independent variable.

Attribute Variables

A great many variables of interest to researchers include the characteristics, or *attributes*, of students, such as sex, anxiety, socioeconomic status, intelligence, learning style, creativity, prior knowledge, exposure to lead paint, musical training prior to kindergarten, level of fat in diet, frequency of exercise, number of siblings, or hunger. Such variables are rarely manipulated in order to function as true independent variables (due to feasibility, practicality, or ethics). These attribute variables contribute to the astonishing array of learner differences, more commonly called *diversity*. Because of the recognized importance of diversity, these variables are rarely ignored in educational research studies. And for good reason: They are important. Their importance is revealed by studies examining how they relate to independent and dependent variables. For example, one approach to teaching a lesson may work

ATTRIBUTE VARIABLE: A measured characteristic of research participants (e.g., learning style) presumed to be related to a dependent variable and part of the research hypothesis (If A, then B qualified by C, where C refers to the attribute variable).

extraordinarily well for low anxiety students but fail miserably for high anxiety students. Some students may have to hear a lesson, others may have to see it, still others may have to feel it. Some learn best in larger groups, others learn best in smaller groups. Ambiguity may frustrate some students, others may thrive on it. The answer to many research questions investigating the effect of a particular teaching method is "It depends." What it depends on are attribute variables (and differences across dependent variables).

Failure to consider attribute variables in the design of educational research may render the research meaningless. For example, let us suppose that two different teaching methods (the independent variable) were compared: lecture versus discussion. Achievement test scores functioned as the dependent variable. The results showed no difference overall between the two groups; both scored 70%. If students had been assessed and classified in accordance with their anxiety level (high versus low), a dramatic difference could have resulted. High anxiety students could have scored 90% and 50% in the lecture and discussion groups, respectively (averaging 70%). Low anxiety students could have scored 50% and 90%, respectively, essentially reversing the findings of the high anxiety group, but still averaging 70%. The finding of "no difference," of course, would not have been accurate since the anxiety groups functioned to essentially cancel the strong teaching method effect.

The best answer, then, to the question "What is the effect of lecture versus discussion methods on achievement?" is "It depends on anxiety." (This is simply a hypothetical example.) Admittedly, it is probably rare that the influence of an independent variable like teaching method would be wiped out so completely by failing to consider attribute variables. The point is that the influence of an independent variable could be masked by unattended learner characteristics. Attribute variables are not limited to student characteristics. Teachers, classrooms, schools, families, and many other variables all have characteristics that may function in this "it depends" manner. (More will be said about this idea in Chapter 10, where the concept of interaction is described.)

HIGHLIGHT AND LEARNING CHECK 5-6

Attribute Variable

An *attribute variable* is a measured or classified preexisting quality of research participants (e.g., birth weight, special education status, age, sex, motivation, aptitude, etc.). Attribute variables defy manipulation, hence they cannot function as independent variables. Presume a researcher studied three methods of teaching math using high-interest and low-interest learners to see its influence on retained learning after 6 months. What is the attribute variable?

One final note about attribute variables: They may also be referred to as *subject* variables, or possibly *moderator* variables. To make matters even more confusing, they may also be referred to as a type of independent variable, namely a *measured* or *selected* independent variable. Differences, hence confusion, in terminology is unfortunate, but it is a reality in research. (Do you see why I could not refer to attribute variables as a type of independent variable? Independent variables are *manipulated* ones, something that is not possible with learner or teacher characteristics. How could one be assigned randomly, in the case of a true independent variable, to, say, a male or female group?)

Because I doubt that all researchers will ever use agreed-upon common labels, critical readers of published research must be alert to this variation in terms. This problem is not as frustrating in reality as it may sound, for the type of variable should be obvious in context despite its masquerading under different names. Don't think that all research terminology is clouded by differences in labels. "Types of variables" appears to offer the worst offense in this regard.

Extraneous Variables

This class of variables, unlike the other three, usually number in the hundreds or thousands in any given research study. These variables are sometimes referred to as *nuisance* or *control* variables for good reason: They are a nuisance and must be controlled. They all have in common the potential to influence the dependent variable but are *extraneous* (not relevant or important) to the research question. Because of this, these extraneous variables must be controlled so that their influence does not contaminate the results. For example, in the computer versus handwriting study of spelling achievement described earlier, the following variables might be considered extraneous:

EXTRANEOUS VARIABLE: Any variable external to a research situation that is impacting the research and requires control so that its influence is neutralized.

- Time of day students practiced spelling
- Amount of students' physical exercise
- Noise level in the room
- Motivation level of the students
- Alertness of the students
- Charisma of the teacher
- Learning styles of the students
- Prior knowledge of the students
- Lead poisoning levels
- Prior experience with computers

This list could go on and on. All of these variables—unless they are independent or attribute variables—must be controlled so that their influence does not jeopardize the meaningfulness of the study. Fortunately, many extraneous variables can be controlled by a single action—random assignment of students to conditions. This simple but powerful technique can neutralize the influence of countless extraneous variables that are related to the student, such as motivation, prior knowledge, lead levels, and so on. The extraneous variables related to the teacher and environment often require special procedures in order to neutralize or control their influence. These control techniques are described in Chapter 7. For now, this category of variables should be recognized as *virtually all sources of influence on the dependent variable other than true independent, quasi-independent, and attribute variables.*

The differences between the four major types of variables are summarized in Table 5.2.

HIGHLIGHT AND LEARNING CHECK 5-7

Extraneous Variable

An *extraneous variable* is an influence in research other than the independent, dependent, and attribute variables factored into the study. Because extraneous variables can influence the dependent variable, their influence must be controlled to avoid confounding ("mixing up") its influence with that of the independent variable. Presume a researcher studied the effects of online versus traditional delivery of instruction on learning gain in math, using students who selected their preferred approach to instruction. What is one extraneous variable and what might be confounded with what?

TABLE 5.2 Four Major Types of Variables Used by Researchers

An Experimental Test of the Proverb "An Apple a Day Keeps the Doctor Away"

Variable	Key Characteristic	Examples
Independent	Manipulation (presumed cause)	Eating apples (none or one per day)
Dependent	Measured outcome (effect)	Number of doctor visits for colds or flu
Attribute	Subject characteristic	Male versus female
Extraneous	Controlled influence	Prior health, other foods

CRITICAL THINKER ALERT 5-5

Different Names

Be on the watch for different terms in research that reflect the same idea. Independent variables might be called *treatment* or *predictor* variables. Dependent variables might be called *response*, *outcome*, or *criterion* variables (among others). Attribute variables might be called *ex-post-facto* or *subject* variables. Extraneous variables might be called *nuisance* or *controlled* variables. There are several other substitute terms as well (e.g., a *moderator* variable might refer to a type of attribute variable).

Discussion: Consider the proverb "Too many cooks spoil the broth." If this were tested empirically, what would the independent variable be? And the dependent variable? What other labels are possible for variation introduced by the cooks? What terms could be used to describe the broth?

Confounding

When extraneous variables are not controlled, sometimes they exert their influence in a troublesome way. Failure to recognize and control for extraneous variables may result in a form of contamination known as a *confounding*. This special term is described below.

CONFOUNDING: The "co-mingling" of an independent and extraneous variable such that as the levels of an independent variable change, so do differences in an extraneous variable (e.g., 10-, 20-, and 30-minute lectures given in cold, comfortable, and hot classrooms, respectively).

The term *confounding* is used often in educational research, but its meaning is not widely understood. It is used in everyday contexts to mean "confused," "bewildered," or "mixed up." In research, you can think about confounding as "mixed up" results. Specifically, a *confounding* occurs whenever a researcher has allowed two or more variables to change together. The independent variable should of course vary, for this is the treatment or intervention that the researcher has deliberately created in order to change systematically (the manipulation). When any other extraneous variable changes along with the deliberate change in the independent variable, then the independent variable is confounded with the extraneous variable. For example, if two methods of teaching were studied by comparing one method in the fall with the other method in the spring, then the teaching method (independent variable) would be confounded with time of year (extraneous variable). If more able teachers taught one method and less able teachers taught another method, then the teaching method (independent variable) is confounded with teachers' ability (extraneous variable). If less able students were taught using one method and more able students were taught using another method, then the teaching method is confounded with student ability. And if one method was used in a red room and another method used in a blue room, then teaching method is confounded with room color. Figure 5.1

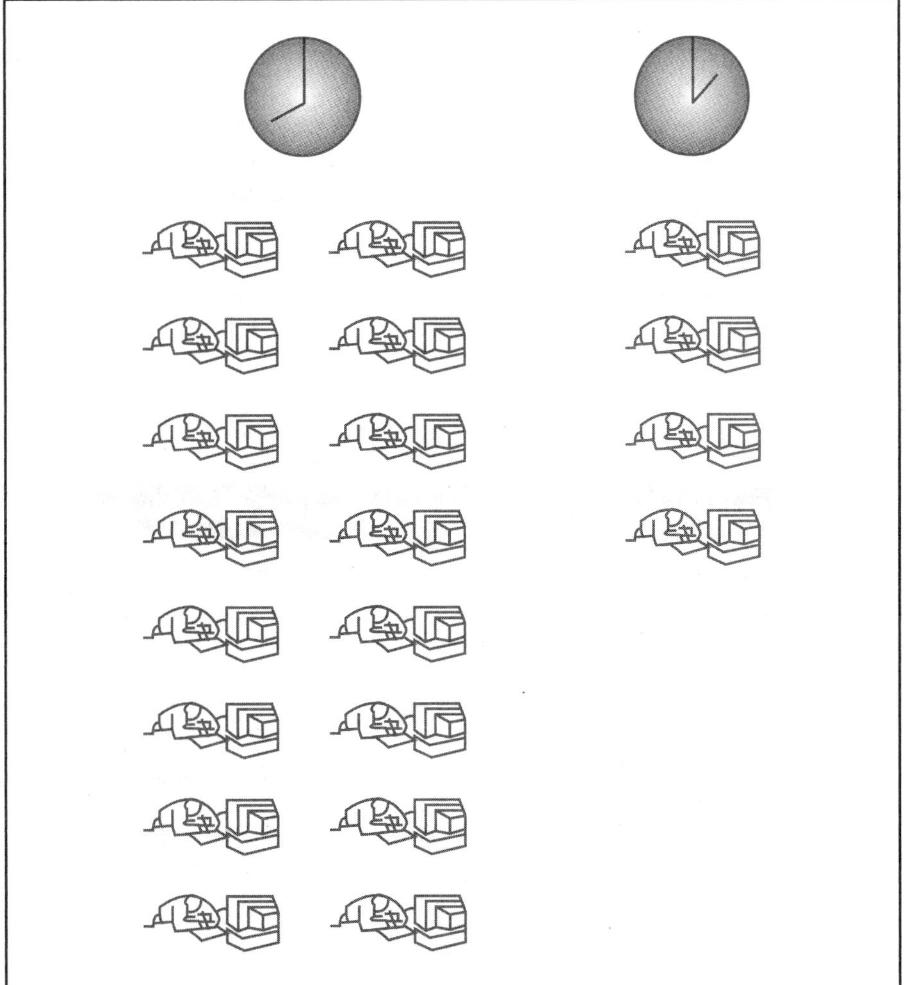

Figure 5.1 Is class size related to achievement? A careless researcher might allow an independent variable, class size, to be confounded with an extraneous variable, time (a large class in the morning and a small class in the afternoon). In this case, achievement differences could be due to variation in the independent variable—class size—or to the extraneous variable—time. The results would be uninterpretable.

Source: Adapted from *Primer of Educational Research* (p. 20), by W. N. Suter, 1998, Needham Heights, MA: Allyn and Bacon.

illustrates how a careless researcher might introduce a confounding variable into a research setting. Examples of other confounded relationships are presented in Table 5.3 below.

CRITICAL THINKER ALERT 5-6

Confounding

The term *confounding* is widely used but poorly understood. It means two variables are changing together. For example, as children's exposure to lead varies, so might their nutrition, making it difficult to disentangle lead and nutrition influences. In this case, it is said that lead exposure is confounded with nutrition. Researchers try to *un*confound variables to learn more about their influences.

Discussion: Our lives appear naturally confounded, so to speak. It's hard to explain fatigue, for example, when loss of sleep at night co-occurs with a poor diet or added stress at school or work. Can you provide an example of hopelessly entangled (confounded) connections in your own life? For instance, is a headache the result of neck or shoulder muscle stress, anxiety, junk food, and/or weak coffee—all of which co-occurred?

TABLE 5.3 **Examples of Confounded Independent and Extraneous Variables**

Independent Variable	Extraneous Variable	Confounding
Amount of sugar in breakfast	Day of week	High sugar on Monday; low sugar on Friday
Length of class	Teacher difference	1-hour class taught by Mr. Smith; 2-hour class taught by Mrs. Woo
Type of teaching	Location	Lecture in Room 102; discussion in Room 812
Use of drug to reduce hyperactivity	Color of room	Drug given students in off-white room; placebo given students in red room
Use of questions in text	Interest level	Interesting text with questions; boring text without questions
School uniforms	Type of school	Uniforms in single-sex school; no uniforms in coed school
School schedule	Type of school	9-month public school; 11-month private school
Type of kindergarten	Parent socioeconomic status	Private school for wealthy parents; public school for less wealthy parents

Note: As the independent variable changes so does the extraneous variable, rendering the results uninterpretable. When this happens, the difference in the dependent variable (which is not stated in this table but can be imagined) could be due to the independent variable *or* the extraneous variable (or some combination of the two).

Notice that the appropriate use of the term *confounding* is in reference to the confounding of independent and extraneous variables; it is *not* the dependent variable that is confounded. Confounded relationships are sometimes eliminated by sound research designs which exert control over the extraneous variables. They are also eliminated with a variety of statistical techniques (e.g., partial correlation). In educational research, they are best prevented with a host of control strategies. These research designs, statistical techniques, and control strategies are described in Chapter 7. Extraneous variables that are successfully controlled through these control maneuvers are sometimes referred to as, quite appropriately, *controlled* variables.

Types of Hypotheses

In addition to the four different types of variables described previously, educational researchers are concerned with the following three different classes of hypotheses:

- Research hypotheses
- Alternative hypotheses
- Null hypotheses

We'll examine each one in turn and then see how they work together.

Research Hypothesis

The *research hypothesis* is what you probably think of as the main hypothesis. It is the researcher's best guess about the outcome of the research study. Expectations about the outcome usually come from the theory that generated the hypothesis in the first place. Research hypotheses are more than vague hunches about the outcome; they are precise statements regarding clear outcomes. They sometimes appear in an If A, then B format where A refers to the independent variable, and B refers to the dependent variable. Some examples are shown below:

- If children are taught to read via whole language, then their reading comprehension will be higher.
- If children watch 3 or more hours of television per day, then their behavior on the playground will be more aggressive.
- If children learn in small cooperative groups, then their social interactions will be more positive.
- If teachers earn master's degrees, then their job satisfaction will increase.
- If young children take piano lessons, then they will have higher math aptitude 10 years later.
- If exercise immediately precedes a geometry lesson, the students will learn faster.

RESEARCH HYPOTHESIS: A predicted outcome based on theory or understanding, which is often stated as If A, then B. It may also be stated as a foreshadowed question in qualitative research.

A research hypothesis may not appear in the If A, then B form. Sometimes it appears as a statement or claim, such as "Young children who take piano lessons will have higher math aptitude 10 years later" or "Exercising immediately before a geometry lesson

HIGHLIGHT AND LEARNING CHECK 5-8

Research Hypothesis

The *research hypothesis* is a predicted outcome, often spawned by theory, an understanding of prior research, or personal observation. If a theory of learning suggests "less is more," what is a reasonable research hypothesis to test the theory?

will result in faster learning." A research hypothesis may even appear as a question, for example, "Will young children who take piano lessons have higher math aptitude 10 years later?" or "Does exercise immediately before a geometry lesson result in faster learning?"

The particular form of the research hypothesis is not as important as its content. It must specify in some form which variables are being studied, and if known, what potential outcome is expected. Educational researchers do not simply gather data on a hodgepodge of many variables in a helter-skelter manner only to fish around aimlessly in the hopes of finding something "significant." The problem with this "shotgun" approach is that "significant" relationships *will* surface, but their significance is illusory because of the workings of mere chance. There will be more about the research hypothesis and the meaning of statistical significance in Chapter 13.

CRITICAL THINKER ALERT 5-7

Research Hypothesis

Research without a clear hypothesis (or at least a "guiding" question) is often criticized for not conforming to a model of scientific inquiry. Good research yields useful information, whether or not the research hypothesis is supported. Lack of support for a research hypothesis in no way suggests a "failure."

Discussion: What drawbacks might be associated with collecting "gobs" of data such as these: birth weight, gender, standardized reading comprehension score, hemoglobin level, body mass index, self-esteem score, frequency of Internet use, knowledge of chess, size of school attended, class rank based on GPA, participation in after school sports, age of mother at birth, number of school days absent, math aptitude, level of sociability, and size of cranial bump above the left ear?

Alternative Hypothesis

Alternative hypotheses are developed or conceptualized by researchers only to be eliminated. They are referred to as *alternative* in the sense that they *rival* the research hypothesis as an explanation for the outcome. In fact, they are sometimes called *rival* hypotheses and are related to alternative explanations for the findings. For example, let's suppose that a new method of teaching reading—Total Immersion—was compared to an existing or traditional method. The research hypothesis might be, "If students are taught to read using Total Immersion, then they will learn to read with greater comprehension." A critic might say, "There is an alternative hypothesis—better teachers used the Total Immersion method—and that is why Total Immersion students read better. Those

ALTERNATIVE HYPOTHESIS: A rival explanation for the research results (often resulting from lack of control or procedural influences). It is an explanation "alternative" to that suggested by the research hypothesis and often "explains away" the findings.

teachers are so good that their students would read better no matter what method they used!" Another critic might say, "There is another alternative hypothesis—more able students were taught using Total Immersion, and those students would read better no matter what method was used." But the careful researcher would have already anticipated these alternative hypotheses and taken steps to rule them out. This could be accomplished by using the same teachers for both the Total Immersion and traditional methods. Further, the researcher could arrange for students to be randomly assigned to each method to assure that the groups are comparable at the start of the research.

Alternative hypotheses are blunders, of sorts, and are avoided by careful researchers for obvious reasons—the findings could be explained away by rival interpretations, rendering the research results difficult to interpret. When critical reviewers of research ask the question "What else could have possibly explained these results?" they are asking for plausible, rival, alternative hypotheses. Cautious researchers anticipate these problems related to potential alternative hypotheses. Then they make certain that they are eliminated, or at least made implausible. There are usually many potential unwanted sources of influence in a research study that must be eliminated in order to permit a clear interpretation of the findings.

HIGHLIGHT AND LEARNING CHECK 5-9

Alternative Hypothesis

An *alternative hypothesis* in research is a counter-explanation for research findings. It opposes the explanation suggested by the research hypothesis, that is, explains the findings by reference to some influence other than the connection between the independent and dependent variables. If a study revealed no difference in self-reported cheating on an exam between proctored and honor system settings, can you think of an alternative hypothesis to consider before concluding that proctoring exams is not necessary?

In short, the alternative hypotheses in a research study include the "interpretation worries" and counter-explanations that researchers attempt to rule out by research designs, control procedures, and careful plans for collecting data. They are answers to the question "How else could these results be explained?" Researchers clearly do not want their findings to be explained away or dismissed because of problems in the way the study was designed and conducted.

An Example: Perceptual Defense

Research in psychology provides excellent examples of alternative hypotheses. Consider the example of the *perceptual defense* phenomenon. McGinnies (1949) attempted to test the credibility of Freudian psychodynamic theory, which suggests that many of our motives stem from unconscious influences and long-forgotten early experiences. The problem with psychodynamic theory, from a scientific point of view, is that the theory (however interesting) does not generate easily testable research hypotheses. Good scientific theories must "stick their neck out" and be vulnerable in the sense that hypotheses spun from the theory can be tested directly. However difficult, McGinnies's experiment attempted to test the notion that the perceptual defense mechanism is capable of recognizing disturbing, anxiety-provoking stimuli at the *unconscious* level. This monitoring device, according to the theory, is constantly on the alert and blocks out environmental threats before they enter our awareness. It is, generally, a protective gateway to our conscious awareness.

This idea of a perceptual defense mechanism was tested in an ingenious (but flawed) way by flashing words on a screen by a machine at speeds much faster than could be recognized. These words were flashed slower and slower by the experimenter until the research subjects could recognize the words, at which point they simply announced the word out loud. The speed at which subjects could recognize and announce the word was called their *threshold.* McGinnies was especially interested in whether thresholds were longer for emotionally threatening (i.e., nasty or taboo) words as compared to neutral words. If the perceptual defense mechanism had been doing its job, it should have prevented, or at least delayed, the threatening words from entering conscious awareness until the force was too strong. The delay, the reasoning goes, would lengthen the threshold. The gate would eventually burst open, allowing the inevitable recognition of the emotionally charged words. The research hypothesis, then, was "If subjects view taboo words compared to neutral words, then their recognition thresholds would be longer." In fact, this is just what McGinnies found—subjects took longer to recognize taboo words than neutral words. This outcome, therefore, provided support for the perceptual defense mechanism and added credibility to the psychodynamic theory which predicted this outcome.

But wait a minute. Recall that alternative hypotheses are rival explanations of the research findings. How else could this result be explained? In several ways. Perhaps subjects recognized the taboo words just as quickly as the neutral words, but hesitated before announcing something embarrassing to the experimenter, especially if they were wrong! Subjects may have "jumped the gun" in their announcement of neutral words (to appear fast, hence intelligent) but delayed somewhat for taboo words until they were absolutely certain that what they actually saw was indeed what they thought they saw. (Would you want to announce nasty words in the presence of a psychologist?) The alternative hypothesis, then, was: "If subjects are shown taboo words and neutral words, then they take longer to announce the taboo words in an attempt to be certain about what they saw."

Researchers have another name for problems such as this: artifact. *Artifacts* are unwanted and unintended sources of bias in the collection or analysis of data; as such, artifacts function as alternative hypotheses. A critic might say that McGinnies's findings were an artifact of his data collection procedure since his subjects may have hesitated before announcing the nasty words, consequently lengthening their perceptual thresholds. Artifacts are common in behavioral research because people's behavior is often influenced by the very process of observation. Subjects may react in unintended ways to the mere presence of a camcorder or clipboard (e.g., they may show nervousness, be better behaved, etc.). In this case, the artifact is also referred to as a *reactive measure* since subjects are reacting to the research procedures required for observation. (A counterpart in medicine might be "white coat fever," whereby blood pressure may skyrocket in response to physicians and all their paraphernalia.) Artifacts are clearly undesirable since they can explain away the findings. To say that specific research findings were an artifact of the data collection procedure is to say that the findings were distorted and not to be trusted.

ARTIFACT: An unwanted source of influence creating a plausible, rival explanation of results. An artifact introduces bias and distorts results.

Here is another example of an artifact that functions as an alternative (plausible, rival) hypothesis: "Standardized achievement test scores increase after an educational intervention." What are other explanations for this finding? What if specific groups, like those with limited English ability, were excluded from the testing after the intervention? This would be a problem if those with limited English ability scored lower than those who remained post intervention. One could not disentangle the intervention effect from the limited English effect. There is, in other words, an alternative explanation for the rise in test scores.

Research studies may be fraught with several alternative hypotheses, not just one glaring one. Another alternative hypothesis in the McGinnies (1949) perceptual defense study might be related to the frequency that neutral and taboo words appear in printed materials (newspapers, magazines, books, advertising signs, etc.). Words that appear more commonly in our language might be recognized faster simply because we are more familiar with them. And if neutral words (compared to taboo words) do indeed appear more frequently in print (hence we are more familiar with them), then another alternative hypothesis would be, "If subjects are shown more frequent and less frequent words, then they will recognize more frequent words faster." You might have recognized this rival explanation as a confounding. The type of word changes as it should since it is the independent variable (neutral versus taboo words), but familiarity (an extraneous variable) changes with it as well (more familiar versus less familiar words). If recognition differences are found between neutral and taboo words, one would not know whether the difference was due to the type of word or the familiarity of the word. Clearly, alternative hypotheses are not wanted, whether in the form of an artifact, a reactive measure, confounding, simple bias, or some other problem.

Problems that function as alternative hypotheses in otherwise well-designed research may be exceedingly difficult to uncover. (Recall the example of The Amazing Randi in Chapter 2.) Those who enjoy solving puzzles will probably also enjoy the dilemmas encountered by an attempt to answer the questions "What else could have possibly caused these results?" and "Was the research hypothesis really supported, or was there an alternative explanation?" This is part of the challenge of critically evaluating research.

CRITICAL THINKER ALERT 5-8

Counter-Explanations

All research is susceptible to alternative hypotheses because there always exists the possibility of counter-explanations for the findings. Good research states explicitly what these alternative hypotheses might be, often in a section of the report titled "Limitations."

Discussion: Presume a researcher recommended that all certified teachers must hold master's degrees, basing the recommendation on a finding that higher standardized achievement test scores were associated with teachers who held master's degrees. What counter-explanations might explain away the finding of a master's degree and achievement link?

Another Example: Learning to Spell

Cunningham and Stanovich (1990) provided another illustration of an alternative hypothesis. They tested whether young students learn to spell best by practicing on a computer, by using alphabet tiles (like those in Scrabble™), or by handwriting. After practicing new words in one of the three groups, students were given a final test, much like a spelling bee, except that the students wrote down each word after it was pronounced by the teacher. The researchers found that the handwriting condition was far better than the computer and alphabet-tile conditions in terms of the students' number of correctly spelled words.

Can you think of an alternative hypothesis? (The clue lies in how the students were tested: all the students were tested using handwriting.) The alternative hypothesis was, "If students are tested with the *same* method used for studying, then they will score higher." Perhaps the computer group would have scored highest if they were tested using the computer; similarly, the alphabet-tile condition might have been superior if they were tested with alphabet tiles. This practice-testing match, therefore, becomes a rival explanation for the findings, since the only condition with the same practice and testing format was the handwriting condition. (This problem was recognized by these researchers and was eliminated in their second experiment. The results, however, were still the same, hence the subtitle of their article: "Writing Beats the Computer.")

It should be clear by now that rival (but plausible) alternative hypotheses are clearly undesirable in the research process. Essentially, these hypotheses are statements about research blunders. Cautious researchers must think carefully about these hypotheses and take steps to avoid them so that they are not rival explanations for the research outcomes.

CRITICAL THINKER ALERT 5-9

Alternative Hypotheses

Careful researchers anticipate problems related to alternative hypotheses beforehand, collect data that might help rule out these rival explanations, and reach conclusions accordingly.

Discussion: Given your response to Critical Thinker Alert 5-8, what additional data could be collected to shed light on this alternative hypothesis?

Null Hypothesis

The third type of hypothesis, the null hypothesis, is used by researchers working under the quantitative tradition and comes into play during the statistical analysis of data. For this reason, the null hypothesis is mentioned only briefly in this section. A more complete explanation appears in Chapter 13 in the discussion of research results and their interpretation.

CRITICAL THINKER ALERT 5-10

Null Hypothesis

Some research reports state their research hypothesis in the null form (e.g., "There will be no difference . . . "). This makes little sense, as the null hypothesis is an assertion about the population. By contrast, the researcher collects data from the sample and believes that a pattern exists in the sample that might generalize to the population. The researcher usually believes the *opposite* of the null hypothesis.

Discussion: Presume a researcher wanted to test the proverb "Practice makes perfect." What is the underlying null hypothesis? What about "Two heads are better than one"? What is the null hypothesis?

The *null hypothesis* is a statistical assumption about the population from which the sample was drawn. The assumption is that there is *no* relationship between the independent and dependent variables—exactly counter to the research hypothesis. Why in the world, you might ask, does the researcher assume there is no relationship among variables in the population? This is a temporary assumption and is believed to be true, so to speak, only while the computer is running during the analysis of the data. The researcher really believes its opposite—the research hypothesis, which posits that there *is* a connection between the variables studied. The computer will then tell the researcher the likelihood (in the form of a *p* value) that the actual findings could be obtained *if* the null hypothesis were true. If the likelihood is very small, for instance, only 1 in 100 chances, the researcher would be entitled to reject the null hypothesis since the outcome is so unlikely (if the null hypothesis were true).

NULL HYPOTHESIS: A statistical hypothesis asserting there is no relationship among variables being studied in the population.

HIGHLIGHT AND LEARNING CHECK 5-10

Null Hypothesis

The *null hypothesis* is a statistical hypothesis asserting there is no connection in the population among variables being studied. Researchers strive to reject the null hypothesis (discard it as not plausible) in an attempt to show there *is* a connection. Presume a researcher collected data to determine whether vitamin B6 improves the retention of learned material. What is the null hypothesis?

What is more likely is that the research hypothesis—the opposite of the null hypothesis—is true and the null hypothesis is false. The researcher then concludes that there is *probably* a relationship in the population from which the sample was drawn. The null hypothesis functions in this temporary way, only to be rejected if the probability of its being true is very low. Most researchers do indeed want to discard (reject) the null hypothesis because its rejection is interpreted as support for the research hypothesis. This is a difficult idea, and some confusion may be unavoidable at this point without greater elaboration. (Many students report that this line of reasoning at first seems "backwards.") The null hypothesis will be explained further in Chapter 13, where its vital role will become clearer.

CRITICAL PERSPECTIVES 5-1

CONSTRUCTS AND VARIABLES

Critical Thinking Toolbox

Educational researchers display critical thinking by honoring multiple perspectives in their work. Consumers of educational research examine beliefs and assumptions of multiple perspectives before accepting or rejecting research conclusions. They avoid a *bandwagon argument*, that is, accepting popular opinion and generalization that may reflect little more than bias (such as "Everyone knows that research shows . . .").

Constructs and Variables in Quantitative Research

The logic used in quantitative research is deduction: An abstract theory or construct (which is general) suggests variables to be investigated (which are more specific, such as dependent variables) with measuring instruments presumed to represent traits or behaviors defined by the variables (which are the most specific). There is a presumption of an objective reality awaiting discovery by objective methods. Constructs and variables are best understood within a context of measurement soundness, control, sampling, and statistical analysis. Methods are usually geared toward understanding cause and effect, with an emphasis on replication.

Constructs and Variables in Qualitative Research

The logic used in qualitative research is *analytic induction*: Specific instances suggest a general theory or social understanding (a construction). Constructs and variables are not imposed on the research design; rather, they emerge from an evolving, flexible design. Participants' experiences and perspectives become situated within greater, more abstract meanings and interpretations. Ongoing methods used in natural settings are usually geared toward meaning and understanding in a broader multidisciplinary context. Variables may be reframed as *observations in context* and *foreshadowed constructs.*

Constructs and Variables in Action Research

The logic used in action research is "reflective" and practical, meaning that ways of thinking here are geared toward identifying and solving problems related to the researcher's own educational practice. Administrators, counselors, and teachers reflect about their practice in an attempt to identify problems and offer possible solutions. The problem is local, personal, and practical (not theoretical). Constructs and variables may be described in terms of ideas, changes, and problem statements.

Critical Thinking Question

How researchers think about constructs, variables, and types of hypotheses across the three perspectives of qualitative, quantitative, and action research reveals very different core assumptions about the nature of "knowing." What differences across assumptions strike you as being most significant? Why do you think that? Do you believe popular opinion about research favors any one of the three perspectives above? Is it possible that researchers themselves may fall victim to a type of bandwagon effect?

Other examples of research, alternative, and null hypotheses are found in Table 5.4.

TABLE 5.4 Examples of Research, Alternative, and Null Hypotheses

Hypothesis	Example
Research	If children watch violent television, then they will act more aggressively at recess.
Alternative	Children prone toward aggression simply watch more violent television.
Null	In a population of school-age children, there is no relationship between television violence and aggressive behavior.
Research	Children who use computers to learn geometry will learn faster than children who use paper and pencil.
Alternative	Children learn faster on the computer because a local news story made them more attentive.
Null	In a population of students, there is no difference in the speed of learning of those who use computers and those who use pencil and paper to learn geometry.
Research	Children will learn to spell better in a spelling bee format than in solo seat work.
Alternative	Children learn better in the spelling bee format because the poor spellers drop out.
Null	In a population of children, there is no difference in the spelling achievement of those who learn in a spelling bee and those who learn in solo seat work.

MORE EXAMPLES

Additional descriptions of published research may help to solidify your knowledge of important ideas related to issues surrounding the research language, namely types of hypotheses and variables. You will find additional descriptions on the Web-based student study site (www.sagepub.com/eic).

Chapter Summary

The research process often begins with a theory—or explanation—of some phenomenon or construct (an unobservable trait). All abstract constructs must be operationally defined before they are researchable; that is, defined in terms of the operations used to produce or measure them (as in the expression "as measured by . . .").

The data collection step in the research process is guided by a research design that manages four different types of variables: independent, or presumed causes; dependent, or presumed effects; attribute, or subject characteristics; and extraneous, or controlled influences. Researchers anticipate biasing sources of contamination or confounding in the research process and use many control procedures to hold them in check.

The whole process is guided further by three different types of hypotheses: the research hypothesis, or predicted outcome; the alternative hypothesis, or rival interpretation of results (such as a confounding); and the null hypothesis, or the assertion that no relationship exists in a population. The null hypothesis becomes relevant only in the statistical analysis phase of the research.

The interpretation of findings may lead to a refinement of the theory and forms the basis for subsequent research.

Application Exercises

1. Describe how you might *operationally* define the following constructs.
   a. happiness
   b. optimism
   c. sociability
   d. cheating
   e. ambition
   f. feeling in control
   g. genius
   h. persistence
   i. authoritarian

2. Consider each of the following scenarios and identify the *independent*, *dependent*, and *attribute* variables. Also name one *extraneous* variable that should be controlled by the researcher.
   a. A group of experienced and "fresh" teachers (with 10+ years and less than 2 years experience, respectively) attended 10 workshop sessions in stress reduction techniques (the treatment). A randomized group of experienced and fresh teachers functioned as a control group. The groups were then compared on a measure of stress (blood pressure). It was found that the treatment was linked to lower levels of stress, with fresh teachers showing a greater effect.
   b. In an attempt to increase the high school graduation rate, a researcher implemented a mentoring program in 10 high schools. Another group of 10 high schools served as a comparison. The researcher found that the mentoring program increased the graduation rate but was more successful for females than males.
   c. A researcher tested whether students' reading comprehension was greater for material read from printed text or from a computer monitor. (The researcher believed that the monitor demanded greater attention, and thus would increase reading comprehension test scores.) The data were analyzed by comparing students with and without home computers. The researcher found no differences between the groups tested.
   d. Are students' grades a function of how much sleep the students get? A researcher wondered about this question and arranged for 100 tenth graders to sleep no less than 9 hours a night for a semester. A control group slept in accordance with their natural habits, which averaged about 6 hours a night. The students were also classified into two groups based on their prior GPAs (3.0 or higher versus less than 3.0). The researcher found that increasing sleep resulted in higher grades during the semester; for the lower GPA students, the effect was more pronounced.
   e. Will students write better if they use a word processor or handwriting? To answer this question, seventh and tenth graders wrote a 3-page essay on a computer with a word processing program or by hand on a writing tablet. (The handwritten essays were transferred to type via a word processor so that the graders, not knowing one group from the other, could not be biased either way.) All essays were rated by independent graders on a 1 to 10 scale reflecting overall quality. The researcher found higher ratings across both grades for the word processing group.
   f. A researcher showed two different videotapes to 50 junior high school classes on the basic principles of electricity. In one condition, the lecture was summarized with a good metaphor. The other condition simply ended without a metaphor. The researcher also tested students' learning styles, and classified each as visual, auditory, or kinesthetic. To measure students' retention of content a month later, the researcher gave a 10-item multiple-choice test. The findings revealed far greater memory in the metaphor groups, but the learning styles made no difference.

3. For each of the following scenarios, describe the confounding that the careless researcher forgot to eliminate.
   a. A researcher tested whether students learn more with visual aids in the form of handouts or slides. Handouts were used during a lecture on the biochemistry of memory and projected slides were used during a lecture on the biochemistry of emotion. Students' comprehension was tested via a 10-item multiple-choice test at the end of each lecture. Students scored higher in the projected slides condition. The researcher concluded that slides were superior to handouts for aiding students' understanding.
   b. A researcher wanted to know whether students write more "from the heart" using handwriting or a computer. Students signed up for the condition of their choice (computer or handwriting), and all students wrote a 3-page essay on "my family." Raters independently and blindly judged the emotional content of each essay on a 1 to 10 scale. The students' essays were clearly more emotional in the handwriting condition. The researcher warned teachers that the use of computers in school will produce robotlike students.
   c. A teacher wanted to know if the color of classrooms affects students' behavior in any noticeable way. This question was prompted by two situations—the school's having been recently painted pale yellow and the fact that many students seemed hyperactive. The teacher checked the conduct reports at the school and compared them to those of another school, one across town that had the same off-white walls that the teacher's school used to have. The conduct reports at the off-white comparison school revealed far fewer instances of misbehavior. The teacher concluded that yellow rooms affect students' behavior in negative ways.

4. For each of the scenarios below, describe the research hypothesis in an If A, then B form. Then offer an alternative hypothesis, that is, a plausible rival explanation for the findings.
   a. A researcher tested whether a new electronic system for monitoring halls would reduce the number of tardies at a large high school. At the same time, a new and somewhat confusing computer system was installed in each classroom for teachers to use in reporting tardies. The researcher found that the electronic system significantly reduced the number of tardies.
   b. A researcher tested a hunch that teachers older than 60 are far happier in their positions than their counterparts in private business. The researcher interviewed 100 older workers from both occupations and found that indeed teachers were happier than businesspeople in their later years. The researcher recommended that older workers seek careers in teaching in order to be happier.
   c. A researcher tested the idea that gymnastic lessons for kindergartners will lead to greater athletic ability in high school. To test this idea, the researcher located two groups of high school students: those who had gymnastic lessons as kindergartners and those who did not. Then their athletic prowess was tested with a battery of physical performance measures. Those who had early gymnastic lessons were clearly far superior as athletes in high school to those who did not have such lessons. The researcher recommended gymnastic lessons to all youngsters in order to improve their adolescent athletic abilities.

5. Can proverbs be tested empirically? Consider each of the following proverbs carefully. Then describe one plausible independent variable (and categories of variation), a dependent variable (operationalized), an attribute variable, and an extraneous variable that you might control. State the testable hypothesis in an If A, then B form.
   a. Too many cooks spoil the broth.
   b. Absence makes the heart grow fonder.
   c. Early to bed and early to rise, make a man healthy, wealthy, and wise.
   d. Laughter is the best medicine.
   e. No pain, no gain.
   f. Practice makes perfect.

g. Spare the rod and spoil the child.
h. The love of money is the root of all evil.
i. Two heads are better than one.
j. Time is a great healer.
k. United we stand, divided we fall.
l. A rolling stone gathers no moss.

6. Browse online journals in your field of interest. Select a research report that states a clear research hypothesis, then answer the following questions.
   a. What was the research hypothesis? Did the authors identify other types of hypotheses, such as an alternative hypothesis or a null hypothesis?
   b. Including independent, dependent, attribute, and extraneous variables, how many types of variables can you identify? List them.
   c. Did the researchers investigate a construct? Can you find an illustration of an operational definition?

ON YOUR OWN

Log on to the Web-based student study site at http://www.sagepub.com/eic for more information about the materials presented in this chapter, suggestions for activities, study aids such as electronic flashcards and review quizzes, a sample research proposal, and research recommendations that include journal article links (with discussion questions and an article evaluation guide) and questions related to this chapter.

6

Theory and Practice

Outline

Overview

The point was made in the last chapter that educational research is best understood as a process, a series of integrated steps with its own language (such as constructs, operational definitions, and different types of variables and hypotheses). This chapter explains how the integrated steps structure the entire research process and how they combine to form an integrated whole. Thinking about research as a connected series of decisions, as opposed to unrelated actions, helps us understand that research results and conclusions are dependent on many factors within the decision chain. Steps in the research process are guided by one of two basic orientations: theoretical or problem based (applied). We will examine the processes relevant to both orientations. We will also examine what may be called *practical research,* a blend of theory and application Let's start with the integrated steps characteristic of theory-based research.

Theory-Based Research

The research process guided by theory usually involves constructs or phenomena that require explanation. Constructs do not exist within a vacuum. The inferred constructs require a theory, or explanation, in order to understand them better. Behind every construct, then, is a theory designed to explain the construct. A theory of intelligence, a theory of motivation, a theory of self-esteem, and a theory of learning would each attempt to explain the construct's origins, development, consequences, or whatever else may be required for a better understanding of the construct.

THEORY: An elaborated explanation for a construct or phenomenon. Theories organize empirical findings and suggest future research.

CRITICAL THINKER ALERT 6-1

Guiding Theories

Theories are explanations that guide future research. They tie together a bundle of research findings and are developed to deepen our understanding.

Discussion: Presume a researcher uncovered relationships between early experience with chess and later achievement in math. How might you explain this finding (that is, theorize about it), and what future research might you suggest as a test of your explanation (theory)?

Although a good synonym for theory is explanation, scientific theories—like the theory of relativity in physics, big bang theory in astronomy, and trickle-down theory in economics—are very broad and encompass many phenomena. Most educational theories, by contrast, are rather narrow and limited by comparison and frequently (but not always) come from outside education, from fields such as psychology and sociology. An example of an education-based theory is Benjamin Bloom's theory of mastery learning (Bloom, 1976), which relates students' characteristics, instruction, and learning outcomes and explains

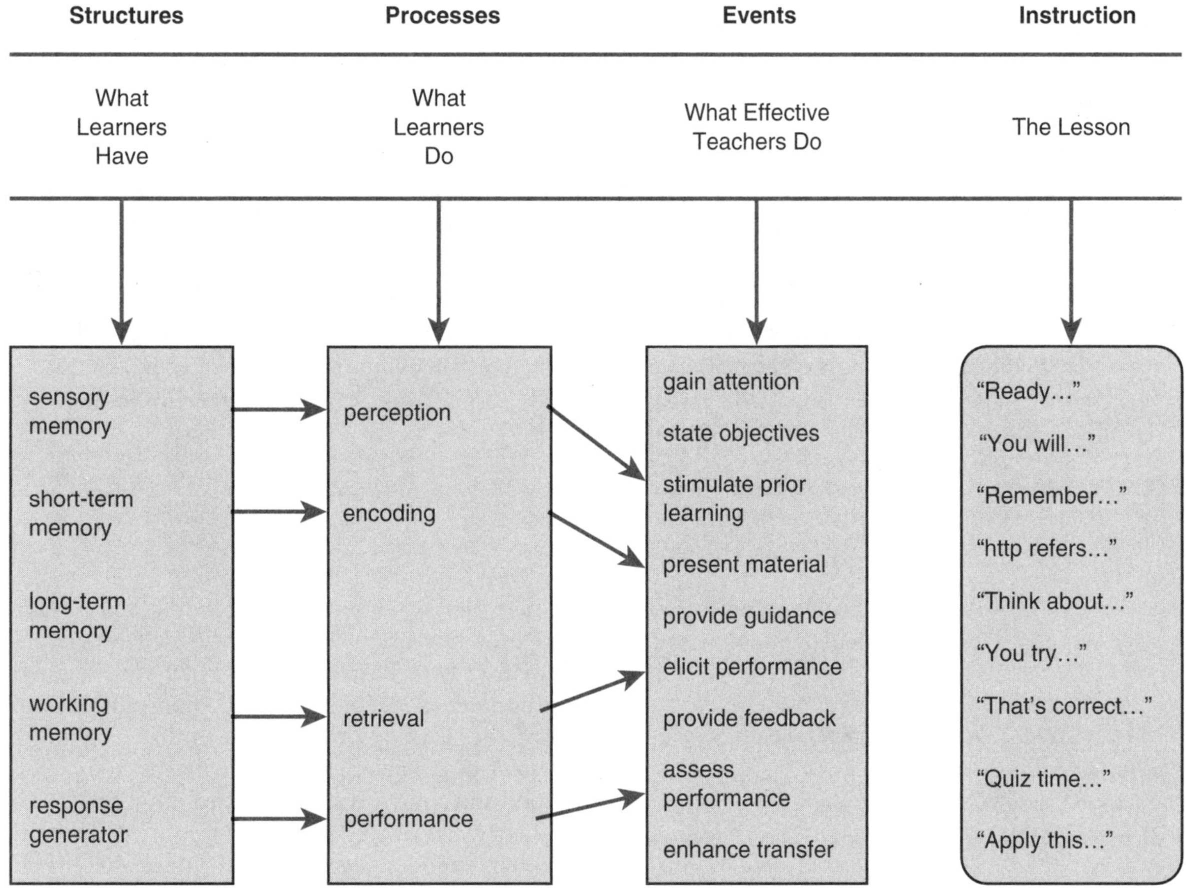

Figure 6.1 Robert Gagne's theory of instruction relating structures, processes, and instructional events. The theory predicts enhanced learning and retention.

Source: Adapted from *Principles of Instructional Design* (4th ed., p. 188), by R. M. Gagne, L. J. Briggs, and W. W. Wager, 1992, Fort Worth, TX: Harcourt Brace Jovanovich.

how all children can reach their full potential in school. Another example of an education theory—an exception since it is so broad and widely generalizable—is Robert Gagne's theory of instruction (Gagne, 1985), which explains the process of effective instructional events in terms of learned outcomes and the underlying cognitive structures and processes. An illustration of Gagne's theory with its full explanatory power is shown in Figure 6.1.

THEORY-BASED RESEARCH: Research aimed at testing the hypotheses spun from a theory with the intention of evaluating the theory (supporting or discarding it) or revising its tenets.

Many theories are best understood when their basic premises are displayed visually using flow diagrams, geometric shapes, and so on. For example, J. P. Guilford's theory of intelligence can be displayed as a cube, Abraham Maslow's theory of motivation as a pyramid, and Robert Sternberg's theory of intelligence as

CRITICAL THINKER ALERT 6-2

Theory Revision

Theories are constantly being challenged and revised as needed based on research results. Many of today's theories about learning and instruction will most likely become mere descriptions (or footnotes) in books on the history of education.

Discussion: As more students learn via the Internet, theories of online or Web-based learning are bound to attract increasing attention. Substantial revisions of these theories over the years, based on research findings, are to be expected. Do you think theories of online learning will dominate the education landscape in 20 years? Will research findings support many of our current ideas about online learning?

a triangle. Many theories utilize metaphors to convey their guiding tenets. One particularly interesting theory of how our brain works is provided by Gerald Edelman (1992), a Nobel Prize winner who rejected the computer model of brain functioning and instead likened the working of our brain to that of a *jungle ecosystem,* or a type of neural Darwinism.

HIGHLIGHT AND LEARNING CHECK 6-1

Theory-Based Research

Theory-based research tests hypotheses derived from explanations (theories or models) of complex constructs or phenomena. Support for hypotheses will add credibility to the theory. What theories have been especially useful in the education sciences?

Good metaphors suggest practical implications of the theory. Sylwester (1993/1994) pointed out that "Edelman's model suggests that a jungle-like brain might thrive best in a jungle-like classroom that includes many sensory, cultural, and problem layers that are closely related to the real-world environment" (p. 50). Theories of memory in particular have made use of many interesting objects to help convey the basic tenets of a theory. Older theories relied on metaphors such as file cabinets, warehouses, storage bins, and so on, whereas more recent theories (e.g., Schank, 1999) use metaphors such as scripts and dynamic workhouses to highlight the importance of concepts such as learning by experience.

Theories explain more than just abstract constructs; they also explain important observable phenomena, such as teenage suicide and depression, gender bias, high school dropout rates, school violence, illegal drug use, boredom with science, and increased absenteeism. Educational phenomena are best understood as trends or observable occurrences. They are different from constructs, as constructs are akin to abstract traits. Because the purpose of a theory is to *explain* constructs or phenomena, it could be said that the purpose of research is to generate and test theories, since the ultimate goal of science is explanation. Examples of older and newer theories that interest educational researchers are shown in Table 6.1.

TABLE 6.1 Examples of Theories Tested by Educational Researchers

Theory	Sampling of Constructs and Ideas
Vygotsky's theory of sociocultural language learning	zone of proximal development
Goldman's theory of intelligence	emotions
Festinger's theory of attitude	cognitive dissonance
Bransford's theory of instruction	situated learning, anchoring
Abelson's theory of learning	scripts
Thorndike's theory of learning	connectionism
Guthrie's theory of learning	contiguity
Reigeluth's learning of instruction	elaboration
Wertheimer's theory of perception	gestalt
Guilford's theory of intelligence	structural cube
Spiro's theory of learning	cognitive flexibility
Schank's theory of memory	dynamic memory; contextual dependency
Miller's theory of memory	information processing; limited capacity
Sweller's theory of instruction	cognitive load
Piaget's theory of cognitive development	schema, equilibration
Bandura's theory of social learning	modeling, efficacy
Atkinson and Shiffrin's theory of memory	stages of information processing; dual-storage
Maslow's theory of humanistic development	needs hierarchy
Bruner's theory of concept learning	scaffolding, discovery; constructivism
Skinner's theory of operant conditioning	reinforcement
Weiner's theory of motivation	causal attributions
Gagne's theory of learning	information processing, instructional events
Slavin's theory of learning	cooperative groups
Carroll's theory of learning	time; minimalism
Bloom's theory of learning	mastery
Atkinson's theory of motivation	expectancy
Gardner's theory of intelligence	multiple intelligences
Sternberg's theory of intelligence	triarchy
Kohlberg's theory of moral reasoning	dilemmas
Erikson's theory of personal development	psychosocial crises
Craik's theory of memory	levels of processing
Paivio's theory of memory	visual and verbal codes
Bransford's theory of memory	transfer-appropriate processing
Ausubel's theory of reception learning	expository teaching
Wittrock's theory of constructive learning	generative teaching
Palincsar and Brown's theory of constructive learning	reciprocal teaching

CRITICAL PERSPECTIVES 6-1

THEORIES AND PRACTICE

Critical Thinking Toolbox

Critical thinking involves searching for evidence to support a belief and noting when evidence is incomplete. Critical thinking includes recognizing that generalizations are often based on incomplete bodies of evidence and therefore are sometimes wrong.

Theories and Practice in Quantitative Research

Quantitative research is usually guided by specific hypotheses deduced logically from a theory developed to explain a construct and is associated with positivism (or logical empiricism). Quantitative and "detached" researchers believe there exist generalized, empirical, and verifiable truths about behavior that are waiting to be found. Finding these laws will enable prediction. Theories can be developed by rigorous scientific methods in ways that separate the researcher from the topic of research. Objective, controlled (unbiased) and formal, predetermined and highly structured methods combined with statistical analysis are designed to support (or refute) theories that generate laws of behavior (and hence prediction). Theories spawn testable hypotheses, measures yield statistically analyzable data, and replicable findings may become "laws" or "principles" (e.g., principles of learning, motivation, etc.). Principles are often translated into practice through lesson plans, the design of instructional materials, classroom management procedures, and the like.

Theories and Practice in Qualitative Research

Qualitative research is often referred to as a *mode of inquiry,* to capture the notion that its methods span a full and unrestricted range of investigative procedures borrowed from many related disciplines. A *phenomenological* study, for example, seeks to understand the essence of a complex (often social) phenomenon without the constraint of a predetermined (perhaps ill-fitting) structure that may either miss its "essence" or change its very nature. Rich narrative descriptions of a phenomenon (e.g., math phobia) are designed to yield deeper understanding and broader explanations (theories). These understandings and new hypotheses tend to emerge after careful exploration of all available data. Practical applications of qualitative research consider the holistic perspective (the whole person in complex interdependencies) and context sensitivity (the sociocultural and historical milieu). Theories are formed inductively, from the "ground up," not deduced logically, from the "top down." A common qualitative research design, in fact, is *grounded theory.* Qualitative inquiries are guided by the worldview (paradigm) called *postmodernism,* which denies the existence of generalized, predictable laws that await discovery by objective methods. Qualitative researchers may generate a new vision (theory) or social construction of reality. New theories are most likely to be generated after total "immersion" with complex data that were gathered naturally.

Theories and Practice in Action Research

Action researchers are concerned less with theoretical constructs and arguments about postmodernism than with "what works." And what does not. Their ideas are likely to come from years of classroom experience and craft knowledge instead of theoretical treatises on cognition and artificial intelligence. Their work is *applied* in the most practical sense. Their *reflective* practice suggests the value of theoretical ideas, but action researchers' main concern is solving everyday problems and improving school practice.

Critical Thinking Questions

Which theoretical and practical orientation—qualitative, quantitative, or action research—has influenced education most significantly over the past decade? What evidence supports your opinion? Can you make a safe generalization about the influence of research on education over the past 10 years?

The Research Process

With this background in mind, you can now see how these research components form an integrated, cyclical process, as shown in Figure 6.2. You'll see how this applies with the three examples below, of which two are fairly simple and one is fairly complex.

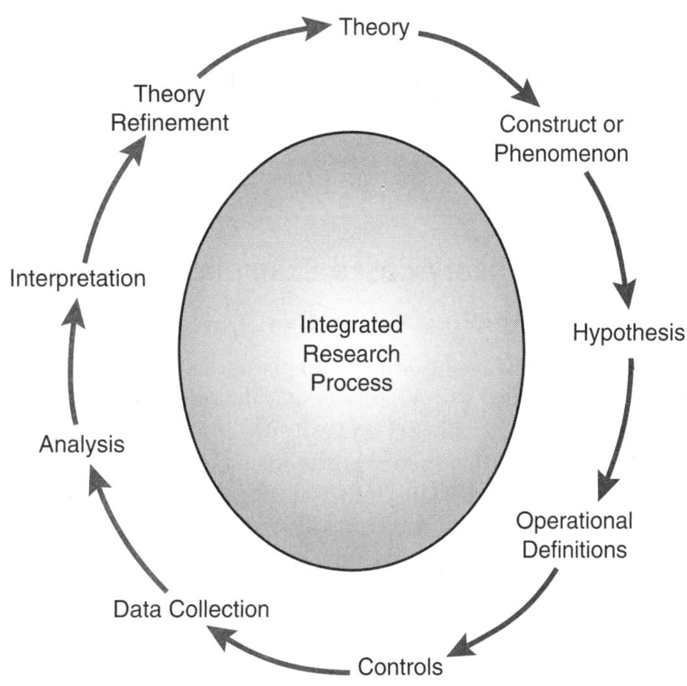

Figure 6.2 The integrated and cyclical nature of the scientific research process.

Source: Adapted from *Primer of Educational Research* (p. 38), by W. N. Suter, 1998, Needham Heights, MA: Allyn and Bacon.

CRITICAL THINKER ALERT 6-3

Useful Theories

Theories in education can never be proven, at least in the same sense that mathematicians prove theorems. A good theory of learning or instruction is a *useful* one, one that guides instructional practice and suggests new hypotheses.

Discussion: Presume my theory of online learning is dubbed the "interdependence discovery" theory. What type of instruction is suggested by this title? Can you offer a research hypothesis based on the constructs suggested by the title?

CRITICAL THINKER ALERT 6-4

Discarded Theories

Although theories cannot be proven in a traditional sense, they can be completely discarded for lack of support (e.g., *phrenology,* the study of mental capacity and personality via surface features of the skull). More commonly, theories are continuously revised in light of new data.

Discussion: Consider my interdependence discovery theory, as mentioned in Critical Thinker Alert 6-3. Presume the highest scoring group in a test of the theory was a control group, one that learned independently and via structured, self-programmed materials. What does this suggest about my theory?

Theory-Based Examples

Spelling Acquisition

In an attempt to explain why some children learn to spell new words quickly and with relative ease while others struggle for a longer time, a researcher develops a new theory and calls it the "multiple sensory modality" theory. An important facet of this theory posits that school learning is enhanced if the learner uses as many sources of sensory feedback as possible to complement the cognitive (thinking) process, including kinesthetic sources (the sensation of body and limb position). This includes fine motor skills like finger movements. The theory suggests that children will learn to spell faster if they practice writing words with their hands (good old-fashioned handwriting) as opposed to passively punching the computer keyboard. Hence, high kinesthesia is defined as handwriting practice, and low kinesthesia is defined as computer keyboard punching. The theory also suggests that large handwriting (big, sweeping letters) will result in the fastest learning of correctly spelled words.

In this example, the *theory* is multiple sensory modality theory, the *construct* being investigated is "learning," and the operational definition of learning is the number of spelling practice trials required to learn a list of 30 words with at least 90% accuracy. This operational definition functions as the dependent variable. The true independent variable is the type of spelling practice (computer keyboard versus handwriting). A reasonable attribute variable (although it is not required in a study like this) would be sex. Because girls mature faster than boys, it would be expected that, according to this theory, girls would outperform boys since their kinesthetic sense (a major factor in this theory) is more advanced at the same age and presumably capable of enhancing their learning of spelling. Two important extraneous variables in this study—ones that require stringent control—are students' prior spelling ability and the spelling difficulty of test words. These extraneous variables would be controlled by using the same words to be learned in both conditions of the independent variable—keyboard versus handwriting—and randomly assigning students to these conditions. This avoids the confounding of type of spelling practice (keyboard versus handwriting) with word difficulty, since both groups would be practicing with the same words. It also avoids confounding type of spelling practice with the prior spelling ability of students. Surely, you would not want the better spellers to practice with handwriting, for then you would not know whether better performance in that group (if indeed that's what the findings reveal) was due to the type of practice or the type of student.

CRITICAL THINKER ALERT 6-5

Research as Process

Scientific research is a process. Decisions made at every stage in the process have implications for findings and interpretations.

Discussion: Consider once again my interdependence discovery theory of online learning mentioned in Critical Thinker Alert 6-3. How might a decision to use a multiple-choice test as the measure of learning influence the findings and their interpretation?

In this example, the research hypothesis is "If students practice spelling new words by handwriting opposed to a computer keyboard, then they will learn to spell faster." One alternative hypothesis is "If students practice spelling with easier words, then they will learn to spell faster." This alternative hypothesis can be ruled out because the difficulty of words was controlled by making sure both groups spelled the same words. The null hypothesis for this study is "In a population of children like these, there will be no difference in the speed of spelling acquisition if they use handwriting versus a computer keyboard." Remember, the null hypothesis comes into play only when the data are being statistically analyzed.

If the results show that the children in the handwriting group learned faster than those in the computer keyboard group, we would state that the research hypothesis was *supported* (not proven). We would also conclude that the theory which generated the research hypothesis is more credible as a result and, at least for now, does not need further refinement. We would not conclude that anything (including the theory) was proven. The word *proof* is best left to theorems in geometry, since it requires a logical argument not well suited to research in the social and behavioral sciences (see Suter & Lindgren, 1989, especially Chapter 2).

Music and Math

Some older children are quite adept at mathematical reasoning and problem solving; others less so. Let's presume that a researcher suspects that early exposure to music is related to math aptitude. The researcher believes so, let's say, because the math and music "centers" of the brain are in close proximity, and enhancing the circuits of one will help to strengthen the circuits of the other. This researcher also suspects that there exists a "window of opportunity" for the neurological development of music understanding, say between the ages of 3 and 6. The earlier the exposure to music, the more profound its effects on mathematical reasoning. Lack of exposure to music during these years, the researcher hypothesizes, takes its toll on the subsequent development of mathematical reasoning. To test this idea, the researcher provides piano lessons and chorus practice to 3- to 6-year-olds for a period of 2 years; a control group receives no such systematic training. Ten years later, the SAT math scores of the two groups are compared. As hypothesized, those children with music experience are more talented in their mathematical reasoning. (This example is hypothetical.)

Let's examine this research as a process, in accordance with Figure 6.2. The construct being investigated is "mathematical reasoning" (some might call this "quantitative intelligence" or simply "math aptitude"). The theory which attempts to explain this construct is the "biology" theory, which details the brain structures and neurochemistry required to explain mathematical thinking. The independent variable is early experience (or lack of it) with music, the dependent variable (the operational definition of mathematical intelligence) is the SAT math scores, the attribute variable is age during first exposure, and one of the many extraneous variables might be the number of ear infections during early childhood. The research hypothesis is, "If young children are exposed to systematic training in music, then they will have higher mathematical reasoning as adolescents (and the younger the age of exposure, the stronger the effects)." One alternative hypothesis is, "If young children are given music lessons, they have higher socioeconomic status, will attend better schools, and will score higher on standardized tests of all types." The null hypothesis is, "In a population of young children, exposure to music will have virtually no effect on later mathematical intelligence."

A major control procedure is the random assignment of children to the music training group (this controls for the extraneous variable of ear infections and greatly reduces the plausibility of the alternative hypothesis concerning socioeconomic status). After the data are collected and analyzed, let us suppose that children with music experience did score substantially higher on the SAT, but the effect was equally strong with all the age groups studied. Because the essence of the research hypothesis was supported, the interpretation, then, offered general support (not proof) for the biology theory. However, some refinement in the "windows of opportunity" concept would be required, since it appears that the earliest exposure to music did not lead to any enhanced effect. After refinement, the theory will be in a better position to generate a new research hypothesis, which if supported, will add to the theory's credibility. The process is continuous: A theory spawns hypotheses, data are collected, the hypothesis is supported (or not), and the theory is refined (or not), spawning new hypotheses.

Gender Bias

Let's consider another example, one that is somewhat more complex. The phenomenon of *gender bias*, as it is usually studied, refers to the preferential attention that boys receive from their teachers. As such, gender bias would be revealed by teachers simply interacting more with boys, calling on them more than girls, asking more follow-up questions of boys, or even waiting longer for boys to answer a question, suggesting a positive expectation in the form of "You can do it." This phenomenon can be explained best by one of several theories. Let's offer a "behavioral" theory of gender bias, as contrasted with, say, an "expectation" theory. According to behavioral theory, a teacher begins by calling on boys more than girls simply because of their demanding behavior, such as wildly waving an outstretched hand, standing up, shouting "Me, me, me, I know, I know." (This might be exaggerated, but you get the idea.) The boys' correct answers reinforce what the teacher is doing, in the sense that the correct answers are satisfying for the teacher, and thus the teachers' behavior (calling on boys) tends to increase in frequency. (The girls would have provided correct answers, too, except they never got a fair chance to contribute because of the boys' more active solicitation of the teacher's attention.)

This behavioral theory denies that teachers' beliefs about or expectations of boys' and girls' school performance are different. (Recall that this is a *behavioral* theory; unobservable constructs such as "expectations" do not play a role.) This theory, then, assumes there is no difference in teachers' expectations for boys' and girls' achievement. Behavioral theory also predicts that the preference of boys over girls tends to increase over the school year (as you would expect with any reinforced behavior). Because behavior can be shaped without awareness, this theory also predicts that teachers will deny treating boys and girls differently. Eventually, the preferential attention given to boys becomes a teacher's habit and will continue until it is extinguished.

Now let's analyze this problem from the perspective of the research process. First, a theory is advanced as an explanation for a phenomenon, in this case, the theory is behavioral theory and the phenomenon is gender bias. This theory then generates research hypotheses about the phenomenon which are consistent with the theory's premises. Several hypotheses could be derived from knowledge of behavioral theory, as described above. First, if beginning teachers are studied, one would expect to see increasing evidence of gender bias in the classroom over the school year, based on the behavioral principle of reinforcement. Second, one would expect to find no differences in teachers' expectations for boys' and girls' success in school learning. Third, one would expect to find that teachers are often unaware of their display of gender bias. More formally, a research hypothesis might be, "If novice teachers are observed over the school year, then they will demonstrate increasing evidence of gender bias without their awareness and without differential expectations for school success of boys and girls."

According to Figure 6.2, constructs and phenomena must be operationally defined (as described in Chapter 5). Here *gender bias* could be defined as the ratio of boys called on versus girls called on (equated for the number of boys versus girls in the classroom), the frequency of follow-up questions that were asked of boys versus girls, and the average wait time for boys versus girls. (Wait time is the number of seconds teachers wait after asking a question of a student before moving on, probing for more information, or simply answering the question themselves.) These measures could be combined to form a composite, with higher numbers indicating greater interaction and attention to boys, that is, greater gender bias. This number, then, becomes the operational definition of gender bias.

Given this complex hypothesis, the researcher must also develop methods for assessing teachers' awareness of gender bias (if it is present) and measuring their relative expectations for boys and girls. These tasks are separate from the measurement of gender bias and require even more complex instrumentation. (To keep this example from becoming hopelessly confused, let's stay focused only on gender bias.)

Figure 6.2 reveals that control procedures must be implemented so that *alternative hypotheses* are eliminated, or at least minimized. (Recall that *alternative hypotheses* are rival explanations of the findings; often they are overlooked sources of contamination or simply research blunders.) For example, class seating charts should assure that boys and girls are spread equally around the room. It would be a problem if boys clustered near the front, because some teachers might be inclined to call on students near the front with greater frequency (it might be easier to see their work, hear their responses, etc.). This would be a problem because according to the operational definition of gender bias, a teacher who did have a preference for the front due to hearing or some other extraneous reason would be misidentified as being gender biased. (If girls preferred the front, then a type of reverse gender bias would be misidentified because of the artifact of girls' preferred seating patterns.) The alternative hypothesis would be, "If teachers are observed over the school year, then they will display increasing preferences for calling on students who sit near the front." Note that this alternative hypothesis, or rival explanation, would be a problem only if more boys than girls sat in the front.

The next step in the research process is to gather data, a step elaborated in Chapters 7 to 9. For now, it is understood that data should be collected from a sufficient number of subjects in a manner that does not jeopardize its meaningfulness. For example, if classroom observers were recording the number of follow-up questions that were directed at boys versus girls, it would be important that the observers not know that boys were expected to receive more follow-up questions. If observers did have this preconceived idea, then it would be too easy to interpret an ambiguous teacher response in a manner that is consistent with what is expected. This technique of keeping data gatherers "in the dark" is called *blinding.*

The end of the cyclical research process involves the analysis of data, followed by the interpretation of findings in light of the theory which generated the research hypotheses in the first place. It may be that the theory needs to be refined, revised, or even abandoned. Quite possibly the theory is supported as it stands. If that is the case, then the theory should be even more useful in the future because of its ability to explain complex phenomena in a way that disjointed guesswork could not. The credible theory, of course, would continue to generate testable hypotheses that might ultimately explain other complex phenomena, or possibly help us understand old problems in a new light. Remember that if this research hypothesis relating level of experience to gender bias is supported, then the findings add *credence* to, but are not *proof* of, the behavioral theory of gender bias.

Curious readers may have noticed that the example of gender bias research did not use a true independent or quasi-independent variable, for there was no experimental manipulation. There was a clear attribute variable (level of teacher experience), a clear dependent variable (a composite measure reflecting gender bias), and at least one extraneous variable to be controlled (seating placement)—but no independent variable. This situation merely reflects the fact that the research was nonexperimental. As you will see in Chapter 11, nonexperimental research can uncover relationships with ease and test hypotheses (and theories) directly. What nonexperimental research lacks, however, is an ability to ferret out *cause-and-effect* relationships. Well-controlled experimental research (as described in Chapter 10), with a researcher manipulation and (especially) a true independent variable, is better suited for uncovering causal connections among those variables being investigated.

HIGHLIGHT AND LEARNING CHECK 6-2

Integrated Research Process

Clear thinking about research in education is enhanced by a model revealing a sequence of integrated, interdependent steps. Decisions at each step in the cycle will affect decisions at the next step. What are the major components of the theory-based research process?

Cooperative Learning Groups

This section describes theory-based research in the published literature. Several hundred research studies in education over decades have demonstrated the value of cooperative learning methods over competitive and individualistic techniques on measures of academic achievement (Johnson & Johnson, 2000). Onwuegbuzie, Collins, and Elbedour (2003) observed that several theories in psychology and education make this prediction, including social interdependence theory, cognitive-developmental theory, and behavioral-learning theory. Each theory highlights the function of several constructs and posits one or more assertions, such as intrinsic motivation and goal seeking, cognitive disequilibrium and knowledge as a social construction, and contingent reinforcement coupled with extrinsic motivation. In addition, Slavin (1990) described his two-element theory of cooperative learning (with the constructs "positive interdependence" and "individual accountability"), and Johnson and Johnson (2000) described their more complicated five-element theory. With such strong and varied theoretical support, a well-designed study that did not reveal the advantages of cooperative learning on achievement would surely create a need to reexamine any or all of these theories.

What piqued the interest of Onwuegbuzie and colleagues (2003) was the role of *group composition* on cooperative learning. Onwuegbuzie and colleagues (2003) wondered whether research findings linking differences among types of groups formed and resultant achievement have implications for theory. They were also interested in *extending* the findings of cooperative learning effects by using graduate students enrolled in a course on research methods in education. To shed light on theoretical orientations and learn more about cooperative learning among graduate students, Onwuegbuzie and colleagues (2003) varied the group size (two to seven students) and group composition, that is, differences in research aptitude, defined as prior achievement. (This variation in group composition is often referred to as *level of homogeneity-heterogeneity,* or *similarity-differences*). Their research tested these three hypotheses: (1) "Cooperative groups with the highest aptitude will have the highest quality of learning"; (2) "The level of group heterogeneity, or spread of aptitude, in a group will be related to the quality of learning"; and (3) "The size of group is related to quality of learning." Notice that the first hypothesis predicted a clear direction (higher quality of learning); the other two hypotheses were non-directional (the outcome might go either way, that is, higher or lower). Notice also that the hypotheses were stated as assertions, as opposed to If A, then B statements or research questions. This format is common in published research studies.

The researchers' outcome measure of learning was the "quality of output," operationally defined as the number of points earned on a written research proposal and a written critique. The research proposal was scored with two rubrics: a content rubric consisting of 145 rating items (on a 5-point scale) and a writing style rubric consisting of 89 rating items (on a 5-point scale). The content rubric evaluated all components of the research proposal (literature review, methodology, etc.), and the writing style rubric evaluated conformity to language usage and APA requirements. ("APA requirements" refers to the writing style described by the *Publication Manual of the American Psychological Association* and demanded by many journals in education.)

As you can imagine, each proposal required careful attention during assessment, but there was ample variation in points earned (145 to 725 and 89 to 445, respectively), which is desirable for statistical analysis. The points were converted into percentages and then combined, giving more weight to the content rubric. The article critique was scored with three different rubrics, each assessing a particular quality (and totaling 235 items on a 5-point scale). These points were also converted into percentages, weighted, and assigned a point value on a 100-point scale. (The researchers reported that both measures of learning required at least 10 hours to score each group. And there were 70 groups!)

Notice also that the researchers' construct "aptitude" in the first hypothesis required an operational definition. It was described as "conceptual knowledge" and operationally defined as the points earned on the (open-ended) midterm and final exams in the course and scored by a 100-point scale using a key that allowed for partial credit.

Like all carefully designed research, Onwuegbuzie and colleagues' research included controls to rule out alternative hypotheses. For example, the same instructor taught all sections of the research methods course in which the cooperative groups were formed. Holding the instructor constant (hence controlled) in this sense prevented confounding the size of groups and their composition with the styles of different instructors. Also, all courses were held at the same time of day, thus avoiding the alternative hypothesis resulting from the confounding of group size and composition with time of day. The 70 cooperative learning groups of two to seven students were formed by "modified stratified random assignment" in an attempt to equalize extraneous sources of influences equally across all groups.

The data collection phase of this research lasted 3 years and involved 15 sections of a research methods course. In addition to the measures of conceptual knowledge (or research aptitude, defined by the midterm and final exam scores) and the primary dependent variables (the scored proposal and critique), the researchers also collected peer evaluations using a rating form to evaluate the level of cooperation of group members as well as information such as the number of previous research courses taken. Finding no relationship between scores on the group projects (proposal and critiques) and the number of previous research courses taken, the researchers were able to conclude that "it is unlikely that students' prior knowledge of research methodology served as a confounding variable" (Onwuegbuzie et al., 2003, p. 227).

The first hypothesis tested by researchers, the link between the level of conceptual knowledge (research aptitude) and the quality of the group projects (proposal and critique), was supported by the data analysis: Cooperative learning groups with the greatest conceptual knowledge produced the best performance outcomes on the proposal and critique. Partial support was found for the second hypothesis: The cooperative learning groups with the greatest heterogeneity (large spread of scores on conceptual knowledge) yielded better research critiques; however, there was no connection between group heterogeneity and the research proposal. The researchers also found partial support for their third hypothesis relating the size of group and the quality of the group project: There was a complex relationship between group size and the article critique but no connection been group size and the quality of the research proposal.

Onwuegbuzie and colleagues' (2003) interpretation and discussion of their results centered on the Matthew effect, "whereby groups that contained high-achieving students on an individual level tended to produce better group outcomes than did their lower-achieving counterparts" (p. 226). The Matthew effect is often summarized simply as "the rich get richer," a type of "fan-spread" where rates of gain on educational outcomes are related to initial levels. The researchers also interpreted their findings in relation to a self-fulfilling prophecy whereby "high individual achieving groups possess higher levels of academic motivation and self-esteem," a type of expectation leading to higher levels of performance output. The researchers' discussion of their findings, for the most part, favors the five-element theory described by Johnson and Johnson (2000), with several refinements. The researchers reached this conclusion, in part, because their findings showed little or no "coattailing" or "social loafing." Their data also supported the recommendation to maximize group output by increasing group heterogeneity (placing low-, moderate-, and high-achieving students in the same cooperative group), preferably using groups of six students. Although this study was based on a theoretical framework, notice that its conclusions are applied, given the recommendations regarding group composition. Many studies in education have a theoretical basis, yet discussion often centers on their application to practical problems, with clear recommendations for practice.

Problem-Based Research

Problem-based educational research, often called *applied* research, above all else is concerned with solving a practical problem, like improving educational practice or evaluating a specific program for the purpose of making sound decisions (like whether the program should be continued). In a sense, all educational research is problem based (applied) if it is not specifically directed at testing hypotheses sprung from a theoretical framework. The distinction between theory- and problem-based research actually represents a rather blurry continuum, and there is no point to pigeonholing all research as either theory or problem based. It would be hard to imagine researchers who test educational theories completely divorced from any ideas about real-world application. Likewise, it would be hard to imagine applied researchers who never thought about the broader implications of their findings in terms of an explanatory framework (theory). The distinction is important, however, in terms of the guidance offered for the integrated steps that comprise the research process. Research based on theory, as described earlier in this chapter, is guided by the cyclical nature of the scientific research process shown in Figure 6.2. Problem-based educational research uses alternative guidance systems, often in the form of what are called *models.*

PROBLEM-BASED RESEARCH: Research focusing on direct application of findings to solve practical problems. It is also referred to as applied research.

HIGHLIGHT AND LEARNING CHECK 6-3

Problem-Based Research

Problem-based, or applied, research is oriented toward application and practice rather than theory, and it attempts to address practical problems in education. Is the distinction between theory-based and problem-based research in education always clear?

Next I will briefly present two types of problem-based research in education—evaluation research and action research—and illustrate how problem-based research differs from theory-based research (which is guided by the cyclical scientific process).

Evaluation Research

Educational evaluations provide data in order to assess (make judgments about) the merit or value of educational programs. (The term *program* is used here in a very general sense, referring to a broad range of instructional methods, curriculum materials, and organizations as well as teachers, administrators, and students.) Most educational programs have specific objectives or more general goals, and their success is usually assessed by how well the objectives and goals were met. A distinction is usually made between two types of educational evaluations: formative and summative (Scriven, 1967). In a *formative* evaluation, data are collected for the purpose of improving specific aspects of a program, like the instructional materials, methods of delivery, and assessment procedures. Recognizing that many educational programs are developed in a trial-and-error manner, formative evaluation research is conducted in the spirit of "forming" a better product or program. Tryouts are followed by revisions (debugging) until the program's outcomes are in line with the program's objectives. In general, formative evaluations are conducted for the purpose of gathering data in order to revise and improve, and thus are an integral part of program development. Current research on DARE, the antidrug education program in many schools, would be an example of this type of evaluation research if evaluators collected data on its program outcomes, all with a focus on improvement in meeting objectives.

EVALUATION RESEARCH: Research concerned with assessing the value of a program or revising it to enhance its effectiveness.

In a *summative* evaluation, by contrast, the purpose is to "summarize" the overall success of a program in terms of reaching its goals or achieving its aims. This is usually done after the program has been developed via formative evaluations. Summative evaluations may be used by policy makers or funding agencies to make sound decisions. One classic example of a summative evaluation is the federally funded Head Start preschool program. The general question posed by evaluators of this program was "Are Head Start children more successful in the later school years than children who do not participate in Head Start?" (The oversimplified answer arising from very complex data is "Yes.") Summative evaluations may also compare two competing programs to determine which is more effective.

Program evaluators, as they are often called, must still grapple with the usual challenges faced by scientific researchers who are theory driven. They must, for example, restate the aims and objectives of a program in terms of operational definitions so that they can be measured. What, for example, would constitute measures of "success" in a DARE or Head Start evaluation? They must also implement controls, often in the form of comparison groups, so that meaningful contrasts can be made between the program and its alternatives. The primary difference between theory-based research and program evaluation is that program evaluators follow models to assess programs (not test theories). All researchers share concerns about measurement, controls, rival explanations, and other challenges that must be overcome in order to meaningfully interpret data.

There is a panorama of step-by-step evaluation models used by program evaluators, and the models are described in some detail by Popham (1993). They range from models emphasizing inputs and outputs to models emphasizing "connoisseurship" and complex appraisal, as in a work of art. They may be objectives oriented,

CRITICAL THINKER ALERT 6-6

Applied Research

Applied (problem-based) research is increasing in importance due, in part, to federal guidelines established by No Child Left Behind that require strong research support ("what works") for programs implemented by schools.

Discussion: What are possible implications of an increasing priority placed on applied or problem-based research as opposed to theory-based research? Might schools become more effective in their mission? How might this affect the advancement of knowledge that can be derived from educational theories?

management oriented, consumer oriented, expertise oriented, adversary oriented, naturalistic, and/or participant oriented (Worthen & Sanders, 1987). Some emphasize discrepancies between an existing state and a desired state (a "needs assessment"), while others emphasize a ratio of cost to benefit. One commonly used model, influencing many program evaluations over the years, is the CIPP Model described by Stufflebeam and his colleagues (1971). The acronym refers to the model's four elements of evaluation: context, input, process, and product (shown in Figure 6.3).

Each facet of the CIPP Model is associated with specific questions; the answers to these questions will help shape sound decisions. The initial facet of evaluation centers on the context (or environment) where problems are identified, unmet needs are assessed, and decisions are made regarding which objectives should be pursued to meet needs. The input stage of evaluation concerns the strategies (plans) and available resources that are required to meet the program's objectives.

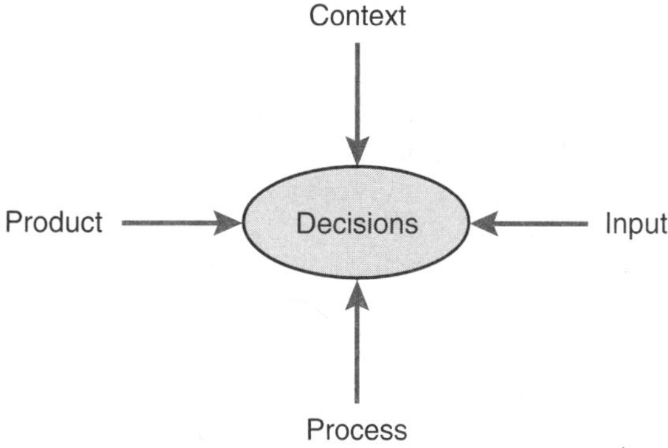

Figure 6.3 The CIPP Model of evaluation research. This model emphasizes questions and decisions and is often used in program planning and operation.

Source: *Educational Evaluation and Decision Making,* Stufflebeam et al. (1971), p. 112.

Important decisions at this point are influenced by information about competing strategies, their effectiveness (and legality) for achieving program goals, and capabilities such as personnel and space. Process evaluation requires the collection of evaluation data, program monitoring, and feedback about program operations while it is under way. Important decisions about data collection methods, record keeping, types of procedural barriers, and the use of materials and facilities will influence how well the program progresses. The last focus in the CIPP Model is product evaluation—the extent to which the goals of the program have been achieved. At this stage, decisions are made with regard to continuing or modifying the program.

HIGHLIGHT AND LEARNING CHECK 6-4

Evaluation Research

Evaluation research in education focuses on determining whether program objectives are being met (summative evaluation) or how to improve specific program areas (formative evaluation). Describe one commonly used program evaluation model.

Program evaluators operating under this model have specific tasks related to each stage of evaluation. They must determine what kinds of information are needed for each stage ("delineation"), obtain the information, and combine all of the pieces ("synthesis"), so that the information is useful for making decisions that affect how (or if) the program will continue.

Although program evaluation research is conceptualized differently than theory-based scientific research, an important point is worth repeating: The major methodological challenges remain the same. These include proper sampling, implementing controls, and using reliable and valid measuring instruments, to name just a few. These topics, among many others, are covered in the chapters to follow.

One program evaluation receiving much attention in recent years is the evaluation of the High/Scope Perry Preschool Program. This program began in 1962 in Ypsilanti, Michigan, to help low-income, at-risk youth gain a positive start in education. What is unique about this program is its comprehensive, well-controlled early evaluation. (This is contrasted with programs that have never planned for systematic evaluations.) It is one of the few programs evaluated by a true experimental design (incorporating the use of a true independent variable). The evaluation involved 123 children (ages 3 and 4), born in poverty, who were randomly divided into two groups: those receiving a quality preschool program (active learning opportunities and interactions influenced by Jean Piaget) and those receiving no preschool. Remarkably, 95% of these original study participants were interviewed at age 27. Operationally defining constructs such as "life success," "social responsibility," or "positive adulthood" is not easy, but the researchers' assessments (dependent variables) included outcome measures such as school achievement, level of schooling attained, arrest records, social service interventions, earnings, home ownership, and commitment to marriage (Schweinhart, Barnes, & Weikart, 1993). The researchers' long-term evaluation revealed positive findings in those areas, and their conclusion suggests that similar programs would be expected to have desirable influence on "protective" factors (such as cognitive skills, self-esteem, social development, and effective communication) and reductions in "risk" factors (such as antisocial behavior, low frustration tolerance, and alcohol use).

CRITICAL THINKER ALERT 6-7

Scientific Research

Federal guidelines under No Child Left Behind demand *scientific* research support for programs in place within reformed schools. Scientific research is empirical, rigorous, and objective and follows established procedures for evaluating program effectiveness.

Discussion: One might argue that some practices in education are simply easier to support than others using rigorous scientific research. And some practices might be impossible to support. Which practices might be relatively easy to support by rigorous research, and what are the implications of guidelines requiring rigorous research support for instructional practices in general?

Action Research

An applied orientation toward research known as *action research* is receiving ever-increasing attention in the professional literature. (Action research is sometimes referred to as *teacher research,* which is discussed separately in Chapter 3.) This type of research is usually conducted by teachers or other educational practitioners (e.g., administrators, counselors, librarians) for the specific purpose of solving a local problem (meaning in the classroom, school, or district) or gathering information so as to make better decisions. Armed with new knowledge or better information, teachers can "take action" by, for example, improving the way a lesson is presented. One strength of action research is that findings are easily translated into practice. By contrast, some approaches to research leave the practical application a mystery, despite buzzwords such as "theory into practice."

ACTION RESEARCH: Research conducted by practitioners in applied fields (teaching, counseling, etc.) for the purpose of solving a specific problem.

Most action research is carried out by teachers for the purpose of improving their practice and understanding it more deeply. As such, action research contributes to the professional development of teachers by increasing their understanding of the conduct of research and the utilization of findings. Because action research often requires several teachers working collaboratively, a side benefit is the formation of collegial networks, leading to better communication among teachers and reducing feelings of isolation ("separate caves"). Action research encourages teachers to reflect on their practice and enhances the profession of teaching as more teachers assume responsibility for evaluating and improving their practice. Teachers should not be excluded from the research loop, nor be viewed as subservient technicians who merely apply the findings of academic researchers. Newkirk (1992) showed how action research is not simply a scaled-down version of formal, scientific research. Its focus on classroom problems is from the heart, so to speak, and its audience consists of like-minded, reflective, curious, and dedicated practitioners. The "spirit" of action research is captured well by Carol Santa (1993):

> I feel that research studies conducted by teachers are the most powerful way to effect change in the educational system. I know that this is a bold claim, but I believe it intensely. Too often teachers use the same methods year after year, without ever questioning their effectiveness. They don't think enough about what they do or take sufficient time to reflect. Therefore, they don't grow and change. The solution to this problem of entrenchment is teacher research. Teachers must think of their classrooms as research laboratories and involve their students as research collaborators. In this way, learning about teaching never becomes static. We remain alive as teachers, and even more important, our students begin to think of themselves as researchers, too. When we involve students as collaborators, they learn about themselves as learners. (pp. 401–402)

A model of the action research process (Sagor, 1992) is presented in Figure 6.4. This model describes sequential steps, where each step leads to the next. Problem formulation requires action researchers to identify the issue of greatest concern,

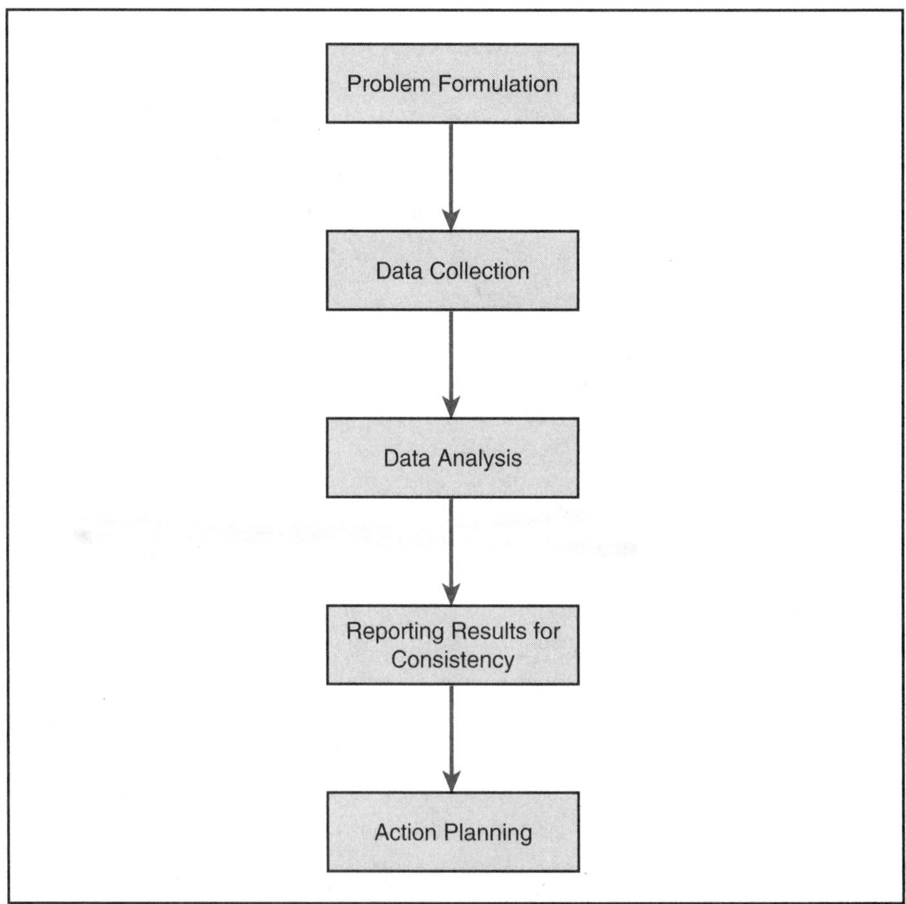

Figure 6.4 Five-step sequential process model of action research.

Source: *How to Conduct Collaborative Action Research* (p. 10), by R. Sagor, 1992, Alexandria, VA: Association for Supervision and Curriculum Development.

what they already know about the issue, and what knowledge is lacking. The problem is then translated into a research question. The credibility of the action research is in large part determined by the data collection step. Sagor (1992) recommends that three sources of data be collected for an adequate answer to each question. *Data analysis* involves the discovery of trends or patterns in the data and the conclusions (if any) that are possible from the analysis. The reporting of action research results is strongly encouraged via as many appropriate forums as possible. Sagor (1992) stated that this step can be especially rewarding, as it gives teachers the opportunity to share what they have learned about their practice. The final step involves translating the findings of the systematic inquiry into ideas for planning and implementing the school or classroom improvement (the "action"). It is this step that has the potential for revitalizing a learning community.

You will probably find that the results of action research are presented somewhat differently than those of theory-based research. The reporting style appears less rigorous than it is in other types of published research. The results are often presented in a quasi-story form, and as such, are more personal and less formal. A story format can be an effective way to share findings and ideas since good stories are memorable. Action research can also be presented in the same manner as large-scale, formal research, following standard publication guidelines such as those in the widely used *Publication Manual of the American Psychological Association* (2001), which is often referred to as the APA manual.

The increasing influence of action research is also revealed by an international journal launched in 1993 and titled, appropriately, *Educational Action Research*, which welcomes accounts of action research studies and articles that contribute to the debate on the practice of action research and its associated methodologies. Other journals founded specifically for the purpose of sharing reports of applied action research and associated ideas include *Networks: An On-line Journal for Teacher Research* (started in 1998) and *The Journal of Action Research in Education* (started in 2002).

HIGHLIGHT AND LEARNING CHECK 6-5

Action Research

Action research in education (e.g., teacher research) is used by reflective practitioners intent on changing (improving) some aspect of their applied practice. Describe one common model of action research.

CRITICAL THINKER ALERT 6-8

Classroom Research

It is a misconception that classroom teachers do not conduct useful research within their own classrooms or schools. As problem-based research becomes more important, so does teacher research geared toward investigating programs and methods and establishing their effectiveness.

Discussion: If you are an educational practitioner such as a teacher, counselor, or administrator, can you think of a problem in your own setting that can be investigated via action research? How would you approach your action research? What type of data would you gather?

An Example: Classroom Connoisseurs

Did you ever wonder how to create a "classroom of connoisseurs"? Seventh-grade language arts teacher Maria Kowal did, and now she has a deeper understanding of classroom connoisseurs that sprung from her action research in the area of reading (Kowal, 2003). Previously, her teaching had an "element of dissatisfaction," for at the end of a typical school year, she could not determine whether or not her students knew they had grown as readers. She wondered whether she could help her students become aware of their progress and identify their needs, and whether this awareness might help them try harder and achieve more. Further, she wondered whether it was possible to involve her students as "co-researchers" in an investigation to shed light on these questions. Kowal's problem was that the concept of "reading growth" was too abstract to work with. What she needed was an "improvable object," like an image or metaphor—something tangible that she could "build and rebuild" with her students.

Maria Kowal and her students arrived at the idea of "connoisseurship" as a way to gauge the complexities of responding to literature in a developmental manner. (We can all evaluate pizza and justify our rating. Why not literature?) Using reading journals, Kowal and her co-investigating students began fine-tuning the process of reflecting on their growth as readers (and writers) and taking a "meta look" at themselves as learners. They developed questionnaires as a group, including questions such as "Why did the teacher ask you to complete this activity?" Students' discussions were videotaped, and the process of "making meaning" from data in the form of discussions was strengthened by students' opportunity to "reflect on themselves in action."

Kowal reported increased vibrancy in her classroom (enthusiasm, amazement, mutual admiration, etc.) as a result of students and teacher together investigating the reading process, assuming the role of connoisseur, and engaging the interactive nature of reading. Evidence revealed that her students could articulate how meaning is created in a poem, short story, or other work of literature, as well as describe a "meta understanding of themselves as learners." Kowal's action research demonstrated the potential of students-as-researchers (not mere subjects) and the potential of a metaphor to expose a complex process such as the interpretation of literature in order to understand it more deeply and chart its developmental progress.

One of the best ways of solidifying your knowledge of the important terms and concepts in this chapter is to describe how these terms are applied in published research, the type you will likely encounter. The next section describes other applications of the process of scientific research in greater detail.

CRITICAL THINKER ALERT 6-9

Question-Spawning Research

Good research often generates more questions than it answers. Teachers, being masters in their own settings, are in a good position to conduct question-spawning action research.

Discussion: Presume a high school math teacher conducts an action research project and discovers that students who finish their exams most quickly often score lowest despite attempts to answer all questions. What follow-up questions does this finding suggest for future action research projects?

Practical Research: A Blend of Theory and Application

Much educational research cannot easily be pigeonholed as theoretical or problem based. In the absence of a theoretical background, a program that requires evaluation, or a specific classroom problem that requires a solution, research that investigates questions relating to educational practices, curriculum, or policy issues might be labeled *practical* research because of its close connection to educational practice and policy. Practical research may investigate constructs without much, if any, attention to the theory that developed the construct (unlike theory-based research). Or it may focus on a problem or program without the pressing need for "action" (as in action research) or recommendations for program improvement or continuation (as in program evaluation). Research in the areas of, for example, homework, instructional delivery systems, teaching styles, scheduling, assessment, ability grouping, and related topics that bear directly on educational practice are all commonly investigated by educational researchers. Such studies cannot be faulted for lack of a theoretical framework or models of evaluation. Theories and models may not be relevant.

PRACTICAL RESEARCH: Research blending aspects of theory-based and problem-based research (as in a test of a "practical theory" such as multiple intelligences).

HIGHLIGHT AND LEARNING CHECK 6-6

Practical Research

Practical research blends theory-based and problem-oriented research. Much contemporary research in education is practical, increasingly so with a federal focus on "what works." Match the research orientation (theory based, problem based, or practical) with these questions: Is the No Child Left Behind Act achieving its goals? What is the optimal amount of assigned homework in sixth grade for maximal learning? Are memories erased or simply inaccessible?

Practical research is also understood best as a process, or series of integrated steps. With less focus on theory, models of evaluation, or immediate classroom problems, practical research centers on discovering relationships that have direct relevance to improving educational practice and creating well-grounded educational policy. One model of practical research is presented in Figure 6.5.

CRITICAL THINKER ALERT 6-10

Aimless Analysis

All research endeavors have a clear purpose, regardless of orientation. An aimless collection of data would not be considered useful research. A table of random numbers, for example, is just that. You could pretend that a portion of the table is real data. Repeated but aimless "analysis" of the numbers will eventually yield "significant" findings, providing convincing evidence that aimless collection of massive data is not useful. Analysis of such data is often meaningless.

Discussion: Evaluation of the meaningfulness of educational research often exposes one's core beliefs and educational values. Which of the following two purposes of research do you think is more meaningful and why: to compare the effectiveness of three different standardized test preparation programs, or to evaluate which of three different teaching techniques appears to spark the greatest interest among students?

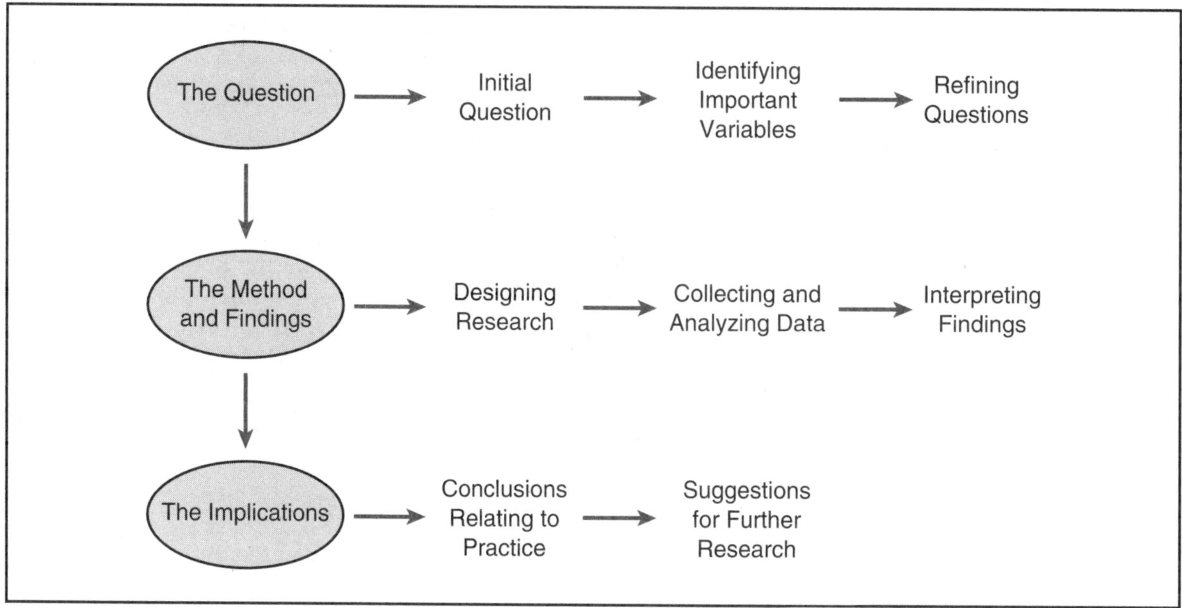

Figure 6.5 One model of practical research. The overarching concern here is the improvement of educational practice.

Practical educational research, of course, adheres tightly to the scientific process that requires safeguards such as operational definitions, empirical measures, controls for biases and unwanted influences, objective data analysis, logical conclusions, and so on.

Applications of Practical Research as a Process

Homework

Illustrations of practical research abound in the literature on many topics in education. Consider Van Voorhis (2003), for example, who observed that "homework is an everyday part of school life" yet often evokes frustration for the student, the student's family, and the teacher who cannot understand why it was incomplete. To complicate matters, research in the area of homework is murky, in part due to conflicting findings. Van Voorhis reported that the relationship between time spent on homework and achievement among elementary school students is negative (more time spent is linked to lower achievement). The relationship tends to become positive, by contrast, among secondary students (more time spent is linked to higher achievement).

Van Voorhis offered one explanation for this changing relationship: Elementary students who struggle in school take more time to complete homework, and secondary students in lower ability classes are assigned less homework compared to those in advanced classes. Van Voorhis also reported that families are involved regularly in the homework process but that there is need for improved communication between the school and home regarding parental help with homework. The research literature on the issue of parental involvement is also mixed, she reported, with many studies reporting both negative and positive findings. Her careful review of the literature thus enabled Van Voorhis to center on the important variables of attitudes, time, and family involvement.

Using Figure 6.5 as reference for understanding the research conducted by Van Voorhis, you can see that her initial but general question was probably akin to "Can schools improve the value of homework assignments?" Her review of the research literature identified several important variables including attitudes, time, and family involvement. This identification led to her refined and answerable research question: "Can weekly, time-efficient, interactive science homework in middle school have positive effects on family involvement in homework, student achievement, and attitudes toward homework?"

Designing practical research, like all scientific research, is challenging. Important decisions must be made about factors such as type of study (for example, an experiment versus a survey), the sample and its selection, materials, measures, methods of control, and strategies for reducing bias. Van Voorhis decided to use 10 sixth- and eighth-grade classes, totaling 253 students. Her chosen research design was quasi-experimental, a type of intervention study using a quasi-independent variable, that is, one not using random assignment to manipulated groups (see Chapter 10). This design allowed her to compare the influence of interactive homework assignments versus noninteractive homework assignments. The interactive homework assignments were carefully designed science activities and permitted ample time for students to involve their families with conversations and other interactions. The noninteractive (control) homework assignments were linked to the science curriculum in the same manner as the interactive assignments and contained the same content and format (but lacked the interactive component). Both types of homework were scored in the same manner.

Data collection lasted 18 weeks, and the dependent (outcome) measures included homework return rates, homework accuracy (points earned), family involvement, time spent on homework, science achievement (report card grade), and attitudes about science. Family involvement was operationally defined as responses to a survey instrument (a rating scale describing the frequency of interaction with family members). Attitudes were operationalized by responses to a survey form with several rating items on an agree-disagree scale. Van Voorhis also collected many variables which functioned as control measures, including prior science achievement, mother's educational level, student aptitude (standardized test scores), class ability grouping, and students' race, gender, and grade level.

Van Voorhis's analysis of data was extensive, yet her major findings can be summarized as follows: Interactive science homework did promote more family involvement as expected, but only with science homework (and not with language arts and mathematics); interactive homework was completed more accurately than noninteractive homework; and students in the interactive homework condition achieved higher grades in science. Van Voorhis concluded her report with two engaging sections titled "Limitations and Recommendations for Future Research" and "Implications for Teaching Practice," the latter focusing on the benefits of well-designed, interactive homework. She concluded, "Educators, policy makers, and families want all children to succeed in school. Part of that solution requires innovative and systematic approaches to current teaching practice. When students complete interactive homework, they report higher levels of family involvement in their school work, report liking this type of assignment, and earn higher report card grades in school" (Van Voorhis, 2003, p. 337).

The Van Voorhis study is practical in its orientation, with clear implications for teaching practice, and it conforms well to the cycle of practical research shown in Figure 6.5. The steps within "The Question" process lead well into the stages within "The Methods and Findings," which in turn flow logically into issues surrounding "The Implications."

Practical research in education is playing an increasingly important role in shaping public policy on myriad issues in education. Topics here might include tracking, distance learning, homeschooling, athletics and academics, grade promotion and retention, high-stakes testing, the standards movement, preschool and child care, teacher retention, charter schools, vouchers, and teacher preparation programs (traditional certification versus alternatives) linked to student learning outcomes. Useful research in areas such as these tends to be large-scale, often involving several thousand students and enormous data sets such as the National Assessment of Education Progress (NAEP), and national (or international) in scope. Nevertheless, policy-oriented, large-scale educational research, like all other types of educational research, conforms to a scientific process with clear guidelines relating to an integrated series of steps (as illustrated in Figure 6.5).

High-Stakes Testing

As one final example, consider the Rosenshine (2003) study of high-stakes testing. High-stakes testing programs attach consequences to scores, perhaps a student's failure to graduate, a teacher's loss of job, or even a school's closure. Rosenshine (2003) first identified the most important factors in an assessment of high-stakes testing programs: a meaningful comparison group and unbiased NAEP scores. (Some states "exempted" students with limited English proficiency, hence inflating state averages.) His refined question became "Is there a difference in the 4-year (Grades 4 to 8) reading and mathematics gain between 12 'clear' high-stakes states and 18 comparison states?" His research method led to data analysis that revealed "much higher" achievement gains in the high-stakes states than in the comparison states. (It should be noted that the NAEP itself is not a "high-stakes" test. The unique statewide tests used by each state were classified as either high-stakes or not. The primary interest was whether the states' use of their own high-stakes tests led to higher achievement—a carryover effect—as measured by a nationally administered test without consequence, that is, the NAEP.)

Rosenshine (2003) was careful not to overstep his bounds in the implications section of his discussion. Because he found that some states showed a greater high-stakes effect than others—and substantially so—he stated, "It would be less appropriate to simply use these results as a hammer and blindly require all states to impose consequences." He also concluded it was "unlikely" that the achievement effect was due to only the consequences and accountability that were introduced in the high-stakes states. He suspected that some states' schools have a stronger academic focus than others, and that other statewide and district policies "facilitated" the achievement gain, hence requiring more research into the influences of other policies. He also suggested an interesting focus for future research: the extent to which the high-stakes consequences act as a motivating or threatening factor.

MORE EXAMPLES

Additional descriptions of published research may help to solidify your knowledge of important ideas related to the research process, namely theory-based, problem-based, and practical research. You will find additional descriptions on the Web-based student study site (www.sagepub.com/eic).

Chapter Summary

The process of educational research is usually guided by two orientations: theoretical and/or problem-based (applied) research. The cyclical nature of the scientific investigation of theories, or explanations, often begins with testing specific research hypotheses generated by the theories and ends with the support or refinement of theory based on analysis. The process is continual, with each step guided by the scientific method and thus emphasizing control. Problem-based research is concerned with solving practical problems and is often guided by models which prescribe how to evaluate program effectiveness or collect data in order to "take action" for the purpose of improving classroom learning. Research that is neither theoretical nor problem based, yet borrows elements from each, may be considered a type of "blend" referred to as *practical* research with clear implications for practice and state or national policy.

Application Exercises

1. Educational and psychological researchers develop theories to explain constructs and phenomena. Consider each of the following and offer your own "theory" (explanation). Then use the ERIC (see Chapter 4) and describe the theories which researchers have advanced as explanations.
   a. The "achievement gap" in education (test score differences by race, ethnicity, or socioeconomic status)
   b. Obesity among elementary school students
   c. The high school dropout rate
   d. Teenage suicide
   e. High school girls' decline in math and science interest
   f. The decline in achievement in the United States over the past 30 years
   g. The rise in IQ scores over the past 50 years (the Flynn effect)
   h. Attention deficit disorder
   i. Learning disabilities
   j. Social anxiety disorder
   k. Self-esteem
   l. Intelligence
   m. Achievement motivation

2. Researchers have tested many theories of learning in education over the past century and derived many principles of instruction from theories that earned scientific support. Use resources on the Internet (such online journals, ERIC, Google searches, etc.) and summarize the core ideas embedded within one theory of your choosing. Then describe briefly the research base that supports the theory you chose and evaluate its scientific support.

3. Drug Abuse Resistance Education (DARE; www.dare.com), the pioneer drug prevention and education program, has operated in many public schools without much formal program evaluation. Only recently have program evaluators turned their attention to DARE. Investigate DARE's goals and objectives. How might you design a program evaluation of DARE? How is DARE currently being evaluated as a program? What are the conclusions?

4. Think about a familiar program in a school or college. What is the purpose of the program? Investigate whether the program has been evaluated, and, if so, describe the data collected, its analysis, and the evaluators' conclusions. If the program has not been evaluated, how might you design a program evaluation that provides useful data?

5. Propose an action research project related to your current educational practice (teacher, counselor, administrator, etc.). Plan your study in accordance with Figure 6.4, attending to at least the problem formulation and data collection steps. Assume your findings have implications for practice. Then discuss how you would accomplish the action planning step in the process. If you are not currently working in an educational setting, propose an action research project related to the course you are taking which uses this text.

ON YOUR OWN

Log on to the Web-based student study site at http://www.sagepub.com/eic for more information about the materials presented in this chapter, suggestions for activities, study aids such as electronic flashcards and review quizzes, a sample research proposal, and research recommendations that include journal article links (with discussion questions and an article evaluation guide) and questions related to this chapter.

Part III Data Collection

The foundation and framework described previously provide the background for Part III. Data collection may be likened to the quality and number of building materials supported by the foundation and reinforcing the framework. Part III describes the core contents of any textbook on educational research methods: control, sampling, and measurement. The meaningfulness of educational research and its quality hinge on these topics related to data collection. Decisions here render data more or less useful and conclusions more or less valid. As before, sensible reasoning about issues related to data collection requires a trek through several interrelated concepts.

Chapter 7 describes numerous ways data can become "contaminated." Some sources of bias are subtle, others are less so. But Chapter 7 makes clear that researchers spend great effort controlling threatening sources of influence, those that question the validity of findings. Chapter 8 covers statistical concepts linked to sample size. Common sampling designs are presented and shown to be related to a researcher's generalization. Chapter 9 unravels the process of instrumentation—that is, collecting sound data. Researchers often equate measurement soundness with reliability and validity, topics covered in depth in this chapter. The three chapters in Part III form an integrated whole. Data collection is especially prone to pitfalls related to muddied thinking; hence Part III deserves careful attention.

7

RESEARCH BIAS AND CONTROL

OUTLINE

OVERVIEW

The previous chapters focused on how educational researchers attempt to understand constructs and complex phenomena by uncovering relationships that may help expose them. Frequently, researchers find that their viewing of these relationships is blocked by unwanted sources of contamination, like smudges on eyeglasses. These blocks are often referred to as biasing effects, examples of which are the experimenter expectancy effect, the Hawthorne effect, and the John Henry effect. This chapter is concerned with understanding these biases and learning how researchers attempt to thwart their contaminating influences.

The chapter also covers methods for establishing control in general. This is important because once extraneous influences are neutralized, researchers are able to interpret their findings without the nuisance of rival explanations or alternative hypotheses (described in Chapter 5). Many procedural methods in educational research introduce threats that can render research findings meaningless. Careful researchers anticipate these sources of contamination and are frequently able to hold these threats in check—that is, control them—through the use of clever research designs, methods, and techniques. Researchers are always thinking (worrying, really) about the threats posed by contamination and bias, many being very subtle and requiring creative solutions.

CRITICAL THINKER ALERT 7-1

Unintended Bias

Unintended bias in research can be very subtle, making it extremely difficult to uncover. A case in point: the necessity for the work of The Amazing Randi described in Chapter 2.

Discussion: Presume a researcher investigated the influence of antidepressants on changes in teenagers' cognitive skills. What bias is apparent in the wording of the previous sentence?

Experimenter Expectancy and Blinding

Perhaps the granddaddy of all troubling effects in educational research is the *expectancy effect,* or the tendency of researchers to bring about the very finding they are expecting. This effect is sometimes referred to as the *self-fulfilling prophecy effect* or the *Pygmalion effect,* after a Greek myth in which a sculptor's statue of a beautiful woman came to life in fulfillment of his hopes. Experimenter expectancy is a serious problem because in its absence the same finding may not occur.

EXPERIMENTER EXPECTANCY: Bias that influences researchers in ways that create conditions favoring expected findings.

Consider once again a researcher who, contrary to previous examples, believes that students learn to spell words faster and easier if they practice on a computer than if they write the words by hand. To test this notion, assume 80 children were randomly assigned to two groups. One group spent five study trials learning 40 new words on the computer, while the other group spent five study trials learning the same words by writing them. Next, the researcher, who is now convinced that

HIGHLIGHT AND LEARNING CHECK 7-1

Experimenter Expectation

Experimenter expectation may create research conditions and bias that favor the expected findings. It is controlled to some extent by blinding, or keeping data collectors or evaluators unaware of conditions that may influence perceptions or behavior. Research participants may also be blinded to prevent response bias due to expectations. Describe how grading an essay from a known skillful writer may influence your perceptions and evaluation of the essay. What steps could be taken to reduce bias?

computers are superior to handwriting, asks each child to spell each word out loud as a test of his or her learning. The researcher then simply scores each spoken spelling as correct or incorrect and compares the overall performance of both groups.

The biasing influence of the researcher's beliefs could bring about the expected result in many ways. Aimee, for example, is known by the researcher to be in the computer group. As she spells "house," she pauses before saying the letter "u" and in fact begins to say "w." Aimee immediately notices a clear but subtle change in the researcher's facial expression, as if to signal disappointment or disapproval. Aimee stops her spelling, thinks about it for a second, then backs up to replace the beginnings of a "w" with a "u." The researcher's face, particularly around the eyebrows, returns to its original "Yes, that's right!" expression. This example, admittedly dramatic, illustrates how just one factor, nonverbal communication, might contribute to the strength of the expectancy effect.

The expectancy effect may be explained in many other ways too. Consider Aimee again, who is less than perfect in her pronunciation. As she spells "turtle," she muddles the last three letters. Although she actually says "t-u-r-*d*-l-e," the researcher misinterprets the "d" for a "t" and consequently scores the spelling as correct. A compounding problem could likewise occur in the handwriting group, where worse spelling performance is expected. The researcher, especially tuned to hear errors where they are expected, may in fact interpret a garbled "t" as an incorrect "d."

Scientific researchers, because they are human, are subject to the same kinds of hopes and wishes that teachers, doctors, parents, and gamblers are subject to. Fortunately, the research process has a built-in control for this type of bias. The control is known as blinding, and it is used whenever and wherever possible by careful researchers. (Recall the story about Clever Hans in Chapter 2.) *Blinding* involves keeping data collectors "in the dark" with regard to information such as into which group a particular subject is assigned (e.g., treatment or control). This is usually accomplished by the use of independent observers who are trained for the specific purpose of collecting data but otherwise have no other knowledge of subjects' grouping, or even the nature of the research question. Blind observers are less likely to be influenced by factors such as expectations or hopes if they have little or no awareness of information known to affect perceptions or judgments.

BLINDING: A control procedure that reduces bias by ensuring that data collectors and/or research participants do not have information that distorts perceptions or influences behavior (such as knowing whether individual study participants are in a control group or an experimental group).

If feasible, blinding is used at all stages of the research process. Consider a make-believe study designed to test the influence of a new drug—let's call it Normid—designed to overcome behavioral problems associated with hyperactivity, such as restlessness and inattention. Further, let's suppose that three different methods of administration were tested: a pill, an injection, and a patch (a Band-Aid-like application that provides a slow release of the drug over time). A control (placebo) group would also have been used, in order to assess the effectiveness of the drug overall. To this end, let's assume that 100 hyperactive students were randomly assigned to one of four groups: control, pill, injection, and patch. The school nurse, who was responsible for the drug's administration, was kept blind and thus unable to influence students' behavior with subtle or nonverbal communications during the administration.

The nurse therefore gave *all* the students (even the controls) a pill, an injection, or a patch. Students in the control group received a saline solution injection, a baking soda pill, and a dry or empty patch. Of course, all pills, injections, and patches were coded somehow in order to be certain all students were receiving their randomly assigned condition. (Notice also that the students themselves were blind to their conditions using this technique, hence controlling for another bias called the *guinea pig effect,* which is described later.) When students' behavior was observed (e.g., fidgeting), it was important to make certain that the observers were blind to conditions as well. This is because ambiguous perceptions and resulting questions (e.g., "Was that a fidget?") could be interpreted in accordance with knowledge of group membership (e.g., "Yes, that probably was a fidget since he's in the control group" or "No, he's in the group that receives injections—presumably the most effective treatment").

Marketing researchers, like educational researchers, are well aware of problems stemming from failure to blind. Consider a taste test of three different types of chocolates, for example. The color of chocolate may influence the taste ratings, yet the marketers are interested in taste, not visual appearance. In this case, the tasters would quite literally be blinded (with a blindfold) so that their ratings would be uncontaminated by the chocolate's visual appearance and reflect only taste.

Teachers who grade essays will probably have little trouble understanding the value of blinding. Knowing that a student is especially able, for example, may lead to quicker reading, less scrutiny, and a faster positive judgment of the essay. Any ambiguity could reasonably be misinterpreted in the student's favor. Unfortunately, the reading and evaluation of a weaker student's essay might be a search for confirming evidence.

Wise educational researchers practice blinding as a control technique at every opportunity. This is true even in situations where bias seems unlikely. The fact is that researchers do not know all of the circumstances that foster expectancy bias nor all the mechanisms through which it operates. Because of this, it is wise to use blinding as a scientific control whenever it is practical. This includes blinding the subjects themselves, as well as using blind raters, observers, data collectors, scorers, and the like.

CRITICAL THINKER ALERT 7-2

Expectations

Researchers naturally have expectations related to research findings, in part due to prior experiences and current perceptions and beliefs. *Blinding,* or keeping data collectors unaware of relevant information related to the research study (like grouping), is often easier to accomplish in medical research (e.g., drug trials) than in educational research. Nevertheless, expectations can be powerful in educational research. Blinding should be used whenever possible, for example, in the scoring of essays.

Discussion: Describe how a teacher's global evaluation of a student's second science project can be influenced by knowledge that the student earned the lowest rating on the first science project.

Hawthorne Effect, John Henry Effect, and Placebos

The *Hawthorne effect,* as you'll recall from Chapter 2, has had a long but controversial history (Adair, Sharpe, & Huynh, 1989; Franke & Kaul, 1978; Rice, 1982). This effect, discovered in the 1920s at the Hawthorne Western Electric Plant near Chicago (Roethlisberger & Dickson, 1939), refers to research participants' behavior changing merely as a result of their awareness of being in a research situation. Participants' behavior could change, for example, simply by knowing the research hypothesis or by receiving special attention in a treatment group. The Hawthorne effect—also known as the *guinea pig effect,* the *novelty effect,* and even the *gee whiz effect*—must be controlled or the researcher will not know whether a change in behavior is the result of a genuine treatment effect or the workings of the Hawthorne effect.

HAWTHORNE EFFECT: Bias that influences research participants' behavior stemming from a treatment's unintended effects related to special attention, novelty, or similar treatment co-occurrences.

How might the Hawthorne effect work? Imagine yourself in an educational research study, one that investigates the effect of using computers in an innovative way to study science. Your classroom is loaded with new computers, many people are peeking in to see all of the equipment, new faces (computer technicians) are present, and a local news crew arrives to complete a story about technology in the classroom. Teachers are a bit bewildered, but they are surely excited. All of the attention paid to your classroom is convincing that your class is truly "special." This, naturally, keeps you attentive and you are eager to begin your introduction to cyberspace.

At the end of the 2-week unit, your achievement level is compared with that of a comparable class that learned the same material by the traditional "talk-and-chalk" method. The results reveal that your computer-oriented class outscored the traditional class by a wide margin. What could explain this finding? Was it the use of computers? Or was it all of the attention that surrounded the computers? Would the traditional class score similarly if it were also in the spotlight? Would the computer class's performance drop once all the hoopla ended (the "honeymoon-is-over" effect)? The difficulty answering these questions highlights the problems related to the Hawthorne effect. Often, one cannot untangle the influence of a treatment effect (e.g., a new method of teaching) from the special attention or novelty associated with its implementation.

Medical research, in the case of drug trials, controls such influences by using a *placebo* group, or a control group treated identically to an experimental group but whose capsules contain only baking soda, for example. Educational researchers have a greater challenge, for their treatments are usually not drugs in capsule form but complicated methods of delivering instruction. The concept of a *placebo in educational research* still exists, however, and it usually takes the form of a second treatment group, one that provides novelty, attention, and related factors but lacks the

PLACEBO: A control condition that preserves the illusion of participants' receiving a treatment.

CRITICAL THINKER ALERT 7-3

Placebos

The phrase *placebo in educational research* should not be taken literally, as educational researchers rarely experiment with drugs. The phrase refers to the use of comparison groups that control for research participants' perceptions related to being in a research study.

Discussion: In an experimental test of virtual education in the middle grades (with all courses delivered online), presume a researcher provided new Apple computers to all students for home use. In this instance, what might be an appropriate placebo in educational research?

critical essence of the first treatment group. In the classroom computer scenario, for example, the traditional "talk-and-chalk" classroom might receive computers in their classroom (along with the media hoopla), but they would not begin using them until after the 2-week unit test. Admittedly, the use of placebos in educational research involves creative challenges.

JOHN HENRY EFFECT: Bias that influences control or comparison groups' performance due to a perceived threat or similar negative perception.

A related bias in educational research is known as the *John Henry effect*, in which the control group "outperforms" itself in a sense by trying to perform as well as the experimental group. The enhanced performance by a control group may be a response to a perceived threat, or even a response to feeling "left out." John Henry, as the legend goes, was a railroad worker who drove spikes in rails by his sheer strength with a sledgehammer. Feeling his job was threatened by a new spike-driver machine, he mustered all his strength and speed to show that he was just as good and fast as the automated machine. In the classroom computer situation described above, it may be possible that teachers in the "talk-and-chalk" control group feel similarly threatened by computers, hence they try their very best to raise achievement scores to the same level as the computer group. Or maybe students in the traditional class, fearing technology or feeling intimidated, put forth extra effort to achieve beyond their usual level. It is in this sense that a control group outperforms itself. The John Henry effect, in this case, would mask the enhanced performance of the treatment group.

HIGHLIGHT AND LEARNING CHECK 7-2

Hawthorne Effect, John Henry Effect, and Placebos

The Hawthorne effect may influence participants' behavior to the extent that they perceive special treatment, attention, or novelty. The John Henry effect may influence control group participants if they become motivated beyond the usual level. Placebos in educational research refer to control groups not receiving a treatment. Such untreated groups are designed to permit comparisons with the experimental groups while controlling for influences such as the Hawthorne effect. Explain how taking a baking soda pill (placebo) might relieve depression or back pain. Explain how the same concept could explain learning among students who believe they are the first students to test, say, a learning-while-asleep method?

Campbell and Stanley Threats and Control Groups

In one of the most influential papers ever published in educational research, Donald Campbell and Julian Stanley (1963) described a handful of commonly appearing sources of bias, or "threats," as they called them, in the conduct of educational research. They are called *threats* because they endanger the internal validity of the study. The term *internal validity,* also coined by Campbell and Stanley (1963), refers to how effectively a research design controls for contaminating influences. Recall from Chapter 5 that researchers are always on guard against alternative hypotheses—those explanations of the results *other* than the research hypothesis. Internal validity is present, then, if no alternative hypotheses exist. If the research design incorporates "tight" controls, then the research is internally valid, alternative hypotheses are absent (or not very plausible), and the researcher can be confident that the results are due to the treatment's influence. When internal validity is lacking, sources of influence other than the treatment could explain the results. These other contaminating and biasing sources, or threats, must be controlled if the research results are to be meaningful.

INTERNAL VALIDITY: The degree to which conditions and procedures establish control. These conditions and procedures rule out rival hypotheses, reduce bias, and neutralize unwanted, potentially contaminating influences. A study has internal validity to the extent that the outcome can be explained by variation introduced by the treatment (and not an uncontrolled variable).

EXTERNAL VALIDITY: The degree to which research results can be generalized beyond the sample and conditions that yielded the findings.

Here is an example of research that lacks internal validity. In a test of learning while asleep, subjects were given a pretest of their knowledge of high energy physics. Then they slept in a laboratory for five nights. While they were asleep, the researcher played audio recordings of five lectures on high energy physics. A posttest after the fifth day revealed that the subjects' knowledge scores had increased. The researcher concluded that the learning-while-asleep treatment was indeed effective. Were the effects in fact due to the treatment and nothing else, hence internally valid? Hardly, and because there are many reasons for the results—other explanations—we would say that the study lacked internal validity. The subjects may have learned more about the topic during their waking hours (possibly the pretest stimulated their interest to seek more information), they may not have been asleep during the lectures, the posttest may have been easier than the pretest, and so on. In sum, internally valid studies are well controlled, consequently one can be reasonably certain that the results are due to the treatment—and nothing else.

CONTROL GROUP: A group not receiving a treatment, one that functions as a comparison so that a treatment effect can be isolated from extraneous influences.

Campbell and Stanley (1963) also described many research designs that controlled for the threats' influence, hence strengthening the internal validity of a study. Many of these designs incorporated the use of control groups. In the next section, I will describe these common but threatening sources of influence and explain how their potentially contaminating effects can be neutralized by research designs.

CRITICAL THINKER ALERT 7-4

Ambiguous Validity

Be alert to the ambiguity of the term *validity* in the research jargon. When applied to establishing control in research, the term *validity* should be preceded by the word *internal.* An internally valid research study, therefore, suggests that major sources of extraneous influences have been well controlled. *Validity* can also refer to measurement soundness (e.g., a valid test) or how well research findings generalize across people and contexts (this is *external validity,* which is described in Chapter 8).

Discussion: If someone were to simply claim that a study is not valid, what follow-up questions are warranted in the probe for more information?

Extraneous Events

Extraneous events (originally termed *history* and *maturation*) refer to outside influences that occur between a pretest and a posttest in addition to the treatment. Let's presume that the treatment is a 10-week workshop designed to increase the SAT scores of graduating seniors. In order to test the effectiveness of this treatment, 100 seniors took the SAT, enrolled in the workshop, then retook the SAT upon completion of the workshop. Sure enough, the seniors' scores increased from 1150 to 1350 on average.

EXTRANEOUS EVENTS: A threat to internal validity that includes influences co-occurring with a treatment between a pretest and posttest.

Although the workshop designers would have liked to conclude that their training was responsible for the increase, they could not easily do so because of other possible events that occurred along with the treatment and might have increased the scores. For example, some students may have purchased a self-study guide describing how to take aptitude tests; others may have seen an article in the newspaper describing how some students can correctly choose the answer on a reading comprehension passage without reading the passage; still others may have already received rejection notices from colleges they applied to and as a result, simply tried harder on the SAT retake after the sobering rejections. Further, others may have learned some test-taking skills from their math instructor, who prepares students to take his difficult tests; and others may have seen a popular program on television concerned with the value of exercise on mental acuity, and, as a consequence, started regular exercise during the workshop (assuming exercise does influence mental prowess).

Some of these influences stem from changes within the research participants themselves simply as a function of the passage of time. For example, many test takers could have been under the weather during the pretesting (which may have been administered during the flu season or a time of high pollen counts) but generally healthier during the posttest and hence scored higher then. One could also argue that the subjects themselves had higher abilities at the posttest because 10 weeks of instruction had elapsed since the pretest. They may have had larger vocabularies, greater knowledge of math and geometry, greater "cultural literacy" that could enhance their reading comprehension, or more knowledge of Latin that could help them with word meanings. You can probably imagine many more extraneous events that could account for the results.

Consider another example. One hundred people with low back pain underwent acupuncture for 10 weeks and found that their pain was greatly reduced. We know that time is a great healer, and these back pain sufferers may have been cured without any treatment. (Remember that backache you had that disappeared after a few weeks without any treatment?) Researchers must consider events that co-occur with the mere passage of time (itself a major influence), including all of the changes within the subjects themselves (even short term, like becoming fatigued) in addition to the changes on the "outside."

Instrumentation

Instrumentation is another class of threatening influences, all of which refer to bias stemming from the process of measurement in the research setting. The threat of instrumentation refers to how taking one test can influence a student's performance on a second test—what Campbell and Stanley (1963) referred to as "testing"—as well as to influences related to the change in the measuring process itself. Using the pretest-posttest SAT training example described above, an increase on the posttest (second test) might be related to the experience of taking the pretest (first test). How could this happen? The concept is simple: You improve with practice. (Have you ever hung wallpaper? Didn't the second room turn out better than the first room?) Simply becoming familiar with the test format or knowing what to expect may lead to a posttest advantage. For example, in the reading comprehension section of the SAT, you know because of your experience with the pretest that the posttest is a race against the clock, with no time to reflect. You may have also learned that geometry was fully represented on the SAT, so you review your geometry textbook before the second test. You might also be more relaxed the second time around, knowing what's ahead. You may have also learned to eat a bigger breakfast the second time around! Instrumentation is a problem because it would be hard to disentangle the workshop effect from the testing effect.

INSTRUMENTATION: A threat to internal validity that includes changes in the measuring device or measuring procedures between a pretest and posttest. It also refers to a process of gathering data with the use of measuring tools such as tests or surveys.

Another type of instrumentation threat is known as *pretest sensitization.* Sometimes the experience of taking a pretest creates an effect by itself, one that might magnify (or wash out) the treatment effect. For example, consider a workshop in human sexuality for high school students. To assess students' knowledge before the workshop, students are given a pretest. After the workshop, they are given a posttest to evaluate learning gain. The pretest might be loaded with interesting questions, such as "Can a young woman get pregnant before she's had her first period?" and "Does a woman have only a 48-hour interval per month when she can get pregnant?" In this case, the pretest itself might stimulate sufficient interest among students that they search out answers before the workshop even begins! It would be difficult to disentangle the amount learned in response to the pretest from the amount learned as a result of the instruction within the workshop.

Or consider a weight loss study in which all subjects are first weighed, then given hypnotherapy for 10 weeks, followed by a final weighing. Quite possibly some subjects have avoided the scales for months, not wanting to face the reality that they have never been heavier. That simple shocking truth—of being, say, over 200 pounds—itself may be sufficient motivation to lose weight by skipping meals. If subjects did lose weight after 10 weeks of hypnosis, how would you know whether it was due to the hypnosis effect or the shocking reality from the initial weighing?

Instrumentation also encompasses problems related to *changes* in the measuring instrument itself between testings. We are aware, for example, that bathroom scales might become inaccurate over time due to corrosion in the components or weak batteries. Or a tape measure can lose accuracy as the little catch at the "0" becomes loose or bent. The same process can occur with educational measures, including human observers who change over time, for example, by becoming careless or more lenient. Consider other illustrations of instrument changes. Periodic recalibration of SAT scores, whereby scores are raised by a specific number of points, may be interpreted as a treatment effect when in fact all scores were simply increased for statistical reasons. Subjects' interpretation of items on a questionnaire could change over time, too. One true-or-false item from a widely used personality inventory—"I like gay parties"—would be interpreted differently today than it was in the 1930s when the test was constructed.

Mortality

Yet another class of threatening biases is *mortality.* Often referred to as *attrition* or simply *loss of subjects,* this problem occurs when research participants drop out of a study. The occasional and haphazard dropping out of a few subjects due to personal reasons such as sickness or relocation does not present a serious bias. The more serious problem is the *systematic* loss of subjects who drop out because of a common reaction to the treatment. In the SAT workshop example, mortality would be a problem if the lowest scoring 20% of the sample decided not to continue with the treatment (workshop) for whatever reasons (fear of failure, embarrassment, assault of self-esteem, feelings of hopelessness, etc.). You can readily see that this would be a problem because, on average, the posttest SATs would be higher than the pretest SATs since the lowest scoring subjects could not contribute to (by lowering) the posttest scores. An average difference between the pretest and posttest scores would emerge even if the workshop had absolutely no effect whatsoever on the raising of SAT scores; the scores would only *appear* to be higher due to a subgroup of subjects dropping out.

MORTALITY: A threat to internal validity that refers to a loss of research participants between a pretest and posttest that stems from an influence of the treatment itself. Also referred to as attrition.

Similar problems occur in other studies as well, including diets that appear to be successful in reducing weight only because those who were not successful (heavier) dropped out. The success rate of a smoking cessation study could also be artificially high because of those failures who simply were not present to be tabulated.

In their description of mortality, Campbell and Stanley (1963, pp. 12–13) have unintentionally provided us with an example of sexism in writing from a previous era. They stated that a study of women in college may show that seniors tend to be less beautiful than freshmen. Why? Not because the harsh 4 years of stress and study ruins beauty, but because beautiful girls drop out of college to marry, leaving the less beautiful ones behind. (Seriously!) The implication here is that young women only go to college to find husbands and, if that's not bad enough, only the prettiest ones are successful! Really!

Regression

Another source of bias is called *regression.* This is a tricky statistical threat which manifests itself whenever research participants with extreme scores (high or low) are retested. Their retest scores tend to be closer to the mean (less extreme) in the absence of any other influence. The shift closer to the mean is relatively small, but it is reliable. (This effect is explained, in part, by large measurement errors, such as very poor luck in guessing, which contributed to the low scores on the first test but are less likely to occur again on the second test.) The only problem arises when a group is selected *because* of their extreme scores (say, a group of low scoring students on the SAT), then given a treatment (a workshop to boost scores) followed by a retest. How much of the increase in scores is due to the workshop effect (if any) and how much is due to the phenomenon of regression? (Remember, the scores naturally move closer to the mean—in this case, increase.) That question is difficult to answer without the use of a randomized control group (as described below). The concept of regression can be seen in other fields as well, including genetics—if, for example, it can be shown that very short parents are likely to have children who are short but, on average, not as short as their parents. In this sense, the children's overall height has moved closer to the mean.

REGRESSION: A threat to internal validity that refers to a tendency of those with extreme scores to score somewhat closer to the mean upon retesting.

Selection

There is one more biasing threat worth describing—*selection.* This problem occurs whenever experimental and control groups are selected in a manner that does not reasonably assure their equivalency (the "apples and oranges" problem). If the experimental and control groups are not comparable to begin with, how would you know whether a difference observed *after* a treatment was, in fact, due to the treatment and not the pretreatment difference? The problem is that you wouldn't know. The threat of selection usually appears when, for example, one school is chosen for participation as the experimental school while another school is chosen as a control (as in a quasi-experiment). Although the control might be chosen because of its apparent comparability with the experimental school, the comparability may be only superficial. There is no better way to create comparable groups than random assignment, as we shall see in the next section.

SELECTION: A threat to internal validity that includes groups of participants who are not comparable before the introduction of a treatment.

HIGHLIGHT AND LEARNING CHECK 7-3

Campbell and Stanley Threats

Campbell and Stanley's term *threats* refers to influences that co-occur with a treatment between a pretest and posttest. They are alternative explanations for a pretest-posttest difference (a treatment effect may be mistaken for these influences). They are *extraneous events* (outside influences like a fire drill or national disaster), *instrumentation* (measurement influences such as becoming test wise), *mortality* (loss of participants from, for example, dropping out after unfavorable reactions to a treatment), *regression* (a less extreme score on a retest, a statistical phenomena), and *selection* (noncomparable treatment and comparison groups, often due to convenient rather than random assignment). These threats are controlled somewhat by the use of cleverly designed control groups, allowing one to "extract" the influence of the threats in order to assess a purer treatment influence. Presume a researcher pretested a group of high school students' attitudes toward military service. A 6-week program was implemented in an attempt to increase interest in military careers. A posttest measure of attitude followed the program. Describe how each of the above threats could exert an influence that would make it difficult to disentangle the program effect from the threat.

Randomized Control Groups

Neutralizing Threats

Fortunately, these sources of bias or threats in research—extraneous events, instrumentation, mortality, regression, and selection—can be controlled (their threat neutralized) through the use of a *randomized control group.* Using the SAT workshop as an example, a randomized control group would be formed by choosing *randomly*—via a random number table—half of the subjects for use as a control group. This group would complete the SAT pretest, but unlike the experimental group, would not be exposed to the workshop designed to boost SAT scores. The control group, however, would be posttested in the same manner as the experimental group. Because of the random process at work, it can be assumed that the groups are essentially equivalent in terms of factors that may affect SAT scores (test-taking skills, aptitude, interests, motivation, attitudes, etc.).

Think about the threat of extraneous events described earlier. Those extraneous sources of bias should affect both groups equally—use of self-study guides, college rejections, exercise habits, pollen, changes in vocabulary, cultural literacy, and so on. Notice that it is not possible to *eliminate* the influence of self-study, exercise, pollen, and all the others; it is only possible to arrange that this influence, whatever it may be, exerts itself *equally* across the two groups. The logic is straightforward: Arrange for only one influence in the control and experimental groups to be different—the workshop in this case—while all the other influences are held constant, or the same, across both groups. Any difference observed in the outcome (SAT posttest scores in this case) could only be attributed to the one factor that was allowed to vary.

CRITICAL THINKER ALERT 7-5

What Is Controlled?

The use of a *control group* in educational research does not necessarily mean that the study is well controlled. The control group may, for example, control only one source of influence, allowing countless others to contaminate the results. It's best to inquire into the sources of influence that are being controlled via the use of a control group (and what sources it does not control for).

Discussion: In a test of physical exercise on volunteer students' math skills (how quickly they solved simple math problems), a researcher used a randomized control group that merely sat for 20 minutes during the other group's exercise. What is being controlled in this case and what is not?

The value of a randomized control group also applies to the problems associated with instrumentation. Remember the practice effect resulting from the SAT retake and the influence linked to expectations, the geometry review, the bigger breakfast, and the change in scoring? The control group effectively neutralizes these threats, again not by getting rid of the influence altogether but by equalizing it across the two groups. If there is a practice effect, for example, linked to an SAT retake, then both groups will be affected similarly by that influence.

The same logic applies to regression bias. Because one would expect that the two randomized groups would contain roughly the *same* number of extreme scorers, the threat is essentially neutralized. Its influence in the experimental group would be offset by an equal influence in the control group. And, as we have seen, we are not concerned about an influence that affects both groups similarly. Above all else, we want to avoid situations where one group is influenced more by biasing factors.

The mortality bias is somewhat more problematic. The influence of subjects dropping out of the workshop haphazardly (due to the flu, relocation, etc.) is not a problem since this influence would similarly affect the control group. The darker side of mortality exerts itself if there is something about the treatment itself that leads to a less haphazard dropping out. For example, if the workshop involves practice tests which threaten the self-confidence of low scorers, then they might be likely to quit sometime during the 10-week treatment, artificially raising the overall average of the workshop group. The control group's low scorers might not feel the same threat and hence might be less likely to quit. Mortality bias of this *non*haphazard type—when it is treatment induced—has no simple solution. This is why researchers try their very best, within ethical boundaries, to discourage dropping out.

Finally, the bias due to selection is easily controlled if—a big if—you can randomly assign subjects to form experimental and control groups. If this is not possible (as is often the case), then the selection bias is always present. Selection bias is especially troublesome because the control group (if not formed randomly) may be different from the experimental group in many ways. The alternative to random assignment is *matching*, whereby control subjects are chosen because of their similarity to the experimental subjects. In educational research, the matching variables are usually age, sex, and socioeconomic status (and often measures of academic achievement, ethnicity, and family background factors). Although this technique can neutralize the influence of those variables, there is no control for the influence of other, unmatched variables, some of which may be dramatic in their influence but hidden from view. In short, matching is never a good substitute for random assignment to groups. Matching can be very useful, however, in other situations (as revealed in the Nun Study described later in this chapter).

Thus far, we have seen how a treatment group is subjected to many influences other than the treatment itself, including all of the sources linked to extraneous events, instrumentation, mortality, regression, and selection. The treatment group is, in actuality, the treatment plus extraneous events plus instrumentation plus mortality plus regression plus selection. By contrast, the control group is merely extraneous events plus instrumentation plus mortality plus regression plus selection. The statistical analysis, therefore, can extract the influences of these biases from the treatment group after examining their strength in the control group. What is left, then, is the relatively pure influence of the treatment itself.

The Random Process

Let me emphasize the value of a *randomly* formed control group. Imagine a group of 100 students formed into two random groups. Choose a variable, any variable.

What about the amount of protein in grams consumed at breakfast? If this could be measured accurately, one would find that the average protein for both groups is *about* the same (though not necessarily identical), hence controlled. Consider another variable: the number of hours of sleep during the previous night. If one group slept an average of 7 hours and 16 minutes, then the other group probably slept *about* 7 hours and 16 minutes. Choose another variable, and the outcome will be the same. Because the two groups are about, not exactly, the same on these extraneous variables, it can be said that their influence is controlled.

RANDOM PROCESS: A control procedure that assures extraneous influences are neutralized by unsystematic scattering across people and conditions.

Random assignment also has a hidden strength. (Do you remember Factor Q, first mentioned in Chapter 3? It was used to illustrate a concept worth repeating for emphasis.) Be futuristic for a moment and consider Factor Q, a factor not discovered until the year 2020 but believed to dramatically affect memory. This factor would not pose a problem in today's research as long as groups are formed randomly. Factor Q, like the protein in breakfasts, would be about the same, hence controlled, across the two groups. In this sense, random assignment controls for all known and *unknown* extraneous variables related to the research participants themselves. That is why it is so powerful.

CRITICAL THINKER ALERT 7-6

Randomized Control Group

One of the most powerful control techniques in research is the *randomized* control group, since it controls for sources of influence related to the subjects themselves. This is because two groups formed via random assignment are comparable on countless participant characteristics.

Discussion: If a large group of (perhaps 60) students was randomly divided into two groups of equal size, would you expect to find an overall difference between the two groups on a meaningless variable such as the value of the last 2 digits of their social security number? What about the proportion of males versus females? Explain.

Many of the threats to internal validity are controlled quite well by the particular research design and the random processes utilized by a researcher. In fact, that is the purpose of the architectural plan (design) of the study—to make sure the findings cannot be explained away by some unwanted, extraneous influence. We will examine research designs in Chapter 10 and see how their features attempt to increase internal validity.

It is important not to confuse *internal* and *external* validity. *External validity* refers to *generalization,* or how well the findings apply to the people and settings beyond the borders of the sample and research conditions (*external,* meaning

HIGHLIGHT AND LEARNING CHECK 7-4

Randomized Control Groups

Randomized control groups neutralize threats so that research findings are more interpretable. They do not eliminate the threats per se. The random process establishes control by distributing extraneous influences evenly over all groups (holding its influence constant). This permits one to isolate a treatment effect from extraneous influences. Explain how a randomized control group can be similar to a randomized experimental group on countless variables (except for the treatment).

"outside" or beyond the sample). External validity will be introduced in Chapter 8 in the discussion of sampling. In this chapter, we have seen that *internal validity* (*internal,* meaning "within" the study itself) refers to the control of unwanted sources of influence, such as the Campbell and Stanley (1963) threats and other effects (e.g., experimenter expectancy). A sharp distinction should be drawn between these types of validity because they refer to very different concerns of researchers. In a sense, internal validity has the highest priority, for if the results are rendered uninterpretable because of contaminating threats and rival explanations, then the generalization of findings becomes irrelevant. If the results are meaningless, no one cares about their applicability.

CRITICAL THINKER ALERT 7-7

Hidden Biases

The Campbell and Stanley (1963) list of threats to internal validity does not exhaust all possibilities of bias. Some biases have probably not yet been discovered.

Discussion: Which of the focus areas—nonverbal communications, sample selection, and theory formation—is a reasonable one for the discovery of hidden biases? Explain.

CRITICAL THINKER ALERT 7-8

Neutralized Influences

Control in research does not mean that a source of influence has necessarily been eliminated; it means that a source of influence has been neutralized so that it no longer affects one group more than the other (its influence is the same, or equated, across groups).

Discussion: Presume a group of 60 male and female students has been randomly divided into two groups of equal size. Has the influence of gender been eliminated or merely controlled (neutralized) by the random process? Explain.

Sequence Effects and Counterbalancing

Let's consider one more bias in educational research, *order effects.* This is a problem when participants receive several tests, treatments, tasks, and so on, and the particular order of their administration affects responses. For example, if you were to complete five tests of cognitive ability, each one lasting an hour, it is reasonable to expect that the last test would be negatively affected by fatigue due to the effort and attention required by the first four. The first one, however, might be negatively affected by your slow mental warm-up and anxiety, to mention a few factors. Your performance might even be affected by *carryover,* or the influence of one test on the other. Possibly, some strategy that you used (and perfected) on the third test could be used successfully during the fourth test. Or maybe some nagging question from the first test negatively affected your performance on the second test. (The same concept can be applied to eating: Does dark chocolate taste as good if it is preceded by milk chocolate? Would you enjoy chocolate more as an appetizer or as a dessert?)

SEQUENCE EFFECTS: Unwanted influences due to ordering (first, second, etc.) and carryover (preceding versus following) of treatments, materials, and so on.

Order effects refer to an influence due to ordinal position (first, second, third, etc.); in contrast, *carryover effects* refer to an influence stemming from a preceding or following condition. Both are instances of the troublesome *sequence effects.*

Order effects and carryover effects could influence all types of measures, including attitudes, interests, and opinions. Your opinion about abortion, for example, might change somewhat depending on whether or not you were just measured on religious commitments. Order effects can also affect your responses to different treatments. For example, imagine being asked right now to remember a list of 20 words without any specific instruction on how to do so (a control condition). Next, imagine learning a new list of 20 words with the specific instructions to form a bizarre image for each word. What do you suppose would happen if you were given the imagery instructions first, followed by the control instructions? Would it be possible *not* to form images in the control condition? Or, consider the spelling of the word *sacrilegious.* If you were asked to spell *religious* first, do you think you would be less likely to spell *sacrilegious* correctly? (Note the transposed *i* and *e.*)

Fortunately, there is a relatively simple way for researchers to neutralize this bias (once again, not eliminate it, just control it). Control is accomplished by a technique called *counterbalancing,* whereby subjects receive a different order of tests, treatments, booklets, words, and so on. This is often accomplished by a random technique, in which each subject is expected to rate a different random order of words, tasks, drawings or whatever is being administered. This technique scatters the influence of order and carryover so that, on average, each word, task, drawing, or whatever is affected positively and negatively in roughly the same amounts. (The greater the number of subjects, the better controlled the effects.)

COUNTERBALANCING: A control procedure that assures order and carryover effects are neutralized by arranging conditions to be equally affected by order and carryover influences.

Randomized counterbalancing is merely one type of counterbalancing, although it is considered by many to be the best because of the random processes at work. A potential drawback of randomized counterbalancing is the practical difficulty of determining and administering a random order of conditions for each subject.

Let's consider one type of *systematic counterbalancing,* called a *Latin Square.* Only four different orders are required in this highly efficient design. Imagine four conditions—call them A, B, C, and D for simplicity (they might be four different background noises administered while subjects are reading). A Latin Square would involve only four different orders, as shown below:

Order 1: A B D C

Order 2: B C A D

Order 3: C D B A

Order 4: D A C B

Notice that each condition (A, B, C, D) occurs in each possible ordinal position (first, second, third, and fourth). Also notice the control for carryover. A B in Order 1 is counterbalanced by B A in Order 3, B C in Order 2 is counterbalanced by C B in Order 4, D C in Order 1 is counterbalanced by C D in Order 3, and so on. This is a clever and efficient design indeed, for it seems to control for so much with only four counterbalanced orders. I would have called it a Magic Square!

Other types and applications of counterbalancing with quasi-experiments are described in Chapter 10.

HIGHLIGHT AND LEARNING CHECK 7-5

Sequence Effects

Sequence effects occur when participants receive multiple treatments or conditions. They include order effects stemming from being first, second, third, and so on and carryover effects stemming from receiving one condition before or after another. These influences are controlled well by counterbalancing, whereby order and carryover effects are spread equally over all conditions (each condition is thus affected similarly). Explain why you would not ask students to rate the interest level of three short stories in exactly the same order. How would you control for the problems you described?

Control by Matching

The rich diversity and enormous variation that makes us so interesting also poses serious challenges for researchers. One might reasonably ask, "What is the effect of a college education?" It is known that college graduates earn more money on average, but are they happier? Are they healthier? Do they live longer? Do they have a greater appreciation for the arts? Are they less likely to be arrested for violent crimes?

MATCHING: A control procedure that equates groups (or materials, etc.) by assuring they are the same or similar on important variables.

One might attempt to answer these questions by comparing two groups: those who graduated from college and those who never attended college. Differences might quickly emerge. Let's say that objective measures reveal college graduates are indeed healthier ("healthier" might be operationally defined as less hypertension, obesity, smoking, and sedentary lifestyles). Other differences might also emerge just as quickly, like college graduates also had parents who were more likely to attend college. Perhaps the college graduates' better health is causally related to parents' healthier habits more than to their college experience. The idea is to isolate the influence of college apart from other co-occurring influences.

A step in this direction involves *matching*. To this end, the two groups (college and no college) could be equated by selecting only those participates in both groups whose parents did not go to college. Because the parents' college backgrounds are the same over all subjects and both groups, it is said that this extraneous variable has been controlled. The next troubling variable would be controlled in the same way, that is, via matching by selection to assure group equivalence on the matched variable.

The ultimate form of matching might be called *twinning*, or the use of identical twins. These unique individuals have provided a treasure trove of data because they are in many ways perfectly matched. Identical twins separated at birth and reared in widely different environments, for example, provide clues about environmental influences such as parenting styles on measured traits such as intelligence. Their genetic backgrounds are well controlled since they are the same across twin pairs. Using twinning in the college education example might involve selecting identical twins who have been raised similarly, with one member of the pair going to college and the other not. This scenario controls for (equates) influences stemming from heredity, parent factors, and family factors. Even these data, however, would be hard to interpret, for the one who did not attend college may have also experienced events which led to that outcome (and also led to differences in the outcome measured by the researcher). The childhood illness or injury (or whatever the events might be) could then be misinterpreted as the "lack of college education effect."

HIGHLIGHT AND LEARNING CHECK 7-6

Matching

Matching is a control procedure that attempts to equate groups on specific variables (often only two or three). The goal is to arrange for two or more groups to be equivalent on each matching variable. It is often used when random assignment is not feasible. If you were to match homeschooled students with their public school "counterparts" to assess achievement differences, which variable would you match and why?

The Nun Study

Sometimes researchers are in a position to match an entire pool of subjects, a type of "cloning," as a control for unwanted, extraneous influences. David Snowdon, a professor at the University of Kentucky, is one example. Snowdon directs the famous Nun Study designed to answer the question "What factors across the lifespan increase the risk for brain diseases (such as stroke and Alzheimer's) and determine longevity and quality of life in the elderly?" Snowdon's research in aging began when he realized that an order of nuns, with hundreds of aging Catholic sisters, was living close by. He recognized a research advantage to relatively uniform backgrounds and lifestyles: their similar socioeconomic status, health care, and living conditions represented a type of natural matching. With little variation, he reasoned, there is less chance of confounded data. With a particular interest in Alzheimer's disease, Snowdon set out to track 678 sisters, who were 75 to 103 years old when the study began. The nuns' contribution to science would continue after their death, for most also agreed to donate their brains for further examination.

At the convent, Snowdon became especially enthused when he found file drawers containing personal records going back many years, including useful measures of the sisters' cognitive abilities such as autobiographies written decades ago by each sister as a requirement to enter the order. The convent's archives were full of objective data for each nun, thus circumventing the need to rely on the aging nun's memory. As you might expect, those with dementia provide poor recall of their personal histories. (Even self-report measures from people without diagnosed dementia are often untrustworthy.)

Because these researchers knew that memory is notoriously unreliable, they could avoid asking the nuns "Were you a good writer at age 18?" and instead they go to the files and find out objectively and truthfully. Similarly, instead of relying on a verbal report that a nun earned a master's degree (which might be fantasy in the mind of anyone with dementia), the researchers could go the the archives and probably find all the facts and documentation they needed. Also enhancing the value of data was the researchers' report that the records were "standardized," that is, they were the same for all nuns (autobiography, school records, family history, etc.). Other documentation provided the researchers with compelling, objective measures of the sisters' cognitive functioning during their early adulthood.

The study has yielded interesting findings, such as those reported by Kemper and colleagues (Kemper, Greiner, Marquis, Prenovost, & Mitzner, 2001). These researchers found that grammatical complexity and "idea density" in the nuns' early writing predicted, to some extent, the onset of dementia 60 years later. In addition, Snowdon (2001) found that positive emotions expressed in writing when a nun was young significantly predicted the nun's longevity. These conclusions were made possible by the very nature of the matched sample.

CRITICAL THINKER ALERT 7-9

Matching

Control by matching participants is a poor substitute for random assignment, but it is often the only realistic substitute method. At least it equates (controls for) differences between groups on matching variables.

Discussion: Why does matching (equating) groups on the important variables of age, sex, and socioeconomic status not control for other important variables?

Researchers often struggle with an external validity (generalization) and internal validity (control) tradeoff. Snowdon (2001) recognized that extrapolation from this unique population of nuns might be limited. But he also emphasized the advantage of nuns: Factors that confound (or confuse) the findings of other studies are eliminated (or at least minimized) due to the similar adult lifestyles and environments of nuns. When researchers say that, for example, diet is confounded with lifestyle, they are saying that those with one type of diet (more fruits and vegetables) may also have a different lifestyle (more exercise, more sleep). Consequently, any difference in overall health could be attributed to diet *or* lifestyle, or a host of other factors. When the Nun Study reports that nuns' economic status, health care, living conditions, and so on are "uniform" (or the same), others take notice since those factors cannot be confounding influences. Anything that stays constant cannot possibly be a confounding factor because confounding requires variation.

Control by Statistics

Recall from Chapter 3 that researchers who do correlational studies fully recognize their limitation for the purpose of establishing cause and effect. (Recall that a correlation between test scores and test-taking speed would not suggest that slow test takers go faster to increase their score.) Fortunately, there exists in correlational studies a powerful control method very different from the type of control used by those who conduct true experiments (e.g., control groups with randomization). The method of control in correlational studies is a type of statistical control, that is, control achieved during the analysis of data. This statistical control technique is known as *partial correlation,* and it is especially useful for uncovering and explaining spurious relationships. A *spurious* relationship between two variables is one that can be "explained away" by reference to a third variable. This idea is explored in the following paragraphs.

During the analysis, the variable that is believed to be a rival hypothesis—the suspected uncontrolled variable—is *partialed* out, which means that its influence is held in check. If a correlation between two variables, say shoe size and spelling ability among elementary school children, remains strong after an extraneous variable, say age, is partialed out, then it can be said that age is controlled for and is *not* an explanation for the link between shoe size and spelling ability.

In this particular case, of course, the correlation between shoe size and spelling ability would vanish when age is controlled, since age is responsible for the spurious correlation between shoe size and reading ability—older children have bigger feet and they are better readers. Even if the correlation did not vanish when age was controlled, there is still the possibility that some other variable, not yet partialed out, is the reason for the correlation. In other words, partial correlation can control for the influence of suspected extraneous variables, but another variable, one not even measured and not part of the analysis, could always be responsible for the correlation originally obtained.

PARTIAL CORRELATION: A control procedure that statistically equates participants on important variables to rule out the variables' confounding influences.

Let's see, at least conceptually, how partial correlation might work in one study. Pretend a researcher hypothesized that radon (a radioactive gaseous element) caused cognitive deficits in children. The researcher tested the IQs of 12 children. (How to plot and interpret correlational data is described in Chapters 9 and 11.) Table 7.1 contains the researcher's fictional data, with the associated scatterplot shown in Figure 7.1.

The correlation between radon and IQ, as you can see from the scatterplot, is negative and very strong, meaning that higher levels of radon are linked to lower IQs (and vice versa). Knowing quite well that correlation does not mean causation, this researcher thinks about other variables that might help explain the finding. Maybe the level of lead in the soil is a confounding factor, resulting in a radon-IQ correlation that could be explained away. Next, the researcher collected soil samples in each child's backyard (where the child plays) and tested them for lead content. (Lead could find its way into soil in a variety of ways, including emissions from motor vehicles.) The lead measure is rather crude, but the researcher enters 1, 2, or 3 into the data set (1 = low level, 2 = medium level, 3 = high level). Table 7.1 contains these data.

When the researcher then correlated radon and IQ while partialing out (controlling for) the lead variable, the correlation dropped to zero; in other words, the radon and IQ relationship disappeared. When two variables are related and the relationship

TABLE 7.1 Radon, IQs, and Lead Levels for 12 Children

Child	Radon	IQ	Lead
A	6	130	1
B	18	85	3
C	9	140	1
D	12	105	2
E	21	75	3
F	15	100	2
G	18	80	3
H	12	110	2
I	6	135	1
J	9	125	1
K	15	115	2
L	21	90	3

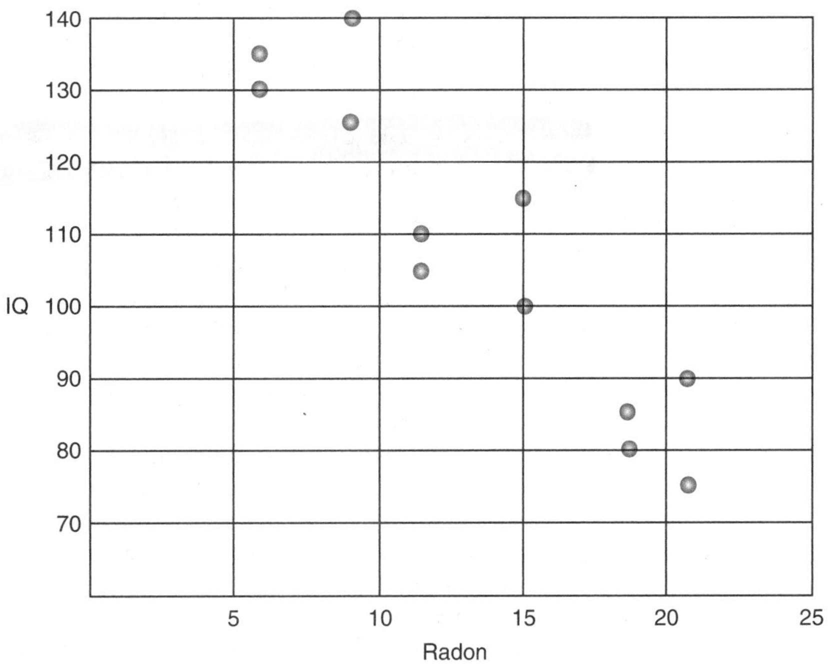

Figure 7.1 Scattergram of hypothetical data. Note the relationship between radon and IQ.

disappears when a third variable is factored in as a control, it is said that the relationship is a *spurious,* or false, one. But what does "control" in this sense really mean? Maybe the best explanation is that the radon-IQ correlation is computed while, quite literally, the lead variable is held constant. That is, the radon-IQ correlation is computed only for those children coded 1 on lead; then it is computed only for those coded 2; and then only for those coded 3. Finally, a type of average is taken over the three correlations. (This is not correct technically, but I think it helps to understand the concept of control by constancy.)

If you examine only the specific cases with lead equals 1—A, C, I, and J—you can see that the higher levels of radon (C and J both with 9 compared to A and I with 6) are associated with both higher and lower IQs (140 and 125) within the simple data set of these four cases. (Both IQs are considered high, but in this subset of data with four cases, they represent the highest and lowest, suggesting no pattern given the same level of radon.) If you examine the other two sets of four cases grouped by their similar values of lead, you'll see that the relationship seems to vanish. In fact, the simple correlation between radon and IQ within each category of lead (only four cases) is zero. This merely reveals that there is no relationship between radon and IQ once lead is partialed out (or some might say "factored in").

In sum, the major point is that an apparent relationship (like that between radon and IQ) can vanish with the statistical control of a third variable. In our example, lead (a controlled variable) was related to both IQ and radon, and because of this, it could explain away the apparent radon-IQ connection.

Multiple Regression

Researchers can extend this type of statistical control to situations where several extraneous variables can be controlled at the same time. This is possible even while examining how several other variables (presumed causes) are related to an important outcome. This widely used technique is called *multiple regression analysis.* Multiple regression analysis, or simply "regression," is not to be confused with regression as a threat to internal validity, as described earlier.

MULTIPLE REGRESSION: A statistical technique using partial correlation as a control that attempts to predict an outcome (a criterion) given two or more predictor variables.

Regression is a statistical maneuver designed to uncover complex relationships among many different variables with the hope of being able to explain, or at least predict, an outcome after establishing statistical control. You can conduct a regression study quite easily by pulling out a file drawer or accessing a database. Let's presume the outcome variable (what you are trying to explain or predict) is class rank at graduation. First you can enter several predictor variables into the equation with the goal of seeing how well you can predict that outcome (since it is already known). If this is successful, you can then use the equation when the outcome is not known, such as with ninth graders, and then you will be able to help those at risk and arrange an environment that favors greater achievement.

The regression might include 25 predictor factors, such as attendance, standardized test scores, membership in the chess club, class math grades, vocabulary test scores, participation in sports, the "Volvo" factor (or socioeconomic status), age at school entry, parent status, sex, and even hat size (!). The regression equation has its own form of statistical control (called partial correlation), so that the independent (separate) influence of, say, age at school entry, can be isolated and studied while its naturally confounding influences, which are already in the equation, are controlled. The equation may pop out of the computer showing that things like age and chess club have no relation to class rank; however, some other variables, like vocabulary knowledge, might be strongly correlated (while controlling for the influence of other variables). The regression also yields an overall summary statistic that shows you how much variation in class rank might be "explained" by all predictors, for example, 60% (with 40% being unexplained).

CRITICAL THINKER ALERT 7-10

Jargon

Research and statistics sometimes employ curious terms, rendering the jargon often uninterpretable by educational practitioners. Some of these terms can be replaced by everyday language (but some cannot). *Regression,* for example, can be referred to as *prediction*. Simple language is preferred over arcane language. Other terms in educational research, such as *reliability,* have common everyday equivalents like *consistency.*

Discussion: In education, in particular, it is important to avoid arcane language when describing research. Can you think of reasons why this is true? (Hint: Think about parents, policy makers, and other consumers of information.)

HIGHLIGHT AND LEARNING CHECK 7-7

Control by Statistics

Control by statistics is often accomplished via partial correlation (and its extension, multiple regression). Its goal is to equate (match) groups statistically by forming similar subgroups between comparison groups. The idea is to "partial out" a variable known to create unwanted differences. If you wanted to test the connection between birth weight and special education referral by fourth grade, what variable might you want to partial out in an attempt to establish control?

In research, it is helpful to have a regression equation yield an important factor that you can influence in some way, like participation in sports, instead of factors like the Volvo effect (predicting achievement on the basis of the cost of vehicles in the driveway) or hat size, factors that you cannot alter very easily. (I recall doing a regression study in a medical setting by including many variables into an equation in an attempt to predict factors related to patients falling in hospitals. My first thought was age—of course older people fall. That was not what the data revealed. And sometime later, as a patient after back surgery in a hospital when I was 32 years old, crash, down I went. Real data often contradict "the obvious" or "the logical.")

One challenge in research is understanding its jargon. Terms often have several meanings, depending on the context. *Regression* is one such term, for this chapter reveals that it also refers to the idea that extreme scores, like those in the bottom or top 10 percentile, will, upon retesting, tend to score closer to the mean (less extreme). You will recall that such scores tend to regress, or "go back to" a level less extreme. *Validity* is another example of a research term with multiple meanings, as you shall see in later chapters.

CRITICAL THINKER ALERT 7-11

Constancy

Researchers often establish control through the use of complex statistical maneuvers. Although the computations might be complicated, the reasoning is simple: Participants are equated on the threatening extraneous variable, hence controlling for its influence.

Discussion: Explain why the concept of sameness, or constancy, is so important in educational research. Is this related to the problem of confounding?

CRITICAL PERSPECTIVES 7-1

CONTROL

Critical Thinking Toolbox

Critical thinkers are always searching rigorously for alternative explanations. They do not assume that their first explanation is the only plausible one. It is a fallacy to think there is just one other alternative explanation (there are likely many others). Critical thinkers search for counter-interpretations, recognizing multiple perspectives, some with insight and some with error.

Control in Quantitative Research

Quantitative research in education favors experimental (intervention) methods and the use of randomized control groups or matching (whenever possible) combined with traditional techniques for reducing bias such as blinding, and so on. Many research designs in quantitative research have been developed with the goal of maximizing internal validity, that is, reducing those influences that "threaten" the ability to establish cause and effect. Pretest-posttest designs have been developed to maximize control over extraneous variables, but the control mainstay in quantitative research remains randomization. Quantitative researchers have developed complex statistical procedures (e.g., multiple regression) as a means for establishing control when more direct methods such as random assignment to groups are not plausible. The concept of control in quantitative research also extends to generalization (external validity), objectivity, and measurement soundness (reliability and validity).

Control in Qualitative Research

Qualitative research in education focuses on collecting and interpreting rich data, with the goal of extracting its meaning for the purpose of understanding complex phenomena. The concept of control centers on a match between explanations and realities. A qualitative researcher may ask, "Do my categories and interpretations reflect actual patterns or are they distorted in some real sense?" Accuracy of observations may become distorted by the researchers' perceptions, despite a focus on disciplined subjectivity. Qualitative researchers use several methods to establish control in this general sense. These include the use of low-inference (but high-detail), concrete (not abstract) descriptions; continuous fieldwork; objective recordings (e.g., videotape); the search for alternative explanations; and triangulation in the broadest sense (use of multiple researchers, methods, measures, etc.).

Control in Action Research

Action researchers use methods of control that enhance the usefulness of their research, methods that enable practical application of their findings. These researchers are less concerned than quantitative researchers with broad, generalized statements about cause; thus many of the techniques in quantitative researchers' arsenals (randomization, blinding, etc.) are less important to them. Much action research is participatory, hence qualitative in nature. This suggests the need for strategies that assure that action researchers' subjectivity does not threaten the credibility of their research. Ultimately, action research is concerned with improving practice. As such, issues of control become less relevant than questions about improving school outcomes on a personal level and enhancing the profession of education.

Critical Thinking Questions

In what sense do researchers' concerns about control illustrate critical thinking? Why are researchers so concerned with alternative interpretations? In what ways do lapses in control invite alternative explanations? Consider this hypothetical claim: All states with the highest standardized achievement test scores have the highest percentage of certified teachers, so we know high achievement is the result of certification standards. What other explanations are plausible given a focus on control?

Commissioned Research

It is risky to think that research studies in any field are commissioned only by so-called disinterested, independent, and impartial researchers with no vested interests in the outcome.

Let's consider a 1993 report published in *JAMA* (the *Journal of the American Medical Association*) (Lesko, Rosenberg, & Shapiro, 1993) and described in the March 8, 1993 issue of *Newsweek* titled "A Really Bad Hair Day". The report suggested that men who have a balding pattern on the crown of their heads are up to 3 times more likely to have a heart attack than men without such a balding pattern. Who commissioned this study? According to *Newsweek*, it was a major pharmaceutical company, one that manufactures a preparation advertised to restore hair. (I am reminded of talk about the study linking a crease in the earlobe to heart disease. If you had such a crease, would you run off to a cosmetic surgeon to have the crease removed in an attempt to stave off heart disease? I hope not.)

Be advised that publishers of instructional materials also commission product evaluations, and may fine-tune research studies with desired outcomes in mind. I am not suggesting fraud, but only noting that some of the hundreds of decisions that must be made in the course of a research study may be guided somewhat by "wishful science." Researchers, after all, are human, with the same hopes and desires all humans share.

HIGHLIGHT AND LEARNING CHECK 7-8

Commissioned Studies

Commissioned studies in education, such as those financed by for-profit curriculum developers, testing or test-preparation corporations, tutoring companies, or private whole-school managers, may be especially prone to bias and "spun" interpretation when the financial stakes are high. How might a profit motive in education enable a fine-tuning of research that "stacks the deck" in a particular direction?

CRITICAL THINKER ALERT 7-12

Impartial Researchers

Completely impartial researchers exist only in theory. Researchers' decisions in the conduct of research and in the interpretations of findings are influenced by researchers' experiences and beliefs.

Discussion: How might researchers' enthusiasm for, say, online courses and Web-based learning influence how they design a study to evaluate important learning outcomes using traditional courses as a comparison?

Control Procedures in a Published Study: Creative Drama

Now let's examine how some of the control procedures described in this chapter have been applied in a published research report.

Freeman, Sullivan, and Fulton (2003) employed several interesting control procedures in their investigation of the benefits of creative drama for third and fourth graders on measures of self-concept, social skills, and problem behavior. These researchers noted that precious few of the hundreds of previous studies on creative drama have used control procedures such as random assignment, control groups, and design features to neutralize commonly recognized threats to internal validity. Their experimental design was particularly interesting: a Solomon Four Group Design. This design incorporates a control for *instrumentation,* in particular *pretest sensitization* (and other threats such as extraneous events), since half the subjects are given the treatment (and half are not) and half the subjects are pretested (and half are not). The configuration is unique in that half the pretested subjects receive the treatment (and half do not), as shown below:

	Pretest?	*Treatment?*	*Posttest?*
Group 1	Yes	Yes	Yes
Group 2	Yes	No	Yes
Group 3	No	Yes	Yes
Group 4	No	No	Yes

Notice in this table displaying the Solomon Four Group Design that all subjects were posttested, but the arrangement of pretesting and treatment permit the researcher to disentangle a treatment effect and a pretesting effect. This concern is especially important in research on attitude change when the measure of attitude itself has the potential to interact with the treatment. (Perhaps completing a pretest "tunes" respondents in to their feelings, hence making them more, or less, responsive to the treatment.) Analyzing these four groups as pairs yields information about a treatment effect among those pretested (Group 1 versus Group 2), a treatment effect among those not pretested (Group 3 versus Group 4), a pretest effect apart from treatment influences (Group 2 versus Group 4), and a pretest effect with treatment influences (Group 1 versus Group 3). Notice that a comparison of Group 1 versus Group 4 would not be informative since an obtained difference could be linked to either the pretest or the treatment (the treatment is confounded with the pretest). Similarly, the comparison between Group 2 and Group 3 is not informative (it also confounds treatment with pretest influences).

Researchers who use the Solomon Four Group Design would likely expect a treatment effect without the contaminating influences of pretesting effects. Such an outcome would increase the generalization of findings because the treatment would most likely be applied without the use of a pretest if used in a nonresearch context. (The use of the pretest merely makes it easier to detect changes due to treatment influences. A pretest is not normally considered an integral part of the treatment.) You can see that these multiple paired comparisons become complex very quickly. Fortunately, there is a method of statistical analysis that greatly simplifies this design. (It is usually analyzed as a *factorial design* and described in terms of *main effects* and *interaction effects,* a topic described in Chapter 10.) You can see, however, that "breaking up" this four-group design into meaningful comparisons tells researchers a great deal about the treatment effect with and without the pretesting influences.

Freeman and colleagues used other techniques for establishing control in their study of creative drama. Their assignment of students to the four groups by use of a table of random numbers effectively created four comparable groups, rendering the threat of *extraneous events* less likely (and controlling for the threat commonly referred to as *selection*). Recall that the threat of extraneous events operates when outside influences, including the mere passage of time and those changes that occur within the subjects themselves, occur between the pretest and posttest in addition to the treatment. This threat was a concern for Freeman and colleagues because their study lasted 18 weeks. The longer the treatment phase, the greater is the concern over extraneous events. The two control groups (Group 2 and Group 4) effectively controlled for extraneous influences over the 18 weeks, such as typical changes in maturation, rapid learning, social factors, family dynamics, world events, and so on. These influences were a concern because of their potential to affect the dependent variables (the third and fourth graders' self-concepts, social skills, and problem behaviors). With the two control (comparison) groups in place that did not receive the creative drama intervention, Freeman and colleagues could essentially assess the treatment's influence above and beyond the extraneous influences by direct comparison with the control groups (which, of course, were influenced by the extraneous factors but not the treatment). In this sense, those extraneous influences can be "subtracted" out in the final analysis.

Furthermore, Freeman and colleagues also addressed the concern over the Hawthorne effect, the tendency of subjects to be affected by being in the research "spotlight." When it is appropriate and feasible, researchers often arrange for control subjects to experience the "special attention" (less the treatment, of course) received by those in the experimental group. Freeman and colleagues attempted to control Hawthorne influences stemming from the pretest by administering to those not pretested a general test in grade-appropriate academic work that was not related to purposes of the study. This procedure at least took the spotlight off the subjects during pretesting, but it could not control for Hawthorne influences that might be traced to the creative drama (treatment) itself. (The usual focus of the Hawthorne effect is the treatment, not a pretest.) It is conceivable that control subjects could have engaged in some other novel activity to control more fully for the Hawthorne effect, but Freeman and colleagues arranged for their control students to engage in "general music activities."

Freeman and colleagues also used blinding as a control technique. They reported that the instructor who implemented the creative drama activities was "provided a description of the activities to be conducted but not advised of the specific outcomes expected or any measurements or instruments involved" (Freeman et al., 2003, p. 134). Furthermore, they reported, "Regular classroom teachers and the district psychometrist [who administered the instruments] were naive with regard to all aspects of the study" (p. 134). "Naive" in this sense means being kept unaware or "in the dark," that is, blind.

Finally, Freeman and colleagues reported that 30 of the original 237 students in the study were not available for data analysis because they transferred to other schools. This information is important for purposes of assessing the threat of *loss of subjects* (also called *mortality* or *attrition*). A 10% (or so) loss of subjects over an 18-week study is not uncommon. The reason for this loss is what is most important for evaluating this threat. Loss due to the treatment itself is a problem. The haphazard loss experienced when students move is not a problem, as in the study by Freeman and colleagues, who reported that students transferred to other schools. (Transferring to other schools because of the creative drama itself is not a plausible alternative hypothesis.) The *nondifferential* (haphazard) loss of subjects is akin to reducing the sample size slightly without introducing serious disruption of the random outcome that created the comparable groups prior to the introduction of the treatment. One rule of thumb is that researchers should not lose more than 25% of their participants (Coalition for Evidence-Based Policy, 2003).

Despite the implementation of strong control features—or maybe *because* of it—Freeman and colleagues' data revealed no treatment effects on students' self-concepts, social skills, and problem behaviors that could be attributed to the weekly sessions of creative drama.

MORE EXAMPLES

Additional descriptions of published research may help to solidify your knowledge of important ideas related to control in educational research. You will find additional descriptions on the Web-based student study site (www.sagepub.com/eic).

Chapter Summary

All researchers must contend with troubling sources of bias and contamination in the conduct of their research. The *expectancy effect,* the tendency to perceive and even bring about the findings that are hypothesized, is controlled by *blinding,* or being kept "in the dark" with regard to biasing information such as whether a subject is in the experimental or control group. Other effects, such as the *Hawthorne effect,* the tendency of subjects to be influenced by their knowledge that they are being studied, may be neutralized to some extent with control (or placebo) groups. There are numerous threats to the internal validity of a study (including extraneous events, instrumentation, mortality, regression, and selection), which contribute to misinterpreting a biasing effect as a treatment effect. Many of these threats can be well controlled with a randomized control group. A well-controlled study is said to be an *internally valid* one. Contamination known as *sequence effects* plagues researchers who arrange for subjects to respond to multiple conditions or stimuli. This bias includes *order effects,* the influence attributed to, for example, a treatment being first or last; and *carryover effects,* the influence attributed to what follows and precedes a condition. Both can be controlled by randomly scrambling orders via *counterbalancing.* *Matching* as a control technique (using either twinning or cloning) can reduce potential confounding in a set of data, though it often presents a tradeoff between internal and external validity. Researchers who conduct correlation studies often achieve control by *partialing,* a statistical control that achieves its effects by removing the influence of a third variable.

Application Exercises

1. For each of the scenarios below, determine whether the researcher inadvertently allowed the influence of the expectancy effect or the Hawthorne effect. Then decide how the researcher should change the procedural methodology so that the influence is controlled.
   a. A researcher tested the idea that students' interest and achievement in world geography could be enhanced by Internet dialogue with students across the globe. A special room in the school was set aside for Internet students; also, specially trained consultants were hired for this research to help students individually make links with foreign peers. The invited consultants were also evaluating their own software (one that automatically translates one language into another), and each of the participating students was interviewed (and tape-recorded) to determine his or her reactions to the experience. The school's principal was eager for others to see this new educational opportunity and invited other educational administrators to visit the "Internet room" during the international exchanges. After 20 Internet-based geography lessons, students were given an interest questionnaire and an achievement test covering the objectives in the lessons. The researcher arranged for a control group of similar students who received instruction on the same material but in a traditional format. The questionnaires and exams were administered and scored by an impartial "outsider" who had no knowledge about the nature of the research.
   b. A researcher was convinced that students could learn complex material much better if they were only provided a good analogy before being exposed to instruction. The topic chosen was genetics; half of the students were given an analogy related to card-playing, and the other half were not. The researcher gave the 15-minute lecture to small groups of about six students. The following day, all the students were asked to write a short essay explaining generally how genetics determine human characteristics. The researcher sorted the essays into two piles (the analogy group and the control group). Next the researcher scored each essay using a global 10-point rating scale to measure the students' general understanding of genetics.

2. Consider each of the scenarios below and decide which of the following threats to internal validity are most apparent: extraneous events, instrumentation, mortality, regression, and selection.
   a. A researcher surveyed high school students to learn more about their practice of smoking cigarettes. The first part of the survey tested their knowledge of the effects of smoking from a medical and physiological perspective, the second part assessed their attitudes toward smoking, and the third part queried their frequency of smoking. Then a group of volunteer smokers participated in a 5-week course after school which was designed to provide knowledge, change attitudes, and (hopefully) reduce smoking. Those students who completed the entire course (about half of the original number) were posttested using the same survey. The findings revealed greater knowledge, more negative attitudes, and fewer smokers among the students as a function of the course. The researchers concluded that the program was successful. The timing was opportune, since many students were completing a driver training course and learning that discounts are provided for nonsmoking drivers by most insurance companies.
   b. A group of second graders scoring at the bottom 10% on a reading test were targeted for intensive instruction daily for 2 weeks. They were retested after the remediation using the same instrument (but with clearer instructions) and scored significantly higher. A comparison group identified at another school as needing—but not yet receiving—remediation was also tested using the same instrument. They scored lower than the remediated group. This finding, coupled with the group's significant gain, led the researcher to conclude that the intensive instruction was effective.

3. For each of the scenarios presented in #2 above, describe how the inclusion of a randomized control group would affect the influence of the threats which were identified.

4. A researcher for a textbook publishing company evaluated five short stories—call them A, B, C, D, and E—by asking sixth graders to read and rate the enjoyability of the stories. All the students read the stories in the order presented above and completed their assessments by rating their enjoyment after each story. What problem is illustrated here, and how would you go about controlling its influence?

5. Imagine a researcher who is planning a correlational study and will use partial correlation as a statistical method of control. Based on what you know about partial correlation and its uses, think about variables that would be prime candidates for control via partial correlation in the following studies.
   a. A researcher investigated the charge that there were sex-salary inequities at the district offices of large urban school districts. As a first step, the researcher calculated the correlation between sex (male, female) and annual salary. What would be an appropriate variable to control via partialing?
   b. A researcher investigated the relationship between vocabulary knowledge and head circumference in a population of elementary school children. What would be an appropriate variable to control via partialing?
   c. A researcher investigated the suspected relationship between IQ and size of family and found lower IQs among later borns (as the number of brothers and sisters increase, the IQ becomes lower). What would be an appropriate variable to control via partialing?
   d. A researcher investigated the relationship between learning disabilities and the consumption of junk foods (the more junk foods consumed by a child, the greater the learning disability). What would be an appropriate variable to control via partialing?

6. Researchers must grapple with many sources of potential bias and contamination in their research, including the Hawthorne effect, the John Henry effect, and expectancy threats (also known as the Pygmalion effect or self-fulfilling prophecy); the threats of extraneous events, instrumentation, mortality, regression, and selection; order effects; and spurious relationships. Some possible solutions to these problems (and related ones) include blinding, placebo groups, randomized control groups, counterbalancing, and the use of partialing in statistics.

   Use an Internet search engine such as Google and key in a term such as "sleep learning," "learn faster," "better memory," or other similar desire related to learning. Be highly skeptical as you sort through the results. Find an especially doubtful claim, one that offers "proof" with a "scientific study." Carefully examine the research evidence. Try to identify one of the problems in the list above that would invalidate the evidence. Then describe how one of the control techniques could be used in a redesign of the study to control for the problem you identified.

ON YOUR OWN

Log on to the Web-based student study site at http://www.sagepub.com/eic for more information about the materials presented in this chapter, suggestions for activities, study aids such as electronic flashcards and review quizzes, a sample research proposal, and research recommendations that include journal article links (with discussion questions and an article evaluation guide) and questions related to this chapter.

8
Sampling in Research

Outline

Overview

The previous chapter focused on important concepts related to control in the conduct of educational research. Researchers face many other weighty issues directly linked to data collection, one of which is sampling. There is little chance of answering the research question, or fairly testing the research hypothesis, without the right quantity and quality of educational data. These concerns about the quantity and quality of data relate to the topics of sampling (Who will provide data?) and measurement (How useful are the data?). This chapter concerns sampling; the following chapter focuses on measurement soundness (reliability and validity). Sampling is especially important in the integrated process of research because pitfalls are common, often leading to faulty conclusions and improper inferences about those in the larger population who were not studied.

One of the most frequently asked questions in the conduct of educational research is "How many subjects do I need?" In fact, this question undoubtedly prompted researchers Helena Kraemer and Sue Thiemann to write a fine little book titled, not surprisingly, *How Many Subjects?* (Kraemer & Thiemann, 1987). The answer to this question is straightforward, but it does require the question asker to know about a statistic called the *effect size.* To understand this important statistic in a truly meaningful way, you must first be familiar with the importance of the *standard deviation.* We now turn our attention to how scores (and other measures) are described. Then we can better answer the question, "How many subjects do I need?" and "How do I acquire my sample of subjects?" These two questions form the basis of what is usually called the researcher's *sampling plan* or *sampling design.*

Describing Data

Central Tendency

In order to make sense out of what may seem an unmanageable array of scores collected during a research project, researchers often list the scores from highest to lowest and tally the number of times each score occurs. As a practical illustration, consider the 25 hypothetical test scores in reading achievement collected by Marlo for a research project and shown in Table 8.1.

FREQUENCY DISTRIBUTION: A plot of scores displayed by their frequency of occurrence (i.e., ranked).

CENTRAL TENDENCY: A characteristic of a distribution of scores that describes where scores tend to center. It is often referred to as an average, the most common one being the mean (the sum of scores divided by the number of scores).

If we rank order these scores from highest to lowest, we will find that they fall into the pattern shown in Table 8.2 under the column labeled "Scores Rank Ordered."

Next to each rank-ordered score in Table 8.2, we find tally marks that reflect the number of students who scored that value. The third column in Table 8.2, labeled "Frequency," is simply the number of tally marks next to each score. The result of this reorganization of scores is a *frequency distribution,* which is simply one way of organizing a larger set of scores into a form that enables us to determine where most scores fall and how they distribute themselves around a midpoint. This pattern of tallies shown in Table 8.2 is typical of ability, achievement, and many other measured traits. This characteristically bell-shaped curve is known as a *normal shape,* simply because it is so common. Many scores bunch up near the middle, and few scores are in the extremes (called *tails*).

Table 8.1 Reading Test Scores From Marlo's Research Project

Name	Score	Name	Score
Daniel	70	Susan	84
Marsha	70	Juan	73
Rujal	89	Bill	73
Steve	76	Karyn	61
Stan	91	Bobbie	73
Rita	69	Stella	73
William	70	Marco	61
Georgette	98	Thom	73
Nabodiri	90	Nancy	76
Maggie	78	Kathy	89
Sam	59	John	78
Gretchen	78	Peter	54
		Linda	69

Source: Adapted from *Primer of Educational Research* (p. 121), by W. N. Suter, 1998, Needham Heights, MA: Allyn and Bacon and *Educational Psychology in the Classroom* (7th ed., p. 540), by H. C. Lindgren and W. N. Suter, 1985, Pacific Grove, CA: Brooks/Cole.

Table 8.2 Frequency Distribution of Scores From Table 8.1

Scores Rank Ordered	Tally	Frequency
98	|	1
91	|	1
90	|	1
89	||	2
84	|	1
78	|||	3
76	||	2
73	|||||	5
70	|||	3
69	||	2
61	||	2
59	|	1
54	|	1

Although the frequency distribution gives us a rough picture of the performance of those who have taken a test and is an efficient method of organizing and summarizing an array of scores, we usually need more information to describe the distribution itself. What, for example, is the score that best represents the group's performance? Logically, the most representative score is to be found where most scores tend to center. The most frequently used index of this tendency is the *mean,* or arithmetic average. The mean is computed simply by adding up all scores in the distribution and dividing by the total number of scores. The mean is usually symbolized as M, and its computation is summarized by $\Sigma X / N$, where Σ (the Greek symbol capital sigma) refers to "sum," X refers to scores, / refers to "divide by," and N refers to the number of scores. (There are other measures of central tendency, such as median and mode, but the mean is by far the most widely used and is the logical companion to the standard deviation, which is described next.) Your calculator will confirm that the sum (ΣX) is 1875, and since there were 25 scores ($N = 25$), the mean (M) = 75 (1875 / 25 = 75).

Dispersion

Although the mean of a set of scores is very helpful for describing the midpoint or central tendency of scores, it tells us nothing about how widely scattered the scores are from the mean. Did all the students in the sample score about the same on the test, or were there great differences among them? In order to answer this question, we need another statistic that tells us the degree of *dispersion,* or spread, of the scores around the mean. One such index of this spread is called the *standard deviation,* which is computed by subtracting the mean from each score, squaring the resulting differences, totaling those differences, dividing that total by the number of scores, and finding the square root of the result. The standard deviation is usually symbolized SD (or S), and we can see how $SD = 10.52$ (11, rounded), given the calculations in Table 8.3.

DISPERSION: A characteristic of a distribution of scores that describes the spread or scatter of scores around the central tendency. The most common measure of dispersion is the standard deviation. The higher the standard deviation, the greater the spread of scores around the mean.

Once we know the standard deviation, we are able to say a great deal about the spread of scores. When scores are distributed normally (bell-shaped, or close to it), scores tend to fall within certain limits or boundaries around the mean. About 68% (two thirds) of the scores fall within the limits formed by the mean plus 1 standard deviation and minus 1 standard deviation. About 95% of the scores fall within the limits formed by the mean plus and minus 2 standard deviations. Finally, about 99% (or nearly all) of the scores fall within the limits formed by the mean plus and minus 3 standard deviations. This suggests that about 68% of Marlo's scores fall between 64 and 86, and about 95% of the cases fall between 53 and 97. (In truth, Marlo's scores do not conform perfectly to these limits—they conform only approximately. This is because the sample is small and contains "sampling error."

HIGHLIGHT AND LEARNING CHECK 8-1

Descriptive Statistics

Descriptive statistics include the mean as a measure of central tendency (the sum of scores dived by sample size) and the standard deviation as a measure of dispersion around the mean (a type of average of the squared deviations of scores around the mean). Which of the following sets of scores appears to have the highest mean? Set A: 4, 2, 5, 7. Set B: 7, 8, 6, 7. Which set has the largest standard deviation?

Table 8.3 Calculation of the Standard Deviation (*SD*) for Marlo's Research Project

Score	Mean	Difference	Difference Squared
70	75	−5	25
73	75	−2	4
70	75	−5	25
73	75	−2	4
89	75	14	196
61	75	−14	196
76	75	1	1
73	75	−2	4
91	75	16	256
73	75	−2	4
69	75	−6	36
61	75	−14	196
70	75	−5	25
73	75	−2	4
98	75	23	529
76	75	1	1
90	75	15	225
89	75	14	196
78	75	3	9
78	75	3	9
59	75	−16	256
54	75	−21	441
78	75	3	9
69	75	−6	36
84	75	9	81

$\Sigma = 2768$

$2768/25 = 110.72$

$\sqrt{110.72} = 10.52$

rounded = 11

A large sample will tend to "round out" the curve so that it matches a bell shape more closely and conforms to the limits formed by the standard deviation.)

To check your understanding of this concept, consider the following: If the average weight of adult females were 135, what would be a reasonable standard deviation—20? This would mean that two thirds of all women weigh between 115 and 155, and that 95% weigh between 95 and 175. This is a reasonable guess for the standard deviation (given those limits). Clearly, a standard deviation of 2 is too small; and a standard deviation of 40 is too high. What would be the standard deviation of rainfall in inches in your city over the past 100 years, if the average were 40 inches—6, perhaps? You simply form boundaries, and then make a judgment.

NORMAL (BELL) DISTRIBUTION: A common shape of score distributions. Normal distributions have common properties, ones that divide a distribution's area in terms of proportions contained within 1, 2, and 3 standard deviations above and below the mean.

With these ideas about normal (bell) distributions, means, standard deviations, and percentages "under the curve" within normal distributions, you can see how easy it is to imagine what a distribution of scores might look like if someone told you, say, that the mean was 83 and the standard deviation was 4. I can envision a bell-shaped distribution with the "hump" above 83, a downward curve toward 79 and 87, and tails beginning around 75 and 91.

CRITICAL THINKER ALERT 8-1

Mean and Standard Deviation

Be advised that there are alternative methods for describing data. The mean and standard deviation, however, dominate statistical analysis. More information on alternatives that may be appropriate for a particular situation can be found under the general topics "exploratory data analysis" and "nonparametric statistics."

Discussion: Presume a researcher found that a large sample of math scores were distributed normally with a mean of 50 and a standard deviation of 8. Given this information, can you determine the approximate cutoff values defining the middle 68% of scores? Can you figure out what approximate score value defines the upper 2% of scores?

CRITICAL THINKER ALERT 8-2

Dispersion

Dispersion of scores, most commonly measured by the standard deviation, is important because it influences researchers' search for relationships. Large dispersion is desirable in correlational studies; small dispersion is desirable in group comparison studies.

Discussion: If my research question examined the relationship between hours slept and reaction time, would I recruit the full range of sleepy and well-rested participants or merely those with average sleep? Why? If my research hypothesis investigated memory differences of those who exercise daily versus those who do not, would I recruit all types of people or restrict my sample to white male college students? Why? Do you see the tradeoff between statistics and generalization? How about the tradeoff between statistics and ethics?

Effect Size

One value of the standard deviation is its use in the calculation of what is known as an *effect size.* The effect size is best understood when it can be applied to a simple experiment. For example, let's consider a study testing the effectiveness of a new method to boost reading comprehension scores. (The treatment was concerned with teaching young readers how to read metacognitively, that is, by asking questions, making predictions, and using other active mental tasks.) Let's assume that the experimental group scored an average of 85 on a reading comprehension test, and the control group scored 75. The standard deviation of the control group was 20. The effect size, called *delta* (and usually written as *d*), is calculated in the following way:

EFFECT SIZE (*d*): An index of a treatment effect expressed as a standardized difference between two means (the mean difference divided by the standard deviation of a comparison group's mean). It is often expressed as a percentile shift, or "boost" from a baseline at the 50th percentile.

$$d = \frac{\text{Treatment Mean} - \text{Control Mean}}{\text{Standard Deviation of Control}}$$

In this case,

$$d = \frac{85 - 75}{20}$$

$$\text{or } d = .5$$

This *d* value of .5 tells us where the treatment group mean falls *in standard deviation units* relative to the control (comparison) group mean. So, we can say that the average treatment reader scored one half of a standard deviation above the mean of those in the untreated control group. This idea is shown in Figure 8.1.

Percentile Shifts

The *d* statistic is usually converted to a *percentile-shift* measure by consulting a statistical table known as the standard normal curve (called the *Z table*). (The details of the conversion of *d* to a percentile are appropriate for a first course in statistics. The *Z* table can be found in most statistics texts; for our purposes, simply be aware that a simple conversion is accomplished with a statistical table.) For example, the *d* of .5 (one half of a standard deviation) in the reading experiment converts to a value at the 69th percentile. We can say, therefore, that the treatment group on average shifted to the 69th percentile of the untreated control group. The baseline measure in this sense is the 50th percentile (or the mean) of an untreated control group, and the treatment's effect is expressed as a shift from this initial starting position.

Think of the *d* as the force or pressure that can boost an entire distribution; think of the percentile shift as the position in the control group where the average of the treatment group has "landed" after its shift. If a shift corresponds to the 79th percentile, for example, you might imagine picking up the entire treatment distribution and placing it over the control distribution so that its average falls to the right at the 79th percentile. Figure 8.2 illustrates the force needed to shift a treatment group far to the right, hence scoring considerably higher than the control group on average.

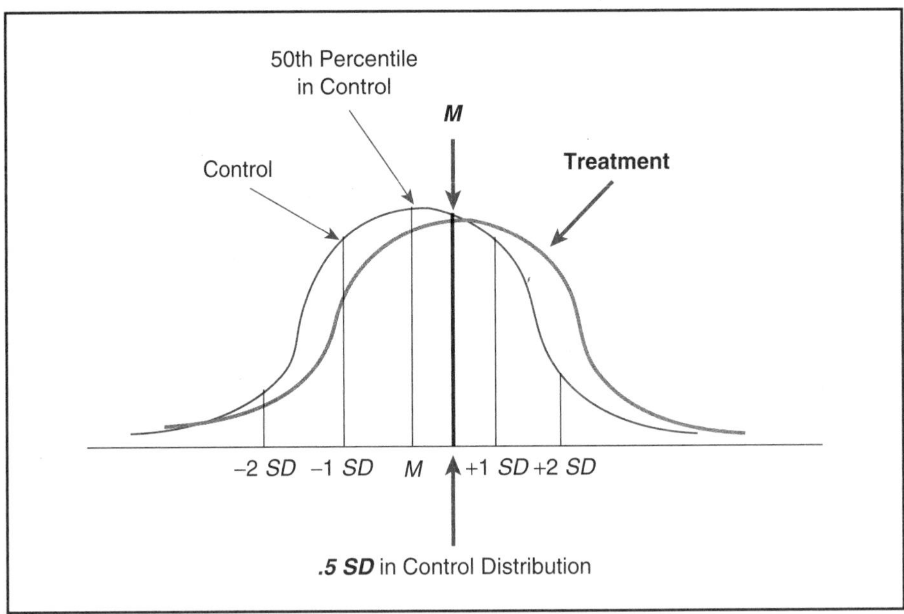

Figure 8.1 Overlapping distributions revealing an effect size of .5. The treatment group (**bold**) scores higher than the control group, shifting to the right and overlapping so that its mean (*M*) falls at the .5 standard deviation (*SD*) mark of the control group. The effect size .5 reveals where the average of the treatment group falls *in relation to the control group* using a standard deviation scale. Keep in mind that the mean of the control group functions as the baseline or starting point; the effect size is the yardstick that measures the distance that the treatment group shifts from the baseline.

Figure 8.2 Overlapping distributions revealing a large effect size. The treatment group (**bold**) has been pushed to the right. Its mean falls closer to the tail of the control group (at the 79th percentile), suggesting a large effect size.

Source: Adapted from *Primer of Educational Research* (p. 125), by W. N. Suter, 1998, Needham Heights, MA: Allyn and Bacon.

TABLE 8.4 Effect Size Measures (*d*) and Related Percentile Shifts

d	Approximate Percentile Shift (compared to control group)
−2.00	2
−1.50	7
−1.00	16
−.80	21
−.50	31
−.20	42
.00	50
.20	58
.50	69
.80	79
1.00	84
1.50	93
2.00	98

The *d* statistic can also be negative, indicating an average treatment group shift *below* the mean of a control group. As an illustration, think about a weight loss group (the treatment is group hypnosis) compared to an untreated control group. Let's assume the treatment group after the hypnosis sessions weighed 120 pounds and the control group weighed 130 pounds with a standard deviation of 15 pounds. The effect size would be (120 – 130) / 15 = –.67. This converts to a percentile of 25, suggesting that the *average* hypnosis group fell at the 25th percentile of the untreated control group. Table 8.4 lists several effect sizes, along with their associated percentile shifts.

Notice that the percentile shifts are symmetrical above and below the average ($d = 0$). The *d* values that fall between those values listed in Table 8.4 have percentile shifts which can be approximated by an interpolation. It should be noted, however, that the interpolated percentile is not a simple linear interpolation (e.g., halfway between *d* values of .50 and .80 is not exactly halfway between percentiles 69 and 79). A standard normal *Z* table should be consulted for the exact values associated with each *d*.

Various effect sizes have been given somewhat arbitrary labels. There is general agreement that a small effect size is .20 (a percentile shift from 50 to 58), a medium effect size is .50 (a percentile shift from 50 to 69), and a large effect size is .80 (a percentile shift from 50 to 79).

HIGHLIGHT AND LEARNING CHECK 8-2

Effect Size (*d*)

The *effect size* (*d*) is a type of standardized difference between two means. It reveals the magnitude of a treatment effect apart from statistical significance and is especially useful for determining the required sample size to uncover effects of varying strength. Its measure can be translated into a *percentile shift,* revealing where the average of one group falls in relation to a percentile in another group. If *d* equals .50, what is the effect size expressed as a percentile? What about if *d* equals 1.00? How is *d* related to standard deviations in a normal distribution?

CRITICAL THINKER ALERT 8-3

Effect Size

Effect sizes are important in research because they influence the determination of sample size. Weaker relationships between variables, if they are to be uncovered, require greater sample sizes. Strong relationships can be uncovered with relatively few research participants.

Discussion: If a researcher found a statistically significant link between hours slept and speed of anagram solutions using only 15 participants, what does this suggest about the strength of the relationship? Would a significant relationship with 2,500 participants suggest anything about the strength of the relationship?

Effect sizes approaching 1.00 (very large) are rather uncommon in education. Such an effect size would be equivalent to increasing the achievement level of students in poverty (about the 20th percentile) to a level beyond the national average of all students (Fashola, 2004; Fashola & Slavin, 1997). Most educational researchers agree that an effect size of .25 or larger is educationally significant.

The values of *d* for small, medium, and large effects may be used in several ways. One important way is described in the following section.

Sample Size Determination

Group Comparison Studies

The effect size measure *d* is vital for determining the appropriate sample size in many types of educational research. Sample size is also determined by factors other than *d*, but fortunately, these factors have standard values which can be preset to generally accepted levels. We will examine these factors in greater detail in Chapter 13, but for now, these factors will be preset to the following values: alpha = .05, power = .80, tails = 2. *Alpha* refers to the probability that a mean difference could arise by chance; .05 is the agreed-upon scientific standard for this value. *Power* refers to the probability of finding a difference when in fact a true difference exists; .80 is considered a desirable standard for power. *Tails* refers to the direction of a mean difference. Two tails allow for an experimental group to be higher *or* lower than a control group; one tail allows for a specific direction of a difference, such as the experimental group scoring higher, not lower, than a control group. Nearly all statistical tests have two tails if two directions are possible, so setting tails = 2 has become the standard.

POWER: A statistical concept used in sample size determination that refers to the likelihood of finding a significant relationship between variables in the sample presuming there is a true relationship in the population being studied.

Given these preset values and knowledge of small, medium, and large effect sizes, one can use the chart in Table 8.5 to arrive at the required number of subjects in a representative sample to uncover a significant difference, if in fact one exists in the population. It should be obvious from this chart that more subjects are needed if the effect size is small. (If an effect size is zero in a population, meaning that there is no difference between groups, then a researcher, of course, would not find a true difference even with an enormous sample size.)

TABLE 8.5 Sample Sizes Needed for Finding a Significant Difference

Effect Size *d*	Required Sample Size in Each Group
.20 (Small)	392
.50 (Medium)	63
.80 (Large)	25

Source: *Statistical Methods in Psychology* (p. 167), by D. C. Howell, 1982, Boston: Duxbury.

Note: This presumes a two-group study with alpha = .05, power =.80, and tails = 2.

The effect sizes and required sample sizes shown in Table 8.5 are appropriate whenever a research question pertains to two contrasted groups, for example, experimental versus control, male versus female, second graders versus third graders, and Teaching Method I versus Teaching Method II. This table can be useful in many different contexts. If a research hypothesis posits a large difference (effect) between, say, males and females in their self-perceived math competency, then it is clear that only 25 males and 25 females would be needed to uncover this difference. Or, if prior research suggests that students taught to read via whole language (the experimental group) will read with greater comprehension than the standard basal group (the control group), but this difference (effect) is small, then the researcher would know that 392 students in *each* group would be needed for a fair test. Or, possibly a researcher is interested in an unexplored relationship, say the effect of exercise on memory span, but only if it is at least medium in strength. It would then be known that 63 subjects would be needed in each group (exercise and control).

Without the information conveyed in Table 8.5, researchers would not know how to interpret a finding of no significant difference. For example, suppose a researcher tested the hypothesis that sugar causes hyperactivity and found that there were no significant differences in hyperactivity between the sugar group and the control group. This finding may reflect the truth: Sugar in fact does not cause hyperactivity (let's presume this is the truth for this example). Or, maybe sugar *does* cause hyperactivity, but the research could not uncover this relationship because of an insufficient sample size. *A finding of no difference is ambiguous without an adequate sample size.* A finding of no difference with an appropriate sample size, by contrast, is fairly easy to interpret—the variables are probably *not* related in the population. In the

CRITICAL THINKER ALERT 8-4

Insufficient Samples

A research finding revealing no significance may be attributable to an insufficient sample size. The larger the sample size, the more likely one is to uncover a significant relationship between variables (presuming one exists in the population).

Discussion: In what sense is sample size in research akin to the power of a microscope?

hyperactivity example, if 400 sugar students were compared with 400 control students and no influence on hyperactivity was found, then the researcher could more comfortably conclude that sugar does not cause hyperactivity. (This conclusion would be warranted only if other aspects of the study were in order, like utilizing the proper control techniques, as described in Chapter 7.)

Before closing this examination of the effect size measure *d*, it should be noted that *d* has uses other than determining sample size. It is also one common measure employed in meta-analysis, a technique described in Chapter 4. Meta-analysis uses *d* in order to summarize the strength of a treatment effect across many studies. Hundreds of separate studies, each one providing a single *d*, can be summarized by one overall effect size.

CRITICAL THINKER ALERT 8-5

Significance and Importance

Researchers frequently report that relationships between variables are "statistically significant" (meaning that they are not likely due to chance factors). These findings can be described further with effect size measures; they reveal how weak or strong relationships are, enabling further conclusions about findings.

Discussion: Presume a researcher found that left-handed students had lower SAT scores than right-handed students. The research was based on 100,000 participants, the SAT difference was statistically significant, and the effect size was .02. What is your conclusion about this finding? Is this an important finding?

Correlational Studies

Correlational studies (which are described in Chapter 11) are not immune from statistical guidelines relating to the proper sample size. These studies are statistically analyzed by the correlation coefficient, usually symbolized *r*. Weak, moderate, and strong relationships, defined as $r = .20$, $r = .50$, and $r = .80$, respectively, have proper sample sizes (total number of subjects) of about 197, 33, and 14 with power = .80, alpha = .05, and tails = 2 (Howell, 1982, p. 167). The effect size measure in correlational studies is often indexed by *r* itself, that is, the correlation coefficient.

Older Rules of Thumb

The sample sizes described above for group comparison studies (392, 63, and 25) for small, medium, and large effects, respectively, may be thought of as *statistically validated* (in the sense they are derived from statistical calculations). By contrast, there are frequently invoked "rules of thumb" for determining sample size. There is widespread consensus (at least in education and the behavioral sciences) that research involving the comparison of two groups should be based on a *minimum per group* size of 30. (You'll notice from Table 8.5 that this value of 30 assumes a fairly large effect size.)

Although this sample size of 30 is a very a common recommendation in reference sources about educational research, it may as well be called a "magic number," for it is a mystery how this number came to be used. It is undoubtedly related to the fact that the mean as a index of central tendency tends to stabilize, or become dependable, when computed on a sample of at least 30 subjects. (A value tends to stabilize when it does not change much when computed across random samples.) One may also find the number 30 in other contexts as well, including business and Wall Street. For example, the widely reported Dow Jones Industrial Average ("the Dow") indexes the movement of leading stocks in several "sectors" by—you guessed it—computing a type of average across the stock price of 30 significant companies.

Having 40 participants per group is also frequently recommended, particularly in the sense of creating comparable groups after random assignment. Randomly dividing 80 people into two groups should create roughly equivalent groups, since individual differences should "wash out." There would be far less confidence about group comparability after randomly assigning, say, 10 people to two groups.

There is another rule of thumb that can be applied to complex correlational research designs. One such correlational design used commonly in educational research is *multiple regression,* whereby more than one variable is correlated with an outcome (called a *criterion variable*). For example, a researcher might investigate how logical reasoning scores are related to a host of personal attributes (called *predictors*), such as the amount of vigorous exercise, early music training, vitamin B6 in the diet, level of secondhand smoke, and even month of birth. This rule suggests one should have "notably" more cases (subjects) than predictors (Tabachnick & Fidell, 1983, p. 379). This means, at the very minimum, having at least 4 to 5 times more people than predictors. Other sources suggest 20 times more cases than predictors. The most common recommendation seems to be to have *at least 10 times as many cases as variables.* The logical reasoning example above would therefore require at least 50 subjects (since there are five attribute variables used as predictors).

Newer Rules of Thumb

Ideas about "rules of thumb" regarding sample size in educational research began to change—become more rigorous—with the passage of the No Child Left Behind legislation in 2001. The Coalition for Evidence-Based Policy (2003) clearly raised the standard with regard to recommended sample size in group comparison studies (particularly for true experiments involving random assignments). Their guidelines are intended to provide information for all educators so that they can identify "scientifically based research" and be in a better position to make sound decisions about program effectiveness as determined by "rigorous evidence." For strong evidence, one should look for the "rough rule of thumb" of 150 participants in *each* group being compared for programs believed to be "modestly effective." If research compares *entire* schools or classrooms (opposed to individual students), the recommended size for rigorous evidence is 25 to 30 schools or classrooms in *each* group. The Coalition also recommends that the dropout rate (loss of subjects for any reason) not exceed 25%.

HIGHLIGHT AND LEARNING CHECK 8-3

Sample Size Determination

Sample size determination varies as a function of statistical requirements (based on effect size measures and power analysis), the type of study conducted (group comparison versus correlation), and rules of thumb (older and newer). There is no one "magic number." What factors are related to a need for larger sample sizes in research? What are the consequences of a sample too small?

CRITICAL THINKER ALERT 8-6

Sample Fairness

Sample size, in large part, influences whether a research finding is significant and "fair" (in a statistical sense). A nil finding with too small a sample yields uninterpretable results. Nothing new is learned.

Discussion: Why do you suppose that poorly designed research in education (small sample size, lack of control procedures, etc.) yields findings that are not interpretable? Can you think of examples of uninterpretable research?

Sample Size and Precision in Scientific Surveys

Most scientific national surveys use about 1,000 or so respondents in their sample. This number produces a "margin of error" around 3%, in other words, a boundary within which a value from the entire population would most likely fall. For example, if a sample size of 1,000 reveals that 66% of parents—plus or minus 3%—favor year-round schooling, then we know that the true percentage in the population of millions of parents will most likely fall between 63% and 69%. Notice that sample size is determined by the desired precision (about a 3% margin of error is customary) and *not* by a certain percentage, say 10%, of the population. If sample size were determined by such a percentage, then polling organizations such as Gallup would have to survey millions of people to assess attitudes toward public education. The Gallup sample size (at least in the survey of attitudes toward education) varies from 1,000 to about 1,300 or so, and the population Gallup generalizes to includes all adults age 18 or older, except those in institutions such as prisons, hospitals, and so on and those in the military. This is over 100 million people!

Also, recent Gallup survey methodology (Rose & Gallup, 2002) is hardly sophisticated. It involves a computer that randomly dials a valid telephone number. When the phone is answered, the interviewer asks to speak to the *youngest male* over age 18 living in the household, and if no male lives there, the interviewer asks to speak to the *oldest female* over 18 in the household. Really! Remarkably, this simple technique, which sounds terribly biased, produces a sample that matches the age and sex distribution in the general population (a "little America"), and their findings generalize to all households in this country, at least within Gallup's defined population, with a very small margin of error. (Recall the Gallup population is enormous, those noninstitutionalized, age 18 or older. And, I may add, those people in households with a working phone.) Their revised methodology (Rose & Gallup, 2003) is hardly more sophisticated, seeking telephone interviews with the household member with the most recent birthday. It is interesting to speculate how the "oldest-male, youngest-female" strategy yields the same representative sample as the "most recent birthday" strategy.

CRITICAL THINKER ALERT 8-7

Large Samples

A large sample size by itself is not impressive. Small samples can mirror the larger population very well if selected in ways that maximize the population's representation.

Discussion: Presume a television news program such as CNN invited e-mail responses to the question "Do you favor year-round public schooling?" Of the 600,000 e-mails received, 75% favored year-round schooling. What factors might limit the representativeness of this large sample? (Presume the population is adults over 18 years of age.)

The "35th Annual Phi Delta Kappa/Gallup Poll of the Public's Attitude Toward the Public Schools" by Rose and Gallup (2003) published in the widely circulated *Phi Delta Kappan* illustrates several key concepts in sampling. Their "magic number" was 1011, admittedly large, but their intended population—the group that they wish to make generalized statements about—is essentially *all adults over age 18 in households with telephones.* In surveys, the overriding statistical concern is precision, or the accuracy of the results. Survey findings are precise when the findings in the sample match very closely the "real" value in the population. Precision is often referred to as *sampling tolerance.* Tolerance is directly a function of sample size and, to a lesser degree, the value of population parameters (e.g., "Is the percentage of respondents in the population who support an issue closer to 80% or 50%?") This precision, or tolerance, in a survey is usually referred to as the *margin of error.* For example, if 60% of the respondents support the idea of homeschooling with a margin of error of plus or minus 3%, we would know that the true percentage in the population is most probably between 57% and 63%, derived simply by subtracting and adding the margin of error to the sample result. These limits, which most likely span the true value in the population, are also referred to as *confidence intervals.* "Most likely" in this case refers to 95 out of 100 times.

MARGIN OF ERROR: A statistical index used in survey results to convey an interval that likely includes the true population value.

Sample sizes for scientific surveys, therefore, are largely determined by how much error you are willing to "tolerate." Table 8.6 shows the required sample sizes for varying levels of sampling error (or margin of error) for the standard level of confidence (.95, or 95 out of 100, as described previously). It also maximizes the sample size ("worst case scenario") by assuming the true split in the population is 50/50; the required sample sizes are smaller for splits like 80/20 or 60/40.

A simple formula, 1 divided by k^2, will also provide a ballpark estimate of sample sizes for surveys, where k is the desired confidence interval. For example, if a margin of error of .04 is acceptable, then 1 divided by $.04^2$ would equal 625. You can see that this estimate is low, but the tabled values are maximized, as described

TABLE 8.6 Required Sample Sizes for Scientific Surveys

Margin of Error	Required Sample Size
13%	100
9%	200
6%	400
5%	750
4%	1000
3%	1500

Source: "The 34th Annual Phi Delta Kappa/Gallup Poll of the Public's Attitude Toward the Public Schools," by L. C. Rose and A. M. Gallup, 2002, *Phi Delta Kappan, 84*(1), p. 56.

Note: The sample size is a function of sampling error.

CRITICAL THINKER ALERT 8-8

Sample Size Guidelines

Several widely recognized guidelines regarding sample size exist in research. Scientific surveys often exceed 1000; experimental and group comparison studies use at least 30 subjects per group and often up to five times that many to uncover significant differences.

Discussion: Given that scientific surveys are often in the range of 1,000 respondents, why do you think a survey might use as many as 50,000 people?

HIGHLIGHT AND LEARNING CHECK 8-4

Survey Precision

Sample size in scientific surveys is largely a function of precision or tolerance, often referred to as the *margin of error.* The required representative sample size for the typical margin of error between 3% and 4% is around 1,000 or more respondents. What other factors affect the required size for a specific level of precision?

previously. If you are conducting a scientific survey, a recommended sample size would fall, most probably, between 600 and 1,000 if you wanted your precision to be within reasonable limits. This may sound like a huge undertaking, but keep in mind that in some surveys, such as the Gallup, the size of the population is enormous, consisting of perhaps 150 million people.

There is *no* strategy for determining sample size in a survey that involves only a specific percentage of the population (e.g., 10% of the population of size 500 is 50). If this were true, then, the sample size of the Gallup surveys would be an absurd 15 million, assuming a 10% sample selection rate.

Sample Size Summary

We have seen that a common sample size for scientific surveys is about 1,000 to 1,300. For group comparison studies (e.g., treatment versus control), the usual sample size is considerably smaller. Sample sizes per group in many areas of research often hover around 30 to 60. With this number, statistics such as the mean, tend to "stabilize" (to be consistent from sample to sample). Sample sizes of 30 to 60 per group are typical in educational research, at least in experimental research, the kind often used to establish cause-and-effect relationships. The appropriate sample size in research is critically important, for an adequate sample size allows for a "fair" test.

If a sample is too small, a statistician might easily miss finding a relationship that, in truth, exists in the population. This is covered in a later chapter, but for now be aware that a "magic number" in research, at least traditionally, appears to be about 30, that is, 30 subjects in *each* group being compared. This number often goes higher, though, like 60 to 70, a number with greater statistical validity. This rule of thumb is also applied to the famed Federal Drug Administration's clinical trials in medicine, at least Phase I, the phase that helps determine the safety of a new drug. (In fact, the sample size for Phase I clinical trials is sometimes as low as 15.)

The Department of Education has established different guidelines (higher standards) regarding sample size, particularly as it applies to practices supported by "rigorous" evidence. The Coalition for Evidence-Based Policy (2003), for example, has determined that a "rough rule of thumb" in randomized experimental studies in education (e.g., treatment versus control) is 150 participants per group for an intervention that is "modestly effective." (These guidelines were established for the purpose of evaluating programs using "scientifically based research" demanded by the No Child Left Behind Act of 2001. These guidelines were modeled after the randomized controlled clinical trials used so often in medical research.) The guidelines, however, do recognize that smaller sizes are appropriate if the intervention is "highly effective." When entire schools or classrooms are compared (opposed to individual students), the recommended sample size is about 25 to 30 schools or classrooms per group. Without regard to "attrition" (loss of research participants due to dropping out), the guidelines established by The Coalition for Evidence-Based Policy (2003) reveal that one should not lose track of more than 25% of the original participants. Generally, you can see that strong evidence in scientific research does not necessarily require thousands of participants for rigorous evidence of program effectiveness.

Sampling Methods

Random Selection

Now that you understand the importance of sample size and how it can affect conclusions, we turn our attention to sampling *methods* (sometimes called sampling *designs*). The concern here is how to select research participants from a larger group. The larger group is called a *population;* it is the entire group which researchers intend to make generalized statements about. A sample, by contrast, provides data and is a subset of the population, one that hopefully mirrors it.

The overarching principle of sampling is concerned with *representativeness*, or the similarity between the sample and the population. Researchers are entitled to generalize their sample findings to a larger population if the sample is similar to, or representative of, the larger population. One of the best methods for assuring that the sample is representative is to select the sample *randomly* from the larger population. Random sampling is accomplished with a table of random numbers, like the one shown in Table 8.7.

RANDOM SELECTION: A method of sampling which assures that each member of a population has an equal and independent chance of being selected for inclusion in a sample. Variants of random selection exist, such as cluster, multiple stage, and stratified.

Random sampling is *not* accomplished with coin flips or drawing numbers from a hat. The use of a random number table assures that each member of the population has an *equal and independent chance* of being selected. To understand this, simply imagine a list of the (let's assume) 5000 teachers in your state. *Equal and independent* means that Person #1 in the population has exactly the same chance of being selected as Person #5000 who has the same chance as Person #2500 who has the same chance as Person #25 who has the same chance as Person #2501. Further, if Person #200 is selected, then Person #201 has the same chance as Person #4592. In a sense, random selection has no "memory," so to speak, and the selection is just as likely to target the neighbor from the previous selection as, say, Person #5000. (Likewise, a random slot machine which has just hit the jackpot is as likely to hit the jackpot on the very next turn as it is on, say, pull #777.)

Let's select a sample randomly from a larger population to see how this is done. A small scale will be used for efficiency, with the understanding that the same procedures could be applied on a much larger scale. In Table 8.8 is a numbered list of students (first names only) in my Introduction to Research course at the University of Arkansas at Little Rock (UALR). Assume these students represent the population, and my task is to select a random sample of size five.

You can enter the Table of Random Numbers (at least a portion, as shown in Table 8.7) anywhere you would like. (I know this doesn't sound scientific, but you

TABLE 8.7 **Portion of a Table of Random Numbers**

69513	93372	98587	64229
24229	23099	96924	23432
45181	28732	76690	06005
75279	75403	49513	16863
89751	63485	34927	11334
06282	75452	26667	46959
69714	28725	43442	19512
10100	43278	55266	46802
08599	32842	47918	40894
93886	57367	78910	38915
94127	99934	35025	50342
97879	92921	68432	68168
43382	28262	10582	25126
91218	49955	01232	55104
89495	00135	27861	39832

TABLE 8.8 Population of UALR Students Enrolled in Introduction to Research

1. Donna	15. Danielle
2. Shandria	16. Tammy
3. Gina	17. Mariella
4. Leslie	18. Sung-Yeon
5. Karen	19. Kimberly
6. Sabrina	20. Arthur
7. Carole	21. Suzanne
8. Michele	22. Melanie
9. Meredith	23. Brooke
10. Paula	24. Maggie
11. Muneerah	25. Elli
12. Adonna	26. Robert
13. Alvin	27. Glenda
14. Tanice	28. Marlo

really can simply close your eyes and point your finger anywhere in the table. It's random!) Let's say that you chose the second column (of five digits) from the left, third row down, last two digits—32. (You need two digits since there are 10 or more people in the "population." If there were 100 or more people in the population, you would simply choose three digits.) Person #32 does not exist in the population, so I choose a direction (down, let's say) and continue until I find numbers which are valid. The next two digits down are 03, hence Gina is in my random sample. Continuing down, we see Person #85 is not valid, likewise Person #52. Continuing, we find Person #25 (Elli) is in the sample, and so is Person #21 (Suzanne). If we continue, we'll reach the bottom of the column before finding valid numbers. So we'll continue in the same spot (last two digits) at the top of the next column to the right (87—do you see this?). Continuing down, we find Person #24 (Maggie) and Person #13 (Alvin). These five students, then, comprise my random sample from the "population."

CRITICAL THINKER ALERT 8-9

Simple Random

Many sampling designs in research are very sophisticated, yet one of the best is very simple. It is called *simple random,* and in this design each member of the population has an equal and independent chance of being selected.

Discussion: Despite its simplicity, a simple random sample is sometimes not practical. Speculate about reasons why an alternative method such as sampling the first 30 names on an alphabetized list of 250 will produce a nonrepresentative sample.

Random selection is a *process,* not an outcome. When it is accomplished with the aid of a random number table (the process), we can say that the resultant sample is random, period. It makes no sense to check the randomness after the fact to make sure it is representative. The use of the table defines it as random; it is not defined by the outcome. This process of random selection is easy, but there is one catch: The members of the population must be numbered so that the table of random numbers can be linked to them. This usually does not present a problem, however, since many lists (paper and electronic) are routinely numbered. (Recall from Chapter 7 that there is another very important type of randomization called random *assignment,* a control procedure that neutralizes the potential contaminating influences of extraneous variables.)

There is one common form of sampling that uses the "every *n*th" system, whereby every 7th (or 10th or 200th) person on list is selected. This type of sampling is a form of *systematic* (opposed to random) sampling. This method clearly does not conform to the definition of random (each member has an equal and independent chance of being selected). Once the 7th (or *n*th) person is chosen, the 8th person has zero chance, but the 14th has absolute certainty of being selected. Also, Person #1 had a zero chance of being selected. In reality, it is unlikely that systematic sampling plans such as this introduce serious bias (but they could, in theory). This form of sampling appears to be used for reasons of practicality and efficiency when no serious bias is suspected with its use (i.e., it is much easier to direct others to choose every 7th name than to explain what a random number table is and how to use it). Systematic sampling is also used when the accessible population is not known (or not truly accessible) or when random selection is not possible. Consider a population of consumers, for example. Surveying every 50th shopper who enters a mall may be the only plausible sampling method, for there could be no list of the population of all shoppers that day from which to randomly select. Although not strictly random, this type of *n*th person sampling is often considered the "next best thing."

CRITICAL THINKER ALERT 8-10

Random Number Table

The use of a random number table, one generated by a computer, guarantees that the process of selection or assignment is random. (Researchers do not flip coins or draw numbers from hats.) Researchers are concerned with the random *process;* it makes little sense to refer to a random outcome. (The outcome is never checked for randomness, in other words, since randomness is a process, not an outcome.)

Discussion: Discuss reasons why it is not appropriate to "fix" a random sample after the fact, that is, to make changes so that the sample "looks" like the larger group (population).

Variants of Random Sampling

Clusters

Researchers frequently encounter intact groups which cannot easily be chopped into small units (or individual students). These unbreakable units are often called *clusters,* and typical clusters in educational research include classrooms, schools, and even districts. (In other disciplines, clusters may be wings of a hospital, city blocks, or counties.) Clusters can be randomly selected in the same way that individuals are randomly selected. Entire classrooms or schools may be numbered using any logical sequence and then selected randomly with the use of a random number table. Such sampling designs are referred to as a *randomized cluster.*

Multiple Stage

Sometimes researchers find it easier to select randomly at two or more stages. For example, 60 schools may be selected randomly in a state, followed by the random selection of 20 classes within each of the 60 schools. This plan would be described as *two-stage random.* A *three-stage random* may start with the selection of 200 large school districts across the nation, be followed by the random selection of 20 schools within each district, and then involve the random selection of 10 classes within each school.

Stratified

Many random sampling designs incorporate subgroups formed on the basis of categories believed to be especially influential. For example, the nationwide Gallup Poll which measures adults' opinions about issues in education will use strata based on four regions of the country and three sizes of community (Rose & Gallup, 2003). The decision to stratify on these factors suggests that attitudes about education vary as a function of geographic region and size of community. Researchers using these *stratified* random sampling designs often arrange for their sample to mirror the entire population on these stratified factors. For example, if 21% of the nation's population resides in the South, then the sample will comprise 21% Southerners. If 40% of the population lives in large cities, then the sample will comprise 40% large-city dwellers. These population values are usually learned from the latest census data. Also, stratified sampling of a large population is more likely to yield a sample group that is representative of the population than is simple (not stratified) random sampling—unless the simple random sample is very large.

HIGHLIGHT AND LEARNING CHECK 8-5

Sample Representation

All sampling methods attempt to comprise a sample that is representative of the population. Simple random sampling assures that each member of the population has an equal and independent chance of being selected. Variants of random sampling exist, including clusters (intact groups), multiple stage (increasing smaller units), and stratified (use of subgroups). How does a technique so simple as random selection accomplish its goal of accurate representation?

External Validity

Educational researchers reserve the term *external validity* to refer to how well the findings in a sample can be generalized, or extended, to a larger population. If a study lacks external validity, then one is not confident that the findings can be applied beyond the narrow confines of the study. One especially common threat to external validity is, to no surprise, lack of random selection. When the sample does not fairly represent the population, external validity is lacking. This is most likely to happen when samples are chosen on the basis of convenience rather than representativeness (this is often called a *convenience* sample). For example, assume you wanted to learn about the opinions held by students at your college or university regarding weekend classes. To this end, you select only those students enrolled in one of your night courses. The findings would almost certainly not apply to students in general. The convenient sample may have been easy to obtain, but it would not be generalizable, thus threatening the external validity of the survey and rendering it useless. Such samples may also be called "captive" samples, for they take advantage of captive audiences such as sophomore college students enrolled in general psychology, parents attending a school meeting, or teachers attending a conference. The samples' poor external validity becomes clear when one attempts to describe the target population of such samples, as a description like "captive audience" or "convenient respondents" hardly makes sense. Convenience samples are common, and this fact highlights the need for caution when attempting to generalize sample findings.

EXTERNAL VALIDITY: The degree to which research results can be generalized beyond the sample and conditions that yielded the findings.

The same problem occurs when opinion surveys are *solicited,* not randomly selected. For example, radio programs may ask their listeners to call a specific number if they agree with a position and a different number if they disagree. Those who choose to call may bare little resemblance to the population at large. Maybe those who agree also feel stronger than those who disagree, hence are more motivated to call. Or consider magazines that print questionnaires and ask readers to return them upon completion. Only those who have a high interest in the purpose of the survey may be motivated to return the questionnaires. The same idea applies to Web and e-mail solicitations to vote. Simply, these procedures are marketing or entertainment, not science.

The failure of research findings to generalize from the sample studied to a larger population, often in a different context, is a chronic problem in education. Programs and instructional materials that might work well in one situation with one specific group of learners may not transfer easily to another group. The variation of learner characteristics is simply huge (cultural backgrounds, learning styles, age, socioeconomic status, and personality are just a few of the thousands of learner qualities). Couple that with the myriad factors that contribute to the context of learning, such as teacher style differences, class size, scheduling variations, school

CRITICAL THINKER ALERT 8-11

Generalization

Generalization of research findings in education (from the participants who supplied data to others who were not studied) is often wishful thinking, due in part to learner, situational (context), and time differences. Adopted (imported) educational programs often fail for these reasons, and what is true in the "lab" often does not hold up in complex classrooms.

Discussion: Is generalization, or widespread application of findings, a reasonable goal in educational research? What factors might explain why a program's success might not transfer from urban Los Angeles to rural Minnesota?

climate, and school resources, to name just a few. The mere passage of time adds to the complexity, for our lives can change quickly in a rapidly changing world with new technologies or changing attitudes.

The idea of finding once and for all "what works" in education, in other words, presumes that the world is static and "one size fits all." This is clearly not the case. Localized interventions may show promise in early trials but fail miserably the following year in a different setting. Many of us experience the counterpart in medicine, for a therapy that works for some people has no effect on others. A drug may affect one person very differently than it affects another person. The thalidomide drug tragedy provides one compelling example. This sedative, introduced in the 1950s and prescribed to pregnant women to combat insomnia and nausea, appeared safe after clinical trials using monkeys. Serious problems followed, including severe birth defects in children whose mothers used the drug early in pregnancy. It was later discovered that similar birth defects were found among one particular species of monkey, but not in the one species used for clinical testing of the drug. This revealed that not only do drug effects not transfer from monkeys to humans, but they may not even transfer from one type of monkey to another. In education (and in heath and medicine), the common observation "It depends" with reference to the effect of some influence (e.g., it depends on time of day, mix of students, style of teacher, previous activity, age or attitude of students, etc.) reveals how difficult it is to discover generalizable laws that are widely applicable across classrooms.

CRITICAL THINKER ALERT 8-12

External Validity

The term *validity* in research has many different meanings, making it difficult to keep straight sometimes. For clarity, the term should always be preceded by another descriptor. For instance, *external* validity refers to how well research findings can be generalized, or extended, beyond the people and settings studied.

Discussion: Some argue that one limitation of research in education is limited external validity. What is unique about processes in education that might explain why research sometimes does not extend beyond the sample and setting to larger groups and to different contexts?

Population and Ecological Generalization

The term *external validity* means generalization, and two types of generalization exist: population and ecological. *Population generalization* refers to people; *ecological generalization* refers to settings—all aspects of the setting, including the physical environment. Ecological generalization is no less important than population generalization, since problems with it can also threaten external validity.

POPULATION GENERALIZATION: The extent to which research findings extend beyond the sample of research participants who provided data.

The type of generalization that focuses on the research participants themselves—apart from the setting—is called *population generalization.* It is concerned with how well people in the sample mirror those people in the population, or the representativeness of the sample participants in relation to the population.

Consider the following study based on educational "seduction" (an idea first described by Naftulin, Ware, and Donnelly, 1973, and later extended by Perry, Abrami, and Leventhal, 1979). Researchers wanted to know if college students' ratings of their professors (in terms of the students' knowledge gain) was affected by a factor such as the professors' enthusiasm. The researchers arranged for an actor on videotape to deliver a 30-minute lecture on some obscure topic. Two versions of the *identical* lecture were given, an enthusiastic one and a boring one. In the enthusiastic presentation, the lecturer was dynamic, eager, excited, and entertaining; in the boring condition, the same lecturer was, well, boring. After the lecture, students in both groups rated how much they thought they learned. The results showed that students who attended the enthusiastic lecture rated their knowledge gain greater than those in the boring one did. The researchers concluded that college students' ratings of their professors are biased, since they can be "seduced" by highly entertaining professors into believing they learned more than they actually did. (But might it be that they, in fact, did learn more, given their greater attention to a dynamic presentation?) This effect also became known as the "Johnny Carson effect," after the late night television entertainer.

Even if the sample in the research described above was large and randomly selected from a population, many people would question its applicability to actual college classrooms. College courses are taught by professors, not actors; lectures are most frequently delivered live by professors, not on video screens by actors; and courses last maybe 50 hours, not 30 minutes. And students are students, so to speak, not subjects who signed up for an experiment to earn course credit. One might question both the ecological and population generalizability of a study such as this.

Consider another example, this one hypothetical. Presume that a researcher studied how young children make sense of reading. In a campus laboratory built especially for this purpose, the subjects in small groups read an experimenter-prepared passage about a summer vacation. A research assistant in each group either asked them funny questions as they read (the experimental group) or said very little (the control group). Results revealed that the experimental group scored higher on reading comprehension tests than the control group did. The researcher concluded that school teachers should make greater use of humor when teaching children how to read. This study may be questioned on grounds that its setting does not match real-world, noisy classrooms staffed by certified teachers using standard materials. Children simply don't learn how to read in sterile learning laboratories within ivory towers staffed by research assistants who use experimenter-prepared reading passages.

The concept of ecological generalization encompasses virtually all aspects of the research setting except the subjects themselves. The method of data collection, for example, is part of the "ecology." Do the opinions expressed over the phone or in e-mails generalize to other settings such as face-to-face interviews and paper-and-pencil formats? While most of us would recognize the size, color, and temperature of a room as part of its ecology, many of us wouldn't readily think of the sex of the experimenter (interviewer) or the readability of materials as part of the ecology (which they are).

ECOLOGICAL GENERALIZATION: The extent to which research findings extend beyond the setting which produced sampled data.

The Coalition for Evidence-Based Policy (2003) provided an example of the failure of research results to generalize even when studies use randomized controlled trials (the "gold standard"). Two multisite studies of the Quantum Opportunity Program (a community-based program that provides assistance for disadvantaged high school students) showed that the program's effectiveness varied greatly among the various program locations. The studies noted that a select few sites, such as Philadelphia (the original site), yielded large positive effects on participants' academic standing and career plans. Yet other sites had virtually no effect on the same outcomes. The coalition concluded that "the program's effects appear to be highly dependent on site-specific factors, and it is not clear that its success can be widely replicated."

HIGHLIGHT AND LEARNING CHECK 8-6

External Validity

External validity refers to how well findings extend, or generalize, beyond the sample to different people (population generalization) and settings (ecological generalization). What factors might influence the external validity of research findings in education?

CRITICAL THINKER ALERT 8-13

Sample Context

When one asks whether research results generalize (that is, whether or not they are externally valid), the issue concerns more than the research participants. The setting, materials, time frame, and implementation are all related to how well results "hold up" in a different environment with different people.

Discussion: Why is "context" so important in education? What other aspects of context (besides those mentioned above) must educational researchers attend to and why do these deserve their attention?

Sampling Shortcuts and Bias

An appreciation of representative sampling might be gained from a brief description of faulty or "curious" sampling. There are literally thousands of ways to introduce a sampling bias. Perhaps the most dramatic blunder (at least in politics) occurred just prior to the 1936 Landon-Roosevelt Presidential election ("Landon, 1,293,669; Roosevelt, 972,897," 1936). This is especially interesting since the survey was one of the largest on record. Nearly 2.5 million potential voters returned surveys through the mail, resulting in a prediction that the Republican candidate, Alf Landon, would defeat Democrat Franklin D. Roosevelt by a wide margin. (The poll was conducted reasonably close in time to the election, and no major influencing event like a scandal occurred between the poll and the election.) Of course, Landon was not elected president, and Roosevelt won by one of the largest landslides in election history.

How can you explain such an error? Like most sampling errors, the problem was a general one: The sample was simply not representative of the population. This lack of representativeness resulted from the pollster's selection of potential voters from, at least in part, automobile registration lists. Who was most likely to own automobiles in the midst of the Depression Era? The wealthy. And were they more likely to be Republicans or Democrats? Republicans. The survey, therefore, was predominantly a survey of Republican voters.

Another notorious case is the 1970 draft lottery. Some of you may have a vivid image of this (I do), for it was televised nationally amid widespread tension. The lottery involved choosing "random" birth dates (366 dates, including February 29) from a large barrel. The first date selected would receive lottery number 1; the second date selected, lottery number 2, and so on. Young men were drafted in accordance with their numbers; those with the lowest numbers were drafted first. This would be a fair sampling procedure if it were truly random (each date having an equal and independent chance of being selected). Clearly, random number (and date) generators were available in 1970, but (probably for public relations) the military opted for an old-fashioned system akin to drawing numbers from a hat. Birth dates were placed in plastic capsules and then dropped into a barrel. Starting with January 1 and systematically working around the calendar, each capsule was added to the others in the barrel and presumably mixed together. This system, of course, guaranteed that December dates would go into the barrel last. But when the lights came on and the television cameras started rolling, the system also guaranteed that the December dates would be the first to come out. December dates, therefore, had low numbers simply because they were the last to go in and the first to come out. Far too many Americans born in December went off to Vietnam as a result, and the military learned a lesson about random sampling: Do it properly with a table of random numbers and forget about displays for public relations.

To borrow an example from medicine, apparently we learned about the dangers of asbestos—in particular, the unique form of lung cancer associated with it—later than we could have. An early survey of asbestos workers in scores of asbestos plants found only one worker out of thousands who had the asbestos-caused lung cancer. The survey, however, was terribly biased because only retirees were surveyed. These people, by definition, had to be reasonably healthy since they lived to retirement age. Most of the workers who got asbestos-caused lung cancer died before retirement, hence they were not part of the study. Of course, a random selection of people who had ever worked with asbestos (within a specific time frame) would have revealed a mortality rate much higher and closer to the truth.

The Lewis Terman longitudinal study of geniuses, though not considered a blunder, also provides an example of unrepresentative sampling. (The late Lewis Terman of Stanford University is credited with revising and standardizing the original test of intelligence developed by Alfred Binet of France for use in this country, hence the

CRITICAL THINKER ALERT 8-14

Representative Samples

Research findings can be applied (generalized) to a larger population only if the sample is an accurate "mirror" (or representation) of that population. Such samples are said to be *representative.*

Discussion: If you surveyed a sample of drivers buying fuel at the closest fueling station to your home, do you think this sample would be representative of registered voters in your town or city? Why or why not? Do you think they would be representative of registered voters across the entire country?

Stanford-Binet scale of intelligence.) In the 1920s, Lewis Terman initiated a lifespan study of geniuses, tracking their development as children and watching their progress as adults until old age. Only about 2% of the population can be labeled "genius" using the traditional Stanford-Binet intelligence quotient of over 132. The test may take an hour to administer and score, so hundreds of hours of testing would have to be done before a handful of geniuses could be found. And Terman wanted to study 1,500 of them! Terman would have had to spend his entire life testing! The solution to this problem of excessive testing (a shortcut, really) involved asking teachers to nominate those few students in their classes who appeared to be geniuses. Then possibly 1 true genius could be found for every 2 children who were tested. It worked! The testing was greatly reduced, and about 1,500 geniuses were selected for study through their entire lifespan. What is the sampling problem, you ask? Teachers were likely inclined to nominate those children who fit stereotyped images of genius—well behaved, studious, quiet, conforming, high achieving, and so on. Quite possibly, another type of genius would be more interesting to study—the creative, funny, bored, troublemaker type who probably never made it to the sample. Of the 1,528 geniuses in the sample (including Terman's own son and daughter!), all but a handful (2 African Americans, 6 Japanese Americans, and 1 Native American) were white, urban, and middle class. Most resided in Los Angeles and San Francisco, and boys outnumbered girls (Leslie, 2000).

The Lawrence Kohlberg study of moral development also provides an interesting example of nonrepresentative sampling (that also is not considered a blunder). Kohlberg tracked how children's moral reasoning changes as they progress through developmental stages (i.e., from "Don't do it because you might get caught and spanked" to "Don't do it because good boys don't do it" to "Don't do it because it's the law"). Kohlberg was able to categorize many children's rationales for particular behaviors in terms of the children's moral development. The problem arose when his early research revealed that girls were somewhat behind boys in their moral thinking. As it turned out, Kohlberg's system of classifying moral responses developmentally was based on boys only. Girls, it was later revealed, are not *slower;* they are simply *different* (and some would argue, more advanced). Whereas boys are concerned about not interfering with the *rights* of others, girls appear to be more concerned about the *needs* of others.

Finally, the study of personality psychology affords at least one interesting sampling blunder. Consider the Minnesota Multiphasic Personality Inventory (MMPI). This test was designed to assess abnormal deviations in personality, such as paranoia and schizophrenia. For a scale on this test to successfully identify schizophrenics and so-called normals, a sample of schizophrenics must answer a set of questions differently than a representative sample of normal personalities did. The sample of hospitalized schizophrenics was obtained from a university hospital in Minnesota. And how was part of the sample of "normals" obtained? From visitors to the hospital (including the schizophrenics' relatives)! (You might recognize this as a convenience sample.) To the extent that friends and family members of hospitalized schizophrenics are not "normal," the normal sample becomes biased.

HIGHLIGHT AND LEARNING CHECK 8-7

Sampling Shortcuts

Sampling shortcuts are very likely to threaten the external validity of research findings since the sample may not mirror the population. Such samples are distortions of the population. What common sampling shortcuts exist, and how do they introduce bias into the sample?

CRITICAL PERSPECTIVES 8-1

SAMPLING

Critical Thinking Toolbox

Critical thinking involves noticing significant—not superficial—similarities and differences. Sensitivity to important differences influences how and why we reason about comparisons (Paul, Binker, Jensen, & Kreklau, 1990). Noting similarities is also aided by the use of analogies, being careful to avoid false or faulty ones.

Sampling in Quantitative Research

Because the overriding concern for quantitative researchers is to select participants who are representative of a larger, target population ("universe"), most techniques used by quantitative researchers are variants of *probability* sampling, so called because the researcher can determine the probability of each member of the population being selected for the sample. We have seen that in a *simple random* sample, each and every member of the population has an equal and independent chance of being selected. There are variations of this basic design, including *stratified* sampling (incorporating blocks or subgroups) and *cluster* sampling (using intact or naturally occurring groups). Quantitative researchers use statistical methods that often assume participants have been randomly selected or assigned to experimental conditions. Samples tend to be large in quantitative research.

Sampling in Qualitative Research

Qualitative researchers often use a variant of *purposive* sampling, the specific type depending on the purpose of the research (Miles & Huberman, 1994; Patton, 2001). Above all else, the sampling strategy in qualitative research is designed to yield "rich" data, with sources including a single person, a small group, and complex organizational sites. Names for different sampling strategies in qualitative research reveal varied purposes, including *extreme case* (unusual, outlying cases), *critical case* (unique, dramatic cases), and *maximum variation* (cases with obvious differences). Other qualitative sampling strategies include *snowball* sampling (participants' recommendations leading to selection of new participants), *opportunistic* sampling (selecting participants during unfolding events, situations, or circumstances), and *typical case* sampling (selection of representative cases). There are others, each providing convincing evidence that qualitative researchers select participants for varied purposes, all of which provide the richness in data that becomes the essential condition in qualitative research. These include *theory* sampling (for the purpose of generating a new theory) and *confirming versus disconfirming* sampling (for the purpose of testing preliminary findings). Samples tend to be small in qualitative research.

Sampling in Action Research

Because action research is centered on practical problems within a personal but applied setting (e.g., a classroom, study hall, counseling room, etc.), sampling presents itself, so to speak, and often includes the researcher's "captive" group of students. Because the action researcher's concern rarely extends to a larger population of students, the sample and population are one and the same. Samples in action research also permit collaboration between teachers (or counselors, administrators, etc.) because action research in education involves the dynamic processes of sharing, self-reflection, data collection, analysis, and action for change. Action research is practical, participatory, and democratic. Those who comprise a sample often participate in selection procedures. Samples tend to be small in action research, often reflecting a subgroup within a teacher's class.

Critical Thinking Questions

What are the most salient differences among the three sampling paradigms represented by quantitative, qualitative, and action research? Are there implications of these differences for research-based conclusions? Can you make any inferences about a researcher's philosophy of education given these different approaches to sampling? What commonalities exist across the three approaches to sampling?

Sampling: Research Examples

Exemplar Teachers

Survey research in education poses several challenges, including defining a population of interest, designing a sampling plan that yields data representative of the population, and minimizing bias due to lack of participation (a low response rate). A population that captured the interest of researchers Lopata, Miller, and Miller (2003) was *exemplar teachers,* those regarded as experts worthy of functioning as models for other teachers intent on improving their practice. Lopata and colleagues (2003) noted that these exemplar teachers are distinguished from their peers because of their depth and breadth of instructional knowledge and "wide and deep cadre of instructional strategies" (p. 233). Lopata and colleagues' (2003) review of the literature suggested that exemplar teachers are also more constructivist in their orientation (less teacher centered), favoring classroom interaction and progressive practices such as cooperative learning. The researchers also noted that despite decades of research support for cooperative learning, details of its application are lacking. They wondered whether exemplar teachers might be "unique" in their preferences for using cooperative learning strategies and whether teacher characteristics (such as years of experience) were related to their *reported* and *preferred* use of cooperative learning. They asked, "Might large discrepancies between reported and preferred frequency of use be linked to teacher characteristics?"

Lopata and colleagues (2003) narrowed their sample to suburban schools in western New York state. They asked 54 schools to participate in their research; all school principals agreed. Each principal was asked to identify 4 exemplar teachers in the building, resulting in 216 potential teacher participants. The researchers then sent surveys to all teachers, hoping for a response rate of at least 70% (but knowing response rates often fall well below 50%). The researchers also knew that a portion of returned surveys cannot be used for a variety of reasons, a common reason being incomplete or uninterpretable responses. (They also knew that some surveys probably never reached their "target" due to delivery problems.) Of the returned 142 surveys, 12 were eliminated due to incomplete responses, leaving 130 usable (analyzable) surveys. The resultant response rate was thus about 60%.

I believe these researchers were probably satisfied with the number of returned surveys (and response rate), in large part because small-scale descriptive surveys (not scientific, national polls) often contain sample sizes around 100 or 200. Many researchers strive for a response rate of 70% or higher and would probably agree that a response rate of 60% (opposed to often-reported rates around 35%) suggests that the findings are minimally different from a target population (all exemplar teachers in western New York state). This seems like a safe assumption, for it is hard to imagine a serious bias introduced by their survey methodology. It is more reasonable to believe that the reasons nonrespondents declined were related to their busy schedules rather than to factors suggesting they could have totally different responses to the survey. The survey, after all, did not solicit personal or controversial self-reported behaviors or beliefs that might differentiate responders from nonresponders. That fact that Lopata and colleagues (2003) did not attempt a second round of mailings to capture a portion of the nonresponders also suggests that, in their judgment, the response rate of 60% did not threaten the interpretation of findings due to serious nonresponse biases.

Researchers faced with substantially lower response rates often send out reminders to nonresponders hoping for a "second wave" of responses to increase the response rate and sample size. (Only the nonresponders or late responders could be targeted, but this requires some type of coding scheme to identify those who have, and have not, responded.) Nevertheless, the possibility of response bias exists with a rate of 60%. The researchers, in fact, acknowledged the possibility that only those who favored the use of cooperative learning responded to the survey. They also recognized another factor that might limit the *external validity* of their study, namely, that the selection procedure relied on principals' nomination of exemplar teachers. Perhaps another method of selection, one based on students' achievement, might have yielded a different sample, returning different responses to the survey. Different methods of selection may have important implications for the external validity of the findings.

The researchers' response rate was reasonably high, undoubtedly due to their careful construction and field testing of the survey. (A field test is trial run, of sorts, designed to uncover correctable problems before the final version of the survey is sent to hundreds of participants.) Lopata and colleagues reported utilizing accepted principles of item construction (e.g., the use of brief, positively stated items) and field testing the survey using a small number of exemplar teachers like those in the population. There is little sense in field testing an instrument using participants who are dissimilar to those in the study. The best practice involves the use of participants for field testing who are themselves potential candidates for being selected in the sample. (Field-tested participants, however, are usually excluded from potential selection once their responses are used to refine the survey.)

My experience suggests that a small number of "pilot" participants in a field test (perhaps 12) nearly always results in a survey's improvement in ways that a developer's scrutiny cannot uncover. It should be no surprise that the researcher's perspective is often different from the participants' perspective, hence creating the need to solicit participants' impressions on an instrument undergoing development. Lopata and colleagues (2003) reported that the results of further field testing "supported item clarity, construction, and relationship to cooperative learning constructs" (p. 235). Their response rate was helped by procedures such as providing a stamped envelope for the return of completed surveys. Further, the surveys were brief and completed anonymously, other factors that undoubtedly contributed to the relatively high response rate.

(Several years ago I developed a survey for nurses that contained these two questions: "How many children do you have? _____" and "What is your age? _____." Next to the age question, I received responses like "3" or "7 and 10." These were not 3-year-old nurses, of course. This illustrates a problem known as *context effects.* My first question led the nurses to think about their children, which led them to quickly misread the second question and write their children's ages. Such responses were quite common, and my blunder led to having to eliminate those questions from the analysis, partly because I could not interpret responses such as "1" and "30." That might have been a 30-year-old with one child—most likely, or a 50-year-old with a 30-year-old son or daughter—a misreading. The moral of the story: Field test surveys before use!)

Lopata and colleagues' (2003) survey contained four elements of cooperative learning. Overall, their findings revealed significant differences between exemplar teachers' reported versus preferred uses of each element of cooperative learning. They reported that exemplar teachers' "actual use of cooperative learning fell below the level at which they would prefer to be practicing cooperative learning" (p. 237). (Here a better word than *actual* might be *reported,* for actual use is determined better by objective observers over time as opposed to teachers' own self-reported beliefs or recollections.) Generally, teacher and school characteristics were not related to reported and preferred discrepancies of use. The researchers suggested that a useful follow-up to their survey would be a study of the reasons for exemplar teachers' less frequent than preferred use of cooperative learning strategies in the classroom.

MORE EXAMPLES

Additional descriptions of published research may help to solidify your knowledge of important ideas related to sampling. You will recognize aspects of the seven dimensions previously described. You will find additional descriptions on the Web-based student study site (www.sagepub.com/eic).

Chapter Summary

Most researchers want to learn something that extends beyond the sample of subjects to a larger, more generalized population. The process of sampling, or how many subjects are sampled and by what method, often determines whether or not this extension is warranted. Central to the notion of sample size is a statistic called an effect size, or *d.* This measures the strength of a relationship between variables; weaker relationships require larger sample sizes to be detected. A medium effect size, defined as a percentile shift from 50 to 69, requires about 63 subjects per group. Common rules of thumb, however, suggest that 30 to 40 (and up to 150) subjects per group is appropriate. The size of sample also determines precision, or margin of error, in a survey study. Large-scale surveys with acceptable precision often require 1,000 to 1,500 respondents.

How subjects are selected often determines the external validity, or general applicability, of the study. Random sampling is one good method of assuring that the sample is representative of the population from which it was drawn. Other methods often introduce bias that can threaten the *population generalization,* which jeopardizes statements about people in the population. The use of unreal settings or materials can threaten the *ecological generalization,* which jeopardizes statements about environmental conditions in the population (such as classrooms, materials, tasks, etc.).

Application Exercises

1. Assume that the amount of time in minutes-per-week high school students spend reading for pleasure is normally distributed with $M = 300$ and $SD = 60$. What can you conclude about the middle two thirds (or 68%) of the distribution, with regard to time spent reading? What about 95% of the students? What percentage read for more than 360 minutes per week? (Hint: Draw a distribution with areas marked off in standard deviation units, and remember that the distribution is symmetrical.)

2. If a researcher found that a treatment designed to boost students' reading for pleasure was described with an effect size $d = 1.00$, what can you conclude about the treatment group's percentile shift? What if $d = .75$? (Hint: You will probably have to *approximate* this answer.)

3. Let's presume that a researcher attempted to uncover a treatment effect of "brain food" on students' memory span. Pretend that we know the concocted meal has a true effect with $d = .20$.
   a. If memory span averages 7 (with $SD = 2$), what can you conclude about the food-boosted memory span?
   b. If a researcher tested this effect with 40 students in the "brain food" group and 40 students in the control group, what type of conclusion would this researcher invariably make?
   c. What conclusion would most likely be made if $d = .50$ and 75 students were in each group?

4. Assume you have a friend who wants to compare males' and females' levels of math anxiety. How would you answer your friend's question—"Is there a usual and customary number of people I'll need in each group for this comparison?"

5. If 50 people were surveyed to assess their opinions about state supported preschools for all children up to age 5, what would you expect in terms of the survey's margin of error?

6. For each of the scenarios below, identify the sampling blunder, speculate about the influence of the bias, and then make a recommendation for ridding the biasing influence.
   a. A researcher wanted to know how people in the local community felt about the use of high-stakes testing in the public schools. The researcher spent the afternoon at Wal-Mart and randomly approached 100 shoppers to ask their opinion (they all agreed to cooperate). The random selection was accomplished with the use of a random number table (the numbers determined which shopper to target, such as the 16th to exit, then the 30th to exit, then the 9th to exit, etc.).
   b. A researcher wanted to know how students at the university felt about mandatory fees from all students to support a child care center for students with children. The researcher set up a table near the dormitory where many different types of students come and go. Those who stopped at the table and seemed friendly were asked to complete the questionnaire.
   c. In order to study differences in occupational aspirations of Catholic high school students and public high school students, a researcher randomly sampled (using school rosters with a random number table) 200 students from the largest Catholic high school and the largest public high school.
   d. In order to learn more about teachers' feelings about their personal safety while at school, a questionnaire was printed in a nationwide subscription journal of interest to many teachers. Teachers were asked to complete the questionnaire and mail it (postage paid) to the journal headquarters for tabulation.

e. In order to study the factors that lead teachers in general to quit the profession, a group of teachers threatening to quit was extensively interviewed. The researcher obtained the group after placing an announcement about the study on the teachers' bulletin board at a large elementary school.

7. Peruse online or e-journals in your field of interest. Locate one research report that uses a survey methodology. What was the sample size? How does that compare to the sample size guidelines for survey research described in this chapter? Was there an attempt to reduce or evaluate nonresponse bias?

8. Peruse online or e-journals in your field of interest. Locate one research report that compares two or more groups. What was the sample size of each group? How does that compare to the sample size guidelines for group comparison studies described in this chapter? Was there a reference to power and its connection to sample size? If so, what did the researcher(s) conclude about power and sample size?

ON YOUR OWN

Log on to the Web-based student study site at http://www.sagepub.com/eic for more information about the materials presented in this chapter, suggestions for activities, study aids such as electronic flashcards and review quizzes, a sample research proposal, and research recommendations that include journal article links (with discussion questions and an article evaluation guide) and questions related to this chapter.

9

MEASUREMENT IN RESEARCH

OUTLINE

OVERVIEW

The previous chapter focused on the important issues related to sampling in the collection of data. Another issue faced by researchers during the process of data collection is measurement soundness. There is little chance of answering the research question, or fairly testing the research hypothesis, without the right quantity (sampling) and quality (measurement soundness) of educational data. This chapter focuses on measurement and provides a basis for answering the question "How useful are the data?" Measurement soundness involves reliability and validity, and it is particularly important because without it, researchers may be studying something different from what they *think* they are studying.

Instrumentation: Collection of Data From Participants

This section addresses one of the most important issues faced by educational researchers: the worth of measured outcomes. Proper sampling of research participants does little good if the quality of measures used is questionable. Just as the strength of a chain is measured by its weakest link, the value of a research study is often compromised by a weak step in the research process. Often one weak step is the measurement process, usually called *instrumentation.* Meaningful research questions, even with strong sampling designs, can be rendered pointless if the researchers' measures, or instruments, are not sound. If the researcher is not measuring what is *supposed* to be measured, then how can the results be meaningfully interpreted? It turns out that measurement soundness is captured by two qualities: reliability and validity. This section looks at the important concerns surrounding the measurement of hypothesized effects in educational research, or B in the expression If A, then B.

INSTRUMENTATION: A threat to internal validity that includes changes in the measuring device or measuring procedures between a pretest and posttest. It also refers to the process of gathering data with the use of measuring tools such as tests or surveys.

Introduction to Reliability and Validity

Recall from Chapter 5 that a researcher's outcome measure is usually referred to as the *dependent variable.* High priority is placed on the dependent variable satisfying at least two criteria: reliability and validity. *Reliability* refers to the *consistency* of the outcome measure; *validity* refers to the *accuracy of inferences* that are made on the basis of the outcome measure.

RELIABILITY: The consistency of measures indexed by an estimate of errors contained within a set of scores.

An example of a reliable (consistent) measure is one that yields the same (or similar) score if a person were tested twice. An example of a valid measure is one where a prediction made from a score is true, as in the case of the (hypothetical) ABC Test of School Attitude if it can be said that Samuel actually dropped out of high school in accordance with a prediction made on the basis of his ninth-grade test score. Dependent variables should be reliable and valid no matter how they were obtained and in what form they were used (ratings, observations, surveys, portfolios, interviews, formal testing, etc.).

This is important for an obvious reason: If the researcher is not measuring what he or she thinks is being measured, then the research question cannot be answered. (Some other research question may be answered, but how would the researcher even know what the question was?) For example, a researcher may think that what is being measured is spelling ability, when in fact it is really hearing ability. Or maybe the researcher thinks that what is being measured is school ability (intelligence), when in fact it is pure motivation to do well in school. Research is meaningless to the extent that the dependent variable fails to measure what it is supposed to measure.

The concepts of reliability and validity are broadly applicable, and there are no measures in educational research that are exempt from meeting the standards imposed by these concepts. This is true despite the huge variation in dependent variables used by educational researchers. Chapter 4 described the of the myriad measures used in educational research, all of which should "measure up" to be useful.

HIGHLIGHT AND LEARNING CHECK 9-1

Instrumentation

Instrumentation involves the use of measuring tools to gather data. Researchers try to maximize the reliability (consistency) and validity (meaningfulness) of their measures. Reliable measures lack error (e.g., haphazard influences due to inattention, carelessness, confusion, etc.), and valid measures permit researchers to make accurate inferences based on a score. Why is it important that researchers' measures be both reliable and valid?

The important concepts of reliability and validity are rather technical, and they are best understood by reference to two statistics: *variance* and *correlation*. These will be briefly explained in the sections that follow. Then we will see how they help explain the concepts of reliability and validity.

CRITICAL THINKER ALERT 9-1

Consistent and Meaningful

The best everyday word for reliability is *consistent;* the best everyday word for validity is *meaningful.*

Discussion: The bathroom scale is an example of a measuring instrument that yields *consistently meaningful* "scores." Can you think of other everyday instruments that can also be described as reliable and valid? Can you think of ones that are inconsistent and less meaningful—very frustrating ones?

Variance

In Chapter 8 we saw how the standard deviation was computed from a set of scores, and how it was interpreted by reference to the normal distribution. *The variance* is the *square of the standard deviation.* (Since the variance is calculated first, it is more precise to say that the standard deviation is the square root of the variance.) If the standard deviation of a set of scores is, say, 3, the variance becomes 9. The variance is not interpreted by reference to the normal curve; in fact, it is not interpreted against any "backdrop." Simply, we can say that if a set of scores

VARIANCE: A measure of dispersion among a set of scores (the square of the standard deviation).

has a variance of 45, and another set has a variance of 66, then the latter set of scores is more variable (scattered or dispersed) about the mean. Like the standard deviation, higher values in variance describe greater scatter among scores. In a very general way, educational researchers study the variance, or differences, in measures, like achievement test scores. The goal of much research effort in education is to explain variance.

What contributes to this variance? How can this variance be explained? If the variance of a set of reading achievement scores were 450, researchers could begin to *partition* (or break up) this value by, for example, attributing 80 units of the 450 units of variance to the completeness of homework reading assignments, 50 units to the method of grouping used during reading instruction, 30 units to the level of parental involvement, 50 units to socioeconomic status, and 10 units to being male or female. You get the idea. In this sense, the study of variance in measures and its partitioning ("explanation") is a primary focus of educational researchers.

Correlation*

In an attempt to explain the variance in a research study, researchers frequently determine what *other* variables are related to scores obtained in a study. We can learn a great deal about the meaning of test scores by determining whether they are related to other variables. The primary method for examining relationships between two or more variables (hence explaining variance) is via a statistical maneuver called the *correlation coefficient.* This technique is best explained by its visual representation, the *scattergram.*

CORRELATION COEFFICIENT: A statistical index of the degree of linear association between two measures (ranging from −1.00 to +1.00) revealing its strength and direction.

SCATTERGRAM: A plot of paired scores revealing a visual display of a correlation. It is also known as a scatterplot or scatter diagram.

By way of illustration, let us consider one class, Ms. Robinson's, and see whether students' reading scores are related to, or correlated with, their scores on a math test as shown in Table 9.1.

Constructing a scattergram of these scores involves finding the intersection of each student's two scores from two axes, or lines, drawn at right angles (with each axis representing a test). Let's see how this is done. One of the students in Ms. Robinson's class, Stan, scored 91 on the reading test and 14 on the math test. Figure 9.1 shows his point as the intersection of his reading score (along the horizontal axis) and his math score (along the vertical axis) using bold lines.

Each of Ms. Robinson's students can be similarly represented on the scattergram shown in Figure 9.1. This is indicated by bold lines revealing the two axes for Stan's scores; you will have to imagine the others. These bold lines do not appear on scattergrams; they are shown here only to illustrate the process.

Note that the plot of intersection points in Figure 9.1 shows that high reading scores are associated with high math scores, and low reading scores are associated with low math scores. Such relationships are said to be *positive* since high scores

*The material in this section was adapted from *Educational Psychology in the Classroom,* 7th edition, by H. C. Lindgren and W. N. Suter. 1985. Reprinted with permission of Wadsworth, a division of Thomson Learning: www.thomsonrights.com. Fax 800-730-2215.

TABLE 9.1 **Ms. Robinson's Students' Paired Reading and Math Test Scores**

Student	Reading Score	Math Score
Daniel	70	6
Juan	73	5
Marsha	70	5
Bill	73	9
Rujal	89	15
Karyn	61	3
Steve	76	8
Bobbie	73	7
Stan	91	14
Stella	73	6
Rita	69	7
Marco	61	3
William	70	7
Thom	73	6
Georgette	94	12
Nancy	76	8
Nambodiri	90	10
Kathy	89	12
Maggie	78	6
John	78	5
Sam	59	3
Peter	54	5
Gretchen	78	7
Linda	69	7
Susan	84	9

Source: Adapted from *Educational Psychology in the Classroom,* 7th edition, by H. C. Lindgren and W. N. Suter. 1985. Reprinted with permission of Wadsworth, a division of Thomson Learning: www.thomsonrights.com. Fax 800-730-2215.

tend to occur together and low scores tend to occur together. When this happens, the scores distribute themselves along an imaginary line running from the lower left to the upper right. You can imagine a straight—but tilted—line running through the points (from the lower left to the upper right). The points themselves are scattered above and below this line. A *negative* relationship, by contrast, occurs when *high* scores on one variable are associated with *low* scores on the other variable. The plot of points in that case would extend from the upper left to the lower right as shown in Figure 9.2. (Clearly, the scores underlying the scattergram in Figure 9.2 are different from those in Figure 9.1 since the relationship is negative. These scores could be reconstructed, however, from the scattergram itself.)

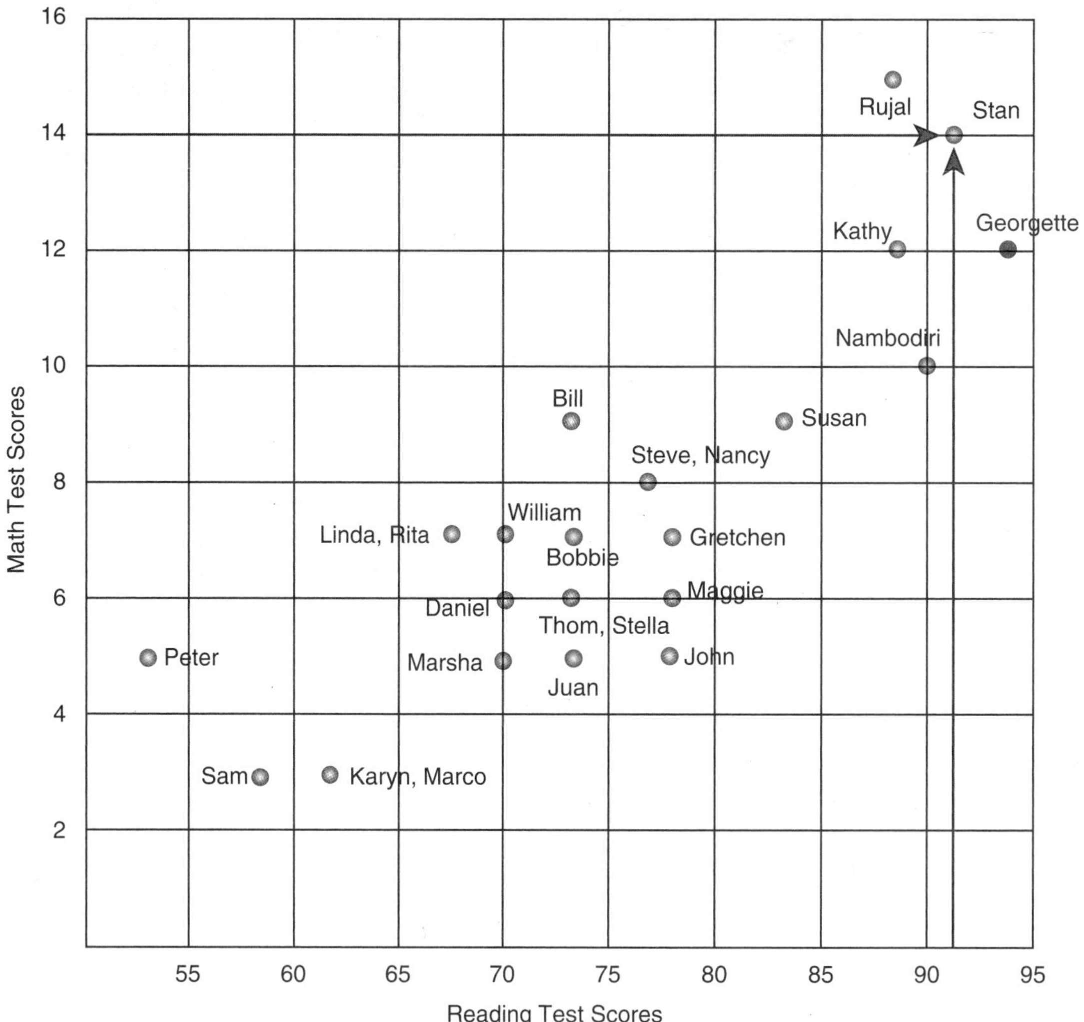

Figure 9.1 Scattergram of reading and math scores. The scores appear in Table 9.1 (students in Ms. Robinson's class). Stan's scores are plotted using bold lines, but the whole plot reveals a positive relationship (scores "swarming" from the lower left to the upper right).

Source: Adapted from *Educational Psychology in the Classroom,* 7th edition, by H. C. Lindgren and W. N. Suter. 1985. Reprinted with permission of Wadsworth, a division of Thomson Learning: www.thomsonrights.com. Fax 800-730-2215.

When there is no relationship between variables, or test scores, then there is no systematic tendency for high scores on one variable to be associated with high *or* low scores on the other variable. If Ms. Robinson's reading and math scores were *unrelated,* then high scores on the reading test would be associated equally often with high, moderate, and low scores on the math test. This lack of relationship would appear on a scattergram as a round cloudburst, or "shotgun" blast of points as illustrated in Figure 9.3.

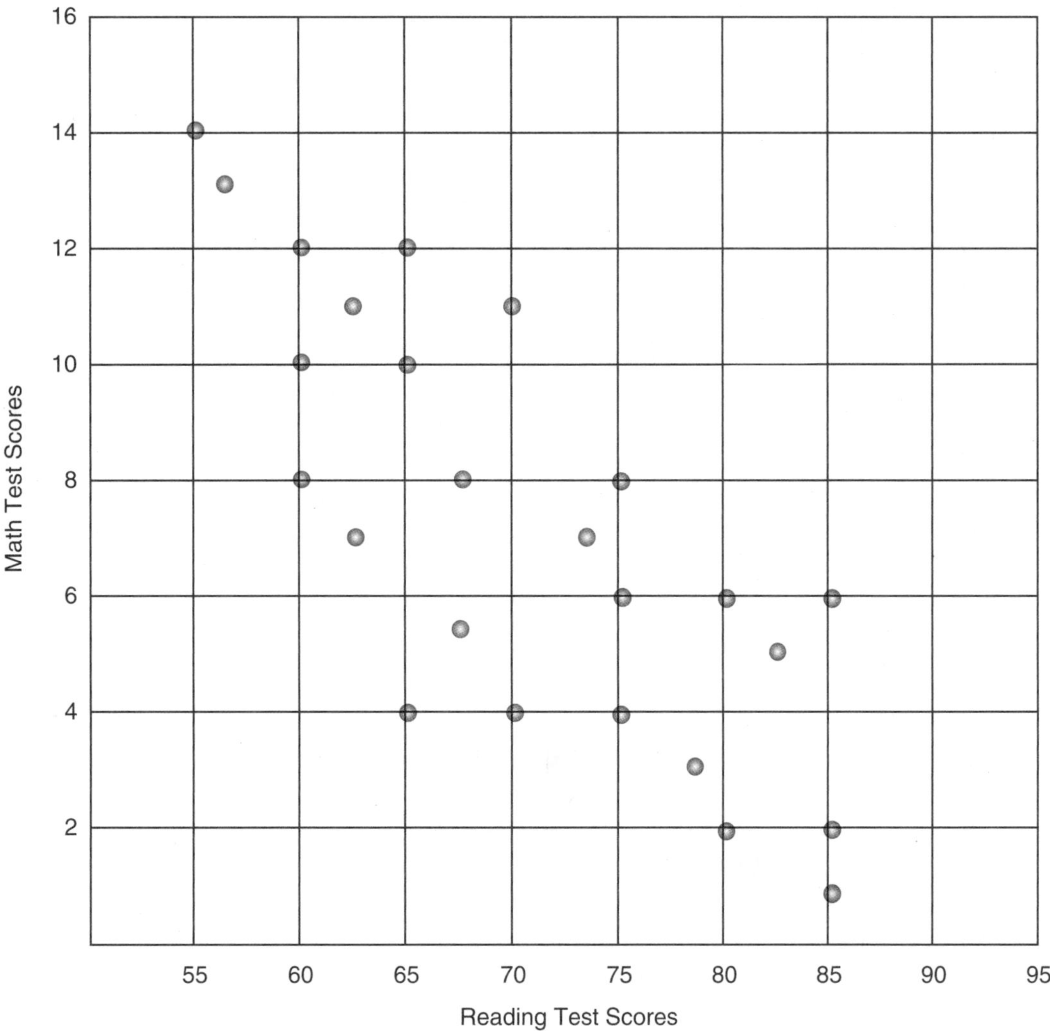

Figure 9.2 Scattergram of scores showing a negative relationship. Notice that scores "swarm" from the upper left to the lower right.

Source: *Educational Psychology in the Classroom* (7th ed., p. 547), by H. C. Lindgren and W. N. Suter, 1985, Pacific Grove, CA: Brooks/Cole.

The exact relationship shown visually on a scattergram can be determined by a *correlation coefficient,* which quantifies the extent to which the variables are linearly related (that is, conform to a straight line pattern). The correlation coefficient, symbolized as r, is a single value, or index, that ranges between −1.00 and +1.00 and describes both the *direction* (negative or positive) and *strength* of the relationship. The higher the r (the closer to 1, either positive or negative), the greater the strength or magnitude of the relationship. Strong relationships on a scattergram will show up as points that appear to fall along a

POSITIVE CORRELATION: A tendency of high scores on one variable to be linked to high scores on another variable (and of low scores to be linked with low scores).

NEGATIVE CORRELATION: A tendency of high scores on one variable to be linked to low scores on another variable (and of low scores to be linked with high scores).

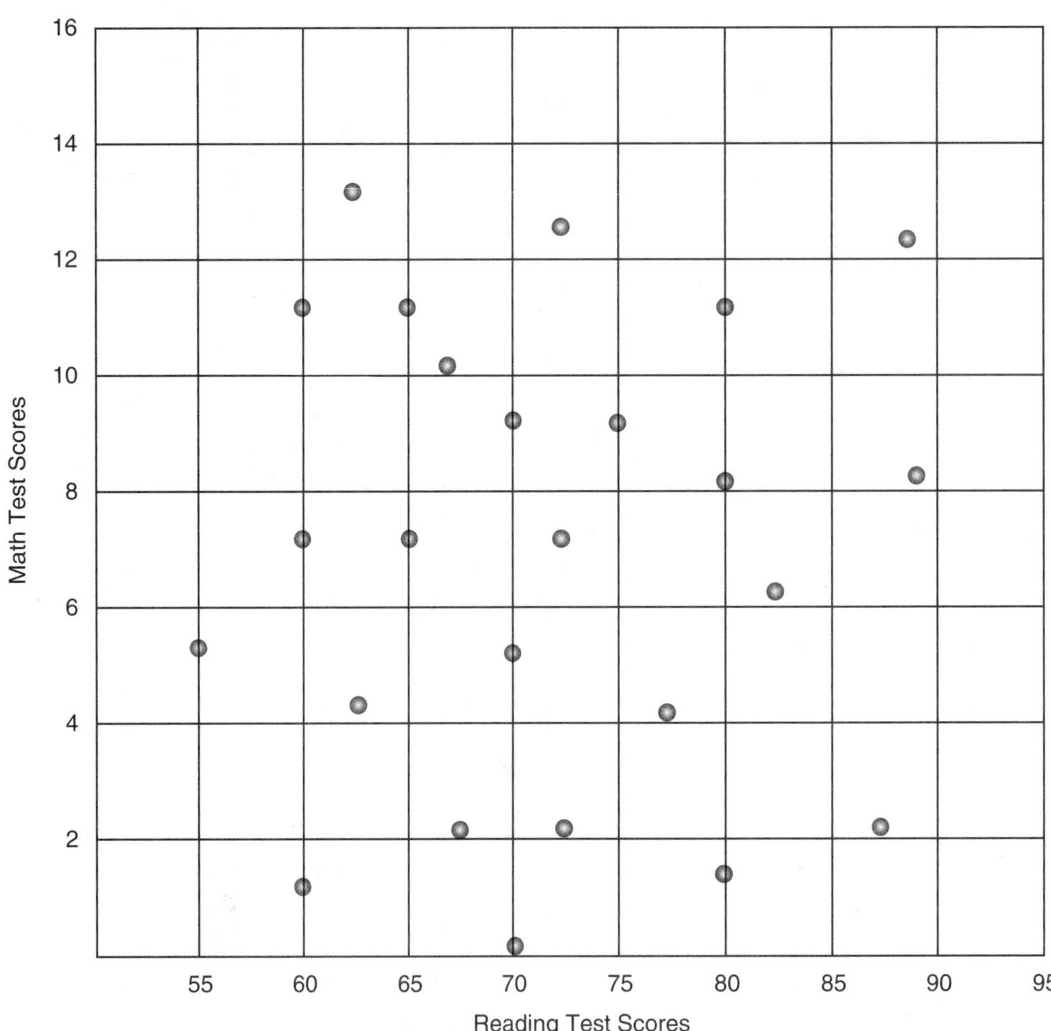

Figure 9.3 Scattergram of scores showing no relationship. Notice the "blob" with no linear pattern.

Source: *Educational Psychology in the Classroom* (7th ed., p. 547), by H. C. Lindgren and W. N. Suter, 1985, Pacific Grove, CA: Brooks/Cole.

tilted straight line, as in Figure 9.1 (positive) or Figure 9.2 (negative); weak or nonexistent relationships appear as a "blob" of points with little or no discernible straight-line pattern, as in Figure 9.3.

Variables which are not related at all (as in Figure 9.3) are summarized with an *r* of zero. Consider the last digit of your phone number and the last digit of your social security number. It is inconceivable that these are related in any way, hence a scattergram would be a round "blob" of points, as in Figure 9.3, and the correlation coefficient *r* would equal zero. (You might try constructing a scattergram with both axes running from 0 to 9, and in your class confirm this "blob" with real data.)

HIGHLIGHT AND LEARNING CHECK 9-2

Variance and Correlation

Variance is the square of the standard deviation, a measure of dispersion in a set of scores. *Correlation* is a measure of the relationship between two sets of scores. Scores are related when one set is predictable, to some extent, from knowledge of the other (e.g., high scores tend to go together; same with low scores). (High scores on one measure may also be associated with low scores on the other measure.) Explain why these two sets of paired scores appear to show a correlation: Set A (10, 4, 8, 13); Set B (22, 3, 17, 40). Which set appears to have the greatest variance?

In sum, positive correlations between Test A and Test B can be interpreted as The higher on test A, the higher on test B; negative correlations can be interpreted as The higher on test A, the lower on test B; and zero correlations can be interpreted as The higher on test A, the higher *or* lower on test B.

Because the test scores in Figure 9.1 tend to be positively correlated, you can predict with greater or lesser accuracy how well a student did on one test if you know the student's score on the other test. The accuracy of this prediction depends on how strongly the variables are correlated. Lower correlations (closer to zero), as we have seen, appear as plots with much scatter (no discernible pattern), hence lower predictability. Higher correlations (closer to −1 or +1), with little scatter on a plot around an imaginary line, permit more predictions. With these ideas of variance and correlation in mind, we can now sharpen our focus on one of the most basic qualities of a good measure, its reliability.

Reliability in Theory

The theory behind reliability is abstract and difficult to understand. Your understanding will be aided, however, with a concrete example. Let's focus on this example first, then we'll look at elements of the theory in reference to the example.

Consider the 10 scores shown in Table 9.2 from a 16-item spelling test. Assume that these 16 words were randomly chosen from a huge pool of 10,000 words, and this particular selection of words is "Spelling Test Form A." The number of words spelled correctly appears under the heading "Obtained Score." The mean and variance of these scores has been computed, and the results are also shown in Table 9.2. (Recall that the *variance* is the square of the standard deviation. See Chapter 8 for a review of the standard deviation and its calculation.)

True Scores

In theory, embedded within each one of these obtained scores shown in Table 9.2 is a *true score,* or the score a student would obtain if there were no measurement error. (True scores are sometimes referred to as *universe* scores.) These true scores are only imagined, but you can think of a true score, in the case of spelling, as the score on a grand test using the huge pool of thousands of words which define the universe of all possible words (hence, the term *universe score*). (This true—universe—score would also contain no error due to inattention, fatigue, hearing factors, or any other influences that might skew the "truth.") For

TRUE SCORE: A theoretical construct referring to a person's score containing no error. It is also defined as one person's average on many tests of the same construct.

ERROR SCORE: A theoretical construct referring to the difference between a true score and an observed score.

TABLE 9.2 Number of Words Correct in Spelling Test Form A

Student	Obtained Score
Merry	8
Paula	7
Craig	9
Keith	8
Bryan	7
David	13
Roger	12
Kathy	12
Hazel	12
Eddie	15

Note: Mean = 10.30; variance = 7.21

example, if the student can actually spell correctly 7,500 of the 10,000 words in the pool, then the student's true score is 75%. You would expect a score of 12 on any of the hundreds of tests formed by randomly selecting 16 words (75% of 16 is 12). This explanation assumes that the obtained score matches the true score on any given test, given no error.

Most obtained scores, of course, will not match the true score in the "real world." But the *average* of thousands and thousands of obtained scores on different forms of the 16-item spelling test constructed by sampling from the huge pool of words would equal the true score. Although *each* score over the many tests would not equal 12, the grand average would equal 12 since positive and negative measurement error balances over the long run. Think of error as being virtually any fluctuating influences that cause obtained scores to differ from the underlying "truth." Because sources of error such as good luck and bad luck (and all others) are random, their positive and negative influences tend to cancel or "wash" out, that is, on balance equal zero.

Of course, you would never expect anyone to actually take thousands of 16-item spelling tests, but you could at least *imagine* this for the purpose of understanding reliability. Reliability is best understood by recognizing that there might be a mismatch between a person's theoretical true score and real-world obtained score on a single test.

Reliability Defined

Test theory defines *reliability* as the "ratio of true score variance over obtained score variance" (true score variance divided by obtained score variance).

You can also think of reliability as the proportion of obtained score variance that is attributed to true score variance. This means that if we could calculate both the variance of obtained scores and the variance of true scores (which are never really known), then we could simply divide the true variance by the obtained variance. The problem is that the true variance can never be calculated directly. The obtained variance, by contrast, is easy to calculate (recall its value appears in Table 9.2).

It turns out that this proportion of obtained variance that is true variance (that is, reliability) can be calculated in a different but real-world way. Researchers need a second score, such as the score on a different set of 16 items (like Form B of the spelling test). These different forms of a test, with each form measuring the same ability or trait but with different items, are also referred to as *parallel* forms. With two scores for all test takers, we can simply calculate the correlation between the scores on both forms. Although the proof of this equivalence is not needed for this conceptual introduction, we thank the original statisticians for discovering that the correlation coefficient between parallel forms of a test equals the ratio of true score variance divided by obtained score variance. This equivalence provides the empirical and theoretical definition of reliability.

CRITICAL THINKER ALERT 9-2

Reliable, Not Valid

Instruments can (and often do) yield scores that are consistent without being meaningful. For example, hat size as a measure of intelligence among college students is a very reliable (consistent) measure but it is not a valid (meaningful) one.

Discussion: Can you offer other examples of consistent yet meaningless scores, ones that are reliable but not valid?

Let's presume that the correlation of scores shown in Table 9.2 with scores on a parallel form of the test was determined to be .58. This is the reliability coefficient, and it is probably easiest to think of reliability in terms of a percentage (although it is typically reported as a proportion): 58% of the variance in obtained scores is attributed to true scores. Think of variance as simply score differences across people—8 versus 13, 9 versus 12, 7 versus 9, and so on. Reliability tells us that 58% of those differences are due to true differences in the trait being measured. The other 42% are attributed to errors such as accidental mistakes, inattention, carelessness, bad luck (in the sense of getting stuck with difficult words), poor guessing, and myriad other influences (including all the counterparts, like good luck, etc.). Given the data in Table 9.2 with the obtained variance of 7.21, we know that about 4.18 of that amount is attributed to true score difference. We know this because the variance was 7.21 and the presumed reliability (or correlation with a parallel test) was .58 ($.58 \times 7.21 = 4.18$).

HIGHLIGHT AND LEARNING CHECK 9-3

True Score

A person's hypothetical true score (e.g., precise weight) contains no error. Conceptually, reliability is the ratio of participants' true score variance (no error) divided by their obtained score variance (true scores plus error). Because true scores are never known, alternative methods for calculating reliability have been developed. What are common sources of errors in measures? If a reliability is .60, about what proportion of the measure is attributable to *error* variance?

Above all else, you can think of reliable measures as those that have closely matching obtained and true scores. When obtained scores are not matched well (correlated) with true scores, the measures are said to be unreliable.

The definition of *reliability* (true score variance divided by obtained score variance) also suggests that reliability is the *square of the correlation between obtained scores and (hypothetical) true scores.* However you look at it, reliability is informative because it tells us what fraction of the "pie" (obtained variance) is linked to the "true stuff," so to speak. Researchers like their measures to contain at least 80% of the "truth," meaning that reliability coefficients above .80 are highly desirable.

Reliability in Practice

Test-Retest Reliability

What good are true scores, you may ask, since we never know true scores in the first place? True scores sound like Fantasy Land—what about the real world? This simple fact renders true scores unnecessary: Theorems in test theory prove that the correlation between obtained scores on Form A of a test and a retested Form B equals the reliability coefficient. (Recall the definition of *reliability*: the proportion of obtained score variance that is attributed to true score variance.) This type of reliability is known as the *coefficient of stability and equivalence.* The term *coefficient* refers to the value of the correlation, *stability* refers to the test-retest procedure, and *equivalence* refers to the parallel forms that were used. If a reliability procedure had used the *same* test as a retest after an interval of time (Form A given twice, the second time after, say, 2 months), the resultant reliability value would be known as the *coefficient of stability.* If a reliability study had used a different but parallel test in an immediate retest procedure, the resultant reliability value would be known as a *coefficient of equivalence.*

TEST-RETEST RELIABILITY: Test consistency determined by correlating test scores and retest scores using the same test (stability reliability) or a similar test (equivalence reliability).

Internal Consistency Reliability: Split-Half, KR20 and KR21, and Alpha

What happens, you may wonder, if a retest with the same or parallel form is simply not possible? There is a solution known as *split-half reliability*. This is a subtype of a more general form of reliability called *internal consistency* reliability. It involves splitting a single test into two equivalent (parallel) halves. An early form of this type of reliability split a test into halves by scoring all even-numbered items and all odd-numbered items. You can think of split-half reliability as a type of retest using two tests (each only half as long) given *without* any time interval between two test sessions. These two (half) test scores are then correlated in the usual way. Split-half reliability involves a statistical adjustment called Spearman-Brown *(SB)* to compensate for the shortened length of the two half-tests. The formula is:

INTERNAL CONSISTENCY RELIABILITY: Test consistency determined by correlating test items within a single test (e.g., coefficient alpha).

$$SB \text{ adjusted reliability} = \frac{2 \times \text{odd even correlation}}{\text{odd even correlation} + 1}$$

More modern versions of this odd-even split take into consideration all possible ways to split to test into two halves, including one random half with the other random half. (What is so special about odd versus even? Nothing.) There are, of course, thousands of ways to split a reasonably long test into two halves, and formulas have been developed which quickly compute the average of all possible split-half reliabilities. One common formula is KR20, named after its developers G. F. Kuder and M. W. Richardson and formula #20 in their article describing this type of reliability. KR20 can be estimated with a simpler formula, KR21, which assumes test item have equal difficulty levels (the KR21 estimate is slightly lower than the KR20 value). The simpler KR21 formula is:

$$\mathrm{KR21} = \frac{k}{k-1}\sqrt{1 - \frac{\mathrm{mean}(k - \mathrm{mean})}{k(\mathrm{variance})}}$$

where k refers to the number of items on the test.

KR20 and KR21 are limited to the extent that test items must be scored on a right-or-wrong (1 or 0) scale. Many measurement scales have other values (e.g., a 1–7 extent of agreement scale or a 1–5 frequency of occurrence scale). Another reliability formula has been developed for more complex scales called *Cronbach's alpha,* after its developer L. J. Cronbach. Alpha, as it turns out, is a general, all-purpose formula because if applied to a right-wrong scale (1 or 0), it is equivalent to KR20. Hence, alpha can be applied to *all* types of scales (including right-or-wrong, 1–7 agree-disagree, etc.), and appears to be the most widely used form for assessing internal consistency reliability. This is because many measuring instruments depart from a simple right-or-wrong scoring system. Furthermore, research studies often take advantage of computing reliability via the internal consistency approach (namely, Cronbach's alpha), eliminating the need for retesting with a parallel form.

All internal consistency reliability coefficients can be interpreted as the expected correlation between one test and a hypothetical parallel form administered without any time interval. As such, these forms of reliability can also be interpreted in terms of the percentage of obtained variance that is true variance. Presuming Cronbach's alpha was .58 given the data in Table 9.2, we can say that 58% of the differences (or variance) in scores can be traced to true (or "real") differences in the ability being measured; the other 42% can be attributed to unwanted random error.

CRITICAL THINKER ALERT 9-3

Cronbach's Alpha

Internal consistency reliability (e.g., Cronbach's alpha) is probably the most commonly reported type of reliability. This type of reliability does not address the consistency of scores over time.

Discussion: Explain the importance of inquiring into the *type* of reliability reported in research. Why is Cronbach's alpha (only) less appropriate than test-retest reliability when researching presumably stable traits such as sociability?

Inter-Rater Reliability

Researchers often use raters to collect information which serves as the dependent variable. Examples here include observers' rating of second graders' hyperactivity, teachers' effectiveness, tenth graders' creativity, eighth graders' writing ability, seventh graders' self-esteem, and a school's climate. Inter-rater reliability can be applied to these situations in order to determine the consistency of observations. Lack of inter-rater reliability would be evident if in scoring a student's essay, one rater awarded it a rating of 7 (on a 1–7 scale) and another rater awarded it a 2. When raters disagree, the researcher cannot be certain about the "truth." This type of inconsistency suggests error, for if there exists a "truth" about the scored essay (let's say it is a true 7), then both raters cannot be correct.

INTER-RATER RELIABILITY: Rater relative consistency determined by correlating two or more raters' ratings.

Inter-rater reliability can be determined by the familiar correlation maneuver. In the case of two raters, a scattergram of both raters' ratings of several essays provides us with a visual display of their consistency. Examine the two plots in Figures 9.4 and 9.5.

As revealed by the wide scatter, it is clear from Figure 9.4 that little or no consistency exists. By contrast, Figure 9.5 shows general consistency as evidenced by the lack of scatter and a clear lower-left to upper-right trend (a low-with-low and high-with-high tendency across ratings). High inter-rater reliability is usually obtainable when raters are sufficiently trained with practice and feedback and can agree on what they are being asked to rate. For example, raters would not be expected to visit

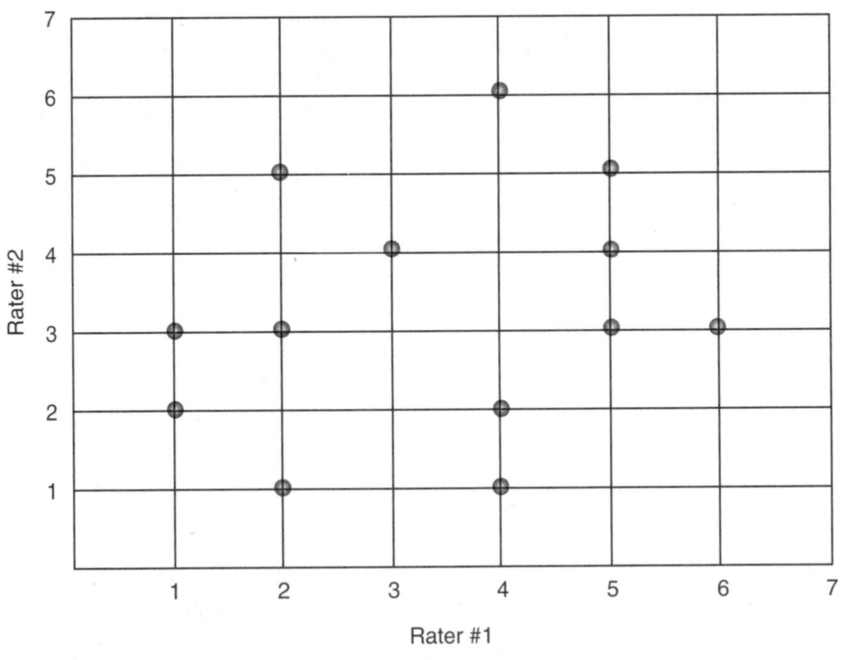

Figure 9.4 Scattergram showing two raters' evaluations and low inter-rater reliability. The reliability is .22, low by any standard.

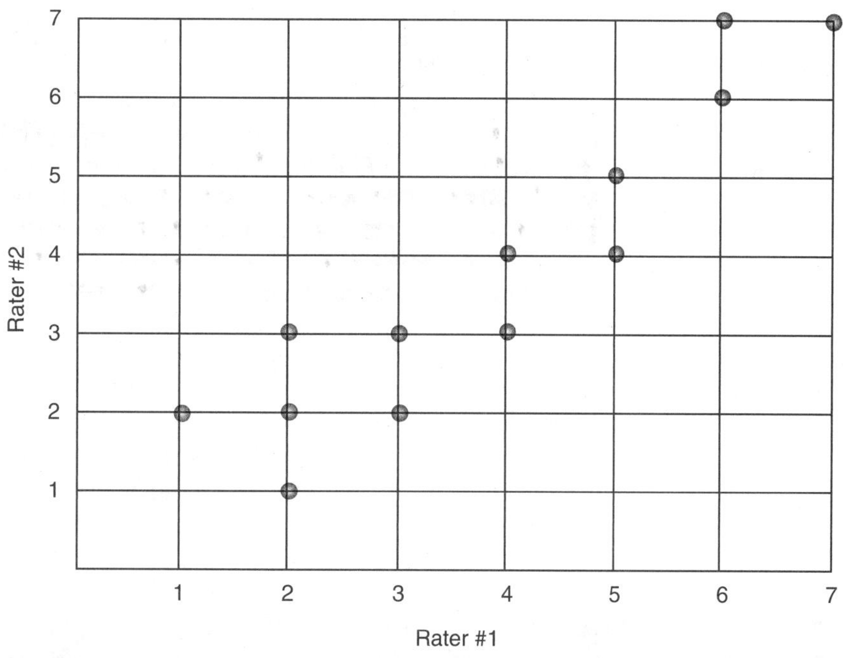

Figure 9.5 Scattergram showing two raters' evaluation and high inter-rater reliability. Its value of .92 reveals overall consistency.

schools and simply rate the overall "climate." They would be asked to evaluate specific dimensions, such as students' behavior, administrators' friendliness, teachers' burnout, or whatever factors are agreed upon as contributors to school climate.

> **HIGHLIGHT AND LEARNING CHECK 9-4**
>
> ## Reliability as Correlation
>
> Reliability computed in practice involves some type of correlation, including *test-retest* (correlating scores on the same or similar test, yielding *stability* and *equivalence* coefficients, respectively), *internal consistency* (correlating item responses on the same test, such as *alpha* coefficient), and *inter-rater* (correlating responses among raters). Each type of reliability is sensitive to different types of errors (time, forms, items, and raters). All types of reliability coefficients yield reliability coefficients between 0 and 1.00, revealing the relative amount of true score variance. Explain why different research situations may require different types of reliability.

There are other formulas that can be used to determine the reliability of more than just two raters (not surprisingly, the formulas are correlation maneuvers called *correlation ratios*). Also, inter-rater reliability coefficients are sensitive to consistency in terms of *relative* agreement; they do not determine absolute agreement. For example, Rater A may rate three essays using ratings of 2, 3, 4; Rater B may rate the same essays 5, 6, 7. Rater B is simply more lenient than Rater A and believes all of the essays deserve higher ratings than those awarded by Rater A. There is perfect relative agreement, however, since the three essays can be rank ordered to show the same ratings. This is a case of perfect reliability but zero agreement (none of the ratings match). An *agreement index* can be calculated by dividing the total number of agreements by the total number of agreements plus disagreements.

Reliability and Types of Error

We have seen that reliability can be explained in terms of true score variance. Reliability can also be described in terms of *consistency* (or *dependability, reproducibility,* etc.). This consistency can be thought of as consistency over four general sources: time, forms, items, and raters. Consistency over time is often referred to as *stability* (or simply *test-retest reliability*); consistency between forms as *equivalence* (or *parallel form reliability*); consistency across items as *internal consistency reliability*; and consistency between or among raters as *inter-rater reliability* (or *relative agreement*). These different types of reliability are sensitive to different sources of error (which appears as inconsistency), and there is *no* reason to expect their equivalence. Because of this, it should not be assumed that, for example, internal consistency (error due to item variation) would be the same as stability (error due to time factors). Although different types of reliability are conceptually similar (all are linked to true variance and are sensitive to error influences), we would not expect them to be equivalent in practice. The different types of reliability are summarized in Table 9.3.

TABLE 9.3 Types of Reliability Using the ABC Test of Spelling

Types of Reliability	Sources of Error	Questions
Stability (Test-Retest)	Time	Are scores similar at both times?
Equivalence (Parallel Form)	Forms	Are scores similar on both forms?
Internal Consistency (e.g., Alpha)	Items	Are responses similar across items?
Observer (Inter-Rater)	Raters	Are raters in relative agreement?

CRITICAL THINKER ALERT 9-4

Types of Reliability

When one refers to the reliability of test scores, it is important to specify a type of reliability. Each type of reliability is sensitive to different sources of error (time, form, items, and raters).

Discussion: Think about instruments designed to measure change over time. In these cases, is consistency over time always desirable?

Reliability of Scores, Not Tests

Perhaps the most misunderstood fact about reliability is that it describes a quality of a *set of scores* produced by a testing instrument and not the instrument itself.

Because of this, it is not technically correct to say that such-and-such instrument has a reliability of .85 (or whatever the value). By contrast, you should say that the *set of scores* from a particular sample in a specific situation can be described with a reliability of .85.

The reliability of scores from a test is influenced greatly by the composition of the sample taking the test. When there is a large variance in scores (a great range of talent, spread in ability, etc.), reliability tends to be *high*. By contrast, when there is small variance (few differences), reliability tends to *decrease.* This is one reason why a test may produce scores with a reliability of .90 in one study and scores with a reliability of .45 in another. It is the amount of variability in a group, not the size of the group per se, that affects reliability. (The size of the sample affects reliability only to the extent that it affects its variability, which it may or may not.)

CRITICAL THINKER ALERT 9-5

Group Variability

Reliability is very sensitive to group variability. The reliability of a set of scores tends to increase with increasing dispersion among scores. Reliability tends to be low when there is little variability among scores.

Discussion: An instrument designed to measure math aptitude was administered to a group of students enrolled in Algebra II and a group of students enrolled in World History. Which group would have scores that are bound to be more reliable? Why?

The introduction of *un*reliability (score *in*consistency) in a set of data lowers the sensitivity or power of a statistical test used to analyze data. This lack of sensitivity or power in a statistical test makes it more difficult to find relationships between variables, when in fact relationships do exist in the population represented by the sample. In other words, unreliability tends to increase the probability of concluding that a relationship does *not* exist in the population when, in reality, it does. All sources of error in measurement tend to contribute to this "missed sighting."

In published research, one typically finds a statement describing the reliability of the instrument being used to answer the research question. (More technically, it is the reliability of scores produced by that instrument.) Unfortunately, this statement often refers to the reliability of the instrument as used in another study. This is unfortunate because reliability is influenced by many factors, and the reliability of scores reported in one research study may be very different from the reliability of scores reported using a different sample. Therefore, in a published research report, reliability coefficients should always be reported describing the data collected from the instrument *as used in the study.*

CRITICAL THINKER ALERT 9-6

Reliable Scores

It makes no sense to refer to "the reliability of a test." Tests don't have reliability. What is reliable or not is the *set of scores* produced by a test. Depending on the characteristics of the group being tested, scores from one group might be far more reliable than scores from a different group.

Discussion: Reliability is a statistical index, computed from scores, not from pages comprising a test or measuring instrument. Given this, identify what is wrong with the following claim: "This instrument is guaranteed to have a reliability coefficient of .80 or higher when used in your school."

Because another researcher's reliable data from a test may not generalize at all to your data from the same test, the computation of reliability in a published study should be routine. This is important because if it were low (for example, below .60), a fair test of the hypothesis would not be possible. How would you know whether a finding of "no difference" was because no relationship exists in the population or because the relationship exists but was missed due to unreliability (error) in the sampled data? You wouldn't know for sure, of course, but information about the reliability of the measures would help you make a more informed conclusion. A different conclusion would be made if no relationships were uncovered with reliable data versus if no relationships were uncovered with unreliable data. (The use of unreliable measures and a finding of "no difference" is clearly ambiguous, for you would not know whether the nil finding was due to there being no relationship in the population, a measuring device that was full of error, or both.)

HIGHLIGHT AND LEARNING CHECK 9-5

Reliability of Scores

Reliability coefficients are computed from sets of measures (data), not from instruments themselves. Because of this, it is appropriate to refer to the *reliability of scores,* not the reliability of tests. Explain how the same test might yield more or less reliable scores depending on the composition of the participants yielding the scores.

The reliability of measures is threatened, as we have seen, by the introduction of countless sources of error. There is one variable, however, that is known to *increase* the reliability of measurements. That variable is test length. With all other factors held constant, it can be shown that reliability increases as test length increases (assuming that the test is not so long that respondents become careless from fatigue). This should make some intuitive sense, for a very short (say, 2-item) test of spelling ability might yield a score of 2 out of 2 correct from a relatively poor speller—thanks to error due to lucky guesses. Error due to luck probably would not explain a good score on a longer test (30 out of 30 correct); the "truth" would more likely come out, maybe as a score of 5 out of 30. In fact, test developers don't worry much about lucky guesses, even on relatively short tests. The probability of scoring 100% by correctly guessing only 5 multiple-choice questions, each with only four choices, is very slim indeed—1 out of 1024!

Standard Error of Measurement

The reliability coefficient is closely associated with another useful measurement statistic, called the *standard error of measurement* (*SEM*). Whereas the reliability coefficient describes a *set* of measures, the *SEM* is more useful for interpreting a *single* score. Given one person's obtained score, we can use the *SEM* to estimate how far away the true score probably lies. About 68% of the test takers on a given test would have true scores that are within one *SEM* of their obtained scores; 95% would have true scores that are within two *SEM*s of their obtained scores. Only about 5% would have true scores that differed by more than two *SEM*s from their obtained scores. In other words, if you double the *SEM*, then add and subtract that value from the obtained score, you have a person's interval that probably includes the true score. This would be true for 95 out of 100 test takers with such intervals; whether it is true for one particular person is not known. We can only say that the interval *probably* spans (includes) the true score for a specific person since it does for 95% of the population.

STANDARD ERROR OF MEASUREMENT: A statistical index that estimates the amount of error in a single score.

Here is another example. If you score 500 on the GRE verbal section, and the *SEM* is 30, then we can say that your true score (in whatever the GRE verbal section measures) probably falls (with a .95 certainty) between 440 and 560. (Taking that test thousands of times would probably earn you a grand average between 440 and 560.)

The *SEM* can also be thought of as the standard deviation of one person's obtained scores around that person's true score. It has an easy calculation, if the reliability coefficient is known. The formula is:

$$SEM = SD\sqrt{1 - reliability}$$

where *SD* refers to the standard deviation of a set of scores.

Let's apply this formula to a set of intelligence test scores. Assume the standard deviation is about 15 and the reliability is about .89; we then have $SEM = 15\sqrt{1 - .89} = 5.00$ (rounded). If Mary scored 115 on an IQ test, her true score would probably fall (chances are 95 out of 100) in the interval 105 to 125.

The *SEM* has a use in classroom tests as well. For example, recent test scores for a course I teach had a reliability of .85 with a standard deviation of about 8, hence an *SEM* of about 3. The lower-bound cutoff for an A was 90%, but I lowered it by 3 points (the value of the *SEM*) to account for unreliability in the form of errors of measurement. A classroom test with a lower reliability, like .60, might warrant an adjusted cutoff two *SEM*s below the original one to account for substantial error of measurement.

HIGHLIGHT AND LEARNING CHECK 9-6

Standard Error of Measurement

The *standard error of measurement* (*SEM*) reveals the amount of error in a *single* score (contrasted with the reliability of a set of scores). Explain why a score of 70 and an *SEM* of 5 might be difficult to interpret given a "cutoff" criterion of 72.

CRITICAL THINKER ALERT 9-7

Standard Error of Measurement

Reliability describes the amount of error in a set of scores. The standard error of measurement describes error within a single score.

Discussion: Individual counseling in schools may involve the interpretation of test scores. What is more appropriate in this context–a reliability index or the standard error of measurement? Why?

Validity

Validity is considered the most important quality of a measured dependent variable. This is because *validity* is concerned with whether the instrument used actually measures what it is supposed to measure. The concern is as basic as these sample questions suggest:

- Do those ratings of hyperactivity really reflect hyperactivity and nothing else?
- Do those scores from the self-esteem instrument actually reflect self-esteem and nothing else?
- Does this test of scholastic aptitude actually predict school achievement?
- Does this test of science knowledge accurately measure the extent to which the course objectives were met?

Validity is the primary concern of all researchers who gather educational data. Reliability plays second fiddle to validity because reliability is of little concern if the measure is not a valid one. Who would care about reliability (consistency) if validity were lacking? There is no value in consistently measuring something that is off target, misguided, or simply the wrong construct. Reliability is a *necessary* condition for validity in the sense that reliability must be present for validity to exist. How can an instrument measure what it is *supposed* to measure if it is full of error? Reliability, though, does not *guarantee* validity. This is because a measure may be reliable but not measuring what it should. It might be reliably measuring something else.

VALIDITY: The meaningfulness of scores, which is often assessed by the accuracy of inferences made on the basis of test scores. It also refers to the extent to which a test measures what it is *supposed* to measure.

Keep in mind that reliability tells us how well an instrument is measuring *whatever it is measuring.* If it is measuring whatever it is measuring with little error, then we know that it is reliable. Reliability does not tell *what* is being measured, only how well it is measuring (whatever it is measuring). The issue of *what* is being measured is the sole concern with *validity.*

An image might help here, as shown in Figure 9.6.

Think about throwing darts at a target. Reliable tosses strike consistenly in one place, but that place may or may not be near the bull's eye. Hitting consistently in the lower left (or upper right) would illustrate reliability without validity—not too impressive. Tosses in the bull's eye, where they are supposed to be, would illustrate validity (and reliability). Like darts which consistently hit in the center, researchers strive for reliable and valid scores with their instruments.

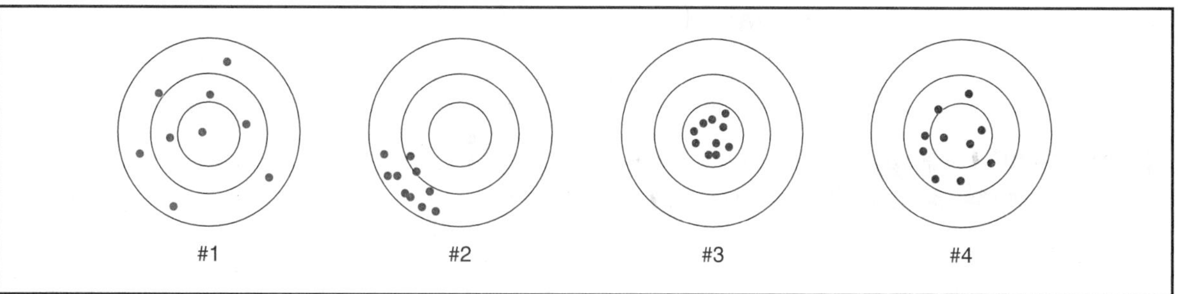

Figure 9.6 Reliability and validity applied to dart throwing. Darts thrown in the bull's eye are valid—that's where they are supposed to be. Darts thrown in a consistent area—anywhere on the target—are reliable. Note that throws can be reliably off target. In the figure above, #1 reveals low reliability and low validity, #2 reveals high reliability but low validity, #3 reveals high reliability and high validity, and #4 reveals fair reliability and fair validity.

Source: *Educational Research: A Guide to the Process* (p. 96), by N. E. Wallen and J. R. Fraenkel, 1991, New York: McGraw-Hill.

It is important to keep in mind the specific purpose for which a test was designed and constructed, or at least the specific purpose for which the test is being used. It makes little sense to discuss a test's validity in a broad sense. *It is far more meaningful to discuss a test's validity for a specific purpose.* (It may have been designed and constructed for a use different from its current use or specific use in a particular study.) Perhaps the best way to think about validity is this: *A measuring instrument yields valid scores to the extent that inferences made on the basis of test scores are in fact accurate.* The meaning of this definition will become clearer as we examine approaches to validity as practiced by educational researchers.

Researchers have found it is useful to approach the issue of validity from three angles, each angle being relevant for the specific purpose the instrument is intended to serve. These three types of validity are:

- Content
- Predictive
- Construct

In fact, there are several other types of validity, but these "big three" appear to cover the major concerns of most researchers. Each of these three types of validity will be described next.

CRITICAL THINKER ALERT 9-8

Validity for a Purpose

It makes little sense to refer to *the* validity of a test. A test has validity *for a specific purpose.* Depending on the purpose for which a test is put, it may or may not be valid. A measuring instrument yields valid scores to the extent that inferences made on the basis of test scores are accurate.

Discussion: Identify what is wrong with the following claim: "This test is guaranteed to be valid in your school." Why is it wrong?

Content Validity

Content validity is of greatest concern for researchers who study achievement. (It is also of prime importance for classroom teachers who construct classroom achievement tests.) As an example, consider the Stanford Achievement Test. This test was designed to guide teaching and learning toward high achievement by helping educators assess what students know and are able to do. A test with such a purpose must assess the extent to which educational objectives are being met, that is, whether students are learning what is being taught (assuming that what is taught matches the instructional objectives). It would be especially informative to determine which teaching methods and techniques, for example, are associated with unusually high achievement.

CONTENT VALIDITY: The extent to which a test reflects the domain of content that it presumably samples.

To meet this end, the constructors of the Stanford Achievement Test first reviewed states' and districts' guidelines and curricula as well as widely used textbooks at all levels. The test objectives were then formulated from a large pool of concepts and skills which were universally taught. At each step in the test construction, curriculum specialists and content area experts reviewed what are called *blueprints* or *curriculum frameworks* for determining the "breadth" and "depth" of tested objectives. Ultimately, the content validity of the Stanford Achievement Test was strengthened by assuring it contained a "representative" and "balanced" coverage of what is termed the *national consensus curriculum.* The developers of the Stanford Achievement Test recognized that content validity is the most important evidence of validity for an achievement battery. It was designed to mirror what is currently taught in schools throughout the United States. The content validity of test items was assured by a careful analysis of newly developed state content standards, curriculum materials, textbooks, instructional materials, and the content standards of many professional organizations (such as the National Council of Teachers of Mathematics).

Less careful test construction would have jeopardized the test's content validity by including mismatches between instructional objectives and test item content. The content validity of tests is important because without it, one would not know whether low achievement test scores were the result of learning deficits or learning-testing mismatches. Assessment of content validity is frequently made by expert judgments with the aid of descriptive statistics, as opposed to complex statistical manipulations. As a student, you've probably experienced the feeling of content *in*validity when you encountered a classroom test item that was not linked to any instructional material. That's not fair!

Predictive Validity

Very often, educational and psychological tests are constructed with the intention of predicting a future outcome. The SAT (previously the Scholastic Assessment Test and the Scholastic Ability Test) was constructed with this purpose in mind. Could high school students' success or failure in their first year of college be predicted on the basis of test scores? If so, then the SAT would have strengthened its validity for predicting academic success. (The SAT was developed for other purposes as well, including the tracking of ability on a national basis over time, since 1941.) Because the SAT was concerned with predicting college success, as opposed to assessing high school achievement, the concern was not with matching

PREDICTIVE VALIDITY: The extent to which test scores accurately predict an outcome (a criterion).

test items with high school curricula. The primary concern was assessing how well students could reason, both verbally and mathematically. The SAT, prior to its overhaul in 2005, sampled verbal reasoning skills in many ways, but most commonly through reading comprehension. The students' ability to answer questions after reading a passage is enhanced not so much by a knowledge base reflecting the high school curriculum as by an ability to comprehend written information and use verbal reasoning skills. One would gather information about the predictive validity of such a test by showing that scores are, in fact, linked to future measures of college success (e.g., grades), the criterion the test was supposed to measure.

As standardized tests evolve over the years, concepts about validity must also evolve. The SAT, for example, completed yet another major "makeover" due, in large part, to criticism about test fairness and concerns related to the value of test preparation. The high school class of 2005 began taking the new SAT in the areas of critical reading (previously titled "verbal"), writing (a new section that includes an essay component and knowledge of grammar), and math. Its validity changed too, for the SAT now reflects what high school students learn in a typical curriculum. It is, in other words, now more closely aligned with achievement testing, as opposed to aptitude testing, suggesting a greater concern with content (not predictive) validity.

One can easily imagine many contexts in which educators could use "crystal balls" in a predictive validity paradigm. Predicting an event like dropping out of high school by use of measures collected in junior high school is one example. This information could be used by targeting high risk students and intervening with appropriate methods shown to decrease the chances of dropping out. Forecasting in this way is valuable because once the dropping out process has begun, it is often too late to stop it.

Predicting which one of several methods of instruction is linked to the greatest probability of success is another application of predictive validity. For example, a student's preferred learning style could be measured on a scale of 1 to 10, reflecting a level of structure (lower scores reflect a preference for less structure and higher scores a preference for more structure). If it can be shown that scores on the learning style test do in fact predict which method of teaching results in the greatest success, then the scores could be used for placement recommendations. The test, therefore, would have predictive validity for that specific purpose.

A test given to kindergartners and designed to predict reading disabilities in the second grade or reading comprehension problems in the seventh grade would have obvious value in education. In many cases, the sooner the instructional intervention, the greater its success.

Construct Validity: Validation as a Process

As you might expect, the construct validity of measures is appropriate whenever the instrument is supposed to measure a construct. Recall from Chapter 5 that a *construct* is a label for an abstract trait or ability that is only presumed to exist—like "intelligence," undoubtedly the single most influential and enduring construct in education. Behind every construct exists a theory to explain it (recall that constructs don't exist in a vacuum). The theory, as we have seen, produces testable hypotheses. If the theory-driven hypotheses are supported using the instrument designed to measure the construct, then it can be said that the *construct validity* of the measure is

CONSTRUCT VALIDITY: The extent to which test scores accurately reflect the trait or ability that the test is presumed to measure.

CRITICAL THINKER ALERT 9-9

Ambiguous Validity

We have seen that the term *validity* in research is ambiguous. When one refers to the validity of a test, one should precede the term *validity* with another descriptor (e.g., *content validity, predictive validity,* or *construct validity*).

Discussion: Explain how the hypothetical test ABC Test of Pedagogical Skill might be valid for each *one* of the three types of validity, but not valid for the other two.

supported, at least partially. Notice that a bundle of three outcomes results from a favorable test of a theory: (1) The research hypothesis is supported, (2) the theory is made more credible, and (3) the construct validity of the measure is supported. Establishing the construct validity of a measure, then, is rather indirect and somewhat convoluted. Thus, construct validity cannot be demonstrated in a one-shot study. It is a slow process and parallels the same tedious path that leads to the eventual acceptance of a theory.

Construct validation can be easily sidetracked. This is because a research hypothesis may not be supported (maybe the theory that spun the hypothesis was wrong), even though the construct validity of the measure was intact. The construct validity of a measure is enhanced if the research hypothesis is supported, but a null research finding sheds no light on the construct validity of the measure. A null finding is ambiguous, because there are many reasons for a finding of no difference, aside from a lack of construct validity with the measure. Some examples of these include inadequate sample size (as we saw early in Chapter 8), poor controls, biases, and, of course, a flawed theory. Construct validation "piggybacks" on the process of supporting a research hypothesis and testing a theory.

HIGHLIGHT AND LEARNING CHECK 9-7

Validity

Validity is concerned with the accuracy of inferences one can make on the basis of a test score. It is also commonly described as the extent to which the test measures what it is *supposed* to measure, that is, its meaningfulness. Content validity is concerned with how well a test samples the entire domain of possible information. It is especially relevant in the construction of achievement tests. Predictive validity is concerned with how well a test score predicts an outcome (e.g., using a test score to predict the risk of failure). Construct validity is concerned with whether a test measures the trait or ability it is presumed to measure. Construct validation is often a complex process of validating the theory that explains the construct. Match these hypothetical test titles with the appropriate validation paradigm: Ace Test of Algebra II, Prime Test of Creativity, and Bravo Test of Teaching Potential.

How, you might wonder, are null research findings ever useful if they could always stem from measures which might lack construct validity? The truth is that construct validation is a *process*. Over time (a long time, usually), the construct validation of an instrument is said to be "established" (at least tentatively). It is conceivable that a researcher could devote a lifelong career to the construct validation of an instrument. The Weschler and Stanford-Binet intelligence scales, for example, are reasonably well accepted as construct valid measures of traditional intelligence (verbal, spatial, and numerical reasoning). (These tests were never intended to assess "street smarts," "people smarts," or introspective, athletic, or musical intelligence.) When these construct validated measures (or "gold standards") are used to test theories about intelligence, and the research hypotheses are not supported, then one can assuredly conclude that the theory which generated the research hypotheses is flawed and should be rejected. (This still assumes adequate sample size, proper controls, and the like.) Needless to say, it is highly desirable to use instruments with at least some level of established construct validity. This position, in its extreme, is dangerous, though, because it encourages scientific "ruts" and an unwillingness to explore new constructs or use innovative measures. (Many educators would argue that the traditional view of intelligence as verbal reasoning is one such rut.)

An Example: Self-Esteem

Let's explore another important construct, "self-esteem," to see how measures of this construct might be validated. At present, there appears to be no measure of self-esteem with established, long-lived validity (no "industry standard"). Researchers working in the area of self-esteem need a theory for guidance, and selection of a theory will further guide the choice (or construction) of an instrument used to measure self-esteem. The choice may center on, for example, the Coopersmith Self-Esteem Inventory (SEI; Coopersmith, 1967), specifically Version A, which has 50 true-or-false questions. If this instrument has construct validity, then it should be sensitive to the generally agreed-upon developmental changes in self-esteem. Berger (1991) reported, "In general, self-esteem, which is usually quite high in early childhood, decreases in middle childhood, reaching a low at about age 12 before it gradually rises again" (p. 396). The Coopersmith Self-Esteem Inventory when administered to children across this age span should show these peaks and valleys in scores if it is indeed measuring the trait (self-esteem) that it presumes to measure. If the scores show this pattern, then one can conclude that the Coopersmith Self-Esteem Inventory has one more notch recorded in support of its construct validity.

Another approach to the inch-by-inch construct validation of the Coopersmith Self-Esteem Inventory would be to match its scores with other measures believed to measure the same construct. The rationale here is simple: Two measures of the same

CRITICAL THINKER ALERT 9-10

Types of Validity

One finds many different terms in the research literature to describe approaches to measurement validity (e.g., criterion-related, discriminant, etc.). Each of these terms is best understood as a specific subtype of validity, subsumed by one of the three *major* types described in this chapter (content, predictive, and construct.)

Discussion: One might argue that all types of validity, despite the diverse collection of terms, are best understood as instances of one of the three general types (content, predictive, construct). Which general type do you think is the most all encompassing? Why do you think that?

"thing" should converge; in this case, they should be in agreement when used to measure the self-esteem of a group of participants. If the two tests reveal discrepant findings then, once again, the results are ambiguous. One (but which one?) or both of the instruments do not measure what they purport to measure, since if they did, the scores would have to be similar.

You may have guessed that there are countless ways to amass evidence in favor of construct validity. One final example will illustrate the range of approaches. The construct "self-esteem," a theory suggests, predicts not only that the self-esteem measure be related to other variables it should be related to but also that it *not* be related to variables it should *not* be related to. For example, "self-esteem" in theory should not be related to, say, "social desirability" (the tendency to portray oneself in a favorable light, even at the expense of honesty). If these two constructs are related, it suggests that the measure of self-esteem might be contaminated, to some degree, by this other personality trait. Such contamination would, of course, threaten the validity of the self-esteem test because it is supposed to measure self-esteem, not social desirability. One could also argue that "self-esteem" should not be related to, say, "preferred learning styles," but should be related to "scholastic achievement" (at least according to the theory that guided the development of the self-esteem instrument). Collecting data by administering the self-esteem, learning style, and achievement tests would provide information to evaluate the construct validity of the self-esteem inventory. Researchers often use the terms *divergent validity* (no relationship when none is expected) and *convergent validity* (a significant relationship when one is expected). Both types of validity may be thought of as subtypes of the more general *construct validity.*

Table 9.4 summarizes the major differences among content, predictive, and construct validity.

TABLE 9.4 Summary of Differences Among Content, Predictive, and Construct Validity

ABC Test of Vocabulary	
Content:	Does it measure the achievement of vocabulary knowledge as reflected in the instructional objectives?
Predictive:	Do test scores predict who will not do well in English next year?
Construct:	Does this test measure what we call verbal intelligence? Are hypotheses born from the theories of this trait supported when using this test?
XYZ Test of Creativity	
Content:	Does the test measure the flexible thinking that was taught in Lesson #1?
Predictive:	Do test scores predict who will earn patents?
Construct:	Does this test measure the trait of creativity? Are hypotheses born from the theories of this trait supported when using this test?

CRITICAL PERSPECTIVES 9-1

MEASUREMENT

Critical Thinking Toolbox

Critical thinking involves "busting apart" reasons into components. An unknown reason for a conclusion carries little weight. Critical thinkers are comfortable explaining their reasoning (Paul, Binker, Jensen, & Kreklau, 1990) and offer careful, reasoned arguments as opposed to using emotionalism.

Measurement in Quantitative Research

Measurement in quantitative research focuses on numeric data (quantities, counts, numbers, statistics, etc.), which are often gathered from formal instruments that are presumed to yield reliable and valid scores. Many instruments are standardized, both in administration and score reporting. The overriding concerns here are score consistency (reliability) and an empirical basis for validity (such as showing scores are significantly linked to important outcomes). Quantitative measures usually conform to scales that are easily transferred to spreadsheets (which are often large) and then imported into data analysis software programs that efficiently "crunch" the numbers. Measuring instruments (tools) in quantitative research are frequently revised until they conform to acceptable levels of reliability and validity (hard data).

Measurement in Qualitative Research

Measurement in qualitative research focuses on verbal descriptions and participants' own words. Data in the form of narratives are often derived from field notes and careful observations in a natural setting. Many data can be derived from documents, photographs, video, and similar rich sources of information. Interviews also provide data in qualitative studies after careful coding during the emergence of meaningful themes. Coding into categories is common, with each category revealing a qualitative difference. Measurement soundness is evaluated by concepts such as credibility, integrity, and confirmation. Further, qualitative researchers rely on techniques such as auditing (a "chain of evidence" reviewed by others) and memo writing (e.g., thinking on paper) to extract meaning from complex sources of data. Measurement in qualitative research is often described as "thick." The credibility of qualitative measures is enhanced by triangulation (the use of multiple yet converging methods, samples, places, times, etc.). The reliability of qualitative data, as compared to that of quantitative data, is less focused on consistency. The accuracy of observations is paramount, and techniques such as *participant review* are used to make certain all recordings and representations are accurate. As you might expect, the scales of measurement in qualitative research are frequently "nominal," meaning that coded values reflect qualitative differences (not numerical dimensions).

Measurement in Action Research

Action researchers in education use both qualitative and quantitative measures. The choice is wide open, as long as the measures conform to the practical and participatory nature of action research. Studying one's own practice poses measurement challenges that Mills (2003) believes are best understood by three *E*s: experiencing, enquiring, and examining. *Experiencing* involves observation of some sort, the result being observation records such as journals, field notes, or videotape samples of interaction. These records have direct implications for measurement, usually in the form of numerical counts (quantitative data) or narrative themes or codes (qualitative data). *Enquiring* involves soliciting information from participants, often during interviews, or by administering instruments such as questionnaires, scales, and tests. Enquiring measures can be either qualitative or quantitative. *Examining* involves extracting meaning from sources such as existing documents and artifacts as well as making new records for assessment and evaluation. Ultimately, these measures will be helpful for developing and evaluating a plan for action.

Critical Thinking Questions

In a famous book titled *The Mismeasure of Man,* Stephen Jay Gould (1981) argued that our urge to rank people is strong but misguided, in part because the mind cannot be reduced to numbers. If Gould had been an educational researcher, what approach to measurement would he have favored? What are your reasons for thinking this? What approach to measurement appears to dominate data gathering in our schools today? What are your reasons for thinking this? Do you think opinions regarding high-stakes assessments in schools are clouded by emotional appeals?

Reliability and Validity in a Published Report on School Climate

This section describes how the important concepts of reliability and validity are applied in a published research investigation of an interesting construct: "school climate" (Brand, Felner, Shim, Seitsinger, & Dumas, 2003).

Brand and colleagues believe that the climate, or social environment, of a school has a "profound and pervasive impact" on students. In order to study school climate and its influences, they set out to construct a reliable and useful (valid) measure of middle and secondary whole school social climate, one developed from a large and diverse but representative sample of schools. To accomplish this research objective, Brand and colleagues used a wealth of data, including surveys or checklists from students, teachers, parents, staff, and administrators; student achievement and demographic data; and school characteristics. Much data came from 2000 K–12 schools across 25 states with unusually high student and teacher response rates (80% to 90%). (The researchers relied heavily on a large data set managed by the Project on High Performance Learning Communities.)

Phase 1 of their instrument development process focused on pilot work, field testing, and "exploratory" analysis. A large pool of potential items was generated from the research literature related to organizational climate and students' adjustment (such as disciplinary harshness, student input in decision making, clarity of rules, safety, etc.). Over 1,000 students' responses to a survey helped revise rating items; a revision was then administered to several thousand other students across 30 schools. Statistical analysis enabled further revision, the result being an instrument with 50 rating items that clustered around 10 distinct dimensions (or factors) of school climate (such as instructional innovation, peer interactions, teacher support, etc.).

Phase 2 involved testing this instrument using a larger and more diverse sample of students and schools (over 100,000 students in 188 schools) for the purpose of establishing the reliability (internal consistency) of the hypothesized dimensions of school climate, assuring consistent student responses within the same school, and determining the stability of climate over time (even with predictable student turnover). Even larger student samples and more schools were obtained for Year 2 and Year 3 comparisons (referred to as *cohorts*, meaning groups that are studied over time). Students and schools were fully representative of the diversity that exists across 16 states.

The purpose of both Phase 1 and Phase 2 data analysis was to describe the structure of students' perceptions of school climate and establish the reliability of those perceptions as measured by their instrument. As we've seen, reliability is concerned with errors of measurement. Researchers seek to maximize reliability so that the differences obtained can more confidently be attributed to true differences in the construct being measured. Notice that Brand and colleagues in Phase 1 did not seek to obtain information on the validity of their instrument (its meaningfulness or usefulness)—they sought only information on its reliability (consistency of responses). There is little sense validating an instrument without first establishing its reliability, or the extent to which the scores differences reflect true differences in whatever is being measured.

Brand and colleagues reported that a large sample of student responses to their school climate instrument provided "moderate to high" levels of scale reliability (on each of 10 dimensions) using the coefficient alpha (the average was .72). You will recognize the coefficient alpha as the general "all-purpose" index of internal consistency reliability. Recall that this type of reliability does not address the stability of climate dimensions over time—it only addresses the extent to which there exists error in items comprising each of the 10 dimensions *at that one point in time*. Given these relatively high alpha coefficients, it appears that these 10 dimensions do, in fact, measure something. *What* is being measured will be their focus of research on its validity.

Brand and colleagues proceeded with establishing the test-retest reliability, or stability, of their newly created instrument, the Inventory of School Climate (ISC). Using large samples of students and schools and 1- and 2-year retest intervals, they reported reliability (stability) coefficients averaging .76 (at the 1-year retest interval) and .52 (at the 2-year retest interval). Thus, it appears that school climate persists over time (is generally stable), despite changes in the student population due to graduation, mobility, and other factors related to transience. Further, these researchers tested the consistency of ISC scores across student subsamples based on gender, race, grade level, and socioeconomic status. This reliability is a type of *interobserver* reliability, or the extent to which raters (in this case having different characteristics) provide consistent ratings. Brand and colleagues' (2003) findings enabled their conclusion that the ISC scales "possess high levels of interobserver reliability and consistency for students from diverse backgrounds" (p. 574).

Phase 3 of the psychometric assessment of the ISC involved its validation (meaningfulness) as a means to check whether it was measuring what it was supposed to measure: school climate. We have seen that validation is a far greater challenge than the determination of reliability. Here the task involved collecting evidence that school climate scores are related to educational outcomes believed to vary as a function of school climate. Brand and colleagues referred to this as "convergent" and "divergent" validity, meaning that climate scores should be related to (converge on) some outcomes and *not* be related to (diverge from) other outcomes. These convergent and divergent predictions are based on what is currently known about school climate from prior research.

Three student adjustment outcomes (often called *criteria*) were selected by Brand and colleagues: *academic* adjustment (measured by standardized achievement scores, grades, and students' ratings of academic aspirations, expectations, etc.), *behavioral* adjustment (measured by teachers' and students' ratings), and *socioemotional* adjustment (students' ratings of self-esteem, depression, and anxiety). The term *ratings* used here is a simplification of more complex instruments used to measure multiple facets of the three types of adjustment. A description of all the instruments used to determine these criteria, more than 10 instruments each comprising many items, is beyond the scope of this discussion. It should be noted, however, that all these outcome measures of adjustment must *themselves* be put to the test of reliability and validity in order to be useful measures of adjustment. These assessments were completed by others in prior research.

Given all these measures of adjustment and each of the 10 scales that are presumed to measure different facets of school climate, you can imagine the complication of their statistical analysis and presentation of findings. Recall that, unlike reliability determination, which often results in a single coefficient, validity assessment is more complex since the *pattern* of many findings must be interpreted and evaluated for meaning. Conclusions are often tempered given this complexity, using words such as *appears*. For example, Brand and colleagues (2003) noted that the ISC "appears to measure a number of dimensions of the school social environment"

(p. 586). Their findings revealed very clearly that school climate cannot be assessed by a single, overall score. Many of their uncovered relationships held for one (or more) of their measured dimensions, but not for all 10 dimensions.

Brand and colleagues summarized their findings related to validity by concluding that multiple climate dimensions of the ISC were indeed related to indexes of academic, behavioral, and social adjustment. They also offered suggestions for possible uses of their instrument designed to measure school climate. Recall from an earlier discussion in this chapter that perhaps the most important criterion for an instrument's validity is the *degree of usefulness, given a specific purpose.*

The research by Brand and colleagues reveals that validation is a complex process requiring an interpretation of patterns of research findings over time and across many studies. It involves clear thinking and sharp judgments. The Brand and colleagues study also shows that educational researchers can measure complex school constructs like climate as well as myriad learner and teacher constructs. Measuring the qualities of whole schools is admittedly complex, but such objective measurement is valuable to the extent that it reveals relationships that help us understand schools' impact on learners and teachers.

MORE EXAMPLES

Additional descriptions of published research may help to solidify your knowledge of important ideas related to instrumentation. You will find additional descriptions on the Web-based student study site (www.sagepub.com/eic).

Chapter Summary

Educational researchers use a wide variety of instruments in the conduct of their data collection, but whatever their form, the measures must satisfy two criteria to be useful: reliability and validity. *Reliability* is an index that is sensitive to errors of measurement (the difference between obtained scores and theoretical true scores) and is best understood as consistecy. Different types of reliability can be computed, each one sensitive to different types of consistency. These include test-retest reliability (consistency over time), parallel form reliability (consistency between two forms of the same test), internal consistency reliability (consistency among items), and inter-rater reliability (consistency among raters). A reliability coefficient does not reveal what the instrument actually measures; it only reveals how well (how much error) it measures. *Validity,* by contrast, is the standard that reflects the meaningfulness of the scores, or what is actually being measured. Valid instruments, then, measure what they are supposed to measure. An instrument yields valid scores to the extent that the inferences made on the basis of test scores are in fact accurate. Three types of validity can be assessed: *content* (the match between items on a test and the instructional content), *predictive* (the match between predictions based on test scores and the actual outcome that the test is trying to predict), and *construct* (the match between test scores and the trait that the test is measuring according to the theory behind the trait). Different types of validity are best understood by reference to the specific purpose to which the test is put.

Application Exercises

1. For each of the scenarios below, determine whether the researcher is assessing reliability or validity. If reliability, then determine whether it is an instance of test-retest, internal consistency, or inter-rater reliability. If validity, then determine whether it is an instance of content, predictive, or construct validity.
   a. A researcher administered the new Test of Teaching Potential to graduating Education majors and then correlated the test scores with principals' ratings of teaching effectiveness after 1 year on the job to see whether the test scores were related to job performance.
   b. A researcher correlated two observers' evaluations of teachers' effectiveness as revealed on the new Teacher Observation Form to see if the observers' evaluations were similar.
   c. A researcher developed a test of the trait optimism and then compared students judged to be "happy" with those judged to be "not happy" to see if they had the different levels of optimism expected if the happiness theory were credible.
   d. A researcher created an achievement test of geography knowledge and compared the test items with a representative sampling of the knowledge-level objectives from widely used textbooks related to geography.
   e. A researcher tested a sample of students using the Occupational Interest Test. The test was administered again 6 months later to see if interests were fleeting.
   f. A researcher administered the new Test of Stress to teachers and then computed alpha to see how well the items "hung together."

2. Suppose you developed an instrument to measure charisma because you believe this is an important quality in teachers. What would you assess first, reliability or validity, and why? What type of reliability is most relevant? Why? What type of validity is most relevant? Why?

3. Now answer the questions posed in #2 above in reference to an instrument designed to measure teachers' likelihood of changing careers. Answer the questions again in reference to an instrument designed to measure students' knowledge of the Constitution.

4. The SAT college entrance exam was redesigned in 2005 in an attempt to align itself with a national curriculum, hence becoming more achievement oriented than aptitude oriented. Given this redirected focus, what are the implications for assessing the test's validity for use in college admissions? How would you evaluate recent evidence of the new SAT's validity and reliability? A good place to start searching for evidence is the Web site of the College Board (www.collegeboard.com). The National Center for Fair and Open Testing, Fair Test, provides other information useful for the purpose of evaluating the psychometric quality of standardized tests (www.fair test.org).

5. Peruse online journals that publish research in your area of interest. Locate one study that focused on the development and validation of a measuring instrument. What evidence was presented in favor of its reliability and validity? How you would evaluate this evidence?

6. Consider the construct "creativity." Do you believe it is a relatively stable and measurable trait? How have researchers measured creativity? (Hint: Start with ERIC.) How would you evaluate commonly used instruments to measure creativity? Do they "measure up" to the standards of reliability and validity?

7. The American Board for Certification of Teaching Excellence (ABCTE; www.abcte.org) certifies beginning teachers through a package of alternative-credentialing tests. Those who pass the tests earn the Passport to Teaching Certification, designed to assure subject knowledge competence and classroom effectiveness. How would you design a study to evaluate the reliability and validity of the Passport to Teaching examination? What other measures might be needed to validate the examination? Would you expect educators' consensus on the criteria used to define teaching competence? What evidence exists to support the reliability and validity of the current ABCTE licensing examinations?

ON YOUR OWN

Log on to the Web-based student study site at http://www.sagepub.com/eic for more information about the materials presented in this chapter, suggestions for activities, study aids such as electronic flashcards and review quizzes, a sample research proposal, and research recommendations that include journal article links (with discussion questions and an article evaluation guide) and questions related to this chapter.

Part IV Design and Analysis

The four chapters in Part IV span important aspects of the research design (the configuration of variables) that structure data collection and analysis. The skills of an architect, so to speak, come into focus as researchers create a plan that most efficiently answers the research question. The decisions associated with research designs are among the most far reaching of researchers' decisions. They often influence researchers' confidence in their conclusions. The thinking skills related to the analysis of data also are sharpened in Part IV.

Chapter 10 surveys randomized true experimental designs and highlights their strengths and limitations. The chapter also describes widely used quasi-experimental and single-subject designs. Key features of these designs are described with attention to the thinking skills needed to understand their advantages and disadvantages, as well as the implications of their use. Chapter 11 continues the examination of nonexperimental research designs, those that lack an intervention. Nonexperimental designs are used frequently by researchers, and attention is focused on the scientific thinking that enhances their value.

Chapter 12 introduces the need for divergent thinking and creative approaches to research designs and data analyses. Scientific thinking must be coupled with innovative approaches to making sense of the complex, rich data supplied by qualitative designs (e.g., ethnographies and case studies). Chapter 13 presents a conceptual understanding of statistical reasoning, including the logical underpinning of tests of significance, errors, and power. The chapter concludes with a description of statistical software (SPSS). All four chapters in Part IV emphasize the value of scientific clarity in thinking to avoid the cognitive pitfalls associated with designs flaws, data misinterpretation, and unwarranted conclusions.

10

Common Experimental Research Designs

Outline

Overview

Researchers are designers, much like architects. They think carefully about the structure, or configuration, of their variables far before any data collection occurs. This makes intuitive sense, for you would probably not begin a driving vacation without a road map. A landscaper would probably not begin excavating without a design. A contractor would probably not begin construction without a blueprint or wiring diagram. A sculptor would probably not begin without an image in mind. And so it is, a researcher would probably not initiate data collection for a research study without the guidance of a *research design.* This chapter describes the valuable function that research designs provide in the conduct of educational research. Decisions here have huge implications for how researchers, and readers of published research, think about results.

Because of the vast array of research designs, the topic of research design can become overwhelming very quickly. Therefore, I will restrict the discussion here to those research designs which are commonly used by educational researchers. They represent a sampling across different types and complexities of educational research.

There are hundreds of potentially useful research designs, and the choice of one specific research design is guided by many factors. Perhaps the most influential factor is the type of research study undertaken, as described in Chapter 3. Some types of research, such as experimental and quasi-experimental research, offer a vast array of designs. Other types, such as causal comparative research, offer a limited selection. And some types of research, such as correlational research, offer a small number of basic designs but a large number of data analysis techniques. These techniques may be simple, as in a scattergram of raw data, or extraordinarily complex, as in structural equation modeling, which attempts to discover "hidden" variables via correlations and test causal connections between them.

This chapter examines common experimental research designs, those designs with a manipulation (a treatment condition or an intervention). Three types of experimental research designs are covered: true experimental, quasi-experimental, and single-subject. All three types involve an experimental manipulation, but only the true experimental designs use the random assignment that greatly facilitates the ability to uncover cause-and-effect relationships. Quasi-experimental designs lack the critical feature of random assignment, but they are still useful for (cautiously) investigating cause and effect. Single-subject designs also uncover cause-and-effect relationships by involving an intervention, but they use unique control procedures and involve different types of evidence to support cause-and-effect relationships.

The following chapter focuses on common nonexperimental research designs, those that lack a researcher's manipulation. These designs are very useful for uncovering relationships and describing complex phenomena of great interest to educational researchers.

Experimental Research Designs

When a research question or hypothesis suggests an intervention of some type, the researcher will consider common *experimental research designs,* that is, designs that

EXPERIMENTAL RESEARCH: Research involving an independent variable—a manipulation of some type (a treatment or an intervention).

TRUE EXPERIMENTAL RESEARCH: Research involving the use of a manipulated independent variable (an intervention) coupled with random assignment of subjects to groups. Such designs are strong for testing cause-and-effect relationships (e.g., randomized posttest control group design, randomized pretest-posttest control group design, and randomized matched control group design).

offer in their blueprints some type of treatment (known as a *manipulation*). The researcher will often choose one of three different types of experimental designs: true experimental, quasi-experimental, and single-subject. When the researcher's focus is not on any type of manipulation, one of several common non-experimental research designs (correlational, causal comparative, and descriptive) will probably be selected. (Recall that these designs are referred to as *nonexperimental* because they do not incorporate any treatment intervention.)

CRITICAL THINKER ALERT 10-1

True Experiments

True experimental research designs in education are the best method, whenever feasible, for uncovering cause-and-effect relationships. Such designs, coupled with control (placebo) groups, are used by the Federal Drug Administration (FDA) to be reasonably sure that prescription drugs are safe and effective, that is, safely cause the health effect for which they were designed. But schools are not run like FDA clinical trials. Nevertheless, the No Child Left Behind Act favors true experimental designs for strong research-based evidence of program and practice effectiveness.

Discussion: What do you think might be a "downside" of preferring true experimental research as evidence of program effectiveness? Do you consider this preference a type of bias? Might other programs be overlooked simply because of practical problems associated with experimental evidence?

True Experimental Designs

You will recall from Chapter 5 that a true independent variable involves a manipulation coupled with random assignment of subjects to groups. A true experimental design, therefore, is one that incorporates a true independent variable. You will also recall from Chapter 5 that a manipulation refers to the creation of group conditions by the researcher. In its most basic form, a manipulation would include a treatment group and a control group. The presence of a control group itself is not essential for a true experiment, although it is commonly used to rule out threats to internal validity (as described in Chapter 7). A true experiment might utilize just two different treatments without a pure control comparison. Four examples of true experimental research designs include the following:

- Randomized posttest control group design
- Randomized pretest-posttest control group design

- Randomized matched control group design
- Randomized factorial design

These four designs will be described in the sections that follow.

CRITICAL THINKER ALERT 10-2

Cause and Effect

True experimental designs, especially those with clever control groups, are well suited to ferret out cause-and-effect relationships because of the power of random assignment of subjects to treatment and control groups.

Discussion: In a true experimental test of the effect of physical exercise on students' creative thinking, what would be an appropriate control group? While the experimental group engaged in exercise, what would the control group do?

Randomized Posttest Control Group Design

The basic building block of experimental designs is the randomized posttest control group design shown below:

R T Post

R C Post

where R refers to random assignment, T refers to a treatment or experimental intervention, C refers to a control or comparison group, and Post refers to a posttest.

The essential conditions of the randomized posttest control group are the use of a treatment group that receives a specific intervention, a posttest to measure (assess) the influence of the treatment effect (if any), a control group to rule out threatening sources of influence, and random assignment of subjects to the control and treatment groups. This design is one of the simplest yet strongest designs in the educational researcher's arsenal, at least from the perspective of control over biasing influences.

Let's consider an example very similar to the one described in Chapter 7. Suppose a researcher wanted to determine if high school students' scores on the SAT could be increased significantly by 6 hours of training in the use of a novel method for test preparation 1 week prior to the exam. To this end, 1,000 students in the Chicago area who had registered to take the SAT were contacted to obtain permission and approval for their participation in the study. Next, 500 students were randomly assigned to the treatment group, which would receive 6 hours of test-taking tips and strategies in one of many small groups on the Saturday prior to the exam. Each session was led by a teacher-leader who trained students to be "test wise" and offered many opportunities for practice. The remaining 500 students were retained as a control group, and they were simply contacted for permission to use their SAT scores as part of a research project. No attempt was made to eliminate the control group students who had attended other workshops on test-taking skills or who had studied on their own. The control group, therefore, represented a subsample of the population who had received a "control" mixture of other types of training or no training at all. As a result, this design tested whether the novel test preparation program resulted in higher scores compared to the hodgepodge of methods students typically used in the absence of an opportunity to prepare with the new method. Let's assume that all the control and treatment group students who were contacted agreed to participate. Here are the results: control group mean = 480; treatment group mean = 590.

Because this research design is strong for ferreting out cause-and-effect relationships, we could be reasonably comfortable in concluding that the new test preparation program was the cause of the enhanced performance. This is because there exists a control group to assess the effects of extraneous influences. To clarify this, just imagine what would happen if the treatment group were actually a second control group and never received the test preparation training. If both control groups' scores were then compared, we would expect to find similar means—after all, we would be comparing two randomly assigned control groups. This is not to say that there are no extraneous influences in this study, like flu outbreaks, uncomfortable testing environments, emotionally charged news events, advice from friends on taking the SAT, and so on. But the important point is that these influences are not selective, so *all of these influences and biases would affect the two groups equally.* In this sense, we can say that the control and treatment groups' scores reflect weather, news, viruses, and the like, but the treatment group also has the specific influence attributed to the training in test-taking skills. Using this rationale, we can safely conclude that the 110-point difference reflects the unique influence of the treatment program itself.

Here is another example of the randomized control group design. Let's assume that a researcher wanted to test the effectiveness of an educational intervention designed to reduce the number of high school students who smoke. Assume that 1,000 ninth graders were selected to participate, and 500 were randomly assigned to the treatment group, consisting of information about the hazards of smoking, including guest speakers with terminal lung cancer. The remaining 500 students were assigned to the control group and were not targeted in any special way. The posttest measure was collected near the end of high school and was simply a count of the number of students in each group who smoked regularly.

Here are the dramatic results: treatment group = 6% smokers; control group = 20% smokers. These hypothetical results favor the intervention, and there are no obvious alternative explanations for the findings. Even if there were powerful extraneous influences—like the continual release of new studies showing the health consequences of smoking, the implementation of substantially lower car insurance rates for nonsmokers, or the smoking-related death of a teen idol—the findings would still provide a strong causal link between the educational intervention and the reduced smoking rate. This is because the extraneous influences affected the groups equally. The presence of a control group allows the researcher to "subtract out" extraneous influence to arrive at a purer measure of the treatment's effect. If there were no control group, then we would not know whether the low 6% smoking rate in the treatment group was due to the intervention itself, to the smoking-related death of the teen idol, or to a combination of both or any one of the hundreds of other plausible explanations related to extraneous influences.

CRITICAL THINKER ALERT 10-3

Experimental Ambiguity

True experimental designs, despite their potential, can still yield ambiguous findings due to many sources of bias and confounding, poor instrumentation (measurement), inadequate sampling, and so on. In other words, alternative hypotheses may be still be present, and usually are, within true experimental research.

Discussion: Presume that in a true experimental test of a program designed to raise SAT scores among those seeking college admission, 200 students were assigned randomly to a control group or a group that received instruction every Saturday morning for 25 weeks (the treatment). Findings revealed that those who completed the program scored significantly higher than those in the control group. What glaring alternative hypothesis would cast doubt on the conclusion that the program was effective?

Randomized Pretest-Posttest Control Group Design

This strong design is represented below:

R Pre T Post

R Pre C Post

where Pre refers to a pretest.

The design differs from the randomized posttest control group design only in that all participants are pretested before the treatment is implemented. The use of a pretest allows for the assessment of change (gain) and functions as a type of personal baseline. In this sense, each subject serves as his or her own control, and the treatment effects can be evaluated in terms of a shift from the starting point. The control group, of course, allows the researcher to control for extraneous influences such as the effect of a pretest on the performance of a posttest, a change due to the mere passage of time, and many other influences which could mistakenly be attributed to the treatment.

Let's consider an application of this strong design. Assume a researcher wanted to evaluate the effectiveness of a treatment designed to reduce the amount of television watched by eighth graders. The treatment involved a series of interesting activities at home over a 3-month period created specifically to compete with television watching after school, in the evenings, and on weekends. After random assignment to groups, 100 eighth graders in each group agreed to log their television viewing (as accurately as possible) every day for 1 month (the Pretest Phase). Each subject's television watching could therefore be summarized by the average number of hours watched per week during the Pretest Phase (after random assignment but before the treatment was initiated). Then the activities began for the treatment group only (Treatment Phase), lasting 1 month. Neither group logged their television viewing during this phase. Finally, after the treatment ended, both groups logged their television watching for 1 month during the Posttest Phase, the end of which marked the completion of the study. Table 10.1 displays the results, expressed in average hours of television watching during the Pretest and Posttest Phases.

Table 10.1 Treatment and Control Group Results on the Pretest and Posttest

	Phase	
Group	Pretest	Posttest
Treatment	89	42
Control	94	86

Note: The outcome is the average hours of television watched.

Notice that the pretest result for the treatment group is somewhat lower than that for the control group. This is simply an instance of sampling error attributed to the random process. This fact is considered in the analysis of the posttest scores, for a portion of the 42 versus 86 gap in the posttest scores is due to the treatment group's somewhat lower initial baseline. These designs are usually analyzed statistically with a technique called *analysis of covariance*, which adjusts posttest scores on the basis of differences in pretest scores. Also notice that the posttest hours of television in the control group were somewhat lower than the pretest hours. The fact that television viewing declined in the control group is also considered in the analysis; that is, a portion of the rather dramatic decline in the treatment group (89 to 42) is in part explained by the control group's small decline.

The control group serves an especially valuable function in this study, because without it, we would not know how to interpret the decline in the treatment group. Maybe the pretest phase was completed in February and the posttest phase was completed in June; television watching might naturally drop in June because of better weather, frequent reruns, and the like. Or possibly a new water park opened in June, and the students spent less time watching television because they frequently visited the park. Because of the control group, the results provide compelling evidence that the treatment itself was responsible for the decline. If the control group had also declined as dramatically, the researcher would have to attribute the treatment group's decline to some factor other than the treatment, like weather, television programming, family vacations, a novel community program designed to encourage students to read more, or any number of competing explanations.

Randomized Matched Control Group Design

This especially strong design is presented below:

M R T Post

M R C Post

where M refers to matched.

This design is similar to the randomized posttest control group design, but is distinguished by the use of matching prior to random assignment of subjects.

A researcher may choose this design if the sample size is too small (perhaps less than 40 per group) to reasonably assure group comparability after random assignment. Subjects are first rank ordered on a variable closely related to the posttest. Then one of the two highest (the two forming a matched pair) is randomly assigned to T or C, with the remaining one being assigned to the other group. The next highest matched pair is similarly assigned, and this continues until the lowest two matched subjects are assigned randomly.

After assignment is complete, the two case-by-case matched groups formed with this technique are nearly identical on the matched variable, and probably comparable on other variables as well. Less is left to chance when using matching prior to random assignment. The choice of the matching variable is crucial, for nothing is gained if it is not related to the posttest. For this reason, the matching variable is often a pretest version of the posttest measure. (A pretest is probably more highly correlated with a posttest than with any other measure.)

Here is an example. A researcher planned to test whether a new method for teaching reading called Read Now! was more effective than one currently in use. To this end, 60 first graders' reading skills were assessed with a pretest, then rank ordered from most advanced to least advanced. Pairs were formed by coupling the two most advanced, next most advanced, and so on, until the two least advanced were coupled as a pair. One member of each pair was randomly assigned to Read Now! while the other was retained as a control. The two groups, now nearly identical (on average) in their pretreatment reading ability, were exposed to the treatment or control instruction for 12 weeks, followed by a posttest measure of reading achievement. Any posttest difference could hardly be attributed to pretreatment reading differences because they were the same on average. If other extraneous influences (e.g., teachers' skill) are controlled, then the researcher is entitled to conclude that the manipulation (the true independent variable of teaching method—Read Now!) probably caused the difference in the outcome.

A Comparison With Weak Pre-Experimental Designs

In order to emphasize the strength of the true experimental designs described previously, consider two *pre-experimental designs,* or weak designs that do not have the essential characteristics of a true experiment: manipulation and random assignment to groups. An example of a pre-experimental (weak) design is the one-group pretest-posttest design shown below:

Pre T Post

As suggested by its name, this design involves merely pretesting a selected group of participants, administering a treatment, then posttesting the group to determine whether a shift in scores occurred from pretest to posttest. Notice that this design has virtually no control for biasing influences in the form of threats to internal validity, such as those described in Chapter 7 (extraneous events, etc.). Consider one example of this design. Suppose a researcher wanted to test the effects of exercise on the ability to recall a list of words. A group of 30 students was shown 40 common words on a screen. Following this, the students were asked to write down all of the words they

PRE-EXPERIMENTAL DESIGN: A weak research design involving a treatment but no control features (e.g., one-group pretest-posttest design).

could remember in a 3-minute period (the "pre"). Next, the students walked briskly around campus for 45 minutes. They were then shown another list of 40 common words and given another 3-minute period in which to write down all words they could remember (the "post").

Here are the results: pretest average = 11 words; posttest average = 16 words. Does exercise increase our memory span? It may appear that way, but because this weak design does not control for extraneous influences, no such conclusion is possible. Isn't it plausible that students learned how to recall more words just from the pretest experience? They may have realized during the end of the pretest that there is a better strategy for recall, and then applied this strategy during the posttest. If there were a control group of students who did not exercise but were pretested and posttested, then this group may have scored higher because of the *pretest effect,* and its influence would have been subtracted from the exercise group to assess the uncontaminated influence of exercise. The control group in this situation would, of course, control for more than just the pretest effect. It would control for the extraneous influences due to word difficulty, time of day, and literally hundreds of other influences.

The Coalition for Evidence-Based Policy (2003) provides another example of the weakness of the pre-experimental design in a test of a summer program that provided remediation and work experience for disadvantaged teenagers. Research cited by the coalition using a randomized pretest-posttest control group design concluded that the short-term impact of the program was positive. Yet if they had used a one-group pretest-posttest design, the conclusion would have been that the program was *harmful.* This is because the control group members' reading ability eroded a full grade level, whereas the treatment group members' reading level eroded by only half a grade level. Apparently, reading ability erodes "naturally" during the summer vacation months.

Let's consider one more weak pre-experimental design to highlight the value of strong randomized true experimental designs. The second weak design is often referred to as the *static-group comparison design* and is shown below:

T Post

C Post

Notice the deliberate absence of the symbol R, which you will recall refers to random assignment. This is why the design is referred to as *static,* meaning "inactive, passive, or intact." There is no active movement of subjects into groups, as the random assignment procedure would require. With this design, typically one group is located (already intact) and given some type of treatment, while another similar group is located to function as an intact comparison.

For example, suppose a school implements a new system of blocked scheduling, whereby students are exposed to fewer but longer classes. Across town there may be a similar school which retains its traditional scheduling, and because of its comparability, functions as a type of control (albeit a weak one). After 3 years, the standardized achievement test scores of each school are compared and clearly show higher overall achievement at the blocked schedule school. Is this evidence to support blocked scheduling? Yes, but the conclusion should be tempered somewhat in light of the fact that the design that yielded this conclusion is not as strong as a randomized control group design. The two schools may have looked comparable, but because they were not formed with random assignment, group comparability could be illusory. Maybe the blocked scheduling school would have scored higher even if it had retained its traditional scheduling due, in part, to a difference on an uncontrolled extraneous variable. Weak pre-experimental designs can be greatly improved by the technique of *matching,* and as such would be called *quasi-experimental designs,* as explained later in this chapter. Matching would be accomplished by selecting two schools that are initially alike on important factors—like ability, motivation, and socioeconomic status—prior to implementing blocked scheduling. It could then be said that the two schools were matched on ability, motivation, and socioeconomic status. Careful matching may approximate randomness in some situations, and in real life, this may be as close to ideal as possible.

HIGHLIGHT AND LEARNING CHECK 10-1

True Experimental Designs

True experimental designs in education incorporate an independent variable (a manipulation) with random assignment. They are well suited for uncovering cause-and-effect relationships when a research question focuses on testing treatment or intervention effects. Many specific designs exist, yet they all share their defining characteristic: a true independent variable. Those best suited for testing cause-and-effect influences also incorporate one or more control groups. What aspects of true experimental designs enable their power to disentangle causal influences?

You are probably wondering how students could ever be randomly assigned to a school. In truth, they rarely are, but the random process could still exert its control via another level of random assignment. Entire schools, maybe hundreds of schools, could be randomly assigned to a blocked schedule or a traditional format. This, of course, is a much more complex experiment, but it is not impossible. One notable example is a national randomized "field trial" of the reading and school improvement program Success for All (Borman, Slavin, Cheung, Madden, & Chambers, 2005). The large-scale true experimental research design (a "cluster randomized trial") used 38 schools randomized to Success for All or control programs. The true experiment represents a new generation of research studies in education, one more commonly reserved for use in clinical drug trials and medicine. Such designs are not without critics, who cite issues related to cost ($7 million for the Success for All evaluation cited above), ethics, and difficulties capturing classrooms' "inner workings" (Viadero, 2005).

Randomized Factorial Designs: Interactions and Main Effects

The Meaning of Interaction

The term *factorial* in research refers to designs that combine two or more independent variables (or attribute variables) within a single experiment in order to determine their *joint* effect, in addition to the overall effect of each variable singly. (The general term *factor,* then, usually refers to either an independent variable or an attribute variable, or both.) The joint effect of two variables is referred to as an *interaction,* an important but difficult concept. You may be familiar with the concept of interaction already, possibly in the form of warnings about drug interactions. This occurs if two drugs—each one separately having a small effect—when combined have an amplifying effect. For example, some medications may make you slightly sleepy; so might a glass of wine. The combination of medication and wine

RANDOMIZED FACTORIAL DESIGN: A true experimental design that incorporates two or more factors (e.g., an independent variable and an attribute variable), permitting the testing of main effect and interaction effects.

INTERACTION EFFECT: An effect that occurs in factorial designs when the influence of one factor depends on the level or category of a second factor (e.g., a treatment affects males but not females). The keyword here is *depends*.

may, however, make you *very* sleepy (more than the slight effects merely added together).

In a sense, an interaction occurs when the total effect is more than the sum of its parts. Interaction can also work in the opposite way—each of two drugs may have a small effect, but the two drugs taken together may have no overall effect. Here the total is *less* than the sum of its parts. In this sense, it is more accurate to say that an interaction occurs when the total is *different* than the sum of its parts.

Another example of interaction may be found in weight loss. If you diet (but don't exercise), you may lose a few pounds, say 3. And if you exercise (but don't diet), you may lose a few pounds, say 4. But dieting and exercise together may result in a loss of 15 pounds! If diet and exercise did not interact, you would expect a weight loss of 7 pounds (3 for diet and 4 for exercise, a simple addition of the effects). Now let's examine this idea more closely, in the context of a randomized factorial true experiment in educational research. This example will help solidify your understanding of the concept of interaction and introduce the concept of main effect.

CRITICAL THINKER ALERT 10-4

Factorial Designs

Factorial designs in educational research are commonly used, in part because of their ability to uncover interactive relationships.

Discussion: Why do you suppose that interactive relationships (expressed by "it depends") are common among educational research findings? Do you think they are common in other fields, too, like health and medicine?

Interaction and Main Effects: A Hypothetical Example

A researcher wanted to know whether fifth graders learn to spell better by practicing on a computer or using handwriting (yes, once again). The researcher also wanted to compare these two learning strategies on relatively easy versus hard words, believing that handwriting might be better for learning to spell easy words but the use of a computer might be better for harder words. This design, therefore, called for four groups: easy words/computer, hard words/computer, easy words/handwriting, hard words/handwriting.

This type of factorial design is usually called a 2×2 factorial, the numbers referring to the categories (how many) of each factor (variable). Multiplying produces the number of groups required in the design. If the researcher wanted to test for differences across three methods, a 3×2 factorial, or 6 groups, would be required. Also, since there are two factors combined within the same study, this design is

TABLE 10.2 Interactive Results of Spelling Test (by Method and Word Type)

	Method	
Word Type	Computer	Handwriting
Easy	20	26
Hard	16	10

referred to as a *two-way factorial.* To test this idea that the best method of spelling practice (computer versus handwriting) is determined by the difficulty of words, 200 students were randomly assigned to one of the four groups, and they received five practice trials (using the computer or using handwriting) in an attempt to spell 30 new words which were relatively easy (e.g., *harp*) or relatively difficult (e.g., *eighth*). On the final test, each student was asked to spell aloud each practiced word. The hypothetical results are shown in Table 10.2, which shows the number of correctly spelled words out of 30 for each group.

MAIN EFFECT: An effect that occurs in factorial designs when the averages between categories of one factor are different overall (e.g., females averaged over treatment and control groups score differently than males averaged over treatment and control groups). Each factor in a factorial design permits an evaluation of its main effect. The keyword here is *overall.*

HIGHLIGHT AND LEARNING CHECK 10-2

Factorial Designs

Factorial designs in education involve two or more factors (independent or attribute variables), thus enabling the evaluation of main effects and interaction effects. *Main effects* compare the overall influences of each factor (e.g., the average treatment condition of all males and females versus the average control condition of all males and females). *Interaction effects* occur when the influence of one factor depends on the category of the other factor (e.g., the treatment affects females more than males). If males scored 4 and 6 and females scored 4 and 2 in the control and treatment conditions, respectively, is there a main effect of sex? Is there a main effect of treatment? Is there an interaction? Explain.

As expected, the Easy words were learned better than the Hard words in both groups overall. We know this because, on average (overall), students spelled 23 Easy words correctly but only 13 Hard words correctly. These values were obtained by merely computing the average of the Easy words overall, (20 + 26) / 2 = 23, and comparing this to the average of the Hard words overall, (16 + 10) / 2 = 13). The word *overall,* in this sense, refers to the average across all categories of the other variable (the categories of Computer and Handwriting under the variable Method). This overall comparison of Word Type is referred to as a *main effect* of Word Type, and in this case, because the overall averages are different, we would say that there *is* a main effect for Word Type.

Furthermore, the number of words learned with a Computer overall did not differ from words learned with Handwriting overall. Using the Computer resulted in an overall average of 18, derived from (20 + 16) / 2 = 18; using Handwriting also resulted in an overall average of 18, derived from (26 + 10) / 2 = 18. The term *overall,* once again, refers to the average across all categories of the other variable (the categories of Easy and Hard under the variable Word Type). This overall comparison between the two categories of Method is referred to as the *main effect* of Method, and in this case, because the overall averages are the same, we would say that there is *no* main effect for Method.

Here comes the interesting part, the interaction or joint effect of Word Type and Method. Examining the data in Table 10.2 reveals that the answer to the question "Which method is better: Computer or Handwriting?" is "It depends." This is the essence of an interaction between variables—the effect of Method on spelling scores *depends* on whether the words are Easy or Hard. If the words are Easy, then Handwriting is superior, but if the words are Hard, then the Computer is superior. This complex, interactive relationship is best depicted in a graph as shown in Figure 10.1. Interactions between variables always appear with nonparallel lines when graphed. The lack of parallelism is simply another way to illustrate a finding qualified by "it depends."

Let's change the results of our spelling experiment somewhat in order to reveal what a *non*interactive result would look like. The altered findings are shown in Table 10.3.

Notice that there exists a main effect for Word Type: an overall average of 23 for Easy words, derived from (20 + 26)/2 = 23, versus an overall average of 19 for Hard words, derived from (16 + 22)/2 = 19. Furthermore, there also exists a main effect

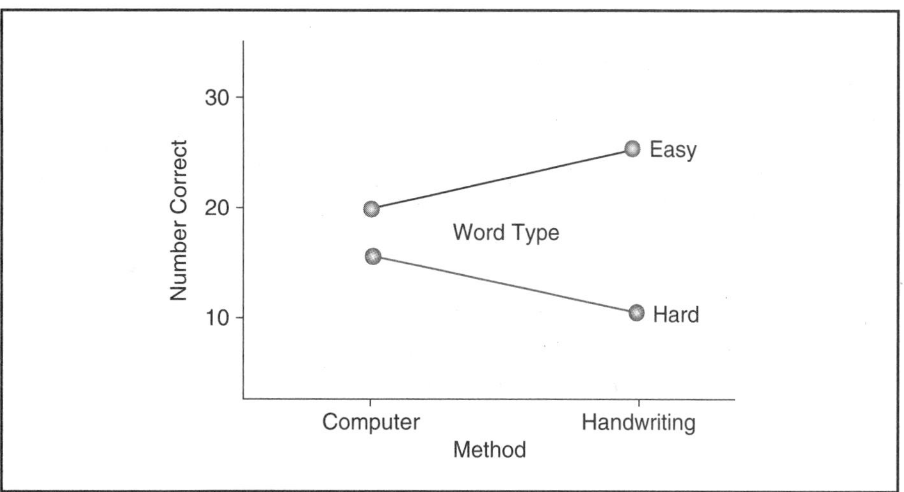

Figure 10.1 Graph of interaction. Correctly spelled words are shown as a function of Method and Word Type. Note the interaction revealed by nonparallel lines.

Table 10.3 **Noninteractive Results of Spelling Test (by Method and Word Type)**

	Method	
Word Type	Computer	Handwriting
Easy	20	26
Hard	16	22

for Method: an overall average of 18 for Computer, derived from (20 + 16)/2 = 18, versus 24 for Handwriting, derived from (26 + 22)/2 = 24. The answer to the question "Which method is better: Computer versus Handwriting?" no longer is "It depends." The answer is "Handwriting" for both Easy and Hard words. The Handwriting condition, when compared to the Computer condition, resulted in a 6-point boost (20 versus 26) for Easy words, and a 6-point boost (16 versus 22) for Hard words. Because of this outcome, we would say that there is *no* interaction between Method and Word Type. This lack of interaction is depicted in Figure 10.2, where the parallelism in the graph is obvious.

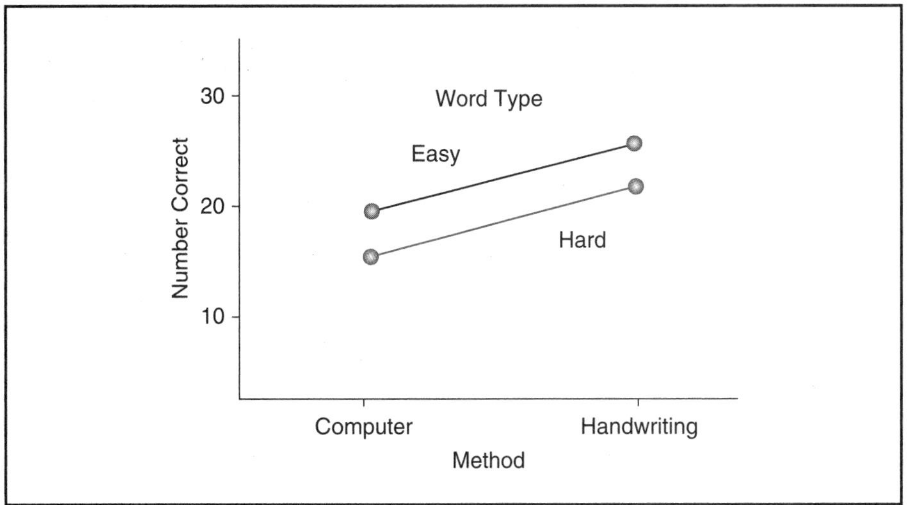

Figure 10.2 Graph revealing no interaction. Correctly spelled words are shown as a function of Method and Word Type. Note the lack of interaction evidenced by parallel lines.

CRITICAL THINKER ALERT 10-5

Interaction

Interaction in research exists when the influence of one variable *depends* on the level of another variable. For example, in a test of reaction time (RT) to a simple perception problem using two factors of age (younger, older) and sex (male, female), one might find an age effect for males only. Perhaps older males are slower than younger males; for females, however, there might be no difference in RT as a function of age. In this case, it is said that age and sex interact in its influence on RT.

Discussion: Presume a researcher studied the influence of class size (smaller, larger) and time of day (morning, afternoon) on students' attentive behaviors. Describe an outcome that reveals an interaction between class size and time of day on students' attention.

CRITICAL THINKER ALERT 10-6

No Interaction

Continuing with the preceding Critical Thinker Alert, if the *same* difference in RT exists between younger and older people for both males and females, it is said that age and sex do not interact in its influence on RT (the age difference does *not* depend on sex).

Discussion: Continuing with the preceding Discussion, can you describe an outcome that suggests no interaction between class size and time of day?

Factorial designs are very common in the practice of educational research for the simple reason that interactions are very common in the classroom (and life outside the classroom). For example, some students, depending on learning style, may thrive in a competitive school climate, others in a cooperative climate. Which climate is best? It depends—on learning style and probably many other variables.

Let's revisit the example of interaction in the context of warnings about drug interactions described earlier in this section, this time with numerical values. In these cases, the effect of a drug *depends* on what other drugs (or food) are consumed. Recall that some drugs may have amplified effects, meaning that when taken in combination they yield an effect stronger than that of each one taken separately. The alcohol and sleeping pill interaction is one of the best known. Let's say on a 1 to 10 scale where 1 is wide awake and 10 is asleep, 1 glass of wine makes you sleepy to the tune of +3 (it increases your sleepiness 3 units regardless of where you are on the scale prior to the drink, from 2 to 5 or 6 to 9, for example). Let's also say that the sleeping pill makes you sleepy to the tune of +2. Taking *both* alcohol and the sleeping pill would make you sleepy in a *compounded* or interactive way—perhaps +7. If they did *not* interact, taking both would affect your sleepiness by +5 (+3 for alcohol and +2 for the sleeping pill). This interaction is revealed by the *non*additive influence of +3 and +2 to equal +7 (not +5). For this reason, some researchers often refer to interactive effects as *nonadditive* and to noninteractive effects as *additive.*

One final point: The interaction between two variables, say A and B, can be described as the AB interaction or the BA interaction. Further, we can say that the influence of A depends on B, or the influence of B depends on A. It's the same relationship. Often, however, it simply makes more sense to describe one variable's influence as being dependent on the other (not vice versa, although it would not be "wrong"). For example, the interaction between type of teaching method (face-to-face versus online) and age (younger versus older) on achievement is best described by saying that the effect of teaching method depends on age (perhaps younger students fare better online and older students fare better face-to-face). That makes more sense than saying that the effect of age depends on teaching method (though it is the same interaction). Invariably, when an independent variable interacts with an attribute variable, it is easiest to understand how the effect of an independent variable depends on an attribute variable (not the other way around).

CRITICAL THINKER ALERT 10-7

Main Effects

Factorial designs in research provide information about main effects (apart from interaction effects). Continuing with the example in the two preceding Critical Thinker Alerts, if older people overall (an average of both males and females) react more slowly than younger people overall (an average of both males and females), it is said that there is a main effect for the factor of age.

Discussion: Continuing with the two preceding Discussions, can you describe an outcome where there is a main effect of class size but no main effect of time of day?

CRITICAL THINKER ALERT 10-8

No Main Effect

Continuing with the example in the three preceding Critical Thinker Alerts, if males overall (an average of both younger and older) react more slowly than females overall (an average of both younger and older), it is said that there is a main effect for the factor of sex.

Discussion: Continuing with the preceding Discussions, can you describe an outcome where there is *no* main effect of class size but there is a main effect of time of day?

CRITICAL THINKER ALERT 10-9

Independent Effects

Main effects and interaction effects exist independently in research outcomes. In other words, whether or not variables interact tells us nothing about whether or not there are main effects. And one variable's main effect tells us nothing about the other variable's main effect or whether or not there is an interaction between variables.

Discussion: Presume a researcher studied the influence of extreme high-stakes testing programs and students' GPAs (above average, below average) on high school dropout rates. If the researcher found that those states with extreme high-stakes testing programs have much higher dropout rates, does this also mean that those with lower GPAs were more likely to drop out? Explain.

CRITICAL THINKER ALERT 10-10

Complex Factorial

Factorial designs become very complex with the addition of a third factor (e.g., A, B, and C). There are three main effects and four interaction effects that are possible: the main effect for A, B, and C; and the interactions for AB, AC, BC, and ABC. The two-way interactions are more easily interpreted than the three-way interaction. With the addition of a fourth factor, the potential interactions are exceedingly complex.

Discussion: Can you figure out which main effects and interaction effects are possible in a four-way (A, B, C, D) factorial design? (Hint: In addition to a four-way interaction, which is uninterpretable, really, there are several two-way and three-way interactions.)

Quasi-Experimental Designs

Recall from Chapter 5 that a distinction was made between two types of independent variables: true and quasi-independent variables. (Also recall that the term *quasi* means "somewhat.") To review, true independent variables allow random assignment to their conditions; quasi-independent variables lack random assignment to their conditions. In the same way, quasi-experimental research designs are experiments, to some degree. What they lack is the critical element of *random assignment to groups.* Quasi-experiments, then, are designs which use quasi-independent variables. There still exists a treatment in quasi-experimental designs, in the sense that the researcher introduces a treatment or experimental program (which is sometimes called an intervention). But control over extraneous variables may be threatened, at least to some degree, with these designs since groups have not been formed using the power of random assignment. This fact frequently leads researchers using these designs to temper their conclusions about cause and effect. Let's examine several common applications of this concept.

QUASI-EXPERIMENTAL DESIGN: A research design that incorporates a quasi-independent variable (an independent variable manipulation without random assignment).

Matched Comparison Group Design

This design involves one group that receives a treatment and another group, usually chosen because of its similarly with the treatment group, that functions as a baseline comparison group. The two groups, however, are intact (they already existed before the intervention), so they are probably not comparable. (And they most surely are not comparable in the strict sense that random assignment would provide.) This design is shown below:

M T Post

M C Post

This type of quasi-experimental design is used often, and its strength rests on how well the extraneous influences have been controlled through matching. When, for practical and ethical reasons, students (because they are not like mice in a laboratory) simply cannot be assigned to random groups, the next best thing is matching them. But once again, matching is less desirable than the true random process as a control procedure. Don't get the idea that random assignment is a magic potion; well-conceived matching designs, at least in some situations, can approximate the level of control provided by random assignment.

MATCHED COMPARISON GROUP DESIGN: A type of quasi-experimental research design that arranges for group similarity.

Matching involves the selection of a comparison group (or individual participants) similar to the treatment group on one or more important variables (the matched variables) that have a bearing on performance. For example, let's suppose that a new program—Operation Stop Dropout—designed to reduce the dropout rate was implemented at North Hills High School, a large inner city school plagued by a 40% dropout rate. The program involved the use of small group discussions and guest speakers. In order to evaluate its effectiveness, a comparison school was selected because of its similarity to North Hills—a current dropout rate of 40%, a majority of low socioeconomic status (SES) students, and standardized achievement test scores in the bottom 25%. One could argue that even in the absence of a comparison group, if a dropout rate decreased from 40% to 15%, then it would be obvious that the program was effective.

But wait. A television spot (unrelated to Operation Stop Dropout) that encouraged students to stay in school aired frequently during the same year that the new program was implemented. And Toyota announced it would begin construction of a new assembly plant just 30 miles away that would be hiring at least 1,500 high school graduates for top paying factory jobs. Furthermore, the army started another promotional blitz to attract capable high school graduates for specialized training.

Now what do you think about the dropout rate reduction from 40% to 15%? Is it due to Operation Stop Dropout? Or is it due to the other, coincidental influences just described? Or, is it due to a combination of the program and other influences? The point is that without a carefully matched comparison group, one could not reasonably attribute any change in the dropout rate to the new program itself. The matched comparison group, in other words, shows us what probably would have happened to the treatment group had the treatment not been implemented. It is an attempt to control for the other plausible explanations, such as the threats to internal validity described in Chapter 7. Ideally, from a research point of view, one would like to find North Hills' dropout rate decline after the treatment while the comparison school's dropout rate remained steady.

The decision concerning which variables of the treatment and comparison groups should be matched centers on those variables most closely related to the measured outcome (dependent variable), in this case the dropout rate. This would suggest that the current dropout rate, SES, and standardized achievement test scores (the matching variables) are all related in a substantial way to future dropout rates. In fact, undoubtedly the three most common matching variables in educational research are age, sex, and SES, for the simple reason that they are related to many educational outcomes. Matching on irrelevant variables, such as astrological sign (on a case-by-case basis) or the color of the school desks, would have essentially no effect on the control or interpretability of the research results. More meaningful matching variables might include school size, average class size, the use of mentoring programs, or any other variable believed to be related to dropout rates.

Time Series Quasi-Experiments

Sometimes a comparison group is simply not feasible for a variety of reasons such as cost, ethics, practicality, and so forth. In the absence of a comparison group, a design known as a *time-series quasi-experiment* can be used that derives its control from observations over time instead of the comparison of one group against another. A *time-series design* is shown below:

Pre Pre Pre Pre Pre T Post Post Post Post Post

In this design, the object is to link a break in the trend revealed over time to the introduction of the treatment. The break in the trend should occur at the same time as or shortly after the treatment introduction. For example, let's say that a large urban school district has observed that a small but worrisome number of new teachers resign after their first year. Records

TIME-SERIES DESIGN: A type of quasi-experimental research design that attempts to establish control via multiple observations of one group before and after treatment.

have been kept on this problem for the past 10 years, and they reveal a consistent baseline: 11, 12, 10, 10, 12, 9, 10, 11, 11, 12. Now assume that the district implements a program for all first-year teachers which offers them a hotline to call with problems, pairing with an experienced teacher, and monthly therapy sessions to discuss anxieties, doubts, and other undesirable emotions.

To evaluate the effectiveness of this program after 5 years, the preprogram trend is compared to the following postprogram trend: 4, 5, 2, 3, 4. Further analysis reveals that such a drop in the attrition rate could hardly be explained by chance. In other words, the drop is probably real, but one must be cautious in attributing the decline to the program, for there may have been other new influences (such as a large pay increase, reduction in class size, six new schools, etc.) that could explain the resulting decline. In the absence of other explanations, the break in the trend over time corresponding to the onset of the program is fairly convincing evidence that the program was the causal mechanism.

Some of the difficulties associated with time series interpretations are revealed in Figure 10.3.

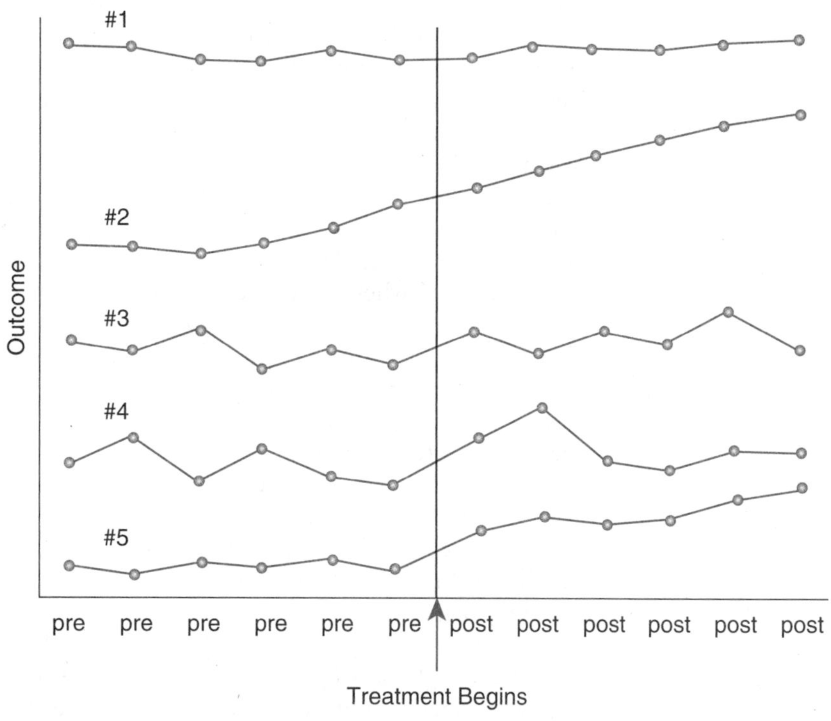

Figure 10.3 Possible outcomes in a time series quasi-experiment. Evidence that the treatment caused a shift over time is strongest with outcome #5. Outcome #1 appears flat, #2 reveals an upward trend before the treatment, #3 is "jerky" both pre and post, and #4 has an upward "blip" that is temporary. Only in #5 are all the post outcomes higher than the pre outcomes.

Source: *Educational Research: A Guide to the Process* (p. 204), by N. E. Wallen and J. R. Fraenkel, 1991, New York: McGraw-Hill.

Counterbalanced Quasi-Experiments

Some educational research questions may be answered by comparing the same participants' responses across all categories of an independent variable. In this type of design, all participants receive *each* of the treatment and control conditions; each subject acts as his or her own control (a perfect "cloning" control, in a sense). Here is an example. A researcher posed the following question: "What type of background noise results in the greatest reading comprehension—silence, dull hum of a motor, or nature sounds (ocean, river, birds, etc.)?" To answer this question, 100 students read a 500-word excerpt from a book on one of three relatively obscure topics: the history of Siberia, history of Greenland, and history of Korea. All three excerpts were judged to be equally interesting and equally difficult.

COUNTERBALANCED QUASI-EXPERIMENT: A type of quasi-experimental research design that establishes control by using a single group to test all treatment and control conditions. It is also called a repeated measures or within subjects design.

All the subjects read the excerpts in all three background noise conditions. The researcher, though, was careful to avoid confounding the noise conditions with excerpts and with orders. To accomplish this, each noise condition was determined randomly to be first, second, or third for each subject. Also, for each subject, a random excerpt was selected for each noise condition, creating a type of double random assignment. For example, the first participant, Bob, received the following randomized order of noise conditions: motor noise, nature sounds, silence. Furthermore, in the motor noise condition, he read about Siberia; in the nature sounds condition, Korea; in the silence condition, Greenland. Then the second participant, Susan, received the following randomly determined noises and topics: nature sounds while reading about Greenland, silence while reading about Korea, and motor noises while reading about Siberia. This design is said to be *counterbalanced,* a term you will recall from Chapter 7, where the concept of control was discussed. It was counterbalanced in the sense that any advantage motor noise might have being first (for Bob) is offset by it being second for, say, Tim, and third for Susan. Similarly, any advantage that might exist for Siberia being first and being paired with motor noise, as with Bob, is offset by its being second or third for other participants and being paired with silence and nature sounds.

This type of randomized counterbalancing establishes control by having each noise condition, on average, occur first, second, or third and having each noise condition preceded and followed by the other two conditions, on average, an equal number of times. The same principle holds for the three different excerpts. Over many participants, the random process equalizes order effects (the advantage of being first or the disadvantage of being last) and carryover effects (the advantage Greenland might have by following Siberia or the disadvantage Korea might have by following Siberia). You can probably understand these order and carryover effects better by imagining being in a market research study providing taste ratings after sampling chocolate Brands A, B, and C, in that order. The ratings of Brand C chocolate might suffer because it was tasted last, if subjects' overstimulated taste buds begin to tire out (an order effect) and as a result of contamination from the two preceding samplings (a carryover effect).

Problems stemming from order and carryover effects are solved by clever systematic counterbalancing techniques. The Latin Square, discussed in Chapter 7, is one such technique.

Research designs that arrange for all subjects to experience all treatment conditions are often referred to as *repeated measures* designs or *within subjects* designs. They are called "repeated measures" because subjects are measured repeatedly (once in each condition) and "within subjects" because comparisons are made within the same subject (across all conditions) instead of between subjects (as in a study where each group consisted of different subjects). Such designs are also called *counterbalanced designs,* after the control technique described above.

Counterbalanced designs are considered to be very sensitive, in the sense that they are more apt to show a treatment effect (if one exists) than are designs that use groups of different subjects. Because of this, counterbalanced designs are usually considered to be more powerful. The drawback is that in many situations, counterbalanced designs are inappropriate because order and carryover effects render meaningless results. For example, if you wanted to know which of two methods for teaching psychology—lecture or self-paced programmed instruction—was best, it would make no sense for subjects who first learned about psychology in the lecture condition to then be exposed to the same content in the self-paced programmed instruction. They have already learned the material. In this case, only two randomly assigned separate groups could be compared. One research alternative might involve students completing, say, 20 units (or chapters) in the study of psychology by learning half of the units via lecture and the other half via self-paced programmed instruction. The units would be randomized across conditions, satisfying the requirements of a randomized counterbalanced within subjects design.

Designs that use separate groups of subjects, in contrast to within subjects designs, are appropriately called *between subjects* designs, or sometimes *independent groups* designs. They appear to be more common in educational research than within subjects designs.

HIGHLIGHT AND LEARNING CHECK 10-3

Quasi-Experimental Designs

Quasi-experimental designs in research involve a manipulation (or an intervention) without the control aspect of random assignment to groups. They establish control in other ways, such as matching (e.g., matched comparison group design), temporal patterns (e.g., time-series designs), and counterbalancing (e.g., repeated measures designs). Matched comparison groups are especially prone to interpretation problems linked to nonequivalence. Explain why matching is important for establishing control (and hence an ability to ferret out cause-and-effect connections), yet is a poor substitute for random assignment.

Single-Subject Experimental Designs

As suggested by their name, these designs involve studying the effect of a treatment on a single subject (or a single group, such as an entire classroom). These designs are considered "experimental" since they involve the introduction of a treatment of some sort, and they accomplish their control through the use of comparisons between baseline observations and treatment observations. These designs, then, involve observing behavior over a period of time as a function of baseline and treatment conditions. Baseline performance in the absence of treatment, which is often labeled A, is compared with treatment performance, which

SINGLE-SUBJECT DESIGN: A type of quasi-experimental research design using one subject to test all treatment and control conditions over time (e.g., an ABAB design).

is often labeled B. These designs, in fact, are typically referred to as ABAB, BAAB, ABA, or some other configuration showing how the baseline and treatment conditions are alternated. Some of these designs, despite their basic simplicity, can be very sophisticated indeed. First, let's consider a hypothetical example of a basic design.

An ABAB Design

In order to determine whether sugar resulted in hyperactive behavior in a 7-year-old boy, a researcher observed the behavior of the student for 2 hours in the morning after he ate his usual high-sugar cereal. The observer recorded the frequency of hyperactive behaviors daily for 2 weeks. These results are shown in Figure 10.4, above Weeks 1–2.

This phase of the design established the baseline, or A, the behavior in the absence of a treatment effect. Next, the researcher began observation after greatly restricting the amount of sugar in the same cereal. The observation was continued for 2 weeks, and the results are shown in Figure 10.4, above Weeks 3–4.

The treatment phase, or B, revealed a clear decrease in the frequency of hyperactivity. Thinking that the decrease might be due to other factors, the researcher reinstituted the high-sugar cereal (the A, or baseline phase) and observed the resultant behavior as shown in Figure 10.4, above Weeks 5–6. As expected, the hyperactive behavior increased with the reintroduction of sugar. Finally, to double check the findings, the researcher withdrew the sugar (B, or treatment) and observed the boy's behavior once more for 2 weeks, as shown above Weeks 7–8 in Figure 10.4.

These findings are rather compelling, especially when all phases are shown together as in Figure 10.4. The visual impact leaves little doubt that hyperactivity is linked to high sugar consumption. Of course, you could not rule out coincidence

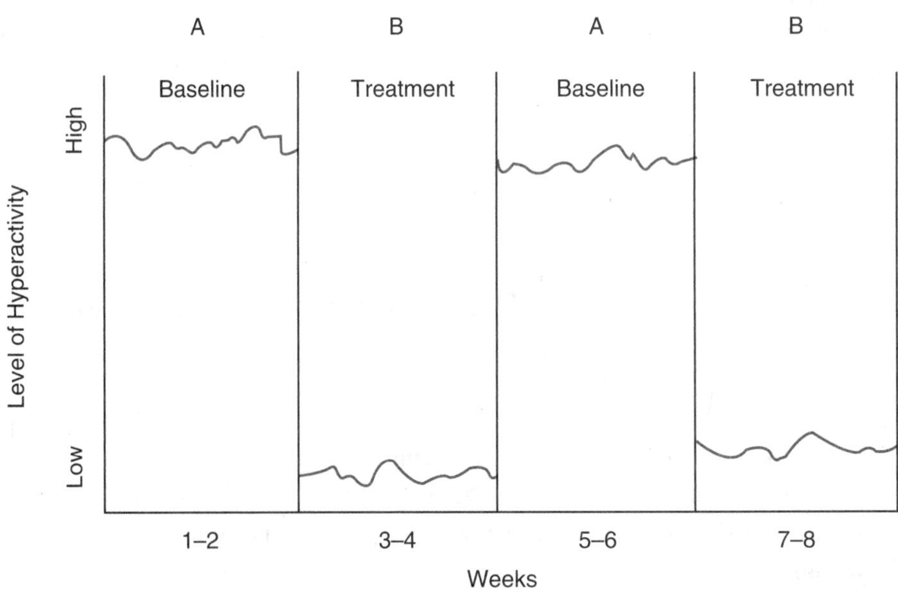

Figure 10.4 Fictional results of an ABAB single-subject design. Here treatment is alternated with baseline (control) to see its effect on hyperactivity.

with 100% certainty. Possibly, some other influence in the classroom occurred at the same time as sugar withdrawal; as a result, the data, although appearing persuasive, would in fact be misleading.

A Multiple Baseline Design

Another, more complex, single-subject design, called the *multiple baseline* design, is probably stronger for ruling out extraneous influences. It may be thought of as an AAAA, BAAA, BBAA, BBBA, BBBB design. Here is how this design might be employed in a sugar-hyperactivity study. The single subject, in this case, is actually a single group. Imagine four students in the same class, Albert, Bob, Carl, and David, all of whom are perceived by their teacher as hyperactive. All four students would be observed for a period of time, say 2 weeks, to establish their baseline level of hyperactivity. Then one student, say Albert, would be withdrawn from sugary cereal while the others would continue to be observed with the baseline high sugar consumption. Next, after 2 weeks, another student (Bob) would be withdrawn from sugary cereal (the treatment) and observed over 2 weeks. (Albert would continue under the treatment as well.) The other two would still be observed under the baseline condition (high sugar consumption). At the next step, Carl would be withdrawn from sugar to join the first two, who had been withdrawn. Finally, David would be observed in the treatment phase for 2 weeks. One possible outcome of this design is shown in Figure 10.5 in phases.

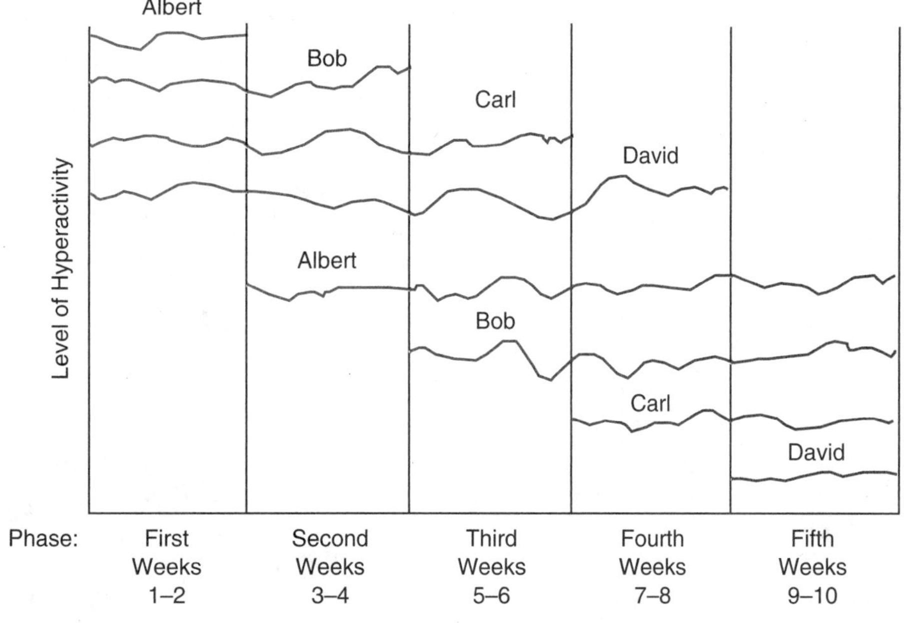

Figure 10.5 Fictional results of a multiple-treatment design. Treatment effects are observed concurrently with controls. The staircase pattern shows convincing evidence for treatment effects while controlling extraneous influences.

Source: Adapted from *Primer of Educational Research* (p. 209), by W. N. Suter, 1998, Needham Heights, MA: Allyn and Bacon.

CRITICAL PERSPECTIVES 10-1

COMMON RESEARCH DESIGNS

Critical Thinking Toolbox

Critical thinking involves pattern recognition—but not at the cost of distortion or misrepresentation (Paul, Binker, Jensen, & Kreklau, 1990). As generalizations are scrutinized, exceptions are sought. Classifications are rarely all-or-none propositions. Critical thinkers avoid the false dichotomy, which is sometimes referred to as the *either-or* fallacy.

Common Research Designs in Quantitative Research

The development of research designs in quantitative research has been heavily influenced by the focus on cause-and-effect relationships and the concern over control. As such, many research designs used by quantitative researchers are true experimental or quasi-experimental, involving some type of intervention. We have seen that these include designs such as the randomized pretest-posttest control group designs and the time series quasi-experimental design. All quantitative research designs (experimental and nonexperimental) are highly structured and influence the data collection procedures linked to the designs (such as structured interviews, observations, and surveys). Quantitative research designs without a manipulation, such as those used in correlational studies, compensate for lack of direct control by using procedures designed to establish statistical control (such as partial correlation and multiple regression). Research designs are set in place before quantitative researchers begin collecting data, often using standardized instruments.

Common Research Designs in Qualitative Research

Qualitative research designs are said to be "emergent," meaning that some components change ("evolve") as the study progresses. This is the spirit of qualitative research, for ongoing data collection and analyses may suggest alternative routes to explore that are perhaps very different from any version of the original blueprint. In this sense, qualitative research designs remain "open" to the twists and turns that findings may suggest. These flexible research designs are deliberate, for qualitative researchers believe that deeper understanding of education processes in context is more likely without the external constraints and controls of imposed designs. The designs also capitalize on natural settings. Common qualitative research designs include ethnographic studies and case studies. It is entirely possibly to design educational research so that an outcome measure is qualitative (e.g., interviews to assess attitude), yet the manipulation or intervention defines a true experiment (e.g., randomized participants assigned to either a control group or a treatment group designed to change attitudes).

Common Research Designs in Action Research

Designs in action research are often described under the general topic "qualitative" research and frequently referred to as either "practical" or "participatory" (or both). Indeed, there is a "spirit" about action research that closely aligns it with qualitative research and its notions of design flexibility. Experimental designs and quantitative measures may also be used by action researchers, although practicing educators might find these imposed structures not well suited for exploring a process in depth, especially in the natural setting of a classroom.

Critical Thinking Questions

The above descriptions are loaded with generalizations. Can you think of exceptions to any of the stated generalizations? Under what situations might typical features of qualitative research designs apply to those in quantitative research? Do you see evidence of any false "trichotomies"?

HIGHLIGHT AND LEARNING CHECK 10-4

Single-Subject Designs

Single-subject quasi-experimental designs establish control and evaluate treatment effects by alternating baseline and treatment conditions while observing patterns over time and across conditions (e.g., multiple baseline design). Can you think of instances where single-subject designs are especially well suited in education? In what situations may such designs be inappropriate?

You can see the obvious staircase pattern in these data. This design is very effective for ruling out co-occurring influence in the environment (or classroom), since you would expect in the Second Phase the hyperactivity of Bob, Carl, and David to decrease if some influence in the classroom, rather than sugary cereal, were responsible for the decline (but it didn't). The same control is also built into the remaining phases. The phases of a multiple baseline design, therefore, have built-in controls and multiple treatment observations, making this design especially strong for ferreting out cause-and-effect relationships. (The findings in Figure 10.5 are for illustrative purposes only. The outcome is perfect for showing a treatment effect, but one would hardly expect real data to reveal themselves so convincingly.)

Experimental Design Examples

Now let's turn our attention to a brief description of experimental designs as they were applied by researchers and reported in published research.

Mathematics Achievement

The experimental research reported by Ysseldyke, Kosciolek, Spicuzza, and Boys (2003) investigated the achievement effects and instructional influences of the learning tool Accelerated Math. This program was designed to raise mathematics achievement scores among fourth and fifth graders in the large urban school district where Ysseldyke and colleagues collected data (three schools, eight classes, and 157 students). At the time, the entire school district was using the program Everyday Math. The research question posed by Ysseldyke and colleagues, then, can be paraphrased, "Are there achievement differences between classes using Everyday Math alone (the control) and Everyday Math plus Accelerated Math (the treatment)?" The researchers were also interested in how the coupling of Accelerated Math with Everyday Math might change the "instructional ecology" (teacher and student behaviors) in the classroom. The intervention (or treatment) is best described as Accelerated Math Plus Everyday Math.

Ysseldyke and colleagues (2003) chose not to assign students to instructional groups; instead they "maintained their natural classroom assignments" (p. 165). Lack of random assignment of subjects to groups combined with a treatment or intervention of some sort are the hallmarks of a quasi-experiment. The researchers' use of the terms *treatment group, control group,* and *intervention* makes it clear that the research design they used is experimental and that they intended to investigate cause-and-effect relationships. Yet this chapter makes it clear that true experiments, opposed to quasi-experiments, are better suited for establishing causal connections between instructional programs and achievement outcomes. Nevertheless, with other control procedures in place, such as matching, Ysseldyke and colleagues were able to learn more about the instructional effects of Accelerated Math. Because their design lacked the power of random assignments, it is classified as quasi-experimental. And because they collected standardized measures across two time periods (pre and post), their design is best described as a "pretest-posttest quasi-experiment."

Because the entire district used Everyday Math as the core curriculum, the researchers were able to create two control groups: a within-school control group and a district-wide control group. The researchers' two control groups strengthened the internal validity of their quasi-experiment. Their within-school control group was comprised of students using Everyday Math only, matched with the experimental group on grade level, gender, ethnicity, and socioeconomic status. Students in the district-wide control group were representative of students in general (at least in that district and in Grades 4 and 5). Notice that one researcher's control group, in this case students who use Everyday Math, might be another researcher's experimental group, such as students given traditional math instruction as a control.

In addition to two standardized measures of math achievement as dependent variables—STAR Math scores and Northwest Achievement Levels Test (NALT) scores—the researchers used a computerized observation system to collect data on student and teacher behaviors as part of the "classroom ecology" across the eight classrooms to link behaviors and learning outcomes to differences among the programs. These additional observations are noteworthy because they enabled the researchers to better understand why a treatment effect existed (or did not exist). Both STAR and NALT tests yielded Normal Curve Equivalent (NCE) scores (standardized with a mean of 50 and a standard deviation of 21). Ysseldyke and colleagues (2003) reported that gains of more than three points during a 1-year comparison are considered "educationally significant" (p. 168).

Ysseldyke and colleagues' results of their quasi-experiment revealed strong support for the use of Accelerated Math Plus Everyday Math. Students in that treatment group scored significantly higher than control students in both the within-school and district-wide comparison groups. Further, their objective observations ("ecobehavioral analysis") revealed instructional and learning differences when Accelerated Math was added to the Everyday Math curriculum. The major observational findings revealed that the Accelerated Math addition contributed to greater use of individualized instruction and interaction, as well as greater student academic engagement. (This finding would counter an alternative hypothesis that the treatment simply focused on test skills and practice.)

Ysseldyke and colleagues (2003) concluded that the "implementation of *Accelerated Math* with *Everyday Math* was related to a change in the overall environment of the classrooms in ways that have been identified as contributing to positive academic outcomes" (p. 173), namely, students' increased academic engagement. The positive academic outcome was clearly revealed by significantly higher scores on the two standardized mathematics achievement tests (STAR and NALT).

Notice that these researchers used the word *related* in reference to their conclusion. This word is often selected by researchers to describe findings that may be open to alternative explanations when research designs (such as the quasi-experiments) are used that do not warrant strong cause-and-effect statements. The word *related* means "connected," to be sure, but what is not known is the *basis* for the connection.

You will recall from Chapter 7 that in the absence of strong controls such as random assignment of teachers to instructional strategies and students to classes using large, diverse samples, one cannot be reasonably certain of the causal mechanism. Research in education is often plagued by the natural confounding of instructional treatments and teachers' experience or skill level. Perhaps more skillful teachers choose to adopt innovative instructional programs. If so, researchers might easily misinterpret a true teacher effect as an instructional program effect (when the teachers, not the program, made the difference).

Learning Disabilities

Tournaki (2003) reviewed the body of research literature on mathematics learning among young children with learning disabilities. She concluded that no research focused on comparing young students with and without learning disabilities (LD) using *strategy* instruction versus drill-and-practice when solving simple addition problems and transferring that knowledge to new situations. She stated her hypotheses in the following way: "(a) students without LD will perform significantly higher than students with LD, and (b) all students, with and without LD, will perform significantly higher when taught through strategy instruction than through drill and practice" (p. 450).

The learning disability classification was operationally defined as "an IQ score within the average range concurrent with academic performance two grade levels below expectancy at the time of testing" (Tournaki, 2003, p. 451). The LD versus general education (GE or non-LD) classification of students functioned as an attribute variable. Tournaki's independent variable was Type of Instruction, with the categories of (1) drill-and-practice, (2) strategy, and (3) control. Instruction in the first two categories was delivered by graduate assistants ("who were unaware of the research hypotheses," that is, blinded) over eight 15-minute sessions. The drill-and-practice was essentially just that, and the strategy instruction was *minimum addend* (the smaller value is counted from the larger value). The control group received no instruction to supplement that in the classroom (i.e., no intervention).

All three instructional groups were pretested and posttested using identical 20 single-digit addition items (e.g., 5 + 2 + ___). These items were drawn randomly from the pool of 80 such items, with the resultant tests having an internal consistency reliability of .91 (Cronbach's alpha). Tournaki also arranged for a transfer test, a parallel test of single-digit addition given shortly after the posttest. Her experiment, therefore, consisted of four phases: Pretest, Instruction (one of three conditions), Posttest, and Transfer.

After her LD and GE students were selected, they were *randomly* assigned to one of the three instructional treatments (drill-and-practice, strategy, or control). Because of the random assignment of participants to the instructional treatment groups, her design is *true experimental.* Given the use of her attribute variable (Type of Student), her design is best described as a pretest-posttest, control group, true experimental 3 × 2 factorial design. The "3 × 2" label is derived from three categories of Type of Instruction (drill-and-practice, strategy, and control) and two categories of Type of Student (classified as either LD or GE). Her four dependent variables were the accuracy and latency (speed) scores from both the posttest and transfer tests. (Her pretests were used in the statistical analysis to adjust for initial differences among all students.)

Her research participants included 42 GE second-grade students and 42 second-grade students identified as having LD attending a self-contained special education class at the same school as GE students. Her decision to use 84 participants (total) was not arbitrary. She stated: "With the level of significance set at .05, the power at .80, and the expected effect size set at .40, the sample size for each cell was calculated to be 14, and the total number of participants, 84" (Tournaki, 2003, p. 451). (Recall that sample size determination was described in Chapter 8. I believe that Tournaki's sample size determination was based on her true independent variable and three categories of Type of Instruction, and that it yielded a per-group number equal to 38, derived from 3 × 28 = 84.) The 3 × 2 factorial design yields six cells (3 × 2 = 6), hence 6 × 14 = 84.

Tournaki's findings (only the accuracy scores on the posttest) are summarized in Table 10.4 (values are rounded).

Recall that two-way factorial designs yield information about the *main effect* for each factor (Type of Instruction and Type of Student) and the *interaction* of the two factors. Tournaki's statistical analysis revealed a statistically significant main effect of Type of Instruction. This main effect is evident when the overall means for Type of Instruction are compared: drill-and-practice, 81.5, or (76 + 87)/2; versus strategy, 93, or (96 + 90)/2; versus control, 69, or (69 + 69)/2. The main effect of Type of Student was not significant, meaning that the overall average of LD students—80.33, or (76 + 96 + 69)/3—did not differ from the overall average of GE students—82, or (87 + 90 + 69)/3.

Further, Tournaki reported that the interaction of the two factors was statistically significant. This tells us that the influence of Type of Instruction depends on the Type of Student. Further analysis revealed that strategy instruction (compared to drill-and-practice) benefited the LD students more than the GE students. (Do you see the 20-point difference between drill-and-practice and strategy for the LD students? This compares to a 3-point difference between drill-and-practice and strategy for the GE students.) The strategy effect, then, is stronger for LD than GE students. It is also interesting to note that there were no *significant* differences between LD and GE students in the strategy condition (96 versus 90 was attributed to chance); the strategy instruction appears to eliminate LD and GE differences.

TABLE 10.4 Posttest Accuracy Scores

	Type of Instruction		
Type of Student	Drill-and-Practice	Strategy	Control
LD	76	96	69
GE	87	90	69

Source: "The Differential Effect of Teaching Addition Through Strategy Instruction Versus Drill and Practice to Students With and Without Learning Disabilities" by N. Tournaki, 2003, *Journal of Learning Disabilities, 36*(5), p. 453.

Tournaki (2003) reported very large effect sizes for Type of Instruction, suggesting that the Type of Instruction effect represents educationally meaningful results in addition to being statistically significant. Tournaki also reported similar findings on the transfer scores, the strategy effect (compared to drill-and-practice) being a boost of 15 points for LD students but only 3 points for GE students. She stated that the "analysis of latency data revealed the same pattern as that of accuracy" (p. 455). In fact, she reported that "students with LD in the strategy group became significantly faster than their counterparts without LD" (p. 455).

Tournaki's hypotheses were supported, but they were also complicated by her finding an interaction between Type of Instruction and Type of Student. It appears that she stated her hypotheses as main effects (as described above), but she found that these effects needed to be qualified (by "it depends") based on the finding of an interaction. Her conclusion highlights the meaning of an interaction: "The findings of this study indicate that strategy instruction and drill-and-practice instruction have differential effects on the 'automatization' of addition skills, depending on student characteristics" (Tournaki, 2003, p. 456). It appears that LD students benefit *greatly* from direct instruction in strategy—more so than GE students. Tournaki also emphasized that her conclusions based on her study must be viewed in light of the study's limitations, including the short duration of experimental intervention, its focus on one skill, and the fact that instruction did not occur in a natural classroom setting.

MORE EXAMPLES

Additional descriptions of published research may help to solidify your knowledge of important ideas related to experimental designs in research. You will find additional descriptions on the Web-based student study site (www.sagepub.com/eic).

Chapter Summary

Experimental research is characterized by an intervention of some sort (as opposed to comparisons between groups which already differ). A wide variety of experimental research designs exists, including true and quasi-experimental and single-subject designs. True experimental designs incorporate a manipulation with random assignment to groups (e.g., the randomized posttest control group design). The strength of the true experimental design is highlighted by its contrast to "pre-experimental" designs that have very little control over threatening influences. True experimental factorial designs are especially useful, for they yield information about main (overall) effects as well as interactive (nonadditive, "compounding") effects. Quasi-experimental designs incorporate treatments or interventions, but they lack the key element of random assignment to groups. This characteristic seriously compromises control in these designs. Alternatives to random assignment, like matching, yield quasi-experimental designs such as the matched comparison group design. Single-subject research designs also involve an intervention, and they often achieve their control by alternating baseline and treatment observations over time.

Application Exercises

1. For each of the scenarios below, determine whether the researcher is conducting an experimental study or a nonexperimental study. If it is experimental, decide whether it is a *true* experiment or a *quasi*-experiment. If it is a quasi-experiment, describe both the limitations of the design and the changes required to qualify as a true experiment.
   a. A researcher randomly assigned 120 students to four treatment groups in an effort to learn more about how different types of studying (the treatment) influence achievement.
   b. A researcher randomly selected 100 teachers from a large school district and divided them into two groups: those with a master's degree and those without one. Then the researcher assessed their levels of multicultural awareness to see if it was related to their educational attainment.
   c. A researcher formed three groups of parents: those who demonstrated a parenting style that included a strong emphasis on developing autonomy, a weak emphasis on developing autonomy, and no emphasis on developing autonomy. Then he measured the children's self-esteem and achievement motivation to see if they were linked to the different parenting styles.
   d. A researcher recruited 200 volunteer college students who were self-reported to be test anxious. A random half was instructed on the use of meditation prior to exams; the other half was not (they merely served as a control and were provided with meditation training after the study was over). Students' anxiety level was assessed after the training just prior to final exams.
   e. Identical twins were observed in a study of the influence of college on people's overall satisfaction with life. Fifty twins were located who satisfied this requirement: one twin graduated from a 4-year college and the other twin never attended college. The researcher then compared the two groups on a measure of their overall happiness.
   f. A researcher studied the number of math and science teachers who graduated from state-supported colleges and universities. In an attempt to increase this rate, a special program was implemented that provided partial tuition payment for teachers in training for math and science positions. The researcher compared the trend before and after the implementation to determine whether the program accomplished its goal.
   g. A researcher studied how students' sleepiness after lunch is affected by varying types of illumination (fluorescent, incandescent, and halogen lighting) in a study hall. All the students were observed under each condition in a counterbalanced design.
   h. A researcher investigated how students' attitudes and achievement are affected by pop quizzes. Three randomized groups were formed: pop quiz twice a week, pop quiz once every 2 weeks, and no pop quizzes.
   i. A researcher studied the influence of class size on reading achievement by arranging for all second graders in a district to be in classes of no larger than 15 students. The researcher compared the end-of-year reading achievement in the size 15 classes with similar classes in another district, all with sizes between 20 and 25.

2. Interactions are common in everyday life, in the sense that the influence of one factor on your behavior depends on the level of a second factor. How the weather affects you, for example, might depend on how much sleep

you've had. Or the stimulating influence of coffee may depend on when you ate your last meal. Provide an original example of the interacting influence of two variables on your behavior, being very careful to include the concept of "it depends."

3. a. Presume a researcher tested boy versus girl students on a multiple-choice (MC) or essay exam. The boys and girls were randomly assigned to the multiple-choice or essay conditions, a true experiment. Here are the results (scores are total points earned):

	Test Type	
	MC	**Essay**
Boys	30	20
Girls	10	20

Is there a main effect for sex? Is there a main effect for test type? Is there an interaction?

Double check your answers with the key and explanation below:

Answers: Yes. No. Yes.

Explanation: You must compute overall average for each variable to assess main effects. The overall average for boys is 25 (the average of 30 and 20). The overall average for girls is 15 (the average of 10 and 20). So, 25 does not equal 15; there is a main effect for sex. The overall average for multiple choice is 20 (the average of 30 and 10). The overall average for essay is 20 (the average of 20 and 20). So, there is no main effect for test type since 20 equals 20. There is an interaction since the boys' scores go down by 10 when multiple choice and essay are compared, and girls' scores go up by 10 when multiple choice and essay are compared (−10 does not equal +10). When graphed, nonparallel lines are obvious. (Put multiple choice and essay on a horizontal line; put boys and girls above that line, or on the "face" of the graph.)

b. Here is another:

	Test Type	
	MC	**Essay**
Boys	10	10
Girls	5	15

Is there a main effect of sex? Is there a main effect of test type? Is there an interaction?

Double check your answer with the key and explanation below:

Answers: No. Yes. Yes.

Explanation: Boys overall equal 10 (the average of 10 and 10); girls overall equal 10 (the average of 5 and 15). So, there is no main effect for sex. Multiple choice overall equals 7.5 (the average of 10 and 5); essay overall equals 12.5 (the average of 10 and 15). So, there is a main effect for test type (7.5 does not equal 12.5). There is an interaction since boys' scores do not change from multiple-choice to essay; yet girls' scores go up by 10 (0 versus +10, the difference is different).

c. Here is one more:

	Test Type	
	MC	**Essay**
Boys	10	30
Girls	10	30

Is there a main effect of sex? Is there a main effect of test type? Is there an interaction?

Double check your answer with the key and explanation below:

Answers: No. Yes. No.

Explanation: There is no main effect for sex (the overall average is 20 versus 20). There is a main effect for test type (the overall average is 10 versus 30). There is no interaction since the test type effect for boys (+20) is the same for girls' (+20). (Note: If the girls had been 30 and 50 for multiple-choice and essay, there still would be no interaction, since both boys and girls go up by the same amount, +20.)

4. Assume a researcher used a 2 × 2 factorial design to study how diet and exercise affect weight loss. Here are the results, expressed in pounds lost after 6 months, for the four treatment combinations: both diet and exercise: 10; neither diet nor exercise: 0; diet but no exercise: 2; no diet but exercise: 1.
   a. Form a table showing the means for each "cell."
   b. Graph the results.
   c. Evaluate each main effect and the interaction effect using the guidelines describe in this chapter.
   d. Repeat a through c above, substituting the following cell means, respectively: 10, 0, 0, 10.
   e. Can you enter values into a blank 2 × 2 table above so that the values satisfy this outcome: "No main effect for diet but a main effect for exercise and an interaction"?

ON YOUR OWN

Log on to the Web-based student study site at http://www.sagepub.com/eic for more information about the materials presented in this chapter, suggestions for activities, study aids such as electronic flashcards and review quizzes, a sample research proposal, and research recommendations that include journal article links (with discussion questions and an article evaluation guide) and questions related to this chapter.

11

Common Nonexperimental Research Designs

Outline

Overview

Recall from the last chapter that a researcher would probably not initiate data collection for a research study without the guidance of a *research design.* The preceding chapter described a sampling of commonly used experimental designs in educational research. This chapter continues a sampling of research designs, but the focus is now on *nonexperimental* designs, those designs that lack an intervention (i.e., treatment) component. This difference is crucial, for nonexperimental research designs do not lend themselves well to the interpretations about cause and effect of interest to so many scientific researchers. Yet they do uncover relationships of interest to all educational researchers. We'll examine three broad classes of nonexperimental research designs—causal comparative, correlational, and descriptive. You will see that researchers think about nonexperimental designs a bit differently than experimental ones. This often requires creativity.

Scientific Research

The No Child Left Behind (NCLB) Act of 2001 makes many references to "scientifically-based research" favoring the use of rigorous randomized trials using control groups (like those described in Chapter 10). Yet few educational researchers define *science* in terms of research designs. And fewer would permit a research design to "drive" a research question. Meaningful research questions should always influence the design of a study, not vice versa. The American Educational Research Association (AERA) adopted by unanimous resolution the declaration that a "fundamental premise of scientific inquiry is that research questions should guide the selection of inquiry methods" (AERA, 2003). Their statement also made clear that there are *multiple* components of quality scientific research. The resolution cautioned against the "singular attention" to the tool of randomized trials and emphasized that a broad range of research problems in education is best addressed through alternative methods. The AERA Council that adopted the resolution urged the framers of the NCLB Act to "expand its current conception of scientifically-based research" and promote a "broader understanding of the range of scientific methodologies essential to quality research" (AERA, 2003).

HIGHLIGHT AND LEARNING CHECK 11-1

Science Defined

Scientists agree that a research question should guide the research method (not vice versa). Scientists use different tools and designs in their work, yet what defines their work as science is a collection of procedures and reasonable ways of thinking. They are concerned with controls and empirical evidence. What do you think distinguishes educational philosophy from educational science?

Science involves an astute chain of reasoning, procedural controls, and empirical evidence. History's brightest scientific minds (e.g., Einstein, Newton, Darwin, Galileo, Edison, Franklin, Curie, Edison, da Vinci, Aristotle, and many others) would hardly be labeled "unscientific" because they did not use random number tables and placebo groups. We saw in Chapter 10 that experimental designs using randomized control groups are effective for evaluating treatment or intervention effects. Yet many of these designs do not tell us how or why a program worked—or didn't work. Many nonexperimental, qualitative, and descriptive designs are well suited for answering questions about "how and why." Further, many experimentally validated treatments are developed by extensive research using nonexperimental designs prior to formal program development. Educational research is best served by the power of complementary research data. The most compelling data in educational research are often generated by the many designs described in Chapters 10 to 12, and they come from studies conducted by researchers who "experiment" themselves by using "alternative designs" during their years of professional work.

Common Nonexperimental Research Designs

The Basic Causal Comparative Design

Recall from Chapter 3 that educational researchers must frequently study phenomena as they naturally occur, without intervention of any sort. This is because it may not be practical, ethical, or feasible to arrange for the occurrence of a factor believed to cause some effect. The influence of divorce, for example, on the educational achievement and motivation of young students can only be studied without intervention. (Can you imagine randomly assigning married couples to a divorce group or high school students to a dropout group?) We also saw in Chapter 3 that researchers who study group differences (attributes) that are preexisting refer to their designs in general as *causal comparative*. They are so-named because the researcher is *comparing* different groups in an effort to explain the *causes* (or effects) of such differences. Examples of attribute variables that are nearly always studied with causal comparative designs are differences in sex, ability, personality, socioeconomic status, parenting styles, family structures, classrooms (such as single-sex versus coed), and, in general, schools and teachers. There are hundreds more, of which all are considered important but not all are readily amenable to experimental manipulations with random assignment.

NONEXPERIMENTAL RESEARCH: Research using designs that do not involve an intervention or a manipulation.

CAUSAL COMPARATIVE RESEARCH: Nonintervention research aimed at uncovering relationships by comparing groups of people who already differ on a variable of interest. It uses designs that search for causes or effects of a preexisting factor of interest. The preexisting factor differentiates groups and permits a meaningful comparison (e.g., examining achievement differences between children in one-parent and two-parent families).

An Example: LD and Self-Esteem

Consider the research reported by Gans, Kenny, and Ghany (2003) in a study of self-concept in children with learning disabilities (LD). Gans and colleagues reported that "the research literature on self-concepts in children with LD shows mixed findings and is often contradictory" (p. 287). (A common observation!) Using middle school students from primarily Hispanic backgrounds, Gans and colleagues hypothesized that students with LD would have lower self-concepts related to intellectual and school matters than their peers without LD, but would not differ from students in general education classes on a measure of global self-concept. They also predicted that girls with LD would have lower self-concepts than boys with LD.

"Self-concept" was operationally defined by scores on the Piers-Harris Children's Self-Concept Scale, an 80-item "yes-no" instrument designed to measure six dimensions of self-esteem (including "Intellectual and School Status") as well as global (or total) self-esteem. The researchers reported that Cronbach's alpha, the internal consistency index of reliability, in their data was .84 for the total self-concept score and between .66 and .79 for the subscale scores. This assures that something, presumably self-concept, is being measured with an acceptable amount of error. (You will recall from Chapter 9 that the calculation of measurement reliability on the data reported within the study is informative yet not routinely practiced. This information is especially useful in the interpretation of nonsignificant findings.)

The Gans and colleagues study is clearly causal comparative, the hallmark of which is inclusion of groups of research participants formed by a classification difference that already exists (defying random assignment to groups). Gans and colleagues used two attribute variables to test their predictions: LD classification (LD students versus non-LD students) and sex (male versus female). "LD" was operationally defined prior to the study by school administrators as a gap of 1.5 standard deviations (or more) between a student's measured intelligence and achievement in math, reading, or written expression. The researchers' hypotheses were tested with 50 students classified as LD and 74 students classified as non-LD (general education). There were approximately equal numbers of boys and girls. (Note: There is no requirement in educational research that sample sizes be equal in experimental and nonexperimental research. Often, however, comparisons are made more sensitive with equal sizes; hence equal group sizes often result in more powerful tests, statistically speaking. For that reason, equal group sizes are more desirable.)

HIGHLIGHT AND LEARNING CHECK 11-2

Causal Comparative Classifications

Causal comparative research searches for causes or effects of group classifications formed by preexisting differences, that is, by participant attributes, not treatments (e.g., being high school dropouts). If most individuals who become high school dropouts also have elevated levels of lead in their blood, why is it risky to conclude that lead causes school failure?

The researchers' hypothesis relating to an LD difference in academic self-concept was indeed supported (LD students scored lower), as was their hypothesis predicting no global self-concept differences. Gans and colleagues (2003) noted that "the students in the LD did not [extend] their feelings of academic weakness to more generalized self-concept perceptions" (p. 292). They also reported that "contrary to our hypothesis, there was no difference between boys with LD and girls with LD on self-concept" (p. 292). Thus, the Gans and colleagues causal comparative research design revealed no evidence that lowered self-concept relating to intellectual skills and school performance among middle-school students causes a generalized (and more disturbing) lowering of overall self-concept. Had they discovered generalized, lowered self-esteem across all dimensions, interpretation would have been more difficult. One could correctly conclude from this research that LD students (at least in this particular study) can be described as having lowered self-concept, yet the cause of this observed difference, given the research design, is open for debate. A simple explanation, such as a shift downward in self-esteem as a consequence or cause of an LD label, may not be correct. There may be other events, perhaps biochemical changes, that lead to both shifts in self-concept and challenges during learning. Simply, causal comparative studies are not well suited to disentangle cause-and-effect relationships. They are comparative (in procedure) but not causal (in logic), despite the design's label.

CRITICAL THINKER ALERT 11-1

Causal Comparative Research

Causal comparative research compares groups that differ on a preexisting attribute (not independent) variable. As such, this type of nonexperimental research is *not* well suited for establishing cause and effect, despite the word *causal* in its label.

Discussion: Presume a researcher compared the SAT scores of students who took Latin in middle school and those who did not. Finding having taken Latin was linked to higher scores, the researcher recommended more Latin courses be offered as a method to better prepare students for college. What is wrong with this conclusion?

Causal Comparative Design Considerations

Forming Groups

The basic causal comparative design is sometimes referred to as an *ex-post-facto design*. As implied by its name (*ex post facto* means "retroactive," "prior to," or "going back to"), this design involves a comparison between groups whose differences are preexisting, or exist prior to the researcher's observations. (Recall that this design feature was first introduced in Chapter 3.) A researcher might classify students into groups according to how much television they watch (a preexisting "condition" or attribute, really) and then compare their academic achievement (GPAs) to learn whether television watching is related to achievement in school. Consider a researcher who classifies high school students according to gender (another preexisting "condition") to see whether they differ in terms of strength of career aspirations. Or consider a researcher who classifies high school girls by their school type (all girl versus coed) to see whether there are differences in academic aptitude (SAT scores).

Notice that the designs described above focus on a presumed *cause* (television, gender, coed schools) of some effect (achievement, aspiration, aptitude, respectively). The grouping (attribute) variable in these examples was a hypothesized cause, while the measured outcome (dependent) variable was the hypothesized effect. Other ex-post-facto designs may focus a presumed *effect* of some cause. For example, a researcher may form two groups on the basis of whether their members dropped out of high school (the effect), while searching for the influence regarded as the cause (e.g., lack of a mentoring relationship, socioeconomic factors, etc.). Or a researcher might group students according to their difficulty in learning to read (the effect), and then search for the presumed cause (e.g., little exposure to written materials prior to kindergarten as a result of rarely being read to by an adult).

Whether the researcher is forming groups out of an interest in a cause or an effect, the basic design is the same. Groups are formed on some basis (a presumed cause or a presumed effect), then compared on another variable to shed light on cause-and-effect relationships. This simplicity is counteracted by the resulting difficulty with interpretation. To repeat this for strong emphasis: Despite the general name for these types of designs—*causal* comparative—such designs are far weaker than true experimental designs for the purpose of establishing cause and effect.

CRITICAL THINKER ALERT 11-2

Uncovering Relationships

Causal comparative research *is* well suited for uncovering relationships and forming theories that might be tested in follow-up studies using experimental or quasi-experimental research to better illuminate causal connections.

Discussion: As a follow-up to the discussion in Critical Thinker Alert 11-1, how might you design research that would illuminate a causal connection between studying Latin in middle school and college success?

Design Controls

Causal comparative designs are often labeled by the techniques used to create the groups used for comparison. For example, a *matched group* design would involve selecting two groups that are dissimilar on the hypothesized cause, say, bottle-fed and breast-fed babies, but are the same on a matching variable believed to be a rival explanation, say, the age and socioeconomic status of the mother.

An *extreme groups* design would involve the selection of groups which represent maximum differences on the hypothesized cause (or effect), for example, those who watch 60 or more hours of television per week and those who watch very little or no television. Such extreme groups could also be matched (equated) on a variable believed to be a rival explanation, for example, exercise. This would be a *matched extreme groups design.*

Strong Inference

We know that the basic causal comparative design frequently lacks strong controls for alternative hypotheses. This design can, however, be greatly strengthened by testing a plausible, rival explanation against the research hypothesis. The concept of a design that tests a research hypothesis against an alternative hypothesis (or one that "pits" two explanations against each other) is called *strong inference* (Platt, 1964) and is one mark of a good research design. Consider each one of the causal comparative examples above, and upon reflection, alternative explanations will probably come to mind.

STRONG INFERENCE: A concept referring to the test of a research hypothesis against an alternative (rival) hypothesis. Strong inference designs permit the elimination of at least one competing explanation (while supporting another).

As an illustration, focus on the example of children who had trouble learning to read and were found to have parents who rarely read to them. Does failing to read to children *cause* learning-to-read difficulties? Maybe, maybe not. Quite possibly, children who have trouble learning to read have lead poisoning (assume for this illustration that this is the real culprit). Perhaps the parents who spent little time reading to their children were predominantly lower social class and living in older homes which contained peeling lead paint. These older homes might also be adjacent to freeways and expressways and surrounded with soil contaminated by cars' leaded pollution over the years. This suggests that lead removal—not reading to children—would be most helpful in ameliorating the problem these children have in learning to read.

A strong inference design would illuminate this rival interpretation by collecting data on both social class *and* lead poisoning in addition to data on reading skills and early reading experiences. In truth, any one effect, like difficulty learning to read, most likely has multiple, complex causes.

Consider another relationship described previously: the television and achievement link. If the group of students with the highest level of television viewing also has the lowest GPAs, does this mean that watching television *causes* lower achievement? No. Maybe lower achievement causes more television watching, in that school failure lowers the motivation to pursue school-related activities (like homework, special projects, etc.), which in turn simply frees up more time for television watching. Could the real culprit be lack of exercise? Lack of exercise may deplete the brain of chemical transmitters, making school learning more difficult (hence, a lower GPA), and it may also encourage lethargic behavior, itself very compatible with television watching. The television, then, gets turned on because the lethargic student simply sits on the couch. The researcher would know this only if data on exercise were collected as part of the design.

Further, imagine (once again) a study which determined that young children who had formal training in music (e.g., piano lessons at age 6) had much greater math ability 10 years later than those who did not have training in music. Were the music lessons the cause of greater math ability? Maybe, maybe not. Possibly, parents who encouraged their children to take music lessons also tutored them more frequently during math homework assignments years later. The cause in this case would be the achievement orientation of the parents, not the music lessons per se. Again, a solid causal comparative design using strong inference would examine data on the achievement orientation of parents as well as music experience and math ability. The supplemental analysis might render the alternative hypothesis less likely (or possibly temper the conclusion if the rival explanation is supported).

HIGHLIGHT AND LEARNING CHECK 11-3

Causal Comparative Techniques

Several design considerations greatly enhance the usefulness of causal comparative research in education, including how groups are formed (selected), how control procedures (e.g., matching) are used, how persuasively alternative explanations are ruled out (e.g., strong inference), and how well spurious relationships are uncovered and controlled. If a researcher wanted to investigate the relationship between divorce during early childhood and adolescent adjustment using casual comparative research, what groups might be formed for comparison? Can you think of design features that might aid the interpretation on findings?

CRITICAL THINKER ALERT 11-3

Strong Inference

Strong inference is a very useful concept in research. It strengthens one's ability to interpret research findings by collecting data relevant to *both* a research *and* an alternative hypothesis (the plausible, rival counter-explanation). If data can rule out an alternative hypothesis while supporting the research hypothesis, one can be more confident in a correct interpretation.

Discussion: As a follow-up to Critical Thinker Alert 11-1, what additional data could have been collected to rule out an alternative hypothesis in the reported causal comparative study?

Spurious Relationships

The counter-explanations suggested by the previous examples may not seem plausible, but I hope that the point is clear: Causal comparative studies uncover links, but the *reasons* for the links may be open to many different interpretations. Variable A may cause Variable B, Variable B may cause Variable A, or Variables A and B may be caused by Variables C, D, E, F, G, H, I, J, . . . Z. When the relationship between Variable A and Variable B is caused (or explained) by Variable C, it is said that the relationship between A and B is *spurious,* or "not real" in a sense. For example, the relationship between early music lessons (A) and math ability in high school (B) is spurious if it is known that the cause of *both* early music exposure and later math ability was the priority the parents placed on achievement (C).

SPURIOUS RELATIONSHIP: A relationship than can be "explained away" by reference to another variable. When a connection between A and B is due solely to both being related causally to C, it is said that the relationship between A and B is spurious (or "false").

HIGHLIGHT AND LEARNING CHECK 11-4

Correlation Is Not Causation

Correlational research is nonexperimental research that seeks relationships via statistical connections between continuously scaled measurements (e.g., test scores and speed; memory capacity and hours slept). Design features and statistical controls help the interpretation of correlations. Researchers always remind themselves that *correlation is not causation.* What various ways might you interpret a negative correlation between class size and student achievement (e.g., larger classes, lower achievement)?

Here is another example: A relationship between balding and heart disease in men may be spurious if it is known that both balding and heart disease were caused by a third variable, like hormone levels. Spurious relationships can be explained away by a hidden factor. One would conclude not that balding per se caused heart disease, only that the linkage between the two was the result of some other influence. (Hair restoration products would not reduce the likelihood of heart disease.)

Or consider another research report: Short men are more likely than tall men to have heart attacks. Height per se does not cause heart attacks (short men would not take growth hormones to ward off heart attacks). A third variable, like poor nutrition in childhood, might cause both lack of growth and a weaker cardiovascular system.

CRITICAL THINKER ALERT 11-4

Spurious Relationships

The term *spurious* is curious! Often misunderstood, it refers to a relationship between two variables that is not "real," in the sense that it can be "explained away" by reference to a third (control) variable. (This idea is related to partial correlation.) For example, the correlation between hat size and vocabulary knowledge among young children can be explained away by age differences. Many spurious relationships, however, do not easily reveal such an obvious third variable.

Discussion: Explain why a connection between height and salary among high school principals (if it exists) is probably a spurious one.

The important point to remember is that two variables may be strongly related without one of them causing the other. Indeed, most relationships of interest to educational researchers are probably a tangled web of many other variables. Fortunately, researchers who use causal comparative research designs often have statistical procedures that allow for greater confidence in cause-and-effect interpretations. These procedures help rule out competing or rival explanations. You may have encountered the expression "controlled for statistically." This general collection of procedures for statistical control—partial correlation—was described briefly in Chapter 7.

Correlational Research Designs

Correlational research is a very close cousin to causal comparative research. They both suffer from the same inherent limitation: lack of intervention and resultant loss of control. The main difference between causal comparative and correlational research, you'll recall from Chapter 3, is the type of scale used in the analysis. Correlational research uses variables that are scaled *continuously,* like number of hours of television watched per week. The values of such a scale have no break, so to speak, in that they can be any number from 1 to, say, 60 (they may run continuously, 1, 2, 3, 4, 5, 6, 7, 8, 9, 10, 11, 12, 13, 14, 15, and so on to 60). This continuously scaled variable can then be related to (correlated with) another continuously scaled variable, like scores on a test of vocabulary knowledge, ranging continuously from 0 correct to 50 correct, the maximum possible score.

CORRELATIONAL RESEARCH: A type of nonexperimental research using one of several designs that measure individual differences in an attempt to uncover relationships between variables.

Contrast these continuous scales with what are called *discrete* scales, those values that are unconnected and distinct, such as type of teaching method, type of study method, school climate, learning style, and gender. Causal comparative research, as we have seen, typically employs one *discrete* (grouping) variable (e.g., male versus female, presence or absence of early music lessons, or breast fed versus bottle fed) and one continuously scaled variable (e.g., score on a test of the ability to "read" faces). Correlational research, by contrast, usually employs two continuously scaled variables such as age and reaction time.

Many complex statistical methods have been developed to analyze and help interpret research findings based on two or more continuously scaled variables. For the purposes of this discussion, these techniques may be described in terms of correlational designs. Let's examine a few common designs.

Basic Bivariate Design

This correlational design is the most fundamental of all correlational designs. The concept of a correlation was introduced in Chapter 9 (in a discussion of reliability) but will be reviewed here briefly. Two variables are measured from a sample of subjects, their data points are plotted, and a statistic is calculated to summarize the overall strength and direction of the relationship, or correlation. Here is a hypothetical example. A group of 20 adult learners enrolled in an intensive 2-week course on accounting principles and

BIVARIATE DESIGN: A type of correlational research design that assesses relationships using two measures.

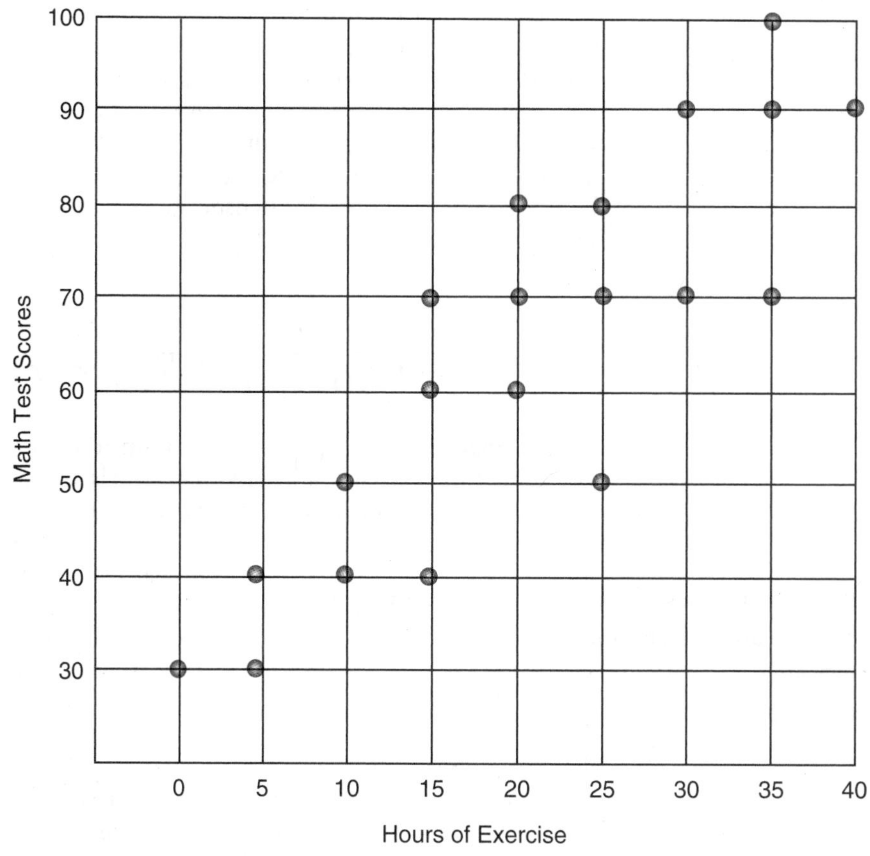

Figure 11.1 Scattergram showing the relationship between Scores and Exercise. (These data are hypothetical.)

completed a 100-item multiple choice test as a measure of their overall learning. At the end of the test, students also estimated how many hours of aerobic exercise they engaged in during the same 2-week period of time as the course. The researcher then plotted the 20 data points showing the relationship between test scores and hours of exercise. The plot, which is often called a *scattergram* (or *scatter diagram or scatterplot*), is shown in Figure 11.1.

The trend is clearly visible in this plot, as the points tend to "swarm" in a specific direction: from the lower left to the upper right. (You may want to review Chapter 9's introduction to the concept of creating and interpreting a scattergram.) Low scores on the test, therefore, tend to be associated with few hours of exercise, and high test scores tend to be associated with more hours of exercise. This is the defining characteristic of a *positive* relationship (low with low, high with high). If the pattern had been different, for example if the "swarm" had moved from the upper left to the lower right, a *negative* relationship would have been revealed. In this case, few hours of exercise would have been associated with higher test scores, and more hours of exercise would have been associated with lower test scores.

How closely the scores resemble an imaginary straight line defines the strength of the relationship—the closer the points are to the line (i.e., the "tighter" they are), the stronger the relationship. (This imaginary line is referred to as a *regression line.*) The statistic which defines the relationship's strength (and direction) is called the *correlation coefficient.* You might remember from Chapter 9 that it is symbolized *r.* Its value can range from −1.00 (a maximized negative correlation) to 1.00 (a maximized positive correlation; the "+" sign is usually deleted in a positive relationship). An *r* value of zero reflects no correlation, or a case in which few hours of exercise are associated with both low and high test scores (and more hours of exercise are also associated with low and high test scores). This lack of correlation would reveal itself as a circular (not linear) pattern (i.e., a "cloudburst" or "blob") of data points. The actual correlation coefficient, *r,* describing the data points shown in Figure 11.1 is .87, positive and quite strong.

As was true with causal comparative studies, the simplicity of this correlational design comes with a price: What does this correlation mean? It is open to many interpretations. Does it mean that exercise is causally related to achievement scores, maybe through changes in brain chemistry? If those with low test scores had exercised more, would they then have had higher scores? Or is this correlation *spurious,* meaning that it is explained by reference to a third variable, such as time, that was not measured by the researcher? Maybe those with more time available are able to study the textbook more and are also able to set aside time for exercise. Maybe the correlation, if spurious, is explained by yet another variable, physical health. Perhaps those who did not exercise very much have chronic health problems requiring medication, and the medication also interferes with attention and memory. Those who exercise more, by contrast, tend to be in better health (they exercise more because they feel better) and require no drugs which impact mental acuity.

Consider the positive correlation between spelling ability and shoe size—those with bigger feet spell better. (Do you remember this from Chapter 3?) How is this possible, you ask? Recall that the answer lies in the sample used to calculate the correlation: students in Grades 6 through 10. Older kids have bigger feet than younger kids,

CRITICAL THINKER ALERT 11-5

Spurious Correlations

Correlational findings are often spurious (see Critical Thinker Alert 11-4), meaning that the linkage between two variables might disappear with the introduction of another variable. A correlation does not imply causation, though a cause-and-effect relationship *is* possible (the link between smoking and longevity being one such example).

Discussion: Can you think of a correlational finding that is probably cause and effect? (Perhaps lead exposure and cognitive functioning in children?) And one that clearly is not? (Perhaps size of house and student GPA?)

and older kids spell better too. This is another example of a spurious relationship; spelling ability and shoe size are both connected causally to a third variable, age. Correlations are sometimes very difficult to interpret because of this "hidden" variable problem. Remember, simply because one variable is *correlated* with another, it is not safe to assume that it *causes* the other.

Correlations between variables abound, and because the world is a tangled web of complex relationships, it would be a surprise if two correlated variables represented, in fact, a simple and direct causal chain. For example, the correlation between watching television and school grades has been the focus of thousands of studies. Does watching too much television lower school grades? Do lower grades lead to watching more television? Is there a third variable responsible for the correlation? Does inactivity (lack of exercise) lead to both lower grades and more television? If one finds a correlation between headaches and neck and shoulder muscle tension, does the head pain cause muscle tension? Does the muscle tension lead to headaches? Or does another variable, like blood chemistry, lead to both headaches and muscle tension? Simply, a correlation between A and B might mean that A causes B, B causes A, or, what is most common, that C (or some complex interplay between C, D, E, and F) causes both A and B. Those who enjoy solving puzzles will enjoy the challenges faced by researchers who must explain the relationships that are discovered.

Educational researchers find it relatively easy to uncover correlations between all sorts of variables, but what the connections mean or how to interpret them is far more challenging. For example, what does a correlation between teachers' verbal ability and their students' achievement scores mean (Walsh, 2001)? Does it mean that smarter teachers produce smarter students? Or do teachers with higher socioeconomic status (family wealth) teach in schools with students who have higher socioeconomic status? A simple correlation, it turns out, is nearly impossible to meaningfully interpret without more information. It is a mistake, for sure, to assume a causal connection between variables (in either direction), for the correlation might be a function of another variable.

CRITICAL THINKER ALERT 11-6

Types of Correlations

Many different correlation coefficients have been developed. Their use depends on the type of data collected and patterns that exist in the relationships uncovered. The most common one is r, or the Pearson correlation coefficient, and it is most appropriate for assessing *linear* (straight-line) relationships. The Pearson r will underestimate other types of relationships, such as those described by curves. The alternatives to the dominant Pearson correlation coefficient are covered in most comprehensive texts in statistics.

Discussion: Can you think of a relationship that is probably *not* linear (straight-line)? Perhaps one with a large "bend" in the middle, reversing its direction?

CRITICAL PERSPECTIVES 11-1

CORRELATIONS

Critical Thinking Toolbox

Be on guard against the "appeal to ignorance" in educational research and among policy makers. This cloudy thinking focuses on what is not known as support for a claim, the tip-off being an assertion of little or no knowledge. For example, "No research results have shown that online education is inferior to onsite instruction; therefore, online instruction must be effective," which is a poor argument in favor of technology.

Correlations in Quantitative Research

Nonexperimental quantitative research makes frequent use of correlational designs in educational research. These designs are revealed visually via mechanisms such as scattergrams, and the primary method of data analysis becomes the correlation coefficient (one of several varieties). These designs are very efficient for uncovering relationships, but they often mask the basis for such relationships (cause and effect, spurious, etc.) The term *correlation* in quantitative research refers to a linkage between variables, one that is revealed by any one of several different non-experimental designs. It does not necessarily suggest a correlational design, as the researcher may uncover a correlations (linkage) with a fourfold, cross tabulation design using tallies, counts, or frequencies.

Correlations in Qualitative Research

The terms *correlations* and *relationships* carry somewhat different meanings for quantitative researchers and qualitative researchers. For qualitative researchers, a correlation (linkage) or relation may include connections such as typologies, sequence charts, hierarchies, tables, and a variety of matrices, networks, and displays. (See Miles and Huberman, 1994, for a discussion of these methods for connecting variables and constructs.) Nonexperimental correlational designs used in qualitative research are broadened to include visual structures that may connect ideas as well as variables.

Correlations in Action Research

Action research borrows nonexperimental, correlational designs from both quantitative and qualitative traditions to the extent that they assist reflective practice and "actionable" research. The correlation may be a coefficient revealing a connection between hours spent on homework and final exam score, or a matrix showing how teaching methods are linked to observations of student engagement.

Critical Thinking Question

Evaluate this argument: Correlational research in education has not revealed that watching violence on cable television leads to aggression at school, so we know that it does not. Can you explain why this argument is faulty?

Examples of Correlational Research

SAT

The simple association, or correlation, between the SAT score and college success (as measured by grades) has been the subject of thousands of research studies, nearly all of which are plagued by difficulties in interpretation. Many studies, for example, report a correlation of .2 or .3 (on a 0 to 1 scale) between test scores and freshman GPAs. But what does this mean? Many believe that the SAT appears to measure "family resources," such as income. (See Bradley and Corwyn, 2002, for a research summary of the relationship between socioeconomic status and a wide array of cognitive outcomes, including those that begin prior to birth and continue into adulthood.) A reliable finding is that for each block of $10,000 in family income (e.g., $20,000 to $30,000), the SAT increases a concomitant amount, revealing a classic stair-step pattern (more or less). Some might even refer to the SAT as the "Wealth Test" (Zwick, 2002). (See Yeung, Linver, and Brooks-Gunn, 2002, for discussion of "how money matters" in children's cognitive development.) The acronym SAT referred originally to the Scholastic Aptitude Test and then to the Scholastic Assessment Test. Now, the SAT refers to nothing but the SAT. This fact does not help us understand what the SAT actually measures. Its revision in 2005 aligns it more closely with a typical school curriculum (including grammar), hence making it more of an achievement test than an aptitude test (Cloud, 2003). Future research will determine whether the scores on the "new" SAT are as closely linked to family income as were the scores on the previous SAT.

CRITICAL THINKER ALERT 11-7

Coefficient of Determination

Squaring a correlation coefficient yields a *coefficient of determination* that tells the researcher the proportion of variance in one variable that is accounted for by the other variable. For example, if the correlation coefficient between SAT scores and class ranking based on GPAs in high school were .30, we would know that 9% of the variance (differences) in class rank is linked to SAT scores (or vice versa). It is said that the other 91% remains "unaccounted for." The squared correlation coefficient (coefficient of determination) is in some sense a more useful statistic than the simple correlation coefficient, for it describes the *strength* of the relationship using a familiar percentage scale (which always shrinks when compared to the correlation coefficient, except when the correlation is 1.00 or −1.00).

Discussion: If the correlation between class size and final exam performance were −.80, what percentage of the variation in exam performance is *unaccounted* for by class size?

CRITICAL THINKER ALERT 11-8

SAT Predictions

The SAT as a predictor of anything is shrouded in controversy. Research findings can be interpreted differently, and reasonably, by different people. You can expect research on the "new" SAT to generate opposing findings and counter-interpretations, especially in a climate of strong ideological and political views.

Discussion: Tests are often used to predict important outcome in education, such as success in college. Why are such tests controversial? Why can't people agree on definitions of "success"?

The Stroop Effect

Imagine being asked to quickly read the word *green* printed in red ink or describe the print color of the word *blue* printed in brown. Invariably, your speed would be slower in such a situation than in any naming condition that does not include this type of dramatic interference. The interference observed in tests such as this is known as the *Stroop effect* (Stroop, 1935).

Johnson and colleagues (2003) noted that the Stroop effect captured the imagination of researchers immediately after its discovery in 1935, generating hundreds of studies in the decades that followed. This impact was attributed, in part, to the fact that the speed score differences between Stroop-type stimuli and comparison conditions (with no interference) revealed stable (highly reliable) measures. Some people consistently experience much greater interference (slower speeds) than others. Pronounced and reliable individual differences usually attract much interest among researchers in the search for others measures (correlates) linked to those differences.

Psychologists, in particular, are curious whether consistent and striking individual differences like the Stroop interference measure (or the granddaddy of them all—intelligence) are shaped largely by genetic or environmental influences (or a complex interplay between the two, as is often the case). The curiosity is understandable, for Stroop interference measures might be correlated with personality traits or other cognitive measures such as reading skills or perceptual and memory measures. Connections such as these would beg for new theoretical formulations that might explain, for example, learning disabilities. Other correlational findings might have implications for classroom assessment or instructional practice.

Johnson and colleagues were especially interested in investigating the Stroop effect with a very unique sample of participants: twins reared apart. Their sample included over 100 either identical or fraternal twins who had been reared apart (with most having been separated in infancy). A correlational study, of course, requires at least two measures in the computation of the correlation coefficient to reveal the magnitude and direction of the correlation. Johnson and colleagues used the Stroop Color-Word Test interference score along with a battery of other measures derived from several instruments, including (1) an inventory that assesses 11 primary personality dimensions, (2) two scales that measure adult intelligence, (3) several tests of perceptual speed and accuracy, (4) a measure of memory span, and (5) two measures of reading skill.

Johnson and colleagues' results revealed no correlation between the Stroop interference scores and personality measures, and generally low correlations with intelligence, perceptions, memory, and reading scores. Of special interest, however, was the comparison of correlation coefficients computed on Stroop interference measures comparing identical and fraternal twins. Johnson and colleagues reported a correlation coefficient (r) of .34 between Stroop interference scores using identical twins, but only .19 using fraternal twins. The unique nature of this twins-reared-apart research design enabled the researchers to conclude that the data suggest "sizable heritabilities" and a "biological basis" for differences assessed by the Stroop test. This conclusion followed from finding higher correlation coefficients with identical twins than with fraternal twins.

This study also shows that researchers can use correlation coefficients in several ways, including the direct assessment of a relationship between two measures and the comparison of two or more correlation coefficients computed on different subsamples. Differences between correlation coefficients may have implications for theory or practice. For example, some instruments may have greater diagnostic value or predictive validity for specific subpopulations. Correlation coefficients may be negative or positive depending on the attributes of a subpopulation. It is also conceivable that when two subpopulations (e.g., males and females) are considered together, a positive correlation for one group combined with a negative correlation with another group may mix together to yield a correlation near zero. (This is probably easier to understand if you imagine two scattergrams, one negative and one positive, being combined in an overlay to form a "blurry X" pattern that looks more circular than linear—indicating no relationship.)

Descriptive Research Designs

Frequently our understanding of educational phenomena is enhanced greatly by the process of careful description. For example, knowing how thinking changes among first-year teachers may help us design better teacher education programs. What are first-year teachers' most prominent anxieties and greatest disappointments? What information gained in teacher preparation courses do they feel is most valuable? What are the most frequent reasons cited among first-year teachers who quit after their first year? What are beginning teachers' attitudes about mainstreaming? What expectations do these teachers have regarding low socioeconomic students? What do they know about the interpretation of standardized test scores? Questions such as these are best answered with a widely used research method: the survey. Let's examine this method more closely.

DESCRIPTIVE RESEARCH: Research aimed at describing the characteristics of a population without generalizing or testing statistical hypotheses.

Survey Designs

Surveys are typically used by researchers when they want to gather information from a group for the purpose of describing characteristics of that group. The survey may take many different forms, but the most common form is probably the written questionnaire very familiar to most of us. The format of the questionnaire may vary from rating items to be passively checked by respondents to more engaging open-ended essay questions. (Examples of some commonly used questionnaire formats and scales were presented in Chapter 4, Table 4.7.)

One especially useful survey design is the *total design method,* as described by Dillman (1978). An updated discussion of the total design method is provided by Salant and Dillman (1994) and is also useful for designing and conducting your own survey. Furthermore, valuable information on conducting surveys is provided by the Phi Delta Kappa Center for Professional Development and Services in the form of PACE (Polling Attitudes of the Community on Education) materials designed for nonspecialists who want to design scientific surveys on attitudes and opinions on education. These materials provide guidance in questionnaire construction, sampling designs, and analysis of data. (For more information, see Rose and Gallup, 2003, p. 52.)

CRITICAL THINKER ALERT 11-9

Survey Responses

Survey responses are easily prone to respondent bias. A survey of drinking habits, for example, may not yield information that matches what is found in household garbage. Other examples of bias include students underreporting their cheating behavior and parents overreporting the learning experiences afforded their children at home.

Discussion: Consider your own personal experiences with surveys. Can you remember any little white lies?

Longitudinal and Cross-Sectional Surveys

Surveys may be administered at a single point in time, or they may be administered many times over a longer period of time. The *longitudinal* survey, for example, is well suited to describe the process of change, or trends over time. With this design, the *same* participants provide data at specific intervals across time. For example, if you wanted to learn how teachers' attitudes change over a 20-year period in the classroom, you might ask the same teachers for their opinions every 5 years. The major drawback here, of course, is the length of time required to completely describe changes (20 years!) An alternative, the *cross-sectional* design, by contrast, can be completed at one point in time by surveying different teachers, say those with 1 year, 5 years, 10 years, 15 years, and 20 years of experience in the classroom. For studying change, however, this cross-sectional approach has its shortcomings.

LONGITUDINAL SURVEY DESIGN: A descriptive research design that collects data from the same group of respondents over a period of time. Such designs often focus on the process of change.

The reason for this is not so obvious: Cross-sectional designs confound time with subject differences. This is because as time changes (5 years to 10 years to

15 years, etc.), so do naturally occurring differences in people. Let's presume that a cross-sectional study shows that reading teachers' beliefs about reading are more phonics-based with increasing years in the classroom. Does this mean that teachers become more phonics oriented with increasing experience in the classroom? Not necessarily. It may be that teachers attitudes don't change at all with increasing experience. Teachers with 15 and 20 years of experience simply learned how to teach reading using phonics when they were in teacher training programs 15 or 20 years ago, and they have been using phonics ever since. And the more recently trained teachers (those with 1 or 5 years of experience) learned to teach reading using whole-language methods more than phonics, and quite possibly, they will continue to use this method even after they have 20 years of experience. In other words, it may be that teachers' methods and attitudes don't change at all over time; it only looks that way in a cross-sectional design because participants at each time interval are different.

CROSS-SECTIONAL SURVEY DESIGN: A research design that describes changes over time using respondents who reflect temporal differences such as age (but data collection occurs at one point in time).

HIGHLIGHT AND LEARNING CHECK 11-5

Descriptive Research Designs

Descriptive research designs describe a population or phenomenon of interest. Descriptive designs often use the survey method (e.g., questionnaire or interview), including longitudinal surveys (studying the same people over time) and cross-sectional surveys (studying different age cohorts at the same time). Both types of survey methodologies have serious limitations. What are these limitations?

In a similar way, it would be misleading to study groups of people in their twenties, fifties, and nineties at the same time (a cross-sectional design) and then project the course of changes of the younger group as they age into their nineties. This is because people in their nineties have had experiences that those in their twenties (and fifties) have not had (and probably never will have), including World Wars I and II, economic depressions, famine, or environmental risks. In this way, it would be hard to disentangle age effects from experience effects.

CRITICAL THINKER ALERT 11-10

Types of Surveys

Learning about developmental changes is best accomplished by longitudinal surveys (but they are time consuming, lasting as long as the period being studied). Cross-sectional surveys can be conducted at one point in time (e.g., with the current ages of respondents being 20, 40, and 60), but they confound age differences with life experiences (e.g., those who are now 20 will not have the same experiences as those who are now 60).

Discussion: Consider today's 10-year-old children and today's 25-year-old young adults. What experiences might the young adults have had over the last 15 years that would cast doubt on current 10-year-olds' following the identical path of psychosocial development?

Combining Longitudinal and Correlational Designs: Hybrids

Researchers who use nonexperimental designs often combine related designs to better enable an answer to their research question (or sometimes even permit a question to emerge). The following section shows how two research designs can be meaningfully integrated.

An Example: The Home Environment

Decades of educational and psychological research tell us that environmental influences, particularly at home, are related to measures of intellectual skills. Molfese, Modglin, and Molfese (2003) set out to extend this knowledge by conducting a nonexperimental study of early home influences and their linkage (correlation) to children's later scores on reading achievement tests. The home environment was operationally defined by scores on the Home Observation for Measurement of the Environment (HOME) developed by Bradley and Caldwell (1984). The HOME inventory involves interview questions at home (usually with the mother) as well as observation items (e.g., extent of reading materials apparent within the home). The researchers used two versions of the HOME inventory, one for early childhood (EC HOME) and one for middle childhood (MC HOME). Both have eight subscales, such as Learning Materials, Academic Stimulation, Emotional Climate, Aspects of the Physical Environment, and so on.

Molfese and colleagues' (2003) research design is considered longitudinal because the *same* children were studied at age 3 and again at 8, 9, or 10. A total of 113 children were studied using measures of socioeconomic status, HOME scores, and reading scores. Socioeconomic status was operationally defined by a composite of numerical scores reflecting level of formal parental education, type of parental occupation (scaled according to professions), and family income. Molfese and colleagues (2003) reported that these "marker variables" were averaged (given equal weight) to provide a single socioeconomic status (SES) measure.

Reading skill was operationally defined by commonly used standardized reading tests in the schools (such as the Stanford Achievement Test Series) as well as widely used laboratory-administered, standardized reading tests (such as Woodcock Reading Mastery Test—Revised). Because this research is nonexperimental, there was no experimental intervention of any sort. Research participants were merely measured twice, and the measures of socioeconomic status, the home environment, and skill at reading were statistically analyzed. Patterns of correlations—and hence the correlational design—were interpreted to better understand the factors that might affect developing reading skills.

The longitudinal-correlational research conducted by Molfese and colleagues (2003) revealed interesting relational patterns, the most obvious being that "the SES measures at 3 and 10 years of age and the EC HOME total and Reading subscale scores were correlated with all reading achievement scores" (p. 63). Another noteworthy pattern in the correlations revealed that the EC HOME (early childhood version) correlated more strongly and consistently than the MC HOME (middle childhood version) with reading scores 5 to 7 years later. Although not especially high (around .35), these statistically significant correlations do suggest the important role of *early* home influences on the development of reading skills. The findings also reveal the importance of assessing the family environment for the purpose of understanding children's cognitive development.

Because these findings of Molfese and colleagues (2003) are correlational, one cannot make cause-and-effect inferences about specific home factors that invariably lead to children's having better (or worse) reading skills several years later. The longitudinal component to correlational research designs, however, strengthens the researcher's ability to disentangle cause-and-effect relationships. An effect of a cause cannot come *prior* to the cause; it must come *after* its cause. For example, aggressive behavior as a young adult cannot cause excessive viewing of violence on television as a teenager; if it is causal, it must be the other way around. Temporal (time) information can be used in sophisticated correlational designs and analyses across several periods, sometimes years or decades, to test the plausibility of a directional causal link (the subject of an advanced course in statistics). These designs are usually referred to as *cross-lagged panel designs;* the method of analysis is often called *path analysis.*

MORE EXAMPLES

Additional descriptions of published research may help to solidify your knowledge of important ideas related to nonexperimental designs in research. You will find additional descriptions on the Web-based student study site (www.sagepub.com/eic).

Chapter Summary

Researchers often uncover relationships in the absence of any intervention or treatment. Such nonexperimental research designs often yield findings that are difficult to interpret. One class of nonexperimental research designs is called *causal comparative,* and these designs compare groups which differ on some important dimension (e.g., heavy versus light television watchers). Researchers who use these designs are usually interested in the effects (or causes) of such differences. Interpretation problems abound since the groups may differ in other important ways (e.g., heavy television watchers may also get less exercise or have poorer diets than those who watch less television). Researchers use *correlational* designs when subjects can be measured on a continuum (e.g., level of exercise in hours per week and speed of mental processing) as opposed to in discrete (category) groupings (as in causal comparative research). Otherwise, correlational and causal comparative designs do not differ in fundamental ways. They suffer from the same inherent interpretation problems. The difficulty with interpreting correlational findings is lessened to some extent with statistical control. Researchers use *descriptive* research designs such as cross-sectional and longitudinal *surveys* to learn more about the characteristics of a particular group. Careful description often precedes the development of new theories and the search for relationships. Many descriptions are accomplished best with qualitative approaches to research that integrate key features of several nonexperimental designs. These are described in the following chapter.

Application Exercises

1. For each of the scenarios below, determine whether the researcher is conducting a nonexperimental study or an experimental study. If it is nonexperimental, decide whether it is causal-comparative, correlational, or descriptive.
   a. A researcher studied the influence of class size on reading achievement among fourth graders. Three randomly formed class sizes were studied (of 12, 18, and 24 students) using a total of 30 schools.
   b. A researcher designed, implemented, and studied the influence of a new Spanish Immersion program at a large urban school. Achievement across several subject areas in the immersion school was compared with achievement in a school across town that was similar in student population but more traditional in its foreign language programs.
   c. A researcher studied how spanking as a punishment in childhood is related to criminal activity in adolescence. Three groups of adolescents were formed: those whose parents used spanking frequently, infrequently, or not at all. Arrests records were then compared across the three groups.
   d. A researcher wondered how adults' reading to children was related to the children's later reading achievement. The reading achievement levels of two groups of sixth graders were compared: those who were read to frequently as young children and those who were not.
   e. A researcher wondered how the general trait of happiness was related to intelligence. Young adults' intelligence was measured using a traditional IQ scale; their level of happiness was also measured on a scale ranging from 1 to 20. The researcher found no association (link) between the results on these two measures.
   f. A researcher wondered whether the time required to complete a multiple-choice test was related to performance on the test. One hundred college students enrolled in General Psychology took an untimed 120-item test; their tests were marked with a ranking reflecting the sequential order they were turned in. The researcher found no association between the test scores and the time spent completing the exam.
   g. A researcher wondered whether principals' effectiveness, as determined by teachers' perceptions, was related to their level of educational attainment. The researcher found that principals with doctorates were perceived to be more effective than those without doctorates.
   h. A researcher wondered how much time parents spend per week helping their children with homework. A questionnaire was administered to a sample of parents in representative school districts across the country.
   i. A researcher wanted to learn more about the moral thinking of contemporary high school students. About 1200 high school seniors were interviewed and asked to provide judgments about hypothetical moral dilemmas. According to the researcher, most students' moral development had not progressed beyond the "conventional."
   j. A researcher studied master teachers in their classrooms and did a narrative summary of field notes which revealed that most master teachers view teaching as a type of "heartfelt artistic expression."
   k. A researcher studied the extraordinary accomplishments of ten 75-year-old full-time teachers and was convinced that the "mind is a muscle."
   l. A researcher wondered if children breast fed as infants had better memories than those who were bottle fed. Two groups of 10-year-olds (one breast fed, the other bottle fed) were compared, and the groups' members were found to have the same memory capacity.

2. Can you conduct your own correlational study? Sure you can. Here is one suggestion. Randomly sample 15 states using the methods described in Chapter 8. (List all the states, number them, and then use a random number table to select 15. You could use all 50 states, of course, but a selection of 15 makes this exercise more manageable.) Then decide what variables might provide an interpretable correlation. State-level information is readily available online at trustworthy Web sites such as the National Center for Education Statistics (http://nces.ed.gov/) and the Nation's Report Card (http://nces.ed.gov/nationsreportcard/). You might consider collecting data on population size, school expenditure, NAEP (or ACT) scores, dropout rates, going-to-college rates, or many others. You could also collect noneducation state data—such as average income, health indexes, crime rates, political measures, or even average number of sunny days—from other sources. Form a scattergram as illustrated in Figure 11.1. Is there a discernible pattern among your data points reflecting a relationship between the variables you chose? If so, how would you interpret this correlation?

ON YOUR OWN

Log on to the Web-based student study site at http://www.sagepub.com/eic for more information about the materials presented in this chapter, suggestions for activities, study aids such as electronic flashcards and review quizzes, a sample research proposal, and research recommendations that include journal article links (with discussion questions and an article evaluation guide) and questions related to this chapter.

12

Qualitative Design and Analysis

Outline

Overview

Recall from the two previous chapters that researchers seek the guidance of a *research design*, or a blueprint for collecting data to answer their questions. Those chapters described commonly used experimental and nonexperimental designs in educational research. This chapter continues a sampling of research designs with a focus on common qualitative research. It examines three broad classes of these designs—*ethnographies, case studies,* and *historiographies.* We will see that researchers think about qualitative designs a bit differently than they do about experimental and nonexperimental ones, often requiring creativity. Such divergent ("outside the box") thinking is apparent in the task of analyzing qualitative research. This will become clear later in this chapter when we focus on how researchers analyze qualitative studies to extract the most meaning.

In the case of qualitative data analysis, we will see that a major task involves coding and pattern seeking using analytic induction. Making sense of data in the form of graphics, video, audio, and text requires clear thinking that is aided by theory, models, constructs, or perhaps metaphor. Because qualitative data analysis is less prescribed than statistical analysis, many would argue that it presents a greater creative challenge. Fortunately, techniques, strategies, and procedures have been developed to help qualitative researchers to extract meaning from their data (including software) and interpret it in ways that enhance our understanding of complex phenomena.

Ethnographic Designs

Sometimes researchers investigate phenomena that do not lend themselves to straightforward quantitative approaches; researchers may not even know just what it is that should be measured or if, in fact, what should be measured could be measured with any degree of meaningfulness. A researcher in this case might use an *ethnographic* design, one of many used in qualitative approaches to educational research.

ETHNOGRAPHIC DESIGN: A nonexperimental descriptive research design that is usually participatory and extends over a period of time in a natural setting. It often uses observational methods, interviews, and a variety of other qualitative methods.

Ethnographic research has been associated with the study of anthropology in situations where the researcher observes, or even becomes part of, a group whose culture and sociology are described. For example, maybe a colony of gorillas is observed in order to understand its social network or a recently "discovered" tribe in Brazil is observed to better understand its culture.

Ethnographic researchers may pose a variety of questions. For example, they may ask, "What is it like to teach in a high school that has many students with behavioral problems?"; "What is the home environment like for an at risk preschooler?"; "What is an all-girls school like?"; "In what ways does typical Catholic education differ from typical public education?"; or "Is there such a thing as a typical home school, and if so, what is home schooling really like for elementary school children?"

Design Features

The design of ethnographic research often centers on the extent to which the researcher participates within a group or merely observes a group. The participant or observer role is not a simple dichotomy. Ethnographic designs may fall anywhere on a participant-observer continuum. An ethnographer studying the lives of teachers in inner city schools may participate in teaching activities or may become involved with conflict resolution in the classroom but be a strict observer during faculty meetings.

Ethnographic research designs usually specify procedures and guidelines for taking field notes. These notes often form the backbone in the analysis of ethnographic data. The *field notes* may take many forms, including detailed observations and general interpretations, reflections, and summaries of recorded interviews. Ethnographic designs in educational research (and case study designs, which are described later in this chapter) frequently employ *triangulation*, a type of qualitative cross-validation (corroboration) or data cross-checking procedure whereby multiple data sources or data collection procedures are expected to agree (converge). For example, a researcher might uncover a pattern in interviews, then check to see whether the same pattern holds up in written correspondence, in printed materials, in minutes of a meeting, in personal journals, or among observers. The researcher can also check to see whether the same pattern using the same data collection technique is consistent over time. If the multiple sources of data collection are in agreement, the findings are believed to be more credible. Triangulation greatly enhances the validity of qualitative findings.

TRIANGULATION: A method used in qualitative research that involves cross-checking multiple data collection sources and procedures.

HIGHLIGHT AND LEARNING CHECK 12-1

Ethnographic Triangulation

Ethnographic research designs often use rich qualitative measures over an extended period of time in a natural setting (a "culture"). They may be "participatory," in the sense that the researcher joins a group (to a greater or lesser extent) to understand its social dynamics and meaning. Triangulation (convergence of measures) enhances the meaningfulness of data, and the findings are often revealed in a story. Which of the following titles is more likely to reflect ethnographic research: "The Social Work of Teaching" or "Correlates of Teaching Satisfaction"? How might sources of data in either study become triangulated?

Published reports of educational ethnographies reflect the rich detail of the blueprints used to carry them out. They are mostly narrative in form, and a better understanding of the phenomenon studied is often conveyed by a good *metaphor* or illuminating story instead of a pie chart or bar graph. Fine examples of ethnographic studies in education can be found in two premiere journals (among others): *American Educational Research Journal* and *Qualitative Studies in Education.*

CRITICAL THINKER ALERT 12-1

Ethnographic Case Studies

Ethnographic and case study research designs may combine, yielding rich, detailed analysis that is not possible with simpler surveys. Ideas that spring from ethnographic and case study research sometimes generate new areas of research or new ways to think about old problems.

Discussion: What research topic would you like to pursue using an ethnographic case study? Can you explain why its rich, detailed analysis might lead to new areas of research?

An Example: Dyslexia

McNulty (2003) wondered, "What are the life stories of adults who were diagnosed with dyslexia as children?" (p. 365). His rationale for selecting a qualitative ethnographic research design is well stated: "Rather than approaching the study with a specific set of questions or variables, a more open-ended inquiry into the events and emotions related to living with diagnosed dyslexia over the course of life was thought to be a useful way to authentically articulate participants' experiences" (p. 365). McNulty (2003) described his nonexperimental research design as the "life story method of narrative analysis," a method of qualitative research that "articulates the experiences" of a group by describing the "qualities within a type of life in a manner that is accurate, relevant, and compelling as determined by those who are familiar with it" (p. 365). The *life story research design,* then, refers to the study of a phenomenon by comparing and contrasting accounts of people's lives who share the same experience.

McNulty (2003) began by defining dyslexia by its primary symptoms: difficulty reading and spelling attributed to a problem with the phonological coding of written language. He selected 12 adult research participants (age 25 to 45) and interviewed them extensively (using audiotapes). Using transcriptions, he determined common and contrasting elements of the shared story, created a typology (or classification scheme) that fit all cases, and eventually created a *collective* life story based on participants' own words. Validation of the life story was accomplished by a "self-validation circle" whereby the participants reviewed the collective story and judged whether it was an "accurate, relevant, and compelling depiction of the experience" (p. 365). Further, McNulty (2003) sought others (none were original participants) who had undergone the shared dyslexia experience for the purpose of reviewing the collective story's accuracy and generalization. This enabled McNulty to revise the collective life story from the perspective of the wider community similarly affected by the phenomenon of dyslexia. McNulty's (2003) analysis was aided by a structural framework that used the elements of a story (such as prologue, exposition, plot, subplot, resolution, etc.).

The life stories as reported were indeed fascinating. The interpretive analyses of the narrative life stories in context enabled McNulty (2003) to characterize dyslexics' attempts to compensate on functional, emotional, and psychological levels. McNulty's creative life story research design effectively uncovered the experiences of dyslexics over the course of life. It revealed what he labeled "LD trauma" and the importance of a "niche" for overcoming problems related to lowered self-esteem.

Case Study Designs

Some descriptive-oriented questions in education can be answered by intensive study of a single person (or single group). For example, one may wonder (as did Jean Piaget) what are the most prominent qualitative changes in children's thinking as they progress through the school years. Piaget answered this question (in part) by very extensive, extraordinarily detailed study of his own children. As it turned out, Piaget's findings based on his case studies generalized remarkably well to ther children. Different case studies,however, may not be so widely applicable.

Let's suppose that Mrs. Rogers is immensely popular with her math students, and that her students outscore others by a wide margin on standardized tests of quantitative reasoning. A case study of this phenomenon may reveal charismatic personality factors coupled with very innovative and highly effective cooperative learning strategies. Yet, another very popular and stellar teacher (in terms of student achievement) may share none of the charisma factors nor teaching strategies of Mrs. Rogers. The other teacher may display great humor and give highly entertaining lectures.

CASE STUDY DESIGN: An approach to qualitative research that focuses on the study of a single person or entity using an extensive variety of data.

Those who conduct case studies, however, are probably interested not so much in generalizing their findings to others as in telling a story. The story is often full of rich narrative detail and may offer insights about complex processes not possible with, for example, the simplistic rating scales used in a large survey. Good case studies are usually fascinating to read; they are engaging and often speculative. Readers of case studies often find useful ideas within the rich descriptions; they may also be stimulated to look at old problems in new ways. Researchers who use case study designs often find that their research "generalizes" to the extent that others can *use* ideas embedded within the descriptions in some other, often personal, context. In this sense, usefulness may be more important for case studies than wide generalization.

The following section describes two qualitative case studies that appeared in the published literature. Both illustrate the challenges and value of qualitative case studies.

Classroom Climate

Pierce (1994) investigated the importance of classroom climate for at-risk learners in an interesting study which she described as a "qualitative case study." (You will, however, also recognize elements of an ethnography.) Descriptive qualitative research often uses blended research designs; in fact, an "ethnographic case study" is quite common in the research literature. Pierce's study is clearly not experimental; it is descriptive, as the purpose was to describe in a natural environment how one teacher created a climate that enhanced learning. Her chosen teacher taught middle school (social studies) and had 24 years of experience.

Inspection of Pierce's research design section reveals that participant observation was the method of data collection, and that students were used as *key informants* (those who provide data) to increase the accuracy of the recorded data (which were mostly observations in the form of audiotapes and field notes). Both participant observation and the use of key informants are hallmarks of ethnographic research designs. Pierce also described the use of "triangulation" in her case, referring to the convergence of observations and conclusions from the teacher, her students, and herself. Other data were collected from interviews, field notes, and archival records—note the appearance of triangulation once again. The accuracy of her data was increased to the extent that all three sources were in agreement.

Pierce (1994) stated that "collected data were categorized, analyzed, and interpreted . . . according to the context in which they occurred" (p. 38). The *context* provides an important backdrop for all descriptive studies. One cannot fully understand the case (in a case study) without analyzing how it is embedded within its setting. Ethnographic case study designs are *holistic,* in the sense that the person is *total* (unified) and cannot be fragmented into independent parts. Holistic description also suggests that the naturalistic setting must be preserved and interpreted in a richly complex social context.

Pierce (1994) reported that "from the initial classroom observations, questions were generated that tended to focus subsequent observations on specific classroom interactions and behaviors" (p. 38). She continued, "Repeating patterns of behavior began to emerge, creating specific categories and subcategories that were used to develop a working hypothesis tentatively explaining how this specific classroom operated" (p. 38). Notice how the design of the study shaped her "working" (tentative) hypothesis. This is radically different from experimental designs used in quantitative research whereby hypotheses are often arrived at deductively from theory, as explained in Chapter 4. Hypotheses derived from theory are fixed for the duration of the research in quantitative, experimental research.

Hypotheses derived from qualitative observations in descriptive research, by contrast, are flexible. Descriptive (qualitative) research questions can be developed and refined as they study progresses. You will not find any level of statistical significance in a report such as Pierce's. Findings are often presented as an "assertion," as was the case with Pierce's (1994) qualitative study: "The classroom ambiance developed through the behaviors and interactions of the teacher and students was one in which the threat of failure was diminished . . . [and] students were provided a 'safe-haven' atmosphere that enhanced learning outcomes" (p. 39).

As you can imagine, "ambiance" is a difficult quality to describe. Her task was aided by the use of student and teacher quotations to capture its essence. Her use of the "safety-net" metaphor also helps the reader understand her conclusions. Such metaphors are invaluable communication devices for qualitative researchers. Pierce continued with an assertion that the climate was created with three identifiable components, undoubtedly the result of her careful process of categorization in her analysis. Qualitative data are often categorized in some form or another to aid description and assertion.

Pierce used *vignettes* in her results and discussion. Vignettes are very brief stories or incidents, and they are used commonly by qualitative researchers to support an assertion. Careful readers of Pierce's report probably feel they know the teacher of this case study without ever having met her; this familiarity is one mark of a good case study. Any reporting of her numerical test scores from a battery of measuring instruments would pale by comparison.

HIGHLIGHT AND LEARNING CHECK 12-2

Case Study Designs

Case study designs rely on extensive data collection, usually over time, with a singular focus on one person or entity (e.g., a school). A variety of qualitative methods, including narrative vignettes, may be used to capture rich description and explanation. Which of the following titles is more likely to reflect case study research: "Social Phobia: A Journey Through High School" or "Birth Weight, Social Skills, and Graduation Rates"?

The Art of Teaching

Flinders (1989) provides a fine example of qualitative case study research. His study received the Outstanding Dissertation of the Year award bestowed by the Association for Supervision and Curriculum Development in 1987. It also contributed to a conceptualization of "responsive teaching" (Bowers & Flinders, 1990), whereby the context of teaching and learning is best viewed as a complex ecology of inseparable language, culture, and thought. His published study begins this way: "Penelope

Harper quickly takes roll, steps out from behind her desk, and glances around the classroom. Her eyes meet those of her students" (Flinders, 1989, p. 16). These opening sentences reveal quickly how the reporting of a qualitative study can differ from that of a quantitative one. Instead of describing relevant theory or summarizing reviews of the research literature, Flinders chose to "tell a story." In fact, Flinders (1993) reported that he found his "inspiration" for this research by "going 'back to school.'" Many qualitative researchers use *metaphor* as a mechanism for sharing findings. Flinders chose the "teacher as artisan" metaphor to describe his findings, referring to a "beautiful lesson" or "well-orchestrated class discussion."

Flinders collected a large amount of data, mostly in the form of interviews, extensive field notes from observations (in which he "shadowed" or followed teachers for entire days), and written documents. His findings, in part, took the form of four artistic dimensions. These findings, or focused themes, did not spring from a computer after statistical analysis. Rather, like most qualitative findings, they more likely "emerged" from the researcher's system of categorizing and making connections among all types of data. Flinders could not simply enter interviews, observations, and written documents into a computer, sit back, and watch his findings flash on a screen.

The analysis of such complex forms of qualitative data, such as extracting prominent themes, is a daunting intellectual experience for many beginning researchers. The artistic dimensions of teaching Flinders described were the result of his insight and keen perception more than a "crunching" of numbers. Behavioral observation scales (like the type found in quantitative studies whereby observers rate the frequency of occurrence of specific behaviors), or stopwatches (used to measure how long teachers wait before answering their own questions), or structured personality inventories (used to measure already established dimensions of personality) would not likely capture the essence of the art of appreciation in the classroom. Flinders, like most qualitative researchers, used memorable prose in his analysis; in this case, he referred to the idea of teachers putting "signatures" on their work as support for his model of teaching as an art or a craft.

Qualitative researchers may not close their reports with a simple summary. They often punctuate their reports in a provocative way, maybe by asking challenging questions or upsetting our traditional thinking about something. The mark of a good qualitative study, in addition to how well it stimulates the reader's thinking, is its persuasiveness.

In short, the Flinders case study is presented as an example of descriptive, qualitative, nonexperimental research; it is neither causal comparative nor correlational, and most would consider it a type of single-subject research. (He studied a small group of six teachers, akin to six single-subject studies.) It is closer to a traditional study (as opposed to teacher research), although his creative qualitative methodology might also be thought of as being somewhat nontraditional. It is also small scale, designed to influence our thinking about the practice of teaching, not offer sweeping suggestions for changes in policy.

The Flinders study represents a blending of ethnographic and case study designs. The study is clearly descriptive and ethnographic, as its goal was to experience classrooms in an attempt to describe through the eyes of classroom teachers how they view professional life. The researcher's concern about an image which failed to capture the artistry suggests that teachers' views might be described best by a descriptive metaphor, in this case borrowing from fine arts. (Evidently, rating scales could not capture the essence of teachers' perceptions.) Flinders was able to describe teachers' perceptions well because he had conducted extensive interviews; his questions were very effective for the purpose of understanding the art of teaching. Flinders also made careful classroom observations—his field notes—and reviewed classroom documents.

Since Flinders described teaching as an art, which is an insightful description, others can now understand how a lesson could be "beautiful" or a class discussion could be "well orchestrated." New ideas will undoubtedly emerge from this model of teaching, and thus the descriptive research done by Flinders will have made a valuable contribution, one that would not be possible without a descriptive qualitative research design.

There are literally dozens of qualitative designs used by educational researchers. Some are simple; others are complex. They may be formal and not modifiable, or informal and dynamic. All of them, however, serve an important guidance function in that they structure the plan for collecting data and determine how the data will be organized. Most generally, qualitative research designs help the process of research by assuring that the research question (or hypothesis) can, in fact, be answered (or tested) in a most efficient way with a minimum number of rival explanations. As is true with many qualitative research designs, most ethnographic designs have built-in flexibility and allow for adjustments as the research progresses. In fact, qualitative research designs are often referred to as *working* or *emergent* designs. Qualitative designs are also well suited for blending several different types of research, such as case studies and action research, as the following study illustrates.

Minority Teachers

Consider another example of a qualitative research design best described as an action research case study. Kauchak and Burbank (2003) observed that a "critical problem facing educators today is the inability of our teacher education system to produce substantial numbers of teachers from racial, ethnic, and language minority groups" (p. 63). Given the context of this problem statement, these researchers sought to answer these two questions: "What knowledge, attitudes, and beliefs influence the student teaching experiences of minority candidates?" and "What influences do the school contexts and teacher preparation programs have on the teaching experiences of minority teacher candidates?" These researchers realized the value of rich or "thick" qualitative data and chose to explore these questions using the in-depth study of two minority preservice teachers. To answer these questions, Kauchak and Burbank (2003) conducted intensive interviews with the two candidates and analyzed a "series of assignments designed to identify the interplay between belief systems and how those belief systems manifested themselves in instructional and curricular choices" (p. 64).

The researchers focused on transcripts of interviews, work samples, and professional development portfolios in an attempt to create categories for coding the complex data. Once meaningful categories were created, the researchers could begin to interpret the emerging themes that helped answer their research questions. They discovered that these two candidates held very different beliefs about teaching. For example, one candidate saw the curriculum as "malleable and responsive" and assumed that it must be connected to students' lives. The same candidate viewed classroom management as a method for "establishing relationships with students, making connections to them as individuals" (p. 71). The other candidate had opposing views and perceived the curriculum as fixed and classroom management as a "struggle" and "obstacle." Kauchak and Burbank identified five possible factors to explain candidates' differences on these important dimensions of teaching (for example, match with students' culture and different stages of professional development).

Kauchak and Burbank's major findings were that minority teachers bring unique voices and perspectives and sometimes dramatically different background experiences to a teacher education program and are shaped by those factors in complex ways. The answer to their research questions, it turned out, was far from simple. They used their five emerging factors arising from their multiple sources of data to conclude that very different attitudes influence teaching in unique and dramatically different ways. They also learned that differences in school contexts and teacher preparation programs can also influence teaching experiences in various ways, depending on teachers' unique background experiences.

Kauchak and Burbank (2003) observed that "like most exploratory research, these case studies raise more questions than they answer" (p. 72). New questions include the following: What attitudes do we want our minority teachers to possess? Do minority teaching candidates interact differently with same-culture students? What placement settings permit the exploration of unique background experiences? These researchers recognized that their study was "clearly exploratory," and because of the limitations of case study methodology, attempts to generalize beyond these teachers and settings is not warranted. Their study, however, does call attention to an important source of new hypotheses to be tested by future research: the exploratory action research case study.

Historical Research

Whether or not history repeats itself is open to debate, but there is little doubt that complete description of the past may help our understanding of the present and future. Learning from the past has the potential to help with present-day problems and forecast trends. Historical description and analysis is the focus of *historical research*, which is also called *historiography.* Historical research may answer specific questions such as "What is the relationship between how teachers have been portrayed in the media over the past 75 years and trends in teacher shortages?" and "Is there a linkage between U.S. war years and changes in social studies curricula over the past 100 years?"

HISTORICAL RESEARCH: The collection and objective study of documents and artifacts related to a past event, often including a description of patterns or trends, in an attempt to explain a phenomenon or test a hypothesis with present-day relevance.

Answers to other historical questions, interesting in their own right, often suggest ideas for future research using nonhistorical methods. For example, learning about instructional trends in homeschooling and their outcomes over 100 years may have research implications for large group instruction in public schools. Historical research may also answer questions that arise from basic curiosity, such as "How did the Civil War interrupt schooling in the South?" Historical researchers can also provide information to educators who might wonder about adopting innovative teaching methods or techniques, particularly those with modern names for older concepts. Historical research might reveal that such methods—whatever they may be called at the time—at the core have a clear track record of success or failure.

The diversity of topics researchable by historical methods is apparent by a simple search of the ERIC database. Topics include African American teaching in the South during the years 1940 to 1960 (Walker, 2001), contributions of intelligence ("past, present, and possible") to dance education (Warburton, 2003), parents and the politics of homework between 1900 and 1960 (Gill & Schlossman, 2003), testing efforts (Shepard, 2003), adult learning disabilities (Gerber, 2003), teacher reflection (Fendler, 2003), and women educator activists (Martin, 2003).

Studying past history for contemporary understanding involves the collection and careful analysis of data that often span decades. History has witnessed many forms of communication, such as print, audio, visual, and digital. Yet communication may be subtle, too, as in artwork, music, images, or nonverbal gestures having different meanings over the years and decades. These sources of data, however, are often complex and threatened by challenges to their authenticity. Historical accuracy requires that many sources of information be *primary sources*—the original documents, records of witnesses, diaries, newspapers, school transcripts, meeting minutes, and varied artifacts that shed light on history. (Even a primary source such as the *New York Post* may err, as in the July 6, 2004 front-page headline that presidential candidate Kerry had chosen Gephardt as his vice-presidential running mate.) The firsthand accounts provided by primary sources, because of their historical accuracy, are trusted and preferred over secondary sources. *Secondary sources* are one or more steps removed from the actual event, and as such, are threatened by lack of authenticity. These include sources of data such as past recollections (with memory and perception, in the face of uncertainty and ambiguity, often altered by assertions of "what must have been"), an author describing the educational views of John Dewey (as opposed to Dewey's own words), and principals' verbal reports of attendance trends (as opposed to inspection of actual attendance records). Researchers focus on *external criticism* when evaluating the authenticity of historical documents and artifacts (whether or not they are genuine). Clearly, any document found to be not genuine would cast serious doubt on the validity of historical conclusions based on it. Given purportedly genuine documents, researchers wonder about their accuracy and use the term *internal criticism* to describe this concern. Past records such as teacher salaries or student test scores may not be correct. Strongly biased authors or past systems of data collection are other sources of serious distortion that may impact the internal criticism of the research.

It is exceedingly difficult to accurately ascribe beliefs and values to those who lived in years gone by. This fact often limits the generalizability of historical research. The search for "what really happened" by specially trained "detectives," or *historiographers,* and its synthesis from a historical perspective usually involves hundreds of hours of document analysis. This process of interpretation or "making sense" is often aided by qualitative techniques such as coding as well as basic descriptive statistics or sophisticated graphic displays. Like all other research endeavors described in this book, historical research follows one of several

HIGHLIGHT AND LEARNING CHECK 12-3

Historical Research

Historical research seeks to describe and explain a past event, often with present-day relevance. Which of the following titles is more likely to reflect historical research: "Intelligent School Design" or "Paddles in the Schoolhouse"?

models and is characterized by a systematic, integrated process. Contributions from historical research play an important role in education. The reader is referred to sources such as Tuchman (1994) and McDowell (2002) for more information.

Let's now turn our attention to methods used by researchers who answer their research questions with qualitative data.

Qualitative Data Analysis

The Challenge

The process of qualitative data analysis is concerned with the *qualities* exhibited by data more than with their *quantities.* As such, many researchers believe that qualitative data analysis is a far more challenging, time-consuming, and creative endeavor than quantitative data analysis. Qualitative data analysis is less technical, less prescribed, and less "linear" but more iterative ("back and forth") than quantitative analysis. In fact, qualitative data analysis is often performed *during* data collection with emerging interpretations—a working hypothesis—guided by a theoretical framework. It is probably accurate to say that qualitative data analysis *evolves* throughout the whole research project and is clearly *not* summarized by a single number such as a *p* value, as is the case with quantitative studies.

Interviews often produce hundreds of pages of transcripts, as do detailed field notes from observations. All of this information requires critical examination, careful interpretation, and challenging synthesis. A good qualitative analysis discovers patterns, coherent themes, meaningful categories, and new ideas and in general uncovers better understanding of a phenomenon or process. Some qualitative researchers prefer to use the term *understanding of data* instead of *analysis of data.* The analysis of rich descriptions occurring throughout the course of a project often provides new perspectives, and its analysis of interconnecting themes may provide useful insights. The depth afforded by qualitative analysis is believed by many to be the best method for understanding the complexity of education in practice. Qualitative analysis is also well suited for exploration of unanticipated results. Above all else, it is concerned with finding *meaning* embedded within rich sources of information.

Good qualitative data analysis often impacts readers through powerful narrative such as stories. Thus Clark and colleagues (1996) began the data analysis section of their qualitative study of teacher-researcher collaboration by stating "Our story comes from the words and voices of the people involved" (p. 203). Miles and Huberman (1994) stated that "words, especially organized into incidents or stories, have a concrete, vivid, meaningful

HIGHLIGHT AND LEARNING CHECK 12-4

Qualitative Data Analysis

Data analysis in qualitative research focuses on *qualities* more than *quantities.* The statistical focus on the *p* value in quantitative research is replaced in qualitative research with pattern seeking and the extraction of meaning from rich, complex sources of linguistic (narrative) or visual (image) data. Much effort is directed toward the creation of categories. Words, symbols, metaphor, vignettes, and an entire array of creative linguistic tools or visual displays may be used instead of "number crunching" in qualitative data analysis. Qualitative data analysis is far less "linear" and prescribed than the statistical analysis used so commonly in quantitative data analysis. One common goal is to establish the credibility of the qualitative research findings and conclusions. Describe the different skills required for being proficient in each type of data analysis.

flavor that often proves far more convincing . . . than pages of summarized numbers" (p. 1).

Researchers with a qualitative orientation often view their work as a challenging craft or art, and this shows in their writing. The Clark and colleagues (1996) study presented data in the form they call "Readers Theater," a written script based on the dialogues and interactions during the meetings of 10 teacher-researchers. A good qualitative analysis often yields stimulating conclusions and sometimes affords a new and useful way to view old problems.

CRITICAL THINKER ALERT 12-2

Qualitative Data Analysis

The types of thinking and skills needed for qualitative data analysis are different from those needed for quantitative data analysis. Creativity, divergent thinking, keen perception of patterns among ambiguity, and strong writing skills are helpful for qualitative data analysis. Qualitative analysis is less dependent on computing software. Whereas statistical analysis often centers on the *p* value, qualitative data analysis involves more time-consuming extraction of meaning from multiple sources of complex data.

Discussion: In what way is creativity an important skill in the analysis of qualitative data? Does this suggest that the quantitative analysis of data is not creative?

Credibility

The most important criterion for judging a qualitative study is its *credibility* or trustworthiness. To assess credibility, one would zero in on the data, its analysis, and resultant conclusions. Any weak link here would threaten the usefulness of the study. According to Miles and Huberman (1994, pp. 11–12), qualitative analysis includes three streams of activity: *data reduction* (simplifying complex data by, for example, extracting recurring themes via coding); *data display* (e.g., matrices, charts, graphs, even stories); and, finally, *drawing conclusions* and verifying them as a means for testing the validity of findings. Qualitative researchers often rely on the use of triangulation to enhance the credibility of the study. Recall that this refers to the use of multiple sources of data and collection strategies, all of which should converge.

CREDIBILITY: A criterion for judging the trustworthiness of qualitative data analysis.

Essentially, the daunting task for qualitative researchers is to take massive amounts of data, often in the form of interviews or detailed field notes from extensive observations, and communicate what the data reveal in a credible way. The interpretation of qualitative data depends on the background and creativity of the researcher far more than interpretation of quantitative data does. Also, there are no agreed-upon, 10-step procedures which all qualitative data interpreters use. Nevertheless, in some way or other, most interpreters will face the task of organizing the data to enhance the study's credibility. This task nearly always involves *coding*, a modifiable system for categorizing the information in the data.

The following section contains a description of a representative qualitative analysis using coding for the purpose of making some of these abstract ideas more concrete.

Emergent Methodology

Many models of qualitative data analysis have been proposed to help guide researchers. In education and psychology, perhaps the most influential has been grounded theory (Glaser & Strauss, 1967; Glaser, 1998). Grounded theory helps the researcher understand the multiple sources of data, which are often observations, conversations, and interviews that themselves combine during the task of note taking. Grounded theory is an example of *emergence* in research. This term suggests an approach that is counter to hypothesis testing, where a preconceived idea about a relationship is tested, or *forced,* by a statistical model (such as the *t* test). An emergent approach to data analysis seeks to understand the situation and discover a theory implicit in the data itself. Instead of crunching numbers to arrive at a *p* value, a grounded theory researcher uses note taking and coding to find categories or themes (akin to variables), sorts information into meaningful patterns, and writes persuasively and creatively about whatever it is that has been discovered in the data.

EMERGENT METHODOLOGY: An approach to qualitative data analysis that relies on inductive reasoning and a continual interplay between data and developing interpretation.

GROUNDED THEORY: An approach to qualitative data analysis using emergent methodologies, such as constant comparison, that permits a theory to develop from the data (from the ground up) without preconceived or inflexible ideas.

The process of constant comparison plays a central role in grounded theory. Here is an example. Suppose that you have conducted interviews with 20 high school teachers related to the topic of classroom challenges. Consider the first interview only. Dick (2002) recommended that you ask yourself these questions: "What is going on here? What is the situation? How is this person managing the situation?" Perhaps the construct of "civility" as a label comes to mind. Next, you code the second interview using the first as a frame of reference. Dick (2002) referred to this as "constant comparison," for one is comparing data set to data set and, eventually, data set to theory.

All the while, theoretical ideas should be surfacing ("emerging") in your thinking as an explanation for patterns that might explain references to civility and related categories (or whatever theme is being expressed). Eventually, categories and their properties become *saturated,* meaning further interviews will probably add little to what is known about an emerging category. As properties of the categories become well defined, linkages between them become more sensible. Eventually, a theory or explanation of category relationships will surface as ideas are compared ("constantly") with actual data.

HIGHLIGHT AND LEARNING CHECK 12-5

Emergent Methodology

Emergent methodology (induction) is used by qualitative data analysts as they gradually build a structure for understanding their findings. They constantly compare a construction of their understanding against data (from the ground up), all the while revising their models as needed without inflexible preconceptions. As each new finding and possible explanation emerges, it is checked against other sources of data until a point of saturation is reached, thus completing the analysis. Explain why qualitative data analysts may not feel "finished" in the same sense that statistical analysts might.

The literature, or published ideas and findings in related fields, is also treated like data in a constant comparison process. It emerges as well; in fact, the relevant literature is probably unknown at the beginning of the study. Dick (2002) summarized the search for meaning this way: "In short, in using grounded theory methodology you assume that the theory is concealed in your data for you to discover" (Memoing section, para. 4).

Examples of Qualitative Data Analysis

Parent Involvement in Early Education

Neuman, Hagedorn, Celano, and Daly (1995) described teenage mothers' beliefs about learning and literacy in an African American community as revealed in a series of peer-group discussions. The researchers identified the beliefs of 19 low-income adolescent mothers, hoping to use this knowledge to enhance the literacy opportunities of the mothers' children. All the mothers lived in impoverished areas and had toddlers enrolled in an early intervention program. The mothers had dropped out of high school and were attempting to complete adult basic education. The researchers noted that parental beliefs have been described using a variety of empirical, self-report instruments that are problematic since they tend to reflect mainstream culture and solicit "it depends" type reactions. Neuman and colleagues (1995) opted for open-ended interview discussion formats in the hope of extracting "far richer and more accurate understandings of beliefs" (p. 807). The 10 hours of discussion were videotaped while observers took notes in an adjacent observation room.

The researchers' task of converting data into codeable categories was guided by the *constant comparative method* (Glaser & Strauss, 1967), a continuous process of category identification and clarification that results in well-defined categories and clear coding instructions. The research team viewed tapes and read transcripts independently and began to identify themes (categories) by "highlighting particular words or phrases—their tone and intensity—which reflected these themes" (Neuman et al., 1995, p. 809). Examples of categories which emerged from the data included "how children learn" ("being told" versus "experience or interaction") and the mother's role and responsibility in schooling.

The next phase of the analysis was directed toward finding linkages among categories that reflect similar views. Neuman and colleagues found, for example, close ties among all of the following categories: "learning is telling," "teachers' role is training," "teachers' method is drill and practice," and "learning is demonstrated by recitation." This was a different perspective from that pertaining to categories linked by play, imagination, and meaningful activities. The mothers' views of themselves as teachers were also examined via comparisons and contrasts of categories which fit a common perspective (what the researchers called "typology"). This was followed by an assessment of the credibility of the categories and representations by members of the research group who had not been involved with the data reduction (coding into categories).

The researchers then presented their analytic categories and interpretation to knowledgeable outsiders for examination and revision. The researchers wanted to be certain that their reconstructions accurately reflected the reality of their subjects. Finally, Neuman and colleagues (1995) "derived a set of theoretical propositions within and across categories and perspectives that seemed to best encompass parents' beliefs about learning and literacy for their children" (p. 810). They concluded that mothers' beliefs fall on a continuum of perspectives on learning (what they labeled "transmissive," "maturational," and "transactional") and that "through a better understanding of parental beliefs, parental involvement programs may be designed to enable culturally diverse parents to realize their aspirations for their children" (p. 822).

Studies such as that of Neuman and colleagues illustrate the challenge of qualitative data analysis. Good interpreters must tolerate ambiguity as they search for recurring regularities in complex data. Their thinking must be flexible; they must attend to counter-evidence as well as evidence as they clarify categories and themes. They must also present their findings in ways that preserve the findings' validity and full meaning and show how a better understanding afforded by the data can be useful for readers.

Detracking

An ethnographic case study by Rubin (2003) illustrates many of the advantages—and challenges—of qualitative data analysis. Rubin's (2003) focus was *detracking*, or "the conscious organization of students into academically and racially heterogeneous classrooms" (p. 540) as a countermeasure to the practice of sorting and grouping students by ability. Her review of the literature revealed an absence of research on the "close consideration of students' experiences with detracking in the nested contexts of school and classroom . . . embedded in a larger social, political, and economic framework that is marked by race- and class-linked inequalities" (p. 543). Her efforts directed toward the "unpacking" of the detracked classroom were "an attempt to probe the mystery of how daily events and interactions often add up to large patterns of inequality" (p. 543).

After providing a detailed context for the study, Rubin (2003) described her methodological orientation as both "interpretive" and "critical," meaning that she retains a perspective that reality is a "social construction" and that our social world is best understood as one "dimension of inequality." Overall, her concern was "eliciting the perspectives of student participation in detracking" and answering the central question "How do students and teachers enact detracking in the classrooms of a racially and socioeconomically diverse urban high school?" (p. 545). She also listed four subquestions "directed at better understanding the experiences of the various participants and the interlocking contexts of detracking at the study site emerging as data collection proceeded" (p. 545). You can readily see that her analysis was not aimed at simply computing a p value and rejecting a null hypothesis.

Rubin's research participants included two teachers and five "focal" students selected as key informants. Her data collection occurred in four phases: first-semester classroom observations, initial interviews, "shadowing" (or following), and end-of-year classroom observations and interviews. These sources yielded a wealth of field notes, but she also collected many written documents ("artifacts"), including e-mail, class handouts, student portfolios, and school newspapers. As with most qualitative studies, Rubin's (2003) data analysis was ongoing and "iterative." She began her analysis by composing "analytical memos" on topics that emerged as significant, thus forming the basis of her initial assertions. More formal data analysis included creating a "coding scheme based on the constant comparison and grouping of data chunks" (p. 549).

Two categories emerged: the "official" world of detracked classrooms (such as expectations established by teachers) and the "unofficial" world (such as students' social and academic desires and the meanings they constructed from the official practices). Her findings essentially described the "collision" (clash and tension) between these two worlds in a rich way, often extracting quotations for illustration. Her "unpacking" (unraveling) of detracked classrooms led Rubin (2003) to conclude that "the use of progressive pedagogies within detracked classrooms, while well intentioned, cannot alone resolve the inequalities permeating that setting and may in some ways reinforce them" (p. 567).

There has been an explosion of interest in qualitative research and analysis in recent years. As a result, there are many valuable sources available for those wanting to learn more about qualitative research and analysis in education. Sage Publications in Thousand Oaks, California, publishes a wide variety of qualitative research books (their 2004 qualitative methods catalogue lists over 200 titles, including software to help analyze qualitative data). Many other publishers include qualitative research references in their offerings, and one of the most widely cited references is Bogdan and Biklen (2003).

Data Analysis Software

Many software programs exist for the benefit of qualitative researchers. One popular one is HyperRESEARCH, which is well designed for self-instruction with its own tutorials and sample studies. (It is also one of the few programs that supports both Macintosh and Windows.) The Appendix by DuPuis (2002) in Schutt (2004) described its essential features: coding and retrieving, report generation, multimedia support, and theory-building tools. Its flexible structure and point-and-click interface enable a multitude of coding schemes, coding manipulations, and searches for relationships—major tasks in qualitative data analysis. Its Study Window and Codes Menu combined with Source Windows will integrate graphics, video, audio, and text information. Its other tools include the Annotation Window for creating memos and coded references, and the Report Window for generating custom reports or exporting them as data in another program (including a statistical package). HyperRESEARCH includes many advanced functions, including autocoding, code searches, coding maps, and a hypothesis tester. The latter is described by DuPuis as an "expert" system for building theories and testing them via coding schemes applied to data.

The Basic Interface in HyperRESEARCH is shown in Figure 12.1. Its menu-driven set of tasks becomes clear. It is well designed for self-teaching, given its tutorial programs, help functions, and many other user-guided features.

HIGHLIGHT AND LEARNING CHECK 12-6

Qualitative Data Analysis Software

Data analysis software is essential for the statistical analysis of quantitative data and is becoming increasingly popular for qualitative data management and analysis. SPSS appears to be a leading program for statistical analysis; it is also very easy to use (including a spreadsheet format, guided menus, etc.). HyperRESEARCH is a popular program for qualitative researchers; it enables retrieval of complex sources of data, permits a variety of coding, and enhances category recognition. Explain how a qualitative software program could facilitate a common task such as constant comparison.

CRITICAL PERSPECTIVES 12-1

DATA ANALYSIS SOFTWARE

Critical Thinking Toolbox

Concept maps represent knowledge and ideas graphically, often shown as networks with "nodes" and links (relations). They are especially useful for communicating complexities and enhancing learning by integrating new and old knowledge into more complex cognitive structures. The new structure itself may help thinkers identify assumptions and avoid blind acceptance of messages such as political pitches, commercial advertisements, and so on. Avoidance of blind acceptance is a marker of critical thinking.

Data Analysis Software in Quantitative Research

Statistical analysis of quantitative data is made possible by two main vendors, SPSS and SAS. Data for analysis may be inputted directly into a data window or imported from another source (e.g., a spreadsheet program from a word processor such as Word). Both SPSS and SAS have become increasingly user-friendly (especially SPSS), given their ease of use with pull-down menus, help functions, and tutorials. Both programs contain an extensive array of statistical tests and maneuvers and permit easy management and recoding of data. Graphs, charts, and tables can accompanying most statistical procedures, greatly assisting with interpretation and report generation. Some statistical procedures also include annotations on the output. One of the most popular and economical statistical software programs remains SPSS for Windows (Student Version) on a single CD, which is easily installed on a desktop or laptop computer.

Data Analysis Software in Qualitative Research

Qualitative computer programs replace more than the hand-analysis tasks of marking, color coding, and literally cutting and pasting information onto index cards. Software programs store data for retrieval in ways that are not practical any other way. The digitized storage permits data organizing and management, coding and searching, ease in developing and connecting themes, exploring data by "memoing" ideas, and presenting and reporting findings. Making sense of data, of course, is an interpretive task reserved for human cognition. The software cannot replace human creativity, but it surely manages with great efficiency those tasks more likely to lead to an insightful recognition of the data's meaning. Qualitative data analysis programs manage all types of data, including text, audio, image, and video. Widely used programs include ATLAS.ti ("The Knowledge Workbench"), QSR N6 (the latest version of NUD*IST), QSR NVivo, The Ethnograph, MAXqda, QDA Miner, and HyperRESEARCH (which was described briefly earlier in this chapter).

Data Analysis Software in Action Research

Teacher action researchers often find that desktop computers have all the software they need to analyze classroom data, present findings, and put what they learn into action. Spreadsheet programs embedded in word processing programs (Word, AppleWorks, etc.) have limited, but often sufficient, statistical and graphic capabilities. Qualitative analysis and many statistical analyses may also be accomplished with the functional capabilities of Word and Excel.

Critical Thinking Questions

What might a concept map of data analysis software used in educational research look like? How might it be connected to what you have learned previously? Could it reveal assumptions that might not be acceptable? (Hint: Think about limitations of menu-driven choices, assumptions built into the software, etc.) How might such a map assist your critical thinking about data analysis in general?

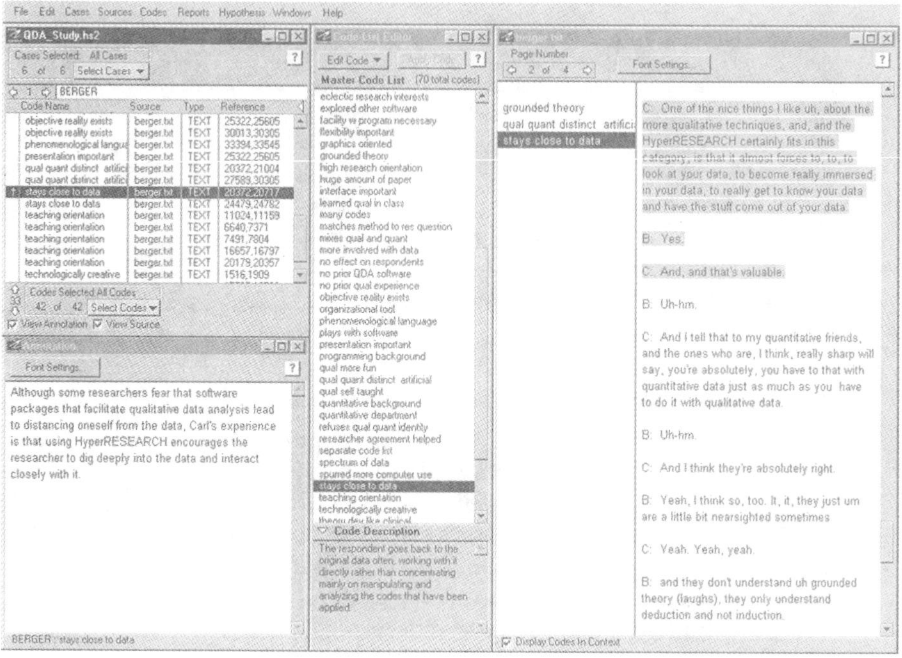

Figure 12.1 The basic interface of HyperRESEARCH. The interface permits navigation to a variety of windows, including Study, Source (text, graphic, movie, and audio), Code List, Code Map, Annotation, Report, Hypothesis Testing, and Autocoding.

Source: Courtesy of ResearchWare, Inc.

Mixed Methodology

Chapter 3 introduced the idea of *mixed method designs,* those that incorporate components of qualitative and quantitative designs and analyses. Indeed, mixed methods designs appear in the published literature with increasing frequency. Two brief descriptions of mixed method studies will help you "ground" important ideas related to qualitative design and analysis.

An Example: Scaffolding

Researchers Ge and Land (2003) provide a fine example of mixed methodology, the blending of a qualitative case studies with a quantitative quasi-experiment. We saw in the previous chapter that many educators value complex problem-solving tasks, especially those designed to "help students see the meaningfulness and relevance of what they learn and to facilitate transfer by contextualizing knowledge in authentic situations" (Ge and Land, 2003, p. 21). The problem is that many students fail to transfer knowledge across contexts. After a review of published research reports and theoretical ideas, Ge and Land believed that "scaffolding" strategies could help students' problem-solving performance. (*Scaffolding* is a term coined by the

Russian theorist Les Vygotsky and refers to the guiding help of a more capable peer, particularly in the "zone" where a learner is close to performing a task independently.) *Scaffolding* was operationally defined by Ge and Land as the use of question prompts (e.g., "What do we know about the problem so far?") and peer interaction (e.g., collaborative learning requiring the sharing of information).

With a solid theoretical background and review of relevant empirical studies, Ge and Land (2003) derived three research hypotheses: (1) "If students receive question prompts (compared to those who do not), then they will perform better on a problem-solving task"; (2) "If students work in collaborative peer groups (compared to those who do not), then they will perform better on a problem-solving task"; and (3) "If students receive question prompts *and* work in collaborative peer groups (compared to those who do not), then they will perform better than all other comparison groups." Ge and Land were also interested in answering a separate research question: "How does using question prompts and peer interaction influence students' thinking during problem solving?" They chose mixed methodology (both qualitative and quantitative approaches) to test these research hypotheses and answer their research question. They stated that this multimethod approach "helps a researcher to seek a triangulation of the results from different data sources; examine overlapping and different facets of a phenomenon; discover paradoxes, contradictions, and fresh perspectives; and expand the scope and breadth of a study" (p. 25).

A quantitative quasi-experimental design was used to test Ge and Land's three hypotheses; a qualitative case study design was used to answer their research question. The quantitative tests of hypotheses were quasi-experimental since students had already been placed into intact ("natural setting") classrooms (they couldn't be assigned on a case-by-case basis to the treatments). Further, the groups of size three to four could not be determined randomly; they were preexisting, formed previously by the course professors for the purpose of completing class projects. (Had the subjects been assigned randomly to each of the four conditions, their quantitative design would be described as "true experimental," which is a far better design for the purpose of uncovering cause-and-effect relationships.) With intact groups, the researchers were nevertheless able to implement their four treatment conditions within a 115-minute laboratory session. The treatment combinations were formed by their two quasi-independent variables, Question Prompts (yes versus no) and Peer Interaction (yes versus no).

The case study design was chosen to supplement findings from the tests of hypotheses and to "gain insights into students' problem-solving processes through think-aloud protocols, interviews, and observations" (Ge & Land, 2003, p. 25). The problem being solved by students in the quasi-experiment was related to customers having difficulty finding what they need in a large supermarket. Students' problem-solving reports were scored by a systematic rubric that awarded points across four dimensions of the solution. These reports were then analyzed as a function of the four treatment groups formed by the two quasi-independent variables (prompts with peer interaction, prompts without peer interaction, no prompts with peer interaction, and no prompts without peer interaction). The three hypotheses were tested by four dependent variables functioning as the operational definition of problem-solving performance. (The four dependent variables reflected a different facet of problem-solving, including problem representation, developing solutions, making justifications, and monitoring and evaluation.)

A total of 117 undergraduate students provided data for the quasi-experiment; 8 students participated in the "comparative, multiple-case studies." Ge and Land (2003) reported that case-study participants were selected "based on informed consent, level of verbal interaction (with peer conditions), and willingness to be audiotaped or videotaped for think aloud protocols, observations, and interviews" (p. 28). (A *protocol* is simply a written record, in this case of subjects' thinking out loud.) The protocols, observations, and interviews formed the basis of the qualitative case studies aimed at answering the research question. The interview questions, as you would expect, were directed at understanding the effects of question prompts and peer interaction (the independent variables or treatment conditions).

Ge and Land's (2003) quantitative data analysis revealed that the use of question prompts resulted in better problem-solving performance across all four dependent measures. By contrast, the peer interaction influences were less striking, with only one of the four measures (problem representation) being significantly higher in the interactive peer collaboration condition (compared to the individual condition). Thus, their data supported the first hypothesis, did not (generally) support their second hypothesis, and did not support their third hypothesis. The qualitative data (think-aloud protocols, observations, and interviews) were analyzed via a process of data reduction, data display, and conclusion drawing and verification. Ge and Land began by "reading and jotting marginal notes on transcripts; identifying patterns and labeling concepts; organizing labeled concepts into data display matrixes; identifying themes; and drawing conclusions" (p. 29). Their qualitative conclusions, as is customary, were supported by clear examples. Far more complex than quantitative data, the examples revealed information (or insight) that "numbers" data could not.

The answer to Ge and Land's research question, based on qualitative analysis, showed that students' thinking benefits from question prompts by engaging in one or more metacognitive activities (four were described). Students' thinking benefits from their peer interactions as students build on each other's ideas by eliciting explanations, sharing different perspectives, and taking full advantage of each other's knowledge. It was clear that the qualitative component of this study revealed these positive influences of peer interactions that the quantitative data did not, illustrating why researchers often use several research designs within the same study (mixed methodologies).

The Ge and Land study also illustrates how an inferential study can be combined with a descriptive one. Because Ge and Land's quantitative outcomes were all associated with tests of significance (as revealed by their p values and the consequent acceptance or rejection of their null hypotheses), we know that they intended to generalize to a larger population similar to those who comprised the sample and provided data. (Recall from Chapter 5 that each research hypotheses is associated with an underlying null hypothesis suggesting no difference in the larger population.) Ge and Land's research question was directed at learning how thinking is influenced by question prompts and peer interaction and was answered by a descriptive (not inferential) portion of the study. This is because their goal was a description of the sample participants' thinking; there were no associated tests of significance and associated p values. Their answer did, however, reveal ideas for future research that might use inferential statistics.

In addition, their study illustrates how single-subject research can complement group research. The tests of three research hypotheses (quantitative findings) clearly represented group research; the research question (qualitative findings) was answered with a type of multiple single-subject design (what they referred to as a "multiple-case study.") Ge and Land's single-subject orientation was most apparent in their results and discussion in reference to the ideas expressed by a single case (not a group consensus). Their research was also traditional, with formal tests of hypotheses and an interest beyond a single classroom. Recall that teacher research focuses on a specific problem facing a classroom teacher with the intent of taking "action" to improve practice.

In summary, the Ge and Land study is best described as quantitative and qualitative (mixed), descriptive and inferential, quasi-experimental (not true experimental), neither causal comparative nor correlational, single-subject (multiple) and group, traditional, and relatively small scale (with its purpose closer to evaluating theory than gathering evidence to influence policy).

MORE EXAMPLES

Additional descriptions of published research may help to solidify your knowledge of important ideas related to qualitative design and analysis. You will find additional descriptions on the Web-based student study site (www.sagepub.com/eic).

Chapter Summary

Many descriptions and explorations of hypotheses are accomplished best with qualitative approaches to research, including ethnographic designs, case study designs, "blended" or hybrid designs that integrate key features of several descriptive research designs, and historical research. Field notes often form the backbone of the analysis of ethnographic data. They may be detailed observations and general interpretations, reflections, and summaries of recorded interviews. Ethnographic designs in educational research frequently employ *triangulation,* a type of qualitative cross-validation (corroboration) or data cross-checking procedure whereby multiple data sources or data collection procedures are expected to agree (converge). Some descriptive-oriented questions in education can be answered by intensive study of a single person (or single group). Such qualitative case studies provide rich, often fascinating data and suggest new areas for research. Historical description and analysis is the focus of *historical research,* which offers the potential to help with present-day problems and forecast trends. Qualitative data analysis usually requires coding of categories and themes, and the analysis itself evolves throughout the course of a study. This process is far less mechanical than statistical analysis. It is a creative endeavor, akin to an art, and the result is often powerful narrative in story form. One influential model of making sense from qualitative data is *grounded theory,* which emphasizes the *emergence* of meaning concealed in data.

The most important criterion for judging a qualitative study is its *credibility* or trustworthiness, which is enhanced by emergent methodology, or the continual interplay between data and developing interpretation (constant comparison). Qualitative data analysis is enabled by software programs such as HyperRESEARCH that are invaluable for functions such as pattern seeking.

Application Exercises

1. Consider each of the following research questions. Do you think each is answered best by a descriptive survey, an ethnography, a case study, or a historical study? Why do you think that?
   a. How does Ms. Overton consistently close the gender gap in her AP Chemistry classes?
   b. How does high school mentoring affect students' aspirations and career decisions?
   c. How many hours per night do sixth graders report working on homework assignments?
   d. How did the Soviet launching of Sputnik affect U.S. school textbooks and the national curriculum?
   e. How do tribal educators differentiate instruction to meet varying learning styles?
   f. What do reading instructors know about reading research?
   g. How does a student with severe social anxiety cope with social demands in high school?
   h. How did the first public charter school influence the charter school movement?
   i. What do teachers know about defining characteristics of sexual harassment in schools?
   j. What is it like to teach at a private progressive school?
   k. How did the media interpret events during the integration of Little Rock's Central High School in 1957?
   l. Why does a teacher teach for 70 years?

2. Locate a recent published report of qualitative research in education in a premiere journal such as the *American Educational Research Journal.* Focus on the data analysis section and summarize how the researchers established the *credibility* or trustworthiness of their findings.

3. Ask five other students enrolled in another education course to write a brief essay titled "How Students Learn." Carefully analyze the essays for a common theme. Is there one? How might you describe this theme? Can you justify this theme? Do you think someone else would extract a similar theme after studying the essays?

On Your Own

Log on to the Web-based student study site at http://www.sagepub.com/eic for more information about the materials presented in this chapter, suggestions for activities, study aids such as electronic flashcards and review quizzes, a sample research proposal, and research recommendations that include journal article links (with discussion questions and an article evaluation guide) and questions related to this chapter.

13
Statistical Data Analysis

Outline

Overview

This chapter focuses on data analysis in quantitative research and the logic of statistical inference. Making sense of numbers is enabled by commonly used statistical procedures and inferential "tests." The goal of these statistical tests is to make an inference about the hypothesis being tested and reach a conclusion about a larger population represented by the sample. The procedural details have been worked out in great detail. Statistical packages that "crunch" the numbers make portions of this task easy, yet there remain many challenges in the proper interpretation of data manipulated by complex formulas. Much statistical analysis is directed toward the computation of the *p* value, that little number that permits logical inference.

Statistical Inference: An Introduction

This chapter concerns an elegant form of thinking commonly called *inference.* This form of thinking permits educational researchers to reach conclusions that have implications far beyond the sample being studied. Inferential thinking helps educational researchers solve an interesting problem after they collect numerical data to answer questions or test hypotheses. The essence of the researcher's problem is this: "What can I conclude about the population from which my sample was drawn?" Researchers ask this question because they are usually more interested in relationships that exist within the population from which the sample was drawn than in relationships within the actual sample studied. After all, if findings do not generalize beyond the sample, then researchers could never apply their findings beyond the narrow confines of the sample of subjects studied. One could reasonably ask, "Who cares about the small number of people studied? What can I say about the larger population?" The process of inferring from the sample to the population involves elegant statistical reasoning. Let's examine this reasoning in some detail.

POPULATION: A large well-defined group that generates a sample (often randomly). Data from the sample are used to make inferences about the larger population.

INFERENCE: A form of logic used in statistics that permits a conclusion about a population based on data collected from a sample.

STATISTIC: A characteristic of a sample. Sample statistics are often used to estimate population parameters.

Coin Flips and Probability

Let's suppose that I claim to possess psychic abilities, that is, that I can affect the outcome of physical events by sheer concentration. Consider a coin flip. My abilities can influence this physical event and are evidenced by the number of heads that will appear during a test of 100 coin flips. My claim is this: As I concentrate on the coin landing "heads up" during 100 flips, you will find that more heads appear than tails. Ready? Here we go. . . . The results are in: After 100 flips, the coin turned up heads 55 times. I say, "I told you so! I'm psychic!"

Your best response as a critical observer is to say, "Well, 55 heads could be a chance occurrence; maybe it would have come up heads 55 times if I—with no such abilities—tried to influence the number of heads." This is the crux of the problem: What are the reasonable limits of chance? Of course, the long run, theoretical expectation is that the coin will turn up heads 50 times after 100 flips (assuming that the coin has not been tampered with). But would you actually expect such a perfect result if you were to flip a coin 100 times? Probably not. What if the coin turned up heads 51 times? Would you dismiss this event as merely the workings of chance? Yes, probably. What about 52 heads? Or 53 heads? Or 54? What about 55, 56, 57, 58, 59, 60, 61, 62, 70, or 80 heads?

Clearly, you need to draw the boundary line somewhere, and if the number of heads crossed the boundary, then you would conclude that the occurrence was *probably* not due to chance. (Of course, even if the result were *not* due to chance, there may be explanations other than psychic ability, such as a trick coin or other extraneous influences.) Fortunately, scientists have worked out a rule to follow in order to avoid being wishy-washy ("Maybe it was due to chance, maybe not, well, I don't know, looks like chance to me, sort of"). The rule is this: Determine what to expect by chance 95% of the time; if the occurrence would be expected less than 5% of the time by chance (outside the 95% boundary), then it was probably *not* due to chance.

In the coin flip example, statisticians have figured that the 95% chance boundaries for the number of heads after 100 tosses is 43 to 57. Here is what that means. Let's say 100 flips of a coin is one trial. After 100 trials, you would expect 95% of the trials to yield between 43 and 57 heads, according to the laws of chance. This is very useful information, for now you can conclude that 55 heads is likely the workings of chance. Clearly, you shouldn't be impressed with 55 heads. This is within the range that you would expect by chance 95% of the time.

But what if the test of my psychic ability had produced 59 heads instead of 55 heads? A very different outcome indeed, since this is more than what you could reasonably attribute to chance. Scientists have a special name for this event: It is called *statistical significance.* One would say, therefore, that 59 heads is a statistically significant outcome since it is expected to occur less than 5% of the time by chance. The shorthand way of stating *statistically significant* is simply $p < .05$, where p refers to probability. This literally means that the probability is less than 5 out of 100 that the results were due to chance. Always keep in mind that the results *may* have in fact been due to chance; statistical significance only means that the results were *probably* not due to chance. Remember, p refers to *probability,* not proof!

Sometimes, research results are presented as $p < .01$ to convey the idea that the probability is less than 1 out of 100 that the findings were due to chance. Or, findings may be presented as $p < .001$, suggesting that the likelihood is less than 1 out of 1000 that chance could be responsible for the results. Statistical significance begins when the threshold of .05 is crossed, and, of course, includes any level of probability less than .05, including .01, .005, .001, or even .00000001.

Educational researchers, of course, do not spend their time challenging psychics with the coin flip test. But they do apply exactly the same logic in the analysis of educational data. Here is the logic: First, determine the boundaries to expect by chance 95% of the time. Second, compare the finding (a mean difference, a positive correlation, etc.) against the 95% chance limits. If the results fall within the boundary, then they *are* probably due to chance and are *not* statistically significant. If the results fall beyond the limits imposed by chance, then they are probably *not* due to chance and are referred to as statistically significant, or $p < .05$.

***p* (*p* VALUE):** An abbreviation for *probability, p* refers to the likelihood that chance factors, or statistical error, could explain a relationship found in a sample.

STATISTICAL SIGNIFICANCE: A concept referring to a finding that cannot easily be explained by the workings of chance factors. Statistical significance is usually triggered when the p drops below .05.

Reading Faces

Let's see how this logic is used in a more realistic research setting. Presume I believe that emotion plays a greater role in learning than is generally believed. Furthermore, I believe that learning is more difficult without an emotional component, and that our "emotional IQ" may influence success in school (and life). Finally, I recognize that there is a long held belief that females are more emotional than males. Let's suppose that being emotionally "with it" involves correctly reading emotional expressions in faces and using this information to communicate more effectively. Given all this information, I might wonder whether girls can read faces better than boys can.

To answer this question, let's suppose that a valid and reliable Face Reading Test had been developed. It involves making judgments about the emotions underlying facial expressions, such as fear, surprise, joy, anger, sadness, and so on. (You have to assume that emotional expressions are universal, and that the test was developed so that there exists a correct emotion for each expression.) Imagine that the boys and girls were shown 20 faces and asked to choose the correct emotion as revealed by the expression (let's assume a multiple-choice format for simplicity). Furthermore, imagine that 30 boys and 30 girls from seventh and eighth grades were given the Face Reading Test. Here are the results, expressed as an average score on the 20-item test:

	Mean
Boys	12.5
Girls	15.0

You can see that girls scored higher than boys, but could this—like 55 heads out of 100 coin flips—be due to chance? Sure, even if boys and girls (in the population) did not differ on this ability, you would not expect to find *exactly* the same mean for them. That's too perfect, akin to getting 50 heads and 50 tails in 100 coin flips. The crux of the problem is chance once again. To demonstrate chance, just imagine 60 girls being randomly divided into two groups and then taking the Face Reading Test. You would not expect exactly the same means for both groups since chance could have easily placed a few more high scorers in one group. The means should be *about* the same, give or take a few points. This "give or take," of course, is what most people simply refer to as "chance."

The problem of determining whether the mean difference of 2.5 points between boys and girls is larger than what you would expect by chance is solved in much the same way that the problem of chance was solved in the coin flip illustration. Let's suppose that the limits imposed by chance 95% of the time were 3.00 points, either way (plus or minus). That is, if you repeatedly compared two groups' average scores on the Face Reading Test (in a situation where the groups did not differ, as in the case where they were formed

HIGHLIGHT AND LEARNING CHECK 13-1

Statistical Significance

Quantitative data analysis is often concerned with making inferences about a population given data collected from a sample of the population. The crux of the problem is chance (or sampling error), for even when no differences exist between groups in a population, sampled data (containing sampling error) will yield differences to some extent (like 6 heads out of 10 flips of a coin). Concepts of probability are used to determine whether the sample difference is larger than one might expect due to chance factors. When the likelihood of chance drops below .05 ($p < .05$), it is said that the findings are *statistically significant* and probably reflect a true difference in the population. In this sense, the expression $p < .05$ means "probably not due to chance." Could a research finding reported as $p < .0001$ ever be due to the working of chance? Explain.

by random assignment), you would find that 95% of all mean differences would not be greater than 3.00 points. So, what do you make of the 2.5 difference obtained in the boy versus girl face reading example above? Clearly, the difference is not significant and could have arisen, quite reasonably, by chance. You would have to conclude that girls do not have a *significantly* greater face reading ability. If the mean difference had been 3.5 (girls = 16.0, boys = 12.5), you would have to reach a different conclusion (one that suggests girls really do have better face reading abilities, since the difference would be statistically significant).

The Null Hypothesis

Recall from Chapter 5 that researchers work with three different kinds of hypotheses: *research* (their prediction about the findings), *alternative* (the "something else" that may have influenced the results), and *null.* The null hypothesis comes into play during the data analysis, and it is used along with the logic I have been describing in order to reach a sound conclusion. The null hypothesis is a type of hidden—behind the scenes—hypothesis whose function waits for number crunching to begin. The null hypothesis has the following two essential characteristics:

- It is a statement about a population (not a sample).
- It is a statement that there is no difference (or relationship) between the groups studied.

In the face reading case, the null hypothesis is "In the population of seventh and eighth graders, there is no difference between boys' and girls' ability to read the emotional expressions on faces." (Notice the enormity of the population, perhaps a size of 1 million.) Why would you want to presume such a thing, especially when you really believe the opposite? The answer is that the use of this null hypothesis enables a clever strategy for making an *inference* about the population, given only data from a sample. An inference is a type of specific-to-general reasoning, one that allows us to make a statement about something general—the population—from something specific—the sample. Let me explain.

We have seen that chance likelihood is presented as a *p* value, but it is important to note now that this *p* value is calculated with the assumption that the *null hypothesis is true.* If we pretend, just for the moment, that the null hypothesis really *is* true, and calculate the *p* value with that in mind, we essentially have determined whether the null hypothesis probably is or is not true. When the *p* value drops below .05, as we've already seen, the results are statistically significant, but more importantly, we then know that the null hypothesis, therefore, is probably *not* true. Scientific researchers use the phrase *reject the null hypothesis* whenever obtained relationships are statistically significant. Researchers, in a sense,

HIGHLIGHT AND LEARNING CHECK 13-2

Rejecting the Null Hypothesis

The null hypothesis asserts that there is *no* relationship among the variables being studied in the population. Although a researcher usually believes its opposite (there is a relationship), the null hypothesis is presumed to be true only for the purpose of "rejecting" its plausibility when the p value is below .05. A "rejected" null hypothesis ($p < .05$) entitles a researcher to conclude that the research hypothesis is supported (there is probably a relationship among variables in the population). This reasoning is linked to the fact that it is possible only to directly calculate chance probabilities. Explain why this reasoning appears to reflect "reverse" logic.

set up the null hypothesis in order to knock it down. They pretend, only while the computer is analyzing the data, that the null hypothesis really is true, but hope in reality to discard it as probably not true. Because the null hypothesis is (usually) the opposite of the research hypothesis, its rejection allows the researcher to logically accept its opposite—the research hypothesis. In this case, we would say that the research hypothesis was *supported*, not proven, since there always exists the possibility that the difference did occur by chance (a fluke), even though that likelihood is small (less than .05).

The Role of the Null Hypothesis

Let's review the role of the null hypothesis. The researcher assumes that the null hypothesis is true: There is no difference between the groups in the population. (There still exists a *distribution* of variables in the population; it is the difference between them that is zero.) If one finds a difference between the groups in the

CRITICAL THINKER ALERT 13-1

Rejecting the Null Hypothesis

The null hypothesis is an assertion that there exists *no* relationship among variables being studied in the population. Researchers only temporarily assume this is true (during the data analysis). They usually hypothesize its opposite (there *is* a relationship). By conducting a statistical test, they determine whether or not the null hypothesis is probably true. If the null hypothesis is probably not true, it can be "rejected." The researcher then concludes that the research hypothesis has been supported.

Discussion: In a test of the difference between online versus face-to-face learning on long-term retention of algebra among ninth graders, what is the null hypothesis?

CRITICAL THINKER ALERT 13-2

Indirect Logic

Many students view the logic described in the preceding Critical Thinker Alert to be "backwards." It is not backwards, but the double negative (i.e., reject the null) can be confusing, to be sure. This is due to the fact that statisticians can compute the probability that the null hypothesis is true given the laws of chance probability. They cannot directly compute the probability that the research hypothesis is true. The logic is more *indirect* than backwards since researchers must try to "shoot down" (reject) a premise that is opposite of what they believe. Think about it this way: Either A or B is true (but not both). We can show that A is probably not true, so then we conclude that B probably *is* true (where A and B are the null and research hypotheses, respectively).

Discussion: If someone were to ask you "Isn't hypothesis testing in research 'backward'?" how would you answer using simple language?

sample drawn from the population, the question for the researcher becomes, "What is the probability of finding a difference this large, if in fact there is no real difference in the population?" It is this probability that the results reveal: the likelihood that the obtained findings could be attributed to the workings of the random process. And when that likelihood is less than .05, the researcher concludes that the findings are statistically significant.

The *p* Value Determination

You can think of the *p* value simply as being the probability that the null hypothesis is true. But how does the computer and its statistical software determine the *p* value? This is accomplished with the famous bell curve, or normal distribution, as it is usually called. Let's see how this curve can help us determine the *p* value in the boy versus girl face reading study. The ideas presented in this example can be logically extended to different situations, like those involving more than two means, or to different types of data, like those needing correlations or frequency counts. We will not examine all of these applications, but you can be assured that their conceptual basis is very similar.

Figure 13.1 shows an idealized version of a normal distribution.

Recall from Chapter 8 that this shows how scores "stack up" when their values are plotted against their frequency of occurrence. Recall further that in addition

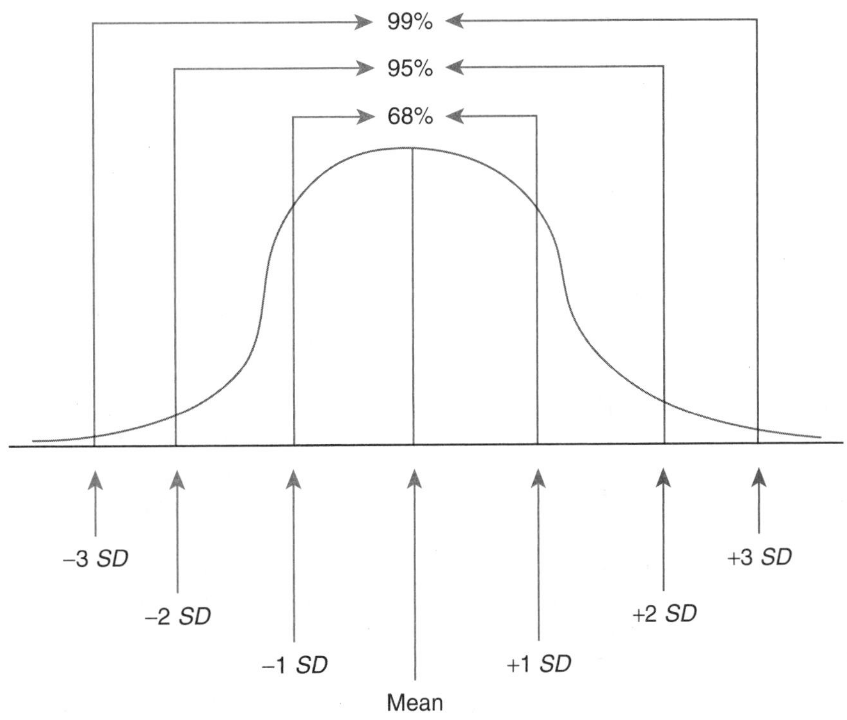

Figure 13.1 An idealized normal (bell) curve. Note the symmetry in the bell and the standard deviation (*SD*) points defining areas of the curve in percentages.

to the shape of the distribution (a bell), the distribution can be described in terms of its central tendency (the mean) and its variability (the standard deviation). The mean falls under the hump of the bell, and the standard deviation corresponds to a specific "cutoff point" in the distribution such that 68% of the cases in the distribution fall between the mean plus and minus 1 standard deviation, 95% fall within 2 standard deviations, and 95% fall within 3 standard deviations.

Mean Differences

Think again about the null hypothesis in our example of boys' versus girls' face reading ability: "In the population of seventh and eighth graders, there is *no* difference between boys' and girls' ability to read faces." If this is true, you can imagine sampling 30 boys and 30 girls, testing them, computing their means, and, finally, finding a mean difference. Here's a concrete example, again emphasizing, for the moment, that the null hypothesis is true. The boy mean = 14.9, the girl mean = 15.2, the mean difference (boy minus girl) = −.3. Imagine doing this again: The boy mean = 13.5, the girl mean = 13.0, the mean difference = .5. Imagine again: The boy mean = 15.6, the girl mean = 15.2, the mean difference = .4. Imagine again: The boy mean = 14.1, the girl mean = 15.2, the mean difference = −1.1. Imagine again: The boy mean = 15.0, the girl mean = 13.5, the mean difference = 1.5. Imagine again: The boy mean = 15.0, the girl mean = 16.00, the mean difference = −1.00. Thus far, we could imagine these mean differences:

−.3

.5

.4

−1.1

1.5

−1.0

Let your imagination run wild and pretend that this study was replicated 1,000 times, that each time a new sample of boys and girls was chosen from the population, and, most importantly, that each time the null hypothesis was presumed to be true. We would have a long, long string of mean differences, and the *mean of these mean differences would equal to zero if in fact the null hypothesis were true.* All of the chance differences, positive and negative, would "wash out" and balance to zero. It is important to understand that the mean of this make-believe sampling of 1,000 mean differences would be zero assuming the null hypothesis is true. Do you see why?

Furthermore, there is a theorem in statistics—the *central limit theorem*—which states that the *shape of this distribution of mean differences will be normal.* In other words, the bell curve would be duplicated in this hypothetical situation of 1,000 mean differences, with most of the differences hovering around zero and increasingly fewer mean differences approaching the extremes. The distribution would therefore look like the one shown in Figure 13.2, a normal "bell" with mean = 0.

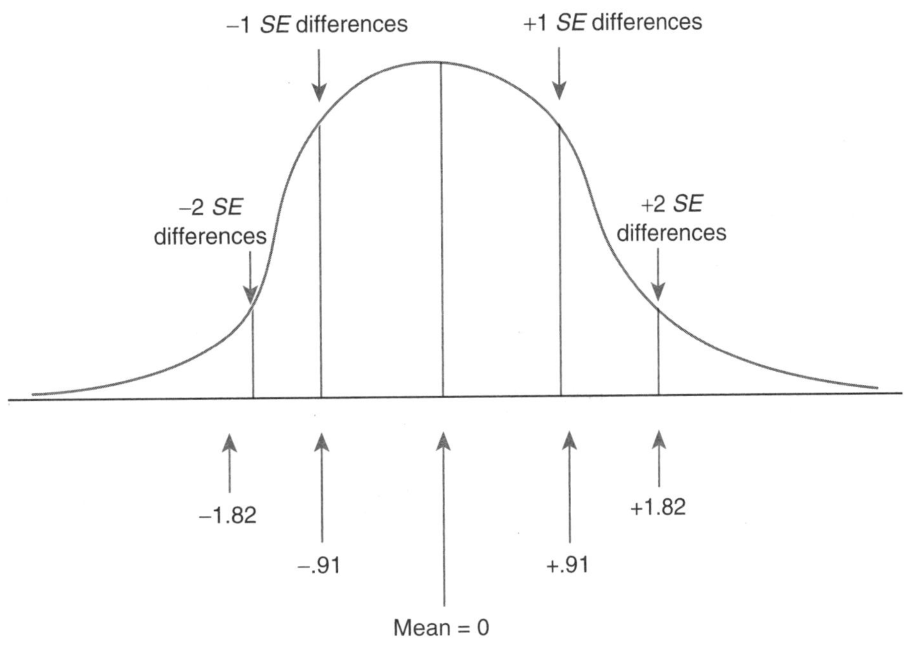

Figure 13.2 A sampling distribution of mean differences. It retains a bell shape with a mean of zero (if the differences reflect sampling error only) and a standard deviation equal to a value shown as the *standard error of mean differences* (or *SE* differences), .91 in this case). Mean differences that fall within an interval formed by *about* two times the value of the standard error of mean differences, positive or negative (2 × +/− .91, or −1.82 to +1.82, in this case) are believed to be due to chance (and are not statistically significant). (See the text for an explanation of this.)

Note: SE differences = standard error of mean differences

CRITICAL THINKER ALERT 13-3

Statistical Logic

Statistical inference involves making generalized statements about the population given a smaller subset of observations in the sample. Inference as a form of logic entails going from specific (the sample) to general (the population).

Discussion: Do researchers *always* intend to make generalized statements about larger populations? Is this always desirable?

Standard Error of Mean Differences

The missing piece of information thus far in the distribution of 1,000 mean differences is the standard deviation. Not to worry, for this information can be estimated quite accurately. The standard deviation of this sampling distribution of mean differences has a special name: the *standard error of mean differences,* and its calculation is based on the standard deviation of the two sample groups. Let's see how this is done.

STANDARD ERROR OF MEAN DIFFERENCES: A measure of sampling error contained within a mean difference. Conceptually, it is the standard deviation of a hypothetical sampling distribution of many mean differences drawn from a population.

Assume that the standard deviation of the boys' face reading scores was 3.0 (with a mean of 12.5) and the standard deviation of the girls' face reading scores was 4.0 (with a mean of 15.0). Also, the sample size was 30 per group. The calculation of the standard error of mean differences is as follows:

$$\sqrt{\left(\frac{3}{\sqrt{30}}\right)^2 + \left(\frac{4}{\sqrt{30}}\right)^2} = .91$$

This value of the standard error of the mean differences, .91, is a very important statistic. Because it is the standard deviation of the sampling distribution of mean differences (assuming the null hypothesis is true), it tells us the reasonable limits of chance differences. Approximately doubling the value of this statistic ($2 \times .91 = 1.82$) will, when added to and subtracted from the mean, form the boundaries of a distribution (in the tail) in such a way that 95% of the cases are contained within that boundary (recall that this is a basic property of the normal distribution). Figure 13.2 shows the sampling distribution of mean differences with the standard error of mean differences marked in the same manner as standard deviations.

TAILS: A statistical concept referring to the direction of an anticipated outcome (e.g., less than, more than). Most statistical tests are "two-tailed," permitting an outcome that could fall either way (like an increase or a decrease). A tail also refers to the outer 5% limits in a normal distribution.

Therefore, if the null hypothesis really *is* true, we would expect mean differences between boys and girls that are attributable to chance not to exceed 1.82 (in either direction). We have essentially solved the problem related to the interpretation of the mean difference of 2.5 between boys and girls in our example. Since the obtained mean difference is larger than 1.82, we must conclude that the difference is statistically significant, and as a result, *reject* the null hypothesis since it is probably not true.

Because the difference falls outside of the 95% chance limits, we can say that the probability of obtaining a mean difference as large as 2.5 (or larger) is less than 5 out of 100, or simply $p < .05$. The value of p itself is often referred to as the *level of statistical significance.* Its rejection logically entitles us to conclude that there is probably a difference in

HIGHLIGHT AND LEARNING CHECK 13-3

The *p* Value

A mean difference between two samples is evaluated by the standard error of mean differences. It determines the chance limits one would expect between means (a mean difference) 95% of the time when the null hypothesis is true. When the mean difference is determined to be too large given the "wobble" (the sampling error permitted by a true null hypothesis), the null hypothesis is "rejected," and the mean difference is statistically significant. The researcher concludes there is probably a relationship in the population. If a *p* value is determined to be .15, what is the researcher's interpretation and conclusion?

face reading ability in the population of boys and girls from which the sample was drawn. This, then, is the basic logic of our statistical tests.

Recap: The Null Hypothesis

To review, researchers temporarily assume the null hypothesis is true, even though they usually believe otherwise. Then a calculation is made (assuming that the null hypothesis is true) to determine how large a difference chance could reasonably explain (e.g., due to chance alone, 95% of sample differences will fall within the boundaries marked by such-and-such to such-and-such). Then the obtained difference is cast against this backdrop of chance differences; if it is larger, then the results are statistically significant (shown as $p < .05$), the null hypothesis is rejected, and it is concluded that there probably exists a true difference in the population. By contrast, if the results are within the chance boundaries, the findings are attributed to chance, they are *not* statistically significant, the null hypothesis is accepted, and researchers conclude that there is no true difference between groups in the population.

CRITICAL THINKER ALERT 13-4

Chance Defined

Researchers have defined "probably not true" to be a likelihood of less than 5 chances out of 100 ($p < .05$). Hence, any likelihood with $p < .05$ is probably not true since the likelihood is so low. A null hypothesis with a $p < .05$, then, can be considered probably not true and rejected, triggering statistical significance and support for the research hypothesis.

Discussion: Can you think of instances where researchers might want to "bump up" the trigger for statistical significance to perhaps .10 from .05? Why might they want to do this?

CRITICAL THINKER ALERT 13-5

Probability and Delta

Because the value of p in a study is influenced by sample size, it is incorrect to conclude that very low p values (e.g., .001) suggest very strong effects. (Very low p values may also suggest a very large sample size.) It is recommended that all reported results from statistical tests (that is, the p values) also include the associated measure of effect size. (More information about effect size measures, such as delta–d, which was introduced in Chapter 8–for a t test and omega square for the F test, are described in statistics texts. Statistical tests, such as the t and F, are described later in this chapter.)

Discussion: Explain why p and d (probability and delta) provide different but useful pieces of information in a statistical analysis.

Correlation Coefficients

The same logic used to test a mean difference for statistical significance is applied to the correlation coefficient, and many other types of statistics as well. Let's consider an example—the relationship between the ability to read the emotional expressions on faces and GPA. Assume that 30 randomly selected college seniors were studied by being administered the Face Reading Test (with scores ranging from 0 to 20, and high scores reflecting greater emotional intelligence). The seniors' GPAs were also retrieved from the school records. The calculation of the correlation coefficient yielded $r = .30$. (Recall from Chapter 9 that this statistic ranges from −1 to 1 with $r = 0$ indicating no relationship.)

CORRELATION COEFFICIENT: A statistical index of the degree of linear association between two measures (ranging from −1.00 to +1.00) revealing its strength and direction.

HIGHLIGHT AND LEARNING CHECK 13-4

Significant Correlation Coefficients

A correlation coefficient, like a mean difference, must be evaluated against a backdrop that reveals the limits of chance if the null hypothesis were true. If statistical reasoning suggests that 95% of all correlation coefficients fall between, say, −.20 and +.20 when the null hypothesis is true, then an obtained correlation coefficient of .30 would be tagged $p < .05$. The researcher would interpret .30 to be statistically significant and conclude there likely exists a correlation in the population. The "chance limits" of a correlation coefficient are determined by the sample size–the larger the sample, the closer the limits are to zero (smaller correlation coefficients are statistically significant with larger sample sizes). Given this, does a "statistically significant" correlation tell you much about its size?

As is customary, the null hypothesis is formed and assumed for the moment to be true. It asserts that in the *population* of college students, there is zero correlation between face reading ability and GPA. Next, a calculation is made to determine how high correlation coefficients would go in many samples drawn from the population *when the null hypothesis is true.* (These calculations have already been done by statisticians; their findings appear in tables found in most statistics books.)

In this case, the calculation reveals that if 100 samples were drawn from a population where the correlation were zero between face reading ability and GPA (the null hypothesis being true), then 95% of them would fall between −.36 and +.36. Only 5% of the samples would yield correlation coefficients outside that range.

Next, the obtained correlation of .30 is compared to this boundary expected by chance. Because it falls *within* the 95% chance boundaries, it is concluded that the correlation is *not* statistically significant and the null hypothesis is *accepted* as probably being true. Hence, in the population of college students, there is probably not a correlation between face reading ability and GPA. The correlation of $r = .30$, it would appear, is a reasonably likely sample finding in a population with $r = 0$.

The r of .30 may as well be interpreted as $r = 0$, since its departure from zero was probably the working of chance. Nonsignificant findings, as in this case, are sometimes written as $p > .05$, meaning the probably of the null hypothesis being true is *greater* than 5 out of 100, which, we have seen, is the scientific definition of "most likely due to chance."

Common Statistical Tests

Thus far we have seen how researchers go about interpreting their findings with a *p*, its value determining what should be done with the null hypothesis—accept it or reject

STATISTICAL TEST: A statistical maneuver applied to sampled data that yields *p* and permits a decision about the null hypothesis (i.e., whether to accept or reject it).

NULL HYPOTHESIS: A statistical hypothesis asserting there is no relationship among variables being studied in the population.

it. There are literally hundreds of statistical tests, but they all have in common their bottom-line calculation: the *p* value. Each one of these statistical maneuvers yields what is called a *test statistic* (often symbolized by a letter, such as *t* or *F*). It is this test statistic that is translated into the *p* value, and interpreted as the probability that the null hypothesis is true.

The variation in statistical tests arises from the diversity of research designs and types of data collected. Fortunately, educational researchers do not have to sort through hundreds of statistical tests. This is because many research applications in education have similarities which are appropriately analyzed with only a handful of techniques. These are described below.

The *t* Test

t TEST: A common statistical test that determines whether a mean difference is statistically significant.

The *t* test is one of the most common statistical tests. It is used to compare two means (one mean difference). Common applications include testing the difference between experimental and control groups, the difference between males and females, the difference between two teaching strategies, and the difference between a pretest and a posttest. As a mean difference increases (all other things being equal), the value of the *t* increases and the *p* level decreases.

As a general rule, *t* values greater than 2.00 are associated with *p* values that drop below the .05 level. When the value of the *p* drops below this scientifically established threshold (.05), the mean difference is significant (and probably not due to chance). (A *t* of 2.00 or greater doesn't always push the *p* value below .05; it varies somewhat as a function of sample size. The *t* value of 2.00, however, should make conceptual sense, for any standardized mean difference that is more than 2 standard errors corresponds to the tail of a normal distribution. In statistics, tails are usually defined as the most extreme 5% area of a distribution.) The *t* statistic, then, is merely a mean difference that has been *standardized* so that it can be evaluated against the normal curve of chance differences.

Two types of *t* tests are used by researchers: *independent groups t* and *correlated groups t* (which is also referred to as *paired t*). The independent groups *t* is undoubtedly the most common application of the *t* test and is used when the subjects in each group are different, as in male versus female, ninth graders versus fifth graders, or visual learners versus auditory learners. (The subjects are *independent* in the sense that the two groups are separate and not connected.) By contrast, a correlated groups *t* is used when there is a linkage between the two groups, as in the case where the same subjects are tested before and after a treatment (pre-post) or when matched subjects in two groups are being compared (every subject in one group has its matched pair in the other group). Another application of the correlated groups *t* test is found in twin studies that compare the talents of identical twins reared apart (in this case the linkage is genetic).

The *t* test usually appears in a published research report in the following way (but here the data are fictional): The treatment group ($M = 93.56$, $SD = 5.32$) scored significantly higher than the control group ($M = 81.67$, $SD = 6.21$), $t(75) = 5.93$,

$p < .01$. The descriptive statistics, means and standard deviations (*M* and *SD*, respectively), reveal that the treatment group scored higher than the control group and that they have about the same scatter of scores around their mean. It is the mean difference of 11.89 (93.56 – 81.67) that has been "standardized" by the *t* test, that is, recast against the normal curve backdrop.

The *t* value itself of 5.93 is an inferential statistic since it permits a decision about the null hypothesis (recall that this is a statement about the population). This *t* value, being a standardized mean difference, tells us that the mean difference of 11.89 corresponds to 5.93 (almost 6!) standard errors in a distribution of chance differences where 95% of those differences are contained within plus and minus 2 standard errors.

The number in parentheses after the *t* statistic refers to the approximate sample size. More precisely, it refers to an adjusted sample size commonly referred to as *degree of freedom* (*df*) in statistics. (Degree of freedom is routed in a complex mathematical argument, but the concept is explained in greater detail in most basic statistics textbooks. It is a technical adjustment that rids a specific type of statistical bias.) All statistical tests are associated with varying degrees of freedom depending on factors such as sample size and the number of calculated statistics required for the test. The correct degree of freedom is not intuitively obvious, but in the case of the *t* test, it is usually the number of subjects less one or two. Fortunately, all statistical software programs determine the appropriate *df* and report it alongside other relevant information. (The term is derived from the idea that once a statistic is calculated, there is an imposed restriction on other calculations, a "loss of freedom," if you will.)

DEGREE OF FREEDOM: A mathematical concept used in statistics that conveys information about size (sample size, number of groups, etc.).

Finally, the bottom line information is conveyed by the *p* value itself, which in this case is less than .01. Because it is less than the cutoff of .05 (the scientific standard), the researcher is entitled to reject the null hypothesis and conclude that it is probably not true. The mean difference in the sample, therefore, probably reflects a real difference in the population. The value of *p* itself is often referred to as the *level of significance*. It also tells us the probability that the null hypothesis is true (in this case, there is less than 1 out of 100 chances that the null hypothesis is true).

Although the *t* can be calculated in a wide variety of situations involving two groups, statisticians have found that the *p* value generated by the *t* test is most accurate when several conditions, or *assumptions*, exist. These are (1) that the populations from which the scores are drawn are normally distributed, as in a bell curve; (2) that the variances of scores (SD^2) in the populations are equal; and (3) that the samples are randomly selected from their populations. In truth, the *t* test is used frequently when some (or all) of these conditions do not exist. Yet it is generally believed that the *t* test is *robust*, meaning that the test yields reasonably accurate *p* values even when the data clearly do not meet the three assumptions. When researchers are not comfortable about the assumptions behind the *t* test, they frequently turn to *nonparametric* statistics, which are explained later in this chapter.

The *F* test

The *F* test, which is usually referred to as the analysis of variance (ANOVA), is probably the most widely used statistical test in educational research. (The test derived the letter name from its developer, Sir Ronald A. Fisher, and is sometimes called

F TEST: A statistical test also known as the analysis of variance (ANOVA) that determines the statistical significance of two or more mean differences.

Fisher's F ratio.) This test is appropriate for testing the significance of two or more means. As such it could be used in place of the *t* to test two means, but it could also be used to test for differences among many means, like those that result from very complex (factorial) research designs involving several main and interaction effects.

As is true with the *t* test, this technique yields an *F* statistic, which is then translated into a *p* so that the researcher can make a sound decision about the null hypothesis (as with the *t* test, reject it if the *p* value drops below .05). This test, like all other inferential tests, has an underlying null hypothesis.

Consider the case of a test to determine differences in teacher attitudes toward technology in the classroom with five different levels of experience (teachers in training, first-year teachers, and teachers with 2–5, 6–10, and 11–20 years of experience). The null hypothesis would be that in the *population* of teachers, there are *no* differences in attitudes toward technology in the classroom among teachers with varying levels of experience. The resultant *p* value, then, tells us how likely it is that the null hypothesis is true. And a rejected null hypothesis tells us that there are significant attitude differences toward technology among teachers with varying levels of experience.

The results of ANOVA usually appear in published research reports in the following way (but here the data are fictional): The analysis of variance revealed there were significant differences among the five groups, $F(4, 95) = 7.90$, $MSE = 3.60$, $p < .05$. (The reader is usually referred to a table which presents means, standard deviations, and sample sizes.) The two numbers in parentheses next to *F* refer to the number of groups and the number of subjects used in the test. (Actually, it is the number of groups less one; and the number of subjects in each group less one, times the number of groups.) The next value is the *F* itself, which is translated into a *p* value. The *MSE* (mean square error) is a measure of average variability within the five groups (akin to a standard deviation). The *p* value is, once again, the bottom line. The reason for conducting the *F* test is to permit a sound decision regarding the null hypothesis. In this case, the null hypothesis can be rejected on the basis of the low *p* value (less than .05), revealing that the mean differences are statistically significant.

As is true for the *t* test, the accuracy of the *F* test depends to some extent on statistical assumptions. The assumptions underlying the *F* test are the same as those underlying the *t* test: normality, equal variances, and random sampling. Like the *t*, the *F* is believed to be robust. Small departures from these assumptions are not likely to greatly affect the accuracy of the *p* value.

The Test for *r*

Researchers commonly test the significance of a correlation coefficient, as was shown earlier in this chapter. The correlation coefficient, or *r*, can be tested with a *t*, the same test statistic used to test two means (but with a different calculation). This test is known as the *test for r*.

TEST FOR *r*: A statistical test that determines whether a correlation coefficient is significantly different from zero.

Another example is a test of the relationship between high school students' "test wisdom" and their scholastic aptitude. The null hypothesis would be "In a *population* of high school students there is *no* relationship between level of test wisdom and scholastic aptitude." Is the null hypothesis probably true? Only the *p* value can tell (not for sure, but probably).

In a published report, the significance of *r* is usually shown simply as, for example, $r = .59$, $p < .01$. The researcher would conclude that the correlation coefficient of .59 is statistically significant and therefore probably *not* zero in the population.

The Chi-Square Test

Quite often, researchers also test for relationships involving *frequency* data in the form of tallies (counts) or percentages. This is accomplished with a statistical test called *chi-square* (symbolized χ^2). For example, a researcher might test whether there is a relationship between a decision to quit teaching after 1 year (yes or no) and the type of teacher training program that prepared the teacher (traditional versus nontraditional). Or a researcher might test whether there is a difference in teachers' preference for 50-minute versus 90-minute classes. The corresponding null hypotheses for the first example would be "In a population of first-year teachers, there is no relationship between a decision to leave the profession and type of training program." The corresponding null hypothesis for the second example would be "In a population of teachers, there is no difference in their preference regarding 50- or 90-minute classes."

The chi-square test usually appears in a published report in the following way: χ^2 (4, $N = 90$) = 9.34, $p < .05$. Recall that the statistical symbol for chi-square is χ^2 and the numbers in parentheses following the chi-square symbol refer to the number of groups (adjusted somewhat, but often the number of groups less one) and the number of subjects (*N*). The chi-square value itself is shown, followed by the all-important *p* value. In this case, given the low *p* value (less than .05), the researcher who used chi-square would decide to reject the null hypothesis since there existed a statistically significant relationship in the sample.

CHI-SQUARE TEST: A statistical test that determines significant relationships using data in the form of frequencies (counts, tallies, etc.).

HIGHLIGHT AND LEARNING CHECK 13-5

Statistical Tests

Educational researchers use statistical tests that yield *p* values to enable sound decisions about the null hypothesis (whether to accept or reject it). Such tests vary depending on the nature of the data (e.g., scores versus frequencies) and the research design (e.g., the number of groups or whether there are groups at all). Common statistical tests include the *t* test (comparing two groups), the *F* test (or ANOVA, comparing two or more groups), the test for *r* (evaluating a correlation coefficient), and the chi-square test (assessing relationships via frequency counts). All these tests produce *p* values that are interpreted similarly with regard to the null hypothesis. Explain why researchers need statistical tests, that is, why they cannot simply look at descriptive statistics and reach a conclusion.

Parametric Versus Nonparametric Tests

Most statistical tests used by researchers are classified as *parametric* because they hold certain assumptions about population characteristics (known as

NONPARAMETRIC TESTS: Statistical tests and indexes (e.g., chi-square test, Spearman rank order correlation) that make few assumptions about the value of parameters.

PARAMETER: A characteristic of a population.

SCALE OF MEASUREMENT: Distinguishing features that identify adjacent values on a measuring device (includes nominal, ordinal, interval, and ratio scales).

HIGHLIGHT AND LEARNING CHECK 13-6

Parametric Versus Nonparametric Tests

Researchers often decide between the use of parametric and nonparametric statistical maneuvers and tests. The decision is largely a function of the chosen scale of measurement and believable assumptions, with nonparametric tests used more commonly with nominal and ordinal scales and when the populations are not presumed to be normal in shape. The nonparametric tests such as the Mann-Whitney U and Spearman rank order correlation have their counterparts in the realm of parametric statistics (the t test for independent groups and the Pearson product moment correlation, respectively). Explain how a researcher's choice of statistical tests might contribute to inconsistent research findings.

parameters). For example, we have seen that the t and F tests assume that samples are drawn randomly from populations that are normal with equal variances. For researchers who are uneasy about these assumptions, another class of statistical tests is available. Appropriately termed *nonparametric*, these tests are appropriate when a researcher believes that the assumptions about the underlying parameters are probably not true ("violated").

Nonparametric tests are also appropriate when the type of data being analyzed (called the *scale of measurement*) is *nominal* or *ordinal* as opposed to *interval*. Nominal scales simply use numbers as labels with no implied order, as in 1 = male, 2 = female. Ordinal scales imply a ranking or continuum, as in 1 = fastest, 2 = next fastest, and so on. Interval scales imply an equal distance between values on a continuum from low to high, as is a temperature scale where 30° to 40° represents the same difference as 90° to 100°. Parametric tests such as the t and F are most appropriately applied to interval data. Statisticians appear split on the type of data used in many educational research studies (such as achievement test scores), as they appear to fall somewhere between ordinal and interval. In reality, many researchers treat most educational data as interval, hence the widespread use of the parametric t and F.

Most parametric tests, however, have nonparametric counterparts for use when parametric assumptions appear in doubt or when the type of data is clearly not interval scaled. Three widely used nonparametric tests are the Mann-Whitney U (the counterpart to the t for independent groups), the Wilcoxon Matched-Pairs Signed-Ranks T (the counterpart to the t for correlated groups), and the Kruskal-Wallis H (the counterpart to ANOVA with one independent variable). The chi-square test for frequency data described earlier is also a nonparametric test, as frequency data are usually associated with nominal scales.

Nonparametric tests yield p values in the same manner as parametric tests, and they are used in the same way with the same rules (if less than .05, reject the null hypothesis). Finally, measures of relationships such as correlation coefficients have parametric and nonparametric counterparts. The widely used *Pearson (product-moment) correlation coefficient* (r) is parametric, and the *Spearman (rank order) correlation coefficient* is nonparametric.

Statistical Errors

Type I

The researcher's decision to accept or reject the null hypothesis may be wrong. A sampling oddity may lead to a decision to reject the null hypothesis when it is in fact true (and should have been accepted). Consider the Face Reading Test once more, and assume for the moment that there are no differences whatsoever in the population between males and females in their face reading ability; that is, the null hypothesis is true. A researcher's sample of females, albeit random, may simply be overrepresented with skillful face readers. The sample of males, likewise, may contain a disproportionate number of people with less skill in face reading. This is simply a fluke, like flipping a coin 7 times only to find it landing on heads each time. Rare events, like being struck by lightning or winning a lottery, do in fact happen. Researchers call this problem *sampling error*. It is not a mistake resulting from confusion or anything like that. In statistics, the term *error* does not connote blame, since it only refers to a variability or fluke in sampling.

TYPE I ERROR: A statistical fluke in sampling that permits an incorrect rejection of the null hypothesis (concluding there is a relationship in the population when there is no relationship).

There is a name (though not a very creative one) for this type of sampling error when the null hypothesis is wrongly rejected: a *Type I error*, which is sometimes called *alpha* or *alpha error*. (This term is totally unrelated to Cronbach's alpha described in Chapter 9.) *Type I error* refers to mistakenly rejecting a true null hypothesis, that is, concluding there is a relationship in the population when in fact there is not. The likelihood of such an error is determined by the *p* value itself. For example, if you reject the null hypothesis, as you should, with a *p* value of .001, then you know that the likelihood of this Type I error is simply .001. This is very unlikely indeed, but a Type I error is still possible (like winning a lottery). Researchers never know for certain whether or not they fell victim to a Type I error. (The strongest evidence of its existence would be a series of replications of the original study that produced the significant finding, all of which, by contrast, accepted the null hypothesis.) Remember, it is not the type of mistake that a researcher could be faulted for; researchers have no control over random oddities.

Type II

There is another type of error in statistical reasoning called a *Type II error*, which is sometimes called *beta* or *beta error*. With this mistake, the researcher would wrongly accept the null hypothesis when in fact it was false, that is, conclude wrongly that there is no relationship in the population. The only explanation for this occurrence is, once again, chance or sampling error. In the face reading example, it may in fact be true that in the population, females really do have better ability to read the emotional clues on faces than males do. But the sample may have simply overrepresented females with poor ability in face reading; conversely, the sample may have been overrepresented by males with good ability in face reading. Once again, this could result from a random oddity in the random number table.

TYPE II ERROR: A statistical fluke in sampling that permits an incorrect acceptance of the null hypothesis (concluding there is no relationship in the population when in fact there is a relationship).

HIGHLIGHT AND LEARNING CHECK 13-7

Statistical Errors (Type I and Type II)

Statistical errors occur when decisions about the null hypothesis are wrong, stemming entirely from the laws of chance. A Type I error (set at .05) is wrongly rejecting the null hypothesis (a "false alarm"); a Type II error is wrongly accepting the null hypothesis (a "missed sighting"). In what sense is the word *error* used? Is it related to sampling error or reasoning error?

The true difference in the population, therefore, would be masked (eliminated) in the sample. In this case, the researcher, based on a *p* value greater than .05, would have no choice but to accept the null hypothesis (wrongly) and be unaware that a mistake was made. In a sense, this Type II error might be more serious than the Type I error, since the Type II error is a "missed sighting." For example, a drug may really be a cure for a disease, but the results of research on the drug may be nonsignificant due to a Type II error. This overlooked cure may go unnoticed because other researchers may not replicate the study. Replicating nonsignificant findings is less exciting, usually, than replicating exciting and significant findings. Type I errors would be discovered during replications of a significant finding, whereas Type II errors would almost certainly not be double-checked with the same frequency. (Why double-check findings showing no relationships?)

The relation between Type I ("false alarm") and Type II ("missed sighting") errors and the null hypothesis is summarized in Table 13.1.

Table 13.1 Type I and Type II Errors

		Null Hypothesis Really Is	
		True	**False**
Your Decision	**Accept**	No error	Type II (Missed Sighting)
	Reject	Type I (False Alarm)	No Error

CRITICAL THINKER ALERT 13-6

Statistical Errors

Two types of statistical errors are possible given the random fluctuations of the sampling process. A Type I error occurs when the null hypothesis is mistakenly rejected (a false alarm); a Type II error occurs when the null hypothesis is mistakenly accepted (a missed sighting).

Discussion: Describe what is meant by *error* in statistical analysis and why Type I and Type II errors are not blameworthy mistakes.

CRITICAL THINKER ALERT 13-7

Statistical Power

The probability of a Type I error ("alpha") is usually "preset" by statistical software to .05. The probability of a Type II error is left to vary, and is largely a function of sample size. Ideally, statistical power should reach .80 or higher, making the probability of a Type II error .20 or less.

Discussion: Why do researchers try to avoid situations where the power of a statistical tests drops below, say, .50?

The Accuracy of *p*

The calculation of *p*, in order to convey accuracy, assumes that "all else is fine." By this I mean that subjects were selected randomly from a population and then assigned randomly to groups, and there were no threats to the internal validity of the study—no blunders, biases, artifacts, confounding, and so forth. The *p* value cannot fix blunders. In the case of serious flaws in the methodology, the *p* value may not be at all accurate, and the inference about the population may be completely wrong. Such flaws are far more serious and blameworthy than a Type I or Type II error.

Consider an example of a researcher testing whether there are sex differences in aerobic exercise frequency (measured in the form of hours of exercise, on average, in 1 week). Assume for this example that there are in fact no differences in the population between males' and females' exercise frequency (that the null hypothesis is indeed true). Let's assume further that the male researcher is a frequent exerciser (this seems reasonable since he is interested in research on exercise).

For convenience, the researcher samples 25 of his male friends ("birds of a feather flock together") and determines that they exercised 4.6 hours per week on average. Furthermore, he samples only a few of his female friends, and must rely on "shopping mall" tactics to complete the survey of 25 females (by just walking up to agreeable looking shoppers and soliciting the information). Pretend that the (mostly solicited) females, on average, exercised 2.6 hours per week. Upon analysis the researcher finds a *p* value of .001, revealing a significant difference between the two samples.

HIGHLIGHT AND LEARNING CHECK 13-8

The Accuracy of *p*

The accuracy of the *p* value depends on many factors, including many issues related to sampling and control procedures. Explain why the accuracy of *p* might be related to the need to replicate findings in educational research many times before considering their practical application.

Remember that the null hypothesis is true in this scenario, and the usual interpretation—there is less than 1 out of 1,000 chances that one would find a mean difference that big in the sample if the null hypothesis were true—is patently false. The sampling was very biased, and the conclusion was wrong.

The major point here is that there is nothing in the statistical analysis that fixes or compensates for procedural blunders prior to the analysis. For the *p* value to be accurate, the researcher should have *randomly* sampled men and women from the population and obtained true (valid) information with little or no loss of subjects. Otherwise, the problem is akin to the old adage: Garbage in, garbage out.

CRITICAL THINKER ALERT 13-8

Statistical Tests

All statistical tests yield *p* values, yet their accuracy depends on the assumptions built into the statistical test. Different statistical tests have different assumptions about the population. If the sample that yielded data for the statistical test does not represent the population, then inferences about the population based on the *p* value may not be at all accurate. In other words, there is nothing about a statistical test that "fixes" sampling blunders.

Discussion: In a test of differences between middle school boys and girls in attitudes toward science, explain why the statistical analysis of a boys' sample obtained from baseball leagues and a girls' sample obtained from music courses might yield misleading *p* values.

The Importance of Power

The statistical power of a test is akin to the power of a microscope or telescope. (The concept of power was first introduced in Chapter 8 in the context of sample size.) Strong power in a microscope allows biologists to see differences between cells very clearly. Strong power in a telescope allows astronomers to see clearly the differences between planets. Likewise, researchers want to be able to see differences between groups or correlations between variables very clearly.

STATISTICAL POWER: A statistical concept referring to the likelihood of correctly rejecting the null hypothesis (concluding there is a relationship in the population when, indeed, one exists).

The *power* of a test more formally is defined as "the ability to uncover relationships in the sample if there are, in fact, true relationships in the population." Powerful statistical tests, then, enable researchers to find relationships when they are present. Power is indexed as a probability, and as such falls between 0 and 1. Think of it as the probability of detecting a relationship—if there is one to detect. Strong power is obviously desirable, and most researchers want to arrange for power to be about .90. This means that if there is a relationship present in the population, the probability of detection in the sample with the statistical test is .90, a very good bet.

Power is calculable in the planning stages of a study. Its value is determined by several factors, such as the strength of the effect (which researchers usually have little control over) and the sample size (which researchers can adjust). Statistical power always increases with increasing sample size. The answer to the question "How many subjects do I need?" is usually determined in large part by the level of power that is desired. (See Chapter 8 for a review of sample size estimation.)

Sample size determination is especially important prior to carrying out a study, for it might be determined that power (as planned) is low, say .15. One could reasonably ask, "Why carry out the study when there is only a .15 probability that a relationship (if one existed) would be detected?" It is easy to see the futility of conducting a study with such low power, yet many researchers are unaware of the low statistical power of their own studies.

Studies with low power (e.g., less than .50) are very difficult to interpret, for a *non*significant finding could be due to *either* low power *or* a true absence of a relationship in the population. The crux of the problem is that there may, in fact, be a relationship in the population, but a statistical test with low power will likely lead to nonsignificant findings. Thus, one who uses a low-power test and accepts the null hypothesis really has not learned very much. The conclusion after the analysis is the same as the proposition before the research: There may or may not be a relationship in the population.

The calculation of power prior to data collection, if it is low, may lead to a revision of plans and an increase in the number of subjects required for a fair test of the hypothesis. But power analysis could also yield other useful information. It might reveal, for example, that the power as planned is .99, and a reduction in sample size to save time, money, and other resources may still yield a very acceptable power of .90. Why use 200 subjects when a fair test is possible with 100?

HIGHLIGHT AND LEARNING CHECK 13-9

Statistical Power

Statistical power refers to the ability of a statistical test to uncover a relationship in the sample—if one exists in the population. It might be said that research is "doomed" if the statistical test has, for example, a power of only .20. This suggests there is only a 20% likelihood of finding a significant relationship (presuming there is one). Power increases with increasing sample size. Explain why "low-power" research in education is difficult to interpret when findings reveal no significant relationships.

Power is defined statistically as 1 minus beta (recall beta is the probability of a Type II error, or mistakenly accepting a false null hypothesis). Hence, power calculation involves computing beta, and easy methods have been developed for accurately estimating beta (see, e.g., Kraemer & Thiemann, 1987). Beta decreases as sample size increases; hence, as previously described, one simple and direct way to increase power is to increase sample size.

CRITICAL THINKER ALERT 13-9

Power and Sample Size

The power of a statistical test (1 minus the probability of a Type II error) is largely determined by sample size. A statistical test that accepts the null hypothesis with very low power is inconclusive. This is because a low-power test is not statistically fair, for even if the null hypothesis were false, the test has little chance of rejecting it. Without knowing the reason for accepting the null hypothesis (low power versus its being true), one has learned very little. By contrast, accepting the null hypothesis with high power suggests that the null hypothesis is indeed true.

Discussion: There are many facets to a "fair" test of a relationship in educational research. Explain why a very low-power test in research might generate this reaction: "But that's not fair!"

Quantitative Data Analysis in Published Reports

Assessment and Motivation

Stefanou and Parkes (2003) observed that educators' dissatisfaction with large-scale, high-stakes "bubble" tests led to a performance-assessment movement that shifted focus to the evaluation of students through the application of more authentic, context-oriented tasks (such as projects and the use of portfolios to display capabilities and learning over time). Teachers often claimed, with little documentation, that learner-centered performance assessments that require deeper level processing strategies in useful contexts were linked to greater motivation in the classroom compared to passive multiple-choice tests. With a theoretical framework in place to support teachers' anecdotal experiences, Stefanou and Parkes arranged for an experimental test of three different formats of classroom assessment and their effects on fifth-grade students' motivation.

Using 79 students in three science classes, these researchers created three types of assessment methods for each of three different instructional units. The three types of assessment were paper-and-pencil (multiple-choice, true-false, matching, etc.), laboratory (with prescribed steps and conclusions based on observations), and a more open-ended, performance-based assessment requiring several tasks. The researchers also used three different dependent variables as outcome measures of motivation: science attitudes, goal orientations, and cognitive engagement. (All three were operationally defined as scores from the Science Activity Questionnaire, with higher scores reflecting more positive experiences with science, a more learning-mastery orientation, and greater self-regulation and engagement, respectively.) Higher scores on these measures, therefore, indicated higher levels of motivation.

All the students were given all three instructional units, experienced all three types of assessment, and completed all three measures of motivation (attitude, orientation, and engagement) in a systematized, counterbalanced manner to avoid confounding type of assessment with time of year and topic of unit. (They did not permit the unit on salt water, for example, to be assessed using only paper-and-pencil.) You will recognize this type of research as an example of an experimental within subjects design.

The means (and standard deviations) for each type of assessment and each measured outcome in Stefanou and Parkes's (2003) study are shown in Table 13.2.

Scanning the means as a function of assessment type reveals no dramatic differences. They all look "about the same." But wait. Only a statistical test can determine for us whether or not these differences likely reflect sampling error only. Stefanou and Parkes used the *F* test, or analysis of variance (ANOVA), to test for the statistical significance of these mean differences.

Indeed, they reported that ANOVA yielded a *p* value greater than .05 ($p > .05$) across means for the Attitude measure and for the Engagement measure. The *p* value for the Orientation measure, by contrast, was statistically significant, $p < .05$. The researchers therefore rejected the null hypothesis relating to the Orientation outcome but accepted the null hypotheses for the other two measures. The null hypothesis for the Orientation measure was likely: "In a population of fifth-grade

TABLE 13.2 Statistical Findings From a Study of Assessment and Student Motivation

	Measure					
	Attitude		Orientation		Engagement	
Assessment	Mean	(*SD*)	Mean	(*SD*)	Mean	(*SD*)
Paper-and-Pencil	3.10	(.41)	3.21	(.43)	3.12	(.51)
Laboratory	3.01	(.45)	3.04	(.39)	3.06	(.44)
Performance	3.15	(.39)	3.21	(.43)	3.13	(.44)

Source: "Effects of Classroom Assessment on Student Motivation in Fifth-Grade Science," by C. Stefanou and J. Parkes, 2003, *Journal of Educational Research, 96*(3), p. 156.

science students, there is no difference in goal orientation as a function of assessment by paper-and-pencil, laboratory, and performance assessment methods."

Rejecting this idea, then, logically entitled the researchers to conclude that there probably *is* a connection between type of assessment and level of goal orientation in the larger population. Recall that the *p* value also tells us the likelihood of a Type I error (concluding there is a relationship when, in truth, there is not). In this case, the probability of this type of error is low, less than .05. Recall also that this demarcation is the standard set by science: An outcome with a probability of occurring less than 5 times out of 100 (assuming the null hypothesis is true) probably did not occur by chance.

Researchers use ANOVA when three or more means are being compared, but because ANOVA is a general ("omnibus") test of mean differences overall, it does not "pinpoint" which single mean difference is statistically significant. A follow-up *t* test can be used in a paired-comparison manner to isolate mean differences contributing to the overall effect. Using this special type of *t* test (Bonferroni), Stefanou and Parkes were able to determine that the Laboratory assessment was statistically lower than the paper-and-pencil and performance assessments (and that the latter two did not differ significantly, hardly surprising since the means were identical). The researchers did not provide a measure of the effect size (like delta) for the one statistically significant comparison, and because of this, we do not know if this difference might also be important for practice.

These findings appear difficult to discuss, in part because the researchers did not uncover dramatic differences. The performance assessments should have yielded greater levels of motivation (measures of attitudes, orientation, engagement), especially when compared to paper-and-pencil assessments. The significant finding, one relating to goal orientation, is obscured by the fact that performance assessment did not differ from paper-and-pencil assessment (contrary to the hypothesis). (Although not relevant to our discussion of statistics, higher scores on the goal orientation measure suggest a task mastery orientation and are believed to reflect motivation that is more positive: learning for the sake of increasing competence as opposed to learning for the sake of a obtaining a reward or avoiding a display of incompetence.)

CRITICAL PERSPECTIVES 13-1

APPROACHES TO DATA ANALYSIS

Critical Thinking Toolbox

Critical thinkers recognize implications from statements, that is, what one can reasonably expect given the truth of statements (Paul, Binker, Jensen, & Kreklau, 1990). Accepting a statement leads to accepting its logical implications.

Data Analysis in Quantitative Research

Analysis of data in quantitative research is statistical, as you would expect, and focuses on methods and techniques designed to summarize numerical values (e.g., the mean) or enable conclusions that extend beyond the sample through hypothesis testing and the *p* value. A clear structure is often imposed on the data via spreadsheets (e.g., Excel) and statistical software (e.g., SPSS). Much effort is directed toward "rejecting" the null hypothesis and concluding that there exists a relationship among variables in the population. The particular statistical test used in quantitative data analysis is a function of the types of independent and dependent variables as well as the types of scales used to collect data. The famous "normal curve" and assumptions about data influence how data will be "crunched," but many data in educational research are analyzed by comparing mean differences and testing linear relationships. Established statistical maneuvers and standardized scores in educational research enable relatively easy analysis (computationally) and straightforward interpretation.

Data Analysis in Qualitative Research

Analysis of data in qualitative research involves pattern seeking using inductive analytic strategies. What this means is that the researcher organizes complex data such as narrative text or images into meaningful categories and interconnecting themes that emerge "from the bottom up." This is opposed to a structure imposed on the data beforehand. Generalizations synthesized from the analysis must come "from the ground up," and the analysis may continue concurrently with data collection. Analysis involves much back-and-forth pattern seeking, coding, and recoding for maximum meaning, as well as eventual interpretation that is cast in a larger, abstract context. Pattern seeking usually ends upon data "saturation," at which point no new insights are likely after continued classifying, coding, and note taking ("memoing"). A major task in qualitative data analysis after its organization is description; its "rich" data often result in "thick" descriptions. Qualitative data analysis may produce new ways of understanding a complex phenomenon, frequently with the aid of a metaphor, model, construct, or theory. The nature of qualitative data in the "raw" form of interview transcripts, videotapes, archived documents, or ethnographic field notes often requires creative strategies to enable the interpretation of these data for the purpose of developing or testing theories in education. Many strategies and techniques of pattern seeking have been developed to aid this task (e.g., constant comparison) and gauge data trustworthiness. Ultimately, the methods of analysis must support the overall credibility of conclusions and a construction of reality from the participants' perspective in a natural setting.

Data Analysis in Action Research

Data analysis in action research can be "mixed," combining elements from both qualitative and quantitative approaches. It is usually not very formal and often includes graphs or figures uncomplicated by references to esoteric procedures and techniques. Basic statistics (tallies, means, medians, etc.) often suffice because there is little interest in generalizing beyond one's own classroom or school (requiring an inference based on statistical tests). Qualitative approaches often include creating categories and emphasizing shared characteristics. Above all else, the data analysis (and interpretation) in action research must enable educators to commit to data-driven decisions—actions—in their own practice.

Critical Thinking Questions

Qualitative and quantitative orientations toward educational data and their analysis are very different on many dimensions. The implications of these differences are great. The consequences of one dominating the other are also great. Which paradigm—qualitative or quantitative—appears to be in favor today? What are the implications and consequences of this being the favored approach?

Fortunately, Stefanou and Parkes (2003) also collected qualitative measures of motivation by taping interviews with each class. They asked questions such as "Having experienced all three assessments, which type do you prefer and why?" They collected the qualitative data "to assist in gaining a better understanding of the interplay between assessment and student motivation than what might have been captured by the [quantitative] inventory" (p. 156). In fact, the interview data did help these researchers make sense of their findings overall. (The general topic of qualitative data analysis was covered in Chapter 12.)

The use of "mixed methods" (both numbers and words, quantitative and qualitative) is one mark of good study because often each type of data helps one interpret the other type. Stefanou and Parkes (2003) remarked, "When we combine the quantitative results with the qualitative information, a clearer picture emerges" (p. 158). Their interview data, for example, revealed that students were very grade conscious and their articulated preference for paper-and-pencil measures merely reflected a form they knew best and believed would help them achieve the highest grade. (Only 2 of 79 students preferred performance assessment!) The interviews, therefore, led the researchers to conclude that, quite possibly, motivation was capped with performance assessments, due to its being linked to fears that the "risk-taking" encouraged during the open-ended performance assessments might negatively affect their grades. In other words, students might feel penalized by taking part in an activity that might be more engaging; challenge is fine, as long as it is not "academically costly." Extracting themes from interview data is also a challenge (see "Emergent Methodology" in Chapter 12).

Data Analysis Software

Statistical Analysis: SPSS

There are bundles of software that appear to dominate the Internet and computing, including Windows as a platform, Explorer as a browser, Word as a word processor, Excel as a spreadsheet, and Adobe as a document reader. I might add SPSS as a statistical analysis program. There are others, of course, but the Statistical Package for the Social Sciences (SPSS) is widely used in statistics courses in higher education, in large part because it (in the student and teacher versions for Windows) is easy to use and is affordable. SPSS is well designed for self-teaching since it includes a fine tutorial. There are also many friendly guides for using SPSS, both printed and online. Using SPSS is simply a matter of inserting the SPSS CD, waiting a few seconds for its installation, and clicking icons as prompted.

Consider an example of SPSS, revealing its ease and clear interpretation. Presume a researcher wondered about a connection between aerobic exercise and speed of mental processing. The researcher recruited 20 high school seniors, and one half, selected randomly, agreed to jog 1 mile and then immediately complete a speed-of-mental-processing task. This task required participants to make simple perceptual judgments (like press one key if the color blue appears, otherwise press a different key; press one key if a word contains an "m," etc.). The instructions encouraged a high level of accuracy, but the primary dependent variable was speed (so fast that it was measured in milliseconds). The control group was merely tested without any aerobic treatment. Let's presume the Aerobic group's scores were 269, 205, 420, 206, 320, 256, 275, 300, 165, and 350. Presume further the Control group's scores were 360, 440, 560 289, 320, 204, 295, 345, 367, and 550.

The most time-consuming task in SPSS is entering data into a spreadsheet format (presuming it does not already exist in Excel or some other format easily imported into SPSS). Figure 13.3 shows an SPSS data entry screen (the "SPSS Data Editor"). This data editor screen will accommodate all types of data.

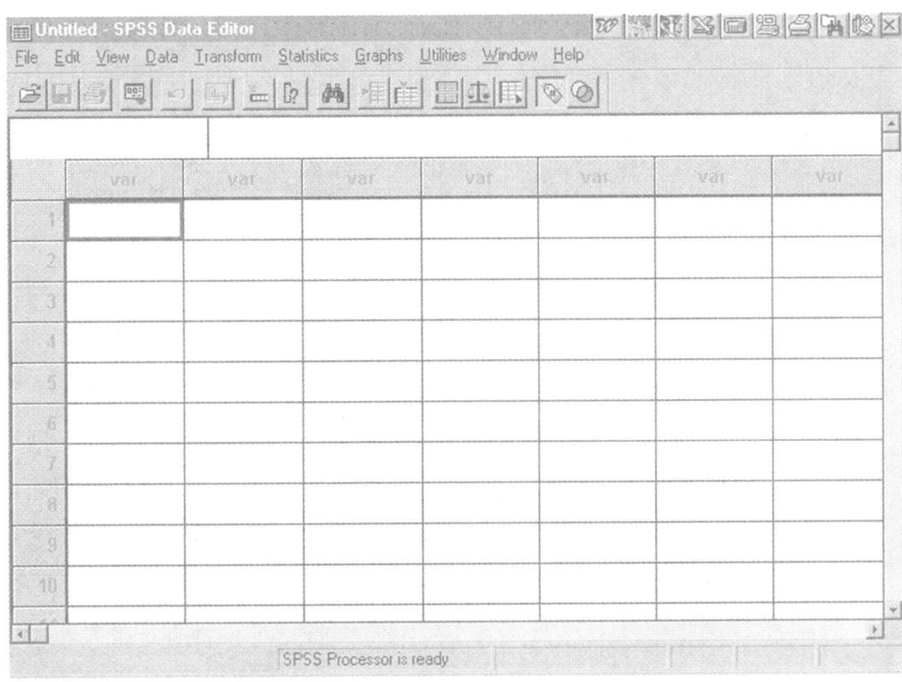

Figure 13.3 A screen image of an SPSS Data Editor. Values are entered in a standard spreadsheet format. Notice the menu-driven choices on the top bar.

There are ample features in SPSS for enhancing the data set such as adding variable names and value labels, recoding variables, computing new variables, handling missing data, and the like. There are many options for creating graphical displays as well. Table 13.3 shows the values from the Aerobic and Control groups as they would appear in an SPSS spreadsheet format. Notice that one variable is labeled "group" with coded values (1 and 2) to distinguish the two groups.

To determine whether the Aerobic group differs significantly from the Control group, you would select "Analyze" on the SPSS menu bar, then "Compare Means," then "Independent Samples *t* Test." SPSS will prompt you for a few other pieces of information (like which groups you want to compare, on what dependent variable,

TABLE 13.3 **Hypothetical Speed Scores in Aerobic and Control Groups**

	Group	Score
1	1	269
2	1	205
3	1	420
4	1	206
5	1	320
6	1	256
7	1	275
8	1	300
9	1	165
10	1	350
11	2	360
12	2	440
13	2	560
14	2	289
15	2	320
16	2	204
17	2	295
18	2	345
19	2	367
20	2	550

Note: This is a printout from an SPSS Data Editor spreadsheet. Under the variable "group," the Aerobic group is coded 1 and the Control group is coded 2. Scores are milliseconds, and lower scores suggest faster mental processing.

etc.). After that point, you simply click "OK" to run the statistical analysis. The results of the SPSS *t* test procedure are shown in Table 13.4.

You will find that the descriptive statistics reveal a mean of 276.60 for the Aerobic group ($SD = 75.60$) and a mean of 373.00 for the Control group ($SD = 113.67$). These statistics leave no doubt that the Aerobic group responded faster in the mental processing tasks. But one must always wonder, "Is it likely that this difference arose by chance factors alone?" Enter the findings of the *t* test. As shown in Figure 13.4, the answer is "Not likely," for this mean difference of

TABLE 13.4 **SPSS Output From the *t* test Procedure**

t-Test

Group Statistics

	Group	N	Mean	Std. Deviation	Std. Error Mean
Score	Aerobic	10	276.60	75.596	23.905
	Control	10	373.00	113.669	35.945

Independent Samples Test

		t-test for Equality of Means			
		t	df	Sig. (2-tailed)	Mean Difference
Score	Equal variances assumed	−2.233	18	.038	−96.40
	Equal variances not assumed	−2.233	15.659	.041	−96.40

Note: The output shows descriptive statistics and *p* values ("Sig."). More information about *t* test assumptions and the interpretation of SPSS output is available from SPSS and basic statistics texts.

nearly 100 milliseconds would occur in less than 5 out of 100 random samples if the null hypothesis were true (there was no connection between exercise and mental processing in the population). Given the results of the SPSS analysis, therefore, you would conclude that there is a statistically significant link between aerobic exercise and mental processing in a population of students like those studied. Of course, more research would be needed to conclude that exercise significantly affects mental processing in a direct causal way beyond the restrictions imposed by this small sample.

Let's presume that the researcher, encouraged by these findings, wanted to test the relationship between exercise and mental acuity using a different sample and in a somewhat different way. Let's presume that 10 students agreed to participate by providing information about their average weekly amount of exercise (in hours) over the course of the concluding semester. The researcher also collected each student's final exam score in Algebra I. These make-believe findings are presented in Table 13.5 (printed from the SPSS Data Editor).

From the SPSS menu bar, you would select "Analyze," then "Correlate," and then "Bivariate" (a two-variable correlation). Table 13.6 shows the SPSS Output Window revealing the correlation coefficient of .74. Its *p* value (level of significance), being less than .05, tells us that the linear relationship between amount of exercise and algebra exam performance is indeed statistically significant. (In the SPSS Correlations output, the *p* value appears as "Sig.")

TABLE 13.5 Data Set Showing Exercise Values and Scores

	Exercise	Score
1	12	88
2	0	50
3	2	42
4	3	38
5	8	99
6	7	90
7	6	76
8	4	80
9	5	88
10	7	70

Note: These data were printed from the SPSS Data Editor in a spreadsheet format. "Exercise" refers to average hours per week of exercise, and "Score" refers to algebra achievement as measured by final exam scores.

TABLE 13.6 SPSS Output From the Correlations Procedure

Correlations

		Exercise	Score
Exercise	Pearson Correlation	1	.739*
	Sig. (2-tailed)	.	.015
	N	10	10
Score	Pearson Correlation	.739*	1
	Sig. (2-tailed)	.015	.
	N	10	10

*Correlation is significant at the 0.05 level (2-tailed).

Note: This shows the Pearson correlation coefficient between Exercise and Score (.74, rounded). Its *p* value is shown as "Sig." and reveals that the correlation is statistically significant.

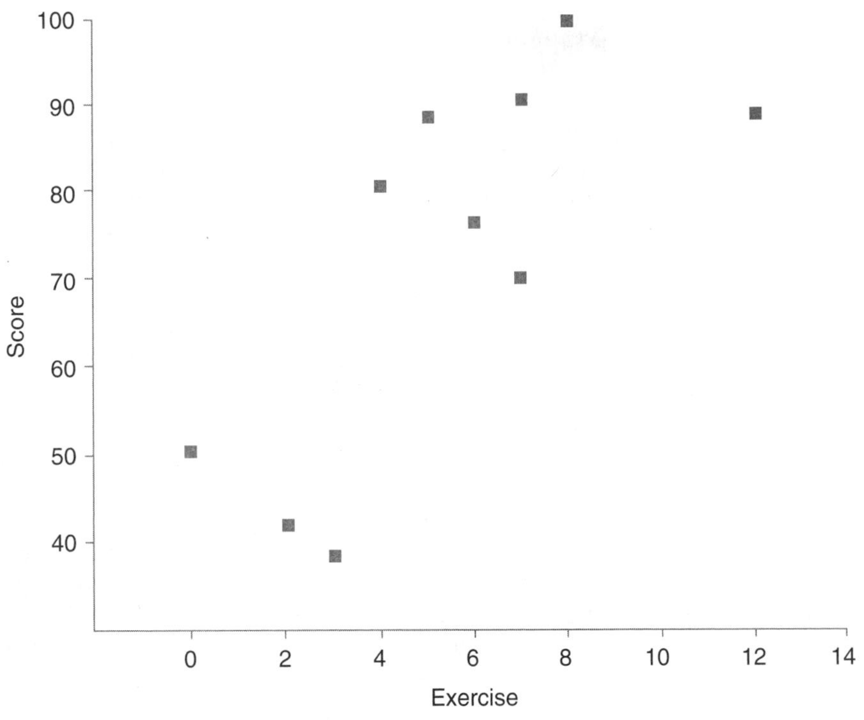

Figure 13.4 Scattergram of the Score and Exercise data in Table 13.5. The correlation is .74 (see Table 13.6). Notice that lower values on exercise tend to be associated with lower scores (and higher values on exercise with higher scores). With a larger sample size, the plot would undoubtedly fill in as values near the middle range of the variables were sampled.

To examine the plot (scatter diagram) of exercise and achievement scores, you would select "Graphs" on the menu choice, then click "Scatter," then "Simple," then "Define" to select the variables for plotting. Clicking "OK" will produce the scattergram as shown in Figure 13.4, revealing a lower-left to upper-right pattern of data points. We have seen that this configuration of points defines a positive relationship.

SPSS is capable of manipulating and analyzing a wide variety of data types using common statistical procedures and tests, both basic and advanced, in education and the social sciences. The two preceding examples only illustrate the ease of SPSS and its general setup.

Chapter Summary

Educational researchers are usually interested in going beyond the sample studied, that is, in making generalizations or inferences about the entire population represented by the sample. This process is accomplished through the use of *inferential* statistical tests. Central to this process is the idea of chance or sampling error. Researchers consider any outcome to be *statistically significant* if it can be attributed to chance with a probability less than .05 (usually symbolized "$p < .05$," where p is sometimes called the *p value* or *level of significance*). The best interpretation, therefore, of statistically significant findings is "probably not due to chance."

Researchers make one seemingly odd but very important assumption during the calculation of the p value: They assume that there is no relationship between the variables being studied in the population. This is referred to as the *null hypothesis* and is assumed to be true for the calculation of the p value. Because this temporary belief is contrary to the research hypothesis (usually), it is set up only to be rejected (hopefully) if the p value drops below .05. Its rejection, then, is synonymous with statistical significance.

In its simplest sense, the p value can be thought of as the likelihood that the null hypothesis is true. Many statistical tests have been developed for researchers (e.g., the t test), and they all have in common the bottom line summary: a p value which tells the researcher whether to reject the null hypothesis ($p < .05$) or to accept it ($p > .05$). This is the basis of the inference that is made regarding the population represented by the sample. For example, if one finds a statistically significant difference between boys' and girls' spatial ability in the sample, one can infer that there is probably a real difference in the population of boys and girls. Such inferences are warranted only when the study is not jeopardized by methodological flaws like biased sampling, threats to internal validity, or any other sources of contamination. Sampling errors also contribute to statistical errors known as Type I (false alarm) and Type II (missed sighting). Type II errors are directly related to power (finding a statistically significant relationship in the sample when there is a true one in the population).

Application Exercises

1. For each research question below, determine whether you think the question could be answered best with quantitative analysis or qualitative analysis. Explain your decision.
   a. How do teachers' implicit theories about students' learning change as they progress from novice to expert?
   b. How do Japanese methods of instruction compare to American methods?
   c. What stages in the development of vocational interests typify high school students?
   d. How does the gap in standardized achievement between students of differing socioeconomic status change during the progression through grade levels?
   e. How would you characterize the ideas of educators with 40 or more years of classroom teaching experience?
   f. Is there a relationship between speed of learning and long-term retention of the learned material?

2. How would you answer the following questions posed by a teacher with no background in scientific research methods?
   a. The null hypothesis seems rather paradoxical to me. Why do researchers hypothesize that *no* relationships exist when they really don't believe that?
   b. The term *statistically significant* when applied to research findings suggests to me that the research findings were important? Isn't this true?
   c. What is meant by the term statistical *test?* Is this like a test that is administered to students?
   d. What do all those *p* letters mean that are littered all over the results section of a published research report?
   e. Why would an experienced researcher make those mistakes called Type I and Type II?
   f. Is the term *statistical power* at all related to the power that might be applied to a telescope or microscope?
   g. What do all those letters like *t, F,* and test for *r* refer to in a published report?

3. Several statistical software sites exist on the Internet. They are Web-based (no download), no cost, and incredibly easy to use. One such site is VassarStats at http://faculty.vassar.edu/lowry/VassarStats.html and another is StatCrunch at http://www.statcrunch.com/. I have used both very reliably for years. Explore VassarStats and then analyze these data from a hypothetical study of sleep's influence on memory. Memory scores for the Eight Hour Group are: 9, 7, 6, 7, 9, 6, 5, 5, 9, 8; memory scores for the Four Hour Group are: 6, 3, 2, 1, 3, 3, 7, 2, 4, 4. Click "*t*-Tests & Procedures" on the VassarStats home page. Then click "*t*-Test for Independent Samples." Enter the scores under "Data Cells" and click "Calculate." What are the means? What was the calculated *t* value (two-tailed)? (Hint: Did you get 4.67, I hope?) What is your decision about the null hypothesis? Are the means significantly different?

ON YOUR OWN

Log on to the Web-based student study site at http://www.sagepub.com/eic for more information about the materials presented in this chapter, suggestions for activities, study aids such as electronic flashcards and review quizzes, a sample research proposal, and research recommendations that include journal article links (with discussion questions and an article evaluation guide) and questions related to this chapter.

Part V Consumer to Producer

The two capstone chapters in Part V integrate the contents of the previous 13 chapters as they facilitate development of the valuable skills of critiquing research and writing research proposals. Each of these skills involves the careful analytic judgments sharpened in the previous chapters. The major ideas and principles of research described in the four previous parts converge in Part V and become tightly focused on the culminating skills associated with writing critical reviews of research and developing research proposals.

Chapter 14 builds on your familiarity with the educational research process and its conceptual foundation, methodological procedures, and scientific ways of thinking. This background enables the reading of published research with comprehension sufficient for thoughtful, critical review. Critical review (critique) is aided by a thorough research analysis, a task that "pulls apart" the research into its important components. More than ever, consumers of educational research are being asked to evaluate research for possible application or implementation. Chapter 14 recognizes this responsibility and offers many practical guidelines for thoughtful research analysis, review, and critique.

Chapter 15 recognizes that you, like many educators (students and practitioners), may be called upon to propose your own empirical research as a program requirement or career position responsibility. This chapter focuses on the practical issues surrounding the preparation of a research proposal. A good research proposal details the procedures needed to answer a research question. It describes what you plan to do, why you plan to do it, and how you intend to carry out your plan. This chapter also describes criteria for evaluating research proposals.

14

Research Analysis and Critique

Outline

Overview

At this point in the study of educational research, you are quite familiar with its process, many methodological procedures, and the scientific way of thinking. This background allows you to read published research with comprehension sufficient for critical review. You are now in a good position to provide thoughtful critical reviews of published research. This chapter will guide you through that process.

It is important to be especially careful to "spot" illogical pitfalls in researchers' conclusions. A fine example of this was provided by Engelmann (2004), who claimed that illogical reasoning occurs with "frightening regularity" and noted that "investigators do not simply flunk Logic 101 . . . [they also] set the stage for a daisy chain of illogic" (p. 48). His example is memorable: "If a dog is a Dalmatian, it has spots. Therefore, if a dog has spots, it is a Dalmatian" (p. 48). Engelmann (2004) emphasized the point that the first statement is true, yet the second statement does not follow logically from the first. (He pointed out that dogs such as English setters, some terriers, and sheepdogs have spots too, but they are not, obviously, Dalmatians.) He provided an example of the same type of illogical reasoning ("medieval logic") in research-based recommendations in the area of reading: "If a beginning reading program is highly effective, it has various features: phonics, phonemic awareness, and so on. Therefore, if a program has these features, it will be highly effective" (p. 48). The important point is that those features in a reading program can be woven into a research hypothesis for empirical testing; logic does not deem them effective. While it is easy for researchers to make recommendations that extend well beyond their data, it is often exceedingly difficult to recognize immediately their flaws in logic. A "critical thinking" research analysis, however, is the first step toward a research critique using sound logic. (Anyone interested in tracing 20 years of illogical reasoning in reading research is well advised to study Engelmann's 2004 article titled "The Dalmatian and Its Spots: Why Research-Based Recommendations Fail Logic 101.")

What Is Research Analysis?

To *analyze* means to break a whole into parts and examine its components methodically. A published research study—the whole—can be dissected into its integrated parts rather easily because of the way it is written (in sections). This is the first step toward being able to evaluate, or critique, its contribution to education and related fields. This section provides practice with the dissection of a published research study, laying it all out, so to speak, so that its integrated parts can be better understood. Sometimes this task is referred to as "unpacking" a research study.

RESEARCH ANALYSIS: The "unpacking" and "dissection" of a published research study for the purpose of laying groundwork for a critical review.

CRITICAL THINKER ALERT 14-1

Research Analysis

A research analysis involves "breaking up" a research study into its integrated components, a dissection of sorts. This permits one to critically evaluate its methodology and assess its contribution.

Discussion: In what way does the format of a published research report facilitate its "unpacking"?

The First Reading: The Big Picture

Reading a published research article with comprehension is not easy. It is a slow, plodding activity, in part because the published report is usually densely packed with information. Careful reading of a 10- to 20-page research report could easily take 1 hour, even longer if you are not familiar with the constructs being investigated and the literature being reviewed.

HIGHLIGHT AND LEARNING CHECK 14-1

Research "Dissection"

The analysis of a research report involves its "dissection" into component parts, a type of "unpacking" or "breaking up." This task sets the stage for a critical review. A quick read of a published report for the "big picture" may help you to better comprehend the report during careful reading later. What aspects of the published report might you attend to during this first reading?

I usually make two passes through an article; the first pass to get my bearings, the second to absorb the detail. Here is an example of that process. I selected a published research study titled "Creating a System of Accountability: The Impact of Instructional Assessment on Elementary School Children's Achievement Test Scores" conducted by Meisels and colleagues (2003). (This is available at http://epaa.asu.edu/epaa/v11n9/).

A published article is easier to tackle if you think about the article in three small chunks: (1) its purpose in context, (2) its methodology, and (3) its findings tied to the conclusions.

Components of a Study

Purpose in Context

Every research study has a purpose, usually in the form of a research question or research hypothesis. Sometimes the research question is contained within the title itself; other times its purpose is stated explicitly in the introduction (and many times at the end of that section). Nevertheless, its purpose should not be embedded in arcane language or buried in extraneous detail.

The purpose of a study is inseparable from the context that produced it. The background literature, therefore, is directly tied to relevant prior studies and current trends. After reading the introduction to Meisels and colleagues' study (while avoiding becoming bogged down in detail), I noted the first chunk of information—the "purpose in context"—for my analysis: to answer the research question "Can the Work Sampling System raise standardized achievement test scores?"

The Work Sampling System (WSS) is an authentic performance assessment procedure that involves the use of portfolios and relies heavily on teachers' observations and perceptions in a variety of classroom situations. It was designed to enhance instruction, having been developed as a counter-reaction to the negative instructional and achievement consequences of high-stakes testing.

Essentially, the "purpose in context" addresses the question "Why was this study done?" Now I know it was done to determine whether a system of teacher assessment (linked to improving instruction) can affect standardized achievement test scores somewhat indirectly without all the problems associated with teaching to the test.

Methodology

Next, I read the published study with the goal of "roughing out" its methodology, that is, how the study was conducted in the most general sense. This is my second large chunk of information. To no surprise, this information is usually found under the section heading "Method." Meisels and colleagues make comprehension of this section easier with clear subdivisions (Procedures, Design, and Sample). Again, without getting bogged down, I am able to pull apart rather complex methodology and summarize it as follows: A sample of fourth graders who used the WSS for 3 years was compared on the Iowa Tests of Basic Skills (ITBS) to a matched sample which did not use it (non-WSS) and a larger sample of other fourth-grade students in area schools.

This scan of the methodology section answers the general question "How did these researchers carry out the study?"

Findings Tied to Conclusions

Finally, my first reading of this research report is concerned with the third and final chunk of information: summarizing the study's "findings tied to conclusions." I usually bypass much of the detailed analysis with the goal of locating the principal findings. My summary of the "findings tied to conclusions" for Meisels and colleagues' study was this: The WSS classrooms' gains in reading on the ITBS far exceeded those of the comparison groups; the gains in math were more modest.

Accountability is not a test; it is a system, one that embeds the curriculum in instructional assessment. Learning is enhanced when the emphasis is on teaching (not testing): "What should I learn next?" replaces "Will this be on the test?"

This third chunk of information answers my related questions "What did the data analysis reveal?" and "How did the researchers arrive at their conclusion?" Notice that this third piece of information, like the first ("purpose in context"), links two ideas: objective results and logical conclusions. These concepts are linked to remind the reader that conclusions should follow logically from the results. This is not obvious, for it is fairly common to see conclusions that stretch well beyond the implications of the data. Weak conclusions are especially common, such as those that are the same no matter what the data analysis revealed. (Why conduct the study if conclusions can be written in advance?)

CRITICAL THINKER ALERT 14-2

The "Big Picture"

Just as many difficult concepts are best understood by a general overview followed by specific instances, research analysis is facilitated by the reading of research to get the "big picture" first. Familiar ideas can function as advance organizers. Linking new ideas gleaned from the big picture to older, familiar ones will undoubtedly increase reading comprehension.

Discussion: Based on your knowledge of principles in education, why does linkage of the new with old enhance reading comprehension of published research?

CRITICAL THINKER ALERT 14-3

Metacognition

Reading comprehension is often increased with metacognitive strategies, that is, actively monitoring your understanding by asking yourself questions (e.g., "Why did the researchers . . . ?" and "How did the researchers . . . ?"). Try to answer these questions as you begin to think like the researchers who reported their study. Think aloud freely and say what you are thinking or wondering as you "learn to learn" about research reports through careful reading.

Discussion: Can you describe any other metacognitive strategies to enhance comprehension that you have learned in the past?

The Second Reading: The Important Details

I usually have many questions after my first reading of a published research article, ones that are answerable with very attentive reading. Reading comprehension is usually higher during the second reading, in part because you have the relevant background going into it (an advance organizer). With the overall picture in mind, the details tend to fall into place much more easily (especially the methodological details). With the "Why?" and "How?" and "What?" questions already answered during the first reading, you can dig a little deeper. With many details understood, you can complete your research "dissection" and be in the position to begin a critical review of published research.

HIGHLIGHT AND LEARNING CHECK 14-2

Components of Research Analysis

The second reading of a published report, a careful one, is necessary for a thorough research analysis. The components of a research analysis are offered in a task-oriented format (e.g., "Describe the sample of research participants"). Do you recognize these tasks as major topics in the preceding chapters?

Guidelines for Research Analysis

Table 14.1 presents a framework for research analysis or "dissection." Answering the questions presented in Table 14.1 requires careful reading of the published research. Published research reports should contain the information that enables your responses to the items in this table. If not, your best judgment will be required.

TABLE 14.1 Components of a Research Analysis

1. State the purpose of the study, including the ancillary, corollary, or secondary purpose. (This statement is often made in the form of a research question or research hypothesis.)
2. Describe the following:
   a. one significant prior study linked to the research
   b. one compelling idea or significant phenomenon related to the purpose of the research
3. Describe whether you believe the research is more theory based or problem based. Why?
4. If applicable, describe the most significant constructs investigated in this study, including their operational definitions.
5. Describe the research in terms of types suggested by the following dichotomies (with an implied continuum):
   a. quantitative versus qualitative
   b. descriptive versus inferential
   c. true experimental versus quasi-experimental
   d. causal comparative versus correlational
   e. single-subject versus group
   f. teacher versus traditional
   g. large-scale policy versus small-scale evaluation
6. If applicable, describe the variables used in the research, including the independent variable(s) (and levels), dependent variable(s), and attribute variable(s).
7. Describe the research design(s) used in the study.
8. Describe the control procedures used by the researchers.
9. Describe the sample of research participants.
10. Describe the reliability and validity of the instruments used in the study.
11. Describe the researchers' attention to alternative hypotheses (rival explanations). For example, how were extraneous variables and sources of bias neutralized?
12. Summarize the following:
    a. the methods of data analysis
    b. the major findings of the study
13. Summarize the most important points in the discussion section of the research report, with particular attention to conclusions and implications.

CRITICAL THINKER ALERT 14-4

Connections

Try to connect as much as possible the major concepts you learned in the preceding chapters of this book to their application in a research article, including types of research, sampling, instrumentation, research design, controls, and so on. Try to answer the questions you generated during your metacognitive activities described in the preceding Critical Thinker Alert.

Discussion: Can you think of questions you might *always* ask yourself about a research study (e.g., "What is its purpose?") despite the vast differences among studies?

Research Analysis: An Example

This section contains an application of the guidelines for a research analysis (presented in Table 14.1) to a published study, the same one used to illustrate a strategy for the first reading and second reading of a research study, Meisels and colleagues' (2003) study of the impact of instructional assessment (the Work Sampling System) on standardized achievement test scores. (Recall that this research study is available online at http://epaa.asu.edu/epaa/v11n9/). Here is the analysis:

1. The purpose of this study was to answer the research question "Can a curriculum-embedded performance assessment, the Work Sampling System, raise standardized achievement test scores more than comparable comparison groups?" A corollary question ("Can this be done effectively?") was related to linking instructional and high-stakes assessment to create a useful system of accountability.

2.a. The most significant prior study was that by Amrein and Berliner (2002), revealing that many current classroom practices may raise test scores but leave general knowledge and important curriculum domains "untouched."

b. A compelling idea is using an alternative to teaching to the test, that is, the use of a new form of assessment that incorporates standards to help make instructional decisions. (The idea here is to link conventional norm-referenced tests, performance assessments, and enhanced instruction to create an accountability system that focuses on instructional assessment.)

3. This research is problem based since it focuses on a type of program evaluation of the Work Sampling System. As such, the reader would expect little connection with theories of learning and instruction.

4. The most significant construct is school learning, or more specifically, "achievement" operationally defined as scores on the Iowa Test of Basic Skills (ITBS).

5. The published research is quantitative (given the outcome is standardized test scores); it is inferential (given the p values that imply generalization to a larger population); it is quasi-experimental (given there is an intervention without the use of random assignment); it is causal comparative, in part (given the comparisons

between "above average" and "below average" students); it is a group study (given the size of the sample groupings); it is traditional (given its focus on a school district and its use of traditional research methods); finally, it is a relatively small-scale evaluation study since it does not involve large, generalizable data sets, the kind often required for making or changing educational policy on a wide basis (although the results do suggest the need for larger scale research directed toward establishing policy in the interest of fair assessment).

6.a. The study's independent variable was the type of classroom assessment, its levels being (1) Work Sampling System (the intervention), (2) Traditional Assessment Group I (matched comparison group), and (3) Traditional Assessment Group II (comparison in district schools).

b. The dependent variable was the change scores on the reading and math sections of the ITBS between third and fourth grade.

c. The attribute variable was the achievement level of students, with levels being above average and below average.

7. The research design was a quasi-experimental, matched group, longitudinal, pre-post design. The researchers described their study as a "natural experiment," a curious term since there is nothing "natural" about experimentation (it involves active experimenter intervention).

8. Several control procedures were used in this study, including matching (WSS students and non-WSS comparison students were matched on race, income, mobility, school size, and number of parents in the home). Statistical control (regression analysis) was also used to control for differences in initial ability; this enables the study of the "trajectory" of change in achievement test scores over time.

9. The sample in this study included 96 third-grade students (the WSS intervention group), 116 comparison students matched to the intervention students (Group I), and about 3,000 similar students districtwide (Group II). A majority of the students in all three groups were African American, nearly 90% of the students received free or reduced cost lunch, and 58% were female.

10. The Work Sampling System is a complex tool that gathers teachers' perceptions and information about students' interactions with materials and other people. Evidence of the reliability and validity of the system is not presented; the reader is referred to other published reports. The reliability of the achievement tests (ITBS) is reported to be high (at least .85); the reader is referred elsewhere for information about the validity of the ITBS.

11. The researchers focused considerable attention on alternative hypotheses. As described, their use of matching ruled out the explanation that the comparison groups were different (had lower scorers) to begin with. Their use of a longitudinal design to study achievement growth within students over time also ruled out the explanation that intervention and comparison students were different in absolute terms (such as lower versus higher achievers overall). This concern was also addressed in their analysis with regression used to rule out the explanation that there were differences among groups prior to the interventions. Further, their regression analysis was related to the concern about floor and ceiling effects—no room to go lower and higher, respectively—in part due to the possibility of bias linked to differences across forms and their administration. Much analysis was

directed toward their concern over attrition, or loss of subjects. A variety of comparisons suggested that missing data could not explain the overall differences among groups.

12.a. These researchers analyzed their data with regression ("covariance models"), *t* tests for mean differences, and effect size measures.

b. Their major finding was that gains in reading, for both above and below average achieving WSS students, far exceeded those of the comparison groups. Smaller gains were found in math.

13. Their discussion emphasized the idea that a well-designed curriculum-embedded instructional assessment can enhance teaching and improve learning within a framework of an accountability system. Students' focus can shift from "What's on the test?" to "What should be learned next?" Higher achievement can be accomplished not by narrowing instruction to test content but by targeting the instructional needs of the learner using standard-based curriculum content.

Research analysis, or unpacking, is not an easy task, I'm sure you'll agree. The research and educational jargon combine for very slow reading (and much back-tracking). Fortunately, there are many fine resources available for educators intent on understanding educational research. (This is undoubtedly due to the emphasis placed on scientific research by the No Child Left Behind Act of 2001.) One useful document is "A Policymaker's Primer on Education Research: How to Understand, Evaluate and Use It" (Lauer, 2004). The primer helps readers of educational research answer these questions: "What does the research tell?"; "Is it trustworthy?"; and "How can the research be used?" These are important questions to keep in mind when unpacking a research study for analysis.

With the research analysis completed, you are now in a fine position to complete the research critique.

What Is a Research Critique?

It should be noted that there is no single accepted or standard format for a critical review of published research (unlike the format required for presenting research findings in a journal article). Nevertheless, there is general agreement about the components of a review. What follows is a recommendation based on other reviewers' suggestions for the content and format of a review and observations of reviews as they are currently practiced.

RESEARCH CRITIQUE: The descriptive review and evaluation of published research.

A *critique* (or critical review) of published research is *not* a closed-minded attack on its worth based on its shortcomings, limitations, or flaws. It is more like a movie review, where the critical reviewer tells us what the movie is about (the plot), general reactions to the movie (e.g., one of the year's best), how the movie achieved its most prominent characteristics (fear, humor, intrigue, etc.), and the movie's strengths (e.g., superb acting, special effects) and weaknesses (e.g., a too-familiar story line, a slow pace), then makes an overall recommendation regarding the movie ("thumbs up" or "thumbs down").

The critical reviewer of published educational research engages in much the same task. A review may provide a description of what the research is all about or its general purpose (the research question or hypothesis and its placement within a broader context, namely, the theoretical framework and literature review), overall reactions to it (e.g., its being a much-needed and well-executed study), how it handled methodological issues (e.g., its research design, control procedures, instrumentation, sampling, etc.), its strengths (e.g., its large sample size, proper control techniques such as blinding, engaging discussion), its weaknesses (e.g., its high loss of subjects, including measures with doubtful validity, being poorly written, having an outdated literature review, etc.), and an overall judgment of the research (e.g., a professor's grade, a journal editor's recommendation to accept it for publication, an administrator's decision to change policy, or a teacher's decision to apply findings to classroom instruction).

HIGHLIGHT AND LEARNING CHECK 14-3

Research Critique

A research critique uses information from a research analysis in order to complete an astute evaluation of the research, including its strengths, weaknesses, methodological features, and overall value. Specific guidelines are offered. How do the skills of critical thinking factor into the task of completing a research critique?

CRITICAL THINKER ALERT 14-5

Critical Review

A critical review is a research analysis coupled with evaluative assessments, that is, judgments about the study's strengths and weaknesses as well as its overall value.

Discussion: In what sense is the research term *critical* akin to *judgment* as opposed to *faultfinding*?

Guidelines for Critiques

Purpose

A critical evaluation of research often begins with an introductory statement regarding its purpose. Why was the research done? What question or questions did it answer? What hypothesis was tested? The reviewer is probably not neutral with regard to the purpose of the research, hence it is appropriate for him or her to evaluate the overall purpose. On the positive side, the research may attempt to answer a question that might yield solutions to very practical problems, shed new light on old problems, provide support for a theory which guides sound decision making, advance our understanding of a complex phenomenon, or test the limits of generalization through replication of others' findings. In a general sense, research is potentially useful to the extent that it has theoretical value via its impact on ideas or applied value through its influence on practice.

The purpose of the research, as we have seen, does not exist in a vacuum. The larger context, or prior research, is relevant to the evaluation of a study's purpose. Issues here might include how well embedded the research is, using prior research findings and ideas as a context. This evaluation is not an easy task, for it involves a type of synthesis, or the creation of a framework for understanding how new research might "fit in." The framework for understanding may be as straightforward as a summary of previous research findings with a statement about a void (gap) in knowledge or understanding that the research is attempting to fill. Or it may be as ambitious as a literature review that culminates in a new theory or model (or a major revision of an existing theory) that is tested by the research. One hallmark of a good research question or hypothesis is that the findings are informative no matter what the outcome. This is especially true if the research compares two competing theories, with one outcome supporting one theory and a different outcome supporting the other theory. This is an application of the concept of strong inference (Platt, 1964) that was described in Chapter 11. Needless to say, the research purpose and its context should discourage any reader from saying "So what?"

CRITICAL THINKER ALERT 14-6

Critical Thinking

Critical thinking involves inquiry into alternative (plausible) explanations for the findings. You should ask questions such as "Are the researchers' interpretations the only plausible ones?"; "Do their conclusions logically follow from the data?"; and "Are their comments data driven, or could they be derived without any data collection and analysis?" It is important that conclusions follow logically from the data and their analysis.

Discussion: What other questions might you pose to enable or sharpen your critical thinking about published research in education?

Overall Reaction

Naturally, after reading a research report, one has an overall evaluation. This reaction, quite reasonably, results from a complex combination of preconceived biases (e.g., an orientation which favors quantitative methodologies or a preference for field studies in a natural environment), an evaluation of purpose in context and methodology, and a weighing of unique strengths and weaknesses. Perhaps the overarching question at the heart of an overall reaction is, "Does the research make any contribution?" The potential contribution could stem from many forms, including, for example, support (or lack of it) for a new or established theory, the application of old models in new situations, the extension (generalization) of others' findings, the generation of empirically based novel ideas, or the reinterpretation of earlier findings based on new data. This list is not exhaustive; it merely describes a few ways that research results may add to our existing knowledge, understanding, and way of thinking about education and the teaching and learning process.

Empirical research may make a significant contribution without being especially strong in its methodology, sampling, control features, and so forth. This may sound paradoxical, but once again, consider the classic case in point: the famous "Pygmalion in the Classroom," a study of the role of teachers' expectation in the determination of students' intellectual development (Rosenthal & Jacobson, 1968). This was a blockbuster idea, to be sure, and it remains one of the most cited educational studies ever conducted in education. You might recall that as it turned out, the validity of the study was seriously challenged by Elashoff and Snow (1971), among others, and today the study is largely discredited. This is not to distract, however, from the study's monumental contribution. There is a widely held belief today that teachers, in fact, do have many expectations of students' abilities based on a large variety of preconceived ideas, and that these stereotyped expectations do affect students in complex ways (but probably not in the simplistic and dramatic way described by Rosenthal and Jacobson).

By contrast, an exceptionally strong study from a methodological point of view (with adequate controls, representative sampling, valid instrumentation, etc.) may leave a reviewer wondering "Who cares?" Other studies may "beat a dead horse" by, for example, replicating an empirical "given," such as the relationship between socioeconomic status and school achievement, without providing any new insight into an older, established relationship.

Methodological Issues

Every research study must grapple with methodological problems. Some problems are relatively easy to overcome; others are more difficult. How a study comes to terms with its methodological challenges often sets it far above (or far below) other studies in a particular area. Consider research design, for instance, and the concept of control. This is a good focal area because nearly all researchers are interested in the *bases* (causes) of relationships which may be discovered. We know that true experimental designs, executed with proper control over extraneous influences, are especially strong for the purpose of ferreting out cause-and-effect relationships. In a research area dominated by correlational findings, such as the link between violence on television and aggressive behavior, any research study using an experimental design should be evaluated with particular attention to its handling of ever-present methodological concerns over controlling extraneous variables.

Another ubiquitous methodological issue is bias. Lack of attention to this issue may be significant enough to completely discredit a research finding. Just as you would probably doubt a research study conducted by a tobacco company showing that smoking does not cause lung disease, you would also probably doubt a drug maker's research-based claim that a particular medication has no side effects, or a book publisher's research-based claim that children learn to read better from books than from computer screens. As we have seen, bias can be very subtle, even "subconscious" (as well as blatant and deliberately distorting), and could affect even the best-intentioned researcher.

Yet another methodological issue that many evaluators focus on is measurement and central concerns of reliability and validity. Studies that employ the strongest designs, the tightest controls, and the best checks against bias may still be rendered questionable if measures are full of error (unreliable) or if they are off target in terms of their purpose (invalid). The process of measurement (instrumentation) is one of the most frequently occurring sources of limitations in educational research.

On the positive side, many studies are noteworthy for their creative methods directed toward solving methodological dilemmas, or at least overcoming inherent weaknesses in research designs. One example here might include *triangulation*, or the use of multiple methods to answer a research question. When the answers to one question all agree (or *converge*), despite the variation in methods used to gather information, the answer is judged to be more believable. The counterpart in a court of law might be evidence from a variety of sources, including eyewitness testimony, fingerprints, and physical evidence such as DNA left at the scene of the crime.

Other methods for overcoming methodological obstacles may involve novel methods of collecting data. For example, if a researcher wants to learn how often high school students worry about family related problems, one possible method would involve asking students at the end of the day to estimate how many times (and for how long) they have episodes of "family worry." We know that memory, being reconstructive, is a very unreliable indicator of "what was" and that people can grossly underestimate or overestimate the frequency of specific behaviors. A more suitable method might involve the students wearing beepers. When beeped at random times throughout the day, each student would immediately write down his or her current thoughts, including descriptions of worrying. Of course, merely telling students what the study is all about before outfitting them with beepers might unintentionally increase the frequency of such worries, as you might expect, since wearing beepers would be a constant reminder of the study's purpose (unless they were merely told the study concerned the nature of thoughts, not particularly family worries). But not informing students of the true purpose of the study would raise ethical issues. Students might also be hesitant to report the true content of their thoughts, thinking that they might be labeled as abnormal and referred to therapy. This is precisely what is meant by an ethical dilemma—one choice of method may introduce bias, and a different choice of method will introduce a controversy, another problem, or a different bias.

Weaknesses and Strengths

One could argue, quite logically, that all studies in education are, at least to some extent, seriously flawed at worst or seriously limited at best. The process of sampling always limits the applicability of generalizations, the instruments are never perfectly reliable and valid, the inferential statistics are never evidence of proof (recall the probability statements arising from the *p* value), randomization never guarantees group equivalency, some respondents do not tell the truth or lack the motivation to perform their best, and so on. Because these criticisms are universal and can be applied to research in all disciplines, they add nothing to our evaluation of specific studies. The following section is concerned with addressing weaknesses that are relatively common and can be applied to specific studies as appropriate.

Educational research cannot easily be faulted for lack of good ideas, useful theories, creative thinking, statistical sophistication, or strong designs. But three of the most common weaknesses in educational research—a big generalization—appear to be poor instrumentation, limited generalization, and alternative explanations and counter-interpretations. These might be good candidates to focus on if asked to discuss a study's weaknesses. Let's take each one of these facets in turn.

CRITICAL THINKER ALERT 14-7

Specific Focus

As you reread the research article, focus on a single element such as *control* in research. Have the researchers utilized effective control procedures? Do their comparison groups (if applicable) make sense? Ask yourself, "How might their control procedures be improved?" In drug research, for example, a drug's effectiveness is usually ascertained by comparing the group that receives the drug to a placebo group (a group that receives only a placebo but that often shows improvement over a "waiting list" control group). The most appropriate control could be either the placebo group *or* the "waiting list" group. It all depends. More appropriate versus less appropriate comparison groups also exist in educational research.

Discussion: What other element in the research process might you focus on? What questions are appropriate to ask yourself?

Instrumentation

At the heart of sound measurement, you will recall from Chapter 9, are the notions of reliability and validity. We have seen the difficulty in measuring well such important constructs as, for example, "self-esteem," "creativity," "motivation," and "emotionality." The construct of "intelligence" stands in sharp contrast to other complex constructs, for there is general agreement that verbal intelligence can, under the right circumstances, be measured reliably and validly, in the sense that intelligence tests seem to yield consistent (stable) scores that can be used to predict school success. It should be emphasized, however, that this apparent success with instrumentation is narrowly confined to traditional *verbal/analytical intelligence* (reasoning with language and symbols) and cannot be claimed for other important facets of intelligence, such as interpersonal, emotional, or practical intelligence. With this in mind, one is wise to scrutinize very carefully those educational research findings investigating constructs which are extraordinarily difficult to measure, such as "creativity" or "character."

The measurement of "school achievement" poses another measurement challenge for researchers. So-called bubble tests, such as the Stanford Achievement Tests, are without question reliable and valid to the extent that their content matches the school curriculum (which it does quite well for most schools in most subject areas). But it is a brief snapshot at best, and it clearly does not assess how students' thinking becomes organized over time and how their knowledge and skills translate into real-world products and activities. Even when they are completed by sufficiently motivated students, the standardized achievement tests tend to measure end-state knowledge of the convergent variety (where there is agreement about a single correct answer). Portfolio assessment, by contrast, tells a story about a student's effort and progress as well as achievement over time. And its focus on products and accomplishments is something that is meaningfully valued by students. The problem with portfolio assessment (besides practicality) from a research perspective is—you guessed it—reliability (in particular, rater agreement).

CRITICAL THINKER ALERT 14-8

Purpose and Linkage

Focus on the purpose of the research, linking it to what you know about education. Relate its purpose to what you think is one of the most significant problems in education (e.g., perhaps you feel it is the achievement gap). Against this "anchor point" or benchmark for context, you might be better able to evaluate its purpose in terms of meaningfulness.

Discussion: What do *you* think are the most significant problems in education? Are they researchable? Have researchers focused on them or have they been ignored?

Generalization

Limited applicability of generalizations, or the failure of research findings to extend beyond the borders of a study (subjects, setting, measures, etc.), appears to be a common weakness of educational research (as is true in many other "inexact" sciences, like health and medicine). Because of this situation, it would not be surprising if in adopting a reading program which had been shown to be effective in a study for one group of first graders, a teacher were to find very different results with her own group. (You might recall that the Coalition for Evidence-Based Policy, 2003, in the document created to guide research critiques under provisions of the No Child Left Behind legislation, also concluded that educational research frequently fails to generalize.) The fact is that teaching and learning are complex processes, most probably characterized by innumerable interactions ("it depends") and very few main effects (see Chapter 10).

One can speculate about reasons for this lack of generalization, but it seems plausible that many educational treatments are complex bundles and not as simple as a label or summary may suggest. Because treatments do not occur in a vacuum, you might think of educational interventions as "treatments with trappings." The trappings (extraneous variables) might include the personalities of teachers, the environmental conditions of the classroom, the climate within the school building, the variation in parental involvement, the presence of teaching aides, class size, and so on. To the extent that any of the trappings interact with the treatment, a different finding may result. The success of any treatment may depend on the context of its implementation. If its implementation is "top down" or mandated by high-level administrators, its success might be unlikely. But if a teacher's "grass roots" movement leads to the adoption of the same treatment, then the treatment's success might be more likely.

In addition to this "treatment as a bundle" phenomenon, there exists the inescapable fact that individual differences among students are simply enormous, and students can react to different treatments in many different ways. This can be explained, in part, by differences in culture, learning style, motivation, interest, and aptitude, to name just a few of the potential thousands of interacting variables.

Alternative Explanations

Undoubtedly, one of the most difficult weaknesses to identify in educational research is the alternative explanations or counter-interpretations of data. Most alternative explanations do not pop out in an obvious way, otherwise they would have been rendered less plausible by the research design and planned control procedures. They often remain hidden, to be revealed only by persistent researchers who dig deeper for the best interpretation. For example, Gerald Bracey (1992), who has written many research columns for the *Phi Delta Kappan,* argued that studies of international achievement comparisons that reveal low U.S. rankings are "fatally flawed" because so many variables were not under the control of the researchers and had not been "factored out" (p. 568). After some digging, Bracey turned up evidence to challenge the assertion that America's public schools are failing. It constitutes what he calls "The Big Lie" (Bracey, 1991). Suffice it to say that nearly all educational research findings have counter-interpretations.

Not considering alternative, yet plausible, interpretations would be regarded as a weakness in any study. Also, a weakness would be evident if a written report of the research did not state the limitations (or problems) with the study as perceived by the researcher. After all, who is in a better position to critique the study than the researcher who actually planned and carried it out? In other words, a stronger study is one which makes a "true confession." This is because all studies in education are, to some extent, limited and prone to methodological problems and a mix of interpretations. Good researchers recognize this fact and make their concerns about alternative explanations explicit in the research report.

Research studies can turn some of these common weaknesses of educational research into strengths: "Trappings" can be built into the design of the study, individual differences can be identified and analyzed as part of the findings, and counter-explanations can be anticipated and evaluated for their plausibility with additional data.

Apart from this, readers of educational research, at least in premiere journals such as the *American Educational Research Journal,* can usually expect characteristic strengths such as a comprehensive review of the literature, a meaningful research question, reasonable controls for obvious biases, proper analysis, and a thought-provoking discussion that is logically related to the actual findings.

Overall Recommendation

After reviewing a research study, reviewers are often faced with the difficult task of recommending whether or not the study should be published, presented, awarded, funded (as in the case of a research proposal), replicated (because of its potential for changes in practice), included (as in a review of the literature, or in a meta-analysis), disseminated (as in the case of influencing public policy), discarded, and so forth. This decision undoubtedly involves a complex weighing of all relevant criteria, inevitable personal bias, a counterbalancing of weaknesses and strengths, maybe even "gut" reactions, and countless other factors. The final decision, though, is often a simple *yes* or *no.* It is no wonder, then, why reviewers of educational research often do not agree on seemingly simple decisions such as "accept" or "reject." (This is merely another instance of poor reliability in educational research.) Of course, all of the research studies used as examples and illustrations in this book have been regarded (at least by some reviewers) as worthy since they have all been published in reputable journals.

The task of critiquing a study is undoubtedly aided by knowledge of what constitutes strong science in the field of educational research. To help readers of research reports in education evaluate whether the reported research is indeed scientific, the National Research Council (2002) derived six principles, ones that underlie the essence of science common to all fields. These are described in Chapter 15 in the section titled "Criteria for Evaluating Research Proposals." You are advised to consult these principles and use them in concert with the guidelines for critiquing a research study described above.

CRITICAL THINKER ALERT 14-9

Muddled Thinking

Clear thinking about research can quickly become muddled, in part as a function of research jargon and complex statistical analysis. Statistical critique requires specialized expertise. But don't lose sight of the fact that statistical analysis is merely a tool designed to help answer the research question. The answer should be clear, despite the statistical analysis being unclear. Keep focused on whether or not the conclusions follow logically from the answers yielded by the statistical analysis. One common flaw in logic, for example, is the faulty conclusion that simply because two variables are related, they must be connected causally. Here is another error in logic: the fallacy of *post hoc ergo propter hoc,* meaning "after this, therefore because of this." Notice the root term *cause* in the word *because.* Reducing class size, then observing higher standardized achievement test scores is an example of this faulty reasoning. There could be many other reasons for higher achievement (e.g., test preparation, exclusion of subpopulations, new curriculum, etc.). Never forget the concept of alternative hypotheses!

Discussion: How might you respond to a researcher who finds no connection between class size and student achievement yet devotes most of the discussion and conclusion to the need to reduce class size?

All types of educational research—including quantitative, qualitative, and action research—are scientific to the extent they conform to established guidelines such as direct, empirical investigation; linkage to theory; coherent reasoning from evidence; replication and generalization; and disclosure for purposes of critique and evaluation (Bracey, 2004). Research is, of course, conducted more and less rigorously and investigates problems that are more and less significant. Nevertheless, the quantitative, qualitative, and action research traditions described in Critical Perspective 14-1 have several unique features that set each one apart, at least to some extent.

CRITICAL PERSPECTIVES 14-1

APPROACHES TO CRITIQUING

Critical Thinking Toolbox

Clear thinking in any field is aided by recognizing logical roadblocks. A *red herring* is one such impediment, or diversion, that is intended to distract. In this context, a red herring is a point made in an argument that is unrelated to the topic and an attempt to distract attention from it, often so that possibly a change in topic or shift from the central focus is seen as evidence. (A red herring is a smoked fish with strong scent; the idiom refers to its use on a trail to confuse tracking dogs.)

Critiquing Quantitative Research

Many of the issues surrounding the evaluation of quantitative research, in addition to the meaningfulness of the research hypothesis, are related to the internal validity (strength of design, controls, etc.), sampling, operational definitions and instrumentation (reliability and validity), statistical techniques, and external validity (generalization). The review of literature in quantitative research is also a common source of scrutiny, as are explicit statements regarding the study's limitations (strong studies make limitations clear).

Critiquing Qualitative Research

It is especially important in qualitative research that the conceptual framework undergirding the study and the chain of reasoning throughout—from data to conclusion to theory—be made abundantly clear. Abstract notions being explored require "grounding" using familiar methods and explicit assumptions. Qualitative data and their themes require sharp focus and scrutiny, including description, organization, and interpretation. The "quality" of data is strongly related to the credibility of conclusions and implications. As with all research, it is important that conclusions follow logically from findings (and are not simply the author's opinions regardless of research outcomes). Critiquing qualitative research poses many of the same creative challenges as conducting it. Help is provided by resources such as that of Shank (2002), who described "standards, virtues, and pitfalls" of qualitative research in the context of avoiding its "seven deadly sins" (p. 180). Qualitative critiques tend to be less "checklist" oriented.

Critiquing Action Research

Because action research is conceptually different from traditional research (action research being done *by* and *for* teachers as part of reflective practice), one would expect the application of different criteria in its evaluation. Mills (2003) suggested that judging action research be guided by asking questions such as "Did the research lead to action?" and "How has the research contributed to a 'reflective stance'?" As you would expect, the value of action research is related to notions such as action, impact, change, and so on, particularly as these notions affect teaching practice, students' learning, and attitudes toward the profession. As such, critiques of action research are often connected to these consequences.

Critical Thinking Question

Consider this claim: Teacher action research is most valuable to the extent it incorporates both quantitative and qualitative outcome measures. Next consider an opposing claim: Teacher research is not valuable in a world where many teachers are overworked, underpaid, and at the mercy of external forces imposed by standardized testing and accountability. In what sense does the opposing argument reflect a type of "red herring"?

Award-Winning Research Ideas

To help anchor notions about research critiques, let's consider the following example of one research report that earned the praise of several reviewers and was judged to be "meritorious."

On occasion, the editors of the *Journal of Educational Research* announce a competition for the Meritorious Contribution to Educational Practice Through Research Award, which recognizes and honors research published in their journal. One award winner was Carolyn M. Evertson's "Training Teachers in Classroom Management: An Experimental Study in Secondary School Classrooms" published in the September/October 1985 issue of *The Journal of Educational Research.* A brief critique of this research follows.

Evertson's award-winning research illustrates many hallmarks of quality research. It has a very clear purpose: to validate principles of classroom management uncovered in correlational research by testing their effectiveness in an experimental study. In her introduction and review of the literature, Evertson recognized that correlational research has yielded potentially useful findings but, by its very nature, is weak with regard to discerning causal relationships. A meaningful research question thus becomes "Can we take correlational findings and demonstrate causal relationships?" It is this type of research that Evertson reported as "rare." Her research attempted to fill this void in the literature. As such her research was very applied; it had immediate and obvious consequences for improving the practice of teaching. It was less theoretical in scope; in fact, no theory was being tested explicitly, as revealed in her literature review. She was answering several applied research questions, not testing research hypotheses born from theory. Her reasons for conducting this study, along with a solid rationale, are clearly stated in the published report.

Several methodological issues in her report are worthy of mention. Her research design was truly experimental, involving a manipulation and random assignment to experimental (workshop) groups and control groups. In fact, she used a technique ("blocked into matched pairs") prior to random assignment which guaranteed equivalence of experimental and control groups on the extraneous variables of experience and grade level. This means that teachers were first sorted into grade levels and ranked in terms of years of experience. A member of each similar pair was then randomly assigned to the experimental or control group. For example, two teachers, both third-grade teachers and each with 5 to 10 years of experience, were considered a matched pair; one was assigned to the treatment group, the other to the control group. This type of paired randomization over 102 teachers was certain to produce comparable experimental and control groups, a most powerful control procedure. Further, the sample size appears adequate, with 51 teachers in each group, and generalizable across all levels.

Another important methodological issue is instrumentation, and Evertson (1985) paid careful attention to maximizing both the quality and array of measures used. Both qualitative and quantitative data were collected, a mark of a good study. A variety of observational measures were collected over multiple observation periods, and Evertson (1985) made certain that their recordings were reliable. Further, observers were also blinded ("not told the identity of trained teachers"), another important control procedure. Overall, this study seems to have been well executed, with appropriate attention to biasing influences and alternative explanations.

HIGHLIGHT AND LEARNING CHECK 14-4

Great Research Ideas

Research in education that is critiqued positively often begins with a meaningful, if not great, research idea. What contributes to a great, award-winning research idea?

Another measure of quality research appears in her report: a recognition of the study's weaknesses. Recall that all research is limited to some extent; most readers need a reminder of this fact. Some limitations may only be recognized from the vantage point of the researcher; it was she, after all, who lived and breathed this study for so long and undoubtedly has deeper insight into some of the problems. The reference to limitations could undoubtedly be expanded into an entire section, not only in this report, but all published research reports. Yet any recognition of a study's limitations, whether subtle or obvious, is clearly a positive feature of the research.

Good Research Analyses and Critiques Take Practice

Writing critiques of educational research is difficult and time consuming. (It takes me several hours to fully dissect published research and complete a comprehensive research analysis; add several more hours to complete a thoughtful critique.) Critique writing is made considerably easier by the completion of a research analysis first (see Table 14.1). To guide you through the process of critiquing research, let's once again consider the study by Meisels and colleagues (2003) that evaluated whether an instructional assessment program (the Work Sampling System) influenced scores on a standardized achievement test (which is available at http://epaa.asu.edu/epaa/v11n9/). (You might want to review the earlier discussion of this study to refresh your memory of the research analysis.)

With my research analysis of the Meisels and colleagues' study in hand, much of the work for the research critique is done. This is because the first section of my critique will summarize the essential components of this study. This includes the purpose, context, constructs, type of research, a brief description of the variables being investigated, the research design, instrumentation, methods of analyses, the major findings, and, finally, the conclusions. (I need not repeat that information here, but suffice it to say that much of this section of my critique could be borrowed directly from the research analysis.)

With an objective description of the study's components complete, my critique can turn to more evaluative comments. Without a doubt, this study combines ideas that are currently receiving great attention in education, namely accountability, authentic assessment, quality instruction, and standardized testing. The authors have done a fine job showing how their study, with its clear purpose, fits into a larger, contemporary, and very significant context.

The reader is left wondering how the Work Sampling System (WSS) actually works in a classroom. Only vague descriptions are provided, probably in large part due to space restrictions. References are provided, however, for those curious about how WSS is implemented in a classroom. Many instructional and assessment programs appear to be adopted by school districts without ongoing evaluation; they become institutionalized as leaders merely take their effectiveness for granted. It is noteworthy that the school system in this study is sharing its resources to evaluate an ongoing program.

Unfortunately, many researchers have not standardized their language as it relates to methodology. This creates confusion, to say the least. Meisels and colleagues are no exception. Their use of the term *natural experiment* is ambiguous, as noted previously. In educational research, the term *natural* is usually reserved for field observations without any research intervention. The term *experiment* is usually short for *true experiment*, whereby the researcher uses manipulation coupled with random assignment. Hence, the two terms combined make little sense. You will recognize Meisels and colleagues' design as an example of *quasi-experimental* research: an intervention without the use of random assignment. The researchers also describe their design as "longitudinal," implying that there are many observations over a longer period of time. Although the students had experienced WSS for 3 years, the researchers' measure of achievement was a single gain score from the third grade to the fourth grade.

This gain score was also described as a "trajectory of children's change in scores." The concept of a trajectory, or change, is desirable because of the enormous "starting" differences in students' achievement (increasing the "error" in measurement). With a change score, students act as their own controls, enabling a more sensitive measure of achievement. Think of it this way: Many of the end-point differences can be explained by the differences at the starting point, with the students comparable to runners in a race who start at different marks. The statistical analysis of change scores essentially brings runners to the same starting line. Additional statistical controls were also used to counteract some of the known problems with change scores, that is, floor and ceiling effects involving little or no room for change. Furthermore, the same statistical analysis controlled for potential problems related to differences in the forms used to assess standardized achievement.

Several control and design features of Meisels and colleagues' study are worth noting. Their use of "trajectory" change scores was already mentioned. Perhaps their most significant method of control was their use of matching as a method to equate their comparison groups and the WSS intervention group. Recall that they matched groups using the demographic variables of race and income (among others). This essentially controls for the influence of those variables, rendering implausible the alternative hypothesis that groups were like "apples and oranges." The method of equating groups, however, does nothing to control for the influence of nonmatching variables.

The researchers were very attuned to problems related to missing data. Recall that *loss of subjects* or *attrition* was one of Campbell and Stanley's (1963) major threats to internal validity. This concern is widespread in research, for the simple loss of data can create significant group differences on a posttest despite the lack of treatment influences. Meisels and colleagues' attention to and analysis of data related to missing scores convinces the reader that loss of subjects is not a serious alternative hypothesis for their observed effects.

The most serious weakness in the methodology used by Meisels and colleagues relates to the contaminating influences of other innovations co-occurring in the schools. This is a serious problem, and it appears to be the greatest threat to the validity of their findings. The problem is recognized fully by the researchers, as they remind the reader that their findings cannot be "definitive" due to their inability to "disentangle" the impact of WSS from that of other programs in existence during the same time frame. Schools and classrooms are complex and dynamic. Because of this, educational research is especially challenging and prone to many problems related to control and rival explanations. A positive feature of Meisels and colleagues' report, however, is that this concern and its potential to distort data and interfere with interpretations is stated explicitly. It is appropriate to remind readers of problems like these in the Discussion section of the report, as they have done.

Meisels and colleagues' sample size appears adequate given standards for sample size in educational research. Recall that a customary group size is perhaps 60 or so, sufficiently large to uncover at least an effect of moderate size. With a sample of 96 WSS students, it can be concluded that Meisels and colleagues' statistical analysis was sufficiently powerful to uncover the program's influence on achievement.

Instrumentation in this study also meets acceptable standards. The Iowa Tests of Basic Skills, the primary dependent variable in this study, has a long history of use in schools and well-documented reliability and content validity.

The findings of Meisels and colleagues were clearly presented and analyzed with an eye toward ruling out rival explanations. (This includes the use of multiple regression, a technique usually covered in advanced statistics.) The researchers' use of an attribute variable, prior level of achievement, enhanced the presentation of findings and enabled their conclusion that the WSS program's influence on reading was equally effective for above and below average students. Their use of *d* as an effect size measure also enhanced the interpretation of their findings. The reader knew, for example, that the influence of WSS on reading was not only statistically significant, it was dramatic in size as well.

In short, I can understand why this study was published. It provided data to reveal how an emphasis on testing can be shifted to teaching and learning, especially in the area of reading (where there were large effects). These data show how educators' concerns over standards, accountability, assessment, and improved instruction might fit into an effective model of curriculum-embedded (instructional) performance assessment. Its major weakness was the use of a comparatively weak design and the inability to disentangle a "pure" WSS effect from other ongoing innovations within the classrooms studied. This was counterbalanced by strengths within the study, including statistical controls in a thorough data analysis, strong instrumentation and sampling, attention to a variety of threats to internal validity, and a discussion which tempered its conclusions but offered an "important lesson."

CRITICAL THINKER ALERT 14-10

Uncritical Acceptance

The thinking skills required to critique research can be enhanced with practice. Often, thinking like a researcher is not a natural inclination. The uncritical acceptance of logical fallacies, unfortunately, appears commonly.

Discussion: Why do you suppose thinking like a researcher may not be "natural"? Is intuition more natural? Why are logical errors (such as correlation and cause) so common?

Research Analyses and Critiques Take More Practice

This chapter concludes with another opportunity to practice your skills in the area of research analyses and critiques. The published research report chosen for this section, Russell and Haney (1997), has received much national attention, and you can access it online (http://epaa.asu.edu/epaa/v5n3/).

The topic of Russell and Haney's (1997) study is familiar, as many examples in this book applied the concept of comparing computers with handwriting. The focus of their comparison, however, was the assessment (testing) of writing skills. I'll begin this critique, as usual, by completing a research analysis following the guidelines suggested earlier: a first reading to get the big picture followed by a second reading to extract the important details. Next I will answer the questions posed in Table 14.1 as a strategy for completing the research analyses; this will form the basis for writing the research critique.

The First Reading Revisited: The Big Picture

The Components of a Study

Purpose

Russell and Haney (1997) investigated the influence of mode of test administration (paper-and-pencil versus computer) on writing performance.

Purpose in Context

These researchers observed incongruous movements in education: Both computer use and authentic assessment have increased in schools. Yet some tests require responses in written form via paper-and-pencil. Their concern was that students' writing skills may be underestimated if they are accustomed to writing on a computer but are tested with paper-and-pencil.

Methodology

Russell and Haney used a true experimental design to test the effect of writing on a computer versus with paper-and-pencil on three different measures of writing performance.

Findings

Students' multiple-choice tests of writing did not differ as a function of the testing being done on a computer or with paper-and-pencil. By contrast, students accustomed to writing on a computer scored significantly higher when tested on a performance writing task (extended written response using a computer) than did those who were tested with paper-and-pencil.

Findings Tied to Conclusions

The validity of tests assessing writing ability may be threatened to the extent that those who are accustomed to writing on a computer are tested via handwriting.

The Second Reading Revisited: The Important Details

This section follows the guidelines for a research analysis (or dissection) provided in Table 14.1.

1. The purpose of the Russell and Haney (1997) study was to experimentally investigate the relationship between mode of test administration (paper-and-pencil versus computer) and measures of writing performance (multiple-choice and written questions).

2.a. Significant prior work includes that of Snyder and Hoffman (1994), who documented the increasing use of computers in the schools.

b. One compelling idea is the potential mismatch between schools' movement toward authentic assessment and tasks that require students to complete work via paper-and-pencil. Thus students' writing skills may be underestimated if they are accustomed to writing on a computer (an authentic task) but are tested with paper-and-pencil.

3. This is clearly problem-based research since no theory is cited as a rationale for the study. The researchers were concerned about a real-world problem: the possibility of invalid assessments of writing ability if there exists a testing medium (paper-and-pencil) that does not match students' usual (authentic) tasks (writing on a computer).

4. These researchers investigated the construct of "school learning performance," operationally defined as test scores on a battery of tests requiring open-ended (short-answer), multiple-choice, and extended written responses. Their particular focus was writing ability, operationally defined as scores on an extended written response ("performance writing assessment").

5. The Russell and Haney (1997) study was quantitative (only numerical scores were used), inferential (evidenced by the level of significance, permitting a conclusion about the larger population), and true experimental (given that the experimental and control groups were formed via the random process). A facet of the study was causal comparative, given the researchers' comparison of males and females (portions of their analysis are also correlational in that they involved intercorrelation of the various assessments and correlational analysis to investigate whether the model of administration effect differed for students with varying writing ability levels). This was a group study (which is obvious from the sample sizes within each group being compared); it was also a traditional study (not a teacher action research project). Finally, I believe this study has the potential to (perhaps broadly) influence policy (if it is replicated several times on a large scale), but the study itself was small scale and evaluation oriented ("blended," in other words).

6. Russell and Haney's independent variable was mode of test administration, with levels being computer (experimental group) and paper-and-pencil (control group). The primary dependent variable was the score on the performance writing assessment (PWAvg); others included the score on the open-ended assessment (OE) and scores on the NAEP subtests (Language Arts, Science, Math). Each NAEP subtest also yielded a multiple-choice score as well as a short-answer score. Furthermore, the primary PWAvg score was also partitioned into a characters score, a words score, and a paragraphs score to study textual responses in greater depth. An attribute variable, male versus female, was also used in one analysis to determine whether the mode of administration effect differed for males versus females.

7. The primary research design used by Russell and Haney (1997) is best described as a true experimental randomized posttest control group design. The design for the secondary analysis using the attribute variable gender can be described as a 2 × 2 factorial (mode of administration by sex). Russell and Haney also reported that this particular study was part of a "larger longitudinal study."

8. Russell and Haney's (1997) sample was a random subsample of sixth-, seventh-, and eighth-grade students from the ALL school in Worchester, Massachusetts. They were part of a larger study to evaluate a school restructuring project (Co-NECT). There were 46 students in the experimental (computer) group, and 68 students were in the control (paper-and-pencil) group.

9. The reliability of measures centered on the process of scoring (inter-rater reliability), particularly the performance writing item. These coefficients ranged from .44 to .62 across three raters, low by most standards. The reliability of the OE and NAEP measures was not addressed. Test validity was also left unaddressed.

10. Russell and Haney (1997) used many control procedures, including the random assignment of subjects to the experimental and control groups. This assured group comparability and control of extraneous variables related to the students themselves. This feature, coupled with the experimenters' manipulation of mode of administration, defined their design as true experimental, the strongest design of its kind for discovering cause-and-effect relationships. (The control group was reported to be a "representative" sample. It is my presumption that the representativeness was achieved via random sampling; they made a later reference to comparisons based on two random samples.) The educational experiences of the groups were held constant—all the students were exposed to the same methods of instruction within the ALL school. Only the method of test administration differed.

The researchers attempted to control for artifacts resulting from the conversion of paper tests to computer tests. Fatigue resulting from reading computer texts might be one such artifact; curiously, they enlarged the font on the computer screen to reduce the impact of screen fatigue (to equalize the fatigue effect). Doing so confounded the mode of administration with print size.

Blinding was used in the scoring of tests to reduce the grader bias that may result from knowledge of experimental versus control group membership. This was accomplished by entering all pencil-and-paper responses verbatim into the computer. Each evaluator was blinded to the student's condition, reducing bias due to expectations. Students' responses within both groups were also randomly intermixed for grading presentation, which also reduced experimenter effects such as warm-up, fatigue, and so on. Furthermore, averaging three raters' evaluations on the writing performance task reduced measurement error. The researchers also used statistical control (multiple regression) to assess the mode of administration effect (controlling for individual ability differences assessed by the open-ended assessment questions completed via paper-and-pencil by all subjects).

11. One alternative hypothesis was the possibility of group differences despite the random selection process (possibly the result of missing data). Multiple regression (statistical control) was used in the analysis to rule out the plausibility of group differences as an explanation for the mode of administration effect.

Another alternative hypothesis is related to the Hawthorne effect (what they refer to as "simple novelty" and "simple motivation"). The researchers argued that the differential motivation of the computer group (as an explanation for their results) is not plausible given the mode of administration effect was not evidenced across all assessments. They also referred to prior studies suggesting the effects of motivation are weaker than the effect of mode of administration.

12.a. Russell and Haney's (1997) data analysis used *t* tests (and effect sizes) to uncover the mode of administration effect. Correlation, regression, and two-way ANOVA were also used to explore this effect further (largely in an attempt to see whether the effect was moderated by subject characteristics).

b. The major finding was what they refer to as a "mode of administration effect" (with a large effect size) most apparent in assessment of extended writing (not multiple-choice responses). Students in the computer condition scored significantly higher on the performance writing assessment (an extended written response) than did students in the paper-and-pencil condition. (Their writing was also longer.) The same was true for shorter written responses on the NAEP tests. No differences were apparent on the multiple-choice tests, and no other subject characteristics appeared to interact with their experimental intervention.

13. Russell and Haney (1997) concluded that students' writing skills may be underestimated if they are accustomed to writing on a computer but are tested with paper-and-pencil. Test validity may be threatened, they believe, to the extent that the media of assessment does not match that of instruction and learning. In short, testing conditions should match learning conditions for maximum validity.

A Brief Critique

A critique of the Russell and Haney (1997) study, like all critiques, should first focus on the objective and descriptive information contained within the framework of the research analysis presented in Table 14.1. Much, if not all, of this information should be presented in a narrative form (without the numbers corresponding to the outline) in the research critique. As before, this is followed by evaluative judgments.

I believe one strength of the Russell and Haney (1997) study is the gathering, analysis, and interpretation of data that reminds readers of an important idea in assessment: the match between learning and testing conditions. Most educators would agree that mismatches between these conditions are a threat to the validity of assessment. This principle might be easily forgotten within rapidly changing, computer-oriented classrooms. Another strength of this study centers on its methodology, namely its randomly selected participants to create comparable groups, use of multiple measures, attention to bias control via blinding raters, attention to alternative hypotheses, thorough analysis of data (such as the analysis of characters, words, and paragraphs to explain the mode-of-administration effect), and clear conclusions.

Weaknesses of this study also center on facets of its methodology. We know that the reliability of the writing assessment was not high and little attention was paid to the validity of measures. It is also likely that their conversion of paper tests to the computer format introduced unwanted, albeit minor, confounding with the extraneous variable print size.

Another weakness of this study was addressed well by these researchers: the potential for the mode-of-administration effect being due to "differential motivation," or a variation of the Hawthorne effect (the novelty of taking tests on the computer). Russell and Haney (1997) also described several weaknesses from their own perspective, including the limited use of extended writing measures and failure to collect data on the important attribute variable of students' level of experience with computers. (Apparently, the assumption was made that most students are comfortable with computers and use them regularly for writing.) This variable may have interacted with mode of administration and led to qualified statements about their major findings. Overall, this study is a fine model of the research process in many ways, and its publication in a fine journal is no surprise.

I trust you will be able to read published research with far better comprehension and be able to discuss it more meaningfully than you would have prior to this tour through educational research. Further, I hope you understand that educational research is truly an integrative *process,* where one step leads to another. Studying educational research in discrete sections does not foster a connective, process-oriented view of research. This is unfortunate. That is why it is important in this chapter to think about all the research concepts and principles you have learned and to try to see how it all "fits together" into a meaningful whole.

Chapter Summary

A critical review of published research involves careful analytic judgment. The review is aided by a thorough research analysis, one which "pulls apart" the research into its important components. Specific questions related to the research analysis were offered in this chapter. Guidelines for critiquing published research were also offered, including the focus on purpose, overall reaction, methodological issues, weaknesses and strengths, and overall recommendations. Educational research could be improved by greater attention to instrumentation, generalization, alternative interpretations or explanations, and explicit descriptions of a study's weaknesses and limitations. Critiquing skills can be enhanced with practice, and the practice itself helps foster a view of research as an integrative process.

Application Exercises

1. Form a small study group of four to six classmates based on your common interests in education. As a group, locate one published research report in your field; then *independently* review the study using guidelines offered in this chapter (including a thorough research analysis and thoughtful critique). Next meet as a group to share your reviews. Discuss areas where there is disagreement and try to understand others' rationale for specific comments in their evaluations. Be prepared for differences in reactions, which can sometimes be radical. Disagreements are common among expert reviewers of manuscripts submitted to journals for publication in education.

2. I know someone who mistakenly sent the same manuscript (a research report) to the same journal but different editors. (There was one editor for the Western portion of the United States and one editor for the Eastern portion.) After having the manuscript reviewed, one editor accepted it (pending revisions) and one editor rejected it outright. Discuss factors that might contribute to the author of same research report receiving opposing publication decisions. (The manuscript was ultimately rejected.)

3. Editors of journals that publish research in education are usually very accessible via e-mail. Select a journal in your field of interest and e-mail the editor with a question such as this: "I am completing a class project for my educational research course. We are interested in knowing about factors responsible for separating accepted versus rejected manuscripts. Can you tell me the single most important factor (or two) that describes those manuscripts accepted for publication? In what way are they different from those manuscripts not accepted? Thank you for your time." Compare your responses with those of other students in your class. Is there consensus among editors about the defining quality of accepted manuscripts?

4. The *Education Policy Analysis Archives* (http://epaa.asu.edu/epaa/) is an online journal with rapid retrieval of full-text articles and research reports in many areas of education. (It is also widely accessed.) Locate one recent report in your field of interest. Write a critique of the research using the guidelines described in this chapter. E-mail your critique to the lead author of the report, explaining that you are a student in an educational research course. Ask whether the author might be willing to evaluate your critique. Share the author's reactions to your critique with other members of your class.

ON YOUR OWN

Log on to the Web-based student study site at http://www.sagepub.com/eic for more information about the materials presented in this chapter, suggestions for activities, study aids such as electronic flashcards and review quizzes, a sample research proposal, and research recommendations that include journal article links (with discussion questions and an article evaluation guide) and questions related to this chapter.

15

WRITING RESEARCH PROPOSALS

OUTLINE

OVERVIEW

Students of educational research often prepare research proposals to satisfy course requirements or to seek approval for a project, thesis, or dissertation. Proposals serve others needs, too, such as securing a grant from an agency or foundation. Yet the general format of a research proposal is roughly the same no matter what the need. This chapter focuses on the practical issues surrounding the preparation of a research proposal. It describes *generic* guidelines for writing proposals, but please keep in mind that the specific requirements for your need (to secure funding, seek approval from a thesis committee, etc.) may not match the recommended generic guidelines perfectly. Particular foundations, universities, and college committees may have specific (and very strict) requirements for a proposal, but they all seek to know *what* you plan to do, *why* you plan to do it, and specifically *how* you intend to carry out your plan.

Students who invest the time and effort required for completing a well-conceived and well-written, comprehensive research proposal will benefit greatly during the next stage of writing: the report of completed research. This is because large sections of the research proposal can be imported—with enhancement, expansion, or revision—for use in the report of completed research. The literature review is often expanded somewhat in the final report, and of course, the data analysis section reveals your actual findings. The discussion is expanded given the findings, as you would expect, but ideas contained within the discussion section of the proposal provide a good start and springboard for a discussion that follows logically from the findings. Portions of some sections might be simply cut and pasted from the proposal to the final report. Careful, dedicated work on the proposal will likely pay off in a big way during the preparation of the final report. You can, if you prefer, view the proposal and final report as essentially one document, the report being a major revision of the proposal. This is because both documents share many of the same sections, such as the problem statement, literature review, and methodology.

Like the research proposal itself, the format of the written report of research will vary as a function of the specific requirements of an agency, a specialized journal considering its publication, or the college and library needs for archiving the final version of a project, thesis, or dissertation. But all reports have the same purpose: the sharing of your findings and conclusions. Many journals (but not all) and university guidelines require that reports of research conform to the style in the most recent edition of the *Publication Manual of the American Psychological Association* (American Psychological Association, 2001), the "APA guide." (Students should always consult the specific submission guidelines of a targeted journal, as the journal may require definite departures from the APA guide. Further, students often find that their university's library has other specific requirements concerning the format of the completed report.) Many students find that the APA guide, written to help authors prepare reports for publication, is also very helpful for the purpose of preparing research proposals. This is because much of the APA guide is concerned with writing style, which applies to research proposals as well as research reports.

Research Proposals

A research proposal, sometimes referred to as a *prospectus,* must be well organized and clear in its communication. There should be no doubt in the reader's mind precisely what you plan to do and how you plan to carry it out. The research proposal must display your clear thinking about the research process and how it relates to your specific purpose. If you are completing a research proposal for a thesis or dissertation, the proposal itself becomes a type of "contract" between you and your committee. Many educators believe that the thesis or dissertation, as a culminating or capstone experience, is the most beneficial of all your learning experiences, in large part due to the powerful "learning in use" principle.

Much of the abstract, sometimes vague, textbook learning about research becomes very real as you apply your new learning to a concrete situation. What was previously "fragile" in your understanding (such as the ideas surrounding the *p* value, operational definition, or interaction among factors in research) becomes much clearer once it is applied to a situation with personal relevance and meaning.

The first step toward this enhanced understanding that comes during the conduct of research is the preparation of a clear research proposal. This clarity, I believe, is entirely possible if you follow generally accepted guidelines for the preparation of a proposal. Table 15.1 presents a "generic" version of the content of a research proposal, meaning that it is derived from generally accepted and widely used formats already in use. (Once again, please keep in mind that the specific requirements for a proposal at your school, college, or university may vary somewhat from those presented in Table 15.1.)

CRITICAL THINKER ALERT 15-1

Anticipated Findings

Think of the research proposal (prospectus) and final report of research as one document (given their common overlap), the final report being a revision of the proposal and the addition of the findings and discussion.

Discussion: A good research proposal may include *anticipated* findings. Do you see any reason why a researcher may *not* want to "anticipate"?

The contents of Table 15.1 represent mere guidelines, and it is understood that not all sections may be relevant to your proposal. Your research proposal may include sections that are not addressed in Table 15.1, reflecting the unique features of your planned research and (possibly) nontraditional approaches.

Components of Research Proposals

Introduction

The Introduction section of a research proposal must specify a clear purpose. The type of proposed research (e.g., quantitative or qualitative, descriptive or inferential, teacher or traditional) makes no difference with regard to the requirement

TABLE 15.1 Components of a Research Proposal

I. Introduction
   A. The problem being investigated (the research question or hypothesis, with a clear purpose provided)
   B. How the planned research contributes to the field of knowledge

II. Brief literature review
   A. Connection of planned research to current status of topic
   B. Description of most relevant theories, models, constructs, or ideas
   C. Summary of most significant prior research related to proposed research
   D. Definitions of key terms

III. Methodology
   A. Ethical and legal safeguards (protecting human subjects)
   B. Research participants and selection procedures
   C. Data collection procedures
      1. Instruments and operational definitions
      2. Scoring and ensuring measurement soundness
   D. Pilot work (if applicable)
   E. Research design and types of variables
   F. Procedures for establishing control
   G. Analysis of data
      1. Methods of data analysis and inferential tests; descriptions of statistical techniques (if applicable)
      2. Methods of data organization and reduction, coding display, and strategies for drawing conclusions (if applicable)

IV. Discussion
   A. Implications of possible findings
   B. Limitations and weaknesses

V. References

VI. Appendixes (possibly instruments used, additional data, and all matters pertaining to the protection of human subjects such as permission letters, institutional review board approval, etc.)

of stating its purpose. Most research purposes can be stated as a problem being investigated, for example, a gap in knowledge, an uncertainty, conflicting research findings, or a disturbing trend. The problem being investigated provides the context for a clear research hypothesis or research question.

For example, a problem being investigated might be the unwanted side effects of high-stakes testing (with research aimed at linking standardized test scores with major consequences). This might be a serious problem if, for example, struggling high school students are pushed off the traditional path to a high school diploma (Viadero, 2003b). The research question might be "Do states with higher stakes testing programs (compared to those with lower stakes testing programs) have a higher high school dropout rate?" Another research question might be "Are first-year teachers in states with high-stakes testing programs more likely to leave teaching than those in states with low-stakes testing programs?"

This section of a research proposal must also state how the planned research contributes to our knowledge and understanding. You might think of this component as a response to a critic who says "Who cares?" Although the rationale for your planned research may be obvious to you, many readers might wonder about its importance when put in the context of more pressing problems in education.

Many students wonder about the length of a research proposal and are surprised to learn that proposals are not lengthy, perhaps 15 to 20 pages total. The Introduction section might only be two well-crafted paragraphs (or about a page).

Brief Literature Review

The Brief Literature Review is just that: a concise, condensed summary of existing knowledge and ideas related to the research problem and a synopsis of key research studies already published. This important component provides a solid framework for the proposal. It reveals what has been done in the area chosen for research and provides clear direction and purpose for the proposal. A good literature review provides clear development of ideas and identifies hypotheses cast away for lack of support, supported with some empirical evidence, or supported to the degree they are considered trustworthy principles. The literature review should precisely define the problem being investigated and place it in a meaningful perspective (historical or otherwise). It must also include what the author believes to be the most significant prior research findings.

Perhaps very few relevant studies are available in the area related to the problem being investigated. More likely, there are dozens if not hundreds of prior studies that are linked to your specific research question. Good research proposals often summarize the bulk of those studies but then highlight the handful of studies directly related to the purpose of the planned research. Perhaps only four to six studies are cited in this section; that is acceptable as long as those few studies provide compelling reasons for your research. These reasons might include the need for replication or follow-up, or possibly improving upon a weak methodology. You may encounter dozens of relevant studies, the challenge being selecting the few that require focus and describing your rationale for selecting and highlighting those chosen few.

Perhaps your research will attempt to explain the discrepancies among prior research studies; in that case, it makes sense to highlight the most significant studies at odds. Or perhaps your study will extend existing knowledge into a new domain. Whatever the purpose of research, the function of the Brief Literature Review is to place your planned study within a context. The reader should know clearly how your study fits into a larger context; there should be no bewilderment about the relevance of prior research and thinking in a specific area. It is also appropriate in this section to define terms that might be unfamiliar to readers. You can assume the reader has a general knowledge of education ideas and vocabulary but may not know terms that are unique to a particular specialty area. A "typical" research proposal might have four to six important terms that require definitions.

Whatever the purpose of the proposed research, a literature review most often begins with careful examination of *secondary* sources for ideas, perspectives, and prior findings. Secondary sources include summaries, reviews, or discussions of original research, and they are found in scholarly books known as reviews, handbooks, yearbooks, and encyclopedias. Examples include the *Review of Educational Research, Handbook of Research on Teaching, Yearbook of Special Education,* and *Encyclopedia of Educational Research.* Especially useful for completing a literature review in any field are published empirical studies known as meta-analyses (which were described in Chapter 4) and best-evidence syntheses. *Meta-analyses* are statistical summaries of quantitative research in a narrow area, and *best-evidence syntheses* are reviews of quantitative and qualitative studies investigating the same topic.

A review of literature must also include the most significant *primary* sources, those articles that report original research. There are hundreds of journals that report original research in education (see Chapter 4), including the print-based *American Educational Research Journal* and the online journal *Educational Policy Analysis Archives.* The Education Resources Information Center (ERIC) described in Chapter 4 (http://www.eric.ed.gov/) is invaluable for the purpose of rapidly locating via enhanced search engines the primary sources most relevant to a proposed study, as ERIC has over a million citations dating back to 1966. Beginning in the fall of 2004, many full-text ERIC documents became available online and without cost. Successful searches of the ERIC databases are dependent on accurate *key terms,* which is explained more fully at the "Search Help" link on the ERIC Web site. Google Scholar (http://scholar.google.com/) became available in 2004 and is yet another method for locating published research in the scholarly and professional journals in education and related fields.

The Internet also affords other primary and secondary sources of information about research and thinking appropriate for a literature review. Especially useful are the federal government Web sites such as those of the Department of Education (www.ed.gov) and its National Center for Education Statistics (http://nces.ed.gov). Further, there are numerous national research institutes and centers such as the Center for the Improvement of Early Reading Achievement (CIERA; www.ciera.org) established by the Department of Education's Institute of Education Sciences. Ten Regional Educational Laboratories also exist (e.g., WestEd, www.wested.org) and provide free online research reports and other Web-based resources. Finally, significant previous research and important conceptual frameworks that might work themselves into a literature review may be found in professional associations such as the American Educational Research Association (www.aera.net), Phi Delta Kappa International, Inc. (www.pdkintl.org), and the Association for Supervision and Curriculum Development (www.ascd.org).

Literature reviews are organized logically by topic (not author) and extend beyond mere summaries of prior research and ideas. They analyze complex studies and integrate or synthesize (pull together) diverse findings. Good literature reviews establish a sound rationale and theoretical framework for the problems and leave little doubt about the significance of the proposed study.

CRITICAL PERSPECTIVES 15-1

LITERATURE REVIEWS

Critical Thinking Toolbox

Critical thinking displays the cognitive skills of analysis and evaluation. It is "clear and careful" as well as simple and flexible (Shank, 2002). Critical thinking is enhanced by breaking up complexities into constituent parts and judging their value or usefulness. One searches for the fewest ideas (keeping it simple) to explain the largest whole, all the while being open to notions never before considered (being flexible).

Literature Reviews in Quantitative Research

A literature review in a quantitative study usually cites many empirical studies in logical support of a specific hypothesis derived from theory. It provides the rationale and backdrop for the research question. The review of previous research may *itself* become a statistical task with use of meta-analysis or similar tools. (Meta-analysis was described in Chapter 4.) This integration and synthesis of previous work is nearly always organized by topic. A good review of literature will leave no doubt in the reader's mind how a particular finding relates explicitly to the research hypothesis. A typical quantitative review objectively summarizes the current status of knowledge on a topic, highlights the recognized gaps within its knowledge base, and connects the present study's hypothesis to the established body of knowledge and thinking.

Literature Reviews in Qualitative Research

A literature review in a qualitative study may be viewed as a preliminary or flexible conceptual framework, or a joining of ideas, often from different disciplines. The use of analogies or frequent use of metaphor is common as a means for understanding complex ideas and their interrelationships and subtle meanings. Many qualitative researchers understand that their literature review is an "argument," or reasons put forth in support of a viewpoint. Good qualitative reviews of the literature convince the reader that a phenomenon is important and that it is not understood sufficiently well. Authors use the literature review to make certain that their themes capture previous work and thinking related to the major constructs being investigated. Literature reviews are often inventive and creative. They convince the reader that the work is not completed within a vacuum. Consistent with the discovery orientation of qualitative research, the literature review often progresses along with data collection and analysis, co-occurring with all phrases of the study.

Literature Reviews in Action Research

Given that action research is practical, it is no surprise that Mills (2003) reminded action researchers that reviewing the literature "could actually save you time" (p. 29). He observed that "taking time to immerse yourself in the literature allows you to reflect on your own problems through someone else's lens" (p. 29). It is in the review of literature that many teachers learn about promising practices. Because most teacher action researchers develop their ideas within their own classrooms, theoretical and conceptual frameworks and others' research findings play a lesser role than their own practical experiences. It is hard to imagine, however, that close attention to others' research findings in a similar situation would not assist an action researcher's interpretation and explanation of findings.

Critical Thinking Questions

After analyzing the differences among the three different types of literature reviews, what simple (single) idea appears to capture the most significant difference across the three orientations? Try to be clear and careful in your answer. What type of literature review might the No Child Left Behind Act endorse most favorably? Can you envision yourself easily shifting between writing both qualitative and quantitative literature reviews? Why or why not?

Methodology

The Methodology section of a research proposal is probably the longest section, perhaps in the range of 5 to 10 pages. It is also the section most likely to change once real-world practicalities set in, such as compliance and response rates of research participants, budget concerns, revoked permissions, and data that do not conform to original plans for analysis, among many other problems that researchers sometimes cannot foresee. Departures from the details of a research proposal are common, and most are likely to be inconsequential.

Plans for the ethical treatment of research participants must be developed with sufficient care that they do *not* change. Areas of concern here are related to issues such as informed consent and privacy rights. Committees that function for the protection of human subjects expect a plan with detailed descriptions that ensure the proposed research conforms to the highest ethical and legal standards. Departures from this plan must usually be approved by the appropriate committee.

CRITICAL THINKER ALERT 15-2

Institutional Review

Institutional review boards (IRBs) are particularly interested in ethical guidelines and legal safeguards—the issues designed to protect human participants. Students' proposals will almost certainly be returned unapproved without sufficient detail in this section of the proposal.

Discussion: If a research proposal described sample selection and recruitment by referring only to "usual and customary ways," do you think the proposal would be reviewed favorably? Why or why not?

The Methodology section must also detail the sample size and subject selection procedures. Whether it is a case study or large-scale survey, a clear rationale for the sample size should be offered. Statistical power analysis is one method for justifying sample size in group comparison studies (whether they are experimental or causal comparative). Desirable precision or tolerance is often used to estimate sample size in surveys. Other justifications include rules of thumb and precedent. Details surrounding subject selection procedures usually consume a paragraph or two depending on the complexity of the plan. Information here is useful to help readers decide whether the selection process was truly random, or perhaps representative, or merely convenient. Decisions here have strong implications for the external validity (generalization) of the study.

The data collection procedures may be simple and straightforward or complex and detailed depending on factors related to the type of study (such as whether it is quantitative or qualitative). Procedures for surveying respondents, too, can be simple or complex depending on whether the survey involves the Internet, mail, phone, or personal contact. It is appropriate in this section to detail how instruments will be scored and describe procedures that are set in place to maximize the reliability and validity of all the measures used. Common descriptions here include procedures for establishing inter-rater reliability, blinding to reduce scoring bias, and techniques for establishing content validity, to name just a few.

Perhaps the proposed research does not require collecting new data. Many projects, theses, and dissertations are completed by accessing the existing data sets often available to responsible members of a school or university. One could argue persuasively for "No new data!" given the vast amount of existing data that sit unanalyzed. School districts often collect data from students, including standardized test scores, and enable others to examine the data in order to answer specific research questions. Large national data sets also exist, for example, the National Assessment of Education Progress (NAEP). Training is usually required to access these large data sets.

If you examine complex data sets, be prepared for ambiguity in the literature, for two researchers entering the same data set with the same research question may in fact reach different conclusions (which is often a function of using different comparison groups). (This is yet another instance of the same research yielding different and often opposing conclusions, as described in Chapter 1.)

In fact, Viadero (2003b) reminded us that such analyses are by no means "the last word." She described how two research groups accessed NAEP achievement data to answer the research question "Do high-stakes testing programs positively affect student achievement?" The researchers reached opposing conclusions. That was no surprise to researcher Audrey Amrein of Arizona State University, who stated, "I've had a lot of people reanalyze our data, and each and every one of them has come up with different results" (quoted in Viadero, 2003b, p. 10). Suffice it to say that those preparing research proposals using existing data sets should have sufficient preparation in handling oftentimes unwieldy computer files and complex data prone to counter-interpretations.

CRITICAL THINKER ALERT 15-3

Existing Data

Give consideration to using an existing data set (international, national, or local) for a research project, thesis, or dissertation. Many data already collected sit unanalyzed.

Discussion: What advantages and disadvantages are apparent in a decision to use an existing data set for a research project?

Pilot work, or a very small-scale "tryout" of the procedures and instruments used in a proposed study, sometimes precedes a formal proposal. The value of a pilot study is to discover potential problems in the methodology and correct them before the actual study begins. Confusing directions, unrealistic time frames, ambiguity built into instruments, and the like are typical areas needing remedies that are uncovered by pilot studies.

Research Design

All research, ranging from the most emerging qualitative and descriptive research to multiway factorial quantitative research, can be described in terms of its "blueprint" or design. The Research Design section of a proposal is often a short paragraph in

CRITICAL THINKER ALERT 15-4

Pilot Studies

Give consideration to conducting pilot studies, those small-scale tryouts designed to uncover problems in methodology and instrumentation. Serious, but correctable, problems could be discovered prior to larger-scale implementation of data collection.

Discussion: Specifically, what types of problems might researchers uncover during pilot studies?

length, but it is packed with important information. Good descriptions of complex research designs permit the reader to visualize the overall plan of the study, such as a $2 \times 3 \times 4$ factorial design or a "thick" triangulated ethnographic design. Many research designs are termed *mixed,* in the sense they combine both quantitative and qualitative components. Complex, mixed designs should be described in sufficient detail to convey the overall plan. Frequently models, figures, or diagrams (often incorporating timelines) are used to convey important facets of a research design.

Procedures

The Procedures section details the process by which participants provide data. This includes the plans in place to gather data that minimizes bias and contamination as well as neutralize threats to internal validity. The length of this section varies greatly as a function of the complexity of data collection. Describing all procedures related to data collection in great detail is usually not necessary unless there are obvious implications for the integrity of data.

Analysis of Data

The planned Analysis of Data section also varies as a function of the type of study planned. The analysis of quantitative studies can often be described in a short paragraph; qualitative studies often require more detail. Well-written data analysis plans usually describe methods for data reduction, strategies for coding, methods for displaying and summarizing data (via tables, charts, graphs, etc.), and the appropriate use of informative statistics such as effect size measures in addition to traditional tests of statistical significance.

Sometimes the actual procedures used to analyze the data do not perfectly match the plan. This is true when qualitative studies take unexpected turns and new types of data are collected that require modified methods of analysis; it is also true in quantitative studies when the actual data collected do not conform to the assumptions required by the statistical tests that were planned. In these cases, for example, nonparametric tests might be used instead of parametric analyses. Researchers often find that additional statistical analyses (or data transformations) are needed to make data more interpretable. Nevertheless, research proposals do require a statement that describes an *anticipated* data analysis plan, often subject to change.

CRITICAL THINKER ALERT 15-5

Flexible Proposals

Don't think of a research proposal as being unchangeable. Often, the realities of ongoing research require departures from the original plan. The data analysis plan, for example, is often revised in accordance with a sample size that falls short of expectations or scores that do not conform to the requirements of the proposed analysis.

Discussion: What components of a research proposal would one be most *hesitant* to modify after approval? Why?

Discussion

The Discussion section is important in the sense that it requires the researcher to think about possible findings in advance—and what they might mean. There is no sense in collecting data that cannot be interpreted. Data are meaningful to the extent that no matter what the outcome, a clear interpretation is possible. Thinking ahead often results in revisions to the methodology so that the data are in fact more interpretable. A study may also benefit from attention to limitations and weaknesses prior to collecting data. Readers of your proposal (most likely members of your thesis or dissertation committee) may recommend changes to your methodology that overcome perceived limitations and weaknesses. Perhaps readers will recognize additional limitations or weaknesses that might have been overlooked. Either way, a study is stronger if its weaknesses are known and stated explicitly in advance.

HIGHLIGHT AND LEARNING CHECK 15-1

Organized Proposals

A good research proposal is well organized and displays clear thinking about the research process. It leaves no doubt in the reader's mind as to precisely what the author plans to do and how he or she intends to carry it out. Its purpose and rationale are abundantly clear. The essential components of a research proposal are described, including the literature review, sound methodology, procedures, and planned analysis of data (among other sections). Its organizing frameworks prove especially useful. How would you describe the preferred writing style for research proposals?

References

The References section deserves great attention to detail. Errors of omission and other inaccuracies are very common—and irritating—for anyone intent on locating a reference. Scanning the references section also provides a quick assessment of the type, scope, and quality of citations in the Introduction and Literature Review. One can also learn how current the bulk of cited studies are, and whether or not a seminal study has been included.

Appendix

Contents within the Appendix (if one exists) vary greatly, once again depending on the type of research being proposed. Common entries include instruments, instructions, findings of pilot studies, and written communications of many types. Other documents are appropriate to the extent they help the reader understand and evaluate the proposal.

CRITICAL THINKER ALERT 15-6

Constant Revisions

Think of the research proposal as a document needing constant revision until it is well organized and clear in its communication. It is important to be certain your proposal displays clear thinking about the research process and how it relates to your specific purpose.

Discussion: What is lacking about this stated purpose of research: "To learn more about why kids struggle in school"?

Writing Style: Clear, Concise, Organized

Writing in educational research, whether for a research proposal or final report of completed research, requires a style that is, above all else, clear, concise, and organized. Of course, it helps when your own ideas have been clarified in your mind. But the mere process of writing seems to clarify ideas. For this reason it makes sense to put your ideas in writing, and then revise them as needed until both your thinking and writing are clear.

I often suggest to my students that they begin their revision process by (1) striking out all unnecessary words, and (2) adding headings (even at the paragraph level, if this is appropriate). Invariably, shorter sentences packed with substance, coupled with headings that automatically force better organization, yield revision that is better understood. Hensen (2003), making recommendations to educators who are writing for professional publications, put it this way: "Just use common words, short sentences, and short paragraphs" (p. 789). Hensen (2005) also noted that "experienced writers are preoccupied not with telling their readers everything they know but with helping readers discover insights" (p. 773).

It appears that most authors in education write in the style required by the American Psychological Association (APA). All requirements for writing in this style are fully explained (with many examples) in the *Publication Manual of the American Psychological Association* (2001). The APA manual provides general advice regarding clear and concise writing style, guidance on grammar and the mechanics of writing, and specific instructions for citing prior research, writing about research methodology, describing statistical tests, creating tables, and avoiding sexism in language (among many other important concerns). The APA manual was originally intended to guide authors in the preparation of research reports, but its value for those preparing research proposals is obvious (in part due to the parallels between and commonalities in proposals and reports).

Perhaps the best advice for students intent on writing a research proposal for a course requirement, thesis, or dissertation is to seek out recently approved proposals

CRITICAL THINKER ALERT 15-7

Writing Style

The writing style of research proposals should be clear and concise. You should reread your proposal at least once for the sole purpose of striking unnecessary words and phrases. Use headings freely—they force organization and enhance readability.

Discussion: What is not clear and concise in the following sentence? "The research participants who were serving in our study of achievement and its relation to motivation were obtained by common selection procedures used on our campus since the College of Education established guidelines about 5 years ago."

from faculty or student peers in the department requiring the proposal. Many departments or graduate offices have guidelines written especially for students approaching this task. Securing guidelines unique to your department or college should be your first strategy. Whatever the format, the overriding concern for authors of research proposals is clear communication related to a research project that can be completed realistically, usually within a narrow time frame and a very limited budget.

Recap

Remember, proposals must be clearly written and well integrated, convey a clear purpose and rationale, set a research problem in context, describe a sound methodology for collecting data and a plan for making sense of it, and persuade the reader that the research will make a contribution to the field of education. Simply and bluntly, readers want to know what, why, and how: precisely *what* it is that you intend to do, *why* you want to do this, and *how* you are going to do it.

Organizing Frameworks

Writing about research ideas (and findings) in education is often enhanced with organizing frameworks, those that help the writer communicate and the reader comprehend. Well-chosen organizing frameworks such as models or principles provide a means for tying ideas together, that is, using a common thread to integrate ideas (or findings). Scattered ideas are hard to understand unless there is some common "anchor" to tie them together. As an example, consider the challenge faced by Rigsby and DeMulder (2003), who were in a position to be ethnographers "listening" to online conversations of 77 teachers over a 3-month period. The online forum, part of a course in a master's program, focused on the language and cultural basis of classroom practice. The researchers' goal was to "make sense of what the teachers were saying" and convey this interpretation to readers.

To accomplish this research objective, they proposed an organizing framework that centered on the five core propositions of the National Board for Professional Teaching Standards (NBPTS), hence providing an interpretation of the concept "autonomous professional." Rigsby and DeMulder (2003) were able to effectively use the NBPTS's principles as a context to analyze the volumes of discussion narratives. (They also used the teachers' essays written to fulfill a final assignment of the course.) They stated, "In order to understand what was happening in the classrooms of [our teachers], we needed a standard of comparison against which to contrast reports of their experience. The NBPTS propositions provide such a framework for comparison."

With the central ideas of standards, assessment, accountability, and the autonomous professional in mind, Rigsby and DeMulder (2003) were able to interpret the teachers' overwhelmingly critical comments. (Teachers were critical of state-mandated testing programs to measure performance relative to new standards. The rich qualitative data, coupled with the NBPTS organizing framework, enabled these researchers to conclude that their state's program had undermined teachers' professionalism, in large part due to the state's ignoring teachers' experience and wisdom in its setting of standards and planning of assessments.)

The point is that organizational frameworks, in a variety of forms, can effectively make sense of data and convince the reader that the plan for data management is meaningful, structured, and coherent. (Readers can easily get lost in a disorganized maze that purports to describe or manage data.)

Research Proposal Ideas

Students of educational research often wonder how researchable ideas are generated. The simple answer is: classroom experience, reading, and talking to other educators. Classroom teachers often report they are swimming in ideas about their practice and how to improve it (or at least understand it better). There has been an explosion of interest in teacher action research as a result. Teachers who are accustomed to evaluating their own teaching, which is often called *reflective practice,* might reasonably ask "How can I improve that lesson?" or "Why did that happen?" Plausible answers to these questions will often form the basis of a researchable idea.

The problem has presented itself; what remains are the *what, why,* and *how* details. In this sense, those who practice reflective teaching are in a natural position to carry out a formal investigation of their ideas. Because many teachers are interested in writing for professional publication, Hensen (2003) advises them to consider using questionnaires and other forms of action research. (Recall from Chapter 6 that there are several journals that publish exclusively action research conducted by teachers.) Hensen (2003) also stated, "Conducting action research helps teachers acquire deeper understanding of how various topics in the curriculum are related, helps them solve classroom problems, revitalizes their teaching, empowers them to make decisions in their classroom, encourages reflective thinking, and makes their teaching less teacher-centered" (p. 789).

Regular readers of publications such as *Education Week* (www.edweek.org), *Educational Leadership* (www.ascd.org), and *Phi Delta Kappan* (www.pdkintl.org) often consider these sources to be a treasure trove of great research ideas. The latter two publications have theme issues or special sections that are especially engaging. A sampling of recent themes from issues of *Educational Leadership* appears in Table 15.2.

Table 15.3 presents a sampling of recent special sections or cover stories published by *Phi Delta Kappan.*

TABLE 15.2 Sampling of Recent Theme Issues of *Educational Leadership*

Supporting New Educators	Redesigning Professional Development
How Schools Improve	Class Size, School Size
Learning From Urban Schools	Schools and the Law
The Adolescent Learner	Understanding Learning Differences
Building Classroom Relationships	What Should We Teach?
Teaching All Students	Making Standards Work
Responding to the Challenges of Accountability	Who Is Teaching Our Children?
New Needs, New Curriculum	Beyond Class Time
Improving Achievement in Math and Science	Helping All Students Achieve
What Research Says About Reading	Evaluating Educators
Leading in Tough Times	The Changing Context of Education
Schools as Learning Communities	The Science of Learning
Keeping Good Teachers	Teaching the Information Generation
The First Years of School	How to Differentiate Instruction
Creating Caring Schools	Keeping Teaching Fresh
Using Data to Improve Student Achievement	Sustaining Change
Equity and Opportunity	Healthy Bodies, Minds, and Buildings
Reading and Writing in the Content Areas	What Do We Mean by Results?
The World in the Classroom	Understanding Youth Culture
Do Students Care About Learning?	The Constructivist Classroom
The Instructional Leader	Redefining Literacy
Customizing Our Schools	Personalized Learning

TABLE 15.3 Sampling of Recent Topics Covered in *Phi Delta Kappan*

Reading Research	Charter Schools
Learner's Bill of Rights	Place-Based Education
Moral Education	Responsible Accountability
Special Education	Reading and Assessment
Achievement Gap	School Leadership
Professional Learning Groups	School Effectiveness
Constitutionality of No Child Left Behind	Block Scheduling
	Middle School Reform
Democracy and Civic Engagement	Standardized Testing
Professional Development	Leaders for the 21st Century
School Reforms That Work	Education Civil Rights
Reorganizing Schools	Alternative Schools
High-Performance School Systems	Early Literacy
School Redesign and Renewal	Success For All
Teacher Education	Passionate Learners
Slow School Movement	Early Childhood Education
Standards and Standardization	Transforming Urban Education
The Condition of Education	The National Reading Panel Report
School Reform	Personalized Instruction

CRITICAL THINKER ALERT 15-8

Research Ideas

Many great research ideas spring from reading journals in education. Online research journals in education enable easy access to reports and often lead to ideas for research projects. Online journals in education are listed on the Web site of the American Educational Research Association (http://aera-cr.asu.edu/links.html).

Discussion: Browse several online journals in your field of interest. Did your reading of these journals stimulate your interest and yield any good ideas?

If you scan the tables of contents of current and past issues of *Educational Leadership* or *Phi Delta Kappan* online, or access a sampling of their full-text articles, you are bound to find a personally relevant topic that piques your research interest. Scholarly reviews of research in specific topic areas within education are also found in *Review of Educational Research* (*RER*), though your reading speed will slow considerably when reading *RER* (compared to the more practitioner-oriented *Educational Leadership* and *Phi Delta Kappan*). Original studies across a wide variety of topic areas are published in the *American Educational Research Journal* (*AERJ*). Both *RER* and *AERJ* are considered premiere journals because they are published by the primary professional organization of educational researchers, the American Educational Research Association (www.aera.net).

These journals, among other fine ones described in Chapter 4, are useful because very often the authors of the published reports describe specific research questions that need to be answered by future research. (Obviously, the most current issues are the most helpful with respect to the need for follow-up research.)

I also find that *ERIC Digests* are especially helpful (www.ericfacility.org). These contain over 3,000 research summaries covering a huge array of topics in education and are bound to stimulate your interest in and pursuit of researchable questions. To convey a sense of the breadth and scope of these summaries, Table 15.4 presents the titles of a recently added collection of *ERIC Digests.*

CRITICAL THINKER ALERT 15-9

Communications

Students of research can benefit greatly from communication with other researchers, well known or otherwise. The preferred mode of communication for most researchers is undoubtedly e-mail.

Discussion: E-mail addresses of many educational researchers can be obtained easily from published journal articles (in print and online) and university directories. Can you think of the "netiquette" that might govern such contacts?

TABLE 15.4 Sampling of Titles From a Collection of *ERIC Digests*

Culturally Responsive Teaching for American Indian Students
Alternatives for At-Risk and Out-of-School Youth
Depression and Disability in Children and Adolescents
Diagnosing Communication Disorders in Culturally and Linguistically Diverse Students
History Standards in Fifty States
Gifted Children With Attention Deficit Hyperactivity Disorder (ADHD)
Promoting the Self-Determination of Students With Severe Disabilities
Integrating the Arts Into the Curriculum for Gifted Students
Early-Decision Programs
Curriculum Reform in the Professions: Preparing Students for a Changing World
Quality in Distance Education
Using Standardized Test Data to Guide Instruction and Intervention
Effect Size and Meta-Analysis
Some Key Concepts for the Design and Review of Empirical Research
Score Normalization as a Fair Grading Practice
Incorporating Family Work Into Individual Counseling
Establishing a Relationship With Families
Working Towards Effective Practices in Distance Career Counseling
Professional School Counselors Can Make Positive Connections With Homeschoolers
Filial Therapy
ADD and ADHD: An Overview for School Counselors
Are Boys Falling Behind in Academics?
New Perspectives on Counseling Underachievers
When Terrorists Strike: What School Counselors Can Do
Scientifically Based Research: What Does It Mean for Counselors?
Bibliotherapy
A Review of Trends in Journalism Education
Literacy Interventions in Low Resource Environments: An International Perspective
Schooling in Mexico: A Brief Guide for U.S. Educators
Small Schools and Teacher Professional Development
Recruiting and Retaining Rural School Administrators
Reliability, Validity, and Authenticity in American Indian and Alaska Native Research
Trends in School Leadership
Thematic Literature and Curriculum for English Language Learners in Early Childhood Education
English Language Learners and High-Stakes Tests: An Overview of the Issues
Nonnative-English-Speaking Teachers in the English Teaching Profession
A New Framework for Teaching in the Cognitive Domain
New Copyright Exemptions for Distance Educators: The Technology, Education and Copyright Harmonization (TEACH) Act
Teacher Preparation and Teacher-Child Interaction in Preschools
Mathematics Standards for Pre-Kindergarten Through Grade 2
Language and Literacy Environments in Preschools
Enriching Children's Out-of-School Time
Developing an International Framework for Education in Democracy
What Federal Statistics Reveal About Migrant Farmworkers: A Summary for Education
Nurturing Resilience and School Success in American Indian and Alaska Native Students
Identification and Recruitment of Migrant Students: Strategies and Resources
Effective Approaches to Teaching Young Mexican Immigrant Children
Can Education Play a Role in the Prevention of Youth Gangs in Indian Country? One Tribe's Approach
Setting the Agenda: American Indian and Alaska Native Education Research Priorities
Using Culturally and Linguistically Appropriate Assessments to Ensure That American Indian and Alaska Native Students Receive the Special Education Programs and Services They Need
Research on Quality in Infant-Toddler Programs
Stress and Young Children
Bullying in Early Adolescence: The Role of the Peer Group
The Prospects for Education Vouchers After the Supreme Court Ruling
Welfare Reform and Urban Children
The Asian and Pacific Islander Population in the U.S.
Teaching the Declaration of Independence
Research on Quality in Infant-Toddler Programs
Stress and Young Children
Using School Board Policy to Improve Student Achievement
Teacher Preparation and Teacher-Child Interaction in Preschools
Bullying in Early Adolescence: The Role of the Peer Group
Class Size Reduction and Urban Students
Strategies for Improving the Educational Outcomes of Latinas
Trauma and Adult Learning
Professional Development for Career Educators
The Impact of Work-Based Learning on Students
The Effects of Competition on Educational Outcomes
Interactive Language Learning on the Web
Model Early Foreign Language Programs: Key Elements
Teaching About Judicial Review
Mental Retardation: Update 2002
Narrative and Stories in Adult Teaching and Learning
Transforming Principal Preparation

Award-Winning Research Ideas and Methodologies

Graduate students in education generate many noteworthy research ideas, undoubtedly a function of their workplace, coursework, reading scholarly journals, and communications with other practitioners in education. Every 2 years Phi Delta Kappa, the professional organization for educators, recognizes outstanding doctoral dissertations by presenting awards for noteworthy contributions to research. The most recent eight awards (corresponding to geographical districts) reveal interesting variation in research ideas and diverse methodologies. These award-wining ideas and sound methodologies used to answer the research questions are briefly described in the paragraphs to follow (see http://www.pdkintl.org/edres/ddwin02.htm).

Karen Wilson Scott at the University of Idaho used a grounded-theory qualitative methodology to investigate her ideas about older adults' resilient beliefs concerning their capabilities (self-efficacy), especially as the beliefs relate to undertaking and persevering with new but challenging pursuits (like obtaining advanced degrees in later life). She developed a theory of "congruous autonomy" from her data to explain older adults' level of commitment and attention to priorities.

John Barry Watson at Claremont Graduate School and San Diego State University used a quantitative true experimental design to test his ideas about the use of metacognitive prompts and probes in a computer-based multimedia tutorial for fifth graders. He concluded that "navigational behavior" and metacognitive awareness can be positively influenced by minimal use of simple, low cost text elements.

K. Michele Ballentine-Linch at the University of Arkansas, Fayetteville used a triangulated qualitative case study to test her ideas about a constructivist, learner-centered leadership academy and its role in professional development. Her detailed study of people's journey of transformation and disposition toward change enabled her to describe characteristics of professional development that act as powerful catalysts for growth.

Sally Rigeman at the University of Iowa observed that the rush to implement technology use in the classroom provides little time to determine whether the new method is better than the method that was replaced. Her ideas centered on comparing microcomputer-based laboratory equipment with traditional equipment to assess its influence on students' learning in chemistry. The quantitative experimental design enabled her conclusion that using technology does not equate to students' learning better.

Nelson J. Maylone at Eastern Michigan University tested his ideas about high-stakes testing programs and students' socioeconomic status using a correlational design. After finding a strong link between family income and test scores, he concluded that high-stakes tests may increase the opportunity gap based on socioeconomic status.

Rose Frances Lefkowitz at St. John's University wondered whether the accommodation of college students' learning styles results in higher achievement when compared to traditional methods. Her quantitative experimental design permitted the conclusion that students' achievement and attitudes benefit from learning-style-responsive instructional strategies.

Pollyann J. Diamond at Valdosta State University used a mixed (both qualitative and quantitative) method to test her ideas about a reading program's levels of implementation and its link to attitudes and achievements among students and teachers. Her research revealed the importance of studying processes as well as outcomes and raised important issues regarding implementation, achievements, and attitudes.

Allison M. Batten at the University of South Carolina also used a mixed method methodology to investigate several interesting ideas centered on first-year teachers and their decision to leave (or not to leave) the teaching profession. Her data analysis and interpretation highlighted the importance of a quality first-year induction program.

On occasion, the *Journal of Educational Research* announces The Harold E. Mitzel Award for Meritorious Contribution to Educational Practice Through Research. One such award went to Nye, Hedges, and Konstantopoulos (2001) for their study "Are Effects of Small Classes Cumulative? Evidence From a Tennessee Experiment." (Another winner of this award, Evertson, 1985, was described in Chapter 14.) A brief overview of Nye and colleagues' study reveals how a fine idea for research can mesh with strong methodology to produce an award-winning study. These researchers observed that some scholars in education argue that the positive influences of smaller class sizes on achievement last only 1 year (the first year). They tested this counterintuitive idea by examining data from Project STAR, the well-known Tennessee 4-year longitudinal experiment (kindergarten through Grade 3) where students and teachers were randomly assigned to a small-class size or regular-class size condition. (They retained the condition for 4 years.) After reviewing the prior research on class size and achievement, much of it nonexperimental, Nye and colleagues (2001) concluded that it was "limited in internal validity" making it "difficult to know if the relations between class size and achievement (controlling for student background) are causal" (p. 337). They stated further that "a plausible hypothesis is that achievement . . . causes students to be assigned to classes of different sizes, not the other way around" (p. 377).

This conclusion and reasoning led them to Project STAR, because the large-scale (79-school) randomized experiment was better suited for causal interpretation since it had "high internal validity" (Nye et al., 2001). Project STAR had been referred to as "one of the great experiments in education in U.S. history" by Mosteller, Light, and Sachs (1996, quoted in Nye et al., 2001). Nye and colleagues' (2001) award-winning idea was to determine whether there existed an *independent* small-class effect on achievement with each passing year, that is, a separate effect in the first grade, apart from any carryover effect from kindergarten; a separate effect in the second grade, apart from any carryover effect from the first grade, and so on.

This was accomplished with a method of statistical control known as multiple regression (it removes via statistical manipulation, say, the Grade 3 achievement effects when evaluating the small-class effect in Grade 4). Nye and colleagues' model for analysis also controlled for the influence of socioeconomic and gender differences among the students who participated in the study.

HIGHLIGHT AND LEARNING CHECK 15-2

Great Research in Education

Research proposals are undoubtedly easier to write once creative and worthwhile ideas are generated. Award-winning research ideas often culminate in new answers to old questions and the discovery of new relationships (and more new ideas) by using existing data sets, thus avoiding the collection of new data. Specific criteria are offered for evaluating a research proposal, including its significance, ethics, instrumentation, and generalization (among other factors). What do you think is the key to great research in education?

Overall, these researchers found that the effect of small classes on standardized achievement tests in reading and mathematics was positive (and statistically significant) in every grade after controlling for achievement in the previous grade. This finding led to their conclusion that the positive effect of small classes on achievement was indeed "cumulative." They also concluded that the additional years in small classes yielded effect sizes that were large enough to be meaningful for public policy.

Nye and colleagues' (2001) award-winning study reveals how clear thinking about prior research can lead to new answers to old questions—even without collecting new data.

Criteria for Evaluating Research Proposals

The criteria for evaluating research proposals and completed research projects are not kept secret. Despite the evaluation criteria that differ as a function of variation in audience, purpose, and context, there is general agreement among researchers (at least conceptually) that high quality research proposals possess these characteristics:

- The problem being investigated and its significance are made crystal clear.
- The conceptualization and development of research questions or hypotheses follow a logical line of reasoning.
- The relevant theoretical and research literature is thoroughly reviewed and then summarized.
- The research design, methods, and instrumentation are most appropriate and rigorously applied.
- The plan for analysis and reporting the findings are well matched to the data collected.
- There is a clear strategy for interpreting research findings with reference to theory, policy, practice, or further research.

Other useful criteria may be derived from the National Research Council's report *Scientific Research in Education* (2002) and its elaboration by Lauer (2004, Appendix B). The council recognized that principles of science do not vary by discipline; the principles underlying scientific research in education are the same as those found in chemistry or economics. Below are the six principles identified by the National Research Council (2002) that form the bases of scientific inquiry (followed by a brief explanation):

- Pose significant questions that can be investigated empirically.
- Link research to relevant theory.
- Use methods that permit direct investigation of the question.
- Provide a coherent and explicit chain of reasoning.
- Replicate and generalize across studies.
- Expose research to encourage professional scrutiny and critique. (p. 52)

In a discussion of the National Research Council's principles, Lauer (2004) noted that "significant" questions are ones that fill gaps in knowledge, search out causes, solve applied problems, test new hypotheses, or expand knowledge derived by prior research. Theories, as we have seen, provide a rationale and guidance for researchers. We have also seen that the appropriate methodology in educational research is closely tied to design, control procedures, and measurement soundness (reliability and validity). The "chain of reasoning" in science is closely tied to the "straight thinking" emphasized in the previous chapters and includes factors such as ruling out alternative (rival) hypotheses and using sound statistical inference. We have also seen that research results become more trustworthy to the extent that they can be generalized across settings and populations. Finally, research in education is also scientific to the extent that it is shared (meaning published or presented), and hence available for critique or evaluation.

Lauer (2004, Appendix B) offered a series of questions to ask yourself when evaluating whether research is scientific, all of which are bound to enhance a proposal in education. These questions include "Does the study rule out explanations for results other than the explanation given by the researcher?"; "Does the study demonstrate how errors or threats to the validity of the results were avoided?"; and "Does the study report on the validity and reliability of the measuring instruments?" Knowing these questions in advance and arranging for their answers within the research design will contribute to stronger science in educational research.

Finally, the frequently-cited APA manual (American Psychological Association, 2001) lists several factors used by journal editors to assess the quality and content of a manuscript for the purpose of deciding whether it merits publication. These same factors may be considered in the proposal stage, for a higher quality proposal is more likely to yield a publishable research once completed. The APA "checklist" suggests that high quality, publishable research has these qualities:

- The research question is significant, important, and original.
- The instruments used to answer the research question are valid and reliable.
- The measured outcome is clearly related to the study's focus.
- The research design clearly answers the research question.
- Research participants are representative of a generalized population.
- The research conforms strictly to ethical guidelines.
- The research is sufficiently "advanced" to permit meaningful results. (APA, 2001, p. 6)

Knowing these criteria for publication at the proposal stage will undoubtedly yield a stronger proposal.

The key to great research in education, the kind that makes significant contributions to theory and practice, deepens our understanding of teaching and learning, and stimulates useful discussion among educators, is a well-integrated research proposal that displays clear thinking and utilizes the most appropriate methodology to meet the research objectives. Most researchers in education believe that the huge variation of approaches to research—from teacher action research to large-scale experiments and from emerging "thick" qualitative studies to completely prescribed quantitative studies—contributes substantially to a more complete understanding of the teaching and learning process. Although there exist "camps" of researchers who argue in favor of one approach or another, few would argue seriously that one approach is best for all problems needing investigation in education. Whatever the purpose and approach, all research in education is strengthened by a research proposal that displays clear thinking and is authored by someone who welcomes critical comments and is willing to make revisions as needed, whether such revisions are slight or significant.

CRITICAL THINKER ALERT 15-10

Publishing

Consider publishing the results of your research in electronic or print journals. Always try to match the type of study with the interests of the journal's readers. Follow the journal's writing style and formatting requirements precisely. Also, consider presenting your research findings at a conference, the most likely outlet for a presentation being the regular meetings of professional organizations.

Discussion: Divisions and Special Interest Groups of the American Educational Research Association (http://www.aera.net/divisions/index.htm and http://www.aera.net/sigs/index.htm) provide opportunities for educators with common research interests to share information, including outlets for publishing or presenting findings. Browse these divisions and special interest groups (especially). Did one or more catch your interest? Do you see the value of joining such organizations, divisions, and special interest groups? Why?

Chapter Summary

A research proposal details the procedures needed to answer a research question. It must be well organized, concise, and clear in its communication. A generic outline of the components of a proposal includes an introduction (how the problem being investigated contributes to the field of knowledge), a brief literature review, methodology (including ethical safeguards, participant selection procedures, data collection methods to include control procedures, research design, and planned analysis of data), and a strategy for interpreting the results—the what, why, and how details. Ideas for proposals come from published journals and other print and online resources, practical experience, communication with others, and clear thinking about prior research. They also come from students' and professors' creative, spontaneous thinking. Completed research proposals often function as useful models (as do other organizing frameworks). Criteria for evaluating research proposals are offered, and knowing these in advance undoubtedly results in higher quality proposals.

Application Exercises

1. Locate a published research study in a bound or online journal in a field of your interest. Work "backwards" by drafting a research proposal using the guidelines presented in this chapter. In other words, your "research proposal" will extract relevant information from the published research; it should resemble a version of the researchers' original proposal (though you will not be able to confirm this).
2. Consider an important, contemporary issue in education. Generate a research question related to that topic. Then write a "skeletal" outline of a research proposal that would answer your research question. Share your proposal with others and ask for constructive comments.
3. Study the Web site of the American Educational Research Association's Grants Program http://www.aera.net/grantsprogram/index .html). Examine the "Funded Research Grants" under the Resources link. Do you see trends or patterns among the funded projects? Examine the "Grant Generated Publications" under the Publications & Reports link. Do you find interesting studies in this collection? What have you learned from your perusal of this Web site?
4. Examine the funded research awards from the U.S. Department of Education (http://www.ed.gov/programs/edresearch/awar ds.html) by clicking each award category. What patterns are apparent among funded research projects? What projects strike you as particularly interesting or noteworthy?

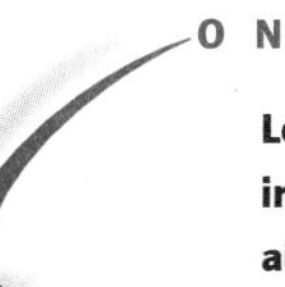

ON YOUR OWN

Log on to the Web-based student study site at http://www.sagepub.com/eic for more information about the materials presented in this chapter, suggestions for activities, study aids such as electronic flashcards and review quizzes, a sample research proposal, and research recommendations that include journal article links (with discussion questions and an article evaluation guide) and questions related to this chapter.

Glossary

Action research: Research conducted by practitioners in applied fields (teaching, counseling, etc.) for the purpose of solving a specific problem.

Affective measures: Educational tests that measure noncognitive constructs such as traits, attitudes, and beliefs.

Agreement index: A measure of the extent to which raters' ratings match in an absolute sense.

Alternative hypothesis: A rival explanation for the research results (often resulting from lack of control or procedural influences). It is an explanation "alternative" to that suggested by the research hypothesis and often "explains away" the findings.

Artifact: An unwanted source of influence creating a plausible, rival explanation of results. An artifact introduces bias and distorts results.

Attribute variable: A measured characteristic of research participants (e.g., learning style) presumed to be related to a dependent variable and part of the research hypothesis (If A, then B qualified by C, where C refers to the attribute variable).

Bivariate design: A type of correlational research design that assesses relationships using two measures.

Blinding: A control procedure that reduces bias by assuring that data collectors and/or research participants do not have information that distorts perceptions or influences behavior (such as knowing whether individual study participants are in a control group or an experimental group).

Case study design: An approach to qualitative research that focuses on the study of a single person or entity using an extensive variety of data.

Causal comparative research: Nonintervention research aimed at uncovering relationships by comparing groups of people who already differ on a variable of interest. It uses designs that search for causes or effects of a preexisting factor of interest. The preexisting factor differentiates groups and permits a meaningful comparison (e.g., examining achievement differences between children in one-parent and two-parent families).

Central tendency: A characteristic of a distribution of scores that describes where scores tend to center. It is often referred to as an average, the most common one being the mean (the sum of scores divided by the number of scores).

Chi-square test: A statistical test that determines significant relationships using data in the form of frequencies (counts, tallies, etc.).

Cognitive measures: Educational tests that measure mental abilities and school achievement.

Confounding: The "co-mingling" of an independent and extraneous variable such that as the levels of an independent variable change, so do differences in an extraneous variable (e.g., 10-, 20-, and 30-minute lectures given in cold, comfortable, and hot classrooms, respectively).

Construct: A label for an abstract trait or ability (such as creativity or intelligence) that is only presumed to exist, as it cannot be measured directly.

Construct validity: The extent to which test scores accurately reflect the trait or ability that the test is presumed to measure.

Content validity: The extent to which a test reflects the domain of content that it presumably samples.

Control: The idea that procedures used in research can minimize bias, neutralize threats to validity, rule out alternative explanations, and help establish cause-and-effect relationships.

Control group: A group not receiving a treatment, one that functions as a comparison so that a treatment effect can be isolated from extraneous influences.

Correlation coefficient: A statistical index of the degree of linear association between two measures (ranging from −1.00 to +1.00) revealing its strength and direction.

Correlational research: A type of nonexperimental research using one of several designs that measure individual differences in an attempt to uncover relationships between variables.

Counterbalanced quasi-experiment: A type of quasi-experimental research design that establishes control by using a single group to test all treatment and control conditions. It is also called a repeated measures or within subjects design.

Counterbalancing: A control procedure that assures order and carryover effects are neutralized by arranging conditions to be equally affected by order and carry-over influences.

Credibility: A criterion for judging the trustworthiness of qualitative data analysis.

Critical thinking: Careful, astute reasoning that includes conceptualization, synthesis, analysis, and evaluation. Critical thinkers reach sound conclusions about the connections between ideas and observations.

Cross-sectional survey design: A research design that describes changes over time using respondents who reflect temporal differences such as age (but data collection occurs at one point in time).

Deductive reasoning: A chain of logic progressing from general (e.g., theory) to specific (e.g., hypothesis) that is often used in quantitative research.

Degree of freedom: A mathematical concept used in statistics that conveys information about size (sample size, number of groups, etc.).

Dependent variable: A variable reflecting the presumed effect of the manipulation of an independent variable (e.g., score on achievement test). It is the B in the If A, then B hypothesis.

Descriptive research: Research aimed at describing the characteristics of a population without generalizing or testing statistical hypotheses.

Discrepant findings: Research outcomes that are inconsistent (or in opposition) across studies. Such findings are often explained by differences in research methods and procedures.

Dispersion: A characteristic of a distribution of scores that describes the spread or scatter of scores around the central tendency. The most common measure of dispersion is the standard deviation. The higher the standard deviation, the greater the spread of scores around the mean.

Ecological generalization: The extent to which research findings extend beyond the setting which produced sampled data.

Effect size (*d*): An index of a treatment effect expressed as a standardized difference between two means (the mean difference divided by the standard deviation of a comparison group's mean). It is often expressed as a percentile shift or "boost" from a baseline at the 50th percentile.

Emergent methodology: An approach to qualitative data analysis that relies on inductive reasoning and a continual interplay between data and developing interpretation.

ERIC: Education Resources Information Center, a database (clearinghouse) of journal and nonjournal education literature and documents.

Error score: A theoretical construct referring to the difference between a true score and an observed score.

Ethnographic design: A nonexperimental descriptive research design that is usually participatory and extends over a period of time in a natural setting. It often uses observational methods, interviews, and a variety of other qualitative methods.

Evaluation research: Research concerned with assessing the value of a program or revising it to enhance its effectiveness.

Experimental research: Research involving an independent variable—a manipulation of some type (a treatment or an intervention).

Experimenter expectancy: Bias that influences researchers in ways that create conditions favoring expected findings.

External validity: The degree to which research results can be generalized beyond the sample and conditions that yielded the findings.

Extraneous events: A threat to internal validity that includes influences co-occurring with a treatment between a pretest and posttest.

Extraneous variable: Any variable external to a research situation that is impacting the research and requires control so that its influence is neutralized.

***F* test:** A statistical test also known as the analysis of variance (ANOVA) that determines the statistical significance of two or more mean differences.

Fourfold table: A method of displaying data to reveal a pattern between two variables, each with two categories of variation.

Frequency distribution: A plot of scores displayed by their frequency of occurrence (i.e., ranked).

Grounded theory: An approach to qualitative data analysis using emergent methodologies, such as constant comparison, that permits a theory to develop from the data (from the ground up) without preconceived or inflexible ideas.

Group research: Research aimed at studying one or more large groups to learn more about relationships among variables or trends over time.

Hawthorne effect: Bias that influences research participants' behavior stemming from a treatment's unintended effects related to special attention, novelty, or similar treatment co-occurrences.

Historical research: The collection and objective study of documents and artifacts related to a past event, often including a description of patterns or trends, in an attempt to explain a phenomenon or test a hypothesis with present-day relevance.

Independent variable: A variable reflecting a presumed cause and the conditions created (manipulated) by the researcher for comparison (e.g., type of teaching method). It is the A in the If A, then B hypothesis.

Inductive reasoning: A chain of logic progressing from specific (e.g., observations) to general (e.g., theory) that is often used in qualitative research.

Inference: A form of logic used in statistics that permits a conclusion about a population based on data collected from a sample.

Inferential research: Research aimed at generalizing to a larger population with data collected from samples of the population.

Inferential statistics: Statistical reasoning that permits generalization beyond the sample to a larger population. Central to this reasoning is the notion of statistical significance, meaning that a relationship found in the sample is probably not due to the workings of chance.

Instrumentation: A threat to internal validity that includes changes in the measuring device or measuring procedures between a pretest and posttest. It also refers to the process of gathering data with the use of measuring tools such as tests or surveys.

Interaction effect: An effect that occurs in factorial designs when the influence of one factor depends on the level or category of a second factor (e.g., a treatment affects males but not females). The keyword here is *depends.*

Internal consistency reliability: Test consistency determined by correlating test items within a single test (e.g., coefficient alpha).

Internal validity: The degree to which conditions and procedures establish control. These conditions and procedures rule out rival hypotheses, reduce bias, and neutralize unwanted, potentially contaminating influences. A study has internal validity to the extent that the outcome can be explained by variation introduced by the treatment (and not an uncontrolled variable).

Inter-rater reliability: Rater relative consistency determined by correlating two or more raters' ratings.

Intuition: A belief without an empirical basis. Research findings often contradict intuitive beliefs.

John Henry effect: Bias that influences control or comparison groups' performance due to a perceived threat or similar negative perception.

Large-scale policy research: Research using large data sets (often standardized measures) with the intention of shaping public policy and influencing reform.

Level of an independent variable: The categories or conditions that define an independent variable (e.g., 10-, 20-, and 30-minute lectures if the independent variable is lecture length).

Longitudinal survey design: A descriptive research design that collects data from the same group of respondents over a period of time. Such designs often focus on the process of change.

Main effect: An effect that occurs in factorial designs when the averages between categories of one factor are different overall (e.g., females averaged over treatment and control groups score differently than males averaged over treatment and control groups). Each factor in a factorial design permits an evaluation of its main effect. The keyword here is *overall.*

Margin of error: A statistical index used in survey results to convey an interval that likely includes the true population value.

Matched comparison group design: A type of quasi-experimental research design that arranges for group similarity.

Matching: A control procedure that equates groups (or materials, etc.) by assuring they are the same or similar on important variables.

Meaningful research: Research conducted with clear value, which is often assessed in terms of positive impact in areas such as social and educational influence. It may also change ways of thinking or suggest new directions for research and theory.

Meta-analysis: A statistical summary of many studies conducted to answer the same research question.

Mortality: A threat to internal validity that refers to a loss of research participants between a pretest and posttest that stems from an influence of the treatment itself. Also referred to as attrition.

Multiple regression: A statistical technique using partial correlation as a control that attempts to predict an outcome (a criterion) given two or more predictor variables.

Negative correlation: A tendency of high scores on one variable to be linked to low scores on another variable (and of low scores to be linked with high scores).

Nonexperimental research: Research using designs that do not involve an intervention or a manipulation.

Nonparametric tests: Statistical tests and indexes (e.g., chi-square test, Spearman rank order correlation) that make few assumptions about the value of parameters.

Normal (bell) distribution: A common shape of score distributions. Normal distributions have common properties, ones that divide a distribution's area in terms of proportions contained within 1, 2, and 3 standard deviations above and below the mean.

Null hypothesis: A statistical hypothesis asserting there is no relationship among variables being studied in the population.

Observational measures: Researcher-recorded data based on personal perceptions of research participants or objects.

Operational definition: An empirical measure of the presumed indicator of a construct or state, such as heart rate as an indicator of "anxiety."

***p* (*p* value):** An abbreviation for *probability, p* refers to the likelihood that chance factors, or statistical error, could explain a relationship found in a sample.

Parameter: A characteristic of a population.

Partial correlation: A control procedure that statistically equates participants on important variables to rule out the variables' confounding influences.

Placebo: A control condition that preserves the illusion of participants' receiving a treatment.

Population: A large well-defined group that generates a sample (often randomly). Data from the sample are used to make inferences about the larger population.

Population generalization: The extent to which research findings extend beyond the sample of research participants who provided data.

Positive correlation: A tendency of high scores on one variable to be linked to high scores on another variable (and of low scores to be linked with low scores).

Power: A statistical concept used in sample size determination that refers to the likelihood of finding a significant relationship between variables in the sample presuming there is a true relationship in the population being studied.

Practical research: Research blending aspects of theory-based and problem-based research (as in a test of a "practical theory" such as multiple intelligences).

Predictive validity: The extent to which test scores accurately predict an outcome (a criterion).

Pre-experimental design: A weak research design involving a treatment but no control features (e.g., a one-group pretest-posttest design).

Problem-based research: Research focusing on direct application of findings to solve practical problems. It is also referred to as applied research.

Qualitative research: Research aimed at explaining complex phenomena through verbal descriptions rather than testing hypotheses with numerical values.

Quantitative research: Research aimed at testing hypotheses with numerical values rather than explaining complex phenomena through verbal descriptions.

Quasi-experimental design: A research design that incorporates a quasi-independent variable (an independent variable manipulation without random assignment).

Quasi-experimental research: Research involving the use of a manipulated independent variable (an intervention) *without* random assignment of participants to groups, weakening the researchers' ability to ferret out cause-and-effect relationships.

Quasi-independent variable: An independent variable that does not permit random assignment of research participants.

Random assignment: Assignment of research participants to groups such that all members have an equal and independent chance of being assigned to each group.

Random process: A control procedure that assures that extraneous influences are neutralized by unsystematic scattering across people and conditions.

Random selection: A method of sampling which ensures that each member of a population has an equal and independent chance of being selected for inclusion in a sample. Variants of random selection exist, such as cluster, multistage, and stratified.

Randomized factorial design: A true experimental design that incorporates two or more factors (e.g., an independent variable and an attribute variable), permitting the testing of main effect and interaction effects.

Reflective teaching: Teachers thinking critically about the art and science of teaching, collecting data to test ideas, and revising their practice to solve classroom problems or improve learning.

Regression: A threat to internal validity that refers to a tendency of those with extreme scores to score somewhat closer to the mean upon retesting.

Relationship: Any connection between variables—though not necessarily cause and effect—whereby values of one variable tend to co-occur with values of another variable.

Reliability: The consistency of measures indexed by an estimate of errors contained within a set of scores.

Replicate and extend: A model of research favoring the repetition of an earlier study with an additional feature that enhances its generalization.

Research analysis: The "unpacking" and "dissection" of a published research study for the purpose of laying groundwork for a critical review.

Research bias: Distortion of data collected in a research study that is explained by unwanted influences stemming from observers, research participants, procedures and settings, or researchers themselves.

Research critique: The descriptive review and evaluation of published research.

Research ethics: Established guidelines that encourage responsible research practices and assure the protection of human research participants.

Research hypothesis: A predicted outcome based on theory or understanding, which is often stated as If A, then B. It may also be stated as a foreshadowed question in qualitative research.

Research problem: The state of affairs or context for research that make clear why data are being collected.

Research question: The purpose of research stated in the form of a question.

Researchable: A research hypothesis (or question) that can be tested (or answered) directly by the collection and analysis of data.

Review of literature: A summary of past and current research and thinking on a specific researchable topic.

Scale of measurement: Distinguishing features that identify adjacent values on a measuring device (includes nominal, ordinal, interval, and ratio scales).

Scattergram: A plot of paired scores revealing a visual display of a correlation. It is also known as a scatterplot or scatter diagram.

Selection: A threat to internal validity that includes groups of participants who are not comparable before the introduction of a treatment.

Sequence effects: Unwanted influences due to ordering (first, second, etc.) and carryover (preceding versus following) of treatments, materials, and so on.

Single-subject design: A type of quasi-experimental research design using one subject to test all treatment and control conditions over time (e.g., an ABAB design).

Single-subject research: Research aimed at studying a single individual (or very small group) to learn more about relationships among variables or trends over time.

Small-scale evaluation research: Research aimed at evaluating local programs or procedures for the purpose of improvement or decision making.

Spurious relationship: A relationship than can be "explained away" by reference to another variable. When a connection between A and B is due solely to both being related causally to C, it is said that the relationship between A and B is spurious (or "false").

Standard error of mean differences: A measure of sampling error contained within a mean difference. Conceptually, it is the standard deviation of a hypothetical sampling distribution of many mean differences drawn from a population.

Standard error of measurement: A statistical index that estimates the amount of error in a single score.

Statistic: A characteristic of a sample. Sample statistics are often used to estimate population parameters.

Statistical power: A statistical concept referring to the likelihood of correctly rejecting the null hypothesis (concluding there is a relationship in the population when, indeed, one exists).

Statistical significance: A concept referring to a finding that cannot easily be explained by the workings of chance factors. Statistical significance is usually triggered when the *p* drops below .05.

Statistical test: A statistical maneuver applied to sampled data that yields *p* and permits a decision about the null hypothesis (i.e., whether to accept or reject it).

Strong inference: A concept referring to the test of a research hypothesis against an alternative (rival) hypothesis. Strong inference designs permit the elimination of at least one competing explanation (while supporting another).

***t* test:** A common statistical test that determines whether a mean difference is statistically significant.

Tails: A statistical concept referring to the direction of an anticipated outcome (e.g., less than, more than). Most statistical tests are "two-tailed," permitting an outcome that could fall either way (like an increase or a decrease). A tail also refers to the outer 5% limits in a normal distribution.

Teacher research: Self-reflective inquiry whereby teachers study their own practice, collect data, and attempt to solve a problem or improve learning in their classrooms.

Test for *r*: A statistical test that determines whether a correlation coefficient is significantly different from zero.

Test-retest reliability: Test consistency determined by correlating test scores and retest scores using the same test (stability reliability) or a similar test (equivalence reliability).

Theory: An elaborated explanation for a construct or phenomenon. Theories organize empirical findings and suggest future research.

Theory-based research: Research aimed at testing the hypotheses spun from a theory with the intention of evaluating the theory (supporting or discarding it) or revising its tenets.

Time-series design: A type of quasi-experimental research design that attempts to establish control via multiple observations of one group before and after treatment.

Traditional research: Formal scientific research using accepted guidelines and an integrated process aimed at testing hypotheses.

Triangulation: A method used in qualitative research that involves cross-checking multiple data collection sources and procedures.

True experimental research: Research involving the use of a manipulated independent variable (an intervention) coupled with random assignment of subjects to groups. Such designs are strong for testing cause-and-effect relationships (e.g., randomized posttest control group design, randomized pretest-posttest control group design, and randomized matched control group design).

True independent variable: An independent variable that permits random assignment of research participants.

True score: A theoretical construct referring to a person's score containing no error. It is also defined as one person's average on many tests of the same construct.

Type I error: A statistical fluke in sampling that permits an incorrect rejection of the null hypothesis (concluding there is a relationship in the population when there is no relationship).

Type II error: A statistical fluke in sampling that permits an incorrect acceptance of the null hypothesis (concluding there is no relationship in the population when in fact there is a relationship).

Validity: The meaningfulness of scores, which is often assessed by the accuracy of inferences made on the basis of test scores. It also refers to the extent to which a test measures what it is *supposed* to measure.

Variable: Any dimension with two or more changing values, such as age or sex.

Variance: A measure of dispersion among a set of scores (the square of the standard deviation).

References

Adair, J. B., Sharpe, D., & Huynh, C. (1989). Hawthorne control procedures in educational experiments: A reconsideration of their use and effectiveness. *Review of Educational Research, 59,* 215–228.

Allen, M., Bourhis, J., Burrell, N., & Mabrey, E. (2003). Comparing student satisfaction with distance education to traditional classrooms in higher education: A meta-analysis. *American Journal of Distance Education, 16*(2), 83–97.

American Educational Research Association (AERA). (2000). *Ethical standards of AERA.* Retrieved April 25, 2005, from http://www.aera.net/aboutaera/?id=222

American Educational Research Association (AERA). (2003). *Resolution on the Essential Elements of Scientifically-based Research.* Retrieved April 25, 2005, from http://35.8.171.42/aera/meeting/councilresolution03.htm

American Psychological Association (APA). (2001). *Publication manual of the American Psychological Association* (5th ed.). Washington, DC: Author.

American Psychological Association. (2002). *Ethical principles of psychologists and code of conduct.* Retrieved August 2, 2004, from http://www.apa.org/ethics/code2002.html

Amrein, A. L., & Berliner, D. C. (2002). High-stakes testing, uncertainty, and students learning. *Education Policy Analysis Archives, 10*(18). Retrieved January 21, 2004, from http://epaa.asu.edu/epaa/v10n18/

Bangert-Downs, R. L., Hurley, M. M., & Wilkinson, B. (2004). The effects of school-based writing-to-learn interventions on academic achievement: A meta-analysis. *Review of Educational Research, 74*(1), 29–58.

Baskerville, T., & Campbell, T. (1999). *Ownership of learning through learning styles.* Retrieved September 8, 2004, from http://gse.gmu.edu/research/tr/articles/Prospect%20Heights%20A/pgs.htm

Bayraktar, S. (2001-2002). A meta-analysis of the effectiveness of computer-assisted instruction in science education. *Journal of Research on Technology in Education, 34*(2), 173–188.

Berger, K. S. (1991). *The developing person through childhood and adolescence.* New York: Worth.

Bernard, R. M., Abrami, P. C., Lou, Y., Borokhorski, E., Wade, A., Wozney, L., Wallet, P. A., Fiset, M., & Huang, B. (2004). How does distance education compare with classroom instruction? A meta-analysis of the empirical literature. *Review of Educational Research, 74*(3), 379–439.

Best, J. (2001). *Damned lies and statistics: Untangling numbers from the media, politicians, and activists.* Berkeley: University of California Press.

Bloom, B. S. (1976). *Human characteristics and school learning.* New York: McGraw-Hill.

Bogdan, R. C., & Biklen, S. K. (2003). *Qualitative research in education: An introduction to theory and methods* (4th ed.). Needham Heights, MA: Allyn & Bacon.

Borman, G. D., Hewes, G. M., Overman, L. T., & Brown, S. (2003). Comprehensive school reform and achievement: A meta-analysis. *Review of Educational Research, 73*(2), 125–230.

Borman, G. D., Slavin, R. E., Cheung, A., Madden, N., & Chambers, B. (2005, April). *The national randomized field trial of Success for All: Second-year outcomes.* Paper presented at the annual meeting of the American Educational Research Association, Montreal, Quebec.

Bowers, C. A., & Flinders, D. (1990). *Responsive teaching.* New York: Teachers College Press.

Bracey, G. W. (1991, October). Why can't they be like we were? *Phi Delta Kappan, 71,* 104–117.

Bracey, G. W. (1992, March). Culture and achievement. *Phi Delta Kappan, 73,* 568–571.

Bracey, G. W. (2004, September). The trouble with research: Part 3. *Phi Delta Kappan, 86,* 91–92.

Bradley, R. H., & Caldwell, B. M. (1984). 174 children: A study of the relationship between home environment and cognitive development during the first 5 years. In A. M. Gottfried & A. E. Gottfried (Eds.), *Home environment and early cognitive development* (pp. 5–56). New York: Academic Press.

Bradley, R. H., & Corwyn, R. F. (2002). Socioeconomic status and child development. *Annual Review of Psychology, 53*(1), 371–399.

Brand, S., Felner, R., Shim, M., Seitsinger, A., & Dumas, T. (2003). Middle school improvement and reform: Development and validation of a school-level assessment of climate, cultural pluralism, and school safety. *Journal of Educational Psychology, 95*(3), 570–588.

Brigman, G. A., & Webb, L. D. (2003). Ready to learn: Teaching kindergarten students school success skills. *Journal of Educational Research, 96,* 286–292.

Bryan, S. (2000). *The colonial times: A learning environment for the 21st century.* Retrieved September 8, 2004, from http://gse.gmu.edu/research/tr/articles/Bryan/colonial.html

Campbell, D. T., & Stanley, J. C. (1963). *Experimental and quasi-experimental designs for research.* Chicago: Rand McNally.

Campbell, F. A., & Ramey, C. T. (1995). Cognitive and school outcomes for high-risk African American students at middle adolescence: Positive effects of early intervention. *American Educational Research Journal, 32,* 743–772.

Campbell, S. K. (1974). *Flaws and fallacies in statistical thinking.* Englewood Cliffs, NJ: Prentice Hall.

Chadwick, B. A., Bahr, H. M., & Albrecht, S. (1984). *Social science research methods.* Englewood Cliffs, NJ: Prentice Hall.

Chambers, E. A. (2004). An introduction to meta-analysis with articles from *The Journal of Educational Research* (1992–2002). *Journal of Educational Research, 98*(1), 35–44.

Chinn, C. A., Waggoner, M. A., Anderson, R. C., Schommer, M., & Wilkinson, I. A. G. (1993). Situated actions during reading lessons: A microanalysis of oral reading error episodes. *American Educational Research Journal, 30,* 361–392.

Clark, C., Moss, P. A., Goering, S., Herter, R. J., Lamar, B., Leonard, D., Robbins, S., Russell, M., Templin, M., & Wascha, K. (1996). Collaboration as dialogue: Teachers and researchers engaged in conversation and professional development. *American Educational Research Journal, 33,* 193–231.

Cloud, J. (2003, October 27). Inside the new SAT. *Time, 162*(17), 48–56.

Coalition for Evidence-Based Policy. (2003). *Identifying and implementing educational practices supported by rigorous evidence: A user friendly guide.* Retrieved January 23, 2004, from http://www.ed.gov/rschstat/research/pubs/rigorousevid/index.html

Coleman, J., Campbell, E., Hobson, C., McPartland, J., Mood, A., Weinfeld, F., & York, R. (1966). *Equality of educational opportunity.* Washington, DC: U.S. Government Printing Office.

Coles, G. (2004, January). Danger in the classroom: "Brain glitch" research and learning to read. *Phi Delta Kappan, 85*(5), 344–351.

Coopersmith, S. (1967). *The antecedents of self-esteem.* San Francisco: Freeman.

Csongradi, C. (1996). *How technology cheats girls.* Retrieved September 8, 2004, from http://www.accessexcellence.org/LC/TL/AR/arcsong.html

Cunningham, A. E., & Stanovich, K. E. (1990). Early spelling acquisition: Writing beats the computer. *Journal of Educational Psychology, 82,* 159–162.

Darling-Hammond, L., & Youngs, P. (2002). Defining "highly qualified teachers": What does "scientifically-based research" actually tell us? *Educational Researcher, 31*(9), 13–25.

Davenas, E., Beauvais, F., Amara, J., Oberbaum, M., Robinson, B., Miasdonna, A., Tedeschi, A., Pomeranz, B., Fortner, P., Belon, P., Sainte-Laudy, J., Poitevin, B., & Benveniste, J. (1988). Human basophil degranulation triggered by very dilute antiserum against IgE. *Nature, 333,* 816–818.

Dellett, K., Fromm, G., Karn, S., & Cricchi, A. (1999). *Developing metacognitive behavior in third and fourth grade students.* Retrieved September 8, 2004, from http://gse.gmu.edu/research/tr/articles/Clearview/Final%20Report.html

Dewey, J. (1933). *How we think: A restatement of the relation of reflective thinking to the educational process.* Lexington, MA: D. C. Heath.

Dick, B. (2002). *Grounded theory: A thumbnail sketch.* Retrieved January 24, 2004, from http://www.scu.edu.au/schools/gcm/ar/arp/grounded.html

Dillman, D. A. (1978). *Mail and telephone surveys: The total design method.* New York: John Wiley.

DuBois, P. H. (1966). A test-minded society: China 1115 B.C.–1905 A.D. In A. Anastasi (Ed.), *Testing problems in perspective* (pp. 29–36). Washington, DC: American Council on Education.

DuPaul, G. J., & Eckert, T. L. (1997). The effects of school-based interventions for attention deficit hyperactivity disorder: A meta-analysis. *School Psychology Review, 26*(1), 5–27.

DuPuis, A. (2002). *How to use a qualitative analysis package.* Randolph, MA: ResearchWare.

Edelman, G. (1992). *Bright air, brilliant fire: On the matter of the mind.* New York: Basic Books.

Ehri, L. C., Nunes, S. R., Stahl, S. A., & Willows, D. M. (2001). Systematic phonics instruction helps students learn to read: Evidence from the National Reading Panel's meta-analysis. *Review of Educational Research, 71*(3), 393–447.

Eisenhart, M., & Borko, H. (1993). *Designing classroom research: Themes, issues, and struggles.* Needham Heights, MA: Allyn & Bacon.

Elashoff, J. D., & Snow, R. E. (1971). *Pygmalion reconsidered.* Worthington, OH: Jones.

Elbaum, B. (2002). The self-concept of students with learning disabilities: A meta-analysis of comparisons across different placements. *Learning Disabilities: Research and Practice, 17*(4), 216–226.

Elbaum, B., & Vaughn, S. (2001). School-based interventions to enhance the self-concept of students with learning disabilities: A meta-analysis. *Elementary School Journal, 101*(3), 303–329.

Engelmann, S. (2004, January 28). The Dalmatian and its spots: Why research-based recommendations fail Logic 101. *Education Week, 23*(20), 34–35, 48.

Evertson, C. M. (1985). Training teachers in classroom management: An experimental study in secondary school classrooms. *Journal of Educational Research, 79*(1), 51–58.

Facione, P. A. (1998). *Critical thinking: What it is and why it counts.* Retrieved September 8, 2004, from http://www.insightassessment.com/pdf_files/what&why98.pdf

Fashola, O. S. (2004, March). Being an informed consumer of quantitative educational research. *Phi Delta Kappan, 85*(7), 532–538.

Fashola, O. S., & Slavin, R. E. (1997). Promising programs for elementary and middle schools: Evidence of effectiveness and replicability. *Journal of Education for Students Placed at Risk, 2,* 251–307.

Fendler, L. (2003). Teacher reflection in a hall of mirrors: Historical influences and political reverberations. *Educational Researcher, 32*(3), 16–25.

Fletcher-Flinn, C. M., & Gravatt, B. (1995). The efficacy of computer assisted instruction (CAI): A meta-analysis. *Journal of Educational Computing Research, 12,* 219–241.

Flinders, D. (1989). Does the "art of teaching" have a future? *Educational Leadership, 46*(8), 16–20.

Flinders, D. (1993). Researcher's comments. In W. Borg, J. Gall, & M. Gall (Eds.), *Applying educational research: A practical guide* (3rd ed., p. 209). New York: Longman.

Flowerday, T., & Schraw, G. (2003). Effect of choice on cognitive and affective engagement. *Journal of Educational Research, 96*(4), 207–215.

Franke, R., & Kaul, J. (1978). The Hawthorne experiments: First statistical interpretation. *American Sociological Review, 43,* 623.

Freeman, G. D., Sullivan, K., & Fulton, C. R. (2003). Effects of creative drama on self-concept, social skills, and problem behavior. *Journal of Education Research, 96*(3), 131–138.

Fukkink, R. G., & de Glopper, K. (1998). Effects of instruction in deriving word meaning from context: A meta-analysis. *Review of Educational Research, 68*(4), 450–469.

Gage, N. L. (1978). *The scientific basis of the art of teaching.* New York: Teachers College Press.

Gagne, R. M. (1985). *The conditions and learning and the theory of instruction* (4th ed.). New York: Holt, Rinehart & Winston.

Gagne, R. M., Briggs, L., & Wager, W. W. (1992). *Principles of instructional design* (4th ed.). Fort Worth, TX: Harcourt Brace Jovanovich.

Gans, A. M., Kenny, M. C., & Ghany, D. L. (2003). Comparing the self-concept of students with and without learning disabilities. *Journal of Learning Disabilities, 36*(3), 287–295.

Gardner, H. (1993). *Frames of mind: The theory of multiple intelligences* (2nd ed.). New York: Basic Books.

Gardner, H. (1999). *Intelligence reframed: Multiple intelligences for the 21st century.* New York: Basic Books.

Gardner, H. (2000). *The disciplined mind: Beyond facts and standardized tests, the K–12 education that every child deserves.* New York: Penguin Putnam.

Ge, X., & Land, S. M. (2003). Scaffolding students' problem-solving processes in an ill-structured task using question prompts and peer interactions. *Educational Technology Research and Development, 51*(1), 21–38.

Gerber, P. J. (2003). Adults with learning disabilities redux. *Remedial and Special Education, 24*(6), 324–337.

Gigerenzer, G. (2002). *Calculated risks: How to know when numbers deceive you.* New York: Simon & Schuster.

Gill, B. P., & Schlossman, S. L. (2003). Parents and the politics of homework: Some historical perspectives. *Teachers College Record, 105*(5), 846–871.

Giovannelli, M. (2003). Relationship between reflective disposition toward teaching and effective teaching. *Journal of Education Research, 96*(5), 293–309.

Glaser, B. G. (1998). *Doing grounded theory.* Mill Valley, CA: Sociology Press.

Glaser, B. G., & Strauss, A. L. (1967). *The discovery of grounded theory: Strategies for qualitative research.* New York: Aldine.

Gould, S. J. (1981). *The mismeasure of man.* New York: Norton.

Greenwald, R., Hedges, L. V., & Laine, R. D. (1996). The effect of school resources on student achievement. *Review of Educational Research, 66*(3), 361–396.

Hass, B. (2004, Fall). The brouhaha surrounding scientifically-based research. *Stanford Educator,* 1–4. Retrieved April 25, 2005, from http://ed.stanford.edu/suse/educator/fall2004/index.html

Hedberg, K. (2002). *Using SQ3R method with fourth grade ESOL students.* Retrieved September 8, 2004, from http://gse.gmu.edu/research/tr/articles/SQ3R%20Method/SQ3R.htm

Hensen, K. T. (2003, June). Writing for professional publication: Some myths and some truths. *Phi Delta Kappan, 84*(10), 788–791.

Hensen, K. T. (2005, June). Writing for publication: A controlled art. *Phi Delta Kappan, 86*(10), 772–776, 781.

Horowitz, J. M. (2002, July 22). What the knees really need. *Time, 160*(4), 62.

Horton, P. B., McConney, A. A., Gallo, M., Woods, A. L., Senn, G. J., & Hamelin, D. (1993). An investigation of the effectiveness of concept mapping as an instructional tool. *Science Education, 77,* 95–111.

Howell, D. C. (1982). *Statistical methods in psychology.* Boston: Duxbury.

Huitt, W. (1998). *Critical thinking: An overview. Educational psychology interactive.* Valdosta, GA: Valdosta State University. Retrieved September 8, 2004, from http://chiron.valdosta.edu/whuitt/col/cogsys/critthnk.html

Jeynes, W. H., & Littell, S. W. (2000). A meta-analysis of studies examining the effect of whole language instruction on the literacy of low-SES students. *Elementary School Journal, 101*(1), 21–33.

Johnson, A. P. (2005). *A short guide to action research* (2nd ed.). Boston: Allyn & Bacon.

Johnson, D. W., & Johnson, R. (2000). Cooperative learning, values, and culturally plural classrooms. In M. Leicester, C. Modgill, & S. Modgill (Eds.), *Values, the classroom, and cultural diversity* (pp. 15–28). London: Cassell PLC.

Johnson, W., Bouchard, T. J., Segal, N. L., Keyes, M., & Samuels, J. (2003). The Stroop Color-Word Test: Genetic and environmental influences; reading, mental ability, and personality correlates. *Journal of Educational Psychology, 95*(1), 58–65.

Kagan, D., Dennis, M. B., Igou, M., Moore, P., & Sparks, K. (1993). The experience of being a teacher in residence. *American Educational Research Journal, 30,* 426–443.

Kauchak, D., & Burbank, M. D. (2003). Voices in the classroom: Case studies of minority teacher candidates. *Action in Teacher Education, XXV*(1), 63–75.

Kemper, S., Greiner, L. H., Marquis, J. G., Prenovost, K., & Mitzner, T. L. (2001). Language decline across the life span: Findings from the Nun Study. *Psychology and Aging, 16,* 227–239.

Kiewra, K. A., DuBois, N. F., Christian, D., & McShane, A. (1988). Providing study notes: Comparison of three types of notes for review. *Journal of Educational Psychology, 80,* 595–597.

Kourilsky, M., & Wittrock, M. C. (1992). Generative teaching: An enhancement strategy for the learning of economics in cooperative groups. *American Educational Research Journal, 29,* 861–876.

Kowal, M. (2003). Creating a classroom of connoisseurs: Grade 7 students and their teachers investigate their growth as readers. *Networks: An On-line Journal for Teacher Research, 6*(1). Retrieved November 20, 2003, from http://www.oise.utoronto.ca/~ctd/networks/journal/Vol%206(1).2003march/Kowal.html

Kraemer, H. C., & Thiemann, S. (1987). *How many subjects? Statistical power analysis in research.* Newbury Park, CA: Sage.

Kramarski, B., & Mevarech, Z. R. (2003). Enhancing mathematical reasoning in the classroom: The effects of cooperative learning and metacognitive training. *American Educational Research Journal, 40*(1), 281–310.

Kroesbergen, E. H., & van Luit, J. E. H. (2003). Mathematics interventions for children with special educational needs: A meta-analysis. *Remedial and Special Education, 24*(2), 97–114.

La Paro, K. M., & Pianta, R. C. (2000). Predicting children's competence in the early school years: A meta-analytic review. *Review of Educational Research, 70*(4), 443–484.

Landon, 1,293,669; Roosevelt, 972,897. (1936, October 31). *The Literary Digest, 122*(18), 5–6.

Larson, L. M., Rottinghaus, P. J., & Borgen, F. H. (2002). Meta-analysis of big six interests and big five personality factors. *Journal of Vocational Behavior, 61*(2), 217–239.

Lauer, P. A. (2004). *A policymaker's primer on educational research: How to understand, evaluate, and use it.* Retrieved April 12, 2004, from http://www.ecs.org/html/educationIssues/Research/primer/index.asp

Lemonick, M. (1998, April 13). Emily's little experiment. *Time, 151*(14), 67.

Lesko, S. M., Rosenberg, L., & Shapiro, S. (1993, February 24). A case-control study of baldness in relation to myocardial infarction in men. *JAMA, 269*(8), 998–1003.

Leslie, M. (2000, July/August). The vexing legacy of Lewis Terman. *Stanford Magazine, 28*(4), 44. Retrieved May 27, 2005, from http://www.stanfordalumni.org/news/magazine/2000/julaug/articles/terman.html

Lindgren, H. C., & Suter, W. N. (1985). *Educational psychology in the classroom* (7th ed.). Pacific Grove, CA: Brooks/Cole.

Lopata, C., Miller, K. A., & Miller, R. H. (2003). Survey of actual and preferred use of cooperative learning among exemplar teachers. *Journal of Educational Research, 96*(4), 232–239.

Lou, Y., Abrami, P. C., Spence, J. C., Poulsen, C., Chambers, B., & d'Apollonia, S. (1996). Within-class grouping: A meta-analysis. *Review of Educational Research, 66*(4), 423–458.

Lovelace, M. J. (2005). Meta-analysis of experimental research based on the Dunn and Dunn model. *Journal of Educational Research, 98*(3), 176–183.

Lykken, D., & Tellegen, A. (1996, May). Happiness is a stochastic phenomenon. *Psychological Science, 7,* 186.

Ma, X. (1999). A meta-analysis of the relationship between anxiety toward mathematics and achievement in mathematics. *Journal for Research in Mathematics Education, 30*(5), 520–540.

Madden, N. A., Slavin, R. E., Karweit, N. L., Dolan, L. J., & Wasik, B. A. (1993). Success for all: Longitudinal effects of a restructuring program for inner-city elementary schools. *American Educational Research Journal, 30,* 123–148.

Martin, J. (2003). The hope of biography: The historical recovery of women educator activists. *History of Education, 32*(2), 219–232.

McDowell, W. H. (2002). *Historical research: A guide.* London: Longman.

McGinnies, E. (1949). Emotionality and perceptual defense. *Psychological Review, 56,* 244–249.

McGlinchey, A. (2002). *Nutrition instruction in the fifth grade classroom: Does knowledge affect eating habits?* Retrieved September 8, 2004, from http://www.fcps.edu/DeerParkES/TR/food.html

McNulty, M. A. (2003). Dyslexia and the life course. *Journal of Learning Disabilities, 36*(4), 363–381.

Meisels, S. J., Atkins-Burnett, S., Xue, Y., Nicholson, J., Bickel, D. D., & Son, S.-H. (2003, February 28). Creating a system of accountability: The impact of instructional assessment on elementary school children's achievement test scores. *Education Policy Analysis Archives, 11*(9). Retrieved November 20, 2003, from http://epaa.asu.edu/epaa/v11n9/

Miles, M. B., & Huberman, A. M. (1994). *Qualitative data analysis* (2nd ed.). Thousand Oaks, CA: Sage.

Mills, G. E. (2003). *Action research: A guide for the teacher researcher* (2nd ed.). Upper Saddle River, NJ: Merrill Prentice Hall.

Molfese, V. J., Modglin, A., & Molfese, D. L. (2003). The role of environment in the development of reading skills: A longitudinal study of preschool and school-age measures. *Journal of Learning Disabilities, 36*(1), 59–67.

Moore, D. S. (2001). *Statistics: Concepts and controversies* (5th ed.). New York: W. H. Freeman.

Moore, M. G., & Kearsley, G. (1996). *Distance education: A systems view.* New York: Wadsworth.

Moseley, J. B. (2002). A controlled trial of arthroscopic surgery for osteoarthritis of the knee. *New England Journal of Medicine, 347*(2), 81–88.

Mosteller, F., Light, R. J., & Sachs, J. A. (1996). Sustained inquiry in education: Lessons learned from skill grouping and class size. *Harvard Educational Review, 66,* 797–842.

Naftulin, D. H., Ware, J. E., & Donnelly, F. A. (1973). The Dr. Fox lecture: A paradigm of educational seduction. *Journal of Medical Education, 48,* 630–635.

National Institute of Child Health and Human Development. (2000). *Report of the National Reading Panel. Teaching children to read: An evidence-based assessment of the scientific research literature on reading and its implications for reading instruction* (NIH Publication No. 00-4769). Washington, DC: U.S. Government Printing Office.

National Research Council, Committee on Scientific Principles for Education Research. (2002). *Scientific research in education* (R. J. Shavelson & L. Towne, Eds.). Washington, DC: National Academy Press.

Neuman, S. B., Hagedorn, T., Celano, D., & Daly, P. (1995). Toward a collaborative approach to parent involvement in early education: A study of teenage mothers in an African-American community. *American Educational Research Journal, 32,* 801–827.

Neuman, S. B., & Roskos, K. (1993). Access to print for children of poverty: Differential effects of adult mediation and literacy-enriched play settings on environmental and functional print tasks. *American Educational Research Journal, 30,* 95–122.

Newkirk, T. (Ed.). (1992). *Workshop by and for teachers: The teacher as researcher.* Portsmouth, NH: Heinemann.

Nye, B., Hedges, L. V., & Konstantopoulos, S. (2001). Are effects of small classes cumulative? Evidence from a Tennessee experiment. *Journal of Educational Research, 94*(6), 336–345.

Oberg, A., & McCutcheon, G. (1987). Teachers' experience doing action research. *Peabody Journal of Education, 64,* 116–127.

Onwuegbuzie, A. J., Collins, K. M. T., & Elbedour, S. (2003) Aptitude by treatment interactions and Mathew effects in graduate-level cooperative-learning groups. *Journal of Educational Research, 96*(4), 217–230.

Painter, D. (2000). *The ThinkQuest challenge: A study of a constructivist learning environment through an after-school computer club.* Retrieved September 8, 2004, from http://www.fcps.k12.va.us/DeerParkES/TR/ThinkQuest.htm

Patton, M. Q. (2001). *Qualitiative research and evaluation methods* (3rd ed.). Thousand Oaks, CA: Sage.

Paul, R., Binker, A., Jensen, K., & Kreklau, H. (1990). *Critical thinking handbook: A guide for remodeling lesson plans in language arts, social studies and science.* Rohnert Park, CA: Foundation for Critical Thinking.

Penny, A. R., & Coe, R. (2004). Effectiveness of consultation on student ratings feedback: A meta-analysis. *Review of Educational Research, 74*(2), 215–253.

Perry, R. P., Abrami, P. C., & Leventhal, L. (1979). Educational seduction: The effect of instructor expressiveness and lecture content on student ratings and achievement. *Journal of Educational Psychology, 71,* 107–116.

Pfungst, O. (1911). *Clever Hans.* New York: Holt, Rinehart & Winston.

Pierce, C. (1994). Importance of classroom climate for at-risk learners. *Journal of Educational Research, 88*(1), 37–42.

Platt, J. R. (1964). Strong inference. *Science, 146,* 347–353.

Poole, B., & Smith, K. (2000). *Finding the links to indpendent reading.* Retrieved September 8, 2004, from http://www.fcps.k12.va.us/DeerParkES/TR/poolesmith/athome.htm

Popham, W. J. (1993). *Educational evaluation* (3rd ed.). Needham Heights, MA: Allyn & Bacon.

Powell, B. (1993, December). Sloppy reasoning, misused data. *Phi Delta Kappan, 75,* 283, 352.

Pringle, R. M., Dawson, K., & Adams, T. (2003). Technology, science and preservice teachers: Creating a culture of technology-savvy elementary teachers. *Action in Teacher Education, XXIV*(4), 46–52.

Rice, B. (1982, February). The Hawthorne defect: Persistence of a flawed theory. *Psychology Today, 16*(2), 70–74.

Richter, R. (2002, July 10). Hormone-replacement therapy study abruptly halted. *Stanford Report.* Retrieved April 25, 2005, from http://news-service.stanford.edu/news/2002/july10/hormone-a.html

Rigsby, L. C., & DeMulder, E. K. (2003, November 18). Teachers' voices interpreting standards: Compromising teachers' autonomy or raising expectations and performance? *Educational Policy Analysis Archives, 11*(44). Retrieved November 20, 2003, from http://epaa.asu.edu/epaa/v11n44/

Ritchie, G. V. (2000). *Playing with history.* Retrieved September 8, 2004, from http://gse.gmu.edu/research/tr/articles/Ritchie/Playinghis.shtml

Roethlisberger, F. J., & Dickson, W. J. (1939). *Management and the worker.* Cambridge, MA: Harvard University Press.

Roller, C. (1998). *Introducing graphing calculators in a trig/math analysis class.* Retrieved September 8, 2004, from http://www.gse.gmu.edu/research/tr/articles/roller/Introcalc.html

Roopnarine, J. L., Ahmeduzzaman, M., Donnely, S., Gill, P., Mennis, A., Arky, L., Dingler, K., McLaughlin, M., & Talukder, E. (1992). Social-cooperative play behaviors and playmate preferences in same-age and mixed-age classrooms over a 6-month period. *American Educational Research Journal, 29,* 757–776.

Rosa, L., Rosa, E., Sarner, L., & Barrett, S. (1998). A close look at therapeutic touch. *Journal of the American Medical Association, 279,* 1005–1010.

Rose, L. C., & Gallup, A. M. (2002, September). The 34th annual Phi Delta Kappa/Gallup poll of the public's attitude toward the public schools. *Phi Delta Kappan, 84*(1), 41–56.

Rose, L. C., & Gallup, A. M. (2003, September). The 35th annual Phi Delta Kappa/Gallup poll of the public's attitude toward the public schools. *Phi Delta Kappan, 85*(1), 41–56.

Rosenshine, B. (2003, August 4). High-stakes testing: Another analysis. *Educational Policy Analysis Archives, 11*(24). Retrieved November 20, 2003, from http://epaa.asu.edu/epaa/v11n24/

Rosenthal, R., & Jacobson, L. (1968). *Pygmalion in the classroom: Teacher expectations and pupils' intellectual development.* New York: Holt, Rinehart & Winston.

Rubin, B. C. (2003). Unpacking detracking: When progressive pedagogy meets students' social worlds. *American Educational Research Journal, 40*(2), 539–573.

Russell, M., & Haney, W. (1997). Testing writing on computers: An experiment comparing student performance on tests conducted via computer and via paper-and-pencil. *Educational Policy Analysis Archives, 5*(3). Retrieved November 20, 2003, from http://epaa.asu.edu/epaa/v5n3.html.

Sagor, R. (1992). *How to conduct collaborative action research.* Alexandria, VA: Association for Supervision and Curriculum Development.

Salant, P., & Dillman, D. A. (1994). *How to conduct your own survey.* New York: John Wiley.

Santa, C. M. (1993). Researcher's comments. In W. Borg, J. Gall, & M. Gall (Eds.), *Applying educational research: A practical guide* (3rd ed., pp. 401–402). New York: Longman.

Schank, R. (1999). *Dynamic memory revisited.* Cambridge, UK: Cambridge University Press.

Schunk, D. (2004). *Learning theories: An educational perspective* (4th ed.). Upper Saddle River, NJ: Pearson Education.

Schutt, R. K. (2004). *Investigating the social world: The process and practice of research* (4th ed.). Thousand Oaks, CA: Pine Forge.

Schweinhart, L. J., Barnes, H. V., & Weikart, D. P. (1993). *Significant benefits: The High/Scope Perry Preschool Study through age 27.* Ypsilanti, MI: High/Scope Press.

Scriven, M. (1967). The methodology of evaluation. In R. E. Stake (Ed.), *Perspectives of curriculum evaluation* (American Education Research Association Monograph Series on Evaluation No. 1). Chicago: Rand McNally.

Scruggs, T. E., & Mastropieri, M. A. (1994). Successful mainstreaming in elementary science classes: A qualitative study of three reputational cases. *American Educational Research Journal, 31,* 785–811.

Severiens, S. E., & Ten Dam, G. T. N. (1994). Gender differences in learning styles: A narrative review and quantitative meta-analysis. *Higher Education, 27*(4), 487–501.

Shank, G. D. (2002). *Qualitative research: A personal skills approach.* Upper Saddle River, NJ: Merrill Prentice Hall.

Shepard, L. A. (2003). The hazards of high-stakes testing. *Issues in Science and Technology, 19*(2), 53–58.

Slavin, R. E. (1990). *Cooperative learning: Theory, research, and practice.* Boston: Allyn & Bacon.

Smart, J. C., & Elton, C. F. (1981). Structural characteristics and citation rates of education journals. *American Educational Research Journal, 18*(4), 399–413.

Snow, R. E. (1969). Unfinished Pygmalion [Review of the use of the book *Pygmalion* in the classroom]. *Contemporary Psychology, 14,* 197–200.

Snowdon, D. (2001). *Aging with grace: What the Nun Study teaches us about leading longer, healthier, and more meaningful lives.* New York: Bantam Dell.

Snyder, T. D., & Hoffman, C. M. (1994). *Digest of education statistics.* Washington, DC: U.S. Department of Education.

Stampfer, M. J., Willett, W. C., Colditz, G. A., Rosner, B., Speizer, F. E., & Hennekens, C. H. (1985). A prospective study of postmenopausal estrogen therapy and coronary heart disease. *New England Journal of Medicine, 313,* 1044–1049.

Stefanou, C., & Parkes, J. (2003). Effects of classroom assessment on student motivation in fifth-grade science. *Journal of Educational Research, 96*(3), 152–159.

Stroop, J. R. (1935). Studies of inference in serial verbal reactions. *Journal of Experimental Psychology, 18,* 643–662.

Stuebing, K. K., Fletcher, J. M., LeDoux, J. M, Lyon, G. R., Shaywitz, S. E., & Shaywitz, B. A. (2002). Validity of IQ-discrepancy classifications of reading disabilities: A meta-analysis. *American Educational Research Journal, 39*(2), 469–518.

Stufflebeam, D. L., Foley, W. J., Gephart, W. J., Guba, E. G., Hammand, R. L., Merriman, H. O., & Provus, M. M. (1971). *Educational evaluation and decision making.* Itaska, IL: Peacock.

Suter, W. N. (1998). *Primer of educational research.* Needham Heights, MA: Allyn & Bacon.

Suter, W. N., & Lindgren, H. C. (1989). *Experimentation in psychology: A guided tour.* Needham Heights, MA: Allyn & Bacon.

Swanson, H. L. (1999). Reading research for students with LD: A meta-analysis of intervention outcomes. *Journal of Learning Disabilities, 32*(6), 504–532.

Swanson, H. L. (2001). Research on interventions for adolescents with learning disabilities: A meta-analysis of outcomes related to higher-order processing. *Elementary School Journal, 101*(3), 331–348

Swanson, H. L., & Deshler, D. (2003). Instructing adolescents with learning disabilities: Converting a meta-analysis to practice. *Journal of Learning Disabilities, 36*(2), 124–135.

Swanson, H. L., & Hoskyn, M. (1998). Experimental intervention on students with learning disabilities: A meta-analysis of treatment outcomes. *Review of Educational Research, 68*(3), 277–321.

Sylwester, R. (1993/1994). What the biology of the brain tells us about learning. *Educational Leadership, 51,* 46–51.

Tabachnick, B. G., & Fidell, L. S. (1983). *Using multivariate statistics.* New York: Harper & Row.

Temple E., Deutsch G. K., Poldrack, R. A., Miller, S. L., Tallal, P., Merzenich, M. M., & Gabrieli, J. D. (2003). Neural deficits in children with dyslexia ameliorated by behavioral remediation: Evidence from functional MRI. *Proceedings of the National Academy of Sciences, 100*(5), 2860–2865.

Thompson, D. (1999, February 22). Real knife, fake surgery. *Time, 153*(7), 66.

Tomchin, E. M., & Impara, J. C. (1992). Unraveling teachers' beliefs about grade retention. *American Educational Research Journal, 29,* 199–223.

Tournaki, N. (2003). The differential effect of teaching addition through strategy instruction versus drill and practice to students with and without learning disabilities. *Journal of Learning Disabilities, 36*(5), 449–458.

Trochim, W. (2000). *The research methods knowledge base* (2nd ed.). Cincinnati, OH: Atomic Dog.

Tuchman, G. (1994). Historical social science: Methodologies, methods, and meanings. In N. K. Denzin & Y. S. Lincoln (Eds.), *Handbook of qualitative* research (pp. 306–323). Thousand Oaks, CA: Sage.

Uribe, D., Klein, J. D., & Sullivan, H. (2003). The effect of computer-mediated collaborative learning on solving ill-defined problems. *Educational Technology Research and Development, 51*(1), 5–19.

Van de Vijver, F. (1997). Meta-analysis of cross-cultural comparisons of cognitive test performance. *Journal of Cross-Cultural Psychology, 28*(6), 678–709.

Van Sledright, B., & Brophy, J. (1992). Storytelling, imagination, and fanciful elaboration in children's historical reconstructions. *American Educational Research Journal, 29,* 837–859.

Van Voorhis, F. L. (2003). Interactive homework in middle school: Effects of family involvement and science achievement. *Journal of Educational Research, 96*(6), 323–338.

Viadero, D. (2003a, January 8). Report finds fault with high-stakes testing. *Education Week, 22*(16), 5.

Viadero, D. (2003b, April 16). Study finds high gains in states with high-stakes tests. *Education Week, 22*(31), 10.

Viadero, D. (2005, May 11). Long-awaited study shows "Success for All" gains. *Education Week, 24*(36), 3.

Vos Savant, M. (2002). *The power of logical thinking: Easy lessons in the art of reasoning . . . and hard facts about its absence in our lives.* New York: St. Martin's.

Walker, V. S. (2001). African American teaching in the South: 1940–1960. *American Educational Research Journal, 38*(4), 751–779.

Wallen, N. E., & Fraenkel, J. R. (1991). *Educational research: A guide to the process.* New York: McGraw-Hill.

Walsh, K. (2001). *Teacher certification reconsidered: Stumbling for quality.* Baltimore: Abell Foundation. (ERIC Document Reproduction Service No. ED460100)

Warburton, E. C. (2003). Intelligence past, present, and possible: The theory of multiple intelligences in dance education. *Journal of Dance Education, 3*(1), 7–15.

Watson, J. D. (1968). *The double helix: A personal account of the discovery of the structure of DNA.* New York: Atheneum.

Weinburgh, M. H. (1995). Gender differences in student attitudes toward science: A meta-analysis of the literature from 1970 to 1991. *Journal of Research in Science Teaching, 32,* 387–398.

Wilson, P. W. F., Garrison, R. J., & Castelli, W. P. (1985). Postmenopausal estrogen use, cigarette smoking, and cardiovascular morbidity in women over 50. *New England Journal of Medicine, 313,* 1038–1043.

Wineburg, S. S. (1987). The self-fulfillment of the self- fulfilling prophecy: A critical appraisal. *Educational Researcher, 16,* 28–37.

Worthen, B. R., & Sanders, J. R. (1987). *Educational evaluation: Alternative approaches and practical guidelines.* New York: Longman.

Yatvin, J. (2003, April 30). I told you so! The misinterpretation and misuse of the National Reading Panel report. *Education Week, 22*(33), 44–56.

Yeung, W. J., Linver, M. R., & Brooks-Gunn, J. (2002). How money matters for young children's development: Parental investment and family processes. *Child Development, 73*(6), 1861–1879.

Ysseldyke, J., Kosciolek, S., Spicuzza, R., & Boys, C. (2003). Effects of a learning information system on mathematics achievement and classroom structure. *Journal of Educational Research, 96*(3), 163–173.

Zwick, R. (2002, December). Is the SAT a "wealth test"? *Phi Delta Kappan, 84*(4), 307–311.

Index

About the Author

W. Newton Suter is Professor in Educational Foundations in the Department of Educational Leadership at the University of Arkansas at Little Rock. He received his PhD in Educational Psychology in 1983 from Stanford University. He is the co-author with Henry Clay Lindgren of the seventh edition of *Educational Psychology in the Classroom* (1985) and *Experimentation in Psychology* (1989), and the author of *Primer of Educational Research* (1998).